NATIONAL GEOGRAPHIC

TRAVELER
India

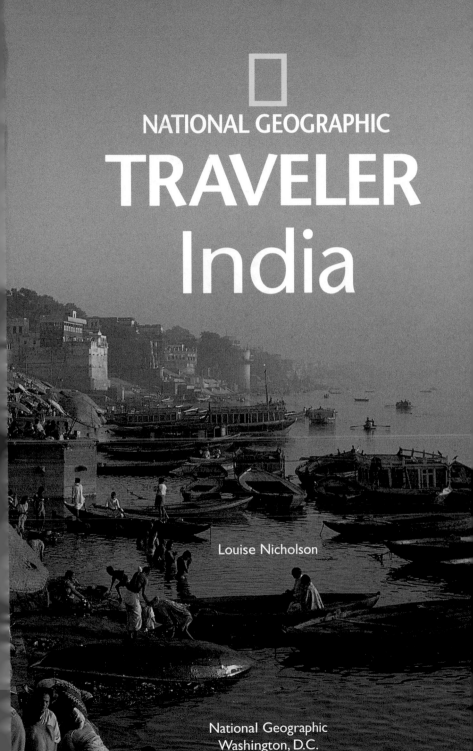

NATIONAL GEOGRAPHIC

TRAVELER
India

Louise Nicholson

National Geographic
Washington, D.C.

Contents

How to use this guide 6–7 About the author 8
The regions 61–334 Travelwise 335–388
Index 389–97 Credits 398–99

Page 1: Indian teenagers at
a temple in Mahabali-puram,
near Chennai (Madras)
Pages 2–3: Brahmans and
pilgrims at Dashashwamedha
Ghat, Varanasi
Left: Film poster suspended
over a busy Mumbai street

How to use this guide

See back flap for keys to text and map symbols.

The *National Geographic Traveler* brings you the best of India in text, pictures, and maps. Divided into three main sections, the guide begins with an overview of history and culture. Following are nine regional chapters with featured sites selected by the author for their particular interest. Each chapter opens with its own contents list.

The regions and sites within the regions are arranged geographically. A map introduces each region, highlighting the featured sites. Walks, drives, and boat rides, plotted on their own maps, suggest routes

for discovering an area. Features and sidebars give intriguing detail on history, culture, or contemporary life.

The final section, Travelwise, lists essential information for the traveler—pretrip planning, special events, getting around, emergencies, and a glossary—plus a selection of hotels, restaurants, stores, and entertainment.

To the best of our knowledge, all information is accurate as of the press date. However, it's always advisable to check at the time of travel.

In India, travel is generally by public transportation or by car and driver. Directions are included to allow you to plan your trip, but detailed driving directions are not included in this guide as your driver should know the best way to get to the sites you wish to visit.

Color coding

Each region is color coded for easy reference. Find the region you want on the map on the front flap, and look for the color flash at the top of the pages of the relevant chapter. Information in **Travelwise** is also color coded to each region.

Taj Mahal
www.tajmahalagra.com
▲ 95 C4
✉ Tajganj
◷ Closed Fri.
$ $

Visitor information

Practical information for most sites is given in the side column (see key to symbols on back flap). The map reference gives the page number of the map and grid reference. Other details are address, telephone number, days closed, and entrance charge in a range from $ (under $4) to $$$$$ (over $25). Other sites have information in italics and parentheses in the text.

TRAVELWISE

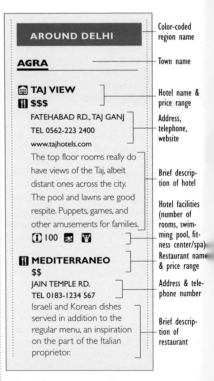

Color-coded region name

Town name

Hotel name & price range

Address, telephone, website

Brief description of hotel

Hotel facilities (number of rooms, swimming pool, fitness center/spa)

Restaurant name & price range

Address & telephone number

Brief description of restaurant

Hotel & restaurant prices

An explanation of the price bands used in entries is given in the Hotels & Restaurants section (see p. 344).

REGIONAL MAPS

State name

Road number

Map reference — **2 ▷**

Adjoining chapter

Important
featured
town

- A locator map accompanies each regional map and shows the location of that region in the country.
- Adjacent regions are shown, each with a page reference.

WALKING TOURS

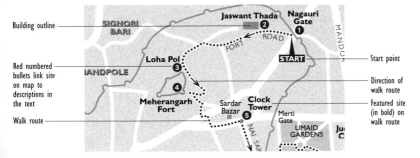

Building outline

Red numbered bullets link site on map to descriptions in the text

Walk route

Start point

Direction of walk route

Featured site (in bold) on walk route

- An information box gives the starting and ending points, time and length of walk, and places not to be missed along the route.
- Where two walks are marked on the map, the second route is shown in orange

DRIVING TOURS

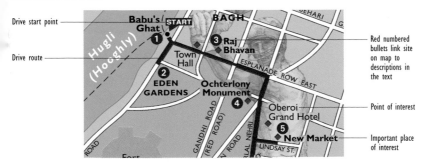

Drive start point

Drive route

Red numbered bullets link site on map to descriptions in the text

Point of interest

Important place of interest

- An information box provides details including starting and finishing points, time and length of drive, and places not to be missed along the route, or tips on terrain.

NATIONAL GEOGRAPHIC

TRAVELER

India

About the author

Louise Nicholson, a British art historian living in New York, catalogued Indian art at the London auctioneers Christie's before spending her honeymoon in India in 1980. Since then she has returned more than 180 times.

Louise finds all aspects of the country endlessly fascinating, from the buildings, traditions, and colorful festivals to the exotic bird life, weaving traditions, and contemporary culture. She has traveled to all parts to lecture and do research for books and journalism—most of her 27 books are about India or London—and was Associate Director for the acclaimed six-part TV series *The Great Mughals.* Louise shares her considerable knowledge and practical experience of India by leading lecture tours, advising private travelers, and taking her family on exciting Indian adventures.

History & culture

**A pink-powdered boy
celebrates the Ganpati
festival in Mumbai.**

India today

INDIA HAS ALWAYS INTRIGUED FOREIGNERS. BACK IN THE FOURTH century B.C., Alexander the Great's men were amazed by the elephants. Later, William Shakespeare (1564–1616), who never visited India, alluded to its exotic trading wealth in his play *A Midsummer Night's Dream.* More recently, in 1897 the well-traveled writer Mark Twain (1835–1910) called India "…the one land that all men desire to see, and having seen once, by even a glimpse, would not give that glimpse for the shows of all the rest of the globe combined." Today, India continues to fascinate with equal force as it mixes tradition and religion with thrusting global enterprise.

LAND OF CONTRASTS

India is a land of sharp contrasts where history and tradition go hand in hand with the dynamic present. It is second only to the United States in information technology, yet home life remains traditional and families eat together, enjoying laboriously prepared fresh dishes rather than convenience fast foods. Examples of this contrast abound throughout the whole of this vast country: A highly skilled silk-weaver from a village near Chennai will confirm his orders by cellular phone, while young students of international law at Delhi University volunteer to have their marriages arranged by their families; in a Rajasthan village a group of women swathed in magenta and saffron saris sits on the ground selling their vegetables next to an Internet café.

Contrasts are obvious from the moment you arrive. On a busy stretch of road outside the capital, New Delhi, you could see a camel, a bullock cart, a bicycle, a herd of goats, a Harley-Davidson motorcycle, an elaborately hand-painted truck, the latest model Mercedes car, a wandering cow, a streamlined, air-conditioned bus, and even an elephant—all somehow getting along together with remarkably few accidents.

And the contrasts extend to huge differences in material wealth. The appalling poverty that was so vividly publicized by Mother Theresa and continues to be a living horror, exists alongside India's less well-known vast wealth in natural resources, wildlife, culture, crafts and skills, and personal affluence. India has more millionaires than the United States, and real estate prices are among the world's highest. And there are regular displays of outrageous extravagance. At some Hindu festivals, intricate images of the gods that take a full year to make are paraded once and then cast into the sea, where they disintegrate in moments. During the wedding season, thousands of families fall into debt in their efforts to put on an impressive show.

From the point of view of the visitor, India assaults the senses, stretching them further than you may have thought possible. You may hear calming religious music, see women dressed in vivid colors, and taste new flavors—not all of them spicy. You will smell fresh coconut milk and jasmine blossoms, and feel the smooth stones of temple floors beneath your bare feet.

India can make you laugh for joy and catch your breath in wonder; it can turn your ideas upside-down and introduce whole new subjects to think about—and, occasionally, it may well make you lose your patience.

People talk of seeing "the real India," when they have taken a local bus or spent time living in a village. This is indeed India, but there is more to it than that. To get anywhere near the real India, you should take advantage of every opportunity available to experience as many different sides as possible of this immensely rich, varied, and stimulating land.

INDIA'S DEMOCRACY: COHERENCE & DIVERSITY

The government of India is, in many ways, a daily miracle in the way that it administers a vast area inhabited by a vast population. This huge land is home to more than a billion people (only China has a larger population), making India the world's largest democracy.

Tradition clashes with modernity in India. Here, a mother swathed in a sari sits proudly with her fashion model daughter.

It has a president as head of state, a prime minister as head of government, and a two-house parliament elected by universal suffrage—Lok Sabha (House of the People, 552 seats) and Rajya Sabha (Council of States, 250 seats). Based on the British Parliament, the political structure also draws on the United States' system and incorporates a bill of rights.

The country is divided into 20 states and 8 union territories, with the northern city of Delhi, the capital since 1911, in a separate category of its own due to its large population. Because the states were created after independence (see p. 50) on broadly historical and linguistic criteria, each has its own distinct character, culture, achievements, and disadvantages, and many have their own language. Looking at the political map of India on the inside back cover of this book, you can see how the states vary in size, from huge Rajasthan to tiny Goa. Their populations vary too: Uttar Pradesh contains more than

166 million people, while remote Sikkim's has about 540,000.

As each state sends its members of parliament to Delhi, so Delhi sends a governor to each state. Each state also has its own administration, called the Legislative Assembly, and elects its own representatives, who can keep in touch with local needs—Delhi can be far away, in thought and culture as well as miles.

Government at all levels is cumbersome. Although India has two national languages,

Bangalore, India's most international city after Mumbai (Bombay), displays a mixture of the traditional and the contemporary.

Hindi (written in Devanagari script) and English, there are 22 officially recognized languages, many with their own script. As you travel, you hear Bengali in West Bengal, Malayalam in Kerala, and Marathi in Maharashtra. Imagine the complexities of a Lok Sabha debate between MPs from several states.

A BILLION PEOPLE

With such a huge population, it's no wonder that the government struggles. The statistics reflect the extent of some of the country's complexities. With more than a billion people, India has 16 percent of the world's population living on 2.42 percent of the world's total area. The population explosion after independence, when it stood at 350 million, was mainly caused by increased longevity thanks to a better diet, control of famines, and treatment of diseases such as malaria, smallpox, and cholera. The average life expectancy has risen from less than 40 years to about 65 years. Population growth is now being curbed by successful family planning programs: India's growth rate has been reduced from 2.5 percent in the 1960s to a current rate of 1.2 percent.

Women are playing a leading role in this effort and in India's impressive literacy campaign, especially in the south. Kerala's literacy is around 93 percent, Tamil Nadu's

65 percent, but in the north, tourist-popular Rajasthan's is only 38.5 percent, and there only 20 percent of women are literate. However, overall, between 1990 and today India's literacy rate has risen from 52 percent to around 65 percent, a huge improvement from the 18 percent at independence in 1947.

Other major changes have come about since independence: Until the 1970s, India's people lived in a mainly rural land; fewer than 20 percent lived in cities. Today, migration and

Seen from afar at night, Mumbai's high-rises, streetlights, and sweeping seafront combine to evoke a Western coastal city.

population growth have increased this number to around 30 percent, straining cities to their limits—16.3 million live in Mumbai (Bombay), 13.2 million in Kolkata (Calcutta), and 12.7 million in the capital. In the country's ten largest cities the average population density is 6,888 per 2.5 square miles (1 sq km).

The liberalization of India's economy since 1991 has turned India from an inward-looking, highly regulated country into one that has taken its part in the global economy. It sustains 24 stock exchanges, from Mumbai to Bhubaneshwar, from Delhi to Chennai.

While India has made huge strides in many areas in recent years—the "green revolution" helped make the country self-sufficient in food with some produce left over to export—some problems persist. Officials calculate that 20 percent of the population still lives below the poverty line (a reduction from 54 percent in the 1970s). This is most acute in the states of Bihar, Madhya Pradesh, and Orissa. Health problems persist, too. The government, in partnership with thousands of nongovernment organizations, is focusing on providing clean water and sanitation to more rural areas and on tackling the persistent presence of malaria, leprosy, and—the most acute problems— AIDS and tuberculosis.

VISITORS IN INDIA

It is important for visitors to be aware that India plays a minor role in world tourism, even though, from the opposite point of view, tourism is India's third largest export industry (after gems and jewelry, and ready-made garments). Tourist activity (and therefore spending) in India is concentrated in the Golden Triangle formed by Delhi, Agra, and Jaipur, and in the increasingly popular towns of Rajasthan. Elsewhere, with exceptions such

India has a population of more than a billion and huge crowds are commonplace. Hindi has special words to describe crowds.

as Ajanta's caves and Varanasi, the more adventurous traveler will find most of India refreshingly quiet.

Traveling around the country is easy. There are good road, railroad, and air networks, and Indian people are particularly helpful and friendly. It is easy to observe and take part in

local life. The host of major festivals (see pp. 379–82) is augmented by thousands of smaller, equally charming ones. You can stop to join in the celebrations of a village deity, inspect the goats at an agricultural fair, and watch the lively wedding processions that dance their way through the streets.

In villages you can find craftsmen practicing ancient skills—making gold jewelry, weaving silk saris, or casting in bronze. The village elementary school usually welcomes a spontaneous visit and an exchange of songs. In the fields you can see the traditional irrigation methods, the planting of wheat and paddy, the gathering in of harvests of cotton, chilies, oil seeds, tea, rubber, lentils, and more—70 percent of Indians depend on agriculture for their livelihood. You will be welcomed into temples, *gurudwaras*, and mosques to observe the faithful and their rituals.

Cities are places for finding top-quality cultural performances, seeing one of India's

Workers harvest tea leaves in a mountainside field in Darjiling. Tea production in India has doubled since independence in 1947.

"Bollywood" movies (the name is a pun on the idea of Hollywood in Bombay), visiting the large markets and high-quality stores, and obtaining information on the surrounding area from the visitor information office.

To find out what is important to Indians now, pick up a copy of the periodical *India Today* or one of many English language newspapers; or explore the many English language television channels. For a glimpse into sophisticated high society, take a look at *Verve* magazine, India's equivalent of *Vogue*.

Gone are the days when travelers had to compromise on their accustomed comforts. India's affluence means that in most metropolitan areas cars are comfortable, hotels efficient, communications streamlined, and stores stocked with international goods. ∎

Land & landscape

INDIA IS VAST, THE WORLD'S SEVENTH LARGEST COUNTRY. IT STRETCHES from 8° to 36° latitude north and from 68° to 97° longitude. The country's diverse landscape of rivers, fields, forests, mountains, and deserts is shaped like a large diamond. To the north, it is cut off from the rest of Asia by the Himalayan mountain range. To the south, the 2,000 miles (3,218 km) of coastline are washed by the Arabian Sea in the west, the Indian Ocean in the south, and the Bay of Bengal to the east.

These mountains and seas separate India from surrounding countries. Pakistan and Bangladesh, which shared India's history until 1947, are the exceptions. Historically, the mountains have been India's natural defense, and only the most determined invaders have penetrated them. The coast, on the other hand, benefited from the east–west sea trade routes and is dotted with ancient trading posts, especially on the Konkani, Malabar, and Coromandel stretches.

Modern India occupies a strategic position in Asia, looking westward to the Middle East and Africa and eastward to Malaysia and the Indonesian Archipelago. Its borders meet, from west to east, Pakistan, Afghanistan, China's Sinkiang Province, Tibet, Nepal, Bhutan, Myanmar (Burma), and Bangladesh. The long strip of the Andaman and Nicobar Islands in the Bay of Bengal and the Lakshadweep Islands in the Arabian Sea are also part of the Republic.

India claims part of the great Himalayan range, the world's highest mountain system and one of its youngest, created when the drifting Indian plate collided with the Tibetan plate of south Asia about 50 million years ago. Mountains, including Everest and 95 other peaks rising above 24,600 feet (7,500 m), were formed well after that, by later movement of the continental plates. Today much of India's forest, which covers 20 percent of the land, is in this region.

India's lesser mountain ranges include the Aravallis, one of the world's oldest mountain systems, in southern Rajasthan, west of which lies the Thar Desert. Here is some of India's mineral wealth, in copper ore, lead-zinc complexes, and rock phosphate. The Vindhya and Satpura Mountains cross central India, a barrier to invaders' southern progress. They rise to the Deccan and Mysore Plateaus, from

which the Sahyadris (Western Ghats) drop sharply to the west coast and the gentler Eastern Ghats to the east coast. Iron ore mined here— in the states of Goa, Karnataka, and Madhya Pradesh—and in Orissa and Bihar make India the world's largest producer of that metal. Gold and diamonds are mined farther south, and rubies and other gems are mined in Kerala.

All of India's mountains help gather the country's precious waters from its two mosoons. The great southwest monsoon begins in Kerala in June and sweeps up north across India through July, August, and September, dumping its final gallons in the Himalayan mountains. The smaller southeast monsoon drenches the east coast intermittently in October and November, enabling Tamil Nadu farmers to harvest three rice crops annually, but sometimes bringing cyclones and destruction, as in Orissa in 1999. After this, the weather is at its best throughout most of India until April, when the heat arrives and the mountains become cool retreats.

Rivers originating from these mountain watersheds nourish India's soil. From the Himalayan mountains you can trace the path of the great Indus, the Ganga (Ganges), and, in the east, the Brahmaputra. The Indus waters the Punjab, India's wheat bowl. The Ganga, Hindus' holiest river, rises near the Gangotri glacier, and with its tributaries, flows through the heartland of rice-growing ancient India to the Bay of Bengal, creating India's largest river basin, which covers 25 percent of the country.

Most of the great rivers of peninsular India meander through flat valleys to the Bay of Bengal. The Brahmani and Mahanadi irrigate Orissa; the Godavari and Krishna flow off the

Coconut palms shade fishing villages here on the Andaman Islands and along India's southern coastline.

Deccan Plateau, and the Penner and the Kaveri (Cauvery) flow from the Mysore Plateau. The great Kaveri benefits from two monsoons and is southern India's holiest river, but siphoning off its waters for irrigation is a contentious issue between Karnataka and Tamil Nadu states. The Narmada—with its controversial dam that threatens to permanently alter the ecology and cultural balance of the area—and Tapti Rivers flow down from the Vindhya and Satpura ranges to the Arabian Sea.

This rhythm of life can, however, go wrong. India's landmass, surrounded by warm oceans, straddles the Tropic of Cancer and is at one of the Earth's major plate junctions. This means that periodically it suffers from violent natural events that may leave disaster in their wake. Tropical cyclones are frequent in the Bay of Bengal, while the relative youth of the Himalaya means that this is a major earthquake region, as exemplified by the devastating earthquake that hit Pakistan in 2005.

Monsoons are relied upon throughout the country to provide water for growing crops. Heavy monsoons, however, can bring floods that often have a high death toll. These floods have been exacerbated by deforestation of the hills for industrial and agricultural purposes. It is a fine balance between having plenty of water to flood the rice fields and having too much so that crops, homes, and even lives are lost. The alternative to the floods may be famines. However, India's infrastructure can

Barren, beautiful Ladakh is believed to have been inhabited first by herdsmen from Tibet, then by early Buddhist monks.

now deal successfully with these: When the monsoon fails in one area, the army is able to move supplies to the drought-stricken area. As a result of this organization, few lives were lost in the Maharashtra famines of 1965–66 and 1974–75, while more than two million people died in the Bengal famine of 1943. ■

Food & drink

CLIMATE, GEOGRAPHY, RELIGION, AND TRADITION HAVE SHAPED THE MANY cuisines of India. There is a huge variety of foods to eat, from the simple to the extravagantly rich. One of the delights of traveling is to sample the dishes of different communities. Even the staple southern Indian meal of rice and *dhal* (pulse—peas, beans, and lentils) varies subtly from town to town; indeed, so many kinds of pulse are grown in India that the financial papers give the pulses stock exchange prices a special section of their own.

India is traditionally associated with spicy food such as curries. The word curry itself has confusing connotations. For many people it implies a highly spiced and rich meat casserole that may well be difficult to digest. In fact, the word comes from Tamil, a southern Indian language: *Kari* simply means "to eat by biting." But curry has for centuries referred to a savory sauce of meat, fish, fruit, or vegetables cooked with a *masala,* a blend of locally available bruised or ground spices. This was traditionally added to the rather bland staple food of grain, either flour, baked into unleavened bread (in the north), or boiled rice (in the east and south). Thus, *karis* gave interest and variety— one fifth-century text describes the hero taking "rice dressed in butter, with its full accompaniment of curries." Today, India's vast array of curries fulfills the same function.

India's sheer size and geographical diversity mean that most foods are produced somewhere in the country. To visit the vast wholesale market outside Delhi is to be at the crossroads of a countrywide food-trading network. Here you see up to 20 kinds of bananas from the south, oranges from the Lower Himalaya, rice from Bengal and Tamil Nadu, and sackfuls of spices.

If you travel to the north, try the breads— *naan, chapatti, roti, paratha,* and the paperthin *romali roti* (handkerchief bread). They go well with mildly spiced lamb or chicken barbecued on skewers in a tandoor (clay oven). In Rajasthan, too, you will find the food is quite gentle, but watch out for the chili peppers. Meat, dhal, and *sabzi* (vegetables) are scooped up with pieces of nutty-textured breads made from maize, millet, or gram. A spoonful of spice-hot *brinjal* (aubergine) or *nimbu* (lime) pickle completes the meal.

In contrast, the dishes inspired by the Islamic courts of Agra, Delhi, Lucknow. and Hyderabad are rich and complicated. Meat is cooked very slowly with cream, almonds, and dried fruits until it is very soft. Vegetables are just as rich, be they *okra* (edible seed pods), *sag* (spinach), *mattar* (peas), or *aloo* (potato). Even the essential dhal has added cream, and breads are sometimes stuffed. So it is essential to have plenty of rice to balance the meal— and to wait until your body is acclimatized before enjoying this kind of feast. Should you wish for some wine with such a meal, India now has vineyards up on the Deccan Plateau. Otherwise, do as the Indians do: Stick to the light local beers and bottled water.

Along the coast, you can relax in the shade over grilled giant shrimp or a pomfret fish cooked with plenty of coconut, which helps to balance the fire-hot spices. As the sun sets in Goa, you might like a glass of *feni*—or a fruit juice, such as mango, papaya, or watermelon. Other thirst-quenching drinks found all over India are *lassi* (thin yogurt drink) and fresh lime juice with either sparkling or still water. The ubiquitous *chai* (tea) is drunk strong with milk and sugar, a surprisingly reviving drink.

Vegetables are popular throughout the country, but it is in the mostly vegetarian south that the vegetable is the star. The best way to sample the variety is to order a *thali* (platter). This circular plate has six or more *katoris* (little dishes) around the edge, each containing a different vegetable or pulse. There will also be *dahi* (yogurt), chutney, and *mighai* (sweet pudding). Start with the *rasam* (clear soup) and work round, mixing boiled rice from the center of the platter into each dish. A thali is utterly delicious, healthy, and always a little bit different to the last one. ∎

In Old Delhi's spice market, you can buy dried chilis, powdered turmeric, cinnamon bark, and other aromatic products.

History & culture

INDIA'S HISTORY STRETCHES BACK SEVERAL MILLENNIA, THROUGH THE RISE and fall of warring states and empires, invasions and conquests. Foreign rulers have pillaged, destroyed, and rebuilt, while rival religions, imported and homegrown, have clashed and merged. Traders from over the mountains and seas have brought their own languages and cultures. But India always remains and retains its uniqueness.

PREHISTORY TO THE CLASSICAL AGE

The subcontinent abounds in uncharted archaeological remains and, therefore, much archaeological activity. The result is that scholars are still reassessing India's early history. The most spectacular group of inhabited rock shelters yet found are the thousand or so strung along a ridge at Bhimbetka (see p. 115), near Bhopal. Half of them are decorated with paintings. Discovered only in 1957, no exact date can be given for these paintings, but estimates of their age range from 10,000 to 40,000 years. Vestiges of human life on the subcontinent go back some 400,000 years. Crudely sharpened stones dating from the period of the Himalayan glaciations (Pleistocene) have been found in India. Stone hammers from the Upper Paleolithic (up to 30,000 years ago) have been found at Pushkar, in Rajasthan, where quartz, agate, and carnelian have been used and arrowheads carved to a beauty and precision far beyond their practical demands.

During these early times, the Upper Paleolithic and Mesolithic periods, early settlements displayed evidence of various lifestyles—fishing, hunting, gathering, simple agriculture and husbandry, and organized trading. Paintings from this era show foreign visitors, and activities such as dancing, hunting, and ambushing. In the Indus Valley, barley and wheat were cultivated; sheep and goats were domesticated; and by 5000 B.C. the familiar humped Indian cattle were the most common domesticated animals. The potter's wheel appeared around 3500 B.C., ushering in mass production, as did grain storehouses built of mud bricks, which are evidence of large, organized communities. Major excavation sites include Banavali and Mitathal (Haryana) and Surkotada (Kachchh). Meanwhile, the Ganga plains reveal evidence of similar but independent developments.

Indus Valley Civilization

Within this widespread cultural network, with its increased use of the floodplains for more productive farming, arose the urbanized Indus Valley Civilization, also known as the Mature Harappan culture, which peaked around 2500 B.C. Its best known cities, Moenjodaro and Harappa, are in Pakistan, but India's sites include fascinating Lothal port (see p. 152) and the spectacular fortress city of Dholavira, both in Gujarat, and Kalibangan in Rajasthan.

These and other cities of this sophisticated civilization were much advanced in comparison with earlier ones. They usually had a clear city plan focused on a high mound, probably a religious-political center. There were special areas for craftspeople, housing for the wealthy, and workers' accommodations. There were large granaries, efficient water and drainage systems, and evidence of international trading.

This intriguing, unified social and political organization extended over present-day Pakistan and much of northern India. Yet two mysteries about the culture remain. Its tantalizing stone seals have not yet been deciphered, and the cause of its final decline around 1700 B.C. is in question. Was it invasion, famine, over-farming, or something else? Whatever the answer, much of the culture was passed down to later Indian society.

Vedic Age: 1500–1000 B.C.

During this period, the Hindu religion and a specific social order known as the caste system (see p. 29) began to be formed—two powerful, cohesive forces that would endure as empires rose and fell over the next 3,000 years.

The gradual migration of Aryan tribes from the Iranian plateau over the mountains

The riotous carvings on the soaring roofs and gateways of Hindu temples can be enjoyed by the faithful outside.

into northern India began between 1500 and 1300 B.C. These seminomadic tribes were pastoralists who formed simple, settled farming village communities quite different from the sophisticated Harappan cities. Each had a warrior chief, called a *raja*, who received tribute in return for being the villagers' protector. Cattle were the main form of wealth, and thus a main reason for war.

The raja's status was confirmed by his priests, called *brahmans,* who compiled the great hymns and verses in Vedic Sanskrit, at first handed down orally but later written down; the *Rig Veda* is the best known. These and other texts, such as the *Upanishads,* the epic *Mahabharata,* and the *Puranas* tell us about Vedic history, life, and thought; the abstract doctrine of *karma* has its roots in Vedic philosophy. The Vedic religion centered on the worship of personified forces of nature and abstract divinities. It emphasized ritual, sacrifice, chanting of hymns, and the

importance of the priest as mediator, and it became the basis of what is known as Hinduism (see pp. 54–57).

As tribal identity became territorial, so royal power was symbolized with coronation and sacrifice, the old tribute became a tax, and trade and agriculture flourished.

Most important of all, a new social order of caste hierarchy emerged, the *varna*. Varna means color, and at first the distinction was between the pale Aryan immigrants and

A group of men sing and dance to celebrate Holi, the arrival of spring, in Jodhpur, western Rajasthan.

darker non-Aryan people of India. The Aryans were divided into priests and teachers *(brahmans)*, warriors and rulers *(kshatriyas)*, and merchants and cultivators *(vaishyas)*, while the non-Aryans and other economically low groups formed the *shudras,* whose purpose was to serve the three superior castes. Ritual

While the caste system officially no longer exists today, it is still exceptional that K. Ramaswamy, born an untouchable, could rise to become a justice of India's Supreme Court.

status and subcastes called *jatis* soon evolved, as did the idea of purity of caste and its opposing pollution. This brought two results: strict caste rules pervading social life, and a fifth caste, the untouchables, whose occupations were considered impure. Mahatma Gandhi later attempted to give these people status by renaming them *harijans* (children of God).

Gradually, Aryan and non-Aryan cultures fused in northern India, creating an Indo-Aryan society whose language groups are the roots of 74 percent of the Indian population today; they include Hindi, Punjabi, Rajasthani, and Bengali. Meanwhile, in southern India, the Dravidian culture remained isolated from Aryan culture, as reflected in its main languages, which predate Indo-Aryan ones: Telegu, Tamil, Kannada, and Malayalam. India never had a common language, but Sanskrit, the most highly developed Indo-Aryan language, remained the language of the educated people until English usurped it during the Raj and became the lingua franca, still used.

Early empires, new faiths
In all, India was unified by its trade routes and by its traders, who enjoyed unprecedented status, patronized the arts, and encouraged the growth of towns. By about 600 B.C., trading had stimulated the rise of port towns (called *puras)* along the rivers, such as Varanasi and Vaishali, marking the start of India's second widespread urbanization, this time in the Ganga Valley.

Economic developments followed, including a common script, coinage, and banking. Meanwhile, invasions from the northwest by the Persian Achaemenid emperor Cyrus in 530 B.C. created a Persian cultural and trading bridge. In this post-Vedic world of republics, monarchies, and powerful traders, the strictures of Vedic Hinduism came into question, and two princes of northern India founded Buddhism and Jainism, instantly successful back-to-basics religions whose practicality and equality appealed especially to the increasingly powerful trading castes.

The kingdom that eventually emerged preeminent was Magadha, whose rulers Bimbisara (543–491 B.C.) and Ajatashatru (491–461 B.C.) founded Rajagriha (Rajgir, near Patna), then Pataliputra (Patna). By the late fourth century, however, the kingdom was in trouble, embroiled in a dispute over succession. The decline of the Magadhan kingdom coincided with the arrival of the Greek general

The magnificent eastern gate of Sanchi's great stupa, carved in the first century B.C., testifies to the attraction of Buddhism for wealthy traders trapped in the Hindu caste system.

Alexander the Great, who invaded the Punjab in 327 B.C. He left garrisons and governors behind when he departed two years later, but his death in 323 B.C. rendered the fledgling Greek province dangerously unstable.

Astute strategist Chandragupta Maurya, who had taken over the weakened Magadhan throne in 321 B.C., threw the Greeks out in 305 B.C.: The powerful Mauryan empire (321–185 B.C.) was born. This, the first of India's many great empires, stretched from Assam to Afghanistan, from Kashmir to Mysore. Its legendary capital was at Pataliputra (Patna). Chandragupta, a Jain, abdicated to join a Jain community in southern India and died by *sallekhana* (slow starvation). His grandson was the greatest Mauryan ruler, Ashoka (R.269–232 B.C.). Ashoka converted to Buddhism and promoted its concept of *dharma*—social responsibility to maintain human dignity and socio-religious harmony. Buddhist edicts on social values and behavior were engraved onto rocks and columns across his empire, usually using Brahmi script and the Pankrit language.

The Shungas and Kanvas succeeded the Mauryas before the focus moved to the northwest. Here the Bactrian Greeks invaded from Afghanistan in 190 B.C. and ruled Gandhara (in modern Pakistan); at its peak their kingdom stretched to Mathura, south of Delhi, only to be supplanted by the Scythians in the first century B.C. and then the Parthians, both central Asian tribes.

India's second important kingdom was the Kushana, which flourished from the first century B.C. to the third century A.D. Its borders encompassed central Asia and northern India, stretching to Varanasi and Vaishali (near Bhopal); its capitals were at Peshawar (now in Pakistan) and Mathura. Under its greatest ruler, the Buddhist convert Kanishka (R.100–120 A.D.), sculpture and other arts flourished, heavily influenced by the Hellenistic art of the Roman Empire. At this time the impressive Buddhist monastery and *stupas* at Sanchi (see p. 116) were built, financed by the traders of nearby Vaishali.

Meanwhile, among the kingdoms of the Deccan (now made up of the states of Karnataka and Andhra Pradesh), the Satavahanas rose in the first century B.C. to enjoy four centuries of preeminence. They maintained a careful mix of Vedic principles, Mauryan political philosophy, and tolerance toward the powerful Buddhist traders. Their

India timeline

B.C.

ca 2,500 Probable peak of Indus Valley Civilization.

327 Alexander the Great of Greece invades.

ca 269–232 Ashoka rules Mauryan empire

190 Greeks from Bactria invade.

A.D.

ca 100–120 Kanishka rules Kushana empire.

ca 335–415 Chandragupta II rules Gupta empire.

ca 600–630 Mahendravarman I rules Pallava empire in southern India.

8th century on Rajputs rise to power in northern India.

805–1278 Chola Empire dominates Tamil Nadu.

1192 Qutb-ud-din-Aibak takes Delhi; in 1206 establishes Slave Sultanate, India's first Muslim kingdom.

1206–1596 The Delhi sultanates: Slave, Khilji, Tughlaq, Sayyid, and Lodi.

1398 Timur (Tamburlaine) sacks Delhi.

1336–1565 Vijayanaga Empire unites southern India.

1509 Alfonso de Alburquerque takes Goa, makes it capital of Portugal's maritime empire.

1526 Babur invades, takes Agra, initiates Mogul empire, crushes Rajput confederacy the next year.

1527–1707 Height of Mogul empire under Emperors Babur, Akbar, Jahangir, Shah Jahan, and Aurangzeb.

1562 Akbar's first Rajput alliance, with Amer (Jaipur).

1616 on Sir Thomas Roe wins trading rights from Jahangir; Portuguese power begins to wane and English power to rise under the East India Company.

1631 Mumtaz Mahal dies and Shah Jahan will build the Taj Mahal as her mausoleum.

1639 Madras founded as English trading headquarters.

1648 Shah Jahan brings the Mughal capital back to Delhi.

1772 British administrative capital moves from Madras to Calcutta.

1799 Arthur Wellesley defeats Tipu Sultan of Mysore; Ranjit Singh takes Lahore and establishes the first Sikh kingdom.

1815–1947 The British government leaves Calcutta for Shimla hill station for six months each year.

1840–1914 India is Britain's most important trading partner.

1857–58 Rebellion against the British at Delhi, Lucknow, and Kanpur. Delhi retaken; Bahadur Shah II deposed, ending Mogul Empire. British power, known as the Raj, is now direct from Westminster.

1869 Suez Canal opens.

1885 National Congress founded, to fight for India's freedom.

1906 All India Muslim League founded, to safeguard Indian Muslims' interests.

1911 King-Emperor George V announces British capital to move to Delhi.

1915 Gandhi returns from South Africa to fight for India's freedom.

1930 Gandhi leads the Salt March protesting against the British salt tax.

1931 Lutyens garden city of New Delhi inaugurated.

1947 Independence for India; East and West Pakistan created.

1950 Republic of India inaugurated. Constitution adopted. Jawaharlal Nehru is India's first prime minister. Gandhi assassinated.

1966–77, 1980–84 Indira Gandhi prime minister.

1971 East Pakistan becomes Bangladesh.

1991–96 Narasimha Rao prime minister; major drive to open India to world market forces.

2001 India's population hits one billion.

2004 Dr. Manmohan Singh becomes prime minister; India's economic upsurge continues

patronage is evident in the rock-cut temples of Karla (see pp. 183-84) and Kanheri (see pp. 170–71), both on trade routes to the Konkan ports.

Farther south, the Chola, Chera, and Pandya chiefs were supreme. Their body of literature, called the *Sangam,* reveals a mainly non-Aryan society whose peasant communities developed ports that thrived. Until the fall of the Roman Empire, trade was brisk in jewels, ivory, fragrant woods, perfumes, and spices, the last an essential part of European culture. When the Visigoth Alaric sacked Rome in A.D. 410, his ransom was 3,000 pounds of Indian pepper, not gold. A Roman cohort was maintained at Calicut on the Malabar coast, and coins, pottery, and other objects testify to foreign trading communities in the coastal ports and at the commercial city of Madurai.

Chola period bronze of Shiva Nataraja

CLASSICAL AGE: 300–650

India's classical age was dominated by the Gupta dynasty (circa 319–circa 467) in northern India, while the Gangas were powerful in Orissa, the Kadambas in the Deccan, and the Pallavas (fourth to seventh centuries) in the deep south.

Chandragupta I (*R.*319–335) brought the Guptas to power, widening his empire's boundaries to the Indus in the west and the Bay of Bengal in the east. His principal cities were on the Ganga at Ayodhya and Allahabad. Their influence stretched southward to the Pallavas' territory around Kanchipuram. Thus, they dominated trade from coast to coast as well as to central Asia and to the old Silk Route between China and Bactria (Afghanistan).

Gupta rulers performed Vedic sacrifices (which sometimes involved animals) to legitimize their rule. They patronized the brahmans and senior courtiers by giving them land

grants and privileges, and they supported Buddhism. During this period, essential elements of Hinduism emerged, such as *bhakti* (see p. 56) and image-worship. So, too, did the importance of the Mother Goddess, the temple as the center of social and religious life, and Vishnu and Shiva, whose complex myths and legends were written in the Purana texts.

Under the Gupta patronage of art and literature, especially under Chandragupta II (*R.*335–415), a new classical style emerged that became the aesthetic yardstick for subsequent artists and craftsmen. Sanskrit poetry reached its apogee in the works of Kalidasa, which include *Raghuvamsa* and *Kumarasambhava.*

Sculpture reached new heights of technique, spirituality, and three-dimensional expression. Architecture witnessed the formative phases of the Nagara and Dravida (see p. 262) temple styles. Coins had fine designs, and the paintings of Ajanta (see pp. 178–79) and Bhaja (see p. 184) influenced Buddhist art across Asia. Formal principles that were followed for centuries were laid down in treatises: Vastu for architecture, Shilpa for sculpture, and Chitra for painting. The 18th-century architect Vidyadhar Bhattacharya looked to these when he was planning Jaipur city (see pp. 131–32).

India was already at the forefront of studies in subjects such as astronomy and medicine. Now, under the Guptas, Aryabhata and Varahamihira pushed the study of astronomy further, while new ideas in mathematics, the cipher, and numerals were exported via the Arabs to Europe. Legal texts abounded, and covered every subject, from social problems to property rights. An almost humanist interest in the ideal citizen preoccupied the philosopher-writers of the time, and Vatsyayana wrote the sophisticated treatise on the art of love, the *Kamasutra.* Only when waves of Huns, then Gurjara, had succeeded in disrupting trade,

did Gupta power wane. Some of these invaders were ancestors of the Rajput clans of Rajasthan (see p. 37).

Down in southern India, most kingdoms of this period followed the Vedic rituals. Kingdoms usually concentrated their worship on either Shiva or Vishnu, and promoted royal-religious power in the Gupta style by giving land grants to both priests and temples. At this time that the temple became the central element in the government of what was an agrarian community, where rice was both the main crop and the standard bartering unit.

Temple architecture blossomed under the early Pallava rulers, who believed they were descended from Brahma. Much of their work survives at their capital, Kanchipuram, and their port, Mamallapuram (Mahabalipuram). Mahendravarman I (R. 600–630), was a

dramatist and poet who converted from Jainism to Shaivism (the worship of Shiva), and under his patronage architecture, literature, and the applied arts began to acquire their distinct Dravidian character.

The Pallavas' arch enemies were the Chalukyas, who ruled in the Deccan, first from Aihole and later from Badami. During the post-Gupta disruptions in the north, Harsha Vadhana eventually lost his kingdom to the Chalukya king Pulakeshin II.

A classical Indian culture developed from the collective achievement of the many remarkable individuals of this period. Its wide scope of learning pushed knowledge forward in a range of subjects, from the development of Sanskrit to the concept of a god-king, from Buddhist philosophy to the *Ramayana* stories. Traders carried this sophisticated culture into

the east, where it profoundly influenced the other cultures that it came into contact with.

FROM THE CLASSICAL AGE TO ISLAM'S ARRIVAL: 650–1206

Post-Gupta northern India saw the growth of regional states, while southern India rose to a new prominence. Here, artistic innovation flourished, as seen in the vigorous sculptures of Elephanta and Ajanta and in the creation of monumental stone temples such as those at Thanjavur, Chidambaram, and Gangakondacholapuram. These temples became a focus for all the arts, especially sculpture, bronze-casting, dance, music, and painting. Patronized by rulers, they played a vital role in endorsing royal power.

During these centuries, autonomous village government was established; it is still

These elephants are part of a huge, lively, and complex relief sculpture cut into the rock at Mahabalipuram.

strong today. Indian merchants' guilds specializing in textiles, gems, and spices expanded to trade with the Jewish, Arab, and Chinese peoples. Sanskrit was the language of officials and high literature. As Buddhism and Jainism waned, Hinduism absorbed local cults to acquire regional characteristics.

In the north, the Ganga Valley and its main city, Kanauj, were under the control of first, the Pratiharas; then, the Palas; and finally the Rashtrakutas, the first Deccan dynasty to reach this area. To the east, the Somavamshis established their capital at Bhubaneshwar, whose fine temples survive.

In the Deccan and far south, wars were

Seated Buddhas, painted in the fifth century with tremendous virtuosity, are just a fragment of the many vibrant, naturalistic frescoes that coat several caves at Ajanta.

fought over the fertile valleys and lucrative trade routes, but in peacetime fine temples were built. The Chalukyas built theirs at Aihole, Pattadakal, and Badami, while the later Hoysalas left intricately carved temples in and around their capital, Halebid.

Farther south, the Pallava rulers, still at loggerheads with the Chalukyas, continued to build temples at their port of Mahabalipuram and their capital, Kanchipuram, one of the seven sacred cities for Hindus, and southern India's largest international textile center. They enjoyed lucrative maritime trade with Sri Lanka, Arabia, and southeast Asia.

In the mid-ninth century, the Cholas (850–1278), longtime chieftains in the area, created the most powerful southern state. Their greatest rulers—Rajaraja I *(R.* 984–1014), Rajendra *(R.* 1014–44), and Kulottunga I *(R.* 1070–1118)—expanded their territories to cover Tamil Nadu, southern Karnataka, southern Kerala, and northern Sri Lanka. From their principal port, Nagappattinam, at the mouth of the Kaveri River, Chola trading extended to China.

Back in the north, Rajput clans were rising to power. These immigrant clans acquired kshatriya (see p. 29) status in the caste system

and traced their lineage to the sun and moon. Some called themselves *Agni-kulu* (Fire Family) and claimed descent from a mythical figure that arose out of a vast sacrificial pit near Mount Abu. These clans included the Kachwahas (Jaipur) and Sisodias (Udaipur) of Rajasthan, as well as the Chandellas (Khajuraho) and the Tomars who founded Delhi around 736. They warred constantly. It was the great Chauhan hero Prithviraj III who took the Tomars' Delhi and managed to fight off an early Islamic invader, Mohammad of Ghor, in 1191.

But even Prithviraj could not stop Islam from taking hold. Arab Muhammad bin Qasim arrived in 711, by sea from Baghdad at a point east of Karachi. Mahmud of Ghazni, a Turk, made repeated raids between 1000 and 1026, his men crossing the Hindu Kush to plunder the northern plains and their rich temples; the Nagda temples near Udaipur are rare survivors (see p. 138). Then, in 1192, the Turkish invader Mohammad of Ghor's slave general, Qutb-ud-din-Aibak, defeated Prithviraj III and took Delhi. When Mohammad of Ghor was assassinated in Lahore in 1206, Aibak assumed control, made Delhi the capital of India's first, if unstable,

A sixth-century triple-headed carving of Shiva in the Elephanta Island cave temple dedicated to Shiva. The right head is feminine while that on the left is fiercely masculine.

Muslim kingdom, and initiated the Delhi Sultanate that would be succeeded by the Mughals. Islam, not Hinduism, would now be the dominant political, social, and cultural force in northern India for six centuries. The capitals, Delhi and for a while Agra, saw the creation of a rich Indo-Islamic culture, much of which survives today in palaces, tombs, cuisine, inlaid marble, and in music and other arts.

THE DELHI SULTANATE: 1206–1526

Until Aibak's own lieutenant, Iltutmish, seized power in 1211, Delhi locals might have been expecting the Islamic presence to be temporary. Iltutmish, however, ruled for 25 years. He consolidated his empire, and his Slave dynasty (he was a Mamluk, a Turkish "slave") (1206–90) was the first of five successive sultanates to rule Delhi. There followed the Khiljis (1290–1320), Tughlaqs (1320–1413), Sayyids (1414–51), and Lodis (1451–1526).

Iltutmish benefited from dramatic events in Central Asia: Ghengis Khan and the Mongols swept through between 1219 and 1222, removing threats to India and ensuring that Muslim India would carve its own history. The Slave usurper was able to annex Sind and Bengal, and his men (known as *mamluks*)

provided the military leadership, provincial governors, and officers of court—a pattern that would be repeated in subsequent dynasties. His richly carved but surprisingly modest-size tomb still stands behind the mosque at Lal Kot.

The Mongols made repeated raids into northern India in the 13th and 14th centuries. Meanwhile, Delhi became the chosen refuge from the central Asian hotbed for many immigrant nobles, bureaucrats, and adventurers. One of these groups, the Turkish Khiljis, succeeded the Slave sultans. Their popular and capable ruler Ala-ud-din-Khilji (R.1296–1315) survived a Mongol siege in 1303, conquered wealthy Gujarat, took the great Rajput forts of Ranthambore and Chittaurgarh, and pushed his empire far southward to Daulatabad, near Aurangabad. His Delhi city, known as Siri, had a great reservoir and a fine university.

Having overstretched themselves, the Khiljis lost out to Ghiyas-ud-din-Tughlaq, a Turko-Mongol. His successor, Muhammad (R.1324–1351), was the most colorful and controversial sultan of all, a mixture of extreme generosity and brutality. He strengthened the Muslim administration by inviting Muslim immigrants to Delhi. One was a

Moroccan, Ibn Battuta, who wrote a detailed account of 14th-century India. Muhammad then moved the capital from Delhi to Daulatabad in 1327 to encourage Muslim colonization of the south, only to relocate back to Delhi in around 1330 to maintain power in the north.

Muhammad's huge empire began to crack. Bengal became an independent sultanate (1335), as did Kashmir (1346) and the Deccan (1347), which went to the Bahmani sultans. Muhammad's impressive successor was the enlightened Feroz Shah Tughlaq (R.1351–1388), whose Delhi was renowned for its beauty, refinement, and intellectual life. Feroz Shah chose to be buried in a fortlike tomb beside Ala-ud-din-Khilji's reservoir. After his death, the empire's disintegration sped up. The Asian conqueror Timur (Tamburlaine) sacked Delhi in 1398. In northern and central India, Jaunpur (1400), Malwa (1406), and Gujarat (1407) went independent, while the Rajput states of Marwar and Mewar emerged.

In the Deccan, the Bahmani state gradually broke up to form five competing sultanates: Gulbarga, Ahmednagar, Bidar, Bijapur, and finally Golconda. South of them lay the bulwark of the last great Hindu power of southern India, the Vijayanaga, which peaked under the rule of Krishnadevaraya (R.1509–1530). By uniting all smaller southern Hindu states, the Vijayanaga Empire (1336–1565) could remain powerful until four of the five sultanates, usually competing against each other, united. At the Battle of Talikota in 1565, the Vijayanaga forces were roundly defeated.

Thus, the territory ruled by Delhi's last two sultanates, the Sayyids and the Lodis, was reduced to just one of many Muslim states in India. In each, power lay with a minority of Muslims and was dependent upon raising land taxes and controlling trade routes and ports. There was relatively little conversion of the local, mostly Hindu, people. At the various courts, with their cosmopolitan mixtures of Muslims and Hindus, the rich Indo-Muslim cultures evolved. You can trace these in surviv-

Hindu and Mughal styles blend in Jai Singh's refined 17th-century additions to Amer Fort, outside Jaipur.

ing buildings, sculptures, and metalwork in the Islamic remains of Delhi, Ahmadabad, Bijapur, Bidar, and a number of other medieval Muslim cities.

In 1502 Sikander Lodi left Delhi, moving his power base 122 miles (196 km) south to Agra. The once legendary capital became nothing but a necropolis surrounding the village of Nizamuddin, where the *durgarh* (shrine) of the Sufi saint Shaikh Nizam-ud-din Chishti (1236–1325) was maintained by the faithful. His royal devotees had included Muhammad and Feroz Shah Tughlaq, and would number several Mughal emperors.

MUGHAL EMPIRE'S GREAT AGE: 1526–1707

Into this fragmented India, Babur, a Burlas Turk, arrived in 1526. He had failed three times in his great ambition to take the Timurid city of Samarkand. Now he looked beyond the Hindu Kush to India's wealth, encouraged by the invitation of disgruntled Afghan chiefs governing Ibrahim Lodi's Punjab territories. Victory over Ibrahim Lodi at Panipat was easy. But when the Rajput clans joined forces under the Sisodia ruler Rana Sanga of Mewar—the only time the quarrelsome Rajputs united under one flag—Babur faced a far greater test. To encourage his men, Babur promised unconquered territories to his own nobles, declared *jihad* (holy war in the name of sacred duty) on the Rajputs, renounced wine, and took a vow to fight to the death. Then, mustering his immense leadership skills and the superior war tactics of Central Asia, Babur crushed the Rajputs in March 1527.

The Mughals had arrived, and they would stay to become the greatest and the last of India's Islamic empires (1526–1858). The first six emperors, known as the Great Mughals (1526–1707), ruled from father to son: Babur, Humayun, Akbar, Jahangir, Shah Jahan, and Aurangzeb. All were great leaders, politicians, and soldiers. All were scholars and highly cultured; all were prone to weaknesses, such as alcohol, opium, or plain superstition; and all oscillated between religious tolerance and orthodoxy. Their diaries, disarmingly frank, reveal their relationship with India (Babur praised peacock meat but missed Persian gardens), their weaknesses (Jahangir has his drinking problem noted glass by glass), and the later stultifying court life (seen in Shah Jahan's opulent Padshahnameh manuscript).

Babur (R.1526–1530) celebrated his triumph with an international gathering and huge feast at Agra. But it was short-lived. After he had defeated a joint force of Afghans and Bengalis near Varanasi in 1529, his health failed. He returned to Agra, and then to Lahore, where he died in December 1530.

Humayun (R.1530–1540, deposed, then 1555–56) inherited an as yet unstable empire and made the decision to move the capital back to Delhi. This gifted soldier matched great his victories with equally great parties and indulgences, a combination which allowed the already superior military and political skills of Sher Shah Sur, the Afghan leader in eastern India, to flourish. Lacking his father's charisma, Humayun lost his supporters, was deposed in 1540, and fled westward across Rajasthan and up to Shah Tahmasp's Persian court.

The brief rule of Sher Shah Sur (R.1540–45), whose handsome tomb lies east of Varanasi, was important for the future of the Mughals. Not only did he develop a strong central army but he also built roads and large travelers' lodgings, including the Grand Trunk Road that stretched from Kabul through Lahore and Delhi eventually to Kolkata. Sher Shah Sur also standardized weights and measures, regularized trade tariffs, and, maybe most important of all, created a tax revenue system that would be the blueprint for the next Mughal emperor, Akbar.

In the chaos that followed the death of Sher Shah Sur's son, Islam Shah (R.1545–1553), Humayun retook his throne in 1555, only to die in Delhi the following year. His teenage son, quickly brought to Delhi from the Punjab, would prove to be the successor to Sher Shah Sur's legacy.

The 14-year-old Akbar (R.1556–1605) first reconquered the Mughal empire, then expanded and consolidated it. Under the guidance of his regent, the able Bairam Khan, he retook most of central India and the Rajput states, including the great forts of Chittaurgarh and Ranthambore in 1567–68. These conquests he cemented with marriage alliances and employment in the Mughal army for the conquered

people. In 1562, on his way to Ajmer, where a revered Sufi saint lay buried, Akbar met with Raja Bihar Mal of Amer (Jaipur's old capital). Akbar agreed to marry Bihar Mal's daughter and take his adopted grandson Man Singh into Mughal service—providing the basis of Jaipur's wealth. Only Mewar, under Rana Pratap and Amar Singh, refused to bow down to Mughal power.

With this stability and his new fort (1567–1575) underway, in 1571 Akbar began to create Fatehpur Sikri, a palace-city emulating the Timurid courts. It was from here that, in 1573, he left to conquer Gujarat, a rich land on the Muslim pilgrimage route to Mecca. To celebrate his victory, he built the Buland Darwaza, the great gate of Fatehpur Sikri's mosque. By 1576 Akbar had completed his victories in eastern India, and in the 1580s and 1590s he extended his empire to the trading cities of Kabul and Qandahar, and to the provinces of Ghazna, Kashmir, Orissa, and Bengal, and to all the land down to the Godavari River.

Akbar now ruled over a large, centralized state defended by nobles of various ethnic and religious groups—Rajputs, Persians, Indians, Muslims, and others. He was a strong, non-sectarian ruler, a soldier and statesman, an art patron, and a liberal philosopher, all of which he used to strengthen his position as emperor.

The administrative framework created during Akbar's rule sustained the empire until the 18th century. It managed to keep the peasantry and nobility happy while filling the state coffers. Akbar was careful to keep close to the ruling Rajput clans and to display religious tolerance. He had Hindu advisers and kept discussions going with the resentful but powerful Muslim orthodoxy in the form of the ulama (learned men). Akbar's liberal views, which annoyed them, led him to lift the jizya (poll tax) on non-Muslims and to welcome the Portuguese missionary Father Monserrat for discussions at Fatehpur Sikri. His ideas on kingship, though, led him to initiate the Mughal tradition of the emperor showing himself to his people at sunrise, thus increasing his power by identifying himself with the ultimate source of energy and endowing himself with supernatural divinity.

From within this prevailing atmosphere of tolerance, India's last great new religion began to emerge. This was Sikhism (see p. 59), whose ten Gurus (teachers) span the 16th and 17th centuries. Their ideas were eventually formalized in 1699.

Akbar's son Salim, born to his Hindu wife from Amer, ascended the throne as Jahangir, or Siezer of the World (R.1605–1627). He was then 36 years old. At a personal level, his intense interest in painting, science, and coins lifted the Mughal court to new cultural heights, but it was matched by a life-long addiction to alcohol and opium. At a political and military level, he ended Mughal–Mewar conflict, expanded the empire into the Himalayan mountains and Kachchh, consolidated control of Bengal and Orissa, and campaigned down in the Deccan.

Ghiyas Beg, a Persian adventurer who had entered Akbar's court, became chief minister, or Itimad-ud-Daulah (Pillar of Government) on Jahangir's accession. His clever, ambitious daughter married Jahangir in 1611 and was soon given the title Nur Jahan (Light of the World). She effectively ruled from behind the veil, even riding into battle carried in a litter slung between two elephants. Her daughter by an earlier marriage was married off to Jahangir's eldest son and heir, Khusrau. Meanwhile, Ghiyas Beg's equally clever and ambitious son, Asaf Khan, had become deputy prime minister and in 1612 gave his daughter, Arjumand Banu, in marriage to Jahangir's third son, Khurram. The couple later rebelled against the emperor and sought refuge at the stoically anti-Mughal Mewar court at Udaipur. When Jahangir's cocktail of drink, drugs, and asthma finally killed him, Asaf Khan triumphed over his sister in the political fallout: Khurram became the next emperor, under the name Shah Jahan (Ruler of the World), and his wife took the title Mumtaz Mahal (Chosen One of the Palace).

For most of the rule of Shah Jahan (R.1627–1658), political and economic stability were sustained throughout the ever expanding empire. The emperor and his vast army, which grew fourfold during his reign, secured Muslim territories in the Deccan, southern Hindu kingdoms, the eastern Assam border, and the northwest frontier to Kabul. Large, cosmopolitan cities emerged—Lahore, Agra, Ahmedabad—whose citizens traded with Asians and newly arrived Europeans, and were the patrons of sophisticated crafts and grand architecture. Meanwhile, land revenue from the now enormous empire sustained the the parasite Mughal nobles and the army; however, dependence on this income would eventually cause the breakup of the empire.

Emperor Akbar passes the crown from his son Jahangir to his grandson Shah Jahan, an image that reinforces Mughal legitimacy.

Shah Jahan's increasingly rich, ostentatious, and unwieldy Mughal court, weighed down with ritual and sheer size, no longer moved from place to place. When not on campaign, Shah Jahan revealed the extent of his grandfather Akbar's devoted attention to his education. At Lahore and Agra he and Mumtaz rebuilt the sandstone royal rooms and state audience halls in marble, showing a new refinement in their proportions and decorating them with floral patterns of semi-precious stone inlay, called *pietra dura* (meaning "hard stone" in Italian).

In June 1631 Mumtaz died giving birth to

their 14th child at Burhampur in the Deccan, while on campaign with her husband. It was a watershed for Shah Jahan and his empire. With his rock gone, he first mourned for two years, giving up music, fine clothes, and celebrations. Then, ill-advisedly putting his campaigns into the hands of his four sons, he threw himself into ambitious building projects. At a personal level, he mixed rigorous orthodoxy with unashamed debauchery. The jizya tax was reinstated on non-Muslims, conversion was encouraged, and building of Hindu temples discouraged.

While Shah Jahan launched into building the Taj Mahal as the mausoleum for Mumtaz, he also began the marble Pearl Mosque in Agra Fort and promoted the building of mosques across his empire. He also laid out an entire new city at the traditional capital, Delhi, calling it Shahjahanabad, today's Old Delhi. The world's grandest emperor and his court moved there in 1648. Today, the palace is forgotten but the walled city outside it buzzes with life, and the great Jama Masjid is the most important mosque for India's Muslim community.

Shah Jahan's sons, meanwhile, watched for their chance. It came in 1657, when the emperor became ill. In Mughal tradition, the sons began plotting and competing for the throne. After a series of false alliances, tricks, and murders, the third son, Aurangzeb, won.

The long rule of Aurangzeb (R.1658–1707) saw the empire stretch to its farthest limit and begin its collapse. Campaigns to keep the northwest and the Rajput princes in line led Aurangzeb unwisely to take control of Jodhpur and later demolish its temples. The result was his loss of all Rajput allies; not one Rajput chief fought for the Mughals in the later Sikh war.

Aurangzeb then turned his attention south. In 1681 he left Delhi for good. His ambition was to control all of peninsular India and to convert its people to Islam. He had already faced the newly strong Marathas of the Deccan, under their hero leader Shivaji (see p. 180). Jai Singh II, the Jaipur ruler who commanded a large Mughal force, captured Shivaji in 1666, but he escaped from Agra and later became king (1674–1680) of his followers. The Marathas would continue to wield their power and, in the 18th century, expand from their base in Pune right across southern India.

Aurangzeb's relentless campaigns, which in some years he unwisely continued through the monsoon, brought depression and illness to his soldiers. Eventually he nominally won almost the whole peninsula, but few of his gains were consolidated. Aurangzeb further weakened his position by doggedly reinforcing his orthodoxy. He called his campaigns jihad, enforced the jizya tax, and replaced Hindu administrators with Muslims.

Aurangzeb, the last of the six Great Mughals died devoutly and quietly in the Deccan. Unlike his predecessors, with their lavish and magnificent tombs at Delhi, Agra, and Lahore, Aurangzeb followed the Koran's demand for simplicity. His unadorned white stone slab lies in the precincts of a modest mosque at Khuldabad, near Aurangabad.

EUROPEAN TRADERS ARRIVE: 1498–1858

While Delhi lost its control and whole tracts of the Mughal Empire became independent, from Bengal and Avadh in the north to Bijapur and Golconda in the south, Hindu rulers and landowners asserted their power. The Jats were able to raid Agra for some of its marble inlay to decorate their palace at Deeg; the Marathas took the wealthy central kingdom of Malwa and started menacing the Rajputs. The Persian despot Nadir Shah had little trouble sacking Delhi of her wealth in 1739. The Afghans sacked Delhi again in 1757. In the power vacuum, new centers of Mughal power emerged: Murshidabad in Bengal, Lucknow in Avadh, east of Delhi, and Hyderabad in the Deccan.

Into this complex readjusting of boundaries and centers of power, with its attendant conflicts, came the European traders.

Trade with the West was not new. In 327 B.C. Alexander the Great's expedition had opened up social and trading links over the mountains. The Romans traded by land and sea, as did Arab and Jewish groups, who settled along the west coast.

The dramatic increase in European trade in the 16th century was stimulated by the desire to break the monopoly of the eastern trade

The Taj Mahal is the tomb of Shah Jahan's wife, Mumtaz Mahal, and a symbol of Mughal power and the might of Islam.

held by Venice and the Levantine. The solution was to bypass Venice, using sea routes around Africa. The Portuguese led the way, spurred on by Prince Henry the Navigator and the Catholic Church's missionary zeal. In 1498 Vasco da Gama (1469–1524) rounded the Cape of Good Hope and sailed across the Indian Ocean to land at Calicut, in Kerala, where Christianity had been flourishing since St. Thomas the Apostle's arrival in A.D. 52.

The second Portuguese expedition arrived in 1503, led by Alfonso de Albuquerque, who built a church and fort at Cochin. In 1509 he came again and took thriving Goa city from the Bijapur rulers. Goa dorada ("golden Goa") was soon a wealthy entrepôt and capital of Europe's largest maritime empire, one that stretched along the coasts of Africa up to Hormuz and included Diu, Daman, Goa, and Cochin on the west coast of India and, on the east coast, Hooghly near modern Kolkata, and on to Malacca in Malaysia. By 1580 Goa's population was 60,000 (Lisbon's was then 110,000), excluding the vast numbers of clergy and slaves. Each year a flotilla of 300 ships laden with spices, gold, and other luxuries

would leave Goa for Lisbon. At a social level, while intermarriage between the Portuguese and the Indians was encouraged, European intolerance revealed itself in the wanton destruction of Hindu temples.

The Portuguese had missionary ambitions, and in 1540 the ideology of the Counter-Reformation arrived in Goa, followed by Francis Xavier (1506–1552) and the Jesuits two years later. Mass conversions began. When Xavier died in China, his body was brought to Goa for burial; in 1560 the Inquisition arrived and not surprisingly banned all non-Christian teaching and ritual. Despite Portugal's position as suppliers of horses to the Vijayanaga empire and as naval auxiliaries of the Mughals, the Portuguese were regarded as cruel, untrustworthy, and intolerant by the Indians.

Furthermore, other European trading eyes were on India. The Dutch, Danes, French, and finally the English set sail for India, each competing to establish factories and trading stations. Eventually, while the English expanded, the Dutch were reduced to Chinsura near Kolkata, and the Danes to nearby Serampore and down on the Tamil Nadu coast

at Tranquebar (modern Tarangambadi). The French kept their main base on the same coast, at Pondicherry, with smaller stations at Mahe in Kerala and Chandernagore in West Bengal.

The British came to India looking for trading opportunities after they failed to break the Dutch trading monopoly in the East Indies. On December 31, 1600, Queen Elizabeth I (R.1558–1603) granted the East India Company its charter "...as much for the honour of this our realm of England as for the increase of our navigation and advancement of trade." A few years later English trade moved forward when Sir Thomas Roe, a senior diplomat, arrived in India from the court of James I (R.1603–1625). In January 1616 Roe finally met the Mughal emperor Jahangir when his itinerant court was at Ajmer. He soon sealed the relationship between England and India that would grow into the greatest trading partnership and cultural exchange the world has known.

Using diplomacy rather than force, the English had established 23 trading factories by 1647, of which Surat (1613) on the west coast and Madras (1639) on the east coast were the most important. However, in 1661 the

View of Calicut (circa 1600). Vasco da Gama, the Portuguese adventurer, landed here on the Kerala coast in 1498.

company acquired the marshy, malarial islands of Bombay (Mumbai) as part of Portuguese princess Catherine of Braganza's dowry on her marriage to Charles II (R.1660–1685). A great cosmopolitan trading city was born under Gerald Aungier, the city's Governor (1672–77).

Already, forays north had led to Calcutta's founding by Job Charnock in 1690. But it was farther south on the east coast, where the climate was healthier, that English trading really flourished. Francis Day founded Madras (now Chennai) in 1639, well-placed for trading cotton. By 1700 its population was 300,000; by 1740 trade with India represented 10 percent of British revenue and much of it passed through Madras.

EAST INDIA COMPANY EXPANDS

British initiatives were gradually transformed into political power. Rivalry between the southern states enabled the two strong Europeans in the area, the British and the French, to play out their rivalry too, but supporting different sides. The young British soldier (later governor of Bengal) Robert Clive (1725–1774), supporting the Nawab of Arcot, defeated the French under the Marquis de Dupleix in 1751, and British supremacy in the south was confirmed nine years later at the Battle of Wandiwash. In the north, Clive's triumph at Plassey in 1757 was confirmed by Hector Munro's decisive victory at the Battle of Buxar in 1764 against the kings of Delhi and Oudh.

The result was a trade boom throughout eastern India. Madras expanded, Calcutta became the headquarters of the East India Company, and from 1774 a string of governors-general, later called viceroys, began with Warren Hastings (1732–1818). European and Indian traders made fortunes from gifts, monopolies, and looting. In the 1780s, with Calcutta's population at 250,000, land revenues and the system of district collectors were fixed, so that, despite famines, the company amassed four million dollars annually.

With its insatiable appetite for profits from trade and land revenue, the company's influence soon expanded across India. From small Benares (Varanasi) kingdom to vast Hyderabad state, the majority of Indian rulers found themselves in debt to the company as a result of trade agreements. There were exceptions. The clever Mysore ruler Haider Ali brought prosperity to the Deccan and wanted, like the British, to benefit from sea trade along their coast. But his son, Tipu Sultan, was finally defeated at Srirangapatnam (1799). In the northwest, the British made a pact with the Sikhs, whose hero king, Ranjit Singh, took Lahore (1799) and established the first Sikh state, which included all of verdant Punjab. The Maratha confederacy, supported by the French and including the Scindias of Gwalior, the Holkars of Indore, and the Gaekwads of Baroda, stretched from Agra down to Karnataka. But their raids on Rajput territories such as Jaipur (1803) and Udaipur (1803) only helped the British win control of major princely states, and during 1816–18 the British finally defeated the Marathas. In the mountains, the Gurkas were defeated (1818) and the

rulers of potentially threatening Persia and Afghanistan were dissuaded from allying with the French or Russians.

The British expanded out of their forts and beyond the open space of the Maidan, then replaced simple houses with grand stucco mansions and public buildings, keeping rigidly to classical designs to satisfy their own aspirations and confirm symbolic order and government over their surroundings. Modifications were made for deeper verandas, or to create cross-drafts. New kinds of buildings appeared: churches, cemeteries, cantonments (military stations), bungalows (which originated in Bengal), and social clubs. This westernization was most evident in Calcutta and Madras, which became elegant neoclassic cities. Soon both Indian rulers and merchants were building hybrid houses mixing Hindu or Muslim traditions with European elements, initiating a new cross-fertilization of styles.

To escape the searing summer sun entirely, the British discovered India's hills. Between 1815 and 1947 the British built more than 80 hill stations (see pp. 278–79), from Shimla and Darjling in the Himalayan foothills to Mahabaleshwar in the Western Ghats above Bombay and Ootacamund in the Nilgiri Hills—the main hill station for Madras and known as "Snooty Ooty." Each was a nostalgic re-creation of British feudal society, whose informal buildings belied a strict social structure within which hunting, jam-making, dog shows, and amateur dramatics all played their part. From 1832 to 1947 the entire government and its hangers-on of families and Europeanized maharajas moved from Calcutta to Shimla annually, governing one fifth of the world's population from a quaint, isolated, hillside town for half the year.

Problems began in the 1830s when, among other things, sales of cotton and opium to China and indigo to Europe dropped, British-made cloth put Indian weavers out of jobs, and famines swept the countryside. Despite social reforms by William Bentinck (1774–1839) and William Macaulay, India was becoming dissatisfied with company rule. Furthermore, the British modernizing projects of the railroads (1853) and telegraph (1865), and the building of irrigation canals and

roads, at first disturbed the conservative basis of Indian society. Small, uncoordinated revolts took place all over India, including grain riots in defiance of revenue payments.

Against this background, the Rebellion of 1857—also known as the Mutiny—is not such a surprise. It was sparked by the Bengal army's irritation at the loss of privileges, the introduction of lower castes, the high local land revenues demanded by the British, and the possible pollution from the pork and beef grease on the new Lee Enfield rifles' cartridges, which the soldiers had to break between their teeth. Starting with the mutiny of the garrison at Meerut on May 10, 1857, uprisings in Delhi, Lucknow, and Kanpur (Cawnpore) spread across Bengal. Although Delhi was retaken in November 1857, the British government was badly shaken. The East India Company was abolished in 1858, and the last Mughal king, Bahadur Shah II, who had encouraged the rebels, was deposed. From then on, the British Crown, and much of British law, administered India directly. The Raj had begun.

BRITISH IMPERIALISM TO INDIAN FREEDOM: 1858–1947

India was now part of the British Empire, with a viceroy as chief executive. Indians were subjects of Queen Victoria. From 1840 to 1914 India was Britain's most important trading partner. In Bombay, the economic boom was further boosted when, during the American Civil War, the Confederacy ports were blocked, temporarily diverting more cotton trade to India. It was during this time that Bombay's Parsee community rose in importance, including the Sassoon, Wadia, Readymoney, Jeejeebhoy, and Tata families, and Bombay acquired the world's grandest set of Victorian Gothic public buildings.

In making Queen Victoria the Empress of India in 1877, Britain saw itself as a grand feudal power controlling the vassals of India. Hence the string of royal visits that peaked in

1911 when the King-Emperor George V visited India. On December 12, he announced to 562 maharajas and other grandees that the capital would move from Calcutta to its traditional and strategic site, Delhi, where an entirely new city would be built. Designed by Edwin Lutyens, assisted by Herbert Baker, it reflected the size and power of the British Empire. At the city's inauguration on February 9, 1931, few people recognized the gathering storm clouds that would bring independence to India in just 16 years.

The pomp and ceremony of these British royal visits were intended to impress the Indian rulers on their own terms and ensure their loyalty in an India that increasingly questioned Britain's presence. The British administrators recognized an uncomfortable link between empire and unequal trade. Their policies to bridge the gap included Indianizing government building styles, promoting English education, building universities and high courts, and including more Indians in government. But only after World War II did the British fully accept that independence was unavoidable and that foreign enterprise could not answer India's problems.

Growing Indian political awareness percolated down from the intelligentsia, who had benefited from the education opportunities, to the masses. Agitation began in the 1870s, seeking a national culture and interests. The Indian National Congress party was founded in 1885, and in 1905 British attempts to weaken the unified National Movement were answered by a countryside boycott of British goods. The next year, Muslims who felt that Congress did not represent them formed the All India Muslim League. While Hindus demanded the recognition of the Hindi language written in Devanagari script, Muslims wanted Urdu in Perso-Arabic script.

India's struggle for freedom entered a new phase in 1915, when Mohandas Karamchand Gandhi (1869–1948)—later known as the Mahatma, or Great Soul—returned from South Africa, where he had experienced racial prejudice. He led a moral protest against oppression (the British presence). Known as civil disobedience, it involved defying laws peacefully and taking punishment willingly. In noncooperation, India had a truly national

and popular political campaign for the first time, promoted by nationalist leaders including Bal Gangadhar Tilak, Sir Sayyid Ahmad Khan, C. Rajagopalachari, Sardar Vallabhbhai Patel, A. K. Azad, and M. A. Jinner.

Gandhi's second civil disobedience movement, in 1930, included his Salt March, protesting the British monopoly on salt production. In the same year Congress, with the young Jawaharlal Nehru as president, adopted the resolution for complete independence for India. The Government of India Act was passed in 1935, giving Indians who met stringent educational and property-owning requirements (about 14 percent of the population) the right to vote to elect representatives. Congress swept the polls. Agitation continued, and in 1942 Congress called for the British to

The Khan of Kelat (seated center) leased the Bolan Pass, linking India with Afghanistan, to the British in the 1930s.

"Quit India." Meanwhile, the Muslim League demanded a separate state for Muslims, to be called Pakistan. Back in Britain, Prime Minister Clement Atlee (1883–1967) and the postwar Labour government encouraged independence.

In 1947 independence and partition came simultaneously. On August 14 the last viceroy, Lord Louis Mountbatten, witnessed the creation of Pakistan—in two parts, 1,200 miles (1,931 km) apart, to be called West and East Pakistan. East Pakistan became the independent country of Bangladesh in 1971. At midnight on August 14–15, 1947, in front of the Red Fort in Old Delhi, Mountbatten formally transferred British power to India's first Prime Minister, Pandit Jawaharlal Nehru (1889–1964), and India's saffron, white, and green flag was flown for the first time. Later, the two leaders toasted each other in Viceroy's House, soon to be renamed Rastrapati Bhavan. Meanwhile, hundreds of thousands of people fled their homelands: Hindus from Pakistan, now a Muslim state, into India; Muslims from what they believed would be a Hindu state, into Pakistan. It is estimated that two million died in communal massacres during this mass cross-migration. Gandhi wept over the violence, the loss of a single India, and the new hatred. On January 30, 1948, he was assassinated by a fundamentalist Hindu.

A YOUNG NATION STEEPED IN HISTORY: 1947–PRESENT

At independence about two-fifths of India, containing about a quarter of the population of 350 million people, belonged not to the Indian government but to the Indian princes. These states—representing Jat, Rajput, Maratha, Hindu, Sikh, and Muslim people—

Nehru and Gandhi at the Indian National Congress committee meeting in Bombay in 1930, when Nehru became its president

were scattered across the country and ranged in size from Hyderabad's 82,000 square miles (212,380 sq km) and 14 million population to tiny Kathiawar's less than half a square mile (1 sq km) and 200 inhabitants. But the autocratic rule and preference for traditional lifestyles displayed by most princes were at odds with those building a new, modern country. Gradually, the princes were absorbed into the new states—which loosely followed geographical, cultural, and linguistic boundaries—and the majority of their lands, palaces, villages, personal wealth, titles, and honors were officially removed. The state of Rajasthan was not completely formed until 1956, nor was Andhra Pradesh, which contains much of former Hyderabad. Today, only a handful of the former rulers and their families maintain their feudal customs and they take their consequent responsibilities seriously.

This is just one example of the massive reorganization that faced the government of Asia's new and huge democracy in 1947. For this, the guiding principle was to maintain national unity and integrity against all potential internal and external threats.

Gandhi's leadership was the model; India's people who had struggled for freedom were its motivation. There was a need to balance modernization with India's strong traditions. Thus, political and judicial equality, a secular state, and improved farming methods were matched with tolerance for all religious practices and some religious law, and recognition of the existing social order, including caste. The ancient custom of Indian rulers holding morning and evening audiences with the people was adopted by the democratically elected politicians—it was at one of these audiences that Prime Minister Indira Gandhi

Students prepare cotton yarn at Gujarat Vidyapith, a school founded by Gandhi in 1920 to produce *khadi,* homespun cloth.

(1917–1984) was assassinated by two of her own guards. At the same time, the new country benefited from some of the practical legacies of British rule—the system of law and administration, the civil service, the railroads, roads and irrigation systems, a nonpolitical army, a free press, and a ready-made capital city. There was also the concept of India as a single country with, most importantly, a unifying language: English.

On January 26, 1950, the Republic of India was inaugurated and the Constitution adopted, an event now celebrated annually with a public holiday and grand parades through Delhi. In the face of major north–south controversies and independence bids from the Punjab, Kashmir, Assam, and other areas, there were two distinct visions of a unified India: Gandhi's decentralized village system and the new leaders' centralized, state-controlled system. The second vision won, modified by the first.

Pandit Jawaharlal Nehru was prime minister from 1947 until his death in 1964, during which time his National Congress Party remained unchallenged. His ideology and

In Mumbai, space is at a premium: Here, four cobblers sit cross-legged in a cubby-hole that opens onto the street, while the client has his shoes resoled.

ambitions for a country as diverse as India were practical and realistic, and they set the tone for the next 50 years. They incorporated a gentle socialism, a secular state (India has no state religion), state-directed economic progress, and nonalignment in foreign affairs.

To these ends, India operated a closed economy until the 1990s, promoting its own industries and products. At the same time, India's high-quality hand loom-weaving and other handicrafts were revived and encouraged, with prestigious national awards and government-run stores to control quality. In food production, India achieved self-sufficiency with some to spare for export. Today, India's principal crops are rice, wheat, other cereals, pulses, oil seeds, cotton, and sugarcane—helped by a gradual doubling of irrigated land. In foreign affairs, India's sheer size and strategic position have forced it to play a sensitive role with its smaller neighbors; internationally, it has maintained its non-aligned position and keeps a careful balance of friendship with China, Russia, and the West.

Nehru can be seen as the head of what, with a few interruptions, has been virtually a dynas-

tic rule over independent India, albeit a democratically elected one. Indira Gandhi, Jawaharlal's daughter and no relation to the Mahatma, dominated Indian politics after her father's death. Prime minister for 15 years, 1966–1977 and 1980–84, she governed in a highly personalized and centralized way, which became dictatorial during the Emergency (1975–77); yet, after a spell out of office, she was reelected. On her assassination, her son, Rajiv, was reluctantly hurled into the job and began to open up India economically before he, too, was assassinated by a suicide bomber in 1991. His widow, Sonia, and his children are now on the political scene.

Recent prime ministers, from Narasimha Rao (1991–96) to the present Dr. Manmohan Singh (2004–) have encouraged India's now unstoppable tide of modernization and the increased determination by individual states to choose their own destinies. This drive for self-improvement is especially true of the southern states (Maharashtra, Karnataka, Andhra Pradesh, Tamil Nadu, and Kerala). Here, progress and prosperity are evident in the cities and villages, in manufacturing and

In Bangalore, traditions are broken as men and women work together for national and international companies at the cutting edge of information technology.

transportation, in education and health. This new wealth is reflected in the increased donations by the faithful to their religious institutions.

This means that, for the visitor, India is as diverse as it always was. But this diversity—in ancient cultures, religions, societies, landscapes, cities, and villages—has a new dynamism. The rise of Bangalore, capital of the southern state of Karnataka, to become the world's third most important information technology center, after Silicon Valley and Israel, has produced a city skyline mixing high-rises with colonial neoclassic buildings, medieval palace remains, and ancient stone temples. Hyderabad, capital of neighboring Andhra Pradesh, is following Bangalore's lead. In the north, however, picturesque Rajasthan looks to quixotic tourism for income, transforming every last palace into a hotel.

INDIA'S PLACE IN THE GLOBAL ECONOMY

It was Rajiv Gandhi who in the mid-80s had the vision of technology-driven India leap-frogging into the 21st century. The real changes came in the 90s though, when India's closed economy opened to the world, most famously in IT software and services (see p. 227). This sector now employs more than 1.3 million people and is the country's top exporter at over $23 billion in 2005–6, with aims to employ 10 million and top $60 billion in exports by 2010.

India's changes have touched almost every village. Farmers check market prices using cell phones; the Internet reaches right into the countryside; there are more than 38 TV news channels—the largest number in any country; and the micro-loan system enables bicycles to be exchanged for motorbikes. Goldman Sachs predicts India's economy will be greater than the United States' by 2020. Yet clean water, basic sewerage, food distribution, and basic health and education remain deplorably unresolved.

With this intense but patchy advancement, India now stands at a fork in the road. Prime Minister Dr. Manmohan Singh and his ministers have to choose between the path of measured advancement that concurrently addresses the fundamental problems of the masses, and the path that surges forward to benefit the few until the bubble bursts. ■

India: Land of many faiths

IF INDIA'S HISTORY SEEMS COMPLEX, THE SPIRITUAL LIVES OF ITS PEOPLE are equally baffling for first-time visitors. India has no state religion, but religion is a vital element in today's India, and integral to its history, monuments, and arts. Hinduism is practiced by the majority of Indians. Out of it were born Buddhism, Jainism, and, much later, Sikhism. With the diaspora of Indians and Indian ideas, all these faiths are now practiced worldwide. India has also absorbed religions—Judaism, Christianity, Zoroastrianism, Islam—whose Indian adherents have given each a regional distinctiveness. In addition, modern movements range from hedonistic ashrams (religious communities) to quasi-political groups. Meanwhile, nature worship and other very ancient practices continue.

To visit India is to encounter several of these faiths, which generally thrive peacefully side by side. A typical fishing village has room for temple, mosque, and church. Pausing to observe the rituals in urban and rural places of worship, or to talk to local people about their faith, is almost always welcome provided customs such as removing shoes are observed. Contact like this can illuminate the various philosophies and dispel preconceptions.

FAITHS THAT EVOLVED IN INDIA
Hinduism

Some 820 million people in India are Hindu—about 82 percent. Yet for all its popularity Hinduism is an elusive religion, and difficult for non-Hindus even to begin to understand. Hinduism has no single sacred text, no dogma, no single prophet, and it demands no formal congregational worship; nor does it oblige the faithful to go to the temple, to tackle its abstract philosophy, to follow specific rituals, or to know its sacred language, Sanskrit. Ideas of rebirth and a plethora of deities add to the confusion.

The beginnings of worship on the subcontinent predate the Indus Valley Civilization and suggest a reverence for natural elements. These were given definition by the pastoral Aryans (see pp. 26–28) who worshiped the sun as "Surya," and introduced ideas of a distinct religion that included precise rituals, sacrifice, and priests *(brahmans)* to mediate between the people and their gods. These ideas were set out in the four Vedic texts, composed in early Sanskrit, sung by heart and passed down through generations orally; writing seems to have begun only about 500 B.C.

Later texts such as the *Upanishads* (philosophical treatises on the soul) and the *Brahmanas* (on ritual) reflect important new ideas: spiritual karma and increased temporal brahman power. *Karma* may be understood to be the power of each person's good or bad thoughts and actions to affect the spirit's movement across generations. The spirit thus endures a series of rebirths with varying degrees of suffering and desire, as the soul progresses or regresses in response to past deeds. The soul makes its final escape either through *nirvana,* when personal identity is extinguished, or through *moksha,* the final release from the cycle of rebirth. Meanwhile, as these ideas became more abstract, ritual more convoluted, and Sanskrit more refined and unintelligible, so brahman power increased. Ordinary people felt excluded and were attracted to new, back-to-basics religions; of these, Buddhism (see p. 58) and Jainism (see pp. 58–59) were the most long-lasting and won merchant and royal patronage.

During and after the classical Gupta period (see p. 33) local spirits, gods, and heroes were absorbed into the central pantheon of gods. Gradually, Hindus began to focus their worship on one of these, with a passionate devotion known as *bhakti.* This encouraged elaborate ritual and the final, very long forms of the great epics (see p. 76): the *Ramayana* and the *Mahabharata.* This last includes the Bhagavad Gita, a discussion between Krishna and Arjuna on the essence of Hindu philosophy: the

A Hindu *sadhu* (holy man) who follows Shiva, god of creative and destructive energy, performs *puja* (worship) at Varanasi.

theory of karma and the human struggle for love, light, and redemption.

Over the centuries, Hindu philosophy, ritual, and myth have permeated almost every aspect of the believer's life. Hindus live, for the most part, in the grip of the caste system (see p. 29), even if modern social and business life seems to deny this. Marriage is usually arranged within the same caste, and dowries require ever spiraling debt as motorcycles and freezers are added to silks and jewelry.

Pilgrimages are the most popular form of Indian tourism, often undertaken in busloads, with much singing and souvenir shopping. The destination may be one of the seven Sacred Cities (see p. 385), or the temple of the believers' chosen deity. This deity is likely to be one form, or aspect, of what may be seen as the extended family of Hindu gods, whose presiding trinity are Brahma (the Creator), Shiva (the Energy, the Destroyer), and Vishnu (the Preserver). The faithful may do *puja*

(worship) to this chosen deity in a corner at home or at the local temple, whose plan follows the ancient *shastras* (treatises). The priest, who receives the worshiper's offering, holds his position by inheritance and ensures the temple receives a steady flow of donations.

For all its vagueness in definition, Hinduism provides a clear pattern for life. There are four stages: childhood and learning, marriage and rearing a family, celibacy and meditation, and finally a renunciation of all

Children sell flowers and tiny oil lamps made of dried leaves for pilgrims to float as tributes on the Ganga at Varanasi.

worldly possessions in the hope of achieving nirvana or moksha. Throughout, the Hindu has four supreme aims: *dharma* (virtue, living the right way), *artha* (wealth achieved in the right way), karma (giving and receiving love and friendship), and, if these three are correctly followed, moksha.

Traditional dancing and music form a key part of Buddhist festivals such as the Ladakh Festival, held in Leh in early August.

Buddhism

India has just eight million Buddhists, yet this is the birthplace of Buddha (Awakened One).

The conventional dates for Buddha's life are 563–483 B.C., but recent research suggests about 450–350 B.C. or even later. A prince of the *kshatriya* caste (see p. 29), Buddha lived at Lumbini, now in Nepal. At the age of about 30, he questioned the point of Hindu austerity and asceticism, renounced his privileged life, and left home. Five years later Buddha attained *bodhi* (enlightenment) after meditating under a pipal (bodhi) tree at Bodh Gaya (see p. 301).

Offering insight rather than divine revelation, Buddha began his lifelong missionary work with his "Setting in Motion the Wheel of Righteousness" sermon preached at Sarnath. It presented life's overwhelming problem— desire—and its solution, The Middle Path (moderation) and dharma (faith as seen in the true nature of the world, human nature, and spiritual attainment). These, with *sangha* (monasticism for men and women), could lead to the goal, nirvana.

Reacting to Hinduism's inaccessibility, Buddha preached a rational, simple philosophy in the vernacular. His dogma was popular, especially among the merchants who, together with rulers from Ashoka Maurya to the Guptas (see pp. 31–35), patronized India's first substantial stone buildings *(stupas)* and sculpture, mostly sited along trade routes. Followers formed monasteries *(sanghas)*, some with adjoining universities such as at Nalanda.

After Buddha's death, the sanghas continued his teachings. Then came the schism. The Hinayana (Lesser Vehicle) sect saw Buddha as the Great Master and spread its ideas to Ceylon, Burma, and Siam. The Mahayana (Great Vehicle) sect considered Buddha to be God and spread its ideas to China, Japan, Tibet, and Mongolia. Buddhism was India's dominant religion for several centuries, but lost out to reformed Hinduism in the seventh century and continued to decline.

Today, India has a growing group of neo-Buddhists, mostly farmers from Maharashtra inspired by the Buddhist convert Dr. Bhim Rao Ambedkar. Dharamsala is home to the Dalai Lama, the head of Tibetan Buddhism and leader of the exiled Tibetan people.

Jainism

India's four million Jains tend to live in the west, near their sacred hills, to which regular pilgrimage is required.

Hari Mandir (Golden Temple)—the Sikhs' most holy *gurudwara*, temple—rises from the Amrit Sarovar at Amritsar. The Sikhs' holy text, *Adi Granth*, is read here daily.

Their founder, Mahavira (Great Hero), is thought to have lived in the sixth century B.C. A religious reformer, like Buddha, he left his birthplace, Patna, to live as a naked ascetic until he achieved spiritual knowledge. He became a *jina* (conqueror), and his followers were known as Jains.

Mahavira taught his followers that the universe is infinite, not created, and that *jivas* (souls) are present in everything. Hence, Jains believe in *ahimsa* (reverence for all life), which demands strict vegetarianism. Adherence to ahimsa, together with the practice of a strict code of behavior can lead to moksha—like Hindus and Buddhists, Jains believe in both reincarnation and salvation. They also reject sacrifice and oppose the caste system, but they do permit *sallekhana* (death by fasting and meditation).

There are two Jain sects. The rigorous "sky-clad" sect, or Digambaras, have no possessions and believe that only men are able to achieve moksha. The white-clad sect, Shvetambaras, are less strict. In today's India Jains are mostly Shvetambaras, who are often commercially successful and may be substantial donors to hospitals, schools, and libraries (see also Ranakpur, p. 138).

Sikhism

Most of India's 20 million Sikhs live in the Punjab and Delhi area and are distinguished by their smoothly wrapped turbans.

Sikhs follow a philosophy founded by Guru Nanak (1469–1539), who was born near Lahore in today's Pakistan. One of several Hindu Sants (poet-philosophers) who introduced Islamic elements into Hinduism, he advocated a single God who is *sat* (truth) and reveals himself through his *gurus* (teachers). He promoted meditation and equality while opposing caste, ritual, superstition, astrology, and sex discrimination.

Nine more gurus consolidated Nanak's teachings. The tenth, Gobind Singh (1666–1708), formalized the new religion in 1699. He began the *gurpurb* (baptism) ceremony, which removed Hindu caste names, and he insisted men adopt the five *kakkars*: *kesh* (uncut hair), *kangha* (comb), *kachha* (shorts), *kara* (steel bracelet), and *kirpan* (sword). He also encouraged military prowess, forbade tobacco-smoking, and declared that henceforth guruship would rest in the Guru Granth Sahib (Sikhs' sacred texts). The most revered copy is kept in the *gurudwara* (temple) at Amritsar (see p. 123).

FAITHS BROUGHT TO INDIA
Islam

India's 120 million Muslims form the country's second largest religious community and the world's second largest Muslim community, after Indonesia's.

The Prophet Muhammad (circa 570–632) preached Islam (submission to God): one God and one community whose *jihad* (sacred duty) is to spread the word, if necessary by war. He proclaimed Mecca to be Islam's pilgrimage center and its Ka'ba (cube-shaped building housing a stone believed to have been given by Gabriel to Abraham) its most sacred shrine. Just 80 years later, Islam reached India, the first of many Islamic incursions that would end with that of the Mughals (see p. 37).

An early doctrinal split over the Prophet's successor created two sects, Sunni and Shia. Most Indian Muslims are Sunni. Many also follow the Sufi path, a mystical thread in Islamic thought that arose in the tenth century in opposition to the militaristic and orthodox mainstream, and whose spiritualism, asceticism, and indulgence of festivals and singing suited Hindu converts.

Muslims believe fatalistically in total surrender to the will of Allah (God) and in equality in life and death—reasons for Islam's early popularity with lower social groups. The Koran, Islam's sacred book, records the Prophet's revelations, much of it similar to the Old Testament. A Muslim has five duties: belief in one God with Muhammad as his Prophet; showing humility by praying five times daily; fasting from dawn to dusk during Ramadan, the month Muhammad received his revelation; doing charitable work; and going on *hajj* (pilgrimage) to Mecca at least once. To avoid the danger of idolatry, no images of Allah are permitted, so *masjids* (places of prostration, mosques) have no figural decoration.

Christianity

India's 25 million Christians belong to a variety of denominations introduced down the centuries.

The Syrian Christians of Kerala, still a powerful force locally, trace their conversion to St. Thomas the Apostle, who landed at Kodungallur (Cranganore) in A.D. 52 and later died at Chennai (Madras) (see p. 258).

The Portuguese traders of the 16th century (see pp. 44–45) brought Roman Catholicism to India, in particular to Goa. Locals underwent mass conversion and, from 1542, received the zeal of St. Francis Xavier (see p. 193), whose Jesuits brought the first printing press to India. Conversion from Hinduism, although often nominal, brought with it the attractive promises of one life and equality in death.

By the 18th century India had congregations of most denominations, from Anglicans and Methodists to Baptists, and these still thrive today.

Judaism

Jewish people have played a significant role in India's past. Refugees arrived in Kerala after the fall of Jerusalem in 587 B.C. Jewish and Arab traders later carried shiploads of spices and luxury goods from India's western ports to the Roman Empire. A Jewish community lived for centuries at Cranganore (Kodungallur), then Cochin, where three synagogues still stand, although only one is used. "White Jews," who did not intermarry with locals, enjoyed high status; "Black Jews," who did, had less status.

During the British period, India had large Jewish communities: Bene Israel, Baghdadis, and Malayalam-speaking Jewish people from Cochin. Most have emigrated to Israel; fewer than 5,000, mostly elderly people, remain.

Zoroastrianism

India's Zoroastrians are better known as Parsees, an elite community that played a key role in building up Bombay.

Zoroastrianism was founded in Iran by the Persian philosopher Zarathustra (Golden Light) sometime between 6000 B.C. and 1500 B.C. Its dual philosophy focuses on the opposing powers of good and evil—the good found in the sacred elements (earth, water, sky, and fire), animals, and plants; the bad in decaying and dead matter. Bodies of the dead are left for the flesh to be eaten by vultures and the bones to be cleansed by the sun and wind, rather than allowed to pollute sacred fire or earth.

Fleeing the Arab Islamic conquests, some Parsees arrived in Gujarat in A.D. 936. Later, in 19th-century Bombay, they shared in the phenomenal business and trading success of the British, whose lifestyles they mimicked. ∎

The capital of the world's largest democracy sprawls across the plains, expanding greedily and unstoppably around the ancient monuments that testify to the attraction of this site for Hindu, Muslim, and British rulers.

Delhi

Independence was declared at Delhi's Red Fort in 1947.

Chandni Chowk, inaugurated in 1648, is still the bustling thoroughfare of Old Delhi.

Delhi

THE CITY OF DELHI IS THE POLITICAL NERVE CENTER OF ALL INDIA AND THE largest commercial hub in northern India. Most of its twelve million and more inhabitants live in the sprawling 580 square miles (1,500 sq km) that surround the historic seven successive cities. Delhi is its own political unit, whose administration has to cope with an alarming recent growth rate and a dry climate with intensely hot summers and cold winters.

There are more than a thousand historic buildings in Delhi, down backstreets, in people's backyards, on golf courses. The flat plain enabled successive conquerors simply to abandon one city and build a fresh one. In theory all monuments are protected, but most are left to take their chances amidst Delhi's burden of humanity. Keeping your eyes open, you can make your very own discoveries in this supremely historic city.

By studying the map opposite you can trace an instant history of Delhi. Begin in the south, at Lal Kot, where tantalizing remains of the Tomar and Chauhan Rajputs' 11th- and 12th-century temples were used by Delhi's first Muslim conqueror, Qutb-ud-din-Aibak, to build his great mosque, begun in 1193. Here, too, is the Qutab Minar, Delhi's landmark tower. Scant remains of Siri, Delhi's second major city, lie to the north.

Next came the three Tughlaq cities. Tughlaqabad's rarely visited fort is 5 miles (8 km) east of Lal Kot, while the remains of Sultan Muhammad's never-completed Jahapanah are near Siri. The citadel of the last and grandest of the Tughlaq cities, Feroz Shah Kotla, stands east of Connaught Place and once overlooked the Yamuna, Delhi's almost forgotten river, which flows on down to Agra and joins the Ganga above Varanasi.

Delhi's sixth city, Purana Qila, was founded by the Mughal emperor Humayun in 1533 and enlarged by his usurper Sher Shah Sur, and it is today the focus of New Delhi's processional route, Raj Path. Farther upstream, Humayun's great-grandson Shah Jahan entered his vibrant Shahjahanabad (Old Delhi) in 1648.

Finally, after Delhi had languished as a backwater for a century or so, the British moved their headquarters here from Calcutta. On February 9, 1931, the British viceroy inaugurated New Delhi, designed by Sir Edwin Lutyens and Herbert Baker to allow for infinite expansion and to encompass all previous Delhi remains without destruction.

Remember that traveling across Delhi takes time. Traffic congestion during the rush hours and at midday slows down all movement. ■

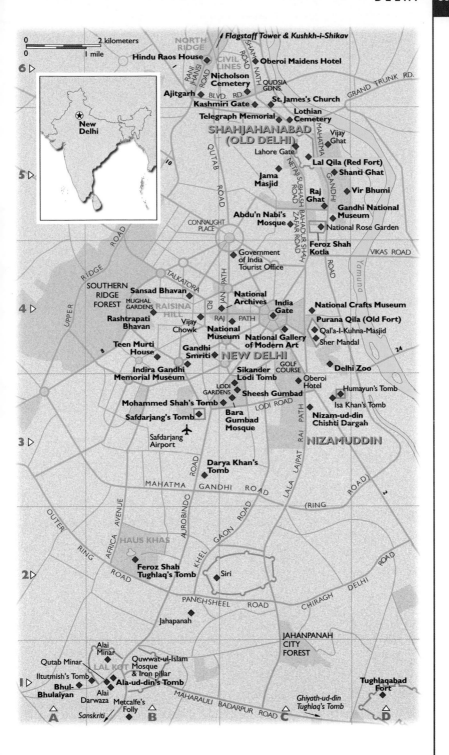

0 — 2 kilometers
0 — 1 mile

Flagstaff Tower & Kushkh-i-Shikav

NORTH RIDGE

Hindu Raos House

CIVIL LINES

Oberoi Maidens Hotel

Nicholson Cemetery

QUDSIA GDNS.

Ajitgarh

BLVD. RD.

St. James's Church

GRAND TRUNK RD.

Kashmiri Gate

Telegraph Memorial

Lothian Cemetery

SHAHJAHANABAD (OLD DELHI)

Vijay Ghat

Lahore Gate

Lal Qila (Red Fort)

Shanti Ghat

Jama Masjid

Raj Ghat

Vir Bhumi

Gandhi National Museum

Abdu'n Nabi's Mosque

National Rose Garden

Feroz Shah Kotla

VIKAS ROAD

New Delhi

CONNAUGHT PLACE

QUTAB ROAD

NETAJI SUBHASH ROAD

BAHADUR SHAH ZAFAR ROAD

Yamuna

Government of India Tourist Office

RIDGE

TALKATORA

SOUTHERN RIDGE FOREST

Sansad Bhavan

National Archives

India Gate

National Crafts Museum

MUGHAL GARDENS

RAISINA HILL

Rashtrapati Bhavan

Vijay Chowk

National Museum

Purana Qila (Old Fort)

Qal'a-I-Kuhna-Masjid

Sher Mandal

JAN PATH

RAJ PATH

National Gallery of Modern Art

Teen Murti House

Gandhi Smriti

NEW DELHI

Delhi Zoo

Indira Gandhi Memorial Museum

Sikander

GOLF COURSE

Lodi Tomb

Oberoi Hotel

Humayun's Tomb

LODI GARDENS

Sheesh Gumbad

Mohammed Shah's Tomb

Isa Khan's Tomb

LODI ROAD

Safdarjang's Tomb

Bara Gumbad Mosque

Nizam-ud-din Chishti Dargah

Safdarjang Airport

RAJ PATH

NIZAMUDDIN

Darya Khan's Tomb

MAHATMA GANDHI ROAD

AUROBINDO ROAD

KHEL GAON ROAD

LALA LAJPAT

(RING ROAD)

OUTER RING ROAD

AFRICA AVENUE

HAUS KHAS

Feroz Shah Tughlaq's Tomb

Siri

CHIRAGH DELHI ROAD

PANCHSHEEL ROAD

Jahapanah

JAHANPANAH CITY FOREST

Alai Minar

Qutab Minar

LAL KOT

Quwwat-ul-Islam Mosque & Iron pillar

Iltutmish's Tomb

Bhul-Bhulaiyan

Alai Darwaza

Ala-ud-din's Tomb

Metcalfe's Folly

Tughlaqabad Fort

Sanskriti

MAHARAULI BADARPUR ROAD

Ghiyath-ud-din Tughlaq's Tomb

A   B   C   D

Shahjahanabad

WANDERING THROUGH THE BACK LANES OF BUSTLING
Old Delhi, it is easy to imagine the great Muslim city built by the
powerful Mogul emperor Shah Jahan to be the new capital of his
secure, vast, and extremely wealthy empire. The lifeless, languishing
Lal Qila, or Red Fort, once its centerpiece, is less convincing.

In 1638, Shah Jahan's fort at Agra,
in need of maintenance and unsuit-
able for the now extensive court ritual, was spilling over with courtiers.
The court was no longer itinerant
and it needed more space. So with
the Taj Mahal (see pp. 100–103) well
under way, the now more orthodox
widower was drawn back to Delhi.
This was the traditional power base
in northern India; it was also the
burial place of Shaikh Nizam-ud-
din Chishti (see p. 70), a Sufi saint

revered by the Moguls. Shah Jahan
intended to associate himself with
previous rulers and holy men, while
totally outshining them with his
new city, Shahjahanabad. If the Taj
Mahal was to be one symbol of
imperial Mogul power, this specially
built city was to be another, even
more impressive one.

To enjoy Shah Jahan's masterpiece, it is best first to visit the old
city and its impressive mosque
opposite the fort, the **Jama**

In 1639 the foundation stone was laid for the great sandstone walls. Fort and city were divided only after the British created an open space that is now a roaring highway.

The fort's great bastion is an addition by Emperor Aurangzeb. Here, Jawaharlal Nehru addressed the people on India's independence day, August 15, 1947, and here the Indian flag was first raised.

Shah Jahan's building begins with **Chatta Chowk,** a covered market that still thrives today and has some interesting art stores at one end. Beyond it, you must use your imagination, as the British destroyed most of the buildings in 1858 (see p. 82).

The **Naqqar-khana** (royal drum house) stands straight ahead, where musicians heralded important arrivals through this official entrance into the **Diwan-i-Am** (public audience hall). The emperor would sit on the magnificent inlaid marble throne for the crowded daily *durbar* (audience). This consisted of music, displays of gifts, dancing, news from the empire, and the meting out of justice.

Only the most favored reached the inner palaces. These lay through high-walled courtyards and gardens that are today just empty lawns. To visit them, start at the right end with **Mumtaz Mahal** (Mumtaz Palace), now the fort's museum. Next comes **Rang Mahal,** the queens' palace, where the cooling Nahar-I-Bahisht (Stream of Paradise) flowing through the palaces broadened out into a marble pool. **Khas Mahal** (private palace) follows: Its modest rooms were where Shah Jahan slept, worshiped, ate, and at sunrise appeared to his people on the balcony.

The **Diwan-i-Khas** (private audience hall) was where favored diplomats and merchants were called before the emperor. ∎

Jama Masjid
 63 C5
✉ Off Netaji Subhash Marg
🕐 Closed to non-Muslims during prayer

Lal Qila
 63 C5
✉ Chandni Chowk
☎ 011-327 3703
🕐 Son-et-lumière times vary

Masjid (see p. 66). This is India's largest mosque, and was finished in 1656. You can see thousands of Muslims offering prayers there today, just as they did in Shah Jahan's time. It is surrounded by busy stores and restaurants, good for souvenirs and exotic food.

LAL QILA

Using his administrative skills, wealth, aesthetic sense, and knowledge of architecture, Shah Jahan laid out a new fort to suit his needs. Its Lahore Gate opened into the main street of a carefully planned adjoining city that thrives almost unchanged four centuries later, and which contains the Jama Masjid.

The site was north of previous cities and beside the Yamuna River, which has since changed its course.

A RICKSHAW RIDE AROUND OLD DELHI

A rickshaw ride around Old Delhi

The best days to enjoy the fun of a rickshaw ride are Monday to Thursday; Jama Masjid (the mosque) is very crowded on Friday. Agree on a price before you start, pay only on completion, and add a tip if appropriate. The driver will wait while you make visits.

Leaving **Lal Qila ❶** (see p. 65) behind you, cross the very busy Netaji Subhash Marg into Chandni Chowk, Old Delhi's main street, which used to run right up to the fort. There are three landmarks on the left. First is the **Digamber Jain Temple** and **Bird Hospital ❷** *(Donation).* The Bird Hospital, located within the precincts of the temple, is where injured birds can be brought for free treatment. Next, behind the busy flower stalls, is **Sisganj Gurdwara ❸,** a Sikh temple dedicated to the ninth guru, Tegh Bahadur. Finally, you come to **Sonehri Masjid** (Golden Mosque) where in 1739 Nadir Shah stood watching the destruction of Delhi and thousands of its inhabitants.

Turn left on **Dariba Kalan,** a narrow street lined with silver and gold shops that locals use as a kind of savings bank.

At the intersection, turn right and follow the road around to the left, past art stores and fireworks suppliers, to the **Jama Masjid ❹,** well worth visiting. At the top of the great steps, leave your shoes, and borrow a cotton overcoat to cover you if your arms or legs are exposed; pay a modest tip afterward. Shah Jahan's last building (1656) proclaims Islam's power and is still India's principal mosque. Designed by Ustad Khlil on Delhi's only mound, it uses glowing red sandstone inlaid with marble and brass, and it has excellent views of the Red Fort from the courtyard. The mosque design, inspired by the Prophet's house at Medina, is simple: a large courtyard with a vaulted hall at one end. The faithful wash ritually in the courtyard's pool, then pray facing the central *mihrab* (niche) of the hall, which indicates the direction of Mecca. The *mimbar* (pulpit) is for the sermon at midday communal prayers on Friday, the Muslims' holy day; the minaret (slender tower) is where the *muezzin* summons the faithful to prayer.

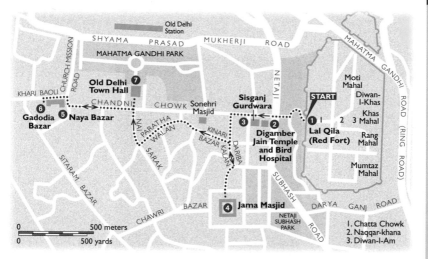

Ride back into Dariba Kalan and turn left for **Kinari Bazar,** Old Delhi's wedding equipment street. Tiny, boxlike stores are filled from floor to ceiling with glittering braids, gold lamé grooms' turbans, currency note garlands, plumes, and tinsel. In October, they also stock the papier-mâché masks for the Ram Lila festival. Almost at the end, bear left along Paratha Walan and Nai Sarak. Turn

▲	See area map page 63
►	Outside the Red Fort
↔	About 2 miles
⏱	1–2 hours
►	Outside the Red Fort

NOT TO BE MISSED
- Jama Masjid
- Kinari Bazar
- Gadodia Bazar

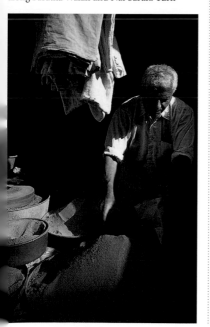

right, passing stores piled with stationery.

Turn left onto Chandni Chowk. At the end, turn right, then left on Khari Baoli. Here is **Naya Bazar ⑤,** the market selling spices, dried fruit, and nuts from Kashmir and Afghanistan. You can taste before buying. The wholesale spice market, **Gadodia Bazar ⑥,** is farther along Khari Baoli, through an arch on the left. Sackfuls of tamarind, ginger, turmeric, and chilis are weighed out on huge iron scales, then humped around by coolies who shout loudly if you are in their way.

Return along Chandni Chowk; the statue in front of **Old Delhi Town Hall** (1860) ⑦ is of the liberal nationalist hero, Swami Shraddhanand, who, like Gandhi (see p. 150), was murdered by a fanatic. ■

Rickshaws (left) are an excellent way to reach the city's markets.

Women & marriage

It may be surprising to learn that for some years India's more privileged women have formed a greater percentage of leading company directors, surgeons, movie directors, and members of parliament than they do in most European countries. This results from a form of backroom emancipation, reinforced by the extended family support system where grandparents and other relatives of a working woman keep house and care for her children.

Indian brides wear a traditional red sari, gold jewelry, plenty of red bangles, and mehndi (henna) patterns on their hands.

But life for the vast majority of Indian women is different, full of inequality and deprivation. Even in India's more emancipated urban areas, tradition remains strong.

This starts at birth—even before birth. The use of illegal prebirth sex-testing in such wealthy states as the Punjab has been linked to the high numbers of private (and illegal) abortions by women carrying healthy female fetuses. After birth, India's children's homes find more unwanted baby girls than boys on their doorsteps. During childhood, girls are often kept back from school to help with the housework, or they drop out altogether. Despite government programs and energetic women's movements, all too often daughters' health, schooling, literacy, and training lag substantially behind their brothers'.

The only incentive parents have to educate a daughter is to improve her marriage prospects. In essence, most Indian parents consider a daughter a burden, who should be married off as soon and as well as possible to remove her as a mouth to be fed and as a responsibility. Unlike sons, who stay at home, a daughter goes to live with her husband's family. Marriage in India is usually more of a contract between two families than a love match. This is clear from the frank advertisements in the Sunday newspapers: Questions of caste, skin color, healthiness, job prospects, virginity, and social standing are paramount.

Most marriages are still arranged, even if more enlightened parents give the couple the right of veto. A teenage village girl may be married to a man she has never met; she moves to his village or town, keeps his mother's house clean, does manual labor in the fields, and bears and raises his children. She has no property rights; divorce is rare; and there is no social security for divorcées or widows. A middle-class woman's lot is not much better, and if she fails to live up to expectations, primarily to produce a healthy son, she may suffer. One of the worst atrocities in India today, despite being outlawed, is "bride-burning"—that is, a "kitchen accident" in which a woman dies from burns caused by flaming "spilled" kerosene.

In almost all cases, marriage is sealed with negotiations over the dowry. To the traditional silks, saris, and jewels, the husband's family may now add demands for such luxuries as freezers, DVD players, or even a car. The wedding, paid for by the bride's family, is usually a spectacular string of processions and parties.

Although apparently invisible, the women in a household wield considerable power in all decisionmaking, from investments and harvesting to the choice of bridegrooms for their own daughters. ■

This child bride from a traditional area of western India endures lengthy Hindu wedding ceremonies and will visit her husband's family home for a few days. She will then return to her own home to live until she reaches puberty.

The exotic bangles and gaily colored saris only emphasize the fate of thousands of women who work as laborers for very low wages in terrible conditions of filth, dust, and heat.

East & North Delhi

DOWN THE CENTURIES, THE YAMUNA RIVER HAS BEEN Delhi's highway and local water source. Its western banks are thus the sites of major ancient monuments and, happily, are being rediscovered. A day spent moving northward along the river takes in a variety of top sights. There should be something to suit every interest: Simply skip the ones that do not appeal.

NIZAMUDDIN TO PURANA QILA

The streets behind the deluxe Oberoi Hotel have a medieval air about them. They form the village of **Nizamuddin,** whose heart is the *dargah* (shrine) of the Sufi saint Shaikh Nizam-ud-din Chishti (1238–1325). One of the great

mystic orders, Sufism was brought to India by Khwaja Muin-ud-din Chishti, who settled in Ajmer (see p. 133). It has been said that the Sufis, whose devotion, piety, asceticism, and tolerance were so attractive to Hindus, were the true missionaries of Islam to India. The Chishti order's influential followers included many of the Sultanate rulers and Mughal royal families.

To visit the **dargah,** follow the streets past stores and stalls selling everything from the Koran to cassettes of *qawwalis,* gentle devotional songs. The shrine itself is surrounded by royal tombs, including those of two Tughlaq rulers and Shah Jahan's daughter, Jahanara (see p. 97) Here, too, lies Amir Khusrau (died 1325), whose poetry includes this couplet: "If there is a paradise on earth, it is this, it is this, it is this"—possibly referring to Shah Jahan's Diwan-i-Am building in the Red Fort (see p. 65). He also wrote qawwalis that you might hear in the daily singing there. All these tombs benefit from the spiritual strength of the saint's presence.

This is why the Mughal emperor Humayun is buried nearby. His is the most magnificent of Delhi's tombs, and it is an essential stop if you are intending to visit the Taj Mahal later, for this is its forerunner. **Humayun's tomb** was built in 1565 by his wife, Bega Begum. She employed the Persian architect Mirak Mirza Ghiyas to design the first great Mughal garden tomb. With his knowledge of monumental Timurid tombs, he created something new using local sandstone, marble, and stonemasons.

Once inside, the visitor moves along through a series of walls pierced by gateways. Inside the first, turn right to Isa Khan's sturdy tomb (1547), already adopting Hindu details such as projecting eaves and domed kiosks. The final wall surrounds a formal *char bagh*

The dargah of **Shaikh Nizam-ud-din Chishti** (above) is the focus of a Muslim burial ground for nobility, including the emperor Humayun, whose tomb (left) stands in a char bagh.

(four gardens) that reflects the Koran's description of paradise. Look at the great tomb on its high platform from here, the double dome making possible a soaring exterior and well-proportioned interior. Through the newly restored gardens, steep steps lead onto the platform to see the emperor's cenotaph (monument) in the mausoleum, and those of his son Dara Shukoh and other Mughal royals. In accordance with Islamic custom, their bodies lie buried at ground level. Before leaving, see if you can spot Purana Qila fort, the next stop.

Delhi Zoo lies between Humayun's tomb and Purana Qila, India's biggest and most important zoo, established in 1959. Through poor management the potentially

Nizamuddin

🅰 63 C3

✉ W of Mathura Rd.

Humayun's tomb

🅰 63 C3

✉ Off Mathura Rd.

💲 $

Delhi Zoo
63 C4
Mathura Rd.
Closed Fri.

fascinating collection, which includes the one-horned rhinoceros from Assam, the Asiatic lion from Gujarat, and other examples of India's rich wildlife, is not always a joy to visit. Better conditions for the animals would greatly enhance this zoo.

A Gujarat basketmaker displays her skills at the National Crafts Museum.

Purana Qila (Old Fort) rises above it. Archaeologists say this spot may have been where Arjuna, one of the five Pandava hero brothers, founded the sacred site of Indraprastha (City of Indra) as recounted in the epic *Mahabharata* (see p. 76). More certainly, the second Mughal emperor, Humayun, brought the capital back here from Agra and in 1533 founded Dinpanah (Shelter of the Faith). The soaring walls and their three gates are his, but his usurper, Sher Shah Sur (see p. 40), erected the two buildings inside: the **Qala-I-Kuhna-Masjid,** with its five great arches and proto-Mughal decoration, and the **Sher Mandal.** It was from the roof of this building that Humayun, having regained his throne in 1555, fell down the stairs and died in 1556.

Purana Qila
63 C4
Mathura Rd.
Son-et-lumière times vary

NATIONAL CRAFTS MUSEUM

Sited in the shadow of the Purana Qila, this is arguably one of the finest museums of its kind and a must for anyone interested in the huge range of fine craftsmanship to be seen all over India. Jyotindra Jain, the museum's inspiration and its director since 1984, constantly commissions pieces and adds to the several thousand quality examples already displayed in a congenial, unstuffy atmosphere.

This is a museum that is guaranteed to bring smiles. A warren of courtyards and rooms designed by Charles Correa houses the primary collection. Do not miss the life-size carved wooden cows and horses, a model of a whole village, tribal metalwork animals of all shapes, and rooms covered with folk paintings. Giant storage pots, plastered walls, a temple chariot, and a carved wooden dovecote lead to the dazzling fabric collection upstairs.

Outside, there are sacred terracotta horses, a group of vernacular painted huts, a good gift shop, and a café. A highlight is watching craftsmen from all over India brought here to spend a three-month period making their own goods. You may find a weaver from Assam, a painter of miniatures from Jodhpur, or a potter from Tamil Nadu. You can buy direct from them; the museum often does

FEROZ SHAH KOTLA & SURROUNDINGS

The centerpiece of this group of site north of Purana Qila is Feroz Shah Kotla, entered from Bahadur Shah Zafar Marg road. It is the ruined citadel of a vast city that, in its heyday under Feroz Shah Tughlaq (*R*.1351–1388), stretched from North Ridge down to Lal Kot and was famed for its palaces, reservoirs, hunting lodges, mosques, and intellectual life. Then, in 1398, Timur (Tamburlaine) sacked it and

Within the complex lies the **National Rose Garden,** usually glorious in February and March. Across the main road you can see **Abdu'n Nabi's Mosque** (1575–76), built by Akbar's ecclesiastical registrar, who, failing to account for money that he had

National Crafts Museum

🏛 63 C4

✉ Pragati Maidan (enter on Bhairion)

🕐 Closed Mon., & July–Sept.

carried off its treasures. His descendant, Babur, later invaded India and founded the Mughal dynasty (see pp. 39–40). Imagine this as you wander the lawns around a ruined mosque, palace, and *baoli* (step-well).

Feroz Shah, a weak ruler but a great builder, intellectual, and antique collector, brought the mysterious carved pillar here from Meerut (and brought another to North Ridge), believing the inscriptions to be a magic charm. In fact, when the scholar James Princep unraveled the pillar's Brahmi script in 1837, it was discovered that the inscriptions were Ashoka's edicts (see p. 31) promoting dharma.

supposedly taken to the poor in Mecca, was summarily murdered.

MEMORIALS TO MAHATMA & OTHERS

The land left behind by the Yamuna when its course altered is now an undulating park devoted to the memory of India's modern heroes. Planted with fine trees and well kept, this is a tranquil and pleasant place for a walk in winter or during cool summer hours.

The first and most visited memorial is **Raj Ghat.** A platform marks the spot where Mahatma Gandhi (see p. 150) was cremated after his assassination on January

The scant but evocative ruins of Feroz Shah Kotla include Feroz Shah's own palace, a mosque, and a baoli (step-well).

Feroz Shah Kotla

🏛 63 C4

✉ Bahadur Shah Zafar Marg

Raj Ghat

🏛 63 C5

✉ Mahatma Gandhi Rd.

A statue of
Mahatma Gandhi
in contemplation,
wreathed with
marigold garlands

**Gandhi National
Museum**
www.gandhimuseum.org
🏛 63 C5
✉ Opposite Raj Ghat,
   Mahatma Gandhi Rd.
☎ 011-2331 1793
🕐 Closed Mon.

Vir Bhumi
🏛 63 C5
✉ Mahatma Gandhi Rd.

**Shanti Van & Vijay
Ghat**
🏛 63 C5
✉ Mahatma Gandhi Rd.

30, 1948. It was then made into an
oasis of peace using Vanu G.
Bhuta's design of a walled, square
garden entered through a simple
arch. For Indians and others, this is
a place of pilgrimage. If you wish
to know more, you can visit the
modest but informative **Gandhi
National Museum** across the
main road, where photographs,
quotes, descriptions, and sometimes documentaries pay tribute to
the Mahatma; literature is on sale
at the gift shop.

Tragedy was to strike Indian
leaders again after 1948. Just north
of here, in a less formal setting, a
string of memorials begins with
Vir Bhumi, where Rajiv Gandhi
(assassinated May 21, 1991) was
cremated. The memorial to his
brother Sanjay Gandhi (died in a

plane accident, June 1980) is nearby. Their mother, Indira
(assassinated October 31, 1984),
was cremated at **Shanti Ghat**
(Forest of Peace), as was her father,
India's first prime minister,
Jawaharlal Nehru (died May 27,
1964). Finally, **Vijay Ghat**
remembers Lal Bahadur Shashtri,
India's second prime minister (died
January 11, 1966). If you get this
far, you can enjoy views of Shah
Jahan's riverside palaces.

**CIVIL LINES & NORTH
RIDGE**
As historians gain a better perspective on the British period in India's
history, so opinions are revised in
the light of greater knowledge and
objectivity. For those interested, a
short trip into the rarely visited

area that was British Delhi from the 18th century until New Delhi was built brings fascinating rewards. (See also Lucknow, pp. 310–313.)

On up Mahatma Gandhi Road and into Lothian Road, the tumbledown **Lothian Cemetery** is on the right, just before an arched ruin midroad. The ruin is the remains of the British Magazine, a huge ammunition storehouse. It was deliberately blown up by the British on May 11, 1857, to prevent the freedom fighters—Indian soldiers in the British Army who had mutinied in Meerut the previous day—from seizing it. The bang was said to have been heard in Meerut, 31 miles (50 km) away. Just beyond, the gray obelisk is the **Telegraph Memorial,** from which the Anglo-Indian operator warned the British Army of the mutineers' approach. On the right, the dilapidated, columned building dates from an earlier time: In 1803 it became Delhi's first **British Residency.**

The distinctive yellow-plastered and domed **St. James's** (consecrated 1836), Delhi's first church, merits a stop. It was built by Col. James Skinner (circa 1778–1841), the son of a Scotsman and a Rajput, who founded Skinner's Horse, crack cavalry regiments distinguished by their yellow uniforms. Skinner family tombs stand in the churchyard. Inside the church, the family pew is at the front, Skinner's tomb is by the altar, and there are monuments to other British men.

Lothian Road now passes a lone survivor of Shah Jahan's many-gated city (see p. 64): **Kashmiri Gate,** so called because the Mughal emperors and their court would leave Delhi's searing summer heat through this gate on their way to the cool Kashmir hills. In September 1857, 5,000 British troops swarmed down from the Ridge, breached the walls, confronted up to 20,000 rebelling Indians and, after six days of fighting, retook Delhi. Brig.-Gen. John Nicholson, who died at the gate, is buried in **Nicholson Cemetery** up the road on the left, across from Qudsia Gardens, now a pale memory of its lush former days.

Here Lothian Road is called Sham Nath Marg. On the right, the spacious and delightful **Oberoi Maidens Hotel** (see p. 347), built in 1900, may be just the place for some refreshment; Sir Edwin Lutyens lived here while his New Delhi was being built.

From here follow Underhill Road, which passes forgotten grand colonial houses set on large, leafy grounds. At the end turn left on Rajpur Road, then left again at the top on Rani Jhansi Marg. This takes you to North Ridge, from which British troops poured down to retake Delhi. **Flagstaff Tower,** on its crest, is where the British women and children gathered five months earlier, before fleeing to Karnal as the mutineers approached.

Near here you can find odds and ends from Delhi's history: first, the remains of one of Feroz Shah Tughlaq's hunting palaces, **Kushkh-i-shikav** (1356), on the right; then, William Fraser's country retreat, on the same side, called **Hindu Rao's House** (1830). Fraser, who had six or seven wives, fathered uncounted children, and knew India better than most Europeans, was Resident of Delhi until his murder in 1835.

On the way down from the ridge you can see the small, tapering Gothic tower of the Mutiny Memorial. Built to remember the British dead, it is now renamed **Ajitgarh** and remembers Indian martyrs who died fighting colonial rule. A left turn on Boulevard Road takes you back to Kashmiri Gate. ∎

Lothian Cemetery
🅜 63 C5
✉ Lothian Rd.

St. James's Church
🅜 63 C6
✉ Lothian Rd.
☎ 011-2296 0873

Nicholson Cemetery
🅜 63 C6
✉ Qudsia Rd.

Kushkh-i-shikav
🅜 63 C6

Hindu Rao's House
🅜 63 B6

Ajitgarh
🅜 63 B6

A good book

Indian literature—written by Indians and non-Indians—is a rich and unending feast of intimate diaries, romantic fiction, matter-of-fact reports, and golden prose. And it keeps on coming: Unknown texts are continually being rediscovered and newly published; familiar favorites such as Rudyard Kipling's *Kim* are reprinted; and new writing on India is as fresh as ever.

It is easy to find good reading material to suit every taste. Moreover, the bigger cities in India have well-stocked bookstores with much lower prices than in the West.

India's literature may be daunting. However, a child's edition, or the children's cartoon strip magazines that recount the main epics episodically, are easy ways of grasping the background stories and a knowledge of these can help you enjoy India's paintings, dance-drama, and sculpture. The *Mahabharata* is an epic poem recounting the civil war between the Pandavas, led by Arjuna, and the Kurus. In a later addition, the *Bhagavad Gita*, Krishna discusses with Arjuna the human struggle for love, light, and redemption. The other great epic is the *Ramayana*, in which good king Rama, helped by monkey and bear allies, rescues his wife, Sita, from Ravana, the multiheaded demon king of Sri Lanka. The ancient Puranas, meanwhile, include the popular stories of Vishnu's incarnation as the vivacious human, Krishna.

Early and classical devotional poetry can be read in sensitive full translations. Try the Penguin editions of *The Kural* by the Tamil writer Tiruvalluvar, or the Sanskrit lyrical poems of Bhartrihari and Bilhana.

The West first learned about India through written accounts. The diaries, travel writing, and letters of early travelers formed the basis of Western knowledge of India until relatively recently. Images of India only became common when the uncle-nephew team of Thomas and William Daniells began publishing series of prints of India in London in the 1790s.

Jawaharlal Nehru wrote *An Autobiography* and *Glimpses of World History*. His contemporaries, equally aware of India's changing state, included Mulk Raj Anand (*Untouchable, Coolie*), Nirad Chaudhuri (*The Autobiography of an Unknown Indian*), and S. H. Manto, whose short stories include *Toba Tek Singh*.

Among recent generations of Indian writers, some of whom live outside the country, are Vikram Seth, whose epic *A Suitable Boy* explores post-independent northern India; Anita Desai, whose novels (for example *Clear Light of Day*) keep mainly to her home city of Delhi, and R. K. Narayan, whose novels are set in the south. Salman Rushdie, best known for *Midnight's Children,* explores Kerala and Mumbai in *The Moor's Last Sigh;* while Rohinton Mistry's *Such a Long Journey* and *A Fine Balance* have a broader base. Among younger writers, Kiran Desai's *Hullabaloo in the Guava Orchard* was followed by *The Inheritance of Loss* which won the Man Booker prize in 2006. Almost all of V. S. Naipaul's candid observations and predictions ring true, beginning with *An Area of Darkness.*

A good way to enjoy a range of writing is to read an anthology. Bruce Palling's *A Literary Companion: India* includes the reactions to India of the 4th-century Chinese Buddhist traveler Fa Hsien, the 19th-century Bishop Heber of Calcutta, and 20th-century English novelist Evelyn Waugh. It is surprising just how many people have written about India—American novelist Mark Twain (1835–1910), the humorist Edward Lear (1812–1888), the poet W. H. Auden (1907–1973), the photographer Sir Cecil Beaton (1904–1980), the explorer Sir Richard Burton (1821–1890), the novelist E. M. Forster (1879–1970)—and many more. ■

Kiran Desai (right), winner of the Booker prize and the National Book Critics Circle Award, and daughter of novelist Anita Desai, is an example of the literary talent that blossoms in India today. Voracious readers of books and newspapers in English as well as in their numerous native languages, educated Indians make full use of their local libraries, bookstores, and newsstands (below).

Feroz Shah
Tughlaq's tomb
looks to Afghan
fort architecture
for inspiration.

South Delhi

INTERESTING REMNANTS OF DELHI'S PRE-MUGHAL CITIES
are scattered over the large area of fashionable and increasingly built-
up south Delhi. To use your time well, it is best to take a taxi or hire a
car and driver for a long morning or, better still, a whole day. The
following route works well; remember to take drinks and snacks.

Lodi Gardens
🅜 63 C3
✉ Lodi Road

Safdarjang's Tomb
🅜 63 B3
✉ Junction of Lodi Rd.
& Sri Aurobindo
Marg
💲 $

LODI GARDENS

A stroll through Lodi Gardens in
the morning is a good start to the
day; your driver will deliver you to
one entrance and collect you from
the other.

Lady Willingdon, whose husband was viceroy from 1931 to
1936, saved this group of majestic
domed tombs from New Delhi
developers in the 1930s, laying out
lawns, shrubs, and shady trees
around them. The tombs were built
during the weak Sayyid and Lodi
sultanates (see p. 39), whose rulers
allowed noble power to grow.
Neither dynasty built a great city,
but both added many tombs and
mosques to Delhi. After Sikander
Lodi (R.1489–1517) moved to Agra
in 1502, the forlorn former capital
was nothing but a great necropolis.

If you enter from Lodi Road,
you come first to the **tomb of
Mohammad Shah,** the third
Sayyid ruler. Built in 1450, its
octagonal plan has sloping
buttresses that contrast with the
soft lotus patterns on the ceiling.
Next comes the **Bara Gumbad
Mosque** (1494), built during the
reign of Sikander Lodi. In addition
to the fine domed gateway, some of
the best plaster decoration in India
survives here; see the delicate
filigree work and elaborate facade.
The contemporary **Sheesh
Gumbad** (glass dome), so-called
because its dome used to have glazed
blue tiles that glittered in the sun,
stands on the hillock; the double-
story room inside has wonderful
stucco and painted decoration.
The **tomb of Sikander Lodi**

preserves its walled enclosure and adjoining mosque. Nearby is the **Athpula,** a seven-arched Mughal bridge built in the 16th century.

SOUTHWARD TO HAUS KHAS

South along Aurobindo Road toward Lal Kot, the first landmark building is the **tomb of Safdarjang,** the Nabab of Oudh (Avadh), a powerful minister to the dissipated, unpopular late Mughal ruler Ahmad Shah. Built in 1754, this is the last of the great Mughal garden tombs, keeping the formal layout of Humayun's (see pp. 70–71), but lacking its grace of style. Half a mile (1 km) farther down Sri Aurobindo Marg, a left turn to Kidwai Nagar reaches the grand tomb of **Darya Khan,** who served all the Lodi sultans.

The city of Siri, begun in 1304 by the popular and able Ala-ud-din Khilji *(R.*1296–1316), lay beyond here, but little remains. To get an idea of it, continue down Sri Aurobindo Marg and turn right into **Haus Khas village,** where many old houses have been renovated into upscale boutiques and restaurants (see p. 346). At the other end of the village street is a walled garden opening onto a huge sunken space. This was the *haus* (reservoir) that provided water for Siri's citizens. To the left are the steps, pavilions, and university buildings added by Feroz Shah Tughlaq in 1354. His austere **tomb** (1390) stands at the corner; its interior has fine plasterwork.

LAL KOT: THE EARLIEST DELHIS

About 7 miles (11km) south of Lodi Gardens down Aurobindo Road is the spot where historical Delhi began. Lal Kot was the Rajput citadel built by the Tomar king Anangpal in about 1060. Enlarged,

fortified, and given 13 gates by the Chauhan king Prithviraj III in 1080, this thriving city was captured by Qutb-ud-din-Aibak in 1192, marking the arrival of Islam in today's India (see p. 37). The next year Aibak began building a mosque, and six years later he began the Qutab Minar.

There is a lot to see in the complex. Through the arched entrance, remains of Ala-ud-din's southernmost Siri buildings survive on the right. Farther ahead, you find the base of **Alai Minar,** an unfinished tower he intended to be twice the size of the Qutab Minar (he died before much was built).

Aibak's mosque lies ahead: the **Quwwat-ul-Islam** (Might of Islam) mosque (1193–97), given additions by Iltutmish (1230) and Ala-ud-din (1315). Delicate stones taken from Hindu and Jain temples were used in the construction—you can see the ropes, bells, cows, and defaced figures on some. Cloisters lead to a courtyard and the monumental screen of the now vanished prayer hall, built by local Hindu masons. You can see how later parts of the magnificent, bold screen carving exchange floral and leaf motifs for more rigorously abstract Islamic arabesques and *suras* (verses) from the Koran. The Gupta **iron pillar** (fourth to fifth century), with its Sanskrit inscription, is a mystery in origins and casting, but legend says that those who encircle it with their arms behind their back will have their wish granted.

To the left of the screen, cross the ditch and turn right to find, at the end of the path, the modest **tomb of Iltutmish** *(R.*1210–1236), Aibak's son-in-law and successor. This is the earliest tomb of an Indian Islamic ruler, with beautifully carved walls. Back along the path, the ruins on the mound

Haus Khas village

- 63 B2
- W off Sri Aurobindo Marg

Lal Kot

- 63 B1
- Junction of Sri Aurobindo Marg & Mehrauli-Badapur Rd.

At Lal Kot, both the Qutab Minar (above) and the tomb of Iltutmish (opposite) used skilled craftsmen for their intricate carving.

Sanskriti
🕍 63 B1
✉ Anadgram, Mehrauli-
   Gurgaon Rd.
   (opposite radio
   station)
☎ 011-2652 7707
🕐 Closed Mon.

Tughlaqabad
🕍 63 D1
✉ Off Mehrauli-
   Gurgaon Rd.

ahead are of Ala-ud-din's unfinished **tomb** and his **college** (university). Leaving them through an
opening on the left, there are views
over the whole complex, including
Aibak's intricately carved, five-story
Qutab Minar (the top two stories
were rebuilt in marble by Feroz
Shah), which served as a tower of
victory and a minaret for calling
the faithful to prayer. The stocky,
square building to the right of it
is **Alai Darwaza** (1311), the
impressive entrance to Ala-ud-din's
now-lost mosque extension. Its
restrained bulk and large panels of
low-relief carving make it the most
Islamic building here. Beyond, the
Gothic-style cupola added to the
Qutab Minar by the British was so
ridiculed that it now stands in a
corner of the lawn.

OTHER SOUTH DELHI SITES

These real treats require a strong
pair of walking shoes, curiosity, and
determination to seek them out.

Take the street at the back of the
Lal Kot parking lot onto the open
plains dotted with Islamic monuments. Right ahead is **Metcalfe's
Folly,** two ruined tombs bought by
Sir Thomas Metcalfe, Delhi's British
Resident from 1835 to 1853, and
turned into a country retreat to
which he would ride on horseback
from Civil Lines (see p. 74).
Jamali-Kamali (1528), the
mosque and tombs of a poet-saint
and his brother, lie beyond; you can
walk or drive to them.

Next, head for Mehrauli village,
half a mile (1 km) west of Lal Kot.
Here you can find **Bhul-
Bhulaiyan** (1562), the double
tomb of Adham Khan and his
powerful mother, Maham Anga,
wet-nurse to the Mughal emperor
Akbar. Just beyond it, a street on the
left leads to a cluster of mosques, a
baoli (step-well), and tombs of three
late Mughal emperors.

If you enjoyed the National
Crafts Museum (see p. 72), then it
is well worth making reservations
to visit **Sanskriti,** which lies south
of Lal Kot. Here O. P. Jain, a collector of Indian crafts, exhibits his
collection of high-quality everyday
objects, terracotta and textiles in
a peaceful garden bordered by
artists' houses.

Finally, head eastward to
Tughlaqabad to find the massive
ruins of the city built by Ghiyath-
ud-Din Tughlaq from 1321 to 1325.
Here you can ramble over the fortifications, the palace precincts, and
the citadel. Across the road stands
Ghiyath-ud-Din's fortified tomb
(circa 1325), once surrounded by a
lake. As with the Sayyid and Lodi
tombs, it contrasts with the garden
tombs of the Mughals. ∎

The rediscovery of India

The British relationship with India's ancient sites and monuments was complicated. Progress in archaeology was pioneered by a few, such as Sir William Jones, who, with a group of fellow enthusiasts, founded the Asiatic Society in 1784. Discoveries were often by-products of military measures. This was true of the Survey of India, begun in 1800, which aimed to map the whole sub-continent from south to north. Teams of surveyors mapped the highest Himalayan peaks in the 1850s, naming the highest of all "Everest," after Sir George Everest, one of the project's superintendents. On this project and others, rediscoveries of overgrown, forgotten monuments abounded—the Chalukyan caves of Badami, the Buddhist *stupas* of Sanchi, the temples of Khajuraho, Ajanta's painted caves.

Ideas of restoration and conservation began in the mid-19th century. But the majority of British administrators still did not appreciate the significance of India's wealth of historical monuments. It took a piece of destruction of their own to kickstart the conservation movement. After Delhi was retaken, the British spent 1858 ransacking the city. They wantonly looted the imperial palaces and desecrated the mosques. Two-thirds of the Red Fort buildings were pulled down. Those remaining became the military garrison, and the area in front was cleared for security reasons. Suggestions for the fate of the Jama Masjid were that it be blown up, sold, turned into barracks or, worst of all, into a Hall of Remembrance to British victims of the war. This provoked an outcry among the enlightened. As the pioneering architectural historian James Fergusson argued, the military excuse for this destruction did not hold up.

The result was the appointment in 1861 of Sir Alexander Cunningham as archaeological surveyor of India. Projects such as the restoration of Sanchi and Gwalior, and the publication of copies of the Ajanta frescoes, followed. Activity increased when Lord Curzon arrived as Viceroy in 1899 and recognized that India had "the most glorious galaxy of monuments in the world," whose maintenance was an imperial responsibility. He reorganized the Archaeological Survey, arranged funds for it, and in 1902 appointed 26-year-old Sir John Marshall as first director-general, a position he held for 29 years. Indian scholars were employed, excavations and drawings made, laws for the protection of ancient monuments passed. While the public's attention was most closely focused on Agra's Mughal buildings, the temples of Kanchipuram, mosques of Bijapur, and other monuments were also cleared, cleaned, and restored.

Since independence, this vast body of knowledge has continued to grow under the aegis of the Archaeological Survey of India. The headquarters is situated next to the National Museum, on Janpath, in Delhi; reliable publications (all too often out of print, sadly) are sold here and at many Archaeological Survey sites.

A more recent conservation group, the Indian National Trust for Art and Cultural Heritage (INTACH), was founded in 1984. This nongovernment organization has area chapters spread right across India, whose enthusiastic, dedicated, and knowledgeable members have already achieved impressive results, including the restoration of Elephanta's cave, work on Jodhpur Fort, fixing some of Varanasi's *ghats,* and creating a heritage plan for Kochi (Cochin) and Mattancherry. For more information on INTACH's work, call tel 011-24692774, or visit www.intach.org. ∎

The British came to India as traders, but many were intrigued by the culture: They revealed India's wonders to the West, from Ajanta's murals (above) and Taj Mahal (below) to Khajuraho's controversial sculptures (opposite).

New Delhi

THE BRITISH HAD THEIR HEADQUARTERS FIRST AT CHENNAI (Madras), then at Kolkata (Calcutta). Delhi, strategic as it had been for past rulers, was a backwater. Agra, not Delhi, was capital of the Northwest Provinces that stretched up to the Hindu Kush.

New Delhi
63 C4

Then, to everyone's surprise, during his royal visit to India in 1911, the King-Emperor George V announced that the capital of British India was to move from Calcutta back to Delhi. Delhi was to rise, phoenixlike, to be the specially built imperial capital of the subcontinent. The King-Emperor and Queen-Empress Mary then laid a foundation stone north of Old Delhi and went home.

In 1913 British architect Edwin Lutyens sailed for India. He and his Planning Commission—Sir Herbert Baker, J. A. Brodie, G. S. C. Swinton, and others—disliked the original site, so they rode around Delhi's scrubland on elephants and settled on another. One night they quietly dug up the foundation stone, put it on a bullock cart, and relaid it on Raisina Hill.

This uncompromising approach was typical of Lutyens, who was responsible for the overall design o

**Above, right:
The two majestic
Secretariat
buildings, North
Block and South
Block, face
each other on
Raisina Hill.**

the new capital, called New Delhi, Viceroy's House (Rastrapati Bhavan), and some designs along Raj Path. His team designed the rest—quantities of public buildings plus more than 4,000 flat-roofed, stuccoed brick bungalows.

To prepare, Lutyens toured northern India. Unimpressed by Mughal buildings (he thought Fatehpur Sikri "the work of monkeys"), he found Sanchi's Buddhist stupas inspiration for his domes. Then he got to work on his plan: classical buildings with Indian details, such as deep shading eaves, set in a gracious garden city capable of endless expansion. He described it as "an Englishman dressed for the climate."

More than 30,000 laborers were employed to transform the hilly, dry site. Glorious red sandstone was brought from Dholpur, as it had been for Shahjahanabad (see p. 64). William Robertson Mustoe, trained at London's Kew Gardens, advised on the planting of 10,000 trees. Costs soared, and the budget passed 15 billion pounds (21 billion dollars). Lutyens fought hard but plans were occasionally modified.

On February 15, 1931, New Delhi was inaugurated by the viceroy, Lord Irwin. Two weeks of festivities included a performance of *Madame Butterfly* in the Red Fort, Scottish dancing, a pageant of painted elephants, and a 21-gun salute to herald the unveiling of Baker's Ashokan columns.

Sixteen years later, New Delhi was one of the most useful, if unintended, legacies the British left to the newly independent India: a ready-made capital.

RAISINA HILL

This is the heart of New Delhi, and India's political center. A good way to see it is to walk from Vijay Chowk to Raisina Hill's controversial gradient: Lutyens accused Baker of making it too steep and blocking the view of his masterpiece, Viceroy's House.

Vijay Chowk is where the military parade known as Beating the Retreat is held each January, at sunset; to the north, the circular building is **Sansad Bhavan** (Parliament House). Moving up the hill, the first pavilion provides breathtaking views. Raj Path sweeps

An elaborate *sarpesh* (turban ornament) made in Jaipur in the 19th century.

down from this citadel of power, crossing Janpath, past India Gate and into the far distance. The grand parade on Republic Day, January 26, moves along here. The area on the right is a vast triangle of once residential buildings; that to the left leads north to Connaught Place, now just one of Delhi's shopping centers.

The brow of Raisina Hill is unashamedly imperial. A wide avenue runs between Baker's **Secretariats,** their design a mixture of English baroque, Mughal doorways, and lotus-decorated domes, and leads to an ornate entrance screen. Beyond lies **Rastrapati Bhavan** (President's Palace, formerly Viceroy's House, *private*). Peer through the gates to see **Jaipur Column,** given by the Maharaja of Jaipur, a close British ally, standing in the courtyard. Behind, Lutyens' masterpiece has a facade 630 feet (192 m) wide and a plan covering 200,000 square feet (18,580 sq m), making it larger than Versailles. It was here, behind the central steps and columns, that Britain's last viceroy, Lord Mountbatten, stood in the Durbar Hall to hand power over to India's first prime minister, Jawaharlal Nehru. Behind the house, President's Estate includes the spectacular **Moghul Gardens.** Inspired by the Moghul Gardens of Kashmir and Gertrude Jekyll's work in England, they are kept in shape by 150 gardeners and are open to the public each spring.

CIVIC NEW DELHI

To get a flavor of the city as it was, drive along Raj Path to **India Gate,** which remembers the 90,000 Indian soldiers who died in World War I and the Afghan War (1919). An eternal flame has been added to honor the Unknown Soldier. Farther along, the graceful sandstone pavilion beyond once held a statue of George V but now stands empty. A clutch of very grand former palaces surrounds it: Hyderabad, Baroda, Bikaner, and Jaipur Houses. The last is now the **National Gallery of Modern Art,** which documents the 20th century emergence of Indian contemporary art and hosts art shows.

Back along Raj Path, the intersection with Janpath was to have a collection of public buildings. It got just two. One is the **National Archives** building, whose exhibits include items from its collection of books and manuscripts on political, social, and economic history. The other is

National Gallery of Modern Art
✉ Jaipur House, India Gate
🕐 Closed Mon.

National Archives
✉ Janpath
🕐 Closed Mon.

National Museum
✉ Janpath
🕐 Closed Mon.
💲 $

the **National Museum** (1955–1960). Founded in 1949, its impressive collection makes a good introduction to Indian art. See especially the stone and bronze sculptures from Mathura, Bharhut, Sarnath, and Kausambi and southern India. They are exhibited in the entrance hall, corridors, and first-floor rooms and are some of India's most glorious artistic achievements. Upstairs are fine miniature paintings, musical instruments, and glittering jewelry.

THREE NEW DELHI HOUSES

Here is a fascinating insider's view of New Delhi. Ask your driver to take you first to the palatial **Teen Murti Museum** (1930) and its flower-filled garden, built for the commander-in-chief. This is where Nehru lived from 1948 until his death in 1964, and his desk, library, and bedroom are as he left them. Next is the contrasting **Indira Gandhi Memorial Museum,** a small bungalow in lush surroundings where Nehru's daughter lived. Photographs lining the walls recount the story of her leadership and the fates of her sons. On the grounds a sculpted river of glass marks the spot

where, on October 31, 1984, she was assassinated. **Gandhi Smriti** (Birla House) is where, on January 30, 1948, Mahatma Gandhi was shot by a Hindu fanatic who believed he was too tolerant toward Muslims. ■

A seated Bodhisattva carved in the first century, found at Mathura, south of Delhi

The Gandhi factor

Politics can turn on a surname. When Indira Nehru, daughter of India's first prime minister, Jawaharlal Nehru, a Kashmiri of the brahman caste, married a Parsee man named Feroz Gandhi, she acquired arguably her most useful political tool.

The very name of Gandhi contained echoes of the greatness of the revered Mahatma, Mohandas Kamarchand Gandhi, although there was no blood connection. Even some Indians would be confused, and no Congress Party campaigners would risk losing votes by putting them right. The hero of the struggle for freedom would be allowed to radiate his influence to the benefit of all, even into the murky waters of politics. Rajiv Gandhi benefited, too, and today, as his daughter rises in the political theater, people throughout India continue to speak not of the Nehru inheritance but of the Gandhi dynasty. ■

Teen Murti Museum
✉ Teen Murti Rd.
🕐 Closed Mon.

Indira Gandhi Memorial Museum
✉ 1 Safdar Jang Rd.
🕐 Closed Mon.

Gandhi Smriti Museum
✉ Hall of Nations Bldg., 5 Tees January Rd.

Creating a modern architecture

When the French architect Le Corbusier (1887–1965) came to India in 1951, he was already 64 years old with a reputation as a brilliant, if controversial, architect and a semi-abstract painter, sculptor, and writer. He turned Indian architecture upside down, and it is only now beginning to find itself again.

Le Corbusier came at the invitation of the Punjab government to be architectural adviser for their new capital. Punjab had been sliced in half when it gained independence and Pakistan's section included the city of Lahore. The Frenchman was impressed by the grand scale of Lutyens' Delhi and by the abstract shapes of the Jantar Mantar there (see p. 92). These ideas he incorporated into his uncompromising designs for Chandigarh (see pp. 120–21), where he employed his modular system and *brises-soleil* (sunbreakers), and placed the emphasis on raw concrete.

Such a total break with the vernacular was welcomed; it underlined the new India's ambition and idealism. Le Corbusier picked up commissions from progressive patrons in Ahmedabad, capital of Gujarat state, where he built Shodhan House, Manorama Sarabhai's houses, and the Mill Owners Association building, all in the 1950s.

A posse of young Indian architects absorbed his tenets; anonymous concrete buildings sprang up all over India. Two exceptional architects were Balkrishna V. Doshi and Charles Correa. Both have early buildings in Ahmedabad, including Doshi's Tagore Hall and Correa's Sabarmati Ashram.

Correa's other public buildings, including arts complexes in Panaji (Goa), Bhopal (Madhya Pradesh), and, most recently,

Though Le Corbusier's large-scale town plans were often rejected, his designs proved very influential.

Jaipur (Rajasthan), show a slow return to Indian traditions but with modern interpretations.

The Jaipur project is the Jawahar Kala Kendra Museum, and it is just one of several major buildings in India that reflect a welcome change. As one writer put it, "Indian architecture is beginning to find its own way again."

The point of inspiration leaves Western philosophy and returns to an ancient Hindu concept, the *mandala*, a representation of the universe that can be used as the mathematical basis for architecture. Correa specifically takes a nine-square mandala, since Hindus believe nine to be the most spiritual and powerful number, which helps connect man to the universe. Two other Indian influences are at play: the Hindu temple design, where open and closed spaces flow in and out of each other, and Jaipur's Jantar Mantar, the giant abstract astrological instruments built by Jai Singh II.

Another powerful and vivid example of India returning to its own roots for inspiration is Satish Gujral's Belgian Embassy in Delhi. Like Correa, Gujral, a painter rather than a trained architect, looks back to the mandala. He also takes inspiration from Delhi's ancient tombs—the sweeping brick arches, the domes, the use of brick and granite. The whole building sits in a large sunken garden, echoing the Mughal emperor Humayun's Persian-inspired garden tomb.

The Jaipur and Delhi buildings are thoroughly modern but sing with the rich song of India's own culture. Furthermore, each has its own clear regional identity. India now has a growing number of architects who are similarly inspired. ■

Above: The vast Secretariat building (1958) in the modern, shared state capital of Chandigarh shows Le Corbusier's obsession with geometric shapes and emphasis on scale. Right: The simple house where Gandhi lived in Sabarmati Ashram, Ahmadabad. Below: The gleaming, white, unfurling lotus shape of the Baha'i Temple in South Delhi has been compared to the Sydney Opera House.

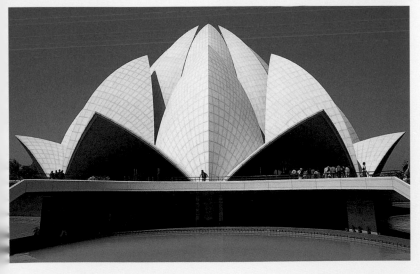

More places to visit in Delhi

ASHOKA'S ROCK EDICT
In 1966 another set of Ashoka's rock edicts (see p. 31) was discovered, this time on a rock in southeast Delhi, proving that a trading center or crossroads had existed in this area as early as Mauryan times.
✉ Off Shaheed Captain Gaur Marg, Srinavaspuri

BABA KHARAK SINGH MARG
This radial road at Connaught Place (see p. 91) is lined with the high-quality, fixed-price official stores of each Indian state, selling state specialties. Halfway along there is a good restaurant for hungry shoppers.
✉ Connaught Pl. 🕐 Closed Sun.

BAHA'I TEMPLE
The nine soaring white marble petals of this lotus-shaped temple make this a landmark in the south Delhi suburbs. There are guided tours of the spectacular central hall.
✉ Kalkaji District Park, Nehru Pl. ☎ 011-444029 🕐 Closed Mon., & services

CHANAKYAPURI
This is the diplomatic area of the city, where foreign nations were given plots of land at the time of independence. It became a showcase for each nation's contemporary architecture. Driving down its main avenue, Shanti Path, you can see the buildings and have fun guessing which style belongs to which country;

Well-stocked shops line the shaded colonnades of Connaught Place.

Pakistan's building is the one with the distinctive blue dome.

CHRISTIAN CATHEDRALS

Both the Anglican and Roman Catholic cathedrals in New Delhi are stunning landmarks, built to the winning designs of British architect H. A. N. Medd. The Anglican Church of the Redemption (1927–1935) is a dignified Palladio-inspired design. The Roman Catholic Church of the Sacred Heart (1930–34) is a bold, Italianate design close to North Avenue.

Church of the Redemption ✉ Church Rd.
Church of the Sacred Heart ✉ Bangla Sahib Rd.

CONNAUGHT PLACE

T. R. Russell's great amphitheater of stuccoed colonnades, which was named after George V's uncle, was originally compared with the city of Bath in England for its modern design, but it took time to win popularity. It eventually became, and has remained to the present day, the hub of Delhi's regular stores, modest hotels, and offices, even if the classy south Delhi colonies (as residential areas of the city are known) have their own commercial centers. If the combination of the eight radial roads running into the three concentric ones (see map p. 63) confuses you, just look for Janpath, which will lead you back to Raj Path. 🅰 63 C5

HAILEY'S BAOLI

This step-well (see p. 386) is thought to have been built during the Tughlaq sultanate and has a tiny mosque at the top of the steps. To find this forgotten relic, head northward up Kasturba Gandhi Marg, turn right on Hailey Road, then take the first lane on the left.

IMPERIAL HOTEL

The Imperial (see p. 346) was built between 1933 and 1935 by the Singh family and furnished with London silver and Italian marble. It is still owned by the same family today. Once the social center of New Delhi, with its majestic palm trees and expansive lawns, it has now been carefully restored.
✉ Janpath, Connaught Pl.

JANTAR MANTAR

Maharaja Jai Singh II of Jaipur was a noted astronomer. He built the first of his five outsize observatories here in 1724, although his principal one was in Jaipur

Ganesh, the elephant god, faces the eye-catching Lakshmi Narayan (Birla) Temple, funded by the Birla family in the 1930s.

(see pp. 131-32). These huge, pink stone, abstract-looking instruments were a gift from the Maharaja to the Mughal emperor Muhammad Shah, for whom he revised both the Muslim calendar and astronomical tables.
✉ Sansad Marg, Connaught Pl.

LAKSHMI NARAYAN MANDIR

Built by the prominent Birla merchant family, who were also patrons of Mahatma Gandhi, this ostentatious, tiered marble temple is appropriately dedicated to Lakshmi, goddess of wealth.
✉ Mandir Marg, W of Connaught Pl.

NATIONAL PHILATELIC MUSEUM

For philatelists, India is an especially interesting country. Yet this collection of rare stamps, first-day covers, and other treats is not easy to find: The best option is to go to the main post office on Sansad Marg, and once there, ask the head postmaster, who will happily direct you. Commemorative stamps are on sale at the main post office, too.
✉ Sansad Marg, Connaught Pl. ☎ 011-371 0154 🕐 Closed Sat.–Sun.

RAIL TRANSPORTATION MUSEUM

This is a railroad buff's delight, an open-air permanent home for some of the great engines and royal coaches that bring to life the great days of subcontinental railroad travel in India. The museum is home to about 30 engines and 20 rail cars, their interiors well-preserved. Those on display include the Maharaja of Baroda's gilt parlor car (1886) and the Maharaja of Mysore's teak car with ivory and gold trim. Here, too, is the car that was used by the Prince of Wales (later Edward VII) during his visit to India in 1876. Inside the museum building itself, you will find a model of India's first-ever train, the steam engine that chugged from Bombay to Thana on April 16, 1853, seen off with a 21-gun salute; there are also models of other famous engines and displays of old tickets.
✉ South end of Chanakyapuri 🕐 Closed Mon.

ST. MARTIN'S CHURCH

Looming over the cantonment (military) area, west of the Ridge, this was the British garrison church. It was designed by Arthur Shoosmith and was built between 1928 and 1930. St. Martin's Church is an extraordinary feat of German Expressionism in British New Delhi, a huge, gaunt monolith with a high, square tower, built using three million bricks. ■

A rich choice of medieval forts and Buddhist *stupas*, riotous Hindu carving and tranquil Sikh temples, tiger country and exotic birds, not to mention the famous Taj Mahal, awaits those who want to escape from the steamy capital.

Around Delhi

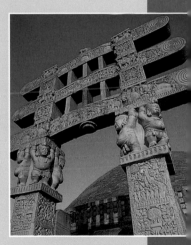

Carved gateway at Sanchi

The Taj Mahal seen from Agra Fort, across a bend in the Yamuna River

Around Delhi

SLIPPING OUT OF DELHI FOR A FEW DAYS CAN BRING GREAT REWARDS. Tempting as it may be to head west to the better known Rajasthan, it is worth considering the riches lying in wait for you to the north and south of India's capital.

This map shows how you can follow the Yamuna as it flows south from Delhi through ancient Mathura to the royal Mughal buildings of Agra. Both cities are just inside Uttar Pradesh, a large state stretching up to the lower Himalayan mountains and eastward far beyond its capital, Lucknow (see pp. 310–13). The contrasting attractions of Fatehpur, Sikri's deserted royal city, and Bharatpur's wondrous bird sanctuary are nearby.

To the south is Madhya Pradesh, India's biggest state; it covers much of central India and has several notable wildlife parks—Panna, Bandhavgarh, and Kanha. Dramatic forest and rocky outcrops are the settings for the forts of Gwalior, Datia, and Orchha and, east of them, the isolated temples of Khajuraho. The capital of Madhya Pradesh is Bhopal, an excellent base for visiting Sanchi and other sites in the area before continuing to Indore and Mandu.

If the weather is hot, a trip north from Delhi might be more comfortable. The Grand Trunk Road runs through Haryana, a small state that takes Delhi's overflow and has the fastest growing economy of all states. It shares its capital, Le Corbusier's specially built Chandigarh (see pp. 120–21), with neighboring Punjab, whose western border meets Pakistan. The unspoiled towns of Patiala and Amritsar stand on either side of Punjab's lush landscape of almost continuous wheat fields.

North of Chandigarh, the cool beauty of the lower Himalayan mountains inspired the British to create their summer capital, Shimla (Simla), here. A trip northeast from Delhi can lead to other cool retreats, such as Mussoorie and Nainital, or join Hindu pilgrims at Hardwar and Rishikesh, ending with a visit to Corbett National Park.

Transportation is easy by car, train, and plane. The Shatabdi Express trains, running from Delhi through Agra, Gwalior, and Jhansi to Bhopal, make travel to this region particularly easy, as does the train up to Chandigarh. There are some particularly delightful hotels in the unspoiled provincial towns. ∎

Ravi

Pathankot 20
HIMACHAL
PRADESH
Gurdaspur
Batala 15   THE HIMALAYA
Amritsar Hoshiarpur
Kapurthala Bilaspur
Jalandhar
PAKISTAN   p. 319
Phagwara Nalagarh 22
Ludhiana Shimla
Firozpur Pinjore Kalka
Moga Khanna Chandigarh
Faridkot Sirhind Dehra Dun
Abohar Patiala Ambala Rishikesh
Bathinda PUNJAB Yamunanagar
UTTARAKHAND
Sirsa Saharanpur Haridwar CORBETT
Kaithal NAT. PARK Ranikhet
HARYANA Karnal Muzaffarnagar Nainital
RAJASTHAN & GUJARAT Jind Panipat Ramnagar
p. 129 Hisar Meerut Haldwani NEPAL
Hansi 10 Sonipat Amroha Moradabad
Bhiwani Rohtak DELHI 24 Rampur Pilibhit
New Delhi Ghaziabad Sambhal
Gurgaon Bareilly
Rewari Faridabad Bulandshahr
Narnaul UTTAR Budaun 24
Aligarh PRADESH
Hathras p. 286
Mathura EASTERN INDIA
Taj Mahal Mainpuri
Fatehpur Sikri Firozabad
KEOLADEO GHANA Agra
NAT. PARK Etawah
Bhind
Morena
Kalpi
Gwalior Hamirpur
Sonagiri Orai 25
Datia Charkhari
Shivpuri 25 Jhansi Nivari Banda
SHIVPURI Orchha Mahoba
NAT. PARK Pichor 26 Chhatarpur
Guna Khajuraho Satna
Tikamgarh PANNA Panna
Lalitpur NAT. PARK
Ashoknagar Pawai
Nimach Bina-Etawa BANDHAVGARH
Mandsaur Sironj Udayapur Sagar NAT.
RAJASTHAN & GUJARAT Rajgarh Damoh PARK Tala
p. 129 Jaora Udaigiri Caves Murwara Umaria
Nagda Shajapur Sanchi Vidisha Sihora
Ratlam Shujalpur Udaipura 12 Patan Jabalpur
Ujjain Dewas Bhopal Bhimbetka Narsimhapur Dindori
Jhabua Dhar Indore Vindhya Range Mandla
Mandu Barwah Hoshangabad Lakhnadon
Narmada Amarwara KANHA
Maheshwar Harda Chhindwara Seoni NAT. PARK
Barwani Khargon Khandwa Betul Waraseoni Baihar
Sendhwa Multai Pandhurna Balaghat
Satpura Range Burhanpur
MUMBAI & MAHARASHTRA
p. 158

0   200 kilometers
0   100 miles

Area of map detail
New
Delhi

A   B   C   D

Qasim Khan,
Akbar's
Superintendent
of Riverine Works,
was responsible
for Agra Fort's
massive sandstone
double walls.

Agra & around

SIKANDER LODI MOVED THE CAPITAL FROM DELHI TO AGRA.
But the Mughal emperors transformed it into the dazzling, fairy-tale
court whose fame reached Europe, and one, Shah Jahan, built the Taj
Mahal here. Today the empty buildings need plenty of imagination to
bring them to life; looking at some jewel-like Indian miniature paintings of Mogul court scenes can help.

Agra

95 C4

**India Tourist
Office**

www.up-tourism.com

191 The Mall

0562-363377

AGRA FORT
After Babur's brief rule, during
which he held a great celebratory
feast at Agra, Humayun took the
capital back to Delhi. But when
Akbar (R.1556–1605) built his fort
between 1565 and 1573, Agra burst
into life. Later, when his grandson
Shah Jahan returned to Delhi in
1648, the fort was left to plunderers
(see Dig, p. 133).

Grand fortifications
Cross the moat to reach the first
great gateway of one of India's
finest riverine forts: Akbar's magnificent double-walled fort beside
the Yamuna. Qasim Khan designed
it, using the glowing red sandstone
that distinguishes many great
Mughal buildings. With soaring
fortifications and the Yamuna
waters lapping its walls, the treasury

It is believed that Jahangir added the long, marble-inlaid facade of the building behind. Through the archway you find a fascinating suite of **Akbar's rooms.** Built by local craftsmen, they are not remotely Islamic. Instead, the stocky proportions, pillar-and-beam structure, and densely carved decoration give them the look of pure Hindu buildings, constructed in stone instead of wood. Look for the central courtyard's square arches, broad decorative brackets, and the Hindu motif of parrots in the carving.

From the courtyard ahead, Akbar watched his elephant fights, a sport only royals were permitted to take part in. Ever superstitious, in 1605 Akbar staged a fight between the elephants of his son Salim and his grandson Khusrau, to see whose would win and thus who would succeed. Salim's elephant won. Later, Jahangir lived in these and other, similar, rooms commissioning paintings and enriching the simple walls with gilt-painted stucco. You can also enjoy your first tantalizing view of the Taj Mahal from here.

Shah Jahan's marble additions

Moving on, the next rooms are a striking contrast. Sandstone is exchanged for white marble, stockiness for elegance. Shah Jahan (R.1627–1658) built them, living here with his beloved wife, Mumtaz Mahal, when not on campaign. After her death and his subsequent move to Delhi, the emperor was deposed by his third son, Aurangzeb, in 1658 and kept prisoner here, tended by his daughter Jahanara until he died in 1666. Shah Jahan's buildings are thus suffused in romance and sadness. **Khas Mahal** is his suite of private rooms, and **Mussaman Burj** is

was safe and the army, court, and citizens could withstand long sieges. Note the battlemented parapets with ramparts and loop-holed merlons. Today's Indian Army still occupies much of the fort. **Amar Singh Gate** comes next, and was built at right angles in order to deflect elephant charges.

Akbar & Jahangir's buildings

At the top of the ramp, a great **stone bath** stands in the gardens on the right, possibly a wedding present from Jahangir (R.1605–1627) to Nur Jahan in 1611. It is said that the rose petals used to scent her bathwater inspired her to develop *attar*, a type of pungent perfume, which is still sold in Indian bazaars; jasmine is one of the lighter ones to try.

State Tourist Office

✉ By Clarks Shiraz Hotel, 64 Taj Rd.

☎ 0562-360517

Festivals

Shardotsav, Oct.: dance and music

Shah Jahan gave the old lanes of Agra this landmark mosque in 1648, the year he forsook the city for Delhi.

Itimud-ud-Daulah's tomb

✉ E bank of Yamuna River, 2 miles (4 km) upstream of Taj Mahal

$ $

decorated raised throne alcove, where the emperor gave his daily audience. As you leave through the arch on the left, imagine the citizens of Agra pouring in through the gate on the right to attend a royal *durbar,* a morning of pomp, ceremony, and entertainment.

AFTER THE MUGHALS
Once the Mughals had moved to Delhi, Agra was occupied successively by the Jats, Marathas, and, from 1803 on, the British. The British cantonment area still has its wide avenues, elegant bungalows, and carefully sited public buildings. Try exploring Mall or Taj Roads, and look for **Queen Mary's Library** and **Central Post Office** at Sadar Bazar. Also, nearby stand handsome **St. George's** cantonment church (1826) and the **Havelock Memorial Church** (1873). In this commercial center, you will find upscale hotels, fine restaurants, and a busy shopping area with local handicrafts and fine leather goods. You may wish to sample some local dishes such as *petha* (pumpkin candy), *dalmoth* (fried chickpeas), and other delicious Mughal-inspired favorites.

North of old Agra city, go past **St. John's Church** the Roman Catholic cathedral with its landmark tower, and Sir Samuel Swinton Jacob's fine St. John's College, to find the **Roman Catholic cemetery** situated on the right. This is one of India's earliest Christian cemeteries. Christians who died in Lahore and Ajmer were brought here for burial. Its impressive monuments include the tomb of John Mildenhall (1614), envoy of Elizabeth I, and a miniature copy of the Taj Mahal built for the Dutchman General Hessing (1803), who was in charge of Agra Fort for the Marathas when the British took it.

the exquisite minipalace inlaid with *pietra dura,* built for Mumtaz. Upstairs, **Diwan-i-Khas** (public audience hall, 1628) is his most elegant building of all. In front of it stand two thrones; the black one was made for Jahangir when, a rebelling prince, he prematurely announced himself emperor in Allahabad in 1603. Underneath here was the treasury; the royal *hamams* (baths) were opposite, and the lawn was laid out with a formal pattern of water channels, fountains and flowerbeds.

Walk around the cloisters to find the tiny **Nagina Masjid** (gem mosque) and then, on the right, steep steps down to the **Diwan-i-Am.** Built by Shah Jahan to replace an earlier wooden version, it has elegant arches in front of a richly

ACROSS THE YAMUNA RIVER

It is worth every effort to visit the **tomb of Itimad-ud-Daulah** (see p. 41), built by his powerful daughter Nur Jahan, Jahangir's empress. The casketlike tomb (1622–28) has its walls coated with polychrome mosaic designs. Find delicate decorations inside, and outside enjoy serene gardens and delightful river views. On the same side of the Yamuna, there are substantial remains of **Ram Bagh** to the north, a Mughal garden that was probably the work of Babur and later Nur Jehan. To the south, the waterside tomb of **Chini-ka-Rauza** (1635) lies behind the market gardens. Further south, the recently rediscovered and renovated **Mahtab Bagh** (moonlit garden) completed the original Taj Mahal complex, and now provides glorious views of the Taj.

AROUND AGRA

At **Sikandra,** 5 miles (8 km) northwest of Agra, visit Akbar's great garden mausoleum. He began it in 1602, on the site of Sikaner Lodi's fort, but after his death in 1605 Jahangir aggrandized it and swapped modest sandstone for marble; Akbar's mausoleum is on the roof. Akbar's huge entrance gateway is impressive; look for Jahangir's floral painted vaults. Beware of the black-faced monkeys, who are quite tame but expect handouts from visitors. East of the complex is Jahangir's fine Kanch Mahal. On the 5-mile (8 km) drive up here, visit the Roman Catholic cemetery (see p. 98); also, spot the *kos minars* (milestones) that guided Mughal travelers, and various tombs.

The ancient city of **Mathura** stands on the Yamuna 39 miles (62 km) northwest of Agra, at the center of the holy land of Braj, and in Hindu mythology was the birth-

Mowing the lawn Indian-style, here at Agra Fort

place of Krishna. As such, Mathura is one of the Hindus' Seven Sacred Cities. Its waterfront is lined with bathing ghats and temples: See especially Dwarkadhish Temple (1914), built by Seth Gokuldass of Gwalior; river trips leave from Vishram Ghat. The town's **Archaeological Museum** has a magnificent collection that reflects Mathura's place as a trading center under the Sunga, Kushana, and Gupta dynasties. It houses ravishing Buddhist and Jain stone sculptures, which often use the distinctive Mathura speckled red sandstone. The collection also includes sculptures made in Gandhara but found locally.

Vrindavan, the most important of a group of Braj villages sacred to Hindus and especially devotees of Krishna, lies about 6 miles (10 km) north of Mathura. Here, Krishna flirted with the milkmaids; at Mahaban, his foster father, Nanda, tended the young god; at Gokul, Krishna was raised in secrecy; at Barsana, his consort Radha was born; and Goverdhan is the hill Krishna lifted to protect the female cowherds from the god Indra's storms. Plan your visit to the villages to coincide with a big Hindu festival (see pp. 379–82). ■

Sikandra
✉ 5 miles (8 km) N of Agra, off NH2
$ $. Free Fri.

Akbar's Mausoleum
☎ 0562-371230
$ $

Mathura
✉ 39 miles (62 km) N of Agra on NH2

Archaeological Museum
✉ Dampier Park, Mathura
🕐 Closed Mon.

Vrindavan
✉ 42 miles (68 km) N of Agra off NH2

Taj Mahal

Taj Mahal
www.tajmahalagra.com

🗺 95 C4
✉ Tajganj
🕐 Closed Fri.
💲 $

SHAH JAHAN'S WIFE DIED IN JUNE 1631 (SEE P. 42) AFTER bearing their 14th child. Mumtaz (Chosen One of the Palace) had been the emperor's wife, companion, adviser, and support for 17 years. Channeling his despair into the creation of her mausoleum, Shah Jahan called a council of top architects and craftsmen and embarked upon his masterpiece. He chose Ustad Isa Khan Effendi, a Persian from Shiraz, as master builder, his pupil Ustad Ahmed for the detailed work, and Ismail Khan for the dome.

Enter through any of the three gates to the complex and you leave chaos for order. The great gate prepares you further for the serenity within, with its inlaid Koran quote known as Al-Fajr (daybreak), which ends: "O Soul that art at rest. Return to the Lord, at peace with Him and He at peace with you. So enter as one of His servants. And enter into His garden."

You then do just that, emerging into a **char bagh** (four gardens), which is how paradise is described in the Koran: a lush, well-planted, walled garden divided symmetrically by water channels. Pause to take it all in.

This **garden tomb** takes to ultimate refinement the Mughal garden tomb built for Humayun (see pp. 70–71). Here, the proportions

A villager fills his water pot from the Yamuna River, seemingly unaware of the reflection of the world-famous local monument, the Taj Mahal.

are more satisfying; luxurious marble is used instead of sandstone, and the whole platform and mausoleum building is pushed from the center of the garden to the end, to benefit from the river light and from being silhouetted against the sky. The dome shape is more elegant and, as close inspection will reveal, the inlay work is finer.

But this memorial is more than a symbol of paradise to reward the faithful. It also symbolizes the royal pleasure garden and a lush oasis in the dry desert heat. To this, Shah Jahan added another, political image: The Taj Mahal symbolizes the might of Islam embodied in the all-powerful Mughal rulers.

It took 22 years to build the Taj. Craftsmen and laborers came from Baghdad, Delhi, Samarkand, Turkey, and from elsewhere in Asia. The marble was from Makrana, near Jaipur; the precious and semi-precious stones from various places—jasper from the Punjab, jade from China, lapis lazuli from Afghanistan, agates from Yemen.

As you wander through the gardens, you see the white marble of the Taj through the contrasting dark green trees; you see it reflected in the long fountain pool. At the front of the platform, railings mark the spot where Mumtaz's body was buried while the Taj Mahal was being built. A **mosque** stands to the left of the Taj. Up on the plat-

form, verses from the Koran, panels of low relief carving, and inlaid designs coat the exterior. Inside, cenotaphs for Mumtaz (central) and Shah Jahan lie surrounded by a finely decorated trellis screen (their real tombs lie in the now closed vault below).

The time of day that you first visit the Taj is important. The hard light of midday flattens it, whereas to enter the precincts midafternoon and slowly explore the gateway views and the lush gardens, ending at the platform as the sun ripens, is a near-perfect experience. You may find yourself inspired to return at sunrise to enjoy the magical and soft morning light. ■

Great Gateway

Char bagh (four gardens)

Above left and right: At the Taj Mahal, a family visits Mumtaz's memorial, while the nearby mosque is silent.

Marble inlay

Mogul patrons lifted the craft of *pietra dura* (hard stone) inlay decoration to new heights. The results are even more impressive if you know a little about this difficult, precise skill and see it being practiced.

Materials are supplied to the *ateliers* of Muslim craftsmen by Hindu merchants. The hard, nonporous white marble comes from Makrana, near Jaipur; coral and stones including turquoise, carnelian, and lapis lazuli come from all over the world. Once the design is agreed upon, a master craftsman draws it on the marble. The stones are selected, cut, and chiseled, then

the beds for each pattern gouged out. Each design is then fitted, fine-tuned, and stuck. Finally the whole surface is polished with fine emery.

Today, more than 5,000 pietra dura craftsmen are working in family-run ateliers in the Agra back lanes. To watch some more easily, visit Subhash Emporium on Gwalior Road. ■

Visitors leave the Taj Mahal gardens through the great gateway, symbolically leaving the garden of Paradise.

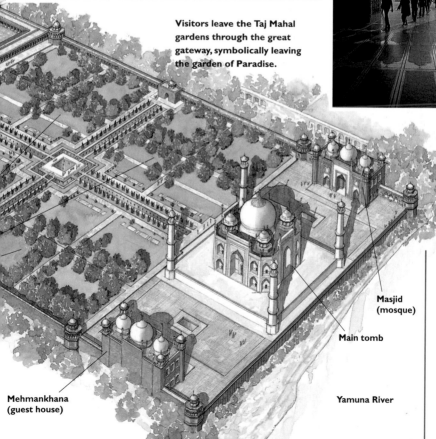

Masjid (mosque)

Main tomb

Mehmankhana (guest house)

Yamuna River

Fatehpur Sikri

FATEHPUR SIKRI IS A PERFECT GHOST CITY. THIS GROUP OF mysterious buildings is all that remains of the city conceived and built by Akbar as his ideal capital. Bursting into life in 1571, it was an instant success; just 14 years later it was virtually abandoned when Akbar was called to defend the northwest frontier of his empire. His court followed him there; he never returned.

Why did Akbar choose this spot? In 1568 the powerful 26-year-old emperor had consolidated his empire but, despite many marriage alliances, had no heir. After his annual pilgrimage to the Chishti tomb at Ajmer, on the way back to Agra he stopped here to visit a living Chishti saint, Shaikh Salim, who predicted that Akbar would soon have three sons. The next year, Akbar's Amber wife, Jadhai Bai, gave birth to a boy, who was named Salim after the saint. The following year Murad was born, and in 1572 Daniyal fulfilled the prediction.

After just two sons had been born, Akbar began to build a new city where the saint lived. He called it Fatehpur Sikri (City of Victory) and envisaged it as the cultural, commercial, and administrative center of his empire; most of his army and treasury stayed at Agra.

A good way to start visiting the buildings is to imagine the bazaars lining the road from inside the gateway up to the ticket office. Remember: There are no contemporary texts or plans, so each building's possible function is pure guesswork. Start by exploring the **Karkhana,** probably the royal workshops. Then see the so-called **Diwan-i-Am** (audience hall), whose built-in throne is decorated with *jali* work, and, behind here, the exquisite palace rooms, treasuries, and discussion halls. Beyond them, several palaces of what was probably the imperial harem have surviving painted decoration. Out

through the back gate, you have to run the gauntlet of peddlers to reach the Jami Masjid and see the saint's tomb, the prayer hall and the soaring Buland Darwaza (Gate of Magnificence) that celebrates Akbar's conquest of Gujarat (1573). ∎

Fatehpur Sikri

- 🗺 95 C4
- ✉ 25 miles (40 km) W of Agra on the Jaipur road in Uttar Pradesh
- ☎ 0562-360517
- 💲 $

Visitor tips

To avoid heat and crowds, go early or in the late afternoon; take drinks and snacks.

The Buland Darwaza is a triumphal gateway that was built to celebrate Akbar's victories in Gujarat during 1573.

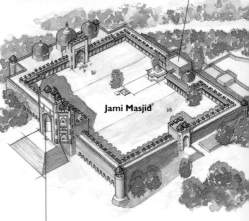

Shaikh Salim's tomb

Jami Masjid

Buland Darwaza

Shaikh Salim Chishti's tomb (above), with exquisite marble *jali* work, stands in the Jami Masjid's huge courtyard.

This intricate stonework in the Diwan-i-Khas has its inspiration in Gujarati wooden carving traditions.

Jadhai Bai's palace

Birbal's house

Maryam's house

Panch Mahal

Ankh Michauli

Diwan-i-Khas

Pachisi Court

entrance

Haran Sara complex

Khwabgah

Anoop Talao

Abdair Khana

Diwan-i Am

Huge, shaggy-feathered painted storks perch precariously high in the trees to nest.

Keoladeo Ghana National Park

TO SPEND A FEW HOURS WALKING IN SILENCE AND watching nature in this park (also known as Bharatpur Bird Sanctuary) is to escape the whirlwind of Agra sight-seeing. It quickly restores the soul.

Keoladeo Ghana National Park
- 95 B4
- 33 miles (53 km) W of Agra, 10 miles (16 km) W of Fatehpur Sikri, in Rajasthan
- $
- No cars; visit by boat, walking, on rented bicycle or by cycle rickshaw

The variety of habitats and climates, and the traditional respect for birds in India, have made the country especially rich in bird life. More than 1,200 of the world's 8,650 species of birds are found here, with 2,000 subspecies among them. This makes India's checklist twice the size of those of North America and Europe. Moreover, the dramatic shapes and colors of many species make bird-watching easy and rewarding for the amateur. For once, patience is not essential, since the birds are everywhere. All you need are sharp eyes, a pair of binoculars, and a good reference book—Bikram Grewal's *A Photographic Guide to the Birds of India & Nepal* (Chelsea Green Pub. Co., 1998) has plenty of helpful photographs. Using this, you will soon find that you are identifying plenty of birds on your own.

Keoladeo Ghana sanctuary takes its official name from the local temple dedicated to Keoladeo (Shiva). Established in 1956, it became a national park in 1981 and is today one of the world's most important sanctuaries for migratory birds and for herons. Although just inside Rajasthan, it is only an hour's drive from Agra, and is best visited from there.

The Maharaja of Bharatpur developed the 11 square miles (29 sq km) of freshwater swamp during the British period as the focus for his grand duck shoots. Viceroy Lord Curzon attended the first one in 1902; Viceroy Lord

Linlithgow was there in 1938 when 4,273 birds were shot, the biggest "bag" ever.

With the guns now put down forever, energetic and enlightened conservation has brought results. There are sometimes more than 375 species of birds to be seen here in winter, when migrating birds arrive from all over Russia, central Asia, and other parts of the world, to join the 120 or so resident species. When the monsoon begins, so does the nest-building. Some 10,000 nests are constructed in the heronries of acacia trees by big birds such as painted and openbill storks, white ibises, spoonbills, and purple herons. Sleek black cormorants, dazzling white egrets, and the common and pond herons play their parts, too. Other species of waterfowl arrive from August to October. Late arrivals to the park include rosy pelicans and flamingos, and, during December and January only, the rare Siberian crane.

By the beginning of March, those chicks who have eluded the vultures and other birds of prey and have become strong and fat begin to depart, bound for their summer homes.

As the land dries, terrestrial birds begin to breed, so even in April there is a rich assortment of birds to spot during a three-hour morning walk. At this time the park's animals—spotted deer, sambhar, blackbuck (small gazelles), mongoose, and others—can also be seen. So can large numbers of rock pythons, especially near the temple and main entrance.

Still, the best time to visit the park is in the morning from September to February. Take a rowboat (and a local ornithologist) out on the lake. As the mist lifts at sunrise, morning birdsong and flapping wings bring the islands of kadam trees alive. Metallic blue kingfishers eye potential breakfast from low branches, eagles glide through the still air, and large painted and black-necked storks stand up to stretch in their precariously balanced treetop nests. As the sun rises and the mist clears, the cacophony of sound rises to a climax: a magical experience. ■

On an early-morning cruise, the local ornithologist identifies each bird's call as it wakes up and welcomes the day with song.

Visitor tips
Best visited at sunrise or sunset; there are several nearby hotels. Binoculars and a field guide recommended, as is hiring one of the excellent local ornithologists, which your hotel or travel agent can arrange for you.

Trains

Ever since the first steam train puffed out of Bombay's Victoria Terminus station to a 21-gun salute on April 16, 1853, the Indian railways have had their own special character. For many British arrivals at Bombay port, their first experience of India was a three-day train ride to their final destination. Soot from the belching smoke blackened the travelers' clothes, there were unaccountable stops between stations, and locals sold their wares at every possible opportunity.

A child traveling by train in Rajasthan in the winter needs a warm pullover and a snug hat.

That first train carried just 400 people along 21 miles (34 km) of track in 75 minutes. Railroads were soon being built by the British to carry valuable trading goods to India's ports, and by the Indian princes to amuse themselves in their princely states: The Gwalior train still runs. Since then, India's railroad system has played a vital role in its economic, industrial, and social development.

Today India is one of the few countries in the world that is expanding its railroad system. The figures are impressive. A fleet of almost 7,000 engines, 34,000 coaches, and 300,000 wagons uses the 39,147 miles (63,000 km) of railroad track, which is punctuated by 7,068 stations. The longest route is Guwahati–Trivandrum, which carries passengers

2,469 miles (3,974 km) from the mountainous northeast to the steamy south. Each year, freight trains carry in excess of a million tons of goods; each day more than 7,500 passenger trains carry 11 million passengers (plus more riding ticketless on the roof). So all-pervading is the railroad that mobile eye hospitals reach isolated rural areas by train, not road.

The Indian railroad employs more than 1.1 million people, making it one of the country's largest employers. At large junctions, such as at Hubli in Karnataka, the workers live in neatly laid-out model towns, each with its houses, stores, churches (many railroad families are Christian), cricket ground, schools, and other public buildings. In India, one can be a railroad man from birth to death.

Gone are the steam engines, except for tourist enjoyment, and the delightful complexities of broad, meter, and narrow gauge are being simplified into broad gauge only. But some trains retain their romantic names—*Himalayan Queen, Pink City Express,* and *Grand Trunk Express.* And buying a ticket and catching a train in India is still a ritual that balances the apparent chaos of the Indian railroad station with the laboriously meticulous requirements of the ticket-selling staff. The process of buying a ticket, reserving a seat, understanding the departures board, and then finding the train and your seat demands plenty of time and possibly some new skills.

Grand new projects are at hand. The fast, reliable, Shatabdi Express train was introduced in the 1980s; its first route was Delhi to Bhopal. The Delhi–Agra stretch takes just over two hours compared to a driving time of four. As India's labyrinth of tracks is simplified and modernized, these trains connect most major cities. The great feat, however, has been the construction of the Konkan Railroad, which runs from Mumbai southward down the west coast to Mangalore (see p. 204). Next on the agenda is a line along Gujarat's long coast. ∎

Steam trains are now very rare in India. This one, which does not carry passengers, awaits its signal outside Agra.

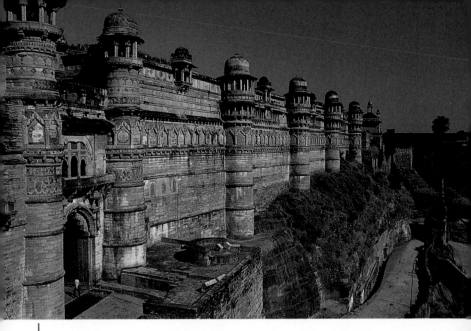

One of the greatest Rajput forts, Gwalior's palace rooms and great outer walls impressed even the fort-weary emperor Akbar.

Gwalior
- 🅰 95 C3
- ✉ Madhya Pradesh

State Tourist Office
www.mptourism.com
- ✉ Hotel Tansen
- ☎ 0751-2340370

Gwalior Fort
- ✉ Gwalior
- 💲 $

Archaeological Museum
- ✉ Gwalior Fort
- ⊕ Closed Fri.
- 💲 $

Jai Vilas
- ✉ S of fort, Gwalior
- 💲 $

Gwalior, Datia, & Orchha

THIS TRIANGLE OF ELEGANT ARCHITECTURAL SITES SET IN a wooded landscape south of Agra (see map p. 95) is easy to enjoy, provided clambering up and down stone steps is not a problem.

GWALIOR

Once the capital of the prestigious princely state of the same name, whose ruler had the title the Scindia, this large town is still dominated by its imposing fort built on top of a huge natural sandstone bluff.

The city's history starts up at **Gwalior Fort,** reached through a series of spectacular fortified gateways. Turn right at the top and you pass two ornate **Sasbahu temples** (tenth century), possibly built by the Kachwaha Rajputs, who founded the fort. **Man Mandir** (1486–1517), built by the Tomar ruler Man Singh, is the fort's centerpiece and one of India's finest early Hindu forts. Note the two courtyards surrounded by suites of rooms, the bold decoration, the variety of roofs, and the glazed tiles on the exterior.

The Tomar Rajputs had seized the fort from Delhi's Tughluq sultan in 1398 and held it until 1516. After the Tomars, the fort passed successively to the Mughals, Marathas, and Jats, and it was the scene of fierce fighting in 1858 between the British, led by Sir Hugh Rose, and the freedom fighters led by a legendary woman, the Rani of Jhansi. Wife of the Raja of Jhansi, she held Jhansi fort against the British with the help of her personal bodyguard when her husband sided with the British in the "Mutiny." When the fort finally fell, she joined the main rebel force at Gwalior, rode into battle dressed as a man with her baby strapped to her back, and was killed. In 1886, Gwalior was ceded to The Scindia.

This brief history helps explain the other monuments here—four more **palaces** lie beyond Man

Mandir, and there is another Hindu temple, some British remains, a Sikh temple and the **Archaeological Museum's** scupltures found in the area. On the way down, look for the Jain statues (7th to 15th centuries, defaced by Babur) cut into the rock. In the city see the **Jami Masjid** (1661) and the grand **tombs** of Muhammad Ghaus (late 16th century)—a Muslim saint who helped Babur win the fort—and Tansen (early 17th century), Akbar's court musician, in whose honor a national music festival is held here annually *(Nov.–Dec.).*

For a flavor of the heights of extravagance reached by India's self-indulgent princes once they allied with the British, visit colossal **Jai Vilas** (1872–74), designed by Lieut.-Col. Sir Michael Filose and now partly a museum. Do not miss the silver model train on the dining room table here, nor the real local one chugging around town.

DATIA & ORCHHA

On the road south from Gwalior to Datia it's worth stopping at **Sonagiri,** a Jain pilgrimage center for the Digambar sect (see p. 59). Take a look at the mirror temple and the white shrines leading up to the hilltop temple.

At **Datia,** a street crosses a causeway and leads through the walled village to the surprising sight of soaring **Govind Mandir Palace** (1620). Inside, dark stairways and labyrinthine corridors rise level by level to reveal a design of such symmetrical clarity and stone carving of such precision and beauty as to make this one of the finest Rajput palaces.

Both this and the grandest of Orchha's palaces were built by Bir Singh Deo of Bundelkund, who sealed his future with Emperor Jahangir by assassinating Emperor Akbar's court historian, Abul Fazl, who disapproved of Jahangir's (then Prince Salim) behavior.

Orchha is a medieval palace city. Its island fort is composed of the **Raj Mahal,** with bright murals of Hindu myths, and the later **Jahangir Mahal** (Bir Singh Deo's addition for Jahangir's state visit). **Sheesh Mahal** stands between them, now a government-run hotel. Other treats include **Rai Praveen Mahal** palace, **Lakshmi Narayan** hilltop temple with its murals, and walks beside the Betwa river to see the royal *chhatris.*

From Orchha you can continue to Khajuraho (see p. 112), Panna (see p. 119), Shivpuri (see p. 119), or Bhopal (see p. 114). ■

**Datia,
Madhya Pradesh**
△ 95 C3
✉ 39 miles (63 km)
S of Gwalior

**Orchha,
Madhya Pradesh**
△ 95 C3
✉ 10 miles (16 km)
S of Datia

A frieze of ducks that enlivens Gwalior Fort's outer walls may have inspired the decoration on Agra Fort's inner gate.

Khajuraho

Khajuraho,
Madhya Pradesh
🗺 95 C3
India Tourist Office
✉ By Western Group of temples

State Tourism Office
www.mptourism.com
✉ Chandella Cultural Centre
☎ 07686 774051

Festival
Maha Shivratri, Feb.–March: dance

FORESTED ISOLATION PROTECTED KHAJURAHO'S CLUSTER of resplendent Hindu temples from Muslim destruction. Created between the 10th and the 12th centuries by the rulers of the Chandella dynasty, a Rajput clan who resisted Muslim invasion, they were then lost until 1819. Their rediscovery is a remarkable story.

In 1819 a British military surveyor spotted the temples in the dense jungle. His report map was unclear: Did the labels read "mines" or "ruins"? Twenty years later, Capt. T. S. Burt was traveling in the area by *palanquin,* heard rumor of the temples, and sought them out. He reported: "I found seven Hindoo temples, most beautifully and exquisitely carved as to workmanship, but the sculptor had at times allowed his subject to grow a little warmer than there was any absolute necessity for his doing."

The eroticism of the sculptures has been the attraction for visitors as much as their fine carving. But they are not a sex manual for voyeurs. New research reveals that Khajuraho was once known as Shivpuri (City of Shiva), and the sculptures decorating the temples recount and celebrate the marriage of Shiva, god of creative and destructive energy, to Parvati. Thus, they portray the consummation of marriage and, at the same time, the highest spiritual experience achievable. According to Hindu theory, lovemaking demands that all the senses be given fully to achieve total physical and mental union.

The structure of each temple lends weight to this theory of marriage, consummation, and procreation. The *jangha* (body) of the temple, between the base and spire, is the celestial realm. Thus, the copulating couples are mostly the divine Shiva and Parvati, and the nymphs are expressing surprise that the god is attending the wedding party. Every Hindu temple mirrors the creation of life: The sanctum or *garbha griha* (womb), is where Shiva's *lingum* (phallus), representing potential creativity, is kept.

Khajuraho's 25 temples may have been part of a nonmonastic center of learning and religion. The most spectacular are in the Western Group, walkable from nearby hotels and the museum.

Today, the car or airplane has replaced the palanquin as the easiest way to reach Khajuraho. To go farther afield, either use a cycle rickshaw or rent a bicycle.

WESTERN GROUP

The added serenity of sunrise and sunset intensifies the surreal experience of seeing these temples. As all nine temples may be overwhelming, here are a few to look at closely.

Pass Varaha Temple, with its sandstone boar, to reach **Lakshamana Temple** *(circa 950),* the oldest of this group, whose riotous carvings of processions, domestic scenes, musicians, and dancers are full of vitality and movement. Next, visit the **Kandariya Mahadeva Temple** (constructed 1025–1050), possibly the finest of all the temples in its architecture, its rising silhouette, and its sublime and fluid

carving. An elaborate wedding garland at the entrance symbolizes the marriage gate; niches along the outside of the sanctum have carvings of the *Sapta Matrikas* (seven mothers) responsible for dressing the bridegroom, Shiva. Finally, pass the three temples of Mahadeva, Devi Jagadambi, and Chitragupta to find **Vishvanatha Temple,** built in 1002 by Dhangadeva *(R. 950–1002).* Shiva's Nandi bull vehicle sits outside, while up on the jangha of the temple the sculptures of amorous couples, sensuous nymphs, and idealized women are especially delicate.

ELSEWHERE ON THE SITE

The simple, old **Matangesvara Temple** stands just outside this complex and is still in daily use. Near it, random Khajuraho artifacts are kept in the **Archaeological Museum,** including a frieze showing how the sandstone for the temples was dug from the Ken River, 20 miles (32 km) away, transported to this area of hard granite, and then cut and carved. The soft river stone then hardened; hence its crispness today. The eastern and southern groups are less spectacular, but nevertheless rewarding. In the first, the early **Parsvanatha Temple** is especially fine; in the second, the isolated **Duladeo Temple** (12th century) shows the Chandellas' decline. ■

Voluptuous Lakshmi nestles against her partner, Vishnu (above), in contrast to the simple shapes of Lakshamana Temple (right), set on a broad, high platform.

Archaeological Museum

✉ Near entrance to Western Group of temples

🕐 Closed Fri.

💲 $ (includes temples)

Bhopal & around

AS THE CAPITAL OF MADHYA PRADESH STATE, BHOPAL benefits from some impressive public buildings. By keeping its rampant modern expansion separate, it remains a delightful provincial town, only now bursting out of its preindependence mix of palaces, mosques, gardens, and lakes.

Bhopal, Madhya Pradesh
⚐ 95 B2

State Tourist Office
✉ Palash Residency, near 45 Bungalow, T. T. Nagar, New Market
☎ 0755-2766750

Rashtriya Manava Sanghralaya (Tribal Habitat Museum of Man)
✉ Shamla Hills, overlooking Upper Lake
🕐 Closed Mon.

The Hindu ruler Raja Bhoj (1018–1085), a scholar of the Paramara dynasty, founded Bhopal in the 11th century. He sited it on a crescent-shaped ridge and created artificial lakes. But Bhopal's present character took shape only from the end of the 17th century. Dost Muhammed Khan, an opportunistic ex-general of the Mughal emperor Aurangzeb's army, took the by then deserted city and laid out a fresh one. Through consistent loyalty to the British, his descendants, including three city-improving *begums* (female Muslim rulers), became major Indian princes and princesses ruling over a happy mix of Hindu and Muslim cultures, a mix that continues today. Tragically, Bhopal's most recent fame came on December 3, 1984, when a lethal cloud of toxic chemicals escaped from a tank at the Union Carbide factory, resulting in death or chronic illness for thousands of local people. The factory is closed, and the site is a wasteland, but the effects continue to haunt locals.

Visitors can stay in Noor-us-Sabah, a delightful converted palace (see p. 350). The **Taj-ul-Masjid** (Mother of All Mosques), built by Shah Jahan Begum (R.1868–1901), is a good place to start exploring the city. The spaciousness of this and **Imam Square,** once the royal heart of Bhopal, contrasts with the smaller mosques and narrow streets of the **Old City,** where ladies wrapped up in *burqa* bargain for silver, silks (local Bilaspur and Chandheri examples are stunning), and jewelry.

Bhopal's museum collections are very impressive. Do not miss the stone sculptures in the **Birla Mandir Museum** (*Next to Birla Mandir, overlooking Lower Lake, closed Wed., $*) and, in the **Rashtriya Manava Sanghralaya** (Tribal Habitat Museum of Man), the tribal homes complete with murals and furnishings. Bhopal's impressive contemporary buildings include Charles Correa's 1982 multi-arts complex, **Bharat Bhavan** (*Lake Drive Rd., closed a.m. & Mon.*), always alive with exhibitions and performances, and his boldly majestic and colorful **State Assembly** (1999).

AROUND BHOPAL

Beyond the industrial suburbs south of Bhopal, a dirt road leads to **Bhimbetka** rocks (see p. 26). These are part of a 5-mile-long (8 km) ridge, where layers of pink, caramel, and cream sandstone have been weathered into fantastical shapes. Under some outcrops early humans left several hundred paintings, which were only rediscovered as recently as the 1950s. Most are line drawings in red or white. They show elephants, antelope, and wild boar, as well as people fishing, fighting, shooting arrows, dancing, and playing the drums. The paintings offer a glimpse of an ancient world and probably span the paleolithic to the neolithic periods. Beautiful and vulnerable, they as yet have no protection.

Best visited with Bhimbetka, **Bhojpur** is where Bhopal's founder dammed the Betwa River to make a reservoir, began his colossal Shiva Temple, and built the nearby Jain shrine with its stone image of Mahavira.

To see the beginnings of monumental Hindu sculpture, seek out the remarkable fifth-century rock-cut Gupta caves at **Udaigiri.**

Climb up the steep steps in the rock face just before Udaigiri village; then stroll among the caves, ending at the best, Cave No. 5. Inside, the 13-foot-high (4 m) composition shows Varaha, Vishnu's boar incarnation, rescuing the earth goddess Bhudevi, possibly an allegory of the Gupta ruler Chandragupta II's unification of northern India.

Nearby at **Besnagar,** find a remarkable survivor: the Column of Heliodorus, a stone pillar erected in 113 B.C. and dedicated to Krishna's father by Heliodorus, a Greek envoy from Taxila, capital of Gandhara (see p. 31).

A marathon but rewarding journey for temple-lovers leads through sparsely populated countryside to the small village of **Udayapur,** clustered around the Udayeshvara Temple (1080). Its ambitious scale, rhythmic proportions, and rich sculpture proclaim its royal patronage, confirmed in an inscription. Its quality, style, dedication to Shiva, and an image of Parvati behind the *lingum* in the sanctum suggest a close relationship with Khajuraho's temples (see pp. 112–113). ∎

Fine *mihrab* patterns decorate a corner of Taj-ul-Masjid.

Bhimbetka
- 95 C2
- 27 miles (43 km) SE of Bhopal

Bhojpur
- 10 miles (16 km) SE of Bhopal

Udaigiri Caves
- 95 C2
- 6 miles (10 km) N of Sanchi

Besnagar
- 4 miles (6 km) N of Sanchi

Udayapur
- 95 C2
- 82 miles (132 km) NE of Bhopal via Sanchi

Sanchi

Sanchi's stupa
itself represents
Buddha, as do the
wheel, trident,
footprint, empty
throne under the
bodhi tree, and
riderless horse.

SANCHI, WHOSE GREAT STUPA, WITH ITS FOUR SOARING gateways embellished with intricate carvings, constitutes one of India's oldest surviving stone buildings and is certainly its finest surviving Buddhist monument.

Monuments spanning the third century B.C. to the seventh century A.D. crowd the hill rising above the plain: *stupas* built to contain holy relics, monastic buildings, elaborate railings, columns, and temples. Yet, despite the size and importance of the site, there may well be so few visitors that you can imagine how General Taylor might have felt when he rediscovered it, completely overgrown, having acted on a tip-off and trekked the 37 miles (60 km) out from Bhopal, in 1819.

Although Sanchi has no known link with Buddha, there are relics here of two of his disciples and of later teachers. Inscriptions indicate that merchants from nearby Vidisha were donors.

It is best to begin with **Stupa I** (third to first century B.C. and fifth century A.D.), whose relatively complete preservation, including railings and gateway sculpture, makes it the most important piece of architecture and narrative art of the Shunga era. The stupa itself is 120 feet (36 m) in diameter and encases an earlier one. Its high terrace makes a good viewing point for the inside faces of the gateways. The surrounding stone balustrade and gateways imitate wood in their structure, but their fully developed motifs (flowers, animals, birds, etc.) and sophisticated iconography narrating the life of Buddha and the *Jataka* tales (stories of his former lives) may be derived from ivory carving. On the stupa, Buddha is never shown in human form (out of respect), but is represented by a wheel, trident, footprint, empty throne beneath the bodhi tree, or riderless horse. ■

Sanchi, Madhya Pradesh

🅰 95 C2

Archaeological Museum

✉ Sanchi

🕐 Closed Fri.

💲 $

Mandu

THE ISOLATED AND EXTENSIVE REMAINS OF THE ONCE magnificent capital of the central Indian kingdom of Malwa make Mandu one of India's most magical forts to visit, especially during or after monsoon lushness. More than 70 handsome Muslim and Hindu monuments built between the 11th and 16th centuries stand amid farming villages on an extensive fortified hilltop, with the Vindhya Mountains as a backdrop.

The powerful Paramara ruler Raja Bhoj (see p. 114) fortified the hilltop, but in 1305 it fell to the Khilji sultans of Delhi. A later Afghan governor of Malwa declared independence from Delhi and moved the capital from Dhar to Mandu. His son, Hoshang Shah, gave Mandu some of its finest buildings (Jama Masjid and his own tomb). Having won the city back in 1436, the Khiljis added more buildings, distinguished for their elegant simplicity, mixing Gujarat and Delhi styles. The Mughals later restored some buildings and in 1617 Jahangir spent his birthday here.

Wandering the palaces, tombs, mosques, and tanks needs time. Here are a few highlights. Beside the modern fort entrance is Hoshang Shah's **Delhi Gate.** The village buildings surround the magnificent pink sandstone **Jama Masjid** and Hoshang Shah's white marble **tomb** (circa 1440), the earliest of its kind on the subcontinent. **Jahaz Mahal** (Ship Palace) is beautiful at sunset.

NEARBY SIGHTS

In contrast, nearby **Indore** (61 miles/97 km from Mandu) is Madhya Pradesh's second largest city and a major center for the steel and car industries. Forty-one miles (66 km) west is Malwa's ancient capital, **Dhar,** whose two mosques, Bhojshala and Lat Masjid, anticipate Mandu's triumphs. ∎

Rupmati, after whom these pavilions at Rewakund, to the south of the main site, are named, was the lover of Mandu's 16th-century ruler, Baz Bahadur.

Mandu, Madhya Pradesh
95 B2

Wildlife parks
of Madhya Pradesh

**Bandhavgarh
National Park**

- 95 D2
- Closed July–Nov.
- $
- Nearest airports Varanasi, Khajuraho; stay at Tala

**Kanha National
Park**

- 95 D2
- Closed July–Oct.
- $
- Nearest airports Nagpur; Jabalpur

THE WILDLIFE SANCTUARIES DEEP IN CENTRAL INDIA ARE exceptional for their wild terrain and abundant animal and bird life, so they are worth the effort needed to get there. Bandhavgarh and Kanha have comfortable accommodations and, moreover, offer a high chance of spotting a tiger.

BANDHAVGARH NATIONAL PARK

The attractive combination of trekking by elephant, the likelihood of spotting a tiger, and the good accommodations sited near the park gates reward you for making the journey. For those devoted to elephants, there is the added bonus of visiting their compound to see them being bathed and fed and to learn how they are reared and trained, using methods unchanged for centuries.

The park was established in 1968 and has since been enlarged. Its 169 square miles (437 sq km) of rugged and hilly landscape stretch across the heart of the Vidhya Mountains and currently harbor the highest density tiger population of any Indian park; next best are

Riding an elephant through Bandhavgarh's wild landscape

Panna National Park

- 95 D3
- Closed July–Oct., best Oct.–April
- $
- Nearest airport Khajuraho; stay at Madla

Shivpuri National Park

- 95 C3
- Open all year, best Feb.–June
- Nearest airport Gwalior

Kanha and Ranthambore (see p. 133). Be on the lookout for tigers, langur, sloth bears, wild boar, *gaur* (wild ox), and porcupine. There are several kinds of deer: *chital* (spotted deer), *nilgai* (blue bull), *sambhar* (small barking deer), and *chowsingha* (four-horned antelope) amid the not too dense *sal* trees of the valleys and mixed foliage of the upper areas.

Serious ornithologists should arrange to watch the park's rich bird life—up to 150 species, including rare hornbills. From the old fort, you will need to hike up a temple-dotted hill.

KANHA NATIONAL PARK

This is one of India's largest and best parks, with more than 770 square miles (2,000 sq km) of land very rich in fauna and gently meandering rivers in the Banjar Valley. Rudyard Kipling's *The Jungle Book* (1894), made into a movie by Walt Disney, is set in this area and depicts the truly idyllic jungle life that you can still experience.

The park was established in 1955 as the start of a successful project to save the almost extinct hardground *barasingha* (Indian swamp deer). Some of the first serious research work was done on tigers here, by American big-cat expert George Schaller, in 1963–65. The park still carries out important Project Tiger work, which serves as a model for wildlife management.

As you travel through the beautiful landscape, you may spot the now flourishing barasingha, and chital deer, langur monkey, gaur, nilgai, wild boar, mouse deer, sambhar, and even the elusive leopard. If you can persuade your jeep driver to stay still long enough, you can glimpse rich bird life through your binoculars, including bee-eaters, black ibises, golden orioles, and serpent eagles.

PANNA NATIONAL PARK

Conveniently close to Khajuraho, this wilderness of valleys and gorges bordering the Ken River is glorious when monsoon rains have given it lushness and copious waterfalls. You may see nilgai, sloth bear, cheetah, sambhar, and *chinkara* (Indian gazelle) in the teak forest, and the rare gharial and mugger crocodiles in the Ken.

But the 210-square-mile (543 sq km) park is best known for its big cats. There is a good chance that patience will be rewarded with sightings of a tiger, leopard, or panther. A good place to wait for one is near the beautiful lake fed by Pandava Falls.

SHIVPURI NATIONAL PARK

This small park of deciduous plains forest was once the summer capital of The Scindias of Gwalior (see p. 110); their grand mausoleums were built in white marble for recent Gwalior royals, with idols lovingly tended by more than 150 people, and are well worth visiting. In the park, ornithologists can enjoy plenty of bird life, including sightings of demoiselle cranes. Animals to see include sambhar, chital, nilgai, and chinkara. ∎

Visitor tips

Accommodations tend to include all meals, guides, jeep rides, and, if an option, elephant safaris; reserving in advance is essential. To experience a park's habitat properly, it is best to stay three nights.

Beware of temperature extremes: It's chilly at dawn and dusk in winter (with occasional frosts) but blisteringly hot after February. All parks offer good animal sightings, especially in the heat and dust between March and June. ∎

Nek Chand's Rock Garden is full of witty surprises, such as these women being drenched by a waterfall.

Chandigarh
🅰 95 B5
Chandigarh Tourist Office
www.chandigarhtourism.gov.in
✉ Interstate Bus
   Terminus, Sector 17
☎ 0172-2704614

Punjab Tourist Office
www.punjabtourism.org
✉ Sector 17
☎ 0172-2699140/711878

Chandigarh

THE FLAT, FERTILE, AND PROSPEROUS LAND STRETCHING from Delhi to the Indus was once all the Punjab. With independence, half was lost to Pakistan and since then further areas have formed two more Indian states: Haryana and Himachal Pradesh. The Green Revolution of the 1960s, introducing modern crop technology and improving on the already substantial British-built irrigation system, transformed the area into the breadbasket of India. A quarter of India's wheat and a third of its milk and dairy foods are produced in this area. Today, Haryana and Punjab share their capital, Chandigarh, a good base for some offbeat sight-seeing.

Independent India's first planned city, conceived by Le Corbusier (see p. 88), was begun in 1952 and, with help from Maxwell Fry and Jane Drew, was completed ten years later. Today, its grid boulevards divided into blocks (called "sectors"), and its grand civic buildings can be judged with some degree of historical perspective, although the initial dramatic effect has been softened by extensive planting.

Le Corbusier envisaged his ideal city as a living organism, with the

Capital Complex *(Guided tours, may be suspended for security reasons; call ahead)* as its "head" and the large green spaces as its "lungs." The capital is one of Le Corbusier's most innovative designs. Set against the Shivalik Hills, his monumental buildings for the High Court, Legislative Assembly, and Secretariat overlook the 1,300-foot-wide (400 m) square. Down the main avenue, Jan Marg, is the **Museum and Art Gallery** *(Sector 10, closed Mon.)*, whose collection reflects the long, rich history and culture of the area, from Gandhara Buddhas to Sikh paintings.

On the city outskirts is the upbeat, witty artwork, the **Rock Garden.** This is retired road inspector Nek Chand's life work: The garden is composed of a succession of open-air rooms, each one individually decorated with colorful mosaics or surreal sculptures of animal and human figures.

AROUND CHANDIGARH

As you head north into the Shivalik Hills along the road to Shimla, **Pinjore** is well worth a stop to visit the walled **Yadavindra**

Gardens. The Mughal emperor Aurangzeb's brother, Fidai Khan, reorganized the ancient gardens, giving them three pleasure palaces and broad terraced lawns; they're good for picnics. From **Kalka,** 2 miles (4 km) farther on, the *Himalayan Queen* and other trains leave for Shimla, a 5½ hour journey. Quaint **Nalagarh** is nearer—37 miles (60 km) from Chandigarh—and quieter, with good walking and the ruined **Ramgarh Fort.**

Southwest of Chandigarh lies **Patiala,** where tourists are hardly ever seen. In this charming, unspoiled city, once the capital of the Sikh state Patiala, do not miss the multistory **Motibagh Palace** with its many painted rooms, nor the busy street markets.

Farther up the Grand Trunk Road toward Amritsar, **Sirhind** has a cluster of Mughal and Sikh monuments you might visit. Then, bypass Ludhiana's wool factories and Jalandhar's bicycle industry to arrive at **Kapurthala,** a Paris-influenced model town and home to the Jalaukhana Palace, built in the 1890s by the French-educated ruler, Jagajit Singh Ahluwalia. ∎

Government Museum and Art Gallery
- ✉ Sector 10, Capital Complex
- ☎ 0172-725568
- 🕐 Closed Mon.
- 💲 $

Rock Garden
- ✉ Behind High Court
- 🕐 Closed a.m. Oct.–March
- 💲 $

Pinjore
- ◭ 95 B5
- ✉ 13 miles (21 km) NE of Chandigarh on Kalka Rd.

Patiala
- ◭ 95 B5
- ✉ 42 miles (68 km) SW of Chandigarh

Motibagh Palace
- ✉ 1.8 miles (3 km) S of Patiala
- 🕐 May be closed to visitors

Sirhind
- ◭ 95 B5
- ✉ 30 miles (48 km) NW of Ambala

Kapurthala
- ◭ 95 B6
- ✉ 113 miles (180 km) W of Chandigargh

Grand Trunk Road

Made famous by Rudyard Kipling in his novel *Kim*, this is one of the world's great ancient roads. It stretches 1,200 miles (2,000 km) across the subcontinent, from mountainous Peshawar on the Pakistan-Afghanistan border to Kolkata on the Bay of Bengal.

Trade has been passing along this route since at least the fourth century B.C., when it was called the Uttar Path (high way). The Mauryan emperor Ashoka gave it paving stones, watchtowers, and some of his edict pillars (see p. 31); portions survive beside the current

road. Sher Shah Sur carried out major maintenance work, built *serais* (medieval motels)—one survives at Sirhind, near Chandigarh—and employed spies at them to report rumor and discontent. The Mughals added wells; the British added asphalt and the present name.

Today, Kipling's "Backbone of all Hind" is India's National Highway 1 (NH1), nicknamed "G.T Road." Trucks, cars, bullock-carts, bicycles, and cows share this great road, perpetuating Kipling's "river of life." ∎

Amritsar, Punjab

🅰 95 A6

**State Tourist
Information**

www.punjabtourism.org

✉ Amritsar
International Hotel

☎ 0183-2555991

Visitor tips

All are welcome at the Hari Mandir, but shoes must be removed and feet washed; no socks are to be worn, heads must be covered, and all tobacco and alcohol must be left outside the complex (there are lockers for this purpose).

Amritsar

THE OLD, WALLED CORE OF PUNJAB'S LARGEST CITY IS A network of bustling bazaars surrounding the beautiful Golden Temple and Jallianwalla Bagh (see box p. 123). These, the gems of Amritsar, are filled with an intense calm and peacefulness, despite their political associations.

Amritsar is the Sikhs' holy city. Every Sikh is required to visit it at least once, so there are usually thousands of pilgrims here. The fourth Guru, Ram Das, founded the trading town in 1577 and enlarged the Amrit Sarovar ("pool of nectar," hence Amritsar) to commemorate a crippled person being cured while bathing there. His son and successor, Arjan Dev, built the first temple (1589–1601) in the lake: the Hari Mandir (Golden Temple).

After multiple Afghan attacks and persecutions in the 18th century, Ranjit Singh led the Sikhs to victory in the Punjab and in 1830 gave 220 pounds (100 kg) of gold to gild the restored temple. In the 20th century, Sikhs saw their dream for Khalistan, an independent Sikh state based on the whole of Ranjit Singh's kingdom, shattered. Nehru made promises; Indira Gandhi offered a reduced version, then withdrew her offer. As a result

of the ensuing conflicts, the Golden Temple was fortified, the Indian Army made an assault on it in June 1984, and Mrs. Gandhi was assassinated in the same year. Rajiv Gandhi drew up the Punjab Accord in July 1985, but the problem remains unresolved.

You need a couple of hours to visit the temple. Start by enjoying your first view of the shimmering **Amrit Sarovar,** on which the Hari Mandir temple appears to float. Then take a slow walk clockwise, right around the tank, following pilgrims as they pause at small shrines devoted to the founding gurus. Along this route, called the Parikrama, are four little booths where devotees take turns to maintain a continuous reading of the *Guru Granth Sahib,* the Sikhs' sacred book. On the east side, up to 6,000 pilgrims a day eat in the Guru-ka-langar (communal dining room) to remind themselves that all are equal.

The climax of your visit is on the west side. Here is the **Akal Takht,** the temple's second most sacred structure. Built by Guru Magolind to house the religious and political governing body of the

Pilgrims make their way along the Guru's Bridge (above) to the Hari Mandir to listen to the continuous daytime reading from the Guru Granth Sahib (right).

Sikhs, it has been immaculately rebuilt since the Indian Army destroyed it during the violent conflicts of 1984.

Before visiting it, worshipers collect their *prasad* (offering) and go along the Guru's Bridge to the highly decorated **Hari Mandir,** which houses a huge copy of the Guru Granth Sahib. You can go there, too, entering through one of its four open doors (symbolizing welcome to all four Hindu castes) to witness the continuous readings, chanting, and music. The book is set on a throne by day, but each evening, in a most moving ceremony, it is paraded to the Akal Takht to the sound of singing and the loud beating of drums. ∎

Jallianwalla Bagh Massacre

On April 13, 1919, without warning, Gen. R. E. H. Dyer and his 150 troops fired continuously for 15 minutes on some 20,000 unarmed people gathered peacefully in a square hemmed in by buildings. The official death toll was 400, with 1,200 injuries. It was one of the worst atrocities perpetrated by the British in India.

The cause was the Rowlatt Act, which empowered the British to imprison without trial any Indian suspected of sedition. A series of one-day strikes in Amritsar

escalated into looting, and Mahatma Gandhi called a mass demonstration for April 13 at Jallianwalla Bagh. No speech or aggressive action had been made when General Dyer ordered his troops to fire.

Today, the square is an extremely touching memorial park, reached through one of the original narrow alleys. A small gallery houses firsthand accounts, contemporary photographs, newspaper reports, and poet Rabindranath Tagore's moving letter, returning his British honors. ∎

Delhi's hill stations

IF THE SEARING HEAT OF THE PLAINS IS UNBEARABLE, THE cooling comfort of the lower Himalayan mountains and their quaint British-founded hill stations (see p. 278) are near at hand. The climate and flowers are best in spring and fall.

SHIMLA (SIMLA), HIMACHAL PRADESH

The capital of modern India's mountainous Himachal Pradesh sustains its position as queen of India's hill stations. Set at an elevation of 7,260 feet (2,213 m) in the pine-forested Shivalik Hills, this was the summer capital of the British administration from 1864 to 1939. Each year, the huge machine of bureaucrats and papers, together with servants, coolies, packhorses, women, and children, made the long journey up here from Calcutta (and later Delhi) until the Kalka to Shimla Railway opened in 1903. From here, for more than half the year, amid the plays, games, dancing, hunting, and gossip, the British governed approximately one-fifth of the world's population.

Shimla's modern mix of mountains, imperial British buildings, Indian town, and wealthy Indian visitors makes it unlike anywhere else in India. To get the most out of it, be prepared to walk, as the center is restricted to pedestrians.

On **The Ridge,** in the town center beside Christ Church (which

has fine stained-glass windows), there are splendid views over the surrounding hills. Walk along The Mall (the main street), past British buildings whose designs range between seaside flippancy and stoic Scottish baronial, past the lavishly refurbished Cecil Hotel, to find **Viceregal Lodge** (*Observatory Rd., partly open to the public, $*).

MUSSOORIE, UTTARAKHAND

At an elevation of 6,561 feet (2,000 m) and a mere 172 miles (277 km) from Delhi, this hill station makes for a good quick break. Discovered by the British in 1823, its popularity is sustained by its spectacular views of the Himalayas and the Dehra Dun valley.

As the town tends to be busy, peace is best found by walking in the beautiful surrounding countryside. **Childers Lodge,** situated above Landour, has the most exquisite views of all, while a walk out to **Tchenchen Choling** *gompa* (monastery) and its gardens is highly rewarding. If you would like to try a more ambitious trek, you can spend four days exploring the Harki Dun valley.

HARIDWAR & RISHIKESH, UTTARAKHAND

As one of the Seven Sacred Cities, **Haridwar** is a busy Hindu pilgrimage center. Here the sacred Ganga River leaves the rugged mountains for the flat plains, and Har-ki-Pairi *ghat* marks the exact spot. All day long the faithful visit the ghats, bridges, and islands; each

Shimla
🅰 95 B5
www.himachaltourism.nic.in
Tourist Office
✉ Railway Station

Mussoorie
🅰 95 C5
Tourist Office
✉ The Mall

Haridwar
🅰 95 C5
Tourist Office
✉ Upper Rd.

Left: Shimla's British area recalls an English seaside town.

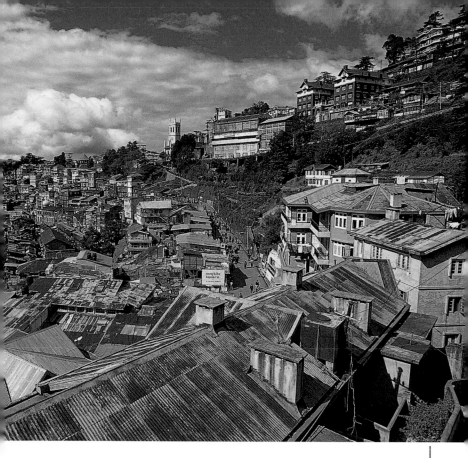

evening, hundreds gather for the Ganga Arati ceremony at dusk, when lights are floated down the river to the sound of gongs and music.

Rishikesh lies within sight, up the mountains of Garhwal. The Beatles put it on the hippie trail with their visit to the Maharishi in February 1968. Today, *ashrams* of all kinds abound, continuing and expanding the spot's ancient tradition as a Hindu pilgrimage stop. Those seriously interested in yoga should reserve in advance at the Shivananda Ashram *(The Divine Life Society, Shivananda Nagar, tel 01364-31140, fax 01364-31196, www.sivananda.org).* For peace, go in winter and spring when the temples are shut and pilgrims fewer. Those wishing to follow the Ganga

to its source can journey on to Gangotri from here (see p. 321).

NAINITAL, UTTARAKHAND
Set in the Kumaun Hills at 6,358 feet (1,938 m), this town overlooking a large, natural lake has sustained its popularity since a sugar merchant, Mr. Barron, discovered its joys in 1841. Find action along The Mall, which runs the length of the lake from Mallital, the colonial area, to Tallital. Try boating on the lake, visiting a Tibetan market, the climbing ropeway to Snow View, and walking longer trails to Naina Peak and China Peak for more views. From Nainital you can visit Corbett National Park (see p. 126), with charming hotels along the route. ■

Shimla clings precariously to the mountainside.

Rishikesh
🅰 95 C5
Tourist Office
✉ Nehru Park

Nainital
🅰 95 C5
Tourist Office
✉ The Mall

More information
For information on places in Uttarakhand (formerly Uttaranchal) state, visit: http://gov.ua.nic.in/uttaran chaltourism/index.html, or www.hill-stations-india.com

Corbett National Park

Corbett National
Park, Uttarakhand

⚠ 95 C5

www.corbettpark.com

✉ Ramnagar

🕐 Open mid-
Nov.–mid-June, after
which monsoons
flood the riverbeds
and cut off the
roads

💲 $

✗ Nearest airport
Pantnagar

ESTABLISHED IN 1936 BY JIM CORBETT (1875–1955), INDIA'S first wildlife sanctuary now preserves a rare expanse of sub-Himalayan wilderness. The dramatic scenery of the 201 square miles (521 sq km) of Kumaun hills, valleys, and rivers makes it particularly beautiful, and especially lush after the monsoon months (November to January), even if much of the core area of 127 square miles (330 sq km) is off-limits to visitors.

Jim Corbett, a hunter turned conservationist and author, was born in Nainital and knew the area intimately. Repeatedly called to save locals by killing man-eating tigers and leopards, Corbett was already concerned about threats to India's wildlife by the 1940s, when he began to champion the conservation awareness of Indians. It was appropriate, then, that in 1973 this

elephant, if you are riding one. Look in the rivers for snout-nosed gharial crocodiles, large mugger crocodiles, and river tortoises. On land, you may see wild boar, sambhar, Himalayan black bear, delicate *chital*, ugly hog deer, porcupine, and trees full of playful rhesus and common langur monkeys.

For ornithologists this park is a paradise, since it attracts an abun-

Lively and intelligent, rhesus monkeys are often seen in Corbett National Park. Watch for them as well in parks, woodland, and scrub throughout India.

Visitor tips
Stay outside the park at Ramnagar, on the Kosi River; the upscale hotels can arrange two- or three-night stays inside the park, taking their own staff and food. Government-run accommodations at Dikhala and elsewhere inside the park are very disappointing.

park was the first Project Tiger Reserve. Ironically, the project's success here has led to overpopulation, as each tiger needs 31 square miles (80 sq km), and there are now regular reports of the man-eating incidents that Corbett tackled.

The park's good infrastructure and its naturalists mean there is a fair chance of sighting the elusive tiger, possibly from the back of an

dance of both plains and hill birds. An hour in a *machan* will be richly rewarded—perhaps with sightings of black-necked stork, honey buzzard, crested serpent eagle, gray hornbill, scarlet minivet, and many different waterfowl, pigeons, parakeets, and kingfishers.

It is best to visit from November to March; after this it gets hotter, but elephant sightings increase. ∎

With vivid colors glowing in the parched land, soaring forts telling of heroic legends, and fairy-tale palaces where, until recently, maharajas lived in untold luxury, this corner of India fulfills a visitor's most exotic dreams.

Rajasthan & Gujarat

A village woman carries her water supply home.

Rajasthan & Gujarat

THESE TWO DRY AND DUSTY STATES IN WESTERN INDIA EXTEND ACROSS THE punishing Great Indian Desert to the Pakistan border and the Arabian Sea, separated from the rest of India by the Aravalli, Vindhya and Satpura mountain ranges. The annual monsoon is crucial: If it fails, the people suffer. Yet the location has brought wealth through trade—a wealth increased in Gujarat because it lies on the pilgrimage route to Mecca used by northern India's Muslim rulers. Today, each state has newly dynamic forward-looking governments. Dramatic modernization moves in parallel with tradition.

Camels are the best form of transport through the dry Thar Desert.

Rajasthan is India's most popular area for visitors. It lies on the doorstep of Delhi and Agra; its former royals were quick to turn their palaces into hotels, and it offers classic romantic India, to be enjoyed easily without having to cope with much of India's complex history.

Most of the feuding Rajput rulers (see p. 37) turned to lives of pure pleasure once they accepted the mantle of British protection. A journey through Rajasthan gives you an idea of that life: visiting forts, shopping in colorful markets, riding painted elephants, spotting wildlife, and staying in one former palace after another.

But there are contrasts. The former states within Rajasthan have stoically held on to their individual characters and traditions. Jaipur, conceived as a commercial hub for the Jaipur princely state, is now the chaotic capital of all Rajasthan. Udaipur was and is distinguished for its lakes, beauty, and proudly defiant Mewar rulers, who poured their energy and vision into creating the most idyllic

Rajput city. Away in the west, Marwar's Jodhpur continues to feel like a royal frontier desert city. It would be no surprise if a camel train arrived in the shadow of the great fort.

Gujarat feels entirely different from Rajasthan. Its coastal trading and agricultural production were so lucrative that Emperor Akbar built the Buland Darwaza at Fatehpur Sikri (see pp. 104–105) when he finally conquered it. Today the many little preindependence kingdoms have metamorphosed into India's second wealthiest state—and one of the country's most enlightened. As an indicator, the literacy rate is 61 percent, compared with Rajasthan's 38 percent. Ahmedabad, its capital, offers a mixture of grand Islamic buildings, fine museums, and strong Gandhi associations: Gujarat was his home state. From Ahmedabad, you can make some journeys to see Harappan sites, Jain monuments, Hindu temples, art deco palaces, and rare wildlife. Hotels are often simple, visitors few, and the rewards considerable. ■

5

SAM SAND DU
(DESERT NAT.)

4▷

Muna

PAKISTAN

3▷

Rann of Kacho

● Lakhpat   Khavd

Naliya   Bhuj
                      Anj
                 Gandhidham
         Mandvi   ● Munc
    Okha   Gulf of Kachchh
                      Jam
2▷   Dwarka
          Kath
△   S
A   Porbandar   8B
Arabian
          Juna
Sea   Som
1▷
          △
          B

200 kilometers
100 miles

Area of map detail

New Delhi

PAKISTAN

Ganganagar
Hanumangarh
Suratgarh
Nohar

AROUND DELHI P. 95

Thar Desert

Sardarshahr
Churu
Mahansar
Bikaner
Fatehpur
Deshnoke
Sikar
Didwana

Jhunjhunun
Shekhawati
Nawalgarh
Alwar
Dig
SARISKA NATIONAL PARK
Bharatpur

GAGNER WIDLIFE SANCTUARY

garh
arh

Phalodi
aisalmer
Pokaran
va

R A J A S T H A N

Osian

Nagaur
Makrana
Sambhar Salt Lake

Jaipur
Amer
Samod
Sambhar
Dausa

KEOLADEO GHANA NAT. PARK
Dhaulpur

Shiv
Shergarh
Jodhpur
Mandor
Saraswati

Pushkar
Ajmer
Raipur
Beawar

Kekri
Tonk
Sawai Madhopur
RANTHAMBHOR NATIONAL PARK

Chambal

Balotra
Pali
Aravalli Range

Devli

Barmer
Luni
Sukri

htan

Jalor
Sirohi
Haldighati
Pindwara
Mount Abu
Shilpgram
Abu Road
Kumbharia
Palanpur

Kumbhalgarh
Nathdwara
Eklingji
Udaipur
Ahah

Banas

Chittaurgarh
Nimbahera

Bhilwara
Bundi
Kota
Baran
Atru
Jhalawar

Sanchor

adhanpur
Siddharpur
Patan
Little Rann
Modhera

Taranga
Mahesana
Himatnagar
Gandhinagar

Dungarpur
Rajsamand Lake
Mahi

Banswara

Gangdhar

E   F

GUJARAT
d
Dhrangadhra
rbi
Surendranagar
Vankaner
8A
jkot
sula
Botad
tra

AHMEDABAD
Sarkhej
Nadiad
Anand
Lothal
Dahod
Godhra

Champaner

AROUND DELHI P. 95

Women gather to chat at the village water pump.

VELAVADAR BLACK BUCK SANCTUARY

eli
Palitana
Alang

Vadodara
Dabhoi

Bhavnagar
Bharuch

ASAN GIR ATIONAL ARK
Mahuva
u & Diu)
Gulf of Khambhat

Surat
Bardoli
Navsari
Ahwa
Valsad

MUMBAI AND MAHARASHTRA P. 158

DAMAN & DIU
Daman

C   D

Aesthete ruler
Pratap Singh built
the Hawa Mahal in
Jaipur in 1799 as a
grandstand for the
palace women.

Amer & Jaipur

A VISIT TO AMER'S MEDIEVAL FORT AND THEN THE NEARBY
walled town of Jaipur, each in turn the capital of the powerful
Kachwaha clan, makes a good introduction to Rajasthan.

Of the 36 proud and warring Rajput
clans, all *kshatriya* caste Hindus, the
Kachwahas of Amer became one of
the greatest. They won Amer fort in
the 12th century when waves of
Muslim invaders controlled nearby
Delhi, Amer's hilltop site. It lay on
the route to the Muslim Chishti
shrine at Ajmer. Thus began a story
of alliance and mutual benefit.
Alliances were strongest with the
Mughals in 1562. The Amer princess
who sealed this alliance gave birth
to Salim, later Emperor Jahangir
(see p. 41).

The results were wealth, prestige,
and the **Amer Fort** and palace
complex you can now visit. Viewed
from the road across Maota Lake, the

left-hand section was built by Man
Singh (*R*.1589–1614), who led
Akbar's troops to repeated victories,
while the right section, which
emulates Mughal buildings at
Agra and Fatehpur Sikri (see pp.
96–105), was built by Jai Singh I
(*R*.1621–1667), who fought for
three Mughal emperors.

The least tiring way to reach the
palace is by car (elephant rides are
now restricted). Once there, don't
miss the **Kali Mata Temple,** with
Jai Singh's elaborately decorated
suites (with good rooftop views)
and the warren of Man Singh's
simpler rooms.

On the way down to the main
road, find **Anokhi Museum of**

Right: Riding up to impressive Amer Fort on an elephant

Jaipur, Rajasthan
129 E4
India Tourist Office
✉ State Hotel, Khasa Kothi
☎ 0141-372200

Rajasthan Tourist Information
www.rajasthantourism.gov.in
✉ Tourist Hotel

City Palace
$ $
🕐 Closed religious festival days
$ $. Free Wed.

Hand-Printing where the local craft's fascinating story is set out in an immaculately restored *haveli* (mansion). (Kheri Gate, Amber, tel: 0141-2530226 www.anokhi.com, closed Mon).

JAIPUR

Fourth in succession after Jai Singh I, the precocious, 11-year-old Jai Singh II *(R.1699–1743)* came to the Kachwaha throne and was awarded the title Sawai (One-and-a-Quarter) to put him above his fellow Rajputs. Having shone on the battlefield, he indulged his love of science and the arts. In 1727 he began to lay out a model palace-city, Jaipur, employing a Bengali called Vidyadhar Bhattacharya as his architect.

Your visit could start with **City Palace** and its collections of fabrics, decorated weapons, paintings, and carpets; the one-and-a-quarter flag flies above. Nearby stands Jai Singh's **Jantar Mantar** (magical

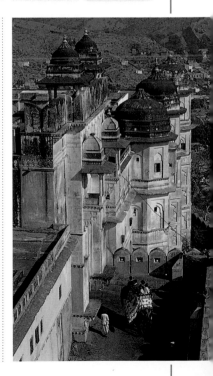

A group of women picnic together on a Jaipur street.

Govinda Deva Temple
- ✉ Jaleb Chowk

Central Museum
- ✉ Ram Niwas Bagh
- 🕐 Closed Fri.
- 💲 $. Free Wed.

Rambagh Palace
- ✉ Bhawani Singh Rd.
- ☎ 0141-2211919

Vidyadhar ka Bagh
- ✉ 4 miles (6 km) E of Jaipur on Agra Rd.

Sisodia Rani ka Bagh
- ✉ 4 miles (6 km) E of Jaipur on Agra Rd.
- 💲 $

instrument), an intriguing set of outsize astronomical instruments, mostly designed to calculate time more precisely. Of the five sets he built, this is the biggest.

Outside the palace complex Jaipur's markets are a riot of color. Find bangles, shoes, puppets, and *attar* (perfume) at Badi Chaupar, in front of the landmark **Hawa Mahal** (Palace of the Winds), cotton cloth and jewelry along **Johari Bazar,** gems and jewels particularly down two lanes of it, Gopalji Ka Bazar, and Haldion Ka Rasta.

If the fervent worship in the Kali Mata temple at Amer (see p. 131) interested you, so will **Govinda Deva Temple.** Jai Singh brought the image of Krishna from Govinda; it is worshiped especially fervently at the 6 p.m. and 8 p.m. *pujas.*

South of the walled city, at the **Central Museum** a delightful collection of puppets, costumes, models, and Jaipur brasswork fills Sir Samuel Swinton Jacob's Albert Hall, begun in 1876 in the spacious lung of Ram Niwas Gardens. The Durbar Hall *(often closed)* contains

spectacular carpets.

Farther south again is the **Rambagh Palace,** built by Maharaja Ram Singh II as a hunting lodge, which Madho Singh II transformed into a royal playground with extensive English gardens. It is now a hotel, but the public can enjoy the gardens, the Lalique fountains, and the Polo Bar of the lodge.

JAIPUR'S OUTSKIRTS

As you leave Jaipur on the road toward Agra, the walled garden **Vidyadhar ka Bagh,** on the right, remembers Jaipur's architect, Vidyadhar Bhattacharya. On the left, **Sisodia Rani ka Bagh** is the country palace built for Jai Singh II's Udaipur queen; there are lively murals and lush gardens. Behind it, troops of langur monkeys are fed daily at 4 p.m. at the **Hanuman Temple.**

On the left, along the Jaipur–Amer road at Gaitor, doors lead to the **Royal Cenotaphs.** Madho Singh II's is the largest; Jai Singh's, found at the back, has columns carved with mythological scenes supporting a marble dome. ∎

Around Jaipur

IF THE CROWDED TOURIST HOT SPOTS OF AMER AND JAIPUR take their toll, seek out some of these quieter, often atmospheric places in the Rajasthan countryside around Jaipur.

Jaipur has a ring of protective forts, the most imposing of which is **Nahargarh,** reached either from the Amer road or by a brisk hike from the city's Nahargarh Fort Road. Sunset is marvelous, when Jaipur's city noises float up through the softening light.

An ideal detour after Amer, the spectacularly sited **Jaigarh** is where Man Singh and his successors stored their treasure. It was expanded by Jai Singh II in 1726, and you can see the great cannon, armory, gun foundry, and palace complex. In times of danger, Amer's royals retreated here.

Moving farther afield, the following sights are listed clockwise around Jaipur from the west. At **Ajmer** (112 miles/135 km from Jaipur) find the Dargarh Sharif (holy shrine) of the Sufi saint Khwajah Muin-ud-din Chisthti, who came to India in 1192 and died here (see p. 70); this is still a popular pilgrimage center, with regular *qawwali* singing. See also Akbar's fort-palace, the finely carved Arhai-din-ka-Jhonpra mosque (1193), and Shah Jahan's marble pavilions. In contrast, the quiet Hindu town of **Pushkar's** draw is its sacred lake. (For the annual Pushkar Fair see p. 385.)

The rugged area of northeast Rajasthan known as **Shekhawati** is dotted with more than 360 villages. During the 19th and 20th centuries, Marwari families, such as the Birlas, Poddars, and Goenkas, made their money in commerce and then lavishly decorated their homes with lively frescoes inside and out. A trip to see these might include Fatehpur, Mahansar, Jhunjhunun, and Nawalgarh.

At Samode (26 miles/42 km NW of Jaipur), descendants of Jai Singh II's finance minister have energetically restored his isolated **Samode Palace,** whose rooms are covered with murals. Nearby, they have also brought the walled royal garden alive again, complete with working fountains.

The **Sariska National Park** (*64 miles/103 km NE of Jaipur*) is a Project Tiger reserve off the Delhi–Jaipur highway, sprawling over 300 square miles (800 sq km); dawn and dusk jeep rides may give sightings of a tiger but will certainly include good birds. **Alwar,** once capital of Alwar state, is dominated by Vinai Vilas (1840), the atmospheric city palace with a top-floor museum; see also the royal *chhatri* and Mughal tomb of Fateh Jung.

In the center of **Bharatpur,** the Jat kings' Lohargarh retains its decayed splendor. Part is now a museum. However, the Bharatpur maharaja's evocative summer palace at nearby **Dig** (circa 1750) survives intact: Wander its gardens, complete with marble swing, and explore the magnificent apartments, some decorated with marble booty from Agra Fort.

Another Project Tiger reserve is **Ranthambhor National Park,** 154 square miles (399 sq km) of deciduous forest rambling over the Aravalli and Vindhya Hills and around Ranthambore's great fort. It provides the ideal habitat for tigers and is popular and fashionable, so it's essential to reserve accommodations (see p. 352) in advance. ■

Nahargarh Fort
✉ 5 miles (9 km) NW of Jaipur on Amer Rd.
$ $

Jaigarh Fort
✉ N of Jaipur on Amer Rd.
☎ 0141-630848
$ $

Bharatpur
▲ 129 F4
✉ 34 miles (55 km) W of Agra

Pushkar has many temples.

Dig
▲ 129 E5
✉ 61 miles (98 km) NW of Agra on NH2
$ $

Ranthambhor National Park
▲ 129 E4
✉ 112 miles (180 km) SE of Jaipur

India's palace hotels

India is awash with palaces. There are thousands of them, huge and unnecessary in today's democratic India. Yet they are the core of every old city and dominate villages; they overlook lakes, perch on hills, and are found down the most unlikely mud lanes.

A stylish waiter looks out from the Rambagh Palace Hotel over its extensive lawns. Maharaja Madho Singh II transformed the hunting lodge into a royal playground.

Before independence, these were great households, often giving employment to several hundred people. They were places of patronage for painters, writers, musicians, and weavers. After 1947, the former rulers and nobles were obliged to give up some of their land, wealth, and properties. With them went the communities they headed. The grandest palaces and forts became landmarks open to the public, while others remained the ancestral homes of nobles, who found their upkeep increasingly difficult to finance. Hundreds more simply fell empty and silent, waiting quietly for their moment to come alive again.

Now, as visitors prefer palaces to high-rises to stay in, these buildings have their chance, encouraged by government tax breaks. All over India, they are being dusted down and opened up as hotels. Some are sensational, others less so; but all have a special charm that adds to a visit to India. The local staff, proud of their area, often ensure that guests have an especially memorable stay.

It was the Maharaja of Jaipur who first saw the potential of renting palace rooms to visitors. He opened the Rambagh Palace Hotel in Jaipur on December 8, 1957; tragically, while other hotels are being lovingly restored, its art deco suites have recently been ripped out. In 1961, Maharana Bhagwat Singh of Udaipur also recognized the end of an era and began to transform Jag Niwas Palace into the Lake Palace Hotel.

His energetic son, Arvind Singh, has continued his work with an attention to quality that is rare. Having restored his own palaces to create the Udaipur hotel cluster of Shiv Niwas, Fateh Prakash, and Dovecote, he now has a palace-hotel network stretching to Jodhpur, Jaisalmer, and Bikaner.

Heritage hotels, as they are known, are not restricted to Rajasthan. They extend from the Himalayan Mountains down to Tamil Nadu. Nalagarh Fort nestles in the Himalayan foothills near Chandigarh. In the west, there is Nilambagh Palace at Bhavnagar in Gujarat, Orchard Palace at Gondal in Saurashtra, and Hingolgadh Castle at Jasden. Central India has Jhira Bagh Palace and Ahilya Fort, both convenient for Mandu; Bhanwar Vilas Palace at Karauli; and Kawardha Palace—convenient for Kanha National Park. Down in the south, Mysore's Lalitha Mahal Palace Hotel is a gloriously extravagant Victorian palace hotel; and there are many more.

Such is the success of heritage hotels that enterprising Indians with flair have started to buy old properties and imbue them with their own, more democratic taste. The team of designer Aman Nath and businessman Francis Wacziac took on the challenge of restoring Neemrana Fort with some friends, then went solo to bring other forts, Raj bungalows, and even a French colonial house in Pondicherry to life. Lekha Poddar has taken the chaotic pile of Devigarh Fort outside Udaipur, stripped it back to its origins and, with immaculate taste, created an uncompromisingly contemporary world-class hotel. For details of these, and more suggestions, see the hotels section of this guide on pp. 344–75. ■

Famous for its school of miniature painting, family-run Deogarh Palace Hotel (above) at Devgarh has finely decorated rooms. Tourists rest beside the sacred Narmada River at Maheshwar (below). Above them rises Ahilya Fort, which contains the 18th century palace of revered ruler Ahilya Bai, now restored into a beautiful hotel.

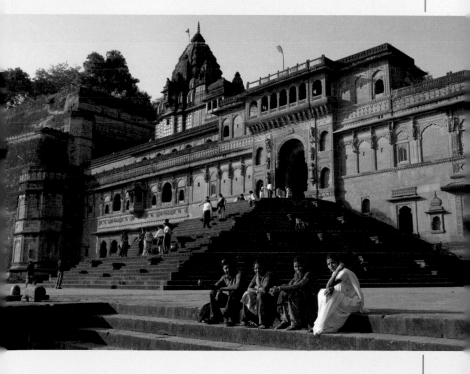

Udaipur

THIS IS RAJASTHAN'S MOST CONGENIAL AND ROMANTIC city, with its gentle light, shimmering lakes, compact center, bustling prosperity, and quantity of sensitively restored palaces. A far cry from the commercial aggressiveness and pollution of Jaipur, Udaipur is a perfect place for a relaxing day or two.

Once the capital of powerful Mewar state, Udaipur has Rajasthan's largest and best-maintained City Palace; it is more than half a mile long and still dominates the city.

Udaipur, Rajasthan

◭ 129 D3

Udaipur Tourist Office

www.rajasthantourism.gov.in

✉ Surajpole

☎ 0294-411535

Choose from a cluster of palace hotels and nobles' *havelis* to stay in; whichever you pick, you can visit the others for meals and drinks.

Start exploring the city by taking the evening boat ride from the main jetty around **Lake Pichola,** dug when Udai Singh fled Mughal danger at Chittaurgarh in 1567 and made this the capital of his state, Mewar. Udai Singh was head of the top Rajput clan, the Sisodias, descended directly from the sun via the god Rama. He and his successors built the huge and very Hindu City Palace. The boat chugs past the **Lake Palace Hotel** (1754, see pp. 134–35 and p. 356), built by Maharana Jagat Singh as a summer retreat, then stops at **Jag Mandir,** the island where Jahangir's son, the future Shah Jahan, sought refuge when he was a rebellious prince; his exquisite little palace (1622) anticipates his later buildings.

On land, there is much to see. The fleet of gleaming royal cars is kept beside the **Garden Hotel** (delicious Gujarati food), opposite **Gulab Bagh** (rose garden). At the **City Palace** *(closed for religious festivals),* with its *jharokas* (projecting balconies), maze of rooms, and wall decorations of inlaid glass, clamber up and down the narrow stairways of the Mardana (men's section), then see the recently restored **Zenana** (women's section). There is barely a touch of Mughal influence here. Finally, visit the restored Durbar Hall and its Crystal Gallery in **Fateh Prakash Palace** *(Tel 0294-528016)* where a fabulous collection of British crystal

is on display, including items from water basins to spitoons.

In the town, the main street leads downhill to the lively bazaars, passing Jagdish Temple and tiny shops selling cottons, wooden toys, and silver jewelry.

Fateh Sagar is an artificial lake. It was constructed in 1678 and Maharana Fateh Singh added the embankment (1889). The pretty shore road leads to well-kept **Saheliyon-ki-Bari** (Garden of Ladies); the island garden is **Nehru Park.** ∎

The twinkling colored glass on this City Palace peacock (right) contrasts with the simple surrounding lanes and traditional houses with carved, overhanging *jharokas* **(balconies).**

Shilpgram

🏛 129 D3

✉ 5 miles (8 km)
W of Udaipur

💲 $

Monsoon Palace

✉ 9 miles (15 km)
SW of Udaipur

Mount Abu

🏛 129 C3

✉ 116 miles (185 km)
NW of Udaipur

Kumbhalgarh

🏛 129 D3

✉ 40 miles (64 km)
N of Udaipur

Ranakpur

✉ 56 miles (90 km)
N of Udaipur; 16
miles (25 km)
SW of Kumbhalgarh

Nagda

✉ 14 miles (22 km)
N of Udaipur

Eklingji

🏛 129 D3

✉ 14 miles (23 km)
NE of Udaipur

Rajsamand Lake

🏛 129 D3

✉ 40 miles (65 km)
NE of Udaipur

Around Udaipur

IF YOU CAN TEAR YOURSELF AWAY FROM THE RELAXING
charm of Udaipur, there is a variety of outings, long and short, to suit
all interests, out across Rajasthan's rugged Aravalli Mountains.

To the west of Udaipur you can
visit the model crafts village of
Shilpgram, founded to preserve
western India's traditional architecture, music, and crafts. The houses
include a carved wooden Gujarat
building; you may see weavers,
musicians, potters, and other
craftsmen at work.

A hike up the hill from Udaipur
to the abandoned **Monsoon
Palace** (1880), now used by the
local radio station, is rewarded with
magical sunset and sunrise views.

To the north of the city are a
number of sites within easy reach of
one another. The rocky outcrops
of **Mount Abu** provide Rajasthan's
only cool retreat from the searing
summer heat. Enjoy the walks,
views, lakes, and the two sets of
temples: the Jains' five finely carved
marble Dilwara temples and the
Hindus' temples at **Achalgarh**
and **Guru Shikar.** See also the
nearby Adhar Devi Temple, which
lies at the top of an extremely long
flight of steps; the views from the
top are magnificent.

Also north of Udaipur, the

spectacular 15th-century ghost
fort-town of **Kumbhalgarh** rises
from rugged countryside, the finest
of 32 forts built by Maharana
Kumbha. Inside the massive ramparts are Jain temples, cenotaphs,
and the citadel, which can be
climbed. Near the entrance, Aodhi
Hotel provides sustenance.

At **Ranakpur,** one of India's
finest Jain temples lies hidden in a
wooded valley—hence its survival.
The main temple (1439) is dedicated
to Adinath, an enlightened Jain
teacher, and built entirely of white
marble, almost every surface of
which is carved. Wander the 29
interconnecting halls and courtyards around the central sanctuary;
two more small temples nestle
among the nearby trees. For a final
Jain temple visit, see Varkana's well-
preserved **Parshvanatha
Temple** (15th century).

Beside the lake at rural **Nagda,**
the exquisite, intricately carved
tenth-century **Sasbahu temples**
bear witness to the scale of Hindu
achievement in northern India and
its destruction by Muslim invaders.

You can walk a
good portion of
Kumbhalgarh's
massive walls,
enjoying views of
the Aravalli
Mountains.

At **Eklingji** village, you can witness *puja* (worship) at two temples: Lakulisha (972) and Ekalinga (15th century), whose elaborately screened Shiva image is highly revered by all Sisodias; major pujas take place throughout the day on Mondays, the special day for Shiva.

Rajsamand Lake was created by Maharana Faj Singh to help prevent drought. Waterside pavilions (1660), carved with Krishna scenes, commemorate his marriage to a Kishangarh princess to save her from Mughal clutches. Enjoy the views from Digambara Jain temple.

Shri Nathji Temple at **Nathdwara** is a pilgrimage center for devotees of Krishna, whose image is from Mathura; there is an elaborate puja here at sunset. The *pitchwais* (cloth paintings) on sale have decorative value only. Nearby, **Haldighati** is where, in 1576, Udaipur's hero, Maharana Pratap Singh, denied the Mughals (led by the Jaipur ruler) their victory.

As you travel east from Udaipur, you come first to **Ahah,** the site of the ancient capital of Mewar. The Sisodias' royal cremation ground has elegant cenotaphs, especially that dedicated to Rana Amer Singh I (1621).

Rajasthan's most spectacular fort-city, **Chittaurgarh** was founded by Bappa Rawal in A.D. 728 on a wide, natural ridge rising from the plains. Three bloody sieges—by Ala-ud-din Khilji of Delhi in 1303, Bahadur Shah of Gujarat in 1535 and Akbar in 1567, when the capital was moved to Udaipur—caused thousands of soldiers' deaths and women's *johar* (ritual mass suicide), but they have only increased its Rajput romance. Inside the massive gateways, see the Palace of Rana Kumbha (1433–1468), the towers of Fame (12th century) and Victory (1457–1468), good temples, lakes, *sati* stones, and other buildings.

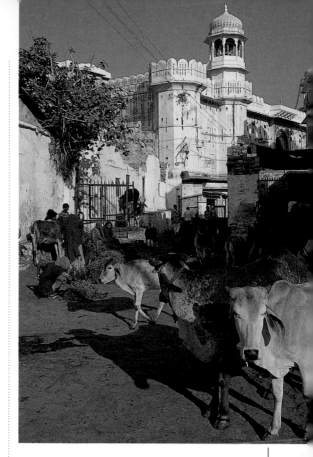

Until recently, **Bundi** seemed frozen in time. Visitors to the hilltop Taragarh Fort (1342), City Palace (begun 1580), Chatar Mahal palace (1660), and Raniji-ki-Baori step-well (1699) in the bazaar, all built by the Hara Chauhan Rajputs, can also see restored *havelis* along the main street, some now housing restaurants and crafts stores.

The thriving industrial town of **Kotah,** on the banks of the Chambal River, has a charming old quarter. City Palace (begun 1625) has remarkable murals and inlay work, and houses the Maharao Madho Singh Museum *(Closed Fri.),* which has a superb collection of deadly looking weapons and royal artifacts. The weaving village of **Kaithoon** and the temples of Jhalrapatan and Baroli are nearby. ■

Nathdwara
🏛 129 D3

Haldighati
🏛 129 D3

Ahah
🏛 129 D3
✉ 2 miles (3 km) E of Udaipur
🕐 Closed Fri.
💲 $

Chittaurgarh
🏛 129 D3
✉ 80 miles (120 km) E of Udaipur
💲 $

A walk around Jodhpur

Rising up from the dusty desert, the great sandstone walls of Jodhpur city enclose a maze of bazaars and lanes crowded with people and camels that huddle around the base of a magnificent fort built on a soaring bluff. In 1549, Rao Jodha made this the capital of his powerful, ever warring Rathore clan's Marwar (Land of Death) state. Today, expanded Jodhpur is Rajasthan's second largest city, after Jaipur.

To explore its ancient core, begin by taking a rickshaw up to the old city and paying the driver's fee. Through **Nagauri Gate ❶**, one of seven in the 6-mile-long (10 km) city wall, a steep, zigzag path leads to the fort entrance. On the way, **Jaswant Thada ❷**, the royal cremation ground, is on the right; the white marble memorial (1899) is to Jaswant Singh II. As you pass through the sixth massive defense gateway, **Loha Pol ❸**, notice the handprints of royal wives who committed *sati* (self-immolation on their husband's funeral pyre).

   Meherangarh Fort ❹ *(Closed 1–2:30 p.m.)* combines serious defense with refined courtly elegance. Beyond Suraj Pol is the palace area, now the Meherangarh Museum. From the interconnecting courtyards you can enjoy fairy-tale views of the sandstone walls, whose windows are carved into such delicate *jali* (lattice) work that they look like lace.

Inside, an organized route takes you through **Moti Mahal** (Pearl Palace, 1581–1595) and **Phool Mahal** (Flower Palace, 1730–1750, decorated 1873–1895), both of which have exquisite painted ceilings and walls, with dancing girls, deities, and proud Jodhpur rulers. **Moti Vilas** (1638–1678) houses the marble coronation seat on which all rulers except Jodha have

- 🅼 See area map pages 128–29
- ▶ Nagauri Gate
- ↔ About 4 miles (6 km)
- 🕒 3–4 hours
- ▶ Umaid Bhawan Palace

NOT TO BE MISSED
- Meherangarh Fort
- Markets around the Clock Tower
- Umaid Bhawan Palace

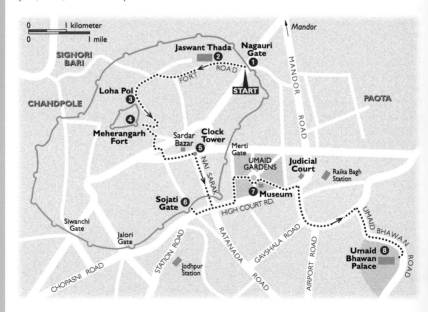

Jodhpur's Meharangarh Fort, built on a natural bluff in the desert, glows in the evening sunlight and offers paternal protection, even today, to the thriving city outside its walls.

been (and continue to be) crowned. This and the adjacent *Zenana* (women's quarters) court have especially fine jali-work. In **Sheesh Mahal** (1707–1724) and **Rang Mahal,** see how inlay and mirrors are used in the decoration. The swords and shields in **Sileh Khana** (the armory) are more works of art than war implements. Finally, the sumptuous interior of **Takhat Vilas** (1843–1873) has jolly dancing-girl murals. Do not miss the splendid silk Mughal tent, booty from a raid on Delhi, nor the terrace with its ancient cannon and magnificent views.

To walk down into the city, take the path beside the painted building at the U-bend above the fort shops. At the bottom, wind your way through narrow alleys to the central Sardar Bazar and its landmark **Clock Tower** ❺—this is not a large area, and you will not get lost—to see street barbers, waterpot sellers, and **Tulahti Mahal** (1638–1681), a palace turned into a women's hospital.

A wide road leads straight to **Sojati Gate**

❻, where good locally made *bandhani* (tie-dye) cotton is sold. From here, take a rickshaw through the New City, pausing to enjoy the Victorian bric-a-brac in the **museum** ❼ in Umaid Gardens, and the crazy Anglo-Rajput style of the **Judicial Court** (1893–96). (Agree on a price with your rickshaw driver in advance, pay on completion, and add a tip if appropriate; he waits while you make visits.)

To end, sweep up the hill to the 347-room **Umaid Bhawan Palace** ❽ (1929–1944). Designed by H. V. Lanchester, it combines beaux-arts with art deco, Western lifestyles with strict *purdah,* and tempers high European 1930s style with Rajput royal taste. It is now divided into private palace, public museum, and deluxe hotel. The massive bronze front doors lead to a grand hall with sweeping marble stairway, circular basement swimming pool, and grand pillared hotel terrace, ideal for refreshment. The **museum** section includes the Durbar Hall, miniature paintings, armor, and fine clocks. ∎

Around Jodhpur

ACROSS THE DRY AND DUSTY THAR DESERT—WHICH CAN BE crossed by car, train, jeep, or camel safari—lie isolated Rajasthani towns whose buildings reflect past wealth accumulated by virtue of their position on one of the world's great east–west trading routes.

Mandor
 129 D4
✉ 5 miles (8 km) N of Jodhpur

Osian
129 D4
✉ 40 miles (64 km) N of Jodhpur

Deshnoke
129 D5
✉ 125 miles (199 km) N of Jodhpur

Bikaner
129 D5
✉ 145 miles (231 km) N of Jodhpur

As you head north from Jodhpur, you soon arrive at **Mandor,** where the Parihar Rajputs ruled Marwar from the sixth century until the Rathores toppled them in 1381. The fort is gone, but Rathore royal cenotaphs stand in lush Mandor Gardens; one is dedicated to Maharaja Ajit Singh (1724), who also built the pleasure palace.

Rajasthan's largest group of early Jain and Brahmanical temples (8th–11th centuries) stands on the outskirts of **Osian**. Most temples stand on a platform, have a curved tower, and are very finely carved.

The Karni Mata Temple at **Deshnoke** may not be a first choice for sightseeing: It swarms with holy rats. Devotees believe departing souls can evade the wrath of Yama, god of death, by reincarnation as a rat. The temple is dedicated to

Bikaner's patron goddess, who is an incarnation of Durga.

To the far north of Jodhpur, reached across arid scrub and sand, **Bikaner** is less picturesque than Jodhpur and Jaisalmer (see p. 143) but just as interesting; it also has fewer visitors and a choice of palaces—hotels in town and lakeside at Gajner. Founded in 1488 by Bhika, sixth son of Rao Jodha of Jodhpur, it quickly benefited from the lucrative trade route. Junagarh Fort (1588–1593), built by Raja Rai Singh, one of Akbar's generals, protects beautiful, treasure-filled palaces: Chandra Mahal has Bhika's bed, exotic Anup Mahal the Coronation Hall enriched with ornamental lacquer work. Inside the Old City's pink sandstone wall, wander the lanes to find the piazza lined with merchants' houses and, in the southeast corner, two Jain temples with brightly colored murals. Don't miss the fine stone carvings at the **Ganga Golden Jubilee Museum** (Closed Sun.), or Sir Samuel Swinton Jacob's Anglo-Rajput **Lallgarh Palace,** begun in 1881 and now a hotel (see p. 354).

Just west of Bikaner, overlooking the artificial lake of Devi Kund Sagar, stand the magnificent, often domed, marble and sandstone royal **cenotaphs**. Farther out, a royal hunting ground is now preserved and protected as the **Gajner Wildlife Sanctuary**. Here you can see *nilgai*, black buck, antelope, wild boar, *chinkara*, gazelles, and in winter, important migratory birds such as the Siberian grouse.

Northeast of Jodhpur, **Nagaur,** is a rich combination of grand mosques and painted palaces that reflect its Muslim and Hindu rulers. The town is the backdrop to a businesslike Cattle Fair (Jan.–Feb.), when thousands arrive to trade cattle, camels, and Nagaur's famously stout bullocks, with time off for dancing and racing.

To the west of Jodhpur, lying on the route to Jaisalmer, is **Barmer's** quiet crafts center. It leaps into life as thousands of Rajasthanis arrive for the annual Tilwara Cattle Fair (Jan.), the largest in Rajasthan and, so far, less commercialized than Pushkar's Camel Fair.

At **Pokaran,** a modest version of Jaisalmer (see below) with fewer visitors, you can explore the ornate, red-sandstone fort and its splendid *havelis* (mansions).

The fortified desert city of **Jaisalmer** is built of fragile, golden sandstone, often exquisitely carved. It has stood isolated in the Thar Desert since its founding by Rawal Jaisal, a Bhatti Rajput, in 1156. Despite its turbulent history, it thrived thanks to the lucrative

trade routes from India to Persia, Arabia, Egypt, Africa, and Europe. More recently, when Western tourists discovered its romantic beauty, it was threatened, first with unsympathetic new buildings, then with an increased water consumption that has brought it to near collapse. Valiant work to save the city is being done by the British-based charity, Jaipur in Jeopardy. You can witness their efforts as you visit the fortifications, fort-palace, and several of the grand havelis. The colorful Desert Festival (Jan.–Feb.) is aimed at tourists.

A camel safari and sleeping under the desert stars around a campfire can be magical. Safaris last from one to four days and usually

head out from Jaisalmer toward the **Sam Dunes,** Amar Sagar lake, and Lodurva's Jain temples or the magnificent royal cenotaphs at Bada Bagh; enthusiasts can ride to Bikaner or Jodhpur. Remember to bring high-factor sun lotion for days and warm woolens for nights.

On a village jeep safari you can learn about desert wildlife and the local Bishnoi tribe: See the tribes thatched huts, learn about their herbal remedies, and appreciate their crafts (often on sale). Trips can be arranged by your hotel. ■

Nagaur
🅰 129 D4
✉ 84 miles (135 km) N of Jodhpur

Gagner Wildlife Sanctuary
🅰 129 D5
✉ 164 miles (263 km) N of Jodhpur

Barmer
🅰 129 C4
✉ 146 miles (233 km) W of Jodhpur

Rajput cenotaphs with Jaisalmer Fort in the background

Pokaran
🅰 129 C4
✉ 116 miles (185 km) NW of Jodhpur

Jaisalmer
🅰 129 C4
✉ 184 miles (295 km) NW of Jodhpur

Sam Dunes
🅰 129 B4
✉ 209 miles (335 km) NW of Jodhpur

The crafts & traditions of Rajasthan

Every town in Rajasthan has its markets, brimful with life, especially toward the end of the day when the heat is less oppressive. Walking through them is a treat, particularly to see all the different crafts on sale. Handsome men, their weatherworn faces framed by magenta turbans, bargain for handstitched leather shoes. Family expeditions choose the embroidered *pilo* (head veil), *choli* (blouse), and *ghaghra* (full skirt) for a bride-to-be. Gaggles of girls buy yet more lacquer bangles.

Peek behind the shops and you see a silversmith or a painter; cast your eyes up and you see yards of tie-dye drying on the rooftops. As night falls, itinerant puppeteers set up their show, certain that they will lure children away from television for one night.

Bold color and a strong sense of pattern distinguish this traditional Udaipur textile decorated with a row of regal Rajput warriors.

Tourism has helped revive several almost lost traditions. In Jaipur the art of block-printing on cotton, whose heyday was the 18th century, thrives once more. Recipes for natural dyes have been rediscovered, blocks of teak are being carved with new and traditional designs, and printers can barely keep up with demand. Another revival is Jaipur pottery, a softpaste pottery decorated with azure blue flowers and patterns.

In Jaipur and Bikaner, you find the best *meenakari* work, the art of enameling that used to depend upon court patronage. The best of these delicate patterns of birds and flowers in ruby red, deep green, and peacock blue often remain hidden on the reverse of gem-studded jewelry.

Jodhpur is known for its *bandhani,* the ancient Indian technique of tie-dyeing fabrics found throughout Rajasthan and Gujarat. Each community has its own designs. The merchant supplies the fabric to a family, usually Muslim. The father draws the pattern on the fabric using tiny dots. The women and children bind the cloth tightly, following the pattern, dye the fabric, then remove the strings. The process may be repeated with a darker color to build up the pattern. Jodhpur is also a center for wooden lacquer work, especially bangles and boxes.

Helped by some dynamic Delhi patrons, miniature-painting is reaching new peaks. Rajasthan's many painting schools declined in the 19th century, but artists are now practicing this very disciplined art using both traditional iconography and innovative designs.

Another joy of Rajasthan is the quantity of traditional entertainment still in evidence: Songs and stories are often so simple that mime is sufficient to explain them. In a land where evening entertainment is minimal, hotels often employ talented families of entertainers to put on a show for their guests. *Bhopas* (balladeers), originally from Marwar, have a visual aid, a *phad* (scroll-painting); while the father sings the story, the mother holds a lantern and they dance. Folk dances often relate to Holi, Gangaur, and other Rajasthan festivals: the *gingad* is accompanied by the big *chang* drum, the *teratali* is more like ritual acrobatics than dancing, and the *ghoomar-gair* is Rajasthan's version of the age-old stick dance. But the puppet show is always the favorite. *Kathputli,* as it is known, is performed by itinerant families. Drawing back the embroidered curtain known as the Taj Mahal, they back up the antics of their beautifully carved, painted, and costumed puppets with music, song, and high-pitched yelps. ∎

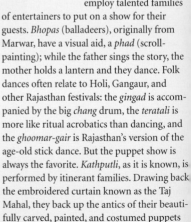

The rich red tones of this densely and laboriously worked cotton patchwork fabric from Jaisalmer (above), which may have been made for a dowry, contrasts with the simplicity of a street tailor from Fatehpur (right), who would be able to run up workaday cotton shirts and pants in a few hours. A group of Jodhpur men (below) swirl their long white robes as they take part in the stick dance, alternately crashing their sticks to the ground and against their partners' sticks.

Ahmedabad

What must once
have been an
impressive
gateway into
Ahmedabad, the
Teen Darwaja
is now barely
noticed among
the congestion.

**Ahmedabad,
Gujarat**
www.gujarattourism.com

 129 C2

**Ahmedabad
Tourist Office**

H. K. House, off
Ashram Rd., S of
Gandhi Bridge

079-26589172

THIS DYNAMIC CITY IS THE CAPITAL OF GUJARAT, A MODERN
state with a very ancient history. It comprises three distinct geographical regions: hilly peninsula Saurashtra, barren Kachchh with its
Rann (desert), and the central, fairly flat portion. As the country's
prime producer of cotton and groundnut oil, and its second greatest
producer of tobacco, Gujarat is India's wealthiest state. A visit to
Ahmedabad's formidable and distinctive Islamic monuments, with
their remarkably fine *jali*-work, and to its many good museums,
makes a perfect springboard for exploring this rarely visited state.

THE OLD CITY

The city's ancient citadel, **Bhadra,**
is a good place to start. When
Ahmad Shah became Sultan of
Gujarat in 1411, he moved the capital here from Patan (see p. 149) and
built this solid, red stone citadel
(not open to the public, but it is

usually possible to climb the staircase inside the main gate to enjoy
good views from the roof). Trade
flourished, boosted by east–west
trade to the ports, and the building
of mosques followed. In this area,
you can see Alif Shah's green-and-
white mosque in front of the citade

Akbar finally absorbed Gujarat into his vast empire in 1572 to benefit from its wealth and its location on the *hajj* (pilgrimage) route to Mecca. The mosque is isolated on a traffic island, but it is well worth risking the traffic to enjoy its ten magnificent, probably unequaled, *jali* (carved latticework) screens, especially those in the western wall (these can easily be seen from outside; the mosque itself is closed to women). Observe how local Hindu and Jain craftsmen have been permitted to carve heroes and animals from Hindu mythology.

Walk along Mahatma Gandhi Road to find more sites dating back to Ahmad Shah. First is his monumental **Teen Darwaja** (triple gateway) in Khas Bazar. Next is his magnificent **Jama Masjid** (completed 1424); go up the great steps with the faithful to see the courtyard, prayer hall (elaborate carving), and Zenana jali screens. Finally, his family **mausoleum** (1442, closed to women) and that of his wives stand in Manek Chowk

and Ahmad Shah's small, private mosque by Victoria Gardens, whose intricate *mihrabs* contrast with Sanskrit inscriptions on stones from an earlier Hindu temple.

Stay in this area to visit **Sidi Sayyid's Mosque** (1573), built shortly after the Mughal emperor

among the streets of jewelers, dyers, and cloth merchants. See the Hindu styles and the fine inlay decoration.

To finish, take three short detours to Rani Sipri's very Hindu **mosque** (1514), the carved wooden **Swaminarayan Temple,** and surrounding traditional **Guajarat havelis**.

This charming mosaic of a pair of doves can be found in the Calico Museum of Textiles.

2001 earthquake; rebuilding

At 8:46 a.m. on January 26, 2001, western India experienced an earthquake that measured 7.7 on the Richter scale. Its epicenter was near Bhuj, a timeless, medieval walled town in the Kachchh (Kutch) region of Gujarat. Shock waves reached as far as Chennai and Nepal. Bhuj and more than 300 villages nearby were wiped out, and the whole state was affected. More than 20,000 people died, and many more were left homeless. In all, 1,016 villages and eight cities suffered substantial damage. In the capital, Ahmedabad, 179 buildings were affected but many of the old wooden *havelis* survived. These are now being conserved. ∎

Thousands of finely tuned kites star in the annual kite festival.

Calico Museum of Textiles
✉ Sarabhai Foundation, Shahibagh
🕐 Closed Wed. Tours only, times vary

Shreyas Folk Art Museum
✉ Near Shreyas Railway Crossing
🕐 Closed Mon.
💲 $

Tribal Research Institute Museum
✉ Gujarat Vidyapith, Ashram Rd.
🕐 Closed Sun.

N.C. Mehta Gallery
✉ Indology Institute, Radhakrishnan Rd., near Gujarat University
🕐 Closed Mon.

Vishalla Vichar Museum
✉ Sarkhej Rd., Vasana

Gandhi Smarak
www.gandhi-manibhavan.org
✉ Sabarmati Ashram, Ashram Rd.
💲 $

Sardar Patel Memorial Museum
✉ Near Shahibagh Rd.
🕐 Closed Mon.
💲 $

Adalaj Vav
✉ 11 miles (17 km) N of Ahmedabad on Ajmer Rd.

OTHER AHMEDABAD SIGHTS

After 1630, Gujarat's run of famines, Marathas, and Muslims turned the city's fortunes. In 1817, under British influence, modern machinery made Ahmedabad the industrial powerhouse of the East. Mahatma Gandhi's arrival (see p. 150) further boosted its textile production and political power. Thus, of Ahmedabad's many museums, the most important is the **Calico Museum of Textiles,** where guides explain a dazzling variety and quality of weaving, embroidery, mirrorwork, tie-dye, printing, and skillful *ikat* weave, all collected by the Sarabhai textile magnates.

For other specialist interests, visit the **Shreyas Folk Art Museum,** displaying Gujarati crafts, the **Tribal Museum,** about the various peoples of Gujarat, the **Kite Museum,** and the **N.C. Mehta Gallery,** with its collection of top-quality Indian miniature paintings. Just outside town, specially built **Vishalla** combines traditional huts, craftsmen, a splendid

museum of Gujarati metalware, and a restaurant. Le Corbusier enthusiasts can see several of his buildings here (see pp. 88–89).

Ahmedabad played a vital role in India's freedom movement (see p. 150). You can visit the Charles Correa-designed **Gandhi Smarak** in Mahatma's Sabarmati Ashram, where Gandhi lived from 1917 to 1930; an excellent exhibition tells the freedom story. To complete the picture, the **Sardar Patel Memorial Museum** remembers the politician and freedom fighter who was deputy to Jawaharlal Nehru.

For a final taste of Ahmedabad's past glory, visit three multi-layered, galleried, and elaborately carved step-wells called *vavs.* In town is **Dada Harini Vav** (1435), and nearby is **Mata Bhavani Vav** (11th century); on the road to Gandhinagar is the best of all, **Adalaj Vav** (1498).

A thirty-minute drive beyond here is **Auto World,** India's finest collection of more than 100 antique cars (Dastan Estate, Sardar Patel Ring Road). ■

North of Ahmedabad

MAKING DAY TRIPS FROM THE CAPITAL, THE INTREPID traveler who ventures into rural Gujarat will be well rewarded by a variety of quality sites.

Gandhinagar, named after the Mahatma, was India's second planned town and, like Chandigarh (see p. 120), was designed by Le Corbusier, assisted by B. V. Doshi. Greenery has considerably softened the impact of this *"cité idéale."*

Continuing farther, to the northwest of Ahmedabad, visit the Surya Temple at **Modhera,** begun in 1027 by Bhimdev I. It was an early achievement of the rich Solanki rulers (11th–13th centuries) and, despite its dilapidation after Mahmud of Ghazni's attack (see p. 37), remains one of Gujarat's great Hindu temples. It was financed by public subscription and built by voluntary labor, and its monumental conception is matched by rich ornamentation. From the huge tank with its double flights of steps, two *mandapas* (halls) lead to the sanctuary; here, note especially the carvings of Agni (south) and Surya (north). Enjoy these in the glow of sunset.

Still farther north you will come to **Anahilvada,** the Solanki capital sacked repeatedly by Muslim marauders, then abandoned for Ahmedabad. Among the remains of the fortifications, temples, and tank is the Solanki queen Udaimati's exquisite Ran-ki-vav (circa 1080), Gujarat's finest step-well. In the Sadvi Wada area of the bustling adjoining city of **Patan,** founded in 1796, watch the *ikat* weave being created in one of its finest forms, the *patola* silk sari; see also carved *havelis,* domes, and Jain temples.

Near here are two good sites. Siddhapur is a time-capsule trading town with grand early 20th century merchants' houses. At **Taranga** you'll find a well-preserved Jain temple (1166), dedicated to Ajitanatha, the second Tirthankara, and built by the Solanki ruler Kumarapala. It's well worth the detour. Join Jain pilgrims for the hill climb. For the explorers, **Kumbharia's,** five Solanki-period Jain temples (1062–1231) rival Mount Abu's; each is built entirely of marble and stands in its own court. ■

Gandhinagar
- 129 D2
- 14 miles (23 km) N of Ahmedabad

Modhera
- 129 C3
- 66 miles (105 km) NW of Ahmedabad

Anahilvada
- 106 miles (169 km) N of Ahmedabad

Patan
- 129 C3
- 106 miles (169 km) N of Ahmedabad

Taranga
- 129 C3
- 84 miles (135 km) NW of Ahmedabad

Kumbharia
- 118 miles (189 km) NE of Ahmedabad

Siddhapur
- 129 C3
- 100 miles (160 km) N of Ahmedabad

A weaver creates the soft pattern of *ikat*-weave silk.

Mahatma Gandhi

One of the most influential men of the 20th century, Mohandas Karamchand Gandhi (1869–1948) was born in Porbandar (see p. 151) in western Gujarat, where his father and grandfather were *diwans* of the princely state. Having trained as a lawyer in London, he worked in South Africa, where his passive resistance against the government's color and race prejudice prompted Bengali poet Rabindranath Tagore (see p. 123) to give him the title Mahatma (Great Soul).

Simple in his lifestyle, Mahatma Gandhi sits cross-legged, wrapped in a shawl, to write.

Returning home in 1915, Gandhi joined India's struggle for freedom and founded the Sabarmati Ashram in Ahmedabad. Two years later he moved in.

Gandhi began a nonviolent moral protest against oppression, known to Indians as *satyagraha* (literally "grasping truth"), and to the British as civil disobedience. It meant peacefully defying laws and willingly taking punishment. Then, appalled by the atrocities at Amritsar generated by his peaceful, national, one-day strike in 1919 (see p. 123), he waged his Non-Cooperation Movement of 1920–22.

Gandhi's aim was to use *ahimsa* (nonviolence) and *satya* (truth) to achieve a united, independent India. When he spun cotton and wove the thread into cloth, it symbolized his vision of an autonomous, self-reliant India free of foreign domination. When he rejected European clothes for the homespun cotton *dhoti* and shawl in 1921, his popularity soared with most Indians. Believing in the equality of all, he tried to give the untouchables dignity by renaming them *harijans* (children of God).

Gandhi had a strong, charismatic character matched by an austere code of living and huge ambitions for India. He campaigned relentlessly, fighting for *swadeshi,* the rejection of the imported cotton that had devastated India's weavers. He also supported the Congress Party president, Jawaharlal Nehru, when, on January 26, 1930, the resolution demanding complete independence was adopted.

That same year Gandhi launched a second civil disobedience campaign, given focus by the mass appeal of his Salt March, protesting against the British monopoly of salt production. On March 12, it left Ahmedabad amid Gandhi's rousing speeches for *swaraj* (freedom); a month later the protesters reached coastal Dandi, where they began to collect water and boil it to make illegal salt, thus expressing their objections to a system that touched every Indian household.

Salt was made illegally, saltworks were raided, government servants resigned, and on May 5 Gandhi was imprisoned. In January 1931, he and the British viceroy, Lord Irwin, signed a pact that led eventually to the Government of India Act of 1935.

During World War II, Gandhi introduced the "Quit India" slogan and worked to keep an undivided, free India. When Jinnah's call for "Direct Action" in 1946 provoked riots in Kolkata, Gandhi fasted until the violence had stopped. He again fasted for peace when, at partition, an estimated five million Hindus and Sikhs came into India, while the same number of Muslims left for Pakistan amid terrible bloodshed. On January 30, 1948, a Hindu extremist angered by Gandhi's tolerance toward Muslims assassinated him in Delhi. Ironically, this dreadful act had the effect of finally quelling the violence. ■

India's last viceroy, Viscount Mountbatten, and his wife flank Gandhi at a meeting at the Viceroy's House, New Delhi, in 1947.

Saurashtra

THIS RURAL AREA OF GUJARAT FILLS THE KATHIAWAR
Peninsula bordered by the Gulf of Kachchh and Cambay and the
Arabian Sea. The ancient ports, forts, and temples recall occupants
of all faiths stretching back to the Harappans (see p. 26). In 1807 the
fragmented land of 220 petty states, many ruled by Rajputs, came
under British supremacy. The sights listed below are arranged in a
clockwise circle from Ahmedabad and are best visited with a car and
driver on day trips or staying overnight.

**Saurashtra,
Gujarat**
🅰 128 B2
**Ahmedabad
Tourist Office**
www.gujarattourism.com
✉ H. K. House,
Ashram Rd., S of
Gandhi Bridge,
Ahmedabad
☎ 079-26589172

SOUTHERN SAURASHTRA
On the road down toward Lothal,
you come first to **Sarkhej,** the site
of the tomb of Ahmad Shah's
spiritual leader, Sheikh Ahmed
Khattu (1445). At Nal Sarovar Bird
Sanctuary you can see migrant
waterbirds (Nov.–Feb.), and at
Dholka (28 miles/44 km south
of Ahmedabad) there are three
monumental medieval mosques
and a beautiful wooden *haveli*
temple to visit. The remarkable and
evocative remains of **Lothal,** an
excavated Harappan port, include
the dock and the town's bazaars.
The site museum has jewelry, seals,
and weights and compasses.
  At **Velavadar Black Buck
Sanctuary,** it's best to pay a guide

to learn more about the elegant Indian antelope (or black buck), traditionally protected by the Bishnoi tribe (see p. 143).

Founded in 1723 by Maharaja Bhavsinghji, the old city of **Bhavnagar,** a cotton-exporting port, has vibrant bazaars for silver, gold, cloth, and *bhandani* (tie-dyed fabrics). Exhibits at the Gandhi Smriti Museum range from Harappan terra-cottas to the story of Gandhi's life. From here you can visit **Palitana,** joining Jain pilgrims to climb their sacred hill of Shatrunjaya, dedicated to the saint Adinath; 900 little temples make its summit India's largest temple city.

The 8-mile-long (13 km) island of **Diu** was, with Goa and Daman, Portuguese until 1962. This is where to relax, enjoy the beaches and cafés, and rent a bicycle to see the old town and fort. Avoid holiday seasons, when Gujaratis flock here to enjoy unrestricted alcohol.

Sadly, there is more myth than reality at **Somnath Temple.** The early versions are part of Hindu mythology; the later ones were successively destroyed by marauding Muslims. Today's temple (1950) was built by Sardar Patel, keeping to the plan of the great Solanki temple at Modhera (see p. 149).

The last of the southern sites is **Sasan Gir National Park,** the final Indian refuge of the Asiatic lion, which roamed northern India's forests until the 1880s. About 300 lions (the numbers are rising) live in 100 square miles (260 sq km), together with panthers and the local Maldhari cattle breeders. It is best to visit from November to mid-June—the later the better for seeing lions.

WESTERN SAURASHTRA

From **Junagadh,** the ancient capital of Gujarat, Jain pilgrims climb their sacred Mount Girnar. Junagadh's old citadel, Uparkot, once a Maurya and Gupta stronghold, is reached through openings in solid rock—three gateways and massive walls; features inside include third- to fourth-century caves with richly carved columns, and two 11th-century *vavs* (stepwells). In town, the Junagadh rulers' mausoleums are some of Gujarat's finest. Out of town, on the way to Mount Girnar's 12th-century temples, a modern building encloses a boulder inscribed with Ashoka's edicts (see p. 31).

Porbandar, now renowned as the birthplace of Gandhi, is a port with ancient trading links to Africa

Sarkhej
- 🄰 129 C2
- ✉ 5 miles (8 km) SW of Ahmedabad

Nal Sarovar Bird Sanctuary
- ✉ 30 miles (48 km) SW of Ahmedabad

Lothal
- 🄰 129 C2
- ✉ 66 miles (105 km) S of Ahmedabad
- 🄢 $

Velavadar Black Buck Sanctuary
- 🄰 129 C2
- ✉ 113 miles (181 km) S of Ahmedabad

Bhavnagar
- 🄰 129 C2
- ✉ 129 miles (204 km) S of Ahmedabad

Diu
- 🄰 129 C1

Somnath
- 🄰 128 B1

Sasan Gir National Park
- 🄰 129 C1
- 🕐 Closed July–Oct.
- 🄢 $

Porbandar
- 🄰 128 B2

Junagadh
- 🄰 128 B2

Climb the hill at Palitana for beautiful views like this one.

Daria Rajmahal

✉ 54 miles (95 km) from Diu Airport

🕐 Closed university holidays

Anut Nivas Khambala

✉ 15 miles (25 km) E of Porbandar

Kirti Mandir

🕐 Closed sunset to sunrise

Dwarka

▲ 128 B2

Jamnagar

▲ 128 B2

Lakhota Fort

🕐 Closed Wed.

$ $

Rajkot

▲ 129 C2

Rajkot Tourist Office

www.gujarattourism.com

✉ Off Jawahar Rd., Bhavnagar House

☎ 0281-234507

Kaba Gandhi no Delo

✉ Off Ghitake Rd., Rajkot

Watson Museum

🕐 Closed Wed., Sat.

$ $

Morbi

▲ 129 C2

Dubargadh Waghaji

🕐 Courtyards only

New Palace

✉ New Palace, Morbi

🕐 Write to request a visit

and Arabia. Under British protection the port prospered. The fine stone was exported to Bombay and Karachi, and the city's rulers added two waterfront palaces: **Daria Rajmahal** and **Anut Nivas Khambala** (1927, museum in the Rajput Room). Gandhi's simple, unfurnished house, the **Kirti Mandir,** is where he lived until his family moved to Rajkot (see below). The neighboring temple, Kirti Mandir (1950), was constructed to commemorate him.

Devotees of Krishna believe he fled Mathura to make **Dwarka** his capital. Pilgrims flock here, especially for the Hindu festivals of Shivratri *(Feb.–March)* and Janmashtami *(Aug.–Sept.),* the latter of which celebrates Krishna's birthday.

Maharaja Ranjit Singh, who played cricket for England with W. G. Grace, gave **Jamnagar** city its first boost into modernity. Head for the old city built beside Ranmal Lake and protected by **Lakhota** and **Bhujia forts.** Inside the walls is Chandni Bazar, with its ancient *havelis* and spectacularly decorated Jain temples dedicated to Adinath and Shantinath; there are glorious murals inside. See also **Ratan Bai Mosque,** with its inlaid doors, Ranjit Singh's sweeping Willingdon Crescent at Chelmsford Market, and enjoy the excellent local *bandhana* work.

CENTRAL SAURASHTRA

The teeming industrial city of **Rajkot,** once the British headquarters of the Western States, is where Gandhi's family moved from Porbandar in 1881. Their home was the modest **Kaba Gandhi no Delo,** which can be found in the old city, among traditional wooden Gujarati houses with carved shutters and stained glass. In the **Watson Museum** (1988), there is

a variety of Harappan, medieval, and Rajput treasures, plus a splendid statue of Queen-Empress Victoria (1899) by Alfred Gilbert, creator of London's bronze statue "Eros." Other colonial buildings include Alfred High School (1875) and Rajkumar College (1870), designed to be Gujarat's equivalent of Eton.

Wankaner was the capital of the former state, where Gandhi's father was once *diwan* (chief minister) to the maharaja. Under British protection, Maharaja Amarshinghi *(R.*1881–1948) transformed the city into a model of self-reforming enterprise and helped the state engineer design his own palace, Ranjit Vilas (1907–1914). This is a landmark building, which manages to combine Victorian Gothic, Italianate, and Mughal styles. Inside is a remarkable marble double spiral staircase. You can stay in the palace's outer buildings.

In this area of Saurashtra, keep a look out for *pallias,* tombstones commemorating bravery. Various images are used to describe the manner of death: A carved hand records a *sati* (self-immolation); a mounted bard with spear indicates a poet who committed suicide because his master defaulted on a loan for which the poet was surety.

Dominating access to the Gujarat peninsula, tiny **Morbi** state was threatened until Thakur Sabhi Waghaji *(R.*1897–1948) gave it stability and modernization, with a streetcar line and railroad. He was also the man responsible for two palaces: **Dubargadh Waghaji** (1880), in Venetian Gothic style, and **New Palace** (1931–1944), a stunning art deco building with an immaculate interior. **Halvad** has a lakeside palace and plenty of pallias, while **Dhrangadhra** is home to herds of wild asses that also live in the Rann of Kachchh. ▪

Kachchh

THE SALT FLATS OF THIS WILD, ARID, AND ISOLATED AREA
dotted with villages are the world's largest breeding area for flamingoes, and a refuge for the prancing Asiatic wild asses. Up in the north,
the marshy Great and Little Ranns of Kachchh (Kutch) flood completely in a good monsoon, making Kachchh an island; in the past
they cut off would-be Muslim invaders. Although nominally part of
various empires, the area has remained highly individual in its traditions and crafts—the women wear fantastic embroidered clothes—
and highly independent in its maritime trading with Africa, the Gulf,
and the Indian coast.

The wealth of Kachchh's second
city, **Mandvi,** mostly came from its
role as the port used by Mughals for
their vast annual *hajj* expeditions to
Mecca—more than 800 ships went
in 1819, and the great *dhows* are
still built here today. You can also
see Vijay Vilas palace, and the
grand, elaborately carved palaces
of the great merchants including
that of Ram Singh's with its later
Dutch facade.

For the adventurous traveler, the
rewards of visiting Kachchh's **villages** should easily compensate for
basic accommodations. Taking a
guide with you from the Bhuj
Tourist Office (and a permit if you
want to travel north), you might
include **Mundra,** near the Jain
temples of Bhadreswar, **Bhujodi,**
with its weavers, or **Anjar,** with its
bright embroideries. Along the way
you can see various tribal communities, each with their distinctive
dress: the pastoral Rabari, known
for their embroidery, the Bharvad,
who came from Mathura, the
nomadic Ahir cattle-breeders, and
the Charans, whose women are
often worshiped for their association with the goddess Parvati. ∎

In Gujarat's
Kachchh area,
famous for its
textiles, women
wear stunning
bandhani or
embroidered
shawls every day.

Festivals
Bhuj, Jan.–Feb.: five-day
celebration of traditional
Kachchh music, dance,
and crafts.

Vadodara & area

Vadodara

🅰 129 D2

**Vadodara
Tourist Office**

www.gujarattourism.com

✉ Train station

☎ 0265-2427489

🕐 Closed Sun.

Lakshmi Vilas

✉ Nehru Rd.

🕐 Closed Mon.

💲 $

**Maharaja Fateh
Singh Museum**

✉ On the grounds
of Lakshmi Vilas

🕐 Closed Mon.

💲 $

THIS STRIP OF RARELY VISITED LAND, SO SIGNIFICANT WHEN
the British established their first trading station at Surat in 1614, is
now a backwater. However, there are several places that make interesting stops for intrepid, seasoned travelers on the way to Mumbai.

On the drive through lush country
from Ahmedabad, stop at pain-
stakingly preserved **Champaner**,
outside Vadodara. After Muhammad
Begada took the Chauhan Rajput
stronghold in 1484, he spent 23
years building it up as his capital,
then abandoned it. Historic walls,
gateways, mosques, and tombs,
and fine views of Pavagadh hill,
rise behind.

    Vadodara (Baroda) is an
ever expanding industrial town,
redeemed by the fine old *havelis* and

bazaars in its old town and by the
well-maintained parks, lakes, and
public buildings added by Baroda
state's enlightened and extravagant
rulers known as Gaekwads ("pro-
tectors of cows"). Start with the
palace, or the reforming Gaekwad
Maharaja Sayajirao's **Lakshmi
Vilas** (1880–1890), reputedly the
most expensive building constructed
by a private individual in the

19th century. Designed by Major
Charles Mant, who went insane, and
completed by Robert Fellowes
Chisholm, this mixture of all Indian
styles also has London stained glass,
Venetian mosaics, and a garden
designed by experts from London's
Kew Gardens. More practically for
his subjects, this Gaekwad built
roads, railways, and hospitals, outlawed child marriage, and made
school compulsory. Nearby, the
**Maharaja Fateh Singh
Museum** houses a large collection
of the influential early 20th century
south Indian artist Raja Ravi Varma
and much European art. See, too,
Pratap Vilas (circa 1910), Makarpura
Palace, the Kalabahavan Technical
Institute (1922), the Vadodara
Museum and Art Gallery's sculptures
and miniature paintings, and the
university's sculptures from Vadaval
and Buddhist monuments from
Devni-mori. Do not miss Naulakhi
Baoli or the royal mausoleum of
Kirti Mandir.

    Drive past Bharuch (Broach) and
Surat, once considerable trading
towns, neither merits a stop. Speed
on to relaxed, quiet **Daman** (131
miles/208 km north of Mumbai) but
be sure to avoid public holidays (see
p. 342) when, like Diu (see p. 153),
it is besieged by locals for its freely
available alcohol. Daman was
Portuguese from 1531 until 1961,
and south of the Damanganga River,
in **Moti Daman,** you will find
grand walls, Portuguese mansions,
and some of the best preserved
churches in Asia. Nani Daman, on
the north bank, has hotels, markets,
and docks. ∎

**Extravagant,
expensive
Lakshmi Vilas
palace is a
romantic cocktail
of Rajput, Mughal,
and Jain archi-
tecture, with
a dash of Gothic
and classical.**

While Mumbai buzzes with talk of futures, mergers, and Bollywood movie budgets, some of India's most spectacular Buddhist caves, early Hindu temples, and historic forts lurk in Maharashtra's dramatic landscape.

Mumbai & Maharashtra

A huge movie poster backs a Mumbai man.

Mumbai & Maharashtra

MAHARASHTRA SWEEPS FROM THE Arabian Sea across the coastal paddy fields and coconut groves of the Konkan, up across the rugged Western Ghats (Sahyadris), and into the heart of peninsular India.

This expansive state, India's third largest in size and population, nevertheless has a unity. Its Marathi-speaking people share a common history, enriched by cultures to the north and south. After a period when Marahashtra was part of the Mauryan Empire (321–185 B.C.), successive Hindu dynasties held power for a thousand years until 1294, when the Yadavas yielded to the first of a string of Muslim rulers. The great port city of Bombay, now renamed Mumbai, rose toward the end of the 17th century, just when the warrior hero Shivaji (see p. 180) was consolidating the Maratha people of the area into a powerful nation. Despite defeat by the British in 1817, Shivaji's inspiration lives on; notice the plethora of statues of modern Maharashtra's founding father in downtown areas.

Visitors often rush through Mumbai and on to other areas of India. This is a shame. Mumbai is not just about trading: Its treasures include remarkable early Buddhist cave sculptures, a deserted Portuguese fort more atmospheric than anything to be found at Old Goa, and a group of world-class, well-preserved High Victorian Gothic public buildings.

Away from the seething life of the city, whose humidity climbs sharply between April and October, the most important trip inland is to the cave temples of Ellora (see pp. 176–77) and Ajanta (see pp. 178–79), whose paintings and sculptures are often said to be some of the greatest achievements in world art. If these and the other Buddhist sites in Mumbai have intrigued you, there are more caves to visit at Karla, Bhaja, and Bedsa, cut into the rock of the Western Ghats (see p. 183). But if you seek Raj charm in the cool hills, take a short train ride up to Matheran, Mahabaleshwar, or Pune, British hill stations now much loved by local

Maharashtrans, set in the heart of what was once Shivaji's Maratha confederacy. For a more adventurous trip, the new Konkan railroad (see pp. 204–205) and the hovercraft crossing Mumbai's harbor make an adventure southward easy; you can go on down to Goa, and extend your journey into a coastal trip right down to Kochi (see p. 207).

AROUND DELHI
p. 95

Tapi

R a n g e

Bhusawal

Jalgaon

Akot

Khamgaon

Akola

Buldana

Ajanta

gaon

Chikhli

S a h y a d r i p a r v a t   R a n g e

Washim

Aurangabad

huldabad

bad

Jalna

Paithan

A R A S H T R A

Godavari

Bid

Parli

B a l a g h a t   R a n g e

Manjra

da

Barsi

Latur

Osmanabad

Udgir

pur

gola

Bhima

13

9

Solapur

Naldurg

9

T H E D E C C A N

p. 222

C

Achalpur

Katol

Gondia

6

Bhandara

6

Amravati

NAGPUR

Sevagram

Wardha

Murtajapur

Hinganghat

Yavatmal

Wardha

Warora

Garhchiroli

Wani

Chandrapur

Pusad

Pengangu

Satmala Range

Parbhani

Nanded

Hingoli

THE DECCAN
p. 222

Sironcha

16

△
E

△
F

△
D

EASTERN INDIA

p. 286

Wainganga

Bhusawal

6

Akola

6

0 ———————— 150 kilometers
0 ———————— 100 miles

Area of map detail

⊛ **New Delhi**

View from the sea-facing rooms of the Taj Mahal Hotel, out over the Gateway of India

Along the way, notice the rich soil. Seventy percent of Maharashtrans work in agriculture, producing India's largest crops of highly prized Alphonso mangoes, seedless grapes, Cavendish bananas, soft-seeded pomegranates, sugar, cashew nuts, and cotton. A convoy of bullock carts bringing in the cotton harvest at sunset is a memorable sight. ■

Mumbai's chief adornments are its billboard movie posters. They are often witty, sometimes hand-painted with great skill, occasionally three-dimensional.

Mumbai

Although Bombay's name was officially changed to Mumbai in 1995, to honor the goddess worshiped by early inhabitants here, the old name sticks. The first time you hear Mumbai used may well be after you arrive in this dynamic business capital of India. Mumbai, home to more than ten million people, houses the headquarters of almost all of India's major banks, financial institutions, insurance companies, and mutual funds. It has India's largest stock exchange, port, and movie industry (see box p. 161). Mumbai even has its own Manhattan-style high-rises, its own offshore oil fields, and *Verve,* its own answer to *Vanity Fair* magazine.

For a city that began as seven boggy, malarial islands, Mumbai has done well. The islands were part of the dowry of Portuguese Princess Catherine of Braganza when she married the English king Charles II, in 1662. In 1668 the British government leased them to the East India Company for £10 a year. The company, which had received its trading charter from Queen Elizabeth I in 1600, could make its own laws and collect all revenue of just under £3,000 per annum (the equivalent of about £300,000 or $600,000 today). Yet the climate was so unhealthy that of the 800 British living there in 1692, 700 died in that year.

fleeing Portuguese oppression in Goa, Arab traders, and others to settle in the city, so that by 1700 its population reached 120,000.

After the company lost its trade monopoly in 1813, the British presence increased. Trade boomed with China in cotton and opium, exchanged for the increasingly popular drink of tea. Fortunes were made. David Sassoon, whose Sephardic Jewish family eventually spread to Europe and America, arrived in 1833 and built up an international trading empire overseen by his eight sons, one of whom was knighted Sir Albert Sassoon of Kensington Gore in 1872.

Meanwhile, steamers brought out boatloads of single British women, known as the "fishing fleet," to supply the empire's men with wives. Bombay's railroad opened in 1853 (reaching the cotton-growing Deccan ten years later); the telegraph arrived in 1865, and the first cotton mill opened the following year. Sir Bartle Frere, governor 1862–67, gave Bombay its spacious streets and great Victorian buildings, and he began the land reclamation program that continues today. During this time the American Civil War closed the Confederacy ports in America, and Bombay traders quickly profited from this by supplying extra cotton to Britain.

When the Suez Canal opened in 1869, Bombay on the west coast became as important as Calcutta on the east. Today, this truly cosmopolitan city has moved with the times and held its position. It is India's most modern and international city, with the inevitable inequalities. Mumbai's rich are India's most ostentatiously rich; Mumbai's Dharavi area is India's largest and worst slum. ∎

However, Bombay was soon the focus of India's west coast trade. Gerald Aungier, known as the "father of Bombay," was governor from 1672–77: He established the Courts of Justice and founded the company militia that became the East India Company Army. Most importantly, he actively encouraged Parsees from Gujarat, Banias (Hindu traders)

Bollywood—the Mumbai film industry

Mumbai's answer to Hollywood is the capital of the all-singing, all-dancing, all-shocking-color, not-much-plot Hindi movie. The huge, hand-painted advertising billboards all over India lure millions into the movie theaters every week to enjoy a sophisticated, slick, and perfectly timed mixture of heroism, romance, and fighting on wildly extravagant sets. Audiences may jeer at the villain, cheer the hero, and sing along with the songs.

Production is complex. Often, money is raised to fund just part of a movie then there is a pause while more financing is sought. Actors may be working concurrently on several movies. The essential music backing may be mimed by the beautiful star but sung by a favorite voice. To immerse yourself in India's foremost popular culture, go to a local movie theater. No one will mind if you do not watch all three hours of escapist entertainment. ∎

Colaba & the Maidan

THIS IS NOT MUMBAI'S OLDEST AREA, BUT IT IS CERTAINLY its grandest, redolent of a vast British empire, with its public buildings the proud legacy of fortunes made from trade with East and West and of men steeped in the Victorian belief in civic pride and duty. The architects of these public buildings mingled Eastern and Western ideas to create some of India's finest Indo-Saracenic monuments.

Mumbai
🅰 158 A3
India Tourist Office
✉ 123 Maharshi Karve
Rd., opposite
Churchgate Station
State Tourist Office
Gateway of India
www.maharashtratourism
.gov.in
☎ 229-3229/2284-
1877

Chhatrapati Shivaji
Maharaj Vastu
Sangrahalaya
(Prince of Wales
Museum)
✉ 159–161 M.G. Rd.
🕐 Closed Mon.
💲 $

The place to start is **Gateway of India** (1927). From the opening of the Suez Canal until the age of airplanes, this end of the Mumbai peninsula is where the ships arrived and passengers stepped ashore into India. George Wittet looked to Gujarat, specifically Ahmedabad (see pp. 146–48), for his honey-colored triumphal arch (1927) adorned with intricate carving, which commemorates the visit of George V and Queen Mary to India in 1911.

On February 28, 1948, after independence, the last British soldier left from here. Today, gaily painted fishing boats and ferries bob in the Arabian Sea, the old ferries ready to take visitors to

Elephanta (see p. 169), the newer hovercraft heading for Mandve (see p. 186).

The red-domed **Taj Mahal Hotel** (1903) stands beside the Gateway of India, overlooking the harbor. Built by Jamshtji Nusserwanji Tata (1839–1904) and equipped with its own Turkish baths, it is still an institution among today's Mumbai rich. Tata, a Parsee trading tycoon, expanded his empire from cotton to include mills, hydroelectric plants, a shipping line, and this memorial to himself designed by Sir Charles Chambers (Tata's descendants went on to found what became Air India and to expand into tea, trucks, and scientific research). The lanes behind the hotel lead to Colaba Causeway, a quality shopping area always buzzing with action.

Wittet, again influenced by medieval Gujarati architecture, designed the **Chhatrapati Shivaji Maharaj Vastu Sangrahalaya**, formerly the **Prince of Wales Museum** (1905–1937), too. It commemorates globe-trotting George V's first visit to India in 1905, when he was Prince of Wales (heir to the throne). Statues of him and of his father, Edward VII, stand in the mature gardens. Inside, beneath the tiled concrete dome, the wide-ranging collection offers something for everyone. Choose from delicate Indian miniature paintings, embroidered Kashmir shawls, or Indian silver, glass, brass, and jade; there are also arms and armor, and top quality Indian sculpture dating from the Harappan period to 18th-century Christian ivory carvings from Goa.

But it is the extravaganza of High Victorian Gothic buildings strung along **Mayo Road** (K.B. Patil Marg), facing the open grass of the Maidan, that take the prize. Many were built of hard, beige Porbandar stone, and most were enriched with skillful, lively, even ebullient, local carving, inspired by Britain's arts and crafts movement. John Lockwood Kipling, Rudyard's father, who was an avid supporter of crafts and ran Mumbai's art school encouraged this unlikely source of inspiration.

Captain Wilkins' **Secretariat** (1874) is really a Venetian Gothic palace. It is 470 feet (143 m) long, with a central arched gable carrying the great staircase window and a soaring 170-foot-high (52 m) tower. Here, the Porbandar stone is enriched with blue and red basalt.

Sir George Gilbert Scott's buildings take a different inspiration. They were designed in England, built under the construction engineer Colonel James Fuller's

watchful eye, and financed by the Parsee benefactor Sir Cowasjee Jehangir Readymoney (his statue is in the gardens). The **University Convocation Hall** (1874) dresses up the 15th-century French decorated style for the tropics and adds some Victorian pomp. There is even a staircase modeled on the Château de Blois. The **University Library** and **Rajabai Tower** (1869–1878), next door, achieve the same success with 14th-century French and Italian Gothic, adding very delicate carving and stained-glass windows. The tower, based on Giotto's campanile in Florence, is decorated with figures representing the castes of western India. The clock used to cheer British residents with its chimes of *Home Sweet Home* and *God Save the Queen*.

Fuller designed the huge **High Court** (1871–79), with its steep, red tiles and skyline figures of Justice and Mercy (and beautiful Minton floor tiles inside). You now jump to the Venetian Gothic of Wilkins's **Public Works Office** (1869–1872), then to the Italianate **General Post Office** (1909), and end with the romantic oriental domes and polychrome stones of Stevens's Byzantine **Churchgate Station** (1894–96). ∎

Mumbai's Maidan is an informal cricket ground.

Visitor tips
Tourist offices and some hotels stock the useful fortnightly listings magazine, "What's On."

Secretariat
✉ Mayo Rd.
🕐 Closed Sat. & Sun.

University
✉ M.G. Rd., Fort

High Court
✉ Bhaurao Patil Marg (entrance on Eldon Rd., off M.G. Rd.)

General Post Office
✉ St. George's Rd.
🕐 Closed Sat. & Sun.

Churchgate Station
✉ Maharshi Karve Rd.
💲 $

A DRIVE THROUGH COLONIAL MUMBAI

A drive through colonial Mumbai

The best days to look at Mumbai's remarkable legacy of classy colonial building are Saturday and Sunday, when there is less traffic and plenty of action on Chowpatty Beach. Tell your driver which places you would like to visit, and he will find the most logical way to reach each building. He will wait while you make visits to these British colonial sites.

The **Gateway of India** ❶ (1927), built to commemorate the visit to India of the King-Emperor George V and Queen-Empress Queen Mary in 1911, overlooks the harbor at Apollo Bunder. Standing in front of it, you have a marvelous view of the **Taj Mahal Hotel** (see p. 162), one of the great hotels of the East, built by the Parsee industrialist J. N. Tata. To the right, a statue of Mumbai's hero, Shivaji (1961), stands in front of the former Yacht Club (1898) with its half-timbered gables.

Drive past the Yacht Club to Wellington Circle (1865). On your left, Phillip's Antiques is a delightful antiques curiosity shop; on your right, the Indo-Gothic Council Hall is the earliest of several Mumbai buildings designed by British architect F. W. Stevens (1870–76). The domed **Prince of Wales Museum** ❷ (see p. 163) is straight ahead, set in lush gardens. Beautiful and evocative **Kenesseth Eliyahoo Synagogue** (see p. 168) is behind Rhythm House.

The next group of buildings to stop and admire is strung out along Mayo Road (K.B. Patil Marg), opposite the open Maidan. This is possibly the world's finest group of High Victorian Gothic public buildings. Their towering confidence and romantic skylines reflect the progressive age in which they were built. The first is Captain Wilkins's **Secretariat** (see p. 163); next is Sir George Gilbert Scott's **University Convocation Hall** ❸ (see p. 163) with its spiral staircases, and his **University Library** and **Rajabai Clocktower** (see p. 163). The group ends with Colonel Fuller's **High Court** (see p. 163), Wilkins's **Public Works Office** (see p. 163), and in Veer Nariman Road (formerly Churchgate Street), James Trubshawe's **General Post Office**. Before leaving, you can enjoy a good view of F. W. Stevens's Byzantine-style **Churchgate Station,** where trains leave for Kanheri Caves and Bassein (see pp. 170–71).

Mumbai ladies stretch out at the Laughter Yoga Club on Marine Drive, with the high-rises of Malagar Hill in the distance.

Farther down Veer Nariman Road, you come to the brightly painted **Flora Fountain** ❹ (1869), which gives its name to this area. There are charming period buildings. On the left, the domed one used to house the publishers Macmillan, and on the right, Handloom House was built as the mansion of the Parsee Sir Jamsetjee Jeejeebhoy. Mahatma Gandhi Road has more period buildings.

Behind **Horniman Circle** (1860) ❺, with the Venetian palazzo of Elphinstone Buildings on the left, lies the old **Fort Area**. Here are two fascinating colonial buildings: the **St. Thomas's Cathedral** (begun 1672) and Col. Thomas Cowper's **Town Hall** (1820–23) ❻, possibly the finest classical building in India, now the Asiatic Library.

From here, take Frere Road past old fort bastions and the Bijapur-inspired General Post Office (1909) to stop and explore Stevens' vast

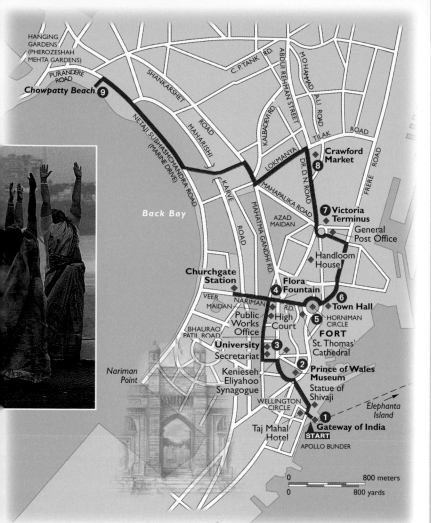

HANGING GARDENS (PHEROZESHAH MEHTA GARDENS)

PURANDERE ROAD

Chowpatty Beach 9

C.P. TANK RD.

SHANKARSHET ROAD

ABDUL REHMAN STREET

MOHAMMAD ALI ROAD

MAHARSHI

NETAJI SUBHASHCHANDRA ROAD (MARINE DRIVE)

KALBADEVI RD.

TILAK ROAD

Crawford Market 8

DR. D.N. ROAD

FRERE ROAD

Back Bay

KARVE ROAD

MAHAPALIKA ROAD

LOKMANYA

MAHATMA GANDHI RD.

AZAD MAIDAN

Victoria Terminus 7

General Post Office

Handloom House

Churchgate Station

VEER MAIDAN

NARIMAN

Flora Fountain 4

Town Hall 6

RD.

Public Works Office

High Court

5

HORNIMAN CIRCLE

BHAURAO PATIL ROAD

University Secretariat

3

FORT

St. Thomas' Cathedral

Nariman Point

Kenieseh Eliyahoo Synagogue

2

Prince of Wales Museum

Statue of Shivaji

Elephanta Island

WELLINGTON CIRCLE

Taj Mahal Hotel

START

Gateway of India 1

APOLLO BUNDER

0   800 meters
0   800 yards

Victoria Terminus (1878–1887, see p. 166) 7, India's finest Gothic building. Stevens's colossal, domed Municipal Buildings (1893) stand opposite; the gable statue represents Urbs Prima in Indis (first city in India). Finally, cruise along Mahapalika and Carnac Roads past schools, hospitals, and colleges bearing the names of their Victorian benefactors. Stop at **Crawford Market** 8 (1865–1871, see p. 167), where mangoes and chilies are sold in a French medieval-styled building. Then head for Marine Drive to take a stroll along **Chowpatty Beach** 9, which runs along beside the Arabian Sea, where locals gather to enjoy food stalls, street entertainers, and sand sculptors. ■

See area map pages 158–59
Gateway of India
8 miles (13 km)
2–4 hours, depending on length of stops
Chowpatty Beach

NOT TO BE MISSED
- Gateway of India
- University Convocation Hall and Library
- St. Thomas's Cathedral
- Victoria Terminus
- Chowpatty Beach

**Chhatrapati
Shivaji Terminus,
(Victoria
Terminus)**

✉ Dr. D. Naoroji Rd.,
Nagar Chowk

💲 $

Victoria Terminus

THE VICTORIAN NOTION OF TRAINS AS A SYMBOL OF
progress was exported to India. The British laid the first Indian train
lines in Mumbai to help move goods to and from their trade capital.
On April 16, 1853, the first train steamed off (see pp. 108–109). Its
station was built later and is, with the Gateway of India, modern
Mumbai's best-known landmark and India's finest Victorian Gothic
building. It is now officially called the Chhatrapati Shivaji Terminus.

F.W. Stevens, a government architect, was commissioned in 1876 to
build a new terminus for the Great
Indian Peninsula Railway, the
largest building project in India at
that time. Stevens looked to George
Gilbert Scott's St. Pancras Station in
London for inspiration. What he
achieved was a grander and more
richly decorated, cathedral-like
monument to the British empire's
progress, symbolized by the railroad. Built in just nine years,
1878–1887, it cost the then-vast
sum of £250,000 (about £15 million
or $20 million in today's money).

If you stand at the great
entrance, the effect is overwhelming. The huge facade has projecting
wings crowned with a colossal,
somewhat un-Gothic dome, on
which a statue of Progress perches

Mumbai combines old and new: Here, an ox-cart shares the road with a public bus in front of the grand Gothic facade of Victoria Terminus.

proudly. Thomas Earp made this, as well as the helpfully labeled stone medallions of imperial worthies on the facade (see if you can find Sir Bartle Frere, governor of the city from 1862 to 1867), and the gorgeous symbolic imperial lion and Indian tiger on top of the gate piers. The whole building is a riot of various colored stones, decorative ironwork, marbles, inlaid tiles, and exuberant sculpture. Most of this ironwork and decorative sculpture was crafted by the Indian students of the Bombay School of Art.

Inside the reservations hall in the left-hand wing, built with pointed arches like a church nave, you can enjoy more glorious High Victorian decoration. The ceilings have gold stars on an azure background, the dado has glazed tiles with rich leaf designs, and the windows are of stained glass or ornamental iron grillwork to reduce the sun's glare. The fixtures are of local woods, the railings are of brass, the floor is tiled, and the stonework is carved with leaves, animals, and birds.

When the building opened, Indians and British alike must have been amazed. Even today, V.T., as it is fondly known locally, adds glamour to a train ride. Furthermore, the Mumbai municipality has honored this colonial building with a new name, albeit rarely used, that links it to the Maratha hero: Chatrapati Shivaji Terminus (C.S.T.). For a truly great Indian train journey, try taking the 24-hour ride on the Punjab Mail from here to Agra, or ride the new Konkan Railway line down to Goa (see pp. 204–205).

Following the success of V.T., Stevens received commissions to build Mumbai's ebullient municipal buildings (1888–1893) opposite the station. Combining Venetian Gothic with Indo-Saracenic styles and dressing them for the city climate, he managed to express imperial and civic pride at the zenith of the empire. Inventive, romantic, and resourceful, Stevens's final great Mumbai building was Churchgate Station. Here, to give a Byzantine character, he used the local red stone from Bassein (see p. 171) to contrast with the white and blue stones. The statue over the entrance, personifying Engineering, is holding symbols of progress—a locomotive and a wheel—in her hands. ■

Mumbai's markets

Mumbai is a rich trading city, great for shopping, either in the comfort of upscale hotel shops or—much more fun—on street after street of stores and stalls. Colaba Causeway, behind the Taj Mahal Hotel, is the place for international fashion, but you may want to be more adventurous. A good place to start is Crawford Market, where Lockwood Kipling's frieze and fountain are the setting for piles of exotic fruit, spices, and vegetables, and a crowded wholesale wing. Stay in the area and take a wander through the streets north of Carnac Road, whose backbone is Abdul Rehman Street. As usual in India, stores of one type tend to cluster together. Cloth can be found on Mangaldas Lane, jewelry in the Zaveri Bazar on Memon Street, near Mumbadevi Temple (dedicated to the titular goddess of Mumbai), and copper and brass on Baiduni Chowk. Farther afield, Mutton Road has stores full of old (and fake) curiosities (see also Bhuleshwar Market, p. 172). ■

Town Hall
- Horniman Circle
- Closed Sat. & Sun.

Cathedral Church of St. Thomas
- Veer Nariman Rd.

Kenesseth Eliyahoo Synagogue
- 68 Worli Hill Rd.
- 022-283 1502

Fort

THE FORT AREA IN SOUTH MUMBAI IS WHERE EUROPEAN
Mumbai began. Here today's crowded commercial streets were once
a large walled fort facing Mumbai Harbor. The Portuguese struck a
deal with Bahadur Shah of Gujarat to trade at Bombay and nearby
Bassein (Vasai, see p. 171). When the Mumbai islands passed to the
British and were leased to the East India Company, the British built
great defensive walls and gates. Although these were mostly destroyed
in 1862, you can trace their path along Mahatma Gandhi and Dr.
Dadabhai Naoroji Roads. As you walk around, look up at the old
facades, some of them dating from the 18th century.

F. W. Stevens's Municipal Buildings embody Victorian and imperial pride.

Begin at the **Town Hall** (1833) at
Horniman Circle, right by the
docks, which were begun in 1860 by
the Wadia family of Bombay. Here,
the great East Indiamen ships were
built of teak, which lasted five times
as long as English oak. Col. Thomas
Cowper's Town Hall, built overlooking a common, is India's finest
neoclassic building. Mostly paid for
by the East India Company, it

reflects the confidence of the rising
British Empire. The windows, with
their wooden shutters and curving
sunshades, are original. Go up the
broad steps and past the fluted
Doric columns shipped here from
England to find a fine set of
marble statues of Bombay governors in the lobby and stairwell,
three of them by Sir Francis
Chantrey. Today, the building is
home to various learned societies.

On the other side of Horniman
Circle, Gerald Aungier began the
**Cathedral Church of St.
Thomas** in 1672. Inside are some
fascinating and beautiful funerary
monuments to rival those in
St. Mary's, Chennai (see p. 258).
They include three by John Bacon:
to Governor John Duncan, to
Katharine Kirkpatrick, whose
sons established British supremacy
in Central India, and to Maj.
Eldred Pottinger.

Down Apollo Street, past surviving old buildings, you find the
simple neoclassic **St. Andrew's
Kirk** (1819) on Marine Street.
Nearby, behind Rhythm House,
stands the 1884 **Kenesseth
Eliyahoo Synagogue**. Funded
by David Sassoon, this is the best
of Mumbai's several once grand,
but now forlorn, synagogues.
The fine upstairs prayer hall is
still in use. ■

Elephanta Island

A VISIT BY BOAT TO ONE OF INDIA'S MOST IMPORTANT early Hindu cave temples is a delight, thanks to the energy of the local branch of the conservation body INTACH (see p. 82). If the sea is calm, the journey itself is a joy, too.

The Portuguese renamed the island, originally called Gharapuri, after the carved elephant they found there (now in Mumbai's Dr. Bhau Daji Lad Museum, see p. 172). Climb up the steps past the souvenir stalls manned by people from the island's three villages, to find a helpful exhibition in the restored custodian's cottage.

The **cave temple** dedicated to Shiva is just beyond. It was possibly the Kalachuri rulers who cut it out of a projecting chunk of the high basalt cliff in the sixth century, possibly with royal patronage. Enter the central opening into a simple, dark hall, whose columns have cushion-shaped capitals.

One spectacular, colossal stone carving of triple-headed Shiva in the center of the back wall dominates the several masterpieces showing the god's different aspects. Only just emerging out of the rock, it subtly combines ideas of male-female and husband-wife; the right head is softly feminine, the left side fiercely masculine. The panels on either side show an androgynous Shiva and his consort Parvati on the left, and Shiva helping the descent of the Ganga on the right.

Continue to the right, past the *lingum* sanctuary with its huge guardian figures, to find first the panel of Shiva's marriage with Parvati and then Shiva spearing Andhaka. Across the courtyard, the panels show Shiva as the Yogi and as Nataraja (Lord of the Dance).

Ahead you find another Yogi and Nataraja flanking the entrance, then two compositions of Shiva and Parvati on Mount Kailasha playing dice. ■

The triple-headed Eternal Shiva at Elephanta displays his full range of powers: male, female, and meditative Mahadera (great god).

Elephanta Island

⚲ 158 A3

🕐 Closed Mon.

💲 $

Ferries

Ferries leave from the Gateway of India regularly from about 9 a.m. until about 2:30 p.m.; the journey takes one hour. Check on the time of the last boat back; if seas are choppy, change your plans. Those not wishing to climb the steps up to the temple can take a train to the site, or be carried in a thronelike chair.

Kanheri Caves,
on the edge of
the city, bring
tranquility and
relief from
Mumbai's hubbub.

Kanheri Caves

158 A3

Take the train to
Borifili Station, then
either a taxi or
rickshaw to Sanjay
Gandhi (Krishnagiri
Upavan) National
Park. From the
north entrance it is
3 miles (5 km) to
the caves.

$

Kanheri Caves & Bassein

KANHERI CAVES AND BASSEIN'S RUINED FORT EACH MAKE
thoroughly rewarding days out of the teeming city and into two very
rural settings going north up the coast. Avoid the long and tiresome
drive through Mumbai's suburbs and, instead, take the local train.
From Churchgate Station you slice up through the central Mumbai
peninsula; the stations are mapped out above the doors of each railway car. Then take a taxi or rickshaw to the site.

KANHERI CAVES

At Kanheri, more than a hundred
Buddhist monuments cut out of a
granite outcrop overlook the
Arabian Sea. For almost a thousand
years, starting with the Satavahanas
of the first century, this was an
important Buddhist community
that lay on trade routes connecting
Nasik, Paithan, Ujjain, Aurangabad,
and other cities to seaports such as

nearby Sopara. As such, it benefited
from donations from merchants,
goldsmiths, and blacksmiths, as
inscriptions reveal. It may also have
been where traveling Buddhist
monks stayed during the monsoon,
when numbers swelled to several
thousand. It was a sophisticated
monastic community and may have
included a university. The caves
were used for study, for meditation,

and as homes, and they reveal both Hinayana and Mahayana Buddhist occupation (see p. 58).

Caves nos. 2 and **3** are the most impressive: No. 2 is a *vihara* with two *stupas;* no. 3 (fifth to sixth century) is a *chaitya* with carvings of Buddha and bejeweled donor couples. Other fine caves abound, some with water cisterns, others with Buddha carvings (Cave no. 67) and ovens for cooking. **Cave no. 11** may have been an assembly hall; **no. 14** contains a carving of the 11-headed Padmapani Avalokiteshvara. At the top of the hill, **Caves nos. 84–87** seem to have been part of a burial ground.

There is a small café on the steep forested hill, where you can relax. The caves are popular with the locals on weekends.

BASSEIN (VASAI)

Spend a wonderful day at the most romantic and substantial Portuguese fort ruins in India, with massive walls and gateways, and soaring 16th- and 17th-century church and convent ruins, all completely overgrown. Rarely visited today, this large city—only Christians lived within its walls, while thousands of other people lived outside them—was Portuguese from 1534 until the Marathas took it in 1739; it was important enough to receive four visits from St. Francis Xavier (see p. 193). By 1818, when it became part of the British Bombay presidency, it was abandoned; today, local fishermen untangle their nets in the old citadel.

The sea gate, complete with its iron doors, is set into massive walls, and the bastions have cannon openings. Inside it, follow the path straight ahead to find the soaring triple-staged tower (1601) of the **Matriz of St. Joseph,** Bassein's cathedral. Next, the now empty **Citadel** on the right retains its stone gate, carved with the Portuguese coat of arms; a warren of rooms lies underground. A five-minute walk farther along the path are the **Church of St. Anthony** (1548), founded by St. Francis Xavier on his third visit, with a grand facade and, to the side, an atmospheric cloister. The climax is the **Church of St. Paul,** a Franciscan foundation whose grand columned portal leads to a vast nave, chancel, a gallery that you can climb up for good views, and a cloister; Portuguese tombstones are set into the floor.

To reach Bassein Fort, take the train to Vasai Station, then take a 20-minute auto-rickshaw journey to the sea entrance, where there is a café. Ask driver to wait, or agree on a time to meet at the other gate. ■

Bassein

🗺 158 A3

✉ 38 miles (61 km) N of Mumbai. Take the train to Vasai, then an autorickshaw to the "qila" (fort) sea gate. Carry bottled water.

💲 $

An unadorned hemispherical stupa stands at the back of the elsewhere elaborately carved Cave no. 3 at Kanheri.

Ganpati Festival

Ganesh, the elephant-headed, sweet-toothed god of prosperity and good fortune, is loved by Mumbai's Hindu businessmen, who celebrate his September birthday with gusto. Huge, gaudy, pink-painted clay images of Ganesh, each with a morsel of last year's figure added to this year's clay mixture, are set up in factories, houses, and on street corners for ten days, decorated with garlands, flickering lights, and even working mini-fountains. On the day of the full moon, they are paraded through the streets to Chowpatty Beach amid music, dancing, and throwing of pink powder. Finally, they are immersed in the sea and bob on the waves until the images dissolve. ■

More places to visit in Mumbai

BHULESHWAR MARKET

This market is found along the streets to the south of C. P. Tank Road, toward Mumbadevi temple. Locals crowd the wonderful vegetable market on Kumbhar Tukda. There are also stores supplying Hindi movie costumes, others supplying idols to temples. Phool Galli ("flower lane") is where temple and wedding flower arrangements are made.

BYCULLA

During the racing season, this area of Mumbai, north of the city center, provides a day's entertainment at **Mahalaxmi Race Course.** Established in 1878, it stimulated India's horse-breeding industry, which is still strong today. During the November to May season, stylish old men, flashy movie stars, and locals of all kinds come to watch the racing on most Wednesdays and weekends. Nearby, among Mumbai's 19th-century cotton mills stands the walled **Maghan Dawid Synagogue** (1861) on Sir Jamsetji Jeejeebhoy Road. North of it, **Dr. Bhau Daji Lad Museum** is a meticulously restored High Victoria 1870s building. Its equally carefully conserved display cases house local crafts and Mumbai history. The ensemble won UNESCO's 2006 conservation award. The Elephanta sculpture (see p. 169) is in the garden; David Sassoon gave the clocktower (1865). **Dr. Bhau Daji Lad Museum** (Victoria and Albert Museum) ✉ Dr. Babasaheb Ambedkar Rd., Byculla ☎ 022-375 7943

KONDVITE

To see more temples, take the train from Churchgate Station to Andheri. Here, 18 cave temples surround a hillock, of which the very early **Cave no. 9** (second century) imitates a thatched hut and **Cave no. 13** (fifth to sixth century) was once a monastery complete with cells and even beds cut out of the rock.

MARINE DRIVE & CHOWPATTY BEACH

Chowpatty Beach and the stretch of beach at the north end of Marine Drive (now called Netaji Subhash Chandra Road) are Mumbai's lung, a refuge from the city's punishing humidity for most of the year. Beside the sea, Mumbai's citizens promenade in the mornings and evenings, and children play cricket at all times of the day. Chowpatty Beach is the city's entertainment center, and is best enjoyed late in the afternoon. You can safely buy Mumbai *chaat* (snacks) from the stalls and wander among the sand sculptors, musicians, astrologers, and other entertainers. The beach is the focus of Mumbai's popular Ganpati Festival (see box above). ■

Karla's Cave no. 8, dating from the first century, has deeply cut columns with boldly carved capitals, mock roof beams, and a stupendous *stupa*.

Maharashtra

Despite its huge size, Maharashtra's principal sites conveniently fall into geographic groups, each with a city base offering good accommodations. To reach them, the most indulgent form of transport is to be driven; this way you can see the landscape, the farms, and the village life and markets. Alternatively, take a train—especially recommended for Matheran—or fly.

Aurangabad, where corporate majors have their industrial sites, has magnificent cave sculptures, and a 50,000-year-old meteorite crater. From here you can visit Daulatabad, Ellora, and, farther away, Ajanta.

Pune is the place to stay if you want to put on your hiking shoes and sun hat to explore the rugged Western Ghats with their spectacular forts associated with Shivaji (see p. 180). From Mahabaleshwar, you can take trips through rural switchback roads with breathtaking views of Shivaji's hill and coastal forts. To see the early Buddhist cave temples of Karla, Bhaja, and Bedsa, stay at the modest hill station of Lonavala.

The stretch between Mumbai and Goa is best visited in a progressive line. Until recently, Maharashtra's coast was among the least developed in India. With the new Konkan railroad and Mumbai–Mandve sea connections, this area is opening up. Accommodations are modest, except for the lovely, characterful hotel at Chiplun, with its lush terraced gardens, but the island fort of Janjira and the two coastal forts of Vijayadurg and Sindhudurg are well worth any discomfort. ∎

At Ajanta, locals
help illuminate
the breathtaking
carvings and
paintings in the
rock-cut caves. In
this case a large,
serene Buddha
sits preaching,
sculpted in high
relief in the
sanctuary.

**Aurangabad,
Maharashtra**
🅰 159 C4
**India Tourist
Office**
✉ Krishna Villas,
Station Rd.
☎ 02432-331217
🕐 Closed Sun.

**State Tourist
Office**
www.maharashtratourism
.gov.in
✉ Holiday Resort Hotel
☎ 02432-331513

Purwar Museum
🕐 Closed Sun. &
university holidays
💲 $

Buddhist Caves
💲 $

Daulatabad Fort
🅰 159 C4
💲 $

Aurangabad & around

TO VISIT THE SCULPTURED AND PAINTED CAVES OF
Aurangabad, Ellora, and Ajanta is to see several wonders of the world.
If your visit to India includes Mumbai, it is well worth flying to
Aurangabad for two or three nights, making it your base for Ellora
and Ajanta.

Despite its newfound business
wealth, Aurangabad retains much
of its Muslim past, and you can
sometimes glimpse an earlier period when the city flourished at the
crossroads of ancient trade routes.
Malik Amber, a former Abyssinian
minister for the Ahmednagar
rulers, founded the city on the
Khan River in 1610. He boosted
trade enough for the Mughal
emperor Shah Jahan to pillage it in
1621 and capture it in 1633. His

son, Prince Aurangzeb, headquartered here when he was governor of
the Deccan (1652–58). He changed
the city's name and built new walls.
Later, as emperor, he moved the
Mughal court here in 1682, making
Aurangabad the imperial city
until his death in 1707. It then languished as a provincial town in the
vast Hyderabad kingdom.
   To see a little of the town, visit
the bazaar area of Malik Amber's
city, where streets converge on

Gulmandi Square. Among the stores and mosques is the **Shah Ganj Masjid** (circa 1720), **Purwar Museum,** housed in a fine old *haveli;* and **Mughal tombs** such as Hazrat Qadar Auliya's, near Jaffa Gate. Out on the plain to the north of the city, the **Bibi-ka-Maqbara** (1679) mimics the Taj Mahal. It was built by Aurangzeb's son, Azam Shah, as the tomb for his mother, Begum Rabia Durani.

Aurangabad's glories are its **Buddhist caves,** built into the rock of the hills to the north and best visited in the afternoon. The groups are close together and date from the Vakataka and Kalachuri periods of the fifth and sixth centuries. The on-site guide lights up the sculptures, but take a flashlight.

Three caves are especially wonderful. In the west group, **Cave no. 3** (fifth century) has fine columns, capitals, and beams and, inside the sanctuary, a composition of devotees kneeling in front of a preaching Buddha. In the east group, **Cave no. 6** (sixth century) has a similar tableau plus traces of a painted ceiling. **Cave no. 7** (sixth century) has bold statues, including Panchika (pot-bellied guardian of the Earth's treasures) with his consort Hariti, plus Buddhas, goddesses, dwarfs, dancers, and musicians.

DAULATABAD

Maharashtra's most spectacular fort surrounds, sits on, and is cut into the huge Balakot rock northwest of Aurangabad, on the road to Ellora (see pp. 176–77). It began as Deogiri (Hill of the Gods), capital of the Yadavas, who lost it to the Khilji sultans of Delhi in 1294. Renamed Daulatabad (Abode of Prosperity), it was the Tughlaq capital from 1327 to 1347, the year the Bahmani governors declared independence. They later moved their capital to Gulbarga. Today's fort is a product of all these periods. One set of massive fortifications leads into **Ambarkot,** the outer fort; the battlements, bastions, guardrooms, and moat of the next set lead into **Kataka,** the inner fort. Through the huge gateways, a street leads between ruined buildings, including the **Jama Masjid** (1318) on the left, and a ruined **Mughal palace** on the right. Across from the Bahmani palace ruins, another imposing gate leads into **Balakot,** the citadel, where a succession of chambers, tunnels, blind alleys, and dark corners lead to the very top.

KHULDABAD

Aurangzeb, last of the six great Mughal emperors, was a religious man. He chose a simple burial in a village where Sufi teachers lived, and he rebuilt the village's walls and gates. If you go into the **Dargah of Hazrat Khaja Seyed Zainuddin** (died 1334), you will find Aurangzeb's tomb in a corner, surrounded by a marble screen added in 1921. ■

Visitor tips
To visit the Aurangabad, Ellora, and Ajanta caves, you will need a minimum of two full days in Aurangabad, preferably more; the day-trip to Ajanta, where there is nowhere comfortable to stay, is long. Flights connect Aurangabad with Mumbai and Udaipur.

Khuldabad
🗺 159 C4

Visitors at Daulatabad inspect the six-yard-long (5.5 m) cannon before clambering up the edifice built into the granite outcrop.

Ellora

**Ellora caves,
Maharashtra**

🗺 159 C4

✉ 18 miles (29 km)
NW of Aurangabad

🕐 Closed Tues.

💲 $

ROCK-CUT ARCHITECTURE IN THE WESTERN GHATS
reached its glorious last phase here at Ellora, with large-scale figure
sculpture, complex compositions, and a wide range of iconographic
schemes. In contrast to Ajanta, where aggressive peddlers and sub-
standard guides try hard to get between you and the art, here you
can wander the long, west-facing basalt escarpment, quietly soaking
up the spirit of this place that has been sacred to Buddhists, Jains, and
Hindus for many centuries.

Visitor tips

It is important to have
enough time to visit the
best of the Buddhist,
Hindu and Jain caves.
For rest, the Kailasha
restaurant has good
food and garden tables.

The caves span the sixth to the
ninth centuries and divide into
three groups: **Caves nos. 1–12,** at
the southern end, are Buddhist;
Caves nos. 13–29, in the middle,
are Hindu, and **Caves nos.
30–33** are Jain. It is best to begin at
the southern end, but be selective in
your visits to avoid confusion.
Try to reach **Cave no. 16** in the

mid-afternoon to see it at its best.
    The Hindu **Caves nos. 21, 28,**
and **29,** of the sixth-century
Kalachuri era, predate the Buddhist
Caves nos. 10–12, which were
built by the Early Chalukyas of the
seventh and eighth centuries.
The Hindu **Caves nos. 15** and
16, Ellora's pinnacle of achievement, were created under the

A large, carved, teaching Buddha lurks in Cave no. 10 at Ellora (right), while a walk on the uncut cliff surrounding Cave no. 16 (above) overlooks the Kailasha temple.

Rashtrakutas of the late eighth century to tenth century, as were the Jain **Caves nos. 30–33.**

Of the dozen Buddhist caves, the first nine are variations on a standard monastic form: columned verandah, central hall, cells to the sides, and a Buddha shrine at the rear. This is seen clearly in **Cave no. 2,** whose guardian figures flank the entrance. **Cave no. 10,** a very fine *chaitya* (worship) hall, is named Vishvakarma after the mythical architect of the gods. It can be found at the end of a courtyard, the two stories set on a basement carved with animals; steps on the left lead up to the richly sculptured gallery. **Cave no. 12** (Tin Thal) has three stories. The top floor (found up steps to the right) is a simple hall with colossal enthroned Buddhas on the side walls, plus rows of meditating and ground-touching Buddhas flanking the sanctum, inside which are goddesses seated on lotuses.

The Hindu group is even more impressive. **Cave no. 15,** named Dashavatara, is a Buddhist monastery later modified for Hindus and partly funded by the Rashtrakuta king Dantigurga *(R.* circa 730–755). Steps lead up to a *mandapa* (pillared hall) profusely sculptured with Shiva and Vishnu images. Moving clockwise, they begin with Shiva killing the demon and end with Vishnu as the man-lion Narasimha.

Cave no. 16, the Kailasha temple, is the spectacular centerpiece of Ellora: a monolithic temple to Shiva entirely sculpted out of the solid rock. In technique, decorative scheme, and quality of sculpture, it is unsurpassed. The Rashtrakuta king Krishna I *(R.* 756–773) began it; his successors continued the royal patronage. If you walk up the cliff on the right, you have a bird's-eye view of the whole complex:

entrance, Nandi pavilion, temple with pyramid-shaped tower, and surrounding courtyard with shrines. Then go down for a closer look. Guardians, the Ganga, and the Yamuna flank the entrance, setting the tone for bold, vibrant sculpture inside. Amid the profusion of decoration, note especially the temple's elephants gathering lotuses on the lower story, compositions from the *Ramayana* and *Mahabharata* on both sides of the steps, and a great Shiva composition in the center of the south side. And do not miss the small hall in the southeast corner,

with its almost three-dimensional figures lounging on a seat.

Finally, there are two late sixth-century Hindu caves, earlier than the others. **No. 21** has remarkably sensuous sculpture: See the female bracket figures on the veranda, the loving couples on the balcony wall, and the river gods Ganga and Yamuna. Interestingly, **Cave no. 29** has a layout and large Shiva wall panels that may be influenced by the cave at Elephanta (see p. 169).

It is a pleasant walk to the Jain group. The finest is **Cave no. 32,** called Indra Sabha. Make your way through the little courtyard, pausing to enjoy the delicate carving of Jina figures; then go upstairs to find exuberantly carved columns and large figures of Ambika (mother goddess) with a child, and Indra. ■

Ajanta

THE MIRACULOUSLY PRESERVED PAINTINGS AND
sculptures that decorate 30 caves cut into the basalt rock of a beautiful crescent-shaped gorge provide the most extensive idea of early
Buddhist artistic traditions in India. They are also the sources for
iconography and styles found in later central Asian and Far Eastern
Buddhist art.

**Ajanta Caves,
Maharashtra**

🗺 159 C4

✉ 64 miles (102 km)
N of Aurangabad

🕐 Closed Mon.

💲 $

The caves date mostly from two
periods: the second and first
centuries B.C., then the late fifth
century A.D., when the Vakataka
rulers, especially Harishena
(R. 460–478), were energetic
patrons. These caves contain the
most impressive sculptures, ranging
from votive images to narrative
tableaus with many figures and an
elaborate decorative motifs.

These later caves also have
India's only extensive series of
Buddhist paintings of such
virtuosity, quality, and wide range
of subjects. They depict Buddha's
life and the stories from the *Jataka*
tales (former lives of Buddha).
These are retold in huge, densely

**Ajanta's caves
are found in the
rocky cliffs of a
dramatic and
beautiful gorge,
fed by a waterfall.**

filled compositions depicting contemporary fifth-century city, court,
and forest life. Tempera was used to
achieve the sinuous lines and har-
monious, soft colors. The rock was
primed, then given a layer of white

lime, on which the outline was
sketched with red cinnabar. The
artists then used lapis lazuli for
blue, glauconite for green, soot for
black, ocher for yellow, and kaolin
chalk for white, thickening it with
glue. Finally, the murals were
polished with a smooth stone.

Abandoned in the seventh century and rediscovered in 1819, most
caves are in fine condition. So, as
with Ellora, selection is essential
because you need time to drink in
the detail. Here are eight to start
you off: All except nos. 9 and 10
date from the late fifth century.
They can be visited in any order, to
avoid the crowds.

Cave no. I is one of the finest
and deserves time. Elaborate sculpture includes flying couples on the
column brackets and the great
Buddha in the sanctum, preaching
the first sermon at Sarnath, his
wheel, deer, and monks on the
pedestal. The murals are some of
Ajanta's best. Two Bodhisattvas
flank the sanctum: Padmapani
(left) and Avalokiteshvara (right).
Jataka tales fill the walls, while to
the right of the outer doorway
some foreigners with caps and
beards offer gifts to a figure who is
possibly Harishena, the Vakataka
king and patron of the cave.

The sculpture of **Cave no. 2**
is more profuse than that in cave
no. 1; see the fat *yakshas* (demi-gods)
and attendants in the left shrine on
the rear walls. In the right shrine,
there are paintings of processions
of female devotees, a very richly

painted ceiling, and *Jataka* and life-of-Buddha stories on the walls.

Now for two early caves, nos. 9 and 10. **No. 9** (first century B.C.) is an elegant *chaitya* hall with plain octagonal columns and a curved vault; the *stupa* on its high drum is the devotional focus. Of the two layers of paintings on the walls, that underneath is contemporary with the building. **Cave no. 10** (second century B.C.) is similar but even earlier, with clearer layers of painting to see; on the left wall, a royal figure worships at a bodhi tree.

One of Ajanta's finest monasteries is **Cave no. 16,** with an inscription dating from Harishena's reign. Its ceiling is carved to imitate wood and there is an image of Buddha teaching. A mural on the left wall shows the conversion of

Nanda, Buddha's cousin. **Cave no. 17** is similar, but the decoration of the shrine's doorway is particularly elaborate. Of the murals here, several are outstanding, including the seated Buddhas over the doorway, the wheel of life on the left of the verandah, and the *Jataka* tales on the inside walls.

Cave no. 19 is an almost perfect chaitya hall with restrained yet elaborate carving. Before entering, see the couple on the left wall; inside, the votive stupa, unusually, has a Buddha image on the front. Finally, wonderful sculpture occupies **Cave no. 26.** The large chaitya hall has a splendid Parinirvana: A 23-foot-long (7 m) Buddha reclines on a couch, his eyes closed in peaceful sleep, his disciples mourning him below. ∎

Frescoes coat the walls of Cave no. 1: This one recounts a *Jataka* tale on the left and shows Padmapani displaying compassion on the right.

Visitor tips
Currently, the caves are closed on Mondays; these closings might increase. Take water and easily portable food such as bananas and cookies, because there is no good restaurant. Weekends are very busy.

Shivaji, the Maratha hero

This extraordinarily able and charismatic leader founded a Maratha polity that gave his people an identity, inspired later generations, and affected Indian history. It is a story worth telling.

Shivaji (1627–1680) was born into war-torn and famine-struck Maharashtra. In 1647, aged 20, Shivaji began subverting local Bijapur authority. He stormed or tricked his way into forts of the *deshmuks* (landed nobles) to carve out an independent and Hindu Maratha zone around Pune, agitating the two powerful Muslim forces that dominated the area, Bijapur and Mughal.

Inspiring and dazzling his people, Shivaji used guerrilla tactics to annoy both enemies. Among his many exploits, in 1659 he killed Bijapur's top general at Pratapgarh Fort and then grabbed Panhala Fort and a tract of the Konkan coast between Mumbai and Goa, where he formed a navy. When Aurangzeb sent Mumtaz Mahal's brother, Shaista Khan, to deal with him in 1660, Shivaji lost many forts and his hometown, Pune, but recovered and promptly sacked Surat in 1664. Mughal pride was wounded. The next year Aurangzeb sent Jai Singh I of Jaipur with 15,000 men. At Purandhar, Shivaji agreed to give up 20 forts, and the next year arrived at Agra to do obeisance to Aurangzeb. Unexpectedly put under house arrest, he promptly escaped to become the ultimate all-Indian hero.

In 1674 the rebel Shivaji underwent a succession of Brahmanical rituals, acquired the ancestry essential to Hindu kingship, and made himself king of the Marathas. Back on his campaigns, he took Vellure and Gingee Forts near Madras, before dying of dysentery in 1680.

The next year, his son Shambhaji gave refuge to Aurangzeb's rebel son, Akbar. This, together with the fear that the Marathas and Rajputs might ally against the Mughal throne, plus the desire to convert peninsular India to Islam, made Emperor Aurangzeb decide to move his entire court and administration—some 180,000 people—down to Aurangabad in 1682. Before his death in 1707, he had killed Shambhaji, besieged his brother-successor Ramjan at Gingee Fort for eight years, and taken and almost immediately lost countless Maratha forts.

It was at this time that the Maratha chiefs, inspired by Shivaji, began to strike out independently. Maratha raiders reached Malwa in central India and sacked the rich cities of Hyderabad and Masulipatnam to control almost the whole peninsula. Then, in 1714, Shambhaji's son made Kanhoji Angria, admiral of the Maratha fleet on the west coast, his *peshwa* (prime minister). Soon the peshwas, not the royals, were ruling the Marathas from Pune.

The scene was set for the Maratha state to become the Maratha confederacy. As the Mughal empire devolved into provincial governments, so the Marathas concentrated on revenue rather than territory. Out of this opportunism emerged the great Maratha princely families of the 19th and 20th centuries: the Gaekwads of Baroda, the Scindias of Gwalior, the Holkars of Indore, the Bhonsles of Nagpur, and the Tarabais of Kolhapur.

Simultaneously, the romantic story of Shivaji inspired Bal Gangadhar Tilak and other nationalists to shake off the British yoke. Conceived in Pune, the first conference of the Indian National Congress was held in Mumbai in 1885. It was to be instrumental in India's winning independence. ■

Shivaji's hero image lives on down the centuries, in miniature paintings (opposite) and in a modern idealized statue (above).

Pune

**Pune,
Maharashtra**
🗺 158 B3
**State Tourist
Office**
www.maharashtratourism
.gov.in
✉ 1 Block, Central
Building
☎ 020-2612-6867
🕐 Closed Sun.

**Raja Dinkar Kelkar
Museum**
✉ 1378 Shukrawar
Peth
🕐 Closed Jan. 26, Aug.
15
💲 $

Viddhant Bhavan
🕐 Closed Sat. & Sun.

**Ohel David
Synagogue**
✉ 9 Dr. Anbedekan
Rd.

**Sassoon
Hospital**
🕐 Call at reception

**Osho Commune
International**
www.osho.com
✉ 17 Koregaon Park
☎ 020-6601-9999
🕐 Tours 10:30 a.m.,
2:30 p.m.
💲 $

HIGH IN THE WESTERN GHATS, ON THE EDGE OF THE
Deccan Plateau, thriving Pune is Maharashtra's second city and offers
striking contrasts: an old city, the spacious British-built new one, and
a controversial *ashram,* more classy resort than religious school.

It was not Shivaji but the later
Peshwas who, from 1750, made
Pune a center of Maratha power.
The British took over in 1818, after
the battle of Khadki (Kirkee). To
see the best of Old Pune, find the
remains of **Shanwar Wada
Fort** and then wander the crowded
lanes of traditional brick houses
and many brightly painted Hindu
temples to reach busy **Mahatma
Phule Market** (1886), opposite
Bel Bagh Temple. A few streets
farther south, at **Raja Dinkar
Kelkar Museum,** there is a vast
collection of everyday arts and
crafts amassed by the poet Kelkar
(1896–1990) from all over India,
displayed on three floors of his
beautiful Peshwa-period mansion.

After 1818, the British, calling
the city Poona, built southern
India's largest cantonment and
attracted commerce, Parsees, and
Jewish people from Mumbai. From
1820 Pune was the summer retreat
of the Mumbai Presidency. Today
the Indian Army keeps the white
colonial houses and their gardens
spick and span. Along the broad,
tree-shaded roads are **Viddhant

Bhavan** (the former Council Hall,
1870) on Manekji Mehta Road and
St. Paul's Church (1863) nearby.
David Sassoon funded the **Ohel
David Synagogue** (1863) on
Laxmi Road, where he is buried;
Sir Jacob Sassoon funded the
Sassoon Hospital, built in the
English Gothic style in 1867.

Pune is best known, however,
for Bhagwan Rajneesh, or Osho
(1931–1990), founder of the **Osho
Commune International.** To
the amazement of locals, thousands
of foreign hippies flocked here to
join the ashram he founded in
1974. Far from promoting the
traditional Hindu ashram aims of
nonmaterialism, peacefulness, and
meditation, its bywords were sexual
liberation, partying, and heady
materialism—at least for the
ashram. When the experiment of
creating a utopian city called
Rajneeshpuram in Oregon, U.S.,
failed, the Bhagwan returned to
Pune, where he died. His ashram
was likened to a spiritual
Disneyland by the *Wall Street
Journal,* and it claims more visitors
than the Taj Mahal. ■

**Above: Devotees
of Bhagwan
Rajneesh, more
often Western
than Indian, share
their emotional
experience with
each other.**

The Western Ghats

A HEADY COCKTAIL OF ROCK-CUT CAVES, FORTS, AND HILL stations excites interest in the rugged Sahyadri ranges of Maharashtra's Western Ghats that climb steeply from the Konkan coast up to the Deccan Plateau. The whole region is linked with the rise of the Marathas, led by their hero, Shivaji (see pp. 180–81). Stay in Pune and make a series of one-day trips.

Sunset at Porcupine Point, Matheran, a popular retreat from the summer heat of Mumbai.

Amarnath is a short detour from Kalyan. Ambaranatha Temple (circa 1060) has a curved tower and, inside, graceful female figures in recesses. Together with the temple at less accessible Sinnar (see p. 188), this is the best surviving monument of the Yadava period, which immediately preceded the Muslim arrival in the south.

People flock to **Matheran** on weekends to enjoy the fresh air, 2,460 feet (750 m) above sea level, at the closest hill station to Mumbai. A delightful way to arrive is by train, first on the Pune Express from Mumbai to Neral, then on the narrow-gauge train up the hill. Even if you go by car, it must be parked 3 miles (5 km) from the center, which does not permit

vehicles. Matheran was popularized by a certain Hugh Malet, who built the first European house here in 1851; Lord Elphinstone, governor of Mumbai, had a road built to his lodge in 1858, sealing its place in fashionable Mumbai society. This is a place to take walks for sensational views down to the plains from Panorama Point and Duke's Nose. For sunsets, try Porcupine Point. Walk to Louise Point for views across the plateau to the ruined hill forts of Prebal and Vishlagarh.

Visitors who like early Buddhist rock-cut temples can take in **Karla, Bhaja, and Bedsa,** found near the popular hill resort of Lonavala, which has plenty of restaurants. Avoid weekends, when crowds disturb the peace.

The "toy train" runs from Neral to Matheran around 281 switchbacks.

MUMBAI & MAHARASHTRA

Amarnath
🔺 158 B3

Matheran
🔺 158 B3

Bhaja
🔺 158 B3

Karla
🔺 158 B3

Rajgurunagar
🔺 158 B3

Purandhar
🔺 158 B3

To see the temples chronologically, begin at Bhaja, where 20 caves date from the early Satavahana period of the second century B.C. **Cave no. 12,** possibly the earliest apsidal rock-cut *chaitya* hall in the western Deccan, once had a teak beam roof; **Cave no. 19** has exceptionally early figural compositions showing, possibly, Surya (left) and Indra (right). At Bedsa, about 6 miles (10 km) away, the chaitya hall of **Cave no. 7** (first century) has a richly carved exterior. Four miles (6 km) north of Bhaja, Karla's caves and cisterns surround the largest and most completely preserved early Buddhist chaitya hall in the area, known as **Cave no. 8.** Built during the brief Kshatrapa rule of the first century, a monolithic column topped with a capital of four lions stands in front of the doors, decorated with the six pairs of donors (the Buddha images were added later); the side walls have splendid elephant sculptures. Inside, see the magnificently carved columns and *stupa.*

If you are traveling on to Nasik (see p. 188), you can pause at **Rajgurunagar** (Khed) to see the mosque and tomb of Dilawar Khan (1613), who had his headquarters here when he commanded the

Ahmednagar forces against the Mughals. Farther along the road, a detour left reaches **Junnar,** renowned as the birthplace of Shivaji, which has various 15th- and 16th-century fortifications, mosques, and tombs. Ancient Junnar's position on a trade route to the Gujarat coast brought patronage for a flourishing Buddhist center during the Satavahana and Kshatrapa periods (second century B.C. to third century A.D.). About 50 simple Buddhist caves are cut into **Shivneri Hill,** 11 more on **Tulja Hill,** 26 on **Lenyadri Hill,** and 50 on **Manmodi Hill.** There is very little decoration, but walking around the hills to seek them out is peaceful and satisfying.

A trio of offbeat places, **Purandhar, Sasvad,** and **Jejuri,** are accessible on a day trip south from Pune. First, head for the great **fort of Purandhar,** perched 4,839 feet (1,475 m) above sea level. You have to walk the final 1,148 feet (350 m) up to the entrance—imagine taking this fort by force as Shivaji did in 1670 and Aurangzeb in 1705. Through the gate, pass the bold Bahmani walls (15th century) and continue up three levels to the ruined buildings; from here there

There are no cars in Matheran, so you either walk, take a rickshaw, or rent a horse to get about town and explore the narrow ridge and its viewpoints.

are good views of Wazirgad, the fortified hill to the east.

The pretty town of **Sasvad** has several of the Peshwas' fortified palaces, some with partly surviving carved wooden structures. **Sangameshvara** and **Changla Vateshvara Temples,** west of the town, are hybrids of Mughal and Hindu architecture with tortoises carved on the hall floors.

Jejuri is a popular pilgrimage center for Maharashtran merchants and farmers who follow the Khandoba cult, and it is especially lively during the April and December fairs. Find the temple through the town and up steps where peddlers sell brass masks of Khandoba. At the top of the steps, four lamp columns stand near a huge brass tortoise.

It's easy to visit the fort at **Sinhagad,** rising 2,296 feet (700 m) above the surrounding plain and once known as Kondhana: The road from Pune almost reaches it. The wonder is to see the walls of the three-pronged fort rising sheer from the steep cliffs, reinforced with ramparts and

towers. Follow the steep path up through three gates. Although little remains inside, you can imagine Muhammad Tughlaq of Delhi trying to besiege it in 1340 and Malik Armad of Golconda taking it in 1486. Shivaji took it in 1647, when he changed its name to Sinhagad (Lion Fort), after which Marathas and Mughals vied for it.

It is worth the journey and the two-hour climb from Vajeghar, where the road ends, to see **Rajgad.** This spectacular fort rises sheer from its three-pronged hill and is so high that, once inside, you have views of Sinhagad, Torna, and Purandhar. Ruined stores, granaries, and halls fill the northern spur. Climb farther to reach Bala Kila (inner fort), 4,320 feet (1,317 m) above sea level, and find Shivaji's impressive palace remains. Having taken Torna Fort in 1646, Shivaji used its treasure to buy arms for Rajgad (King's Fort) and make it his seat of government until 1672, when he moved west to Raigad Fort. It was from there that he left to campaign on the Konkan coast in 1666. ∎

Captured by Shivaji in 1656, Rajgad (Royal Fort) opened up the Konkan routes to him; it became his seat of government (1672) and place of coronation (1674).

Sinhagad
 158 B3
✉ 20 miles from Pune

Rajgad
158 B3

Mumbai to Goa

THIS ISOLATED AND UNSPOILED AREA OF COASTAL Maharashtra has become much more accessible due to new railroads and faster sea transportation. Hovercrafts and catamarans regularly leave the Gateway of India for Mandve; your ticket includes the bus ride on to Alibag, where there are taxi stands. If you are traveling by private car, the driver will meet you at Mandve. Alternatively, make use of the Konkan Railway (see pp. 204–205). Avoid driving out of Mumbai.

Alibag was the headquarters of Shivaji's Maratha fleet from 1662 on. Later, the Angres, who mixed trading with piracy, used it as a base from which to annoy European shipping until the British took it in 1840. You can visit the island **Kolaba Fort** (1820) at low tide or see it while you walk along the

town. As you roam the massive fortifications, guardrooms, cannon, and the four-story *durbar* (audience) hall, imagine its proud history. The Sidis, Abyssinian admirals in the service of the Adil Shahis of Bijapur, built it in 1511 but by 1618 had asserted their independence. Mixing piracy with providing armed escorts for pilgrims on *hajj* to Mecca, they never lost to Shivaji or the British. Today's former royals live in the hilltop palace; the creekside road south from Murud passes their tombs. Because Janjira is isolated, visit it after a night or so at **Chiplun,** a thriving town on the Vashishti River.

Almost as good as Janjira, the magnificent fort of **Vijayadurg** sits at the mouth of the Vaghotan Creek. The Adil Shahis of Bijapur built it but Shivaji took it, renamed it Vijayadurg (Victory Fort), and strengthened it. This, not Alibag, was his base for attacking Janjira, and the Angres later used it as a piracy base. You can explore the three concentric sets of fortifications, the residences, the barracks, and the granary. Continue to **Malvan.** It's well worth the somewhat simple accommodations to enjoy this charming town, its cafés, and cashew nut production. Take a boat ride out to the island **Sindhudurg Fort** to walk along some of the 2 miles (3 km) of fortifications built by Shivaji when he made this his coastal headquarters in about 1665. ■

If you miss the low tide walk from Alibag to Kolaba Fort, you can sometimes take a ferry there to explore its 17 wall towers, teak doors, stables, and storerooms.

beach. The main road goes straight through dusty **Chaul,** reducing the pleasure of seeking out the remains of walls and churches that were once part of a major Konkan port governed by the Bahmanis of Gulbarga, then the Portuguese.

Quite simply India's most spectacular island fort, **Janjira** is reached by rowboat from Murud

Buying fruit from local markets can be a form of entertainment.

More places to visit in Maharashtra

AHMEDNAGAR

Founded in 1494 by Ahmad Nizam Shah, who broke away from the Bahmanis of Bidar (see p. 241), this was the capital of the powerful Nizam Shahi rulers. Wars with Bijapur and Golconda ended when all three states, plus Bidar, formed a Muslim alliance to overthrow the Hindu kingdom of Vijayanagar in 1565 (see pp. 236–39). Later, despite an accord with Goa, Ahmednagar finally lost out to the Mughals in 1636, after which it belonged to Hyderabad, the Marathas, and, from 1808, the British. It was in the splendid **Circular Fort** (1563), with its moat and 22 bastions, that Jawaharlal Nehru wrote most of his book *The Discovery of India* while an imprisoned freedom fighter. See also the exquisitely decorated **Damris Mosque** (1568), the **Jami Masjid,** and **Mecca Mosque** in the heart of the city, the **Kotla** (1537), which was a Shia college of education, and **Ahmad's Tomb** (1509) in Bagh Rauza gardens. Out of town, the **Dargah of Alamgir** (1707) marks the spot where the Mughal emperor Aurangzeb collapsed and died (see Khuldabad, p. 175). Nearby stand two garden palaces: **Farh Bagh** and **Hayat Behisht Bagh.**

🅰 158 B3 ✉ 72 miles (116 km) northeast of Pune, 68 miles (110 km) southwest of Aurangabad, 90 miles (145 km) south of Nasik

KOLHAPUR

This busy commercial city in southern Maharashtra traces its history back to the Satavahana period, when it traded with the Mediterranean. More recently, it was the capital of the breakaway Maratha maharajas of Kolhapur, who commissioned fine Indo-Saracenic buildings by Maj. Charles Mant, better known for his Chennai buildings (see pp. 256–57). In the Old City, find **Rajwada** (Old Palace) and the popular **Mahalakshmi Temple.** Then visit Mant's splendid and influential buildings. There is **Kolhapur Museum** (1872–76, *closed Mon.*), built as the Town Hall, and Chhatrapati Pramila Raja Hospital (1881–84). His masterpiece, though, is **New Palace** (1884, *closed Mon.),* where former royals still live. The basalt and sandstone building has neo-Mughal cusped arches and a *durbar* hall with stained glass illustrating the life of Shivaji. The royal paraphernalia ranges from a silver elephant saddle to a veritable zoo of stuffed animals; one maharaja was an expert taxidermist. Take a look inside the **Shalini Palace** (1931–34), now a hotel overlooking Rankala Lake and furnished with fine Belgian glass. Do not miss the chance to buy Kolhapur leather shoes, to see *kusti* (wrestling) training near the Rajwada, to visit the spectacularly sited **Panhala Fort,** which guarded trade routes to the coast. This is a good base for visits to Vijayadurg and Sindhudurg (see p. 186), and is on the road to Bijapur (see p. 240) and Belgaum.

🏔 158 B2 **Visitor information** ✉ Kedar Complex, Station Road ☎ 0231-652935

MAHABALESHWAR

This is where the sacred Krishna River springs, making it a pilgrimage site for the faithful. The British, after making a treaty with the local ruler in 1829, exploited this lush, wooded site in the Sahyadri Hills as a hill station. Still popular for its views, streams, and fresh air, this is a good base for visiting Shivaji's **Pratapgarh**

Kolhapur's visitors make time to shop for its famous *chappals* (sandals).

(1656), where he murdered the Bijapur commander, and **Raigad,** which he captured in 1636 and made his capital in 1672. He and his son were crowned here. Trips can be made to the island forts of Janjira (see p. 180) and Suvarnadurg, by Harnai, from here. There are more Shivaji sites at Pune.

🏔 158 B3 ✉ 74 miles (120 km) SW of Pune

NASIK

The sacred Godavari River, flowing through this ancient holy city, attracts a continuous stream of pilgrims, swelling to vast numbers every 12 years for the Kumbh Mela festival (last held in 2001, next in 2013, see p. 304). Hindus believe Rama spent part of his exile here, with Sita and Lakshmana. Join pilgrims to visit the riverside temples, including **Rameshvara** (18th century), leaving time to visit three sites out of town. **Pandu Lena** has rock-cut Buddhist caves (second century B.C. to third century A.D.); Nos. 3, 10, and 18 are especially interesting. Within the dramatic cliffs of Trimbak lies the source of the Godavari River, much visited during two annual fairs (*Oct.–Nov. & Feb.–March*). At Sinnar, on the road to Pune, **Gondeshvara Temple** (11th century) was built by the Yadava rulers and is one of Maharashtra's largest and best preserved temples.

🏔 158 B4 ✉ 81 miles (130 km) northeast of Mumbai; 130 miles (209 km) north of Pune **Visitor information** ✉ Golf Club, Old Agra Road ☎ 0253-570059

PAITHAN

This is a treat for archaeology and weaving enthusiasts. The thriving settlement founded by the Satavahana ruler Shalivahana as his capital in A.D. 78 is being unearthed at Nag Ghat: Local weavers create the distinctive Paithan designs in fine silk and cotton.

🏔 159 C3 ✉ 32 miles (51 km) south of Aurangabad

SOLAPUR

Down in southeast Maharashtra, on the road to Bijapur and Gulbarga, Solapur's strategic importance has made it the subject of many battles. Thus, in town there is an impressive **fort** with sloping walls, built by the 14th-century Bahmanis, with inner additions by the Adil Shahis of Bijapur. **Naldurg,** 28 miles (45 km) to the west, has a magnificent fort (16th century) built by the Adil Shahis on a bluff above the Bori River. If your route is to or from Ahmednagar, it is worth detouring to **Parenda** to see one of Maharashtra's most perfect early military forts, built around 1500 for the Bidar sultans.

🏔 159 C2 ∎

With mountains to the east and ancient marine trade routes to the west, this strip of palm-fringed beaches, fishing villages, forts, and ports has a history and culture distinct from the rest of peninsular India.

West Coast: Goa & Kerala

A colorful umbrella shades a bargain-hunter at Mapusa market in Goa.

The lush Goan landscape is complemented by the rich colors of the traditional clothing worn by its inhabitants.

West Coast: Goa & Kerala

A NARROW BAND OF LUSH, VERDANT LAND RUNS DOWN THE WEST COAST of India's peninsula, sandwiched between the Western Ghat mountains and the Arabian Sea. From northern Goa to southern Kerala the visitor can relax on the beaches or take advantage of a variety of water sports. There is here something for everyone, in this mixture of east and west with its easygoing ambience.

The map shows how mountains and sea have played their part in the West Coast story. The mountains have been a barrier crossed more often by traders than by empire-builders, the seas a tool to bring trading wealth and introduce new cultures, peoples, and religions. Arabs, Romans, and, later, Europeans arrived, bringing Judaism, Islam, and various forms of Christianity. Coastal people have tended to look outward across the water, rather than inward to the great empires of the Deccan and Tamil Nadu, and their coast is littered with ancient forts and modern ports—Panaji, Mangalore, Cannanore, Kozhikode (Calicut), Kochi (Cochin), and others—all centers for shipbuilding.

None of India's great rivers empties here, but India's great southwest monsoon hits Kerala in July and soaks the Western Ghats in July and August, so hundreds of little rivers flow down to the coast. They run from the steep Sahyadri Hills to the Konkan coast of Goa and the Kanara coast of Karnataka. They flow from the even higher Cardamom Hills to the Malabar Coast of Kerala, slowed down by such quantities of inland lagoons and rivers that land and water become inseparable.

Today these busy rivers continue to carry the local merchants' traditional sources of wealth (pepper, cardamom, other spices, and quantities of rice) to the ports. They also carry tea from the Nilgiri Hills, coffee from

MUMBAI &
MAHARASHTRA
p.158

5▷
Pernem •
Aguada •
Panaji •
Margao •
Palolem •

Old Goa
Ponda
GOA
Karwar

Gokarn •
Kumta •
Honavar •

W. GHATS
KARNATAKA
THE DECCAN
p.222

Bhatkal •
Kundapura •
(Coondapoor)
Barkur •
Udipi •
(Udupi)

Karkal •

4▷

A r a b i a n
S e a

Mangalore •
• Bantval

48

or Sahyadri

Kasaragod •
Bekal •

0   200 kilometers
0   100 miles

Taliparamba •
Kannur •
(Cannanore)

3▷

• Chetlat

• Kiltan

AMINDIVI
ISLANDS
Kadmat •

Thalassery •
(Tellicherry) • Mahe

L a c c a d i v e

Nilgiri
Hills

Bangaram •
• Pitti
Androth •

Kozhikode
(Calicut) •
• Manjeri

✈ Agatti
⊙ Kavaratti

Tirur • **KERALA**

• Palakkad

Ponnani • • Cheruthuruthi

LAKSHADWEEP

Cheriyam •

Guruvayur • ∧ Anaimali
Thrissur (Trichur) • *Hills* 2695m
Kodungallur • Angamali Anai Mudi

S
e
a

TAMIL NADU
p.255

Suheli •
Kalpani •

Cardamom

2▷ **LAKSHADWEEP**

ERNAKULAM •
Ettumanur • *Munnar*
• Vaikam *Hills*

Nine Degree Channel

Kochi
(Cochin) ✈
Vembanad Lake

🚢 Thekkadi
Periyar Lake

Alappuzha •
(Alleppey) Kottayam •
• Thiruvalla

PERIYAR
NAT. PARK

Kayankulam • • Chengannur

Kollam
(Quilon) •
• Varkala

Thiruvananthapuram ⊙
(Trivandrum) • Kovalam

• Minicoy

Vizhinjam •

Padmanabhapuram
Palace ◆

I N D I A N   O C E A N

△   △   △
A   **B**   **C**

Area of map detail

New
Delhi

Karnataka's plantations, and lucrative rubber
and turmeric (see pp. 214–15).

This coast that depended so much upon
the sea has a new land connection: the Konkan
Railway (see pp. 204–205). Opened in 1998, it
stretches from Mumbai to Kochi and is already
hauling the more isolated, undeveloped parts
of the coast into the modern world. Goa and

Kerala have been quick to respond with some
charming upscale hotels. Visitors can
comfortably explore a beautiful area of mostly
unspoiled India, while enjoying palm-fringed
beaches and outstanding local cuisines. A
week or so spent in this region makes a relaxing and striking contrast to touring India's
great monuments. ∎

Goa is dotted with dazzling, white-washed colonial baroque churches that serve its substantial Roman Catholic population.

Old Goa & Panaji

PANAJI IS THE SLOW-PACED, FRIENDLY CAPITAL OF GOA, A tiny state of 1,429 square miles (3,702 sq km) created only in 1987, its language of Konkani given official status in 1988. Explore Panaji after your visit to Old Goa, the region's former capital, reached by road or by passenger boat up the Mandovi River.

Panaji Goa
🗺 191 B5
State Tourist Office
www.goatourism.org
✉ Trionara Apartments, Dr Alvares Costa Rd.
☎ 0832-226515

India Tourist Office
✉ Communidade Building, Church Sq.
☎ 0832-223412

OLD GOA

The few surviving churches and monasteries, with baroque high altars and encroaching palm trees, evoke Goa's most recent great city, for this ancient river port was used by the Ashoka, Satavahanah, and Chalukya empires. The Kadambas (11th–12th centuries) made it their capital on two nearby sites, attracting Khilji, then Tughlaq forces from far away Delhi. Later, Goa was wrested from the Bahmanis by the all-powerful Vijayanagas, won back (when the port capital was moved to this site), but in 1489 lost for good to the Adil Shahis of Bijapur.

Meanwhile, Portuguese explorer Bartolomeu Dias rounded the Cape of Good Hope in 1488. A decade later Vasco da Gama rounded the Cape and sailed across the Indian Ocean to Calicut, and in 1503 Alfonso de Albuquerque built Fort Cochin. In 1510, Albuquerque sailed up the Mandovi and took Goa on November 25, establishing it as the capital of a fast-growing Portuguese maritime empire.

Goa was an entrepôt for trade up and down the coast, in and out of India, and from the Arabian Gulf across to Malacca. The Portuguese levied taxes on everything—cargoes of indigo, cotton, cinnamon, mace, nutmeg, Chinese silk, porcelain, and the very valuable pepper. For a century Goa was known as *Goa dourada* (golden Goa). It was an international city of churches, convents, palaces, mansions, docks, and markets, swarming with activity. It was a center for Roman Catholicism, for the Portuguese

in 1843 did little to alleviate. Portugal clung to her colony until December 19, 1961, when Nehru's Indian forces liberated the city.

To enjoy Old Goa town, wander through the baroque colonial churches with their ebullient decoration, twisted columns, flying angels, and lashings of gilt. The three major churches (see p. 194) are the **Basilica of Bom Jesus** (1594–1605), the **Cathedral of St. Catherine** (1562–1619), and the **Convent and Church of St. Francis of Assisi** (1521 and 1661), which also includes the town's museum.

PANAJI
Still with a definite Portuguese air, Panaji sits at the mouth of the Mandovi River. It only became the capital of Goa when the port at Old Goa town silted up. It is worth paying a visit to the hilltop parish church, **Our Lady of the Immaculate Conception** (1619), built in Portuguese Baroque style with twin towers; then walk through the old area of Fontainhas to see old public buildings, such as the **Case Modea** (Mint) and **Idalcaon Palace** (Secretariat). The riverside area west of here is home to the colorful municipal market and Charles Correa's splendid **Kala Academy** (1973–1983), decorated with Mario Miranda's monochrome murals. ∎

trading zeal was matched with a missionary zeal. Missionaries arrived early in Goa, closely followed by the Jesuits and their Counter-Reformation (1540) and Inquisition (1560).

But the Portuguese Empire faded. The reasons were many: loss of trade after the fall of Vijayanagar, the proselytizing zeal against Hindus, the taxation of Muslims on *hajj* (pilgrimage) to Mecca, plagues of cholera, deceitful Portuguese business practices, and the arrival of Dutch and English traders in 1595 and 1600. Goa sank into isolation that the removal of its capital from unhealthy Old Goa to Panaji

Old Goa Churches
$ $ for each:

Panaji
⚠ 191 A5

Our Lady of the Immaculate Conception
$ $

Kala Academy
$ $

Festivals
Carnival, week preceding Lent: festivities throughout Goa
Holy Week, Easter, & Christmas, dates vary: grand processions, various churches; contact local tourist offices for specific information.

St. Francis Xavier

Goencha Saiba (Lord of Goa) is the affectionate Konkani title Goan Christians, Hindus, and Muslims give to their local saint. Born in Spain in 1506, Francisco Xavier y Jassu met Ignatius Loyola in Paris, took a vow to convert infidels, and joined the Society of Jesus. The Portuguese king, Dom Joao III, sent Xavier to Portugal's new colony, Goa. He arrived in May 1542, aged 36, and made Goa his base for five voyages to the Far East. After his death on Sancian Island in 1552, his body was returned to Goa in 1553 and carried in triumph from the riverside. St. Francis was canonized in 1662. ∎

A drive through Old Goa, Ponda, & Margao

This gentle day excursion takes in Portuguese monuments and mansions, and some of Ponda's most distinctive temples.

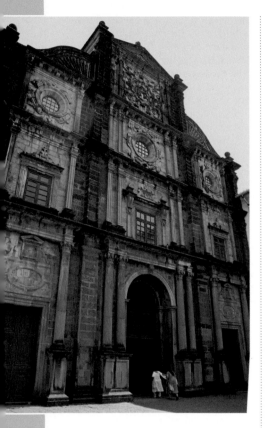

The Basilica of Bom Jesus is a focal point for Goa's Catholic population.

The road to **Old Goa ❶** rises over a hill to give you a first glimpse of the overgrown city with St. Augustine's soaring tower. Head for the center, where the group of big churches stands. In the **Basilica of Bom Jesus** (1594–1605), built by the Jesuits next to their home, the Professed House (1589 and 1633), is St. Francis Xavier's elaborate mausoleum, given by the Duke of Tuscany, Cosimo III. Inside the casket, a light shines on St. Francis's body. Across the square stand the

grand **Cathedral of St. Catherine** (1562–1619), built for the Dominicans, and the beautiful painted **Convent and Church of St. Francis of Assisi** (1521), housing Goa's best museum with a collection of sculptures and portraits of Portuguese governors.

Take a walk west of the Cathedral to see the **Church of St. Cajetan** (1655–1700), whose dome was modeled on that of St. Peter's in Rome. Continue through the **Viceroy's Arch,** built by Francisco da Gama (viceroy 1597–1600), to the silent docks, where more than a thousand ships were loaded each year. From here either walk or drive up Holy Hill to the **Church and Monastery of St. Augustine** (1602), its pink laterite stone lit by morning sun. The 152-foot-high (46 m) church tower, eight chapels, 100 or so carved granite tombstones, and monastic buildings testify to a substantial community. A path across the road leads to the **Church of Our Lady of the Rosary** (1544–49), which overlooks the Mandovi River; here St. Francis preached at evening mass.

Leaving Old Goa, the temples of Ponda are a total contrast (see p. 198). Instead of riverside colonial style, you now have secret temple building in secluded valleys. Driving southward, the road twists and climbs into hills where spreading cashew trees and jackfruit trees grow. Here are three contrasting temples to visit. **Sri Mangesh Temple ❷,** at Priol, has all the distinctive Goan elements and is Goa's richest temple. Up the steps, find the large courtyard with a *tulsi* (basil) pot, a lamp tower, and an elephant on wheels in front of the lemon-yellow and white-domed temple; inside, look for the tiles and Belgian glass. **Sri Lakshmi Narashimha Devashtan Temple ❸,** dedicated to Vishnu and Lakshmi in the gods' abode, stands in an appropriately idyllic woodland setting at Velinga and is probably Goa's most beautiful temple. Finally, **Sri Shantadurga Temple ❹,** near Queula, is Goa's most popular temple, especially crowded with people buying flowers before the main *puja* at 1 p.m., held in a *mandapa* (hall) of baroque splendor.

From here, the road goes through Borim before crossing the Zuari River. A detour left after Camurlim village leads through lanes to **Rachol Seminary** (see p. 202) **⑤**, with its great entrance hall, chapel, and museum.

Margao ⑥ (see p. 196) is southern Goa's main town. Bustling yet rural, it has two good areas to visit. As you drive in along the one-way street, you can already see some of the

A well-maintained Indo-Portuguese house with its *balcao* (veranda)

town's grand old houses. You can stop at **Largo de Igreja** (Church Square), the old central square, to see a cluster of old houses that overlook the gleaming white **Church of the Holy Spirit** (1564, rebuilt 1675), with its baroque and rococo interior. Then visit the **covered market,** where locals buy spices, vegetables, household goods, and, outside, fresh fish. In the Margao outskirts of Borda, reached by taking Agostinho Lourenco Street from Largo de Igreja, find the huge palace of **Sat Burnzam Gor.** ∎

- 🅜 See area map page 191
- ➤ Old Goa
- ↔ 20 miles
- 🕒 5–6 hours
- ➤ Margao

NOT TO BE MISSED
- Basilica of Bom Jesus, Old Goa
- St. Augustine's Church, Old Goa
- Sri Mangesh Temple, Priol, near Ponda
- Largo de Igreja (church square), Margao
- Covered market, Margao

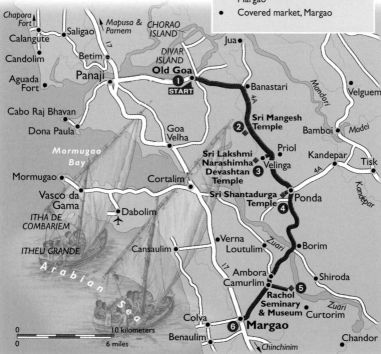

Margao & around

GOA'S SECOND LARGEST TOWN IS A GOOD PLACE TO FEEL the influence of 450 years of Portuguese rule, partly because there are few tourists, partly because it forms part of the heartland of the Old Conquests (the rest of Goa was conquered in the 18th century).

**Margao,
Goa**
191 A5
**Margao Tourist
Office**
✉ Tourist Hotel

As you approach Margao from the surrounding countryside, you notice the whitewashed baroque facades of colonial Catholic churches standing beside the paddy fields and rivers. Women often wear pretty dresses with puffed sleeves, rather than saris. Widows dress in European black, not Hindu white, and sit crocheting on the deep *balcaos* (porches) of their houses. These are painted blue, red-umber, and yellow, with the large windows outlined in white. The cuisine is a mixture of Portuguese and Indian traditions, and wine is readily available. Soccer, not cricket, is the favorite sport. Even the Portuguese siesta is maintained: Everything closes from 2 p.m. to 4 p.m.

When the city of Old Goa declined, the Old Conquests were barely affected. Here, the Portuguese-speaking Christian Goans ran the government and trade, and in due course they formed the local aristocracy in Margao and the villages. Prosperity here peaked in the 18th and 19th centuries, when the great houses were built.

For a breathtaking view over Margao and the Arabian Sea, go up to **Mount Church.** Down in the town, the markets are the hub for trading the fish and farming produce of southern Goa. Behind the big red-and-white Municipal Building you can find the fisher-women, their saris tucked up, crouching beside baskets of shrimp, pearl spot, Indian salmon, and other catches of the morning. Nearby, you can buy fruit from the great piles of bananas, pineapples, chikoos, jackfruits, and, starting in

March, mangoes. Inside the old **covered market** you'll find dried mangoes, flowers, fresh Goan bread, tobacco leaves, and sacks full of turmeric, garlic, Goan red chilies, and the dried tamarind that gives a bitter richness to local dishes. The box-shaped stores stocking wines, jewelry, and hardware form the walls of the market.

To see a good cluster of old houses, go to **Aquerim** district and brave the thundering traffic to walk along the two one-way streets that lead in and out of town and run along both sides of Largo de Igreja (Church Square). These grand town houses with their painted walls, iron balconies, and carved balustrades surround the tall, dazzlingly white **Church of the Holy Spirit** (1564, rebuilt 1675), one of Goa's finest late baroque churches. If it is open, go inside to enjoy the coffered ceiling, grand gilt pulpit, rococo altar, and baroque transept altarpieces.

To see more fine houses, go along Agostinho Lourenco Street behind the church and toward Curtorim. About half a mile along stands the huge palace of **Sat Burnzam Gor,** built around 1790 by Inacio Silva and now lived in by his descendants. As well as a string of grand salons, it has one of Goa's earliest private chapels.

If this has whetted your appetite, you can follow a delightful circular route around the villages of this area, **Salcete,** to see more. Begin at the old Portuguese administrative center, **Loutolim,** found by turning north from Carmurlim on the Margao–Ponda road. The clutch of fine old buildings includes **Case dos Mirandos** (*Contact tourist office to arrange a visit*), still lived in by the Miranda family. Built early in the 18th century, it has a chapel, bedrooms, salon, and deep internal verandah on the first

floor and a great banqueting room, library, and main bedroom upstairs. Two other fine Loutolim houses are **Roque Caetan Miranda House** (1815), a typical Goan country house and **Salvador Costa House,** with its spectacular chapel. Visits to both houses should be arranged through the tourist office.

Continue to Chandor, through undulating land with old houses scattered around and flashy new ones built with money newly earned in the Middle East. You may wish to pause at **Rachol** (see p. 202) or to see Curtorim's splendid church facade. Chandor is dominated by the vast, ornate **Menezes-Braganza Mansion** whose second-floor rooms are furnished with gilt mirrors, four-poster beds, and quantities of elegantly carved chairs. Do not miss the ballroom, with its blue-and white-painted zinc ceiling, Italian chandeliers, Belgian mirrors, and portrait of the mansion's builder, Anton Francesco Santana Pereira. For more villages to visit, see Chinchinim (see p. 202). ∎

The Menezes-Braganza Mansion, part of which dates from the 16th century, boasts historic furnishings.

Sat Burnzam Gor
- ✉ Borda
- 🕒 Visits by written or telephone appointment

Menenzes Braganza Mansion
- ✉ Chandor
- 🕒 Contact tourist office to arrange a visit
- 💲 $

Ponda's temples

WHEN PORTUGUESE MISSIONARY ZEAL SPARKED THE PUBlication of an edict to destroy Hindu temples in 1540, some Hindu priests fled with the temple deity to the forested hills around Ponda, outside the Portuguese territories. Thus, while more than 550 temples were destroyed, many Hindus continued to worship in secret. Today, about 50 of Goa's temples have deities who are, in effect, long-term refugees, still situated close to, but outside, Ponda.

Sri Mangesh Temple, with its soaring *deepastambha* (lamp tower), encapsulates the idiosyncratic Goa temple.

Ponda, Goa

🗺 191 B5

Hinduism flourished freely again under more benign Portuguese rule at the end of the 18th century. Despite the number of churches you see sprinkled across the state, Goa is today 60 percent Hindu. Furthermore, Christians sometimes join Hindus to pay their respects to an ancient deity worshiped by their Hindu ancestors.

Goa's temples have a style all their own. The laterite walls are usually plastered and painted, and there are often domed central roofs, red-tiled side roofs, and tall *deepastambhas* (lamp towers). Inside, you may find Greek-inspired columns and grand chandeliers.

The pick of Ponda's temples is probably **Sri Mangesh Temple** at Priol, whose Shiva *lingum* was brought here for safety from

Cortalim and hidden until the 18th century, when the temple was built. The seven-story deepastambha, elaborate doorway, and Belgian glass testify to the temple's wealth and status. **Sri Mahalsa Temple** lies between here and Ponda, in Mardol village. Do not miss the tall, brass pillar topped by Garuda and set on a turtle's back, signs that the temple is dedicated to Vishnu. At Velinga, **Sri Narashimha Devashtan Temple** is especially beautiful in its peaceful wooded setting and is dedicated to Vishnu and his consort Lakshmi. The gleaming image of Narasimha, Vishnu's fourth *avatar* (earthly form), was brought here for safety from Sancoale in the 1560s. The key features are the original entrance and the tank around the back. ■

Goa's beaches

EARLY MORNING SUN, BARE FEET ON FIRM SAND, FISHER-
men going out to sea, porpoises playing in the frothy waves, and infinite stretches of sand beneath a canopy of blue sky await you. Have
breakfast in a beachside café, go for a swim, and then retreat to the
shade to read until lunch—grilled giant shrimp are popular. After a
siesta, enjoy swimming and strolling along part of the 66 miles
(106 km) of beach until the spectacular sunset over the sea.

Goa

🗺 191 A5 & B5

Goa's dark sand is clean and fine.
Some beaches are very long: The
uba dando ("straight rod") is the
great 12-mile (21 km) stretch in
southern Goa from Velsao to
Mobor. Each beach is named after
the fishing village nestling in the
coconut palms behind it, so the uba
dando has several names. Each
beach has its own character, from
isolated Agonda to sociable and
popular Calangute, or the almost
private coves like Vainguinim.
Different beaches attract different
crowds: Sinquerim Beach is next to
two upscale hotels, Anjuna is a hippie hangout, and Indians arrive in
busloads at Calangute and Colva.

It is easy to beach hop: Simply
walk to the next beach, rent a
bicycle or motorcycle, or take a taxi.
Where you need to cross a river,

your only problem is waiting for
the ferry to arrive; in Goa, there is
always time to wait.

Goa takes an active interest in
ecology. Heated local debates have
resulted in strict laws. New buildings must be 660 feet (200 m) back
from the high-tide line. Sand dunes
and their salt-tolerant vegetation
are encouraged and litter cleared
regularly. These laws particularly
affect the owners of beach cafés,
temporary structures where you
can have a drink. Try local *feni* (see
p. 201) or its lighter equivalent,
urrack; do nothing much and watch
the waves to a soundtrack of old
Motown and Beatles hits. Licenses
are given and taken away seemingly
arbitrarily, but there should always
be some friendly cafés waiting to
serve you.

**Goa's beaches
range from sandy
crescent shapes,
like this, to the
12-mile-long
(21 km) sweep of
uba dando south
of Panaji.**

After a night at sea, fishermen unload their catch on the beach at Colva.

Goa's beach etiquette is simple: Nudity is unacceptable, drugs are illegal, the sea should be checked locally for undertow, and peddlers need fierce bargaining or a polite "no, thank you." To help you find the right beach, here are the best of them, from north to south.

QUIET NORTHERN GOA BEACHES

To reach these peaceful spots, take the ferry from Siolim across the Chapora River into Pernem district, little influenced by the Portuguese. Isolated **Querim Beach** is best reached by a pleasant walk from Arambol (Harmal) Beach past a mixture of palms, fishing boats, Hindu-owned cafés, a handful of hippies, and a good local bakery. Turn left from the Chapora Ferry and follow the riverbank. **Morgim**

Beach (Morji) tends to be very quiet unless a busload of Indians arrives, and there is good bird-watching.

BUSIER NORTHERN GOA BEACHES

Six miles (10 km) of beach stretch from Baga down to Sinquerim along the coast of Bardez district. This is where the action is, with beach parties, a choice of restaurants, bars, and nightlife. Behind the beaches, old Portuguese houses and churches stand among paddy fields. **Anjuna Beach** is a social center for hippies and beach parties, with safe swimming, cafés, and the Wednesday afternoon market with vendors from Rajasthan, Gujarat, and Karnataka; nearby Mapusa's Friday market (see p. 202) is inland. Pretty, crescent-shaped

Baga Beach, in front of some very good accommodations, has tempting restaurants and a lively social life, which is also true of neighboring **Calangute Beach.** **Candolim Beach** is next, with its charming inns and cafés. Finally, **Sinquerim Beach,** lined with palm trees, runs right down to Fort Aguada, where you will find upscale hotels, cafés, water sports, and the inevitable peddlers.

BEACHES NEAR PANAJI

These are small beaches, where the sand has a silver tint because of the iron content. Some of the beaches are private, and thus free of peddlers. **Dona Paula Beach** is reserved for guests of the hotels overlooking it; **Vainguinim Beach** is reached through Cidade de Goa Hotel, whose garden encircles it.

LONG SOUTHERN GOA BEACHES

Uba dando's 12-mile (19 km) stretch is, so far, quieter than the main northern Goa beaches. Its sand is cleaner, and its sea is usually calm. Margao, Ponda, Panaji, and Old Goa (see pp. 192–98) are fairly accessible, but avoid Bogmalo, right on the airport flight path. Beaches run from Velsao to lively **Colva,** with its fishermen, beach cafés, village market, and restaurants. Peaceful **Sernabatim, Benaulim,** and **Varca** beaches are surprisingly little-used by patrons of the nearby upscale hotels. **Cavelossim** fronts the pretty village of Carmona, and **Mobor** is home to a super-chic hotel. You then come to Betul village and the Sal River.

QUIET SOUTHERN GOA BEACHES

To enjoy nearly empty beaches with their wilder scenery, go for the day and take a picnic. **Agonda Beach** is usually particularly quiet, whereas **Palolem's** beauty is threatened by development. South of here are **Rajbag** and **Galgibaga.** ■

Anjuna's busy flea market (right) has a heady mix of goods from all over India, plus little restaurants and, of course, the beach.

Coconut palm

This versatile tree plays an essential role in Goan life. Seaside clumps help protect villagers from the sun, wind, and monsoon storms. Inland, more than half of Goa's agricultural land is devoted to coconut and cashew production, something the Jesuits encouraged: Tended, watered and fertilized, an acre (0.4 ha) of coconut palms will produce 7,000 nuts a year against 1,000 in the wild. The juice of green (unripe) coconuts is a refreshing drink. Ripe nuts have their fibers twisted into ropes, fishing nets, and rigging, or woven into coir matting. Shells become fuel or eating-bowls. Coconut milk and the kernel are used in cooking; dried and pressed, they produce valuable coconut oil. The timber is used for building, its fronds for thatched roofs, fish traps, mats, and baskets. Sap is tapped to make jaggery (raw sugar) or to distill into the alcoholic drink *feni,* which can also be made from the bitter cashew fruits. ■

More places to visit in Goa

AGUADA FORT

Goa's strongest fort, built in 1612, defends Aguada Bay and the mouth of the Mandovi River. Built using the latest Italian engineering theories of low, broad walls, wide moats, and cylindrical turrets, it surrounded Sinquerim

Southern India's fresh, fragrant spices are on sale at village markets, the range tailored to local cuisine.

and Candolim villages and had 79 cannons. Reach it through Betin, Verim, or Nerul fishing villages. The fort archway leads to the church, lighthouse, and citadel which has views across the Mandovi to Cabo promontory and the governor of Goa's mansion.

⊠ North of Panaji

CHAPORA FORT

The fort was a refuge for locals when Shivaji's son Shambhaji swept down here in 1739. The Portuguese treaty won them back this district, Bardez, in exchange for the Marathas having

Bassein (see p. 171). Hike up the hill to see the laterite battlements and bastions (1617) and to enjoy views down over Chapora estuary, past mango and cashew orchards.

⊠ North of Panaji

COLVA, BENAULIM, & CHINCHINIM VILLAGES

These three Salcete district villages, are all situated west of Margao. Colva has a high baroque church, **Our Lady of Mercy** (1630, rebuilt 18th century), and nice old houses. Nearby Benaulim has the baroque **Church of St. John the Baptist** and more charming houses such as **Vincent Correia Fonsecos** (now apartments). Finally, twisting lanes lead through paddy fields and cashew orchards to Chinchinim. In the pretty square, Dr. Alvaro Loyola Furtado's **mansion** stands next to the peppermint green church.

⊠ West of Margao

DIVA ISLAND

This is part of the northern Tiswadi district, but it is easily reached by ferry from near Old Goa. From 1510 on, this was Albuquerque's base, so many of Diva's 8,000 inhabitants are descended from Goa's first Christians. There are beautiful houses near the crossroads, such as that of leading Goan writer Mario Cabral e Sas. You can visit the hilltop church of **Nossa Senhora da Piedade** (1700–1724).

⊠ South of Panaji

MAPUSA MARKET

Every Friday the main square of Mapusa is a hive of activity. Locals buy their fruit, fish, and household goods such as tiffin cans (lunch boxes); visitors look for Goan terra-cotta pottery, and crafts from other states. Stores sell cashews and Mumbai-made accessories.

⊠ North of Panaji

RACHOL SEMINARY

All of Goa's 500 churches need priests, and Rachol Seminary is one of four seminaries devoted to training them. Founded in 1574, the fortlike building has a chapel with an ornately gilded altar and impressive relics, pulpit, and murals. The small **Museum of**

Christian Art, which opened in 1994, has exquisite pieces, including a gilded St. Ursula figure, processional flags, and the Loutolim priest's palanquin.

✉ 4 miles (7 km) east of Margao

SEA & RIVER CRUISES

Locals often run informal sunset boat rides up Goa's many rivers, where you can spot birds such as sandplovers, terns, ospreys, and sea eagles. Trips also go out on the sea to look for schools of humpbacked dolphins.

✉ South of Panaji

SPICE PLANTATIONS

Goa is less famous for its spices than Kerala. However, there are two fascinating spice gardens at Khandepar near Ponda, both well run for visitors: **Savoi Verem Spice Garden** and **Garden of Eden.** See tiny chilis; nutmeg fruits that must be pried open for the lacelike mace surrounding the nut; fragrant cinnamon bark; cloves drying in the sun; vines of black pepper (once known as black gold); and much more.

✉ East of Panaji

TAMBDI SURLA TEMPLE

A one-day trip inland from Panaji takes you to Goa's best building: a beautiful and evocative temple hidden in a clearing in the thick forested hills. Built of basalt stone, the decoration is crisp and deep, the roofs powerfully primitive. This is a rare survivor from the Kadamba empire, which ruled Goa in the 11th and 12th centuries, ran the west coast's major port, and was India's finest maritime power. Turn left at Molem crossroads, then right to Surla. Then take the next right turn; follow this road right to the end, and walk a short distance through the trees.

✉ East of Ponda

MORE NORTHERN GOA TEMPLES

Some of the best temples in northern Goa include **Mauli Temple** at Sarmalem, near Pernem, with graffito decoration and **Sri Bhagavati Temple** at Parcem. Eastward into Bicholim district, **Sri Saptakoteshwar Temple** at Naroa had a refugee deity brought here from Diva Island by Shivaji in 1668.

✉ North of Panaji

MORE SOUTHERN GOA TEMPLES

In southern Goa, near Ponda, you can find two temples in lush valleys near Bandora. **Sri Nagesh Temple** was founded here and has friezes of scenes from the great Hindu epics. At nearby Queula, **Sri Shantadurga Temple** (1738) was partly funded by Shivaji's grandson Shambhaji (see Chapora Fort,

Fruit sellers provide on-the-spot drinks, often either coconut milk or, as here, watermelon juice.

p. 202). At 1 p.m., you can witness the main *puja* of the day, with men standing on the right and women on the left beneath a gilded ceiling. Mirrors outside spotlight the deity for the benefit of the overflow. Down in the south of Salcete district, there are two hilltop temples, founded in the fifth century or earlier, with splendid views. **Sri Chandranath** has its *lingum* carved out of the hill, while **Sri Chandreshwar Bhutnath Temple,** dedicated to Shiva as Lord of the Moon, has a similarly carved Nandi bull.

✉ South of Panaji ■

The Konkan Railway

While other countries abandon their trains, India wisely promotes this low-pollution form of transportation and even builds entirely new lines. The Konkan Railway is the country's most recent triumph, an engineering feat that runs 523 miles (999 km) through three states—Maharashtra, Goa, and Karnataka—from Mumbai (Bombay) down the coast to Mangalore. There it links up to an older railroad line to Kochi (Cochin).

Initiated in 1984, begun in 1990, and opened in 1997, Konkan was the largest railroad project of the 20th century. Billed as "A Dream Come True," it provides a north–south transportation infrastructure that will boost the economy and increase employment of a poor area where the monsoon regularly destroys roads and makes port connections by inland waterways and sea unnavigable.

Along the route, trains cross 143 major bridges, of which the longest is a mile (1.6 km), and 1,670 minor ones. They pass through 75 tunnels, the longest one more than 4 miles (6 km). They cross India's highest viaduct, 211 feet (64 m) high, roll over 85,630 tons (87,000 tonnes) of rails and 1.2 million railroad ties, and stop at up to 53 stations.

The railway has changed the lives of coastal people. They are less isolated; traveling distances and times have been reduced—a train journey from Goa to Mumbai is cut from 20 to 10 hours—and the fare is cheaper.

But ecologists and environmentalists, albeit pleased at the prospect of less pollution from trucks, are anxious. They fear the area's rich mineral resources—iron ore, bauxite, chromite, manganese, and silica sand—and its dense forests will be ravaged. Iron ore is already a major Goa industry. Maharashtra has the last tract of India's untouched coastal forest. They also worry about increased population, urbanization, and industrialization, and the consequent pollution of the coast's fragile ecosystem.

Thermal plants, an oil refinery, and copper-smelting complexes are already planned, and train passengers are expected to reach 21 million each year by 2014.

For the visitor, the Konkan Railway opens up travel along the coast south of Mumbai. The grueling drive out of Mumbai can be avoided by taking a train from Victoria Terminus. Roha makes a good stop for visiting Janjira, and Chiplun for staying in a quaint hotel while exploring the Vashishti River and valley. Farther south, Sawantwadi is the station for seeing the forts at Malvan and Vijayadurg. In Goa, there are stations at Pernem, Old Goa, Margao, and Canacona. The scenic route continues down coastal Karnataka with stops that include Karwar, Coondapur, and Mangalore (see p. 206). Here the Konkan Railway links into the older Southern Railway, built to serve British trading needs, and continues down to Kochi, stopping at such towns as Kozhikode (Calicut) and Thrissur (Trichur).

The current schedule enables you to hop on a train in Mumbai at 4:40 p.m., enjoy a good night's sleep, meals on board, a day's window sightseeing, and arrive at Kochi at 9 p.m the next day. This is a fast train: You do not stop at every station. ∎

Trains chug slowly through Goa along the new Konkan Railway line (right), stopping at stations with smart and useful bilingual signs, as at Chandor (above). The new line crosses many rivers, including the wide Zuari near Cortalim, where fishing families continue to mend their nets (opposite above).

Coastal Karnataka
⚇ Map p. 191

Coastal villages celebrate their temple deities with gusto.

Coastal Karnataka

THE COASTAL STRIP OF GOA'S NEIGHBORING STATE Karnataka is called Kanara. Its landscapes are among the most scenic in India. Laterite cliffs alternate with almost empty beaches and mangrove-lined river estuaries. Tourists are rare; facilities are simple.

Gokarn Tourist Office
www.karnataka.gov.in

Jog Falls
www.karnataka.gov.in
🕐 Avoid monsoon season (Nov.–Jan.)

Mekkekattu Tourist Office
www.karnataka.gov.in

Mangalore Tourist Office
www.karnataka.gov.in
✉ Hotel Indraprestha, Lighthouse Hill Rd.

If you are traveling from Goa down the coast to Mangalore, you pass through **Gokarn** first—an ancient pilgrimage center focused on its **Sri Mahabaleshwar** and **Sri Mahaganpati** temples. Pilgrims shave their heads, take a holy dip in the sea, and then visit both temples to perform their *puja* (worship) and *darshan* (ritual viewing of the deity); the splendid *rath* (temple chariot) is still used for Shivratri, Shiva's festival *(Feb.)*.

A string of perfect beaches follows, some the home of Goa's long-stay beachbums. On down the coast, a detour inland from Bhatkal leads to **Jog Falls,** although the drive there from Kumta is more spectacular. The falls are India's highest and set amid breathtaking hill scenery; hikers can follow the track down to the water, but should take a guide to avoid getting lost.

At Barkur, turn inland to **Mekkekattu** for a fantastic sight: about 170 new, bright red *bhuta* (spirit) images in the Nandikeshvara Temple complex (see also Mysore's Folklore Museum, p. 231).

Farther down the coast you come to **Udupi** (Udipi), famous through India as the birthplace of delicious *masala dosas,* the thin rice pancakes stuffed with vegetables and first made in the town's *brahman* hotels. Having sampled one or two in a café at the Hotel Sharada International or Kediyoor, go to the square to join pilgrims visiting the amazing wooden Krishna temple, with its copper-clad sloping roofs, founded by the Hindu saint Madhva (1238–1317). Look for the colorful temple chariot processions in winter.

Finally, you reach cosmopolitan **Mangalore,** a great port since the sixth century, later owned by the Vijayanagas, Portuguese, Tipu Sultan, and the British. From here, pepper, ginger, and other spices were traded with the Middle East. Today, its exports are coffee, cocoa, cashew nuts, and granite. Sadly, there are scant remains of its past— the **Manjunatha Temple** (tenth century) with its fine bronzes, and **St. Aloysius College Chapel** (1885), with its Italian frescoes and murals, are probably the best. ∎

Kochi (Cochin) & Ernakulum

SPREAD OUT OVER SEVERAL ISLANDS WHERE VEMBANAD
Lake meets the Arabian Sea, Kochi's main center is peaceful, historic
Fort Cochin and Mattancherry; its twin city, dynamic, expanding
Ernakulum, lies across the water to the east.

St. Thomas the Apostle is believed
to have come to the isthmus of
Kochi in about A.D. 50 and created a
Christian community called the
Moplars. Jewish people came, too,
then Syrian Christians, Chinese,
and Persian travelers, and, in 1502,
Vasco da Gama. He established a
Portuguese factory to process spices
for export. The following year,
Albuquerque arrived with friars to
begin the fort and church.

The English set up their spice
factory in 1635 only to lose it in
1663 to the Dutch, who converted
the Catholic church to a Protestant
chapel and the cathedral into a
warehouse. When the Netherlands
fell to the French in 1795, the
British were quick to grab Kochi
and its lucrative and strategic port.

Gentle trading continues. You
can still see spice go-downs (warehouses) in the Mattancherry area of
Kochi, but its character is preserved
thanks to the growth of Ernakulum
on the mainland. Little fishing
boats still bring their catch to the
harbor at sunset, though Kochi's
real wealth is its commercial port,
which handles much of the state's
phenomenal production of rubber,
coconuts, tapioca, bananas, ginger,
coir (coconut fiber), and cashews.

Ernakulum is a fast-growing,
affluent city where flashy jewelry,
silk, and other luxury boutiques
thrive thanks to the wealth generated by spice-growers, rubber barons,
and the many Keralites who work
hard stints for high wages in the
Middle East. ∎

**Kochi &
Ernakulum**
Kerala
🅰 191 C2

India Tourist Office
✉ Willingdon Island,
near the Taj
Malabar Hotel
☎ 0484-668352

**Kerala Tourist
Office**
www.keralatourism.org
✉ Shanmugham Rd.,
Ernakulum (outpost
at main boat jetty)
☎ 0484-353234

Kathakali shows
See p. 380 for information
on shows.

**For the Kathakali
dancer, applying
make-up is part of
the religious
performance.**

Kathakali dance

K erala's distinctive culture has
many traditions in dance,
drama, sports, and religious ritual.
One of the few that is easy to see
is Kathakali, a highly sophisticated
and dramatic dance-drama whose
name means "story-play." Derived
from a form of yoga, the ritual of
the performance begins with the
application of elaborate make-up
and costumes, whose colors are
symbolic. The dance itself is a styl-
ized religious pantomime recounting stories from the great epics and
can last a whole night. For once in
India, the shortened tourist shows
are of a high quality, are clearly
explained, and give a good idea of
the full-length performance. ∎

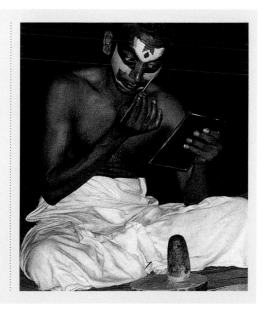

Pulleys and weights lower and raise the teak frames of these huge Chinese fishing nets.

A walk around Kochi (Cochin)

The best days for this walk are Sunday through Thursday, as the Dutch Palace is closed on Fridays and the Pardesi Synagogue is closed on both Fridays and Saturdays. Reach Kochi by ferry from Ernakulum and Willingdon Island, rather than by car; or negotiate for a private boat. At Kochi, if walking is too tiring, hire a rickshaw or rent a bicycle.

The walk begins at **Mattancherry Jetty ❶**, where the shoreline has beautiful old tiled buildings with pastel-colored walls, many still used as go-downs (warehouses). Go to the main road and into the Mattancherry for **Dutch Palace ❷** (1557), in fact built by the Portuguese for the Kochi Raja, Veera Keralavaram *(R.1537–1561)*, to help win a better trading deal; the Dutch merely renovated it in 1663. Inside, there are court dresses, paintings, and palanquins in the Coronation Room and India's most spectacular 16th- to 18th-century frescoes in the other rooms. Upstairs, a rich palette coats the walls with illustrations from the *Ramayana;* downstairs, the later paintings show Shiva and Mohini, and Krishna holding Mount Govardan and playing with the *gopies* (milkmaids).

Turn right on leaving the palace for a little walk through an area that is called Jew Town, past stores selling packaged spices and traders working in their go-downs. Turn right at the end, by the **Indian Pepper & Spice Trade Building,** and peek inside. You will find Synagogue Lane, and at the end is the **Pardesi Synagogue ❸** *(Sun.–Thurs. 10 a.m.–noon & 2–5 p.m.; timings can vary);* enjoy the beauty and calm of its interior. Founded in 1568, then destroyed by the Portuguese, the synagogue was rebuilt in 1664 under Dutch approval and given its prized floor of Cantonese willow-pattern tiles in the mid-18th century by Ezekial Rahabi, who also gave the clock tower. As a result of emigration to Israel, the local Jewish community is so reduced that services are not always possible. The rabbi depends upon

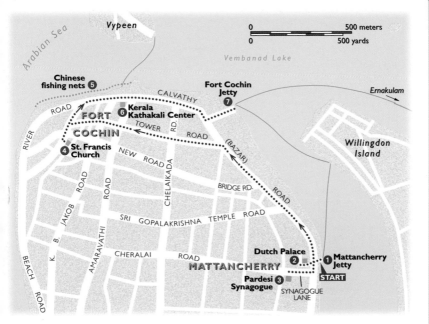

Jewish visitors to make up the required numbers, but he is often there to show them special copper plates. These record the grant of privileges to White Jews (see p. 60), made by King Ravi Varman (962–1020) to the Jewish merchant Joseph Rabban.

To walk to Fort Cochin, go back through Jew Town and along Calvathy (Bazaar) Road; then turn left on Tower Road to pass some old houses and lush walled gardens. You emerge in a parody of an English village: a lawn for Sunday cricket, surrounded by British coir merchants' houses and **St. Francis Church** ❹ (1546). The Portuguese Franciscan friars built the plain, massive structure to replace the earlier wooden one that was probably India's first European church. Inside, the memorial on the far right is to Vasco da Gama (viceroy 1524), who died here on Christmas Day 1524; his body was later moved to Lisbon. There are also fine tombstones of Portuguese, Dutch, and British traders. On Sundays, the congregation overflows and the church is cooled by *punkas,* the manual air-conditioning system.

Turn right out of the church and go down the road past some very handsome colonial traders' houses to the tip of Fort Cochin, finding a handful more on the right, shaded by

> 🅜 See area map page 191
> ▶ Dutch Palace, Mattancherry
> 🔁 2 miles (3 km)
> 🕐 2–3 hours
> ▶ Fort Cochin Jetty
>
> **NOT TO BE MISSED**
> - Dutch Palace, Mattancherry
> - Synagogue, Mattancherry
> - St. Francis Church, Fort Cochin
> - Chinese fishing nets, Fort Cochin

giant rain trees. At the water's edge, the cantilevered **Chinese fishing nets** ❺ were introduced to Kerala by traders from the court of Kublai Khan. Kerala's distinct temple architecture, conical fishermen's hats, paper, and porcelain also evolved thanks to Chinese trading. A complicated system of pulleys and weights lowers and raises each of these huge teak frames.

You are now near the **Kerala Kathakali Center** ❻ for Kathakali performances (see p. 207). Farther on, off Calvathy Road, is **Fort Cochin Jetty** ❼, where you can find boats back to Willingdon Island and Ernakulum, or sunset boat rides in the harbor. ■

The backwaters

Moving by boat through the Kerala backwaters, known locally as Kuttanadu, allows you to glimpse an enclosed world where bountiful nature and simple village life are in harmony.

THE GREATEST PLEASURE IN KERALA IS TO TAKE A BOAT slowly through the shimmering backwaters. You can watch kingfishers dive, boats deliver their goods, children catch water buses to school, boys splash in the water, and women prepare spicy Kerala fish dishes in the shade of towering coconut palms.

Kerala's coastal region is more water than land in places. There are 44 rivers that, with innumerable tributaries, meander their way to the Arabian Sea. Rivers, estuaries, deltas, and man-made canals interlink to create a vast, ancient, and labyrinthine water transportation system still used to carry spices, rubber and rice. The longest canal stretches 228 miles (367 km) from the capital, Thiruvananthapuram (see pp. 212–13), up to Tirur.

BACKWATER CULTURE

The bigger backwaters lie between Kochi (Cochin) and Kollam (Quillon), where **Vembanad Lake** spreads over 77 square miles (200 sq km). Known as Kuttanadu, this area is where life is spent beside, on, and often in the water, on narrow slivers of land. Here, in the dense tropical vegetation, families live in brightly painted houses that appear to float on the water. Tiny grocery stores and tailors

somehow squeeze on, too, as do tightly planted orchards of jackfruit trees, coconut palms, and mango trees, and each homestead's chickens, ducks, and, of course, cows. Everything from the morning newspaper to the sari chest is transported by boat.

Locals may be skimming through the canals using a thick paddle at a furious speed. Or they may punt their narrow dugout boats along with a tall pole, which they plunge into the water, push hard, and then slip out just before it disappears. On bigger boats, carrying coir, *copra* (dried coconut flesh), and piles of coconuts or cashew nuts, locals have small palmyra palm leaf huts as their onboard homes. Lazy boatmen tag on to motor ferries; others put up sails; still others carve the prow.

Coir and fishing are the main industries here; you may see fishermen diving for freshwater mussels or simply dangling a rod and line. Farmers must harvest any paddy growing in the boggy fields before the monsoon, when the whole area is flooded—not surprisingly, since the water level of the canals is often higher than the fields on either side. But when the monsoon ends in August, Keralites celebrate the Onam festival, believing it to mark the return of the benign, mythical King Mahabali from his exile in the underworld. Great boat pageants and races are held, which used to be between rival princes. Today, the best are the snake boat races held near Alappuzha (Alleppey). Having slicked down their great *chandan vallam* (racing boats) with special oil to make them glide faster, a hundred oarsmen each hurtle through the water to great roars from the crowds. For the benefit of visitors, this and the Thrissur Puram (see p. 220) are now repeated in mid-January each year.

Right:
For the boat races, crews of up to a hundred power each narrow snake boat with its lavishly decorated high prow.

ENVIRONMENTAL ISSUES

The big threat to Kuttanadu life—apart from population growth and land reclamation—is African moss. This waterweed grows rampantly and threatens to throttle the waterways entirely. The velvety leaf with its thick cushion of intertwining fibrous roots was introduced about 30 years ago, but it has already had a drastic effect on the ecosystem. The water cannot now be used for drinking or washing. Fish and aquatic life have reduced in numbers because no sunlight reaches them. Boats cannot pass through the blocked rivulets and canals.

HOW TO VISIT THE BACKWATERS

There are various ways of seeing the backwaters. One is to rent a converted country rice boat called a *kettuvallam*, the type that used to transport goods down to Kochi. It comes complete with crew, so you can opt out of "real life" to spend a few days being pampered in this watery paradise.

If this is too exotic, rent a private boat and driver for the day from Alappuzha or Kottayam (the waterscape from Kotch is dull for the first two hours); you can be dropped off at one of two upscale waterside hotels at Kumarakom, overlooking Vembanad Lake. Or simply join locals on a public ferry from one town to another. ∎

Thiruvananthapuram (Trivandrum)

A corner of Shri Padmanabhaswamy Temple exemplifies Kerala's superb woodcarving.

Thiruvananthapuram, Kerala
🗺 191 C1

India Tourist Office
✉ Airport Counter
☎ 0471-502298

State Tourist Office
www.kerala.gov
www.keralatourism.org
✉ Park View
☎ 0471-321132

Puttan Malika Palace
✉ Chalai Bazaar Rd.

Kuthiramalika Palace Museum
🕐 Closed Mon.
💲 $

KERALA'S SEASIDE CAPITAL RAMBLES OVER SEVEN HILLS. IN contrast to other state capitals, it is laid back and easy, with little metropolitan buzz. Leafy parks and traditional red-tiled houses line the wide, quiet streets.

When India won freedom in 1947, the princely states of Travancore and Cochin and British-administered Malabar were amalgamated to form Kerala, whose official language is Malayalam. Since then, the state has enjoyed a radical reputation. In 1957 it was the first in the world to democratically elect a Communist government. Reforms led to a fairer distribution of wealth, much improved education and health care, but little industrial development. Today, its birthrate is India's lowest, its health is among the best, and its literacy rate is an impressive 93 percent, the highest in India.

Thiruvananthapuram, called Trivandrum when it was the capital of Travancore state, took its new name to honor the god Vishnu. It means "holy city of Anantha," and Anantha is the coiled snake on which Vishnu rests in the cosmic ocean. It is in this form, called Padmanabha, that the royal family of Travancore worshiped their principal deity. When Raja Matanda Varma (*R.1729–1758*) moved the capital here in 1750, he dedicated the whole state of Travancore to her and built the temple his descendants still control, the **Shri Padmanabhaswamy Temple,** which stands in the historic heart of the city. Although non-Hindus cannot go inside, you'll find the surrounding area of interest. Walk around the temple, and at the front see the faithful bathing in the tank or buying souvenirs and *puja*

offerings. Here, too, you may see students practicing the special Kerala martial arts exercise, Kalarippayat, in the early morning.

The Travancore rajas moved into nearby **Puttan Malika Palace** when they left Padmanabhapuram (see below). They still live here, visiting their great temple early each morning, but have opened some rooms to the public. The polished floors, delicately carved wooden screens, and royal crystal are superb treasures; see especially the fine murals and columns carved as rampant horses.

Beyond the old quarter, at the far end of M. G. Road, lie the **Public Gardens,** 64 acres (26 ha) of lawns and trees and the home to the **Arts & Crafts (Napier) Museum** (1874–1880). Inside R. F. Chisholm's brightly colored brick building with stained-glass windows, there are fine Chola bronzes and Kerala woodcarvings, masks and puppets, gold jewelry, musical instruments, and various royal memorabilia. The **Shri Chitra Art Gallery** is also in the gardens, as well as the **Natural History Museum** (*Closed Wed. a.m. & Fri.–Mon.*), whose models of the Kerala *taravad* (manor house) and traditional *nalekettu* (four-sided courtyard) house show you what to look for while driving through the countryside.

PADMANABHAPURAM PALACE

Although Padmanabhapuram

Visitors to Kerala can watch a demonstration of Kalariphayat, rigorous martial arts training.

Palace is in Tamil Nadu state, it makes sense to visit the Travancore rulers' former capital from Thiruvananthapuram. The splendid palace, one of southern India's finest royal buildings, dates from 1550, although Raja Matanda Varma (1729–1758) remodeled much of it. The teak rooms with their deep, overhanging roofs are arranged around four courtyards and enriched with elaborate carving, rosewood furniture displaying a strong Chinese trading influence, and spectacular murals, superior even to those in Mattancherry's Dutch Palace (see p. 208). It may still be closed to the public, for preservation purposes.

During your tour with the obligatory and informative guide, note the delicate perforated screens, foliated brackets, and *dhatura*-flower pendants. The many rooms include a carved open hall, where the king addressed his people. The upstairs council chamber has an ingenious air-conditioning system using herbs soaked in water, broad-seated chairs for ministers to sit on cross-legged, and a floor gleaming with polish achieved by mixing burned coconut, sticky sugarcane extract, egg white, lime, and sand. The tower's top room is reserved for the god, complete with bed and murals. There is also the **Ekandamandapam** (Lonely Place), the oldest section reserved for rituals for the goddess Durga. It has a stone-columned dance hall and includes the bedroom of the raja, whose bed was made from medicinal woods. The whole ensemble brings to life the very special Travancore royal house, where succession was matriarchal through the eldest sister's eldest son; the ruler did not marry, to prevent his love being diverted from his state to his children. ■

Arts & Crafts (formerly Napier) Museum
🕐 Closed Mon.
💲 $

Shri Chitra Art Gallery
🕐 Closed Mon.
💲 $

Natural History Museum
🕐 Closed Mon.
💲 $

Festivals
Arat festivals, March–April, Oct.–Nov.: activities and street processions during two ten-day festivals

Visitor tips
Entry to most of Kerala's temples is barred to non-Hindus.

Padmanabha-puram Palace
🗺 191 C1
✉ 34 miles (55 km) SE of Thiruvananth-apuram
🕐 Closed Mon. Best to avoid weekends
💲 $

India's spice box

Spices are essential to every Indian meal, even if the *masala* (blend) varies from region to region. Spices give each dish its distinctive flavor and character. The meat, fish, or vegetables are added after the spices have cooked a little.

From early times, Greeks, Romans, Arabs, and Chinese have paid highly for powerful spices to perfume themselves, improve room odors, help preserve food, act as medicines, and disguise the pungent smells of rancid meat. Southern India was the chief source, and prices could compare with gold.

In the 15th century the urge to break the Arab and Venetian stranglehold on the spice trade led to Christopher Columbus's arrival in America, while looking for a westerly route to India, and Vasco da Gama's discovery of the sea route around Africa. From then on, the Portuguese, Dutch, French, and British began to trade directly with India.

Pepper, once known as black gold, is the king of spices, and Kerala produces 95 percent of India's pepper crop. All over Kerala you can see the pepper vines growing up trees shading other crops, and peppercorns drying in the sun. Most pepper is grown alongside cashew, coffee, coconut, areca nut, tapioca, banana, and rice crops on homesteads lying between the high mountains and the coast.

In fact, most of India's spices are grown in the south of the country on small plantations. More than 60 percent of India's cardamom is grown on the high Kerala hills, alongside tea, coffee, and rubber, and in mountain forests.

Fresh red chilis are sorted for quality and size. They will be sold whole or ground in markets and factories.

The seeds sprout from the base of a big, broad-leafed bush and are picked by women who dry them and keep a few for use as aphrodisiacs. Ginger is part of the same plant family, and about 70 percent of the world's requirement is grown here; it is used in food and as a digestive medicine. *Haldi* (turmeric) is another rhizome, mostly grown in neighboring Andhra Pradesh. As well as being used in cooking, it is used in medicine as an antiseptic and rubbed onto babies' and women's skin to soften and lighten it. Thanks to such attractive properties, the domestic market consumes 98 percent of the 350,000 tons (371,350 tonnes) that are produced in India every year.

Buying these and other spices in the local markets is a lot of fun. Did you know that nutmeg is a fruit, from which we get mace? The kernel of the fruit is the nutmeg that we use in cooking; the strands of mace are wrapped around it. Cinnamon is the inner bark of the lateral shoots of pruned cinnamon trees, and it is sold in tightly curled quills. Chilis come in all sizes: The big ones are eaten as vegetables or are crushed to make mild paprika; the small ones have the "fire" in them.

Cashew nuts, most often ground and used in the gentle sauces of Mughal dishes, grow in a most interesting way. Just one pair of nuts grows outside each large, yellow, bitter fruit. When harvested, they must then be laboriously shelled and skinned by hand, then sorted according to size. This is the reason for their high cost. ■

Above: Peppercorns, here kept in a special wooden box, were once so valuable that they were used by traders as currency.

It is fascinating to visit the wholesale spice market in Jew Town, Kochi (above), where brisk business continues as it has for hundreds of years. Sackfuls of precious and fragrant seeds, pods, and bark are carted off to be sold again before they reach the marketplace (right), where grateful cooks buy them.

India's coastline is dotted with traditional fishing villages; here, Keralites haul their boat up onto the beach.

Kerala's beaches & Lakshadweep Islands

IF IT IS TIME TO CHILL OUT, YOU HAVE SEVERAL CHOICES. Very little of the long, sandy shoreline of the Malabar coast, stretching 342 miles (550 km) from Goa down to Kanya Kumari, is developed by Western standards. Unlike Goa (see pp. 190–203), Kerala has few beachside hotels or cafés, and locals may well be upset by scanty swimsuits. For a complete escape, head for Bangaram Island.

Kovalam, Kerala

 191 C1

Varkala

 191 C2

✉ 33 miles (53 km) N of Thiruvananthapuram, 12 miles (19 km) S of Kollam

Danardhana Swamy Temple

✉ Varkala

Lakshadweep Islands

www.lakshadweeptourism. nic.in

191 A2 & A3

The empty beaches punctuated with cliffs or fishing villages make wonderful places for refreshing and peaceful walks and a quiet swim. The two areas where beach life has developed are Kovalam and, to a lesser degree, Varkala; both are reached from Thiruvananthapuram.

To seek out the best of Kovalam, go to quiet **Samudra Beach,** watch the fishing boats on **Hawah Beach,** discover restaurants on **Lighthouse Beach** (with a nice afternoon walk down to Vizhinjam village), and find peace on **Pozhikkara Beach.**

Varkala is quite different from Kovalam, though it may well change. This pilgrimage center draws

Hindus to the **Danardhana Swamy Temple** overlooking the sea, where they pay respect to their ancestors; after 5 p.m. non-Hindus may enter. A lane next to it leads down to the beach, which so far retains its charm. You can enjoy its white sands and promontory walks. There are also natural springs, the local town's market, and, if you like, you can take an elephant ride into the nearby forest.

LAKSHADWEEP ISLANDS

Coming here is still a total escape because foreign tourism is tightly controlled. To conserve the islands' culture, only Bangaram Island is open to non-Indians. Visitor

Ayurvedic medicine

The ancient medicinal philosophy called *ayurved* has been practiced in India for at least 5,000 years, especially in Kerala. Unlike Western medicine, which seeks to discover and then eliminate what is making you sick, Ayurved considers that disease reveals a body that is totally out of balance. Thus the imbalance, rather than the disease, is treated. First, you must accept that the body is controlled by three forces: *pitta* (the sun's force over digestion and metabolism); *kapha* (the moon's cooling force over the body's organs); and *vata* (the wind's effect on movement and the nervous system). Diagnosis is by considering physical complaints, emotions, family background, and daily habits. Treatment may involve herbal preparations and yoga exercises. Ayurvedic doctors and pharmacies throughout India often have training in both Western and Ayurvedic systems, and can help tackle long-term problems such as migraines and asthma. To find out more, visit one of the many Ayurvedic centers, such as C.V.N. Kalari Sangam by Shri Padmanabhaswamy Temple in Thiruvananthapuram. ∎

Getting to the Lakshadweeps
If you want to visit the Lakshadweep Islands, you will have to fly from Kochi, or alternatively book a cruise through a travel agent.

numbers are limited, prices are high, and there is nothing much to do except relax. A snorkel and mask are essentials.

As you fly in, look down on the 36 coral islands lying in the azure Arabian Sea between 137 miles (220 km) and 273 miles (439 km) off the Kerala coast. They are India's smallest Union Territory: Just 52,000 people live here on the ten habitable islands, with Kavaratti the capital and Agatti the airport. Most inhabitants are Sunni Muslims, speak Malayalam, and live by fishing and coconut cultivation. Other crops here include jackfruit, banana, and wild almond.

Bangaram Island, with a resident population of 61, is reached by a two-hour boat ride from Agatti, 5 miles (8 km) away: Watch the boatman carefully avoiding the coral in the shallow sea. This beautiful teardrop-shaped island is surrounded by white sands and guaranteed warm calm water—about 79° F (26° C), perfect for spending hours watching the exotic underwater world. ∎

The idyllic Lakshadweep Islands may take some effort and expense to reach, but peace and natural beauty are guaranteed after arrival there.

More places to visit in Kerala

As Kerala is so long and thin, the suggestions below are arranged in two sections, each with a good central base.

KOZHIKODE & NORTHERN KERALA
Bekal
Here you will find northern Kerala's best pre-served coastal **fort:** Grand ramparts, walls, and bastions (17th century), were built by Shivappa Nayaka of Nagar and later taken by Haider Ali in 1763.

⛰ 191 B3 ✉ 49 miles (79 km) north of Kannur, 37 miles (60 km) south of Mangalore

Kannur (Cannanore)
This was the capital of the powerful Ali Rajas, Kerala's only Muslim royal dynasty. They used the massive triangular Fort St. Angelo, built by the Portuguese (1505) in their 1770s alliance with Tipu Sultan against the British.

⛰ 191 B3 ✉ 14 miles (23 km) north of Thalassery, 57 miles (92 km) north of Kozhikode

Kozhikode (Calicut)
Make this the base for exploring northern Kerala. Kozhikode is a thriving, modern town trading in spices, timber, coffee, and tea. It is the former capital of the Samutiri rulers, bet-ter known as the Zamorins. They had close ties with Arab Muslim traders, who equipped their army and were threatened by the Portuguese, then the English, French, and Danes. See the **Tali Temple** and mosques with distinctive multi-tiered tiled roofs: **Mithqalpalli** (16th century), **Jama Masjid,** and **Mucchandipalli** (both 15th century).

⛰ 191 B3

Taliparamba
Two of Kerala's finest temples are here, both founded in the ninth century but mostly rebuilt in the 16th and 17th centuries: **Rajarajeshvara Temple,** in town, and **Krushan Temple,** which stands in a pretty grove one mile (1.6 km) to the south and has beautiful friezes recounting the Krishna story.

⛰ 191 B3 ✉ 14 miles (23 km) north of Kannur

Thalassery (Tellicherry)
This attractive coastal town is where the British set up a factory in 1683. See their impressive **fort** (1708) and overgrown **cemetery,** the Mappila traders' traditional **warehouses** and **homes,** and the Kerala-style **Odothilpalli Mosque** (17th–18th century).

⛰ 191 B3 ✉ 34 miles (55 km) north of Kozhikode

AROUND KOCHI & ERNAKULUM
Alappuzha (Alleppey)
This pretty, affluent town, with enough bridges to make it an Indian Venice, owes its character to vigorous development by the Travancore rulers after they took it over in 1762. Merchants flocked here to use the new warehouses, and a shipbuilding industry blossomed, boosting trade with Bombay and Calcutta. Produce was, and still is, delivered here from the hills along the inland waterways, including quantities of coir for matting.

⛰ 191 C2 ✉ 35 miles (56 km) south of Kochi, 52 miles (84 km) north of Kollam

Angamali
Angamali has unusual 17th- and 18th-century Christian monuments: baroque **St. George's, St. Mary's,** with its nave murals showing the Last Judgment and Christ telling St. Thomas to go to India, and, at nearby Kanjoor village, another **St. Mary's,** whose murals curiously include the defeat of Tipu Sultan (see p. 226).

⛰ 191 C2 ✉ 20 miles (32 km) north of Ernakulum

Cheruthuruthi
This town is home to the **Kerala Kalamandalam,** the state's finest academy for classic Keralas Kathakali and other per-forming arts, such as Kutiyattam (an archaic kind of Kathakali). The academy was founded in 1927 by the Malayali poet Vallathol, and vis-itors are permitted to watch the fascinating training sessions and performances in the beautiful theater.

⛰ 191 C2 ✉ 18 miles (29 km) north of Thrissur ☎ 0492-622418

Guruvayur

At Kerala's most popular pilgrimage town, you can join pilgrims to enter the **Krishan Temple** (but not the sanctuary), then drive 2 miles (3 km) east to see the temple's elephants in the compound of the fine mansion at **Punnathoor Kotta.**

🅰 191 C2 ✉ 18 miles (29 km) north of Thrissur

Kayankulam

Kayankulam's **Krishnapuram Palace** is less ornate than Padmanabhapuram (see p. 212) but just as interesting. It was probably built by Ramayya Dalawa, who was governor of northern Travancore under Rama Varma (1758–1798); one room off the small interior courts has a beautiful mural of Vishnu riding on Garuda.

🅰 191 C2 ✉ 30 miles (48 km) south of Alappuzha 🕒 Closed Mon.

Kodungallur (Cranganore)

There's little to see, but the town is historically very important. It was from here that Arabs and Romans imported spices to Alexandria and Oman, and that early Jewish people, Christians, and Muslims arrived to make their first settlements in India. Christians claim St. Thomas arrived at Pallipuram, near here; Muslims claim that Malik bin Dinar, an Arab missionary, founded the Cheraman Mosque here in 630.

🅰 191 C2 ✉ 32 miles (51 km) north of Ernakulum

Kollam (Quilon)

A lively town between the sea and Ashtamudi Lake, the southern point of the backwaters, Kollam was already a port of call for seventh-century Chinese merchants. Traces of its Portuguese, Dutch, Travancore, and British administrators can be found around the town, attesting to Kerala's cosmopolitan history. **Ganapati Temple** stands opposite **Old Tobacco Godown,** while the baroque **cathedral** is a reminder that Kollam is probably the oldest Catholic diocese in Southern India, established in 1328. Also of interest is a **Syrian Church** (1519) with unusual 18th-century murals, the **Valiakada Arikade mosque,** and the **Travelers**

Kerala's ancient canals, their maintenance funded by local rulers, include one that stretches 228 miles (367 km) from the capital, Thiruvananthapuram, up to Tirur.

Bungalow, built as the British Residency.

🅰 191 C2 ✉ 53 miles (85 km) south of Alappuzha, 44 miles (71 km) north of Thiruvananthapuram

Kottayam

This affluent, charming town lies on the Minachil River, which connects with Vembanad Lake. Most of Kerala's hill produce arrives here before continuing to Kochi and Alappuzha, often by boat. You can happily stroll around for a few hours, catch water buses, watch life, and maybe visit the **Syrian Church** in Puthenangadi area. Kottayam is the headquarters of Kerala's Orthodox Syrian and Roman Catholic communities.

🅰 191 C2 ✉ 45 miles (72 km) south of Ernakulum

Munnar

A spectacular drive along a country road follows the ridge of the hills, with panoramic views of rolling tea gardens on either side. British tea, coffee, and cardamom planters created this mini-hill station at 5,000 feet (1,524 m), centered on the **High Range Club** and **Protestant Church** (1910), which appear unchanged since their foundation. While here, go to **Lockhart Gap** for breathtaking views over the Annamalai Hills; serious hikers can tackle **Anai Mudi,** southern India's highest peak at 8,838 feet (2,694 m). From here you can visit Periyar, or continue through the hills to Kodaikanal (see p. 281).

🔼 191 C2 ✉ 139 miles (224 km) east of Ernakulum

Palai

As this is the seat of a bishop of the Syrian Catholic church, the old **Cathedral of St. Thomas** (1002) is one of Kerala's grandest churches, with magnificent gilded altars.

✉ 10 miles (16 km) east of Ettumanur

Periyar National Park

After a beautiful drive up through the Cardamom Hills, you have 270 square miles (700 sq km) of hilltop deciduous woodland and a huge artificial lake to explore. Established in 1934, this is one of the best sanctuaries for watching wild elephants,

At the climax of the Puram and Elephants festivals, mahouts and their helpers dance on top of their caparisoned charges.

especially at either sunrise and sunset. The sanctuary also provides visitors with excellent forest walks and bird-watching for traveling nature lovers.

🔼 191 C2 ✉ 74 miles (119 km) east of Kottayam, 99 miles (159 km) west of Madurai in Tamil Nadu

Thiruvalla, Kaviyur, & Chengannur

Thiruvalla's **Vallabha Temple** is one of Kerala's largest temple complexes, with elaborate tiered gables, porches, and carvings. Also here is the contemporary British architect Laurie Baker's **St. John's Cathedral,** inspired by Kerala traditions. Kaviyur's **Mahadeva Temple** has some of Kerala's finest carved woodwork and, nearby, a Chera period **cave temple** (eighth to ninth century), with fully rounded figures including a proud chieftain. Chengannur's **Narashimha Temple** also has exceptionally beautiful woodwork.

🔼 191 C2 **Thiruvalla** ✉ 17 miles (27 km) south of Kottayam

Thrissur (Trichur)

Thrissur is famous for its magnificent Puram festival *(April–May),* when richly decorated elephants parade through the crowded streets, accompanied by music and fireworks. Their final destination is the huge **Vadakkunnatha Temple** (16th to 17th century) with its walled courtyards, tiered roofs, dancing hall, and several shrines. Thrissur was the Kochi rulers' second city, and the museum complex reflects its rich history. There are superb bronzes in the **Art Museum** and other interesting artifacts in the **Archaeological Museum** *(Closed Mon.)* and **State museums.**

🔼 191 C2 ✉ 43 miles (69 km) north of Ernakulum

Vaikam, Kaduthuruthi, & Ettumanur

These are three places worth visiting on the Ernakulum–Kottayam road. Vaikam is where Mahatma Gandhi's 1925 *satyagraha* movement (see p. 150) resulted in temple roads being opened to all in the then highly caste-ridden Kerala. At Kaduthuruthi you can visit two fine Syrian Christian churches: the baroque **St. Mary's** (rebuilt 1599), with its very elaborate gilded altar (18th century), and the **Forane Church of the Holy Ghost,** one mile (1.6 km) away. At Ettumanur (6 miles/10 km north of Kottayam), the roadside **Mahadava Temple** (1542) has vivid murals painted inside its traditional gateway.

🔼 191 C2 **Vaikam** ✉ 24 miles (39 km) south of Ernakulum ■

Beneath the huge skies of the Deccan Plateau great Hindu and Muslim kingdoms rose and fell, battled for power, and left their magnificent monuments strewn across the dramatic, still rural landscape.

The Deccan

Piles of brightly colored, finely ground spices in Mysore's Devaraja Market

The Deccan

TRAVELING THROUGH THE DECCAN, WHICH COMPRISES MOST OF KARNATAKA and Andhra Pradesh states, can be demanding, but the region's magnificent monuments and stunning landscapes make it one of the most rewarding areas of India to visit. You encounter a succession of utterly different, wondrous sights.

There are two focal points: Bangalore and Hyderabad, the capitals of Kannada-speaking Karnataka and Telegu-speaking Andhra Pradesh states. Bangalore, once an elegant British town now a dynamic state capital, is India's Silicon Valley. Hyderabad, thick with the remnants of its royal Muslim Qutb Shahi and Nizam rulers, is following Bangalore's lead and exploding into the global economy.

Outside these great cities lies a challenging, rural landscape. The great Godavari, Krishna, and Kaveri Rivers and their tributaries, which all empty into the Bay of Bengal, feed the rich soil of the Deccan Plateau, where agriculture accounts for 70 percent of both states' employment. On your travels you will see fields of rice, ground nuts, chilis, cotton, and sugarcane, plus Andhra Pradesh's tobacco and Karnataka's mulberry bushes for its silk industry. One village will be sleepy, the next in the midst of a festival; a single goatherd and his flock will block a road; an empty field will transform into a livestock fair where cattle have been daubed with pink polka dots.

In the west, you can visit British hill stations nestling in the lush Nilgiri Hills and view the protected forests and wildlife of three adjoining national parks. If you feel a lack of romance, you have the palaces of Mysore. To the north, forgotten empires have left some of India's finest temples, from the earliest efforts at Aihole, which imitated wooden structures, to the final glories of Vijayanagar.

North and eastward again, the rulers of the great Bahmani kingdom, Vijayanagar's rivals, built citadels at Gulbarga and Bidar. Then they broke up into rival sultanates, decking their cities with romantic, bulbous-domed mosques and tombs, while facing the inevitable onslaught of Mughal expansion from the north. Finally, there are rarely visited sites along Andhra Pradesh's beautiful 621 miles (999 km) of coast at Tirupati and around Vishakhapatnam port and the Godavari and Krishna Deltas.

Amid all this, heroes abound. You can follow the stories of Vikramaditya, the eighth-century ruler of the Chalukyas, and Krishnadeveraya, who later ruled the Vijayanaga kingdom. You can also see evidence of the enlightened 18th-century expansionism of Haider Ali and his son, Tipu Sultan, which resulted in their clashes with the British. ■

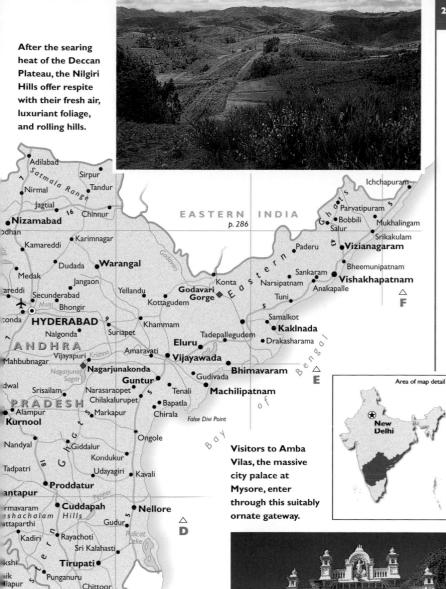

After the searing heat of the Deccan Plateau, the Nilgiri Hills offer respite with their fresh air, luxuriant foliage, and rolling hills.

EASTERN INDIA
p. 286

Adilabad
Sirpur
Satmala Range
Nirmal
Tandur
Jagtial
Chinnur
Nizamabad
odhan
Kamareddi
Karimnagar
reddi
Dudada
Warangal
Medak
Jangaon
Yellandu
Secunderabad
Bhongir
conda
HYDERABAD
Nalgonda
Suriapet
Khammam
ANDHRA
Vijayapuri
Krishna
Amaravati
Mahbubnagar
Nagarjuna Sagar
Nagarjunakonda
Guntur
dwal
Srisailam
Narasaraopet
Tenali
PRADESH
Chilakalurupet
Bapatla
Alampur
Markapur
Chirala
Kurnool
False Divi Point
Nandyal
Giddalur
Ongole
Tadpatri
Kondukur
antapur
Udayagiri
Kavali
Proddatur
Penner
rmavaram
Cuddapah
Nellore
eshachalam Hills
Gudur
ttaparthi
Kadiri
Rayachoti
Pulicat Lake
kshi
Sri Kalahasti
ik
Tirupati
lapur
Punganuru
olar
Chittoor

Godavari
Konta
Godavari Gorge
Kottagudem
Tadepallegudem
Eluru
Vijayawada
Gudivada
Bhimavaram
Machilipatnam

Ichchapuram
Parvatipuram
Bobbili
Mukhalingam
Salur
Srikakulam
Paderu
Vizianagaram
Sankaram
Bheemunipatnam
Narsipatnam
Vishakhapatnam
Anakapalle
Tuni
Samalkot
Kaklnada
Drakasharama

Eastern Ghats

Bay of Bengal

TAMIL NADU
p. 255

0 ——— 200 kilometers
0 ——— 100 miles

Area of map detail
New Delhi

Visitors to Amba Vilas, the massive city palace at Mysore, enter through this suitably ornate gateway.

Karnataka

Karnataka's dramatic landscape ranges from giant boulders, seemingly dropped by the gods onto barren hills, to the bountiful paddy fields and leafy coffee plantations of the undulating Kodagu area. This is the backdrop for stunning monuments that have been the silent witnesses to the heady adventures of great Hindu and Muslim dynasties whose struggles for power survive in local tales. Dynasties rose and fell from the 7th to the 18th centuries, landmark events were the defeat, in 1565, of the last great Hindu empire, Vijayanagar, and the death of the enlightened hero Tipu Sultan in 1799.

Karnataka's capital is the dynamic city of Bangalore, where you may hear just as much English spoken as the official state language, Kannada. As India's foremost center for IT, office buildings, luxurious hotels, and quality shops make a stark contrast with Mysore, just three hours' drive away. This slow-paced historical city is dominated by grand and fanciful palaces. Either city makes an ideal stop between visiting the national parks of Nagarhole, Bandipur and Mudumalai.

The walls of the great Mahanavami Platform at Vijayanagar are coated in vivacious friezes showing dancing girls, horse traders, and hunting scenes.

But less than 30 percent of the state's population lives in the cities. As you travel through countryside irrigated by the great river systems of the Cauvery and the Krishna, you cross the high Deccan Plateau that gives Karnataka its name: it is Kannada for "lofty land." ∎

Neon lights and
billboards on busy
Brigade Road
reflect no
evidence of
Bangalore's more
verdant past.

Bangalore

ONCE KNOWN FOR ITS FRESH AIR, TREES, AND PARKS, which brought relief to visitors from the hot upper plains, Bangalore, capital of Karnataka state, is now a thundering, commercial city whose climate is no longer so benign. But it is still one of India's cleanest cities.

Bangalore,
Karnataka
🅰 222 B2
India Tourist Office
✉ K.F.C. Building,
48 Church St.
☎ 080-5585417

State Tourist Office
www.karnatakatourism.org
✉ No. 49, 2nd Fl, West
Entrance,
Khanija Bhawan,
Race Course Rd.
☎ 080-223 52901
Toll free: 800-425 1414

Cubbon Park
✉ M.G. Rd.

The city was founded by Kempe Gowda, a lord of the Vijayanaga kingdom (see p. 236), who built a mud fort here in 1537. The Wodeyars of Mysore (see p. 230) took the city in 1687. Haider Ali (R.1761–1782) took Bangalore in 1758 and three years later usurped the Wodeyar throne. Keeping Mysore and nearby Srirangapatnam as his base, he made Bangalore a crossroads for east–west southern trading and for exporting cotton and other crops from this rich agricultural area. He and his son, Tipu Sultan (R.1782–1799), whose palace remains are well worth visiting, could thus raise huge taxes. These funded the famous Mysore army of 60,000 men, with its superb light cavalry, Telugu marksmen, and herds of huge, white Deccan cattle. This army was used

to win ports on the Kerala coast, aiming to crush the Peshwas of Pune (see p. 182) and the Nizams of Hyderabad (see pp. 248–49), and to establish trade with Arabia and Persia. Far from being the despot painted by the British, Tipu was imitating their mercantile and expansionist ideology, which is why Arthur Wellesley (later Duke of Wellington) needed to defeat him.

After Tipu's death (see p. 246) in 1799, Bangalore became a flourishing British garrison town and continued to be important up to independence. The British cantonment had everything a homesick servant of the empire could wish for: horse-racing, tennis courts, a pretty park, Victorian Gothic bungalows with herbaceous bordered gardens, the obligatory statue of the Queen-Empress

Victoria, and grand clubs for cards, croquet, snooker (a game similar to billiards), and lavish parties.

These British buildings and the city's two green spaces—**Cubbon Park** and the **Race Course**—give Bangalore its spaciousness and lingering elegance today. It may have highrises, new affluence, a population of almost eight million, and top-quality stores, but you can easily imagine colonial times, not long ago, when servants in white livery and gloves served cucumber sandwiches and chili-cheese toast to *memsahibs* wearing flower-printed dresses. Try driving through Cubbon Park, walking around the High Courts or one of the many churches, or visiting **Lalbagh Botanical Gardens.** Founded by Haider Ali in 1760 and further planted by Tipu, their 240 acres (97 ha) contain rare trees and other plants, British pavilions, and greenhouses. In February and August, the quintessentially British flower shows staged here have dazzling arrays of dahlias, chrysanthemums, and roses.

It is significant that the Karnataka government chose to site its huge neo-Dravadian-style

granite **Vidhana Soudha** (Secretariat and State Legislative) right in the British area, opposite the Law Courts. Winston Churchill, who always opposed India's desired independence, would doubtless have taken this as flattery. He came to live here in 1937 as a young soldier and wrote happy letters home describing his huge bungalow with its two acres (1 ha) of gardens, rose beds, and deep verandas wreathed in purple bougainvillea. He and two of his friends kept about 30 horses and devoted themselves to the serious purpose of life: polo. ■

This splendid Victorian pavilion in Lalbagh Botanical Gardens is the setting for Bangalore's set-piece flower shows.

Information technology

Bangalore is India's information technology (IT) capital and the world's third most important IT city. It is also India's software capital, with exports growing at 46 percent a year, comared to a national average of 30 percent. IT, together with science, has made Bangalore a more international city even than Mumbai (Bombay). Glass skyscrapers rising above the parks and brick buildings indicate a sensational new affluence. Formerly, Indian IT brains went to work for U.S. companies in California. Today,

the tables have turned: They have returned home and set up their own companies. Bangalore is the headquarters of TCS, Wipro and Infosys. Many multinationals, such as IBM and HP, find they now need to finance sleek new office buildings in Bangalore. Meanwhile, their Indian counterparts stock their offices with Indian-made, not American, equipment, proven to be comparable to the products of the best U.S. brands. Hyderabad, with an enlightened state government, is following Bangalore's lead. ■

Race Course
✉ Race Course Rd.
 080-560001

A drive around old colonial Bangalore

Hire a driver for a morning or afternoon to explore British life in Bangalore and to glimpse the town's past as southern India's elegant, relaxed garden city. It is best to go on Saturday or Sunday, when there is less traffic.

Start by going to the **High Courts** ① (Attara Kacheri), a classical, arcaded stone building, painted Pompeian red and originally built in 1868 as the public offices. A statue of Bangalore's commissioner from 1834 to 1861, Sir Mark Cubbon, stands in front. The jacaranda trees to the left add a cloud of contrasting mauve when they blossom in springtime.

Across a ceremonial road that is often the scene of farmers' union protests, the imposing polished granite **Vidhana Soudha** (1956) (see p. 227) stands as the symbol of the fulfillment of the Kannada-speaking peoples' long ambition—to unite in one state. K. Hanumanthaiah, chief minister when the building was completed, said this "people's palace" would "reflect the power and dignity of the people." Certainly, it is India's largest civic structure. Its design takes inspiration from Karnataka's temple architecture: See the projecting balconies, the curving eaves, and the temple-like, curving towers that are added to the huge wings.

Now ask your driver to take you through **Cubbon Park,** almost 300 acres (121 ha) laid out by Cubbon in 1864. You may wish to

get out for a stroll near the **Seshadri Iyer Memorial Hall** ② (1913), built to house the Public Library and named to honor a prime minister of Mysore state. Leave the park at the southern corner and go up R. R. M. Roy Road to glimpse the timeless, stucco **Bangalore Club** ③ *(members only)*, with some nice old houses nearby. Return along Kasturba Gandhi Road to find three public buildings on the left. The middle one is the

> 🗺 See area map pages 222–23
> ▶ High Courts
> 🔄 5 miles (8 km)
> 🕐 2–3 hours
> ▶ Kempe Gowda Road
>
> **NOT TO BE MISSED**
> - Vidhana Soudha
> - Cubbon Park
> - Russell Market

Busy streets in colonial Bangalore

Government Museum ❹ (1876), whose sculpture gallery, hero stones, and Mysore school miniature paintings are worth a look.

At the far end of Kasturba Gandhi Road, an incongruous trio of **statues** ❺ stands at the main gate of Cubbon Park: a memorial statue of Queen Victoria (1906) and statues of Edward VII, and Mahatma Gandhi.

Turn right along Mahatma Gandhi Road to see the neoclassic, domed **St. Mark's Cathedral** (1812) on the right. Then turn left to find the Victorian Gothic **St. Andrew's**

Church ❻ on Cubbon Road (1867). Drive past the church facade and down to **Russell Market** ❼, built so that British *memsahibs* could shop in safety after a scandal concerning a moneylender and an abortion.

From here, drive up across Infantry Road and turn right back on Cubbon Road again to pass the palatial, whitewashed **Raj Bhavan** ❽ (1831), built as the British Residency, and go down Race Course Road to the end. Turn left, and you will find **Kempe Gowda Road,** an excellent place for fixed-price silk stores such as **Karnataka Silk Industries Corporation (K.S.I.C.)** ❾. Helpful assistants advise on the lengths needed for your requirements and the suitability of the various silk weaves—crêpe de chine, georgette, chiffon, soft and spun silk, stone-washed and raw silk.

If you are feeling inspired by this drive, and are energetic enough, you can continue on to see Tipu's Palace and Lalbagh Botanical Gardens (see p. 227). ■

Facade of the High Courts

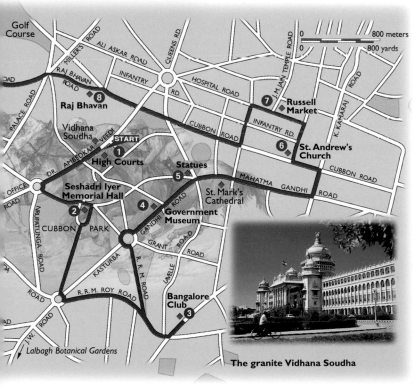

The granite Vidhana Soudha

Mysore

In the pre-traffic early morning, Mysore still appears to be an elegant city of palaces.

THE WODEYARS, ORIGINALLY GOVERNORS OF SOUTHERN Karnataka under the Vijayanaga emperors (see p. 236), rose to be rulers of Mysore and to determine its delightful character, preserved today, partly because the city does not have an airport. The former royal family still lives in a corner of the vast, city-center Amba Vilas Palace, the place to begin exploring the city.

Mysore, Karnataka

⚄ 222 B1

State Tourist Office

www.karnatakatourism.org

✉ Yatri Niwas, J.L.B. Rd.

☎ 0821-423652

Amba Vilas Palace

✉ Entry on south side only; shoes and cameras must be deposited before entering; socks permitted

🕐 Open daily

Extravagant, fantastical **Amba Vilas Palace** (1897–1912), also known as the Maharaja's palace, was designed by Henry Irwin and outstrips most Rajasthan palaces. It takes most of a morning just to follow the route around it and to see the outbuildings. The Wodeyars built a fort here in 1524 while governors, but they moved away when they became rulers. Tipu later razed Mysore, intending to rebuild it; when the British reinstated the young Krishnaraja III as a puppet Wodeyar ruler in 1801, Mysore still needed rebuilding.

After a fire in 1897, Irwin was awarded the commission to rebuild. He created an Indo-Saracenic palace that manages to be simultaneously imperial, traditional, and progressive. On your way through, details to look for include the maharajas' *howdah* (seat used to ride elephants), encrusted with 24-carat gold, and the eight enormous bronze tigers by Robert William Colton. In the octagonal wedding hall, see the long friezes recording the 1930 Dussehra procession, the cast-iron pillars shipped out from Glasgow, and the Belgian stained-glass peacocks. In the Durbar Hall are whole avenues of carved pillars, huge inlaid doors, walls coated in arabesques, and a Mughal-style floor. Before leaving the compound, explore the surviving rooms of the older palace, now housing a museum, and some of the old temples. The palace is illuminated by tiny lights on Sundays and festivals.

Nearby, part of **Jaganmohan Palace** (1900) was transformed into a museum of musical instruments and miniature paintings in 1915 by Krishnaraja IV, who followed tradition in his enlightened and progressive policies, in his energetic building program for his model state, and in his loyalty to the British. You will find the **Sri Chamarajendra Art Gallery** at the back of the building, where Lord Curzon attended Krishnaraja IV's coronation; do not miss the murals of royal pastimes.

Near Amba Vilas are the City Corporation Offices and the Public Offices. Up Siyaji Rao Road are hospitals, schools, and the grand **Government House.** On Kalidasa Road, the **Manasa Gangotri Folklore Museum** has wonderful wooden *bhuta* figures from Mekkekattu (see p. 206). **Dvaraja Market** has sacks of flowers, pyramids of spices, neat arrangements of polished fruits and vegetables, and piles of fresh herbs.

Chamundi Hill makes a pleasant afternoon trip. Drive to the top to see the **temple** (12th century) dedicated to Mysore's titular deity,

Chamuneswari (Durga), which is made of solid gold; then walk down steps past the huge **Nandi bull** (1659) carved out of black granite. End the day with a visit to **Lalitha Mahal Palace Hotel,** built in 1931 for the foreign meat-eating guests of the strictly vegetarian maharaja. It has a wonderful double staircase, a period bar, and dining in the former ballroom. ∎

Shwetavara-haswamy Temple, inside the Amba Vilas compound

Dussehra (Dassera)

Mysore celebrates with gusto this week-long festival of the triumph of good over evil that arrives in September–October and harks back to the annual extravaganza at Vijayanagar. It is symbolized in the goddess Chamundeswari's (Durga's) triumph over the demon buffalo Mahishasura, rather than the northern India version, of Rama's triumph over Ravana. Vijayadashami marks the finale to ten days of pageantry: Caparisoned elephants, horses, and cavalry, plus some movie-starlike deities parade to the Banni Mantap, and everything ends in dramatic fireworks. A cultural festival runs in parallel to honor Saraswati, goddess of the arts. This is a good opportunity to experience the special Carnatic music and dance of Karnataka in the palace's Durbar Hall and grounds—and some *yakshagana* dance-drama. The Mysore royals, famous for their hospitality, would hold their Mysore Week at this time. Events included races at the city's pretty racetrack and an extravagant outing to witness the *khedda* (elephant roundup) in the forest at Nagarhole (see pp. 232–33). ∎

Sri Chamarajendra Art Gallery
- ✉ Back of Jaganmohan Palace
- 🕐 Closed Wed.
- ❓ No photography

Manasa Gangotri Folklore Museum
- ✉ Jayalakshmi Vilas Mansion
- 🕐 Closed Sat. p.m. & all Sun.

Lalitha Mahal Palace Hotel
- ✉ Siddharth Nagar

Nagarhole, Bandipur, & Mudumalai National Parks

**Nagarhole
National Park,
Karnataka**

🗺 222 B1

✉ 60 miles (96.5 km)
SW of Mysore

💲 $. Game viewing
extra

**Bandipur National
Park, Karnataka**

🗺 222 B1

✉ 50 miles (80 km)
S of Mysore

💲 $. Game viewing
extra

**Mudumalai
National Park,
Tamil Nadu**

🗺 222 B1

💲 $. Game viewing
extra

EVEN THOUGH MUDUMALAI IS IN TAMIL NADU, THESE
three parks are treated together, since they border each other. Their
wildlife, notably the herds of Karnataka elephants, roams freely
among them. Furthermore, they are now collectively referred to as
the Nilgiri Biosphere Reserve and constitute India's most extensive
tract of continuous protected forest. To protect the wildlife, access
is limited and visits are usually only permitted at certain hours
each day.

All three parks are relatively easy to
reach from Bangalore (see pp.
226–29), Mysore (see pp. 230–31),
or Ooty (see pp. 280–81). Roads are
good, and the scenery around Ooty
is spectacular. The parks also fit well
into a southern India itinerary, so
be sure to reserve accommodations
in advance. As usual, prices tend to
include all meals, guides, jeep rides,
and elephant and boat rides where

**The rich vista of
Bandipur National
Park, as seen from
Himavadh Gopala
Swami Hill. Ele-
phants and birds
can frequently
be seen amongst
the trees.**

available. The best time to visit is
from October to May, staying at least
three nights to get the full benefit. It
takes time to learn how to spot the
animals and identify the birds. (In
June the heat is punishing; in postmonsoon September the ground
cover is too thick to see game.)

In addition to elephants, you
may come across *gaur* (Indian

bison), sambhar, several other
species of deer, crocodiles, and a
rich selection of birds; lucky and
patient visitors may see a tiger or
leopard. The great variety of bird
life is another bonus.

NAGARHOLE NATIONAL
PARK

Centered on the Kabini River and
the lake created by damming it, this
is one of the best parks in India for
seeing and learning about animals
and birds in a variety of settings.
Accommodations in the maharaja
of Mysore's hunting lodge and
viceroy's buildings add further
charm, as does the team of expert
naturalists and the almost certain
chance of seeing wild elephants.

The 110 square miles (284 sq
km) of mixed deciduous trees,
swamps, streams, and soaring
bamboo clumps are home to
hundreds of elephants. This is
where the maharaja's annual
khedda (elephant roundup) was
held, and where the movie *Sabhu
the Elephant Boy* was made—
movies of both events are shown in
the evenings. To watch a group of
elephants for an hour or so at
sunset simply moving through the
riverside grasses, the baby elephants
frolicking under the watchful eye
of their nanny carers, is a truly
memorable experience.

The drier it is, the better your

animal sightings along the river banks will be. On an evening boat ride you may see fat crocodiles lounging on the banks, while many elephants, bison, and deer arrive to populate this Garden of Eden.

On arrival, plan your itinerary with your naturalist. This might include jeep drives, a sunrise expedition on the lake in coracles (small boats made of buffalo hide), observing a waterhole from a *machan* (blind), and cruising up the Kabini at sunset. At the elephant camp you can see the elephants being bathed and you can feed them their breakfast of lentils and rice hay. Each day includes a siesta period and ends with a simple dinner around a campfire beside the lake.

BANDIPUR NATIONAL PARK

Created in the 1930s by the maharaja of Mysore, then expanded in the 1940s to join the Nagarhole and Mudumalai land, this park covers 340 square miles (880 sq km) of dry, deciduous forest south of the Kabini River.

You may sight elephants anywhere in the forest. Bird-watching is good here, too, and you can enjoy fine views from Rolling Rocks, over the deep and craggy Mysore Ditch, or from Gopalswamy Betta, a high ridge overlooking Mysore Plateau.

MUDUMALAI NATIONAL PARK, TAMIL NADU

This tract of 150 square miles (400 sq km) of forest nestles under and into the Nilgiri Hills and attracts a variety of wildlife. You may see giant squirrels, and bonnet and common langur monkeys, as well as the usual gaur, sambhar, and deer. The bird life includes species of the plains and hills attracted by springtime fruit trees. There are also delightful accommodations and the Kargudi elephant camp to visit. ∎

Within an elephant herd, the young are looked after not only by their mothers but also by special "nanny" elephants.

Badami
🅰 222 B3
💲 $

**Badami Medieval
Sculpture Gallery**
🕐 Closed Fri.

Pattadakal
🅰 222 B3
💲 $

Badami, Pattadakal, & Aihole

THREE CLUSTERS OF EXQUISITE CAVES AND TEMPLES, isolated in the dry but beautiful Malprabha River Valley of rural Karnataka, rival those at Mahabalipuram in Tamil Nadu (see pp. 260–61). Together they form the foundation of the glorious achievements that followed in medieval cities throughout the subcontinent. They are worth every effort to reach them across the open Deccan plains from Vijayangar, Bijapur, or Hubli.

A succession of Early Chalukya rulers were responsible for these masterpieces. From their first base at Aihole, the Chalukyas rose from the fourth century to control most of Karnataka, as well as parts of Andhra Pradesh and Maharashtra, until the Rashtrakutas overthrew them in 757. Pattadakal was their religious center and coronation city.

BADAMI
Pulakeshin I (*R.* 543–566) moved the capital to Badami, doubtless attracted by the soaring, protective bluffs surrounding a beautiful lake. Later, Pulakeshin II (*R.* 610–642) left from here to defeat Harsha of Kanauj, the most powerful king of northern India, and to push the Chalukya boundaries south when he came into conflict with the Pallavas of Kanchipuram. After repeated Chalukya raids on Kanchipuram in 612 and after, the Pallavas retaliated and took Badami in 654. Pulakeshin lost his life, but his successor Vikramaditya I expelled the Pallavas, and his son Vinayaditya (*R.* 696–733) enjoyed a long and peaceful reign. Pallava troubles returned under Vikramaditya II (*R.* 733–744), whose son lost out to the Rashtrakutas.

To enjoy Badami's treasures in their best light, you need to see some in the morning and the rest in the evening. In the morning, see the cave temples cut into the southern cliffs. The morning sun illuminates

both the sculptures and the pinks and purples of the sandstone. Created in the sixth century, their bold and rounded sculptures have a stunning robustness, while the column, capital, and ceiling decoration is a delicate mix of figures, foliage, jewels, and garlands. Find images of Harihare (left) and Shiva with Nandi (right) in **Cave no. 1,** with a magnificent 18-armed dancing Shiva nearby. **Cave no. 2** has images of Vishnu as Varaha (left) and Trivikrama (right), while **Cave no. 3,** inscribed with the date 578, is even richer and has traces of painting; see especially Vishnu on the coiled serpent and the Narasimha composition. **Cave no. 4** is Jain, adorned with restrained images of Tirthankaras.

In the evening, you can take a pony and trap through the narrow lanes of Badami village and then walk along the lakeside to enjoy the sunset from **Bhutanatha Temple** (7th and 11th centuries). To explore further, see the two lakeside temples in town and, up the path behind it, three clifftop temples and gorgeous views. **Mahakuta,** a village not far from here, has a group of four temples built in the years between Badami's and Pattadakal's.

PATTADAKAL
Outside the village, set in manicured lawns beside the Malprabha River, these now isolated eighth-century temples

A sensuous carving adorns Sanameshvara Temple at Pattadakal, the eighth-century royal commemorative and coronation site for early Chalukyan rulers.

mix various styles to achieve the climax of Early Chalukyan building.

Unless you are a true temple addict, be selective here. Go across the lawns, past earlier and simpler temples, to see the two largest and most developed, dedicated to Virupaksha and Mallikarjuna, two forms of Shiva. Built by the queen in about 745 to commemorate Vikramaditya II's victory over the Pallavas, they are decorated with large sculptures full of a vitality that is almost contagious. See especially the panels flanking the east porch of Virupaksha; inside, there are the sensuous courting couples and delicate narrative friezes on the columns.

AIHOLE

The many Hindu and Jain monuments here, both rock-cut caves and temples, span the periods of the Early Chalukyas, the Rashtrakutas, and the Late Chalukyas (10th–13th centuries), who ruled northern Karnataka from Basavakalyan and built splendid temples at Ittagi (see p. 244) and Dambal. Their patrons were kings and merchants, since the town was then an important trading center. Together they display the bold experiments of this period. The best way to enjoy them is to make your base the little government rest house, whose staff can prepare food if asked on your arrival. ■

Aihole
🏛 222 B3

Aihole Archaeological Museum
🕐 Closed Fri.

Badami's soaring cliffs and lake make a dramatic yet peaceful setting for Bhutanatha Temple.

Vijayanagar

**Vijayanagar,
Karnataka**
www.karnataka.com/tourism
🗺 222 B3

Hampi
🗺 7 miles (11 km)
NE from Hospet
$ $

CONSIDERED BY MANY TO EQUAL PETRA IN JORDAN WITH its impressive buildings amid large rocks beside the mighty Tungabhadra River, Vijayanagar's ruins were forgotten until a team of archaeologists started work here in the 1960s. Yet the powerful Hindu rulers of this once huge metropolis controlled all of southern India and provided the unifying power to keep the Muslim threat at bay until 1565. Today, royal, religious, and civic buildings dot the former city, sharing space with banana groves, paddy fields, and villages.

Vijayanagar's rulers rose in parallel, and in rivalry, with the Muslim Bahmanis based at Gulbarga and Bidar (see pp. 240–41). They established their base at Vijayanagar (City of Victory) in 1336, after seizing the waning Hoysala territories in southern Karnataka, then swiftly regained most lands lost to the Delhi sultans. Thus they achieved the allegiance of the newly liberated rulers of the whole region, down to the tip of Tamil Nadu, apart from most of the Malabar coast.

The consequent vast amounts of tribute money and taxes were used by Bukka I (R.1354–1377) and Devaraya II (R.1423–1446), then by Krishnadevaraya (R.1510–1529) and his brother-in-law, Achyutadevaraya (R.1529–1542) to create their imperial capital. Its size, trading

The fine carving of royal Vitthala Temple's granite stone chariot (right) and magnificent mandapa or hall, (left), contrast with the rough, boulder-strewn landscape.

These grand buildings probably housed the royal elephants.

Hospet, Karnataka State Tourist Office

✉ Old Fire Station Building

Visitor tips

The five-hour drive, 209 miles (337 km) north of Bangalore, is relentless and best tackled by leaving very early. Or, you can take the overnight train to Hospet. Otherwise, approach from Badami (93 miles/150 km) or Bijapur (129 miles/207 km). It's best to stay at Hospet and explore Vijayanagar's various sights with a combination of driving and walking. Take a picnic if you are going to be out all day.

wealth, grand buildings, and grandiose rulers were compared to Rome by its visitors.

But on Achyutadevaraya's death the commander of the imperial forces, Ramaraya, took control and kept the rightful successor in prison. It was Ramaraya's high-handedness with the sultans who had emerged from the Bahmani breakup that led to war. In January 1565, at Talikota near Aihole (see p. 235), the combined forces of Bijapur, Bidar, Golconda, and Ahmednagar crushed the Vijayanaga army and then spent a reputed four years sacking the city of its vast wealth, burning the wooden buildings to melt off the gold decoration.

Many buildings survived because they were built of stone and a visit to see the remains of Vijayanagar is still highly recommended. There are two main areas to visit: The sacred and the royal, with extras for those with time.

A very good place to start is Hampi village. Here you can visit **Virupaksha Temple** (13th to 17th century, *$*), the only temple

in the area still in use; its resident elephant helps with the *pujas*. Hemakuta Hill rises above it, a huge slope of granite that provides fine views up the river and has small temples and shrines. Through the great rocks there are two monolithic Ganeshas and Krishnadevaraya's 1513 **Krishna Temple** (*Hemakuta Hill*), built to celebrate a military campaign in Orissa. Just beyond, a lane on the right leads through a banana grove to a huge monolithic Narasimha.

A second walk from Hampi goes up the main street of stores and cafés, then left along a path that passes the riverside Kodandarama Temple, where bus-loads of pilgrims come to worship Rama. Indeed, this is epic country:

Farther along the path, after a detour down a wide bazaar to see the 16th-century **Achyutaraya Temple** *(foot of Matanga Hill),* you pass what is believed to be the cave where Sugriva hid Sita's jewel. The riverside path continues from here to Krishnadevaraya's 16th-century **Vitthala Temple** *($)* and surrounding city bazaars. Roaming the complex, you will find the piers carved into rearing animals and riders, the great stone chariot, and a basement frieze of Portuguese horse traders, who made rich profits from the Vijayanagas.

A third walk starts at the Royal Enclosure. First, see the private **Lotus Mahal** *(Zenana Enclosure, $)* and the amazing elephant stables. Return around the palace walls and go along the road to the **Ramachandra Temple** (15th century). Its outer wall is covered with an incredible relief showing the Mahanavami festival procession; there are more reliefs of Rama stories inside. Beyond the temple lies the area for royal public performance. You can find the platform for the hall of justice, the step-well, and the magnificent **Mahanavami Platform,** entirely covered with friezes of royal hunting, partying, and marching; the platform is thought to be the place where the king sat to watch the Mahanyvami festivities.

Finally, for a special atmospheric outing, choose either sunrise or sunset to climb Matanga Hill: There are a lot of big steps, but the trip is worth the effort. ∎

A view from Hemakuta Hill over Hampi village and the tall *gopura* (gateway) of its Virupaksha Temple, with the Tungabhadra River beyond

Hot pink temple flowers for sale at merchants' booths in Bidar

Southern sultanates

ALTHOUGH SMALL TODAY, EACH OF THE OLD SULTANATE cities of Bijapur, Gulbarga, Bidar, and Golconda were at one time a great medieval fort city, powerful enough to hold back the invading Mughal armies. Each has left monuments, whose romantic designs and silhouettes are a rich amalgam reflecting the peoples who migrated there, initially to Gulbarga. Their rulers, lacking the traditional Islamic passion for recording events, have left a certain mystery: We know little about them. However, we have a number of their artifacts, especially some stunning miniature paintings, whose vivid colors and lyrical lines confirm strong cultural links with Safavid Iran, with the addition of the sensuality found in local southern Indian sculpture.

**Bijapur,
Karnataka**
222 B4

Visitor tip
Bijapur Tourist Office is the only information post in this area, so it is best to collect information there, before moving on.

BIJAPUR
As you wander the streets of this laid-back provincial town, where a pony and trap is still a regular form of transportation, it is only the evidence of the immensely grand buildings and monuments at every turn that convinces you Bijapur was once great. This was the prosperous capital of the Adil Shahi dynasty (1490–1686), established by Yusuf Adil Khan (R.1490–1510). Its rulers tempered their extravagant patronage with an acute aesthetic sense. But protracted and expensive

wars and then decline under Mughal rule finally extinguished Bijapur's power.

GULBARGA
Although little remains to testify to it, the sultanate story begins here, 103 miles (165 km) northeast of Bijapur (see map pp. 222–23). It is a story worth telling, because the history of this part of India, where north meets south, can be confusing.

A succession of incursions into southern India by the Delhi sultans began in 1296 and finally brought the Yadava, Kakatiya, Hoysala, and Pandya dynasties to a close. Muhammad Tughlaq even moved his capital down to Daulatabad (see p. 175) in 1327 to consolidate his triumphs. But when he returned to Delhi in 1334, the Muslim governors of Madurai and Daulatabad proclaimed their independence, and the Hindu Vijayanaga rulers began to liberate their fellow chieftains.

The governors of Daulatabad rose to become the powerful Bahmanis, moving to Gulbarga in 1347, then departing for Bidar in 1424. Their vast territories included Maharashtra, northern Karnataka, and Andhra Pradesh. Gulbarga became a metropolis attracting other Muslims—Persians, Arabs, Turks, and Abyssinians—and its buildings reflect this in their Persian forms and decoration.

Mosques and palaces filled the great circular **citadel,** whose 52-foot-thick (16 m) crenellated walls and 15 watchtowers now surround just one beautiful mosque (1367). Outside the walls the Bahmanis built their tombs and those of saints who boosted their image; see the lively **Dargah of Hazrat Gesu Nawaz** (died 1422), which, with its Persian painted neighbor, attracts many pilgrims but is open only to men. Early royal tombs lie in the fields west of the fort: massive cubic chambers with domes. Find later tombs at Haft Gunbad, near the Dargah.

Gulbarga's fate was to achieve independence and lose out to, first, the Adil Shahis of Bijapur, then the Mughals.

BIDAR

After moving its capital here in 1424, the Bahmani kingdom reached its zenith under Ahmad I (R.1422–1436), Muhammed Bahmani III (R.1463–1482), and Bahmani's able prime minister,

Mahmud Gawan. At its height, the Bahmani kingdom stretched from the Arabian Sea to the Bay of Bengal. Internal rivalries, however, soon broke up the kingdom and five sultanate states emerged. Qasim Barid (R.1488–1504) took control of a much reduced Bidar, and his successors mixed patronage with decline. Three other sultanates—Golconda, Bijapur, and Ahmednagar in Maharashtra—had Shia Muslim rulers, which contributed to their antagonism to the Sunni Mughals.

Today, a visit to Bidar transports you to those distant times, much more so than a visit to Gulbarga. The **fort,** whose massive walls and seven gateways are Baridi work, overlooks the plains. Inside are

substantial remains of the royal palaces, including tiled and inlaid walls, the Solah Khamb Mosque (1327), the Diwan-i-Am (public audience hall), and the throne room. In the walled city, see the **Shihabuddin Ahmad Is Takht-I Kirmani gateway** and the huge **Madrasa** ("place of learning") founded by Mahmud Gawan in 1472 for Shia studies. Its minaret and front arcade have bold calligraphic motifs and, in places, still retain their richly colored tiles. ∎

Gulbarga, Karnataka
▲ 222 B4

Bidar, Karnataka
▲ 222 B4

Muhammad Adil Shah II built his own mausoleum in Bijapur, the Gol Gumbaz, whose huge dome, at 145 feet (44 m) in diameter, is one of the world's largest.

Outside Bijapur's city walls, the early morning sun illuminates the tomb of Ibrahim Rauza.

Bijapur by pony & trap

Bijapur's great black mosques, walls, and tombs look their most impressive in the early morning or late afternoon, and what better way to travel to them than by pony and trap? Women should cover their arms and legs and take a head shawl. Agree on a price with your pony and trap master before you start. Ask him to wait when you want to get down, and pay him at the end with a suitable addition for waiting time.

During your ride, imagine an exotic court of energetic patronage, funded by Vijayanaga booty. It found expression in buildings, miniature-painting, music, and religious Sufi learning and science. Only after the final Mughal onslaught and victory by Aurangzeb in 1686 did the decline set in.

Start at the landmark **Gol Gumbaz ❶** (1655), the majestically simple tomb of Muhammad II, with a huge, hemispherical dome on a cube-shaped base; the interior is almost austere in its simplicity. Hop back on your trap and go straight ahead from the Gol Gumbaz gateway; then turn right on Jama Masjid Road. Here, you will find a **trio of monuments ❷:** the incomplete but nevertheless monumental **Jama Masjid** (1576), **Yusuf's Old Jama Masjid** (1513), and, down a side street, the tiny **Ali Sahib Pir Masjid,** with fine plaster decoration.

Now go toward the citadel and past its entrance to find **Asar Mahal ❸,** built as a hall of justice but later converted into a reliquary to hold two hairs of the Prophet. Its civic origins give us a good idea of the character of Bijapur's palace buildings. Perhaps, like

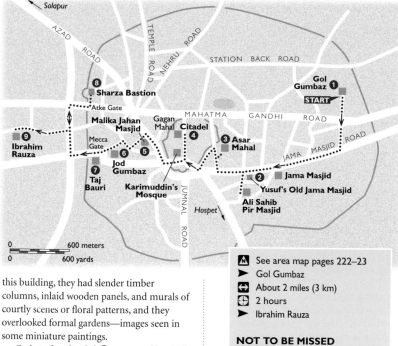

this building, they had slender timber columns, inlaid wooden panels, and murals of courtly scenes or floral patterns, and they overlooked formal gardens—images seen in some miniature paintings.

Go into the **citadel ④**, protected by thick inner walls, to find **Karimuddin's Mosque** (1310), begun when the Delhi sultans were in residence and built with stones from destroyed temples. Gangan Mahal, Ali I's audience hall, is easy to identify: Its great triple arch faces the open area where the people sat.

Outside the west wall of the citadel is the small and finely decorated **Malika Jahan Masjid ⑤**, possibly specially built for women. Nearby, **Jod Gumbaz ⑥** is a pair of tombs with elegant facades and slightly bulbous domes containing the remains of Khan Muhammad, commander of the Adil Shahi troops, and Abdul Razzaq, his spiritual advisor. The large, square tank with stepped sides and arcades is **Taj Bauri ⑦**, where the entrance steps descend to a big arched gateway.

Now go out of the city by the Mecca Gate, turn right, and go in at the next one, Atke Gate. Here, you can climb the wall to see the Malik-i-Maidan, Bijapur's famous gun, which sits on the **Sharza Bastion ⑧**. This is a good moment to look at Bijapur's magnificent **walls** (1565), built by Yusuf Adil Khan. They are 32 feet (10 m) high, reinforced by 96 round

bastions, and equipped with guardrooms and a parapet. You can walk along the broad path on top of them right around the city.

Your ride ends with a visit to the best of all, the Adil Shahi buildings: **Ibrahim Rauza ⑨** (1628). This is a tomb and mosque built by Ibrahim II for his queen, Taj Sultana, but later converted into a mausoleum for himself and his family. You enter through a single gateway and go through a formal garden to reach both buildings, which stand on a plinth. Take time to look carefully at the exterior of the tomb: It rises up in layers, crowned by a bulbous dome that sits on a ring of petals. Now go into the verandah to look closely at its outer walls, doorways, and windows, and enjoy the precision-cut geometric and calligraphic designs. Some are cut through as screens, others are cut in shallow relief. ■

A See area map pages 222–23
► Gol Gumbaz
⟷ About 2 miles (3 km)
⊕ 2 hours
► Ibrahim Rauza

NOT TO BE MISSED
- Gol Gumbaz
- Asar Mahal
- Walking the walls
- Ibrahim Rauza

More places to visit in Karnataka

ARSIKERE & ARALAGUPPE

For more 13th-century Hoysala temple elegance and richness, visit the towns of Arsikere and Aralaguppe. A second Aralaguppe temple, **Kalleshvara** (ninth century), has a beautiful ceiling panel.

⚊ 222 B2 **Arsikere** ✉ 27 miles (44 km) northeast of Hassan

BAGALI, KURUVATTI, & HARIHAR

Bagali and Kuruvatti are villages with Chalukya temples. Bagali's **Kalleshvara** (tenth century) has surprisingly provocative sculptures. Kuruvatti's **Chalukya** (11th century) has masterpiece bracket figures on the east doorway. Harihar town has a splendid Hoysala temple, **Harihareshvara** (1224).

⚊ 222 B3 **Bagali** ✉ 34 miles (55 km) southwest of Hospet

BELUR & HALEBID

The great Hoysala ruler Vishnuvardhana (R.1108–1142) built the Channekashava Temple at his capital, **Belur,** to celebrate his defeat of the Cholas in 1116. The dense, fluent carving riots over the squat yet refined building; note the high plinth, star-shaped plan, lathe-turned pillars, and polished surfaces.

At nearby **Halebid,** visit the incomplete double Hoysalesvara Temple, designed and begun by Kedaroja for the Hoysala ruler Narasimha I (R.1141–1182). Up on the platform you can follow the bands of decoration with their lively carving and precision, showing

rows of elephants, stories from the epics, baroque scrollwork, and scenes from courtly life. Above them, the great sculptures include Shiva dancing with the flayed skin of the elephant demon and Brahma seated on a goose. The sumptuously bejeweled temple-guardian figures are especially fine, as is the fat Ganesh figure. To visit longer at the Hoysala temples, you can stay in Hassan.

⚊ 222 B3 **Belur** ✉ 23 miles (38 km) northwest of Hassan; **Halebid** ✉ 20 miles (32 km) north of Hassan

CHITRADURGA FORT

At the halfway point of the Bangalore–Hospet road, this is a good place to stretch your legs. Go through several great gates to find two Hoysala temples and various tanks, palace buildings, and lamp columns.

⚊ 222 B2 ✉ 124 miles (200 km) northwest of Bangalore

ITTAGI & OTHER TEMPLES

There are some very rural villages on the Hospet–Hubli road; Ittagi makes a wonderful picnic spot. Before this, you can visit the ninth- and tenth-century temples at **Kukkunur,** on the way to Ittagi, where you can enjoy the highly decorated **Mahadeva Temple** (1112). On toward Hubli, the

Every 12 years Jains celebrate the Mahamasta Kabhisheka festival to Gomateshvara at Shravanabelagola.

Silk, the state industry

Karnataka produces 85 percent of India's raw silk, and the industry is closely controlled by the government at every stage. Japanese male moths are mated with local Mysore females, who are carefully checked for disease. Once hatched, the pupa are sold at a fixed price to the mulberry-bush owner or to farmers, who rear them to cocoon stage.

This is when you can see woven mats propped up in the morning sun outside small farms. The worms on them eat mulberry leaves continuously for 26–28 days, during which they molt four times and grow to be 4–6 inches (10–15 cm) long. They then turn from white to yellow and for about four days furiously spin their cocoons with a viscous solution; each one of these will be unraveled to about 4,000 feet (1,200 m) of silk yarn. The cocoons are then sold for boiling, reeling, dyeing, and weaving. You will be made very welcome at most roadside silk-production units, where the managers are usually happy to explain the precise workings of each of the processes to you. ■

temples at **Lakkundi** are Late Chalukya buildings of gray-green schist, all richly carved; this village is especially nice to wander in. Finally, the **Dodda Basappa Temple** (12th century) at **Dambal** is one of the most beautifully carved Late Chalukya temples.
Ittagi ✉ 33 miles (53 km) west of Hospet

KODAGU (COORG)

This beautiful area mixes rugged mountains with cardamom jungle, paddy fields, and orderly coffee plantations established by the British. The tall and graceful people, known as Kodavas or Coorgis, have maintained their distinct culture, including heavy jewelry, very rich saris, ancestor worship, and cuisine. Driving through the area, pause at **Madikeri** (Mercara) with its fort-palace, and **Talakaveri,** where the Kaveri River springs from the wooded slopes of Brahmagiri Hill.
🅼 222 B1 **Madikeri** ✉ 60 miles (96 km) west of Mysore

MALNAD

This wild, forested region offers a combination of waterfalls (for Jog Falls see p. 206), craggy peaks, and monuments created by the Nayaka rulers of the 16th and 17th centuries. Having done well under the Vijayanagas, they became independent, with capitals at Keladi, then Ikkeri. Your base can be **Shimoga,** whose restored **Shivappa Nayaka Palace** overlooking the Tunga River is worth visiting. One outing is to **Keladi** and **Ikkeri's temples,** another to **Nagar, Devaganga's** tanks and pavilions, and **Kavaledurga's** citadel. Take a trip north to **Balligave** and **Banavasi's** Hoysala and Late Chalukya temples, or south to **Amritpur's** outstanding Hoysala temple (1196).
🅼 222 A2 **Shimoga** ✉ 97 miles (156 km) north of Hassan, 120 miles (193 km) southwest of Hospet

RANGANATHITTU BIRD SANCTUARY

An early morning or evening visit to this bird sanctuary near Srirangapatnam is magical. Take a boat out on the lake with an ornithologist for some peaceful bird-watching, looking out for electric blue kingfishers to great

gangling herons, spoonbills, and openbill storks; there are also crocodiles in the water.
🅼 222 B1 ✉ 12 miles (19 km) north of Mysore

SOMNATHPUR

Even if you think you have seen enough temples, you will delight in this little gem found down country lanes, a 90-minute drive out of Mysore. Built in 1268, the **Keshava Vishnu Temple** is the last and most complete of the three great Hoysala temples (see Belur & Halebid). Try asking the guardian if you may go up onto the walls to enjoy fabulous views of the star-shaped plan and the densely carved roofs that top each of the shrines.
🅼 222 B1 ✉ 21 miles (75 km) east of Mysore

SRIRANGAPATNAM (SERINGAPATAM)

The island fortress on the Kaveri River is synonymous with Tipu Sultan (see p. 226), killed here in 1799 when General Harris stormed the citadel, confirming British supremacy in southern India. Get a flavor of the fort's great ramparts and visit the possible site of the breach and the place where Tipu fell. Then find the pretty, Mughal-influenced **Daria Daulat Bagh** (1784), Tipu's pleasure resort, where there are delicate murals and drawings of his sons. A small formal garden surrounds the cenotaphs of Tipu and his father, Haider Ali, who are buried together underneath them.
🅼 222 B1 ✉ 9 miles (14 km) north of Mysore

SHRAVANABELAGOLA

Southern India's most sacred Jain site is believed to have been where the Mauryan emperor Chandragupta died in about 300 B.C. If you are physically fit, the reward of walking up Indragiri Hill is to see the 58-foot-high calm, monolithic figure of Gomateshvara (981) that has been carved out of the rock; or, visit the priest's house with its painted walls.

It is worth arranging a visit to **Nritgram dance village** (Tel 080-8466312), founded by dancer Protima Bedi, to learn about different forms of Indian dance and see dancing.
🅼 222 B2 ✉ 56 miles (90 km) north of Mysore ■

Andhra Pradesh

Andhra Pradesh has much to offer, though few visitors come here. Hyderabad is littered with dilapidated palaces, the backdrop to a dynamic city that today looks to Bangalore's IT success as its inspiration. Its infrastructure is being entirely rebuilt at a furious speed, adding overpasses, new airport terminals, a hi-tech city, and entertainment parks; a film city is already up and running.

In contrast, if you are feeling adventurous, leave the capital and venture into the rugged countryside, where you will be well rewarded with evocative, offbeat sites but expect simple accommodations. Not far from Hyderabad lie the remains of Nagarjunakonda and Warangal, whose ramparts and fort you might have to yourself.

At Tirupati, in southeastern Andhra Pradesh, you can join the seething masses of Hindu pilgrims in their daily *pujas* to Lord Venkateswara in what is believed to be the world's richest temple. Around Vishakapatnam is a rich landscape made up of the Kailasha Hills, Orissan temples, and Buddhist and Dutch ruins. ■

It is always worth climbing up India's forts for an overview of the surrounding city and countryside, as here at **Golconda Fort.**

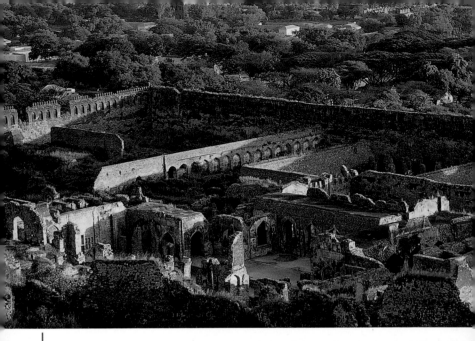

Golconda Fort's many surviving buildings give a vivid idea of medieval fort life.

Golconda & Hyderabad

GOLCONDA FORT IS NOT INDIA'S BIGGEST, BUT IT IS ONE of its most spectacular. Great crenellated walls with round bastions run 3 miles (5 km) around the bottom of a rocky bluff in a forbidding, boulder-strewn landscape. Inside, substantial remains cover the hill, with the royal Durbar Hall at the top. The adjacent city of Hyderabad developed as a result of Golconda's expansion.

Hyderabad, Andhra Pradesh India Tourist Office

✉ 2nd Fl, Sandozi Building, 26 Himayatnagar
☎ 040-7630037

Andhra Pradesh Tourism

www.aptourism.in
✉ Tourism House, Himayatnagar
☎ 040-23262151

Golconda
⚑ 223 C4
Golconda Royal Tombs
✉ Golconda
🕐 Closed Fri.
💲 $

Already in the 12th century, Golconda was a wealthy fort city. Later, it was an important outpost of the Bahmani kingdom, whose Turkish governor, Quli Qutb al-Mulk (R.1494–1543), broke free to establish his own kingdom and Qutb Shahi line of sultans. An outstanding military leader, he consolidated his gains over rival rulers, including those of Vijayanagar and Orissa, putting Golconda on a level footing with Bijapur.

The royal necropolis, near the fort, reflects the magnificence of these rulers. Seven **tombs** stand in a formal garden. Each has an onion dome perched on a cube-shaped mausoleum, surrounded by a richly ornamented arcade, with additional corner minarets. In early morning

or sunset light, the whole ensemble is hauntingly romantic.

The reign of Ibrahim Qutb Shah (R.1550–1580) marked Golconda's peak. Under his successor, Muhammad Quli Qutb Shah (R. 1580–1612), plans were made for expansion despite external threats, and in 1591 the city of Hyderabad was laid out beside the Musi River.

HYDERABAD
Comparative peace followed. Mughals and Marathas watched for opportunities to pounce on Hyderabad's wealth and its stocks of diamonds; in 1687 the Mughals conquered the city. Later, Mughal emperor Muhammad Shah's representative in Aurangabad, Nizam ul Mulk, declared independence and

took the title Asaf Jah I (*R.*1724–1748). Hyderabad, India's largest state (82,000 sq miles), recovered to withstand British, French, and Maratha threats. It finally gave in to the idea of independent India only in 1956.

Today Hyderabad is India's sixth largest city—a chaotic, ever-expanding urban sprawl that takes little care of its heritage. Encompassing Old and New Hyderabad plus Secunderabad, a station for British troops founded in 1853 after the British alliance, and now the high-tech Cyberabad, it is not an easy city to grasp. Here are a few things to look for.

Set the mood with a visit to the **Salar Jung Museum,** a vast and random collection made by the Nizam's prime minister, Salar Jung (1899–1949). Then find the landmark pink **High Court** (1916), designed by Vincent Esch, whose carved Agra sandstone has lapis lazuli–glazed domes and gilded finials. Esch's boys' school is next door. Along Mahboob Shahi Road there is a rare survivor of Quli Qutb Shah's original buildings, the **Badshahi Ashurkhana** (1592–96), the royal house of mourning, with beautiful enamel tile mosaics (1611). The Nizam's prime ministers lived in the **Diwan Deorhi** across the road. Up the road you find the **Charkaman** (four arches, 1594) and Old Hyderabad's focus, the **Char Minar** (four towers, 1591), once the ceremonial gateway to the palace, now constantly threatened by developers.

In this area you can find *bidri* workers, bangles and pearl stores (see box). **Mecca Masjid** (1598) is one of India's largest mosques; **Chow Mohalla** is a well-restored 1860s palace. Further afield, seek out **Falaknuma Palace** (now being restored) and the **Nizam's Silver Jubilee** and **State Archaeological Museums,** which reflect Karnataka's rich history. Fans of Indian film should visit **Ramoji Film City.** ◼

Salar Jung Museum
- ✉ Sardar Patel Rd.
- 🕐 Closed Fri.
- 💲 $

Badshahi Ashurkhana
- ✉ Mahboob Shahi Rd.
- 🕐 May be closed to visitors

Diwan Deorhi
- ✉ Sardar Patel Rd.
- 🕐 May be closed to visitors

Mecca Masjid
- ✉ Sardar Patel Rd.

Chow Mohalla Palace
- ✉ Kilwat

Falaknuma Palace
- ✉ Falaknuma

Nizam's Silver Jubilee Museum
- ✉ Puram Haveli

State Archaeological Museum
- ✉ Public Gardens

Ramoji Film City
www.ramojifilmcity.com

Pearls & *bidri* work

The fabulously rich Nizams of Hyderabad were famous for their love of pearls, which they wore, rubbed on their bodies, and even ate ground up. Hyderabad is still India's pearl market, where every wealthy bride-to-be wants to shop. In little workshops around Char Minar, pearls grown in Japan are sorted, pierced, sorted again, and either sold or re-exported. Many go straight to the shops in nearby Pertheghatty Road, where they are sorted by color, size, and quality. Clients select their pearl type and the required number is counted out, priced by weight, and strung on silk; the family jeweler will add the gemstones and a fancy clasp. In the same area, the special Muslim craft of bidri ware can be seen in the little alleys. This is the technique of decorating metalwork with a very fine silver or brass inlay of arabesque, floral, geometric, or calligraphic patterns. ◼

A Hyderabad craftsman uses tiny pearls to decorate a bangle.

Warangal
🅰 223 C4

Nagarjunakonda
🅰 223 C3
🅰 SE of Hyderabad

Museum
🕐 Closed Fri.

Vijayawada
🅰 223 D4

Victoria Jubilee
Museum
✉ Bundra Rd.
🕐 Closed Fri.

Guntur
🅰 223 D3

Boudhasree
Archaeological
Museum
🕐 Closed Fri.

Amaravati
🅰 223 D4

Museum
🕐 Closed Fri.

Eastern & southern
Andhra Pradesh

TRAVELING FROM HYDERABAD THROUGH THE BARREN
landscape to the northeast is quite a tough trip, but on the way you
can explore the glories of the Kakatiya rulers of the 13th and 14th
centuries, whose territories nudged the Gangas of Orissa to the north
and the Cholas of Tamil Nadu to the south. Use a car and driver.

EASTERN ANDHRA
PRADESH
First stop is the Kakatiyas' second
capital, **Warangal,** laid out by
Ganapatideva (R.1199–1262) and
his daughter, Queen Rudramadeva
(R.1262–1289); see the two rings of
outer earthen walls, the monumental gateways, the massive granite
inner fort walls, and the temple
portals. Two miles (3 km) away, the
fine gray-green basalt **Thousand-
Pillared Temple** (1163) stands at
Hanamkonda, the first Kakatiya
capital. The enthusiastic can
continue 42 miles (68 km) to
Palampet for the superb Ramappa
Temple (1213) and nearby
Ghanapur's shrines; clever Kakatiya
engineers created both lakes.

Travel southwest from
Hyderabad to reach Vijayapuri in
time to catch the morning boat
(usually 9:30 a.m.) to an island in
the Krishna River, to see tantalizing
limestone sculptures that testify to
Nagarjunakonda's former glory.
In the third and fourth centuries
the Ikshvakus, Andhra's most powerful rulers, made this their capital
and patronized fine Buddhist and
secular buildings that extended
over more than eight square miles
(20 sq km). Their monuments were
rediscovered by archaeologists in the
1950s, but in 1960 the Nagarjuna
Sagar Dam opened and almost the
whole area was flooded; the island
you visit was once the summit of
Nagarjuna Hill. It is well worth
visiting, however, to see the fort

remains, the reconstructed stadium
and monastery, *maha chaitya* (great
stupa, third century) and other
stupas, and the amazing sculptures
on display in the museum.

If you follow the Krishna River to
its lush delta, you will come to
Vijayawada, an isolated and fasci-
nating spot best reached by train or
air, because it is a long road journey.
It has been an important commercial
center since at least the fifth century.
In town, the **Victoria Jubilee
Museum** has impressive local
Buddhist finds. Set off to see
Kondapalle's fort and
Undavalli's rock-cut sanctuaries.
Farther away, southward through
tobacco, cotton, and paddy fields,
**Guntur's Boudhasree
Archaeological Museum** has
more local Buddhist finds.
Continue to **Amaravati,** once
known as Maha Chaitya (Great
Stupa), the site of India's largest
and most elaborate stupa (third
century B.C. to fourth century A.D.).
The majority of its sculptures are
now shared between Chennai
Government Museum (see p. 259)
and London's British Museum, but
it is still worth going to this
haunting site beside the Krishna
River; its museum displays the
many recent finds.

The verdant Godavari River
Delta is a historically prosperous
area dotted with fields of rice and
sugar, with immensely beautiful
scenery and fascinating places to
visit. Stay in **Rajahmundry** and

make an outing to see the temples of **Bikkavolu, Drakasharama,** and, best of all, **Samalkot,** an 11th-century temple and the area's largest East Chalukya monument. Alternatively, cross the Godavari to visit **Guntupalle's** Buddhist relics in a wooded ravine. And do not leave without taking the boat trip up the Godavari to visit **Godavari Gorge** in the wooded hills of the Eastern Ghats.

Vishakhapatnam, a huge port founded by the English in 1689, faces onto a fine broad bay that opens into the Bay of Bengal. As India's principal port, naval base, and industrial center on the east coast, it is equipped with good hotels from which to explore the beautiful surrounding rural area. In the nearby forested Kailasha Hills, you can find **Simhachalam's** hilltop Varaha Narasimha Temple (1268) at the end of a winding road; the patron of this pure Orissa temple was commander of the armies of the Eastern Ganga kings

of Orissa (see p. 294). Inside the granite temple enclosure find carved lions, friezes and garlands, royal princes, gods, and life-size prancing horses.

Meanwhile, hilly **Sankaram** is known for its Buddhist remains while coastal **Bheemunipatnam,** a major Dutch settlement, has sandy beaches, a Dutch fort, houses, and grand tombs. Farther up the coast, **Ramatirtham** and **Salihundram** have more Buddhist remains, and remote **Mukhalingam,** the early capital of the Eastern Gangas, has good temples, including the early **Madhukeshvara** (ninth century), with its curved tower and beautiful sculptures.

SOUTHWESTERN ANDHRA PRADESH

Many fine but isolated monuments lie in this rarely visited region. If you are traveling through it on National Highway 7, which runs from Hyderabad to Bangalore, you may wish to stop and see one

This vast monolith, found a mile east of Lepakshi town, shows Shiva's mount regally decked in garlands and bells.

Anantapur
🅰 223 C3

Penukonda
🅰 222 B2

Lepakshi
🅰 223 C2

Alampur
🅰 223 C3

Puttaparthi
🅰 223 C2

Prasanthi Nilaya Ashram
☎ 08555-8758; no advance reservations

Tirupati
🅰 223 C2

or two. For a closer look, stay overnight at **Anantapur.** You can take a walk up to **Gooty's Fort,** dramatically sited on a granite outcrop right beside the highway; east of here, Tadpatri's two major **Vijayanaga temples,** one in town and the other overlooking the Penner River, have very ornate sculpture and even some surviving ceiling paintings.

Back on the highway and beyond Anantapur, **Penukonda** is a convenient stop. After 1565, this fort is where the defeated Vijayanaga rulers fled before they moved on to Chandragiri. Among the ruins you can find the Hoysala-period **Parshvanatha Temple** and the **Rama and Sita Temples,** whose facades are carved with the *Ramayana* and Krishna legends.

Farther south, **Lepakshi** lies 7 miles (11 km) west of the highway. Here, past the huge Nandi monolith, you find the **Virabhadra Temple** (16th century), built by two brothers who were Vijayanaga governors of Penukonda. Its sculpture is glorious, and its ceiling frescoes the best surviving from the period: Note the costumes, faces, rich colors, and the donor brothers worshiping Shiva and Parvati (east side).

At **Alampur,** Andhra Pradesh's earliest large group of Hindu temples has been saved from the Srisailam Dam, a huge hydroelectric project on the Krishna River, which stretches east from here to Srisailam, 53 miles (85 km) away. Built by the Early Chalukyas of Badami in the seventh and eighth centuries, the temples overlooked the Tungabhadra River; now they are protected from the water by a barrage, and other threatened temples have been dismantled and re-erected here.

Restrained and simple, each has enriching sculpture, especially **Svarga Brahma Temple** (689). If you are driving from Hyderabad,

you could pause at Srisailam, where **Mallikarjuna Temple** (14th century), with its wonderful and unusual wall reliefs, overlooks a deep gorge in the Krishna River.

Puttaparthi is a remote, quiet village in the arid rocky hills of southwest Andhra Pradesh. It has leaped to fame because it is the birthplace, and the home from July to March, of one of India's best-known living saints, Sri Sathya Sai Baba. Thousands of disciples visit him each year, staying in the new **Prasanthi Nilaya Ashram,** which is like a model village. Born in 1926, the saint is credited with possessing supernatural abilities. He claims that his miracles are to shock materialists, while his message is really universal love: his image is seen all over India. At the ashram he gives *darshan* twice daily, which anyone may attend.

SOUTHEASTERN ANDHRA PRADESH
With the pilgrimage temple-city of Tirupati as its main attraction, this area is best visited from Chennai (see pp. 256–59). Traveling here from Hyderabad is best done over several days, with stops at some of the sites mentioned on these pages.

If you arrive at **Tirupati** from the rural peace of Andhra Pradesh, it may come as a shock. Every day, overcrowded busloads of pilgrims arrive from Chennai for a one-day visit. From the town they continue through the trees and up the switchback roads to worship at the **Venkateshvara Temple** (tenth century and later), on Tirumala Hill in the Seshachalam Hills. As the temple is open to non-Hindus, this is an opportunity to observe closely many aspects of Hinduism, from the preparatory cleansing head-shave on arrival to the almost intoxicating spiritual ecstasy of the chanting faithful at the sanctum. ∎

This lush land fed by two monsoon seasons is peppered with some of India's prettiest villages, each with ancient stone temples whose soaring and tapered gateways are landmarks across the viridian fields of paddy.

Tamil Nadu

A sacred cow with brightly painted horns

An elaborate *kolam,* a ritual pattern created using colored *muggu* (rice flour)

Tamil Nadu

THE STATE OF TAMIL NADU PULSATES WITH ENERGY AND VITALITY. MOST OF its monuments are busy places, so you can experience the vigor and purity of the great Dravidian culture in huge temple complexes thronged with people (see pp. 262–63). You can visit the British-built High Court of Chennai (Madras), busy with lawyers. Tamil Nadu also presents strong contrasts. Madurai's sprawling temple feels like a medieval temple town; hilltop Ooty is still reminiscent of its British hill station origins; Thanjavur retains some of its regal Chola majesty.

Furthermore, Tamil Nadu is comparatively compact. The relatively short drive from place to place through the clean, quaint villages is pure pleasure. You can easily drive from the British Victorian elegance of Chennai to a simple bronze-casting atelier, from the formal excitement of the Bharata Natyam dance to the bells and smells of Hindu worship aided by the temple's resident elephant. Undoubtedly, Tamil Nadu makes the gentlest introduction to India.

Look at the map, and it is clear why this is so. Tamil Nadu almost fills the southern tip of India. On the east, the Bay of Bengal's surf laps the sandy beaches of the Coromandel coast, which has for centuries brought international trade and cultural exchange with west and east. On the west, the steep and rugged Western Ghats are the barrier between Tamil Nadu and Kerala and Karnataka. British hill stations nestle in the northern Nilgiri Hills. South of here, the Anamalai (Elephant) Hills are a mixture of dense forest and velvet-smooth tea gardens. South again, more tea gardens and the hill station of Kodaikanal sit in the Palani Hills. Thus, as you can see, all the rivers flow eastward, including the great Kaveri (Cauvery), southern India's most sacred river (see p. 265).

Pallava, Chola, and then Pandya empires fueled the distinct and very sophisticated Tamil culture beginning in the seventh century. With

Area of map detail

New Delhi

THE DECCAN p. 222

Pulicat

5▷

Tiruttani
Ambattur
Avadi
CHENNAI (MADRAS)
Arcot
Sriperumbudur
Vrinchipuram
Vellore
Kanchipuram
Ambur
Chengalpattu
Krishnagiri
Vaniyambadi
VEDANTANGAL BIRD SANCTUARY
Mahabalipuram
Tirukkalukkundram
Tiruppattur
Gingee
Tiruvannamalai
Tindivanam
Vettavalam

4▷
THE DECCAN p. 222
Dharmapuri
Panamalai
Auroville
Villupuram
PUDUCHERRY

Yercaud
PUDUCHERRY (Pondicherry)
Cuddalore
Coromandel Coast

Salem
Attur
Neyveli
Bay of Bengal

2636m
Doda-Betta
mandalam (Ooty)
Coonoor
Bhavani
Tiruchengodu
Chidambaram
Nilgiri Hills
Mettuppalaiyam
Erode
Namakkal
Jayamkondacholapuram
Gangakondacholapuram
Tiruppur
Punjai
Perambalur
Kilaiyur
Tarangambadi
Kaveri (Cauvery)
Kumbakonam
Karaikal
Karur
Tiruvaiyaru
PUDUCHERRY
Coimbatore
Srirangam
Darasuram
Nagappattinam
3▷
Tiruchchirappalli (Trichy)
Thanjavur
Thiruvarur
Velanganni
Pollachi
Kodumbalur
Kiranur
Palani
Nartamalai
Pudukkottai
POINT CALIMERE WILDLIFE SANCTUARY
Vedaranniyam
Anaimalai Hills
Palani Hills
Dindigul
TAMIL NADU
Point Calimere

THE WEST COAST: GOA & KERALA p. 191
Kodaikanal
Alagarkoil
Chettinad
Teni
Karaikkudi
Polk Strait
Madurai
Devakottai
Thirupparankundram
Sivaganga
SRI LANKA (CEYLON)
Srivilliputtur
Virudunagar
2▷
Sivakasi
Ramanathapuram
Rameswaram
Rajapalaiyam
Kilakkarai
Dhanushkodi

Kalugumalai
Tenkasi
Tuticorin
Gulf of Mannar
Tirunelveli
Palayankottai
Krishnapuram
Papanasam
Alvar Tirunagari
Kayalpattinam
Tiruchchendur
1▷
Padmanabhapuram
Manapadu
0   100 kilometers
Nagercoil
0   75 miles
Suchindram
Kanniyakumari
Cape Comorin

A   B   C   D

little interference from the Mughals or the British, their monuments and culture survive today in this affluent, culturally rich, traditional, yet dynamic and modern state.

Tamil Nadu's capital, Madras, was renamed Chennai in 1996. Its economy mixes the historically important rice (see p. 266), sugar-cane, and cotton with export business and industrial activity so rampant that Tamil Nadu currently has India's top industrial investment growth rate—even higher than Maharashtra's. As you might expect, literacy is high, and the state language of Tamil is often supplemented with skills in English rather than Hindi. ∎

A view of bustling Chennai, with its wide streets, exotic skyline, and, in the distance, port cranes and the Bay of Bengal

Chennai (Madras)

TAMIL NADU'S SPRAWLING COASTAL CAPITAL IS TUCKED UP in the northern corner of the state, just south of its huge port. With a population of around six million, this is India's fourth largest city, but its seaside position and relative spaciousness make its center pleasant to explore.

Chennai, Tamil Nadu

🗺 255 D5

India Tourist Office

✉ 154 Anna Salai

☎ 044-8524295

🕐 Closed Sat. p.m. & Sun.

State Tourist Office

www.tamilnadutourism.org

✉ 2 Wallajah Rd.

☎ 044-25638358

Visitor tip

Strong currents make it unwise to swim at Chennai.

There is certainly plenty to see while strolling around the very fine streets or taking advantage of the busy beach. Chennai is also the place to prepare for your inland temple tours by watching a performance of Bharata Natyam (see p. 257) and visiting the small but exceptional museum collections. So even if you opt to bypass the city in favor of relaxing at a beach hotel to the south, Chennai deserves at least a long day's visit, possibly two.

Founded on the Cooum and Adyar Rivers in 1639 by the British merchant Francis Day, the city's site was chosen for its cheap local cotton. Despite having no port and ferocious surf, which meant much cargo was lost as it was landed in small boats, Madras grew fast. By 1644 the East India Company was

building its fort and had a work-force of around 400 weavers working in the surrounding villages. This textile trade continues to be vital to Chennai today, as important as its leather and auto industries. In 1688 James II (R.1685–88) granted a municipal charter, India's first, to a city that by then had about 300,000 inhabitants. (The population of London, Europe's largest city by far, was 575,000.) Soon there were twin towns on the site: the Europeans' Fort St. George and the Indians' Chennaipatnam, or Black Town, which was renamed Georgetown in honor of the King-Emperor George V's visit in 1911.

By 1740, British trade in India was so substantial that it represented 10 percent of all

Britain's revenue and made a major contribution to London's Georgian wealth and affluence. Much of this trade passed through Madras, which remained the nerve center of British influence in India until the move to Calcutta in 1772 (see p. 289). The city's established merchants built their famous stuccoed houses outside the walls of the fort and ensured that their departed loved ones were remembered in style in the fort's St. Mary's Church.

Madras was a relaxed, elegant, gleaming garden city cooled by sea breezes. The French occupied it in 1746–49, but the young general, Robert Clive, crushed them at the Battle of Arcot in 1751, consolidating Britain's supremacy in southern India; Britain's position in Bengal was confirmed at Plassey in 1757 (see p. 315). Even when the British focus moved to Calcutta, Madras remained an important city. To give the capital of the Madras presidency a promenade worthy of its status, Governor Grant Duff (1881–86) laid out the splendid 3-mile-long (5 km) **Marina,** which runs right along the waterfront. Soon this classical city was adorned

with a string of spectacular waterfront Indo-Saracenic buildings, several designed by Robert Fellowes Chisholm and Henry Irwin. Today the Marina is one of the most beautiful promenades to be found in any city, and is much loved by Chennai's residents, who come down here in the cool of the evening for a stroll, small talk, a snack of freshly barbecued fish, or a cooling frolic in the waves. ■

An ornately adorned woman performs the traditional Tamil temple dance, bharata natyam.

Bharata Natyam

This is probably India's oldest classical dance, created in the Tamil Nadu temples as a form of worship and now enjoying a vigorous revival. A woman performs the solo dance that begins with *alarippu,* symbolizing the body unfolding to offer itself to the gods. *Nritta* (pure dance) follows, when the dancer uses a combination of formalized face, hand, body, and dance expressions to expound on a poem sung by the *natuvangari* (conductor), accompanied by musicians. Rhythm is all-important, emphasized when the dancer replies to the music by stamping her feet to sound the bells of her ankle bracelets. A dancer's initiation performance should be for the gods in one of the great temples such as Chidambaram (see p. 265). You can find regular performances at Chennai's many *sabbas,* arts societies, and venues, and there are more than 500 dance and classical music performances during the December–January Chennai Festival; the tourist offices carry full details. ■

A drive around Chennai (Madras)

This drive works around Chennai's current system of one-way streets to give you a good introduction to the city. Enjoy a walk on the splendid beach before you start—and maybe another after you finish.

Start with a visit to **San Thome Cathedral ❶** (1547, 1896), where St. Thomas the Apostle's relics are kept. It is believed that he came to India from Palestine in A.D. 52 and was killed in A.D. 78. Around 1100 the saint's remains were moved inland and a new church was built, possibly by the Persian Christian community. It stands in Mylapore, once the Tamil port, where the Portuguese made a settlement in 1522. Nearby **Kapalishvara Temple** is lively with plenty of festivals, singing, and busy bazaars.

Enthusiasts can detour to the southwest to see **St. Thomas's Mount,** believed to be where the saint was stoned to death. **The Old Cantonment** is nearby, with lots of old flat-topped Madras villas; return via the racetrack and **Raj Bhawan** (1817), the former Government House built for Sir Thomas Munro.

The drive follows the Marina, renamed **Kamaraj Road,** for a group of Victorian buildings that are collectively as impressive as Mumbai's (Bombay). Moving up it, pause to see the circular former **Vivekananda House ❷** (1842), once the Ice House, where the Tudor Ice Company used to store blocks of ice imported from America; the Lutyens-style **University Examination Hall;** and **Presidency College.** Its older part was designed by Chisholm (1882) in a style mixing French and Italian Renaissance and various local details.

Next come the **Public Water Works** (1870), **Chepauk Palace** (1768) built for the anglophile Nawab of the Carnatic, with Chisholm's later tower (1870), and Chisholm's university **Senate House** (1873). This time he went for the Gothic-Saracenic style, with polychrome stones and arcades. A Golden Jubilee statue of Queen-Empress Victoria (1887) stands outside. Both she and Chantry's bronze equestrian statue of popular Sir Thomas Munro (1839), seen on the right after crossing the Cooum River, have survived postindependence cleansing of Raj memories.

A group of aspiring advocates in front of Chennai's magnificent High Courts

Continue north to **Fort St. George ❸,** begun in 1644. Drive or walk through it to find **St. Mary's Church ❹** (1678–1680), the spiritual heart of old Chennai and the East's oldest surviving Anglican church. Inside, look for the original, intricately carved teak gallery balustrade and the black Pallavaram granite font where Job Charnock, who would later found Calcutta, had his daughters baptized. A stunning collection of funerary monuments includes several by John Flaxman and John Bacon. Elihu Yale (governor 1687–1692) married here and was later a benefactor to Yale University.

Now for a contrast: the spectacular Indo-Saracenic warren of the **High Courts ❺** (1888–1892), whose design by J. W. Brassington was revised by Irwin and J. H. Stephens. Up the stairs by the statue of Sri T. Muthasamy Iyer, the first Indian judge, the public courts have beautiful stained glass and tiles. Finally, drive past the Gothic arcades of **Chennai Central Station ❻** (1868–1872) to find, on the right, **St. Andrew's Kirk ❼** (1818–1821), considered India's most accomplished neoclassic church; the circular interior

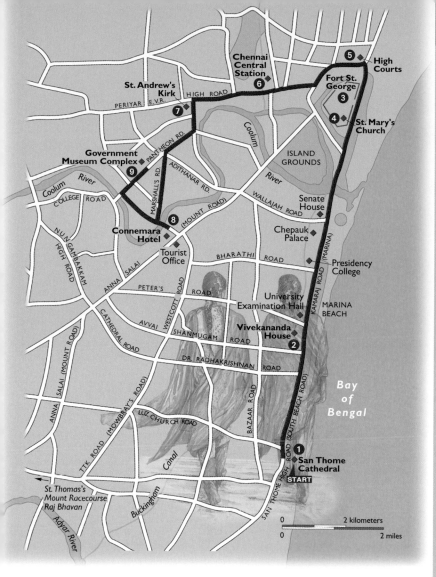

has its original louvered doors and cane pews.

The **Connemara Hotel** ❽ has an excellent lunch buffet of local dishes. You can get dance performance information from the tourist office on nearby Anna Salai.

The **Government Museum Complex** ❾ (closed Fri.), also grandly called The Pantheon, is exceptionally good and deserves a whole afternoon. Founded in 1851, it has three main sections: stone carvings, including the Amaravati sculptures upstairs; bronzes, many from Chola temples; and musical instruments, photographs, and Chettinad carvings. ■

See area map page 255
San Thome Cathedral
About 4 miles (6 km)
Allow a full day, with lunch as indicated
Government Museum Complex

NOT TO BE MISSED
- Strolling up the Marina
- St. Mary's Church
- Government Museum Complex

Mahabalipuram
(Mamallapuram)

GREAT CAVES, ROCKS AND BOULDERS, CARVED STONES AND friezes, and monolithic temples testify to the former importance of Mahabalipuram, port city of the Pallavas, the first great dynasty of southern India. Their royal capital was at Kanchipuram (see pp. 264–65).

Mahabalipuram

255 D4

Tourist Office

✉ North end of the village

🕐 Closed Sat. & Sun.

Visitor tip

There is a huge amount to see here, mostly of very high quality. So, start early, and take a break at a café or hotel.

Rising from local rulers to wealthy emperors, the Pallava dynasts believed in divine right and, in Hindu tradition, traced their ancestry back to Brahma. They called their empire Dravidia and extended it over present-day Tamil Nadu and into the Deccan, coming into repeated conflict with the Early Chalukyas of Badami (see p. 234). The Pallavas created much of the blueprint by which Tamil Nadu would live for centuries and promoted the village and temple culture known as Dravidian. They encouraged agriculture to increase both produce and taxes. Rice was the main crop and bartering unit, but coconuts, mangoes, plantains, cotton, and gingelly (sesame) were also grown. Each village built its own brick-lined tank as its essential water reservoir; many are still in use today. Taxes were levied on everyone and everything, from marriage parties to letter carriers; only weavers to the royal court were exempt.

Mahabalipuram's survivors are Tamil Nadu's earliest monuments. Mostly dating from the seventh and early eighth centuries, they seem to show a relentless thirst for experimentation, and much of the temple carving is sublime. It is best to go early, stopping for drinks in a café.

It was under the politically powerful Mahendravarman I *(R. 600–630)*, a dramatist and poet who converted from Jainism to Shaivism, that some of the earliest rock-cut temples were chiseled. He was succeeded by Mamalla *(R. 630–668)* and later by Rajasimha *(R. 700–728)*.

Here there is a selection of especially wonderful monuments to look for. Start by visiting the so-called **Tiger Cave,** found in the trees about a mile (1.6 km) north of the village. A huge boulder has been carved to create a small portico surrounded by fierce masklike *yali* heads and two elephants. Along a path, find another early temple, a tiny living shrine roofed in coconut leaf. Beside it, a row of upright stones placed in the sand to face the sunrise has its origins in pre-Hindu nature worship.

In the village, clamber up the hill behind the center to find **Varaha Cave Temple.** Colossal, bold, and vigorous sculptures fill the interior: Varaha lifting up Dhudevi (left), Trivikrama (right), and Lakshmi and Durga on the rear wall.

Back in the village center, there are two treats: first, **Arjuna's Penance,** a remarkable piece of top-quality relief carving, whose composition, of great complexity and intellect, coats some 50 feet (15 m) of a rock face. Using delicate modeling and carefully observed detail, mixing naturalism with stylization, and taking advantage of a cleft in the rock, the craftsmen have enriched their story. Today, we interpret it as either the penance of Arjuna (standing on one leg) or the sage Bhagiratha persuading Shiva to receive the Ganga River in his matted locks. Next to this, find the **Krishna Mandapa,** whose back wall has a gentle and bucolic scene

of Krishna protecting the *gopies* by lifting Mount Goverdhana as an umbrella; see the farmer milking his cow.

Now drive past the stone-carvers' workshops and climb the steps up to **Mahishamardini Temple,** whose veranda sculptures are yet more masterpieces: Vishnu sleeping on the serpent (left) and Durga killing the buffalo-headed demon (right).

Beyond the village, standing alone in a sandy enclosure, the **Pancha Rathas** are five monolith temples; that is, they are huge boulders carved to become temples. Their names mean little, but their variety of shapes and their carvings reveal an intensely creative period. See especially the tallest and most elaborate *rath* (chariot), whose

sculptures already have a recognizable iconography; the south side shows Shiva with the royal patron, Mamalla.

Early in the eighth century, later than all these different caves and monoliths, Mahabalipuram's **Shore Temple** was built. Together with Kailasanatha Temple at Kanchipuram, this is the first significant structural temple in Tamil Nadu and provides the blueprint for the Dravidian temple (see pp. 262–63). ∎

Part of the Krishna Mandapa relief at Mahabalipuram, a farmer milks his cow.

Dravidian temples

Tamil Nadu's temples were built by the villagers to be their religious, social, cultural, and political focus—a position many still hold today. Funded by the king or a local man of means, they kept thousands of people employed for life, and still do. Temples remain the bedrock of Tamil Nadu communities.

The temple itself follows a basic format. One principal *gopura* (gateway) through the wall leads into a courtyard and so to the porch, *mandapa* (hall), and main shrine; the mandapas and shrine have increasingly lofty *vimanhas* (roofs). The elements are in line, so the worshiper progresses from the open spaces and their ebullient, symbolic sculpture to the increasingly dark, mysterious, simple, and womblike sanctum.

This pilgrim has rubbed his forehead and arms with ashes as a sign of penitence.

Many temples were founded by the Pallavas and Cholas, then enlarged by the Vijayanagas and Pandyas. They sometimes added subsidiary shrines for the consort or family of the principal deity; thus a temple to Shiva could be given shrines for his consort, Parvati, and his sons, Ganesh and Kartikeya. They might add extra mandapas for dance or special festivals, and around the central core they might build rooms for administration, facilities for cooking, sleeping rooms for the ever growing numbers of temple inmates, and libraries for study. Storage rooms were also needed for the festival chariots and for the coconuts, sugar, flowers, and spices sold in the temple to the faithful as offerings during their *puja* (worship). You can see this arrangement in many temples.

As the temples got bigger, extra and taller walls were built to increase the space for these buildings and to protect the increasingly large treasuries from attack by greedy Muslim armies. Temples at Tiruchirappalli and Madurai have several concentric walls and still function as complete cities. These later walls, whose tops were frequently decorated with Nandi bulls (Shiva's vehicle), have gopuras with higher and higher pyramid-shaped roofs covered with carvings of all the deities of the Hindu pantheon. This was because the untouchables, the lowest caste, were not permitted to enter the temples, and they therefore worshiped by looking up at the gopuras. It was for their benefit, as well as for that of the old and infirm that, at the many festivals, the temple deity was hauled around the village on an elaborately carved wooden *rath* (chariot).

Locals used their temples for much more than just simple worship. Their devotions became increasingly passionate, stimulating the great devotional poetry and music, the Bharata Natyam dance (see p. 257), and the legendary silk-weaving to clothe the deities. Locals went to Sanskrit school in the temple; later they traded, held meetings, and celebrated there, too. Today, a Hindu may well do a special puja before making a journey or opening a store, or after landing a good job. In the past the income of whole villages was given to a temple—the inscriptions running around temple platforms are often a record such donations. Nowadays, wealthy Hindus may pay for special pujas, maintenance work, or meals for the poor. The wealthy industrial Birla family has even completely funded several entirely new temples. ∎

The temple is often still the focus of daily life, which goes on all around a Kanchipuram temple (above), while vendors take up positions outside Madurai's Minakshi Temple (below).

This Vijayanagar-
period temple
sculpture of a
rearing horse
crushing his
enemy symbolizes
good triumphing
over evil, Hindus
over Muslims.

Kanchipuram

🔼 255 C5

A temple odyssey

THIS TOUR FROM CHENNAI (MADRAS) TO THANJAVUR
visits a handful of the many glorious temples, some now empty,
others functioning just as they have done for centuries.

KANCHIPURAM

The only one of the Seven Sacred
Cities dedicated to both Shiva and
Vishnu, Kanchipuram was enriched
by the Pallava rulers (see p. 260),
who made it their capital. Chola,
Vijayanaga, and Nayaka rulers further embellished it. Today this busy
town, 35 miles (72 km) southeast of
Chennai, has 50 or so functioning
temples whose rituals gave birth to

one of southern India's most
important silk-weaving centers.
(Buy here, or, for more choice and
better prices, in the big cities.)

The buildings span a thousand
years of creative and devotional
output. Begin with the simple
sandstone, eighth-century
Kailasanatha Temple (0.5
mile/1 km west of the city center),
the finest of the Pallava ruler

Rajasimha's buildings, dedicated to Shiva as lord of Kailasha, his mountain home; you can see a variety of Shiva images. Late eighth-century **Vaikuntha Perumal Temple** stands to the east, near the train station. Built by Nandivarma II, the temple has one *mandapa* that leads to three shrines dedicated to Vishnu as the boar and lion; the rear wall sculptures illustrate Pallava historic events.

The later **Ekambareshvar Temple** (mostly 16th and 17th century), dedicated to Shiva as lord of the mango tree, is the city's largest temple (north of the center). Built in 1509 by the Vijayanaga emperor Krishnadeveraya, it has a soaring *gopora* (192 feet/58 m high), which leads toward an equally huge mandapa and corridor. The 12th-century **Varadaraja Temple** (1.5 miles/3 km southeast of the city) has a Vijayanaga addition, whose columns are elaborately carved with Vaishnava iconography and rearing horses.

KANCHIPURAM TO CHIDAMBARAM

As soon as you leave Kanchipuram, you're on country roads. On the way to Mahabalipuram,

Uttaramrur has two fine late Pallava temples built by Dantivarman *(R. 796–817)*. If you want to see more Pallava monuments, spend a very quiet but long rural day inland; otherwise drive right down to Pondicherry (see p. 267).

The rarely visited early cave temple at **Mandagappattu,** near Gingee has an inscription that refers to Mahendravarman I *(R. 580–630)*. Continue to the huge but clearly laid out **Arunachaleshvara Temple** (16th to 17th century) at **Tiruvannamalai** (major festival, *Nov.–Dec.),* where Shiva is worshiped as Lord of the Eastern Mountain. Finish with the hilltop temple (early eighth century) at **Panamalai,** 19 miles (30 km) east.

CHIDAMBARAM TO THANJAVUR

Chidambaram's **Nataraja Temple** (12th to 13th century) is like a fair every day. Nataraja is Shiva as the cosmic dancer, the Cholas' favorite form of Shiva. Try to arrive in time to witness the busy and elaborate main morning puja, usually around 9:30 a.m.; temple management and pilgrims' gifts make this one of India's richest

Chidambaram
🏛 255 C3
Chidambaram Tourist Office
www.tamilnadutourism.org
✉ Next to T.T.D.C. Hotel Tamil Nadu, Railway Feeder Road

Visitor tips
Neither Kumbakonam nor Kanchipuram has a tourist office. You can obtain a detailed map of Kanchipuram from the T.T.D.C. Tamil Nadu Hotel. A pleasant way to explore the temples more thoroughly is to rent a bicycle.

Kaveri (Cauvery) River

Southern India's most sacred river rises in Karnataka and carries its life-giving waters into Tamil Nadu. Here its delta is used for intensive rice cultivation before emptying into the Bay of Bengal. For southern Indians the Kaveri is as important as the Ganga, and its banks have many temples and special *ghats* (steps) for death ceremonies—Trichy's Ranganathaswamy Temple occupies a whole island.

Blessed by two monsoons, in July and November, the river usually flows generously—although the governments of Karnataka and Tamil Nadu argue over how much water each may draw off. This is nothing new. Historically, Tamil Nadu harnessed the Kaveri to its advantage. To fund arts patronage, agrarian administrative units called *nadus* (hence Tamil Nadu's name) promoted better irrigation for more efficient farming. Paddy crops increased from two to three a year, creating a surplus of rice that was their most lucrative export. ∎

River and was intended to surpass his predecessor, Rajajraja I's Thanjavur temple. Only a few village names (meaning "watchman's area," "firework makers," etc.) and some brick debris give clues to the extent of Rajendra's city. But the temple is testament enough. It is superb, neither big nor complex: Its glory is the monumental simplicity and its sculpture. Large panels on the outside of the shrine, mostly of Shiva, include one magnificent composition of Shiva garlanding Chandesha.

It is a short drive to **Kumbakonam,** a busy and ancient religious center between the banks of the Kaveri and its tributary, Arasala. Here are bronze-workers, traditional gold and jewelry dealers, and, of course, temples. The ritual core of the city is **Mahamakam Tank,** the focus of the festival held here every 12 years (next one 2004). The finest temple, however, is found just outside the city, across the Arasala at **Darasuram,** where the Airavateshvara Temple (mid-12th century) built by Rajaraja II (*R.*1146–1172) is probably the finest late Chola building; the compact structure is coated in fine sculpture. From here the lanes twist through paddy fields and villages to Thanjavur (see pp. 268-69). ∎

His power and transport combined, a farmer's precious bullocks have their horns brightly painted for Pongal festival.

temples. Then explore the warren of halls and corridors, mostly built in the late Chola period; do not miss the carvings of Bharata Natyam dance positions on the inside walls of the main gates.

The ride to evocatively named **Gangakondacholapuram** goes inland through villages where rope-making is a thriving cottage industry; you can pause to see how it is done. Then, seemingly in the middle of nowhere, you arrive at the windowless wall surrounding **Brihadishvara Temple.** Built by Rajendra I (*R.*1012–1044) in his new capital, it celebrated his victory in eastern India up by the Ganga

Importance of rice

If you are in southern India in early January, you may witness Pongal, the rice harvest festival. Farmers scrub their bullocks and paint their horns. On Pongal morning, each village home boils newly harvested rice amid a complicated ritual. When it boils over it is *pongal,* a sign indicating a rich harvest to follow.

Here, rice is more than a staple part of the diet and economy. It is a fundamental part of life. Before a

child goes to school, there is a rice ceremony to Saraswati, goddess of learning. A bride tips a bowl of rice into her new home to symbolize fertility and prosperity; a mourning family offers rice balls at the *sradh* ceremony to help the spirit find peace. Throughout the state you can see *kolams,* intricate patterns of rice powder made by women to encourage prosperity and happiness and to ward off black ants from their houses. ∎

Puducherry (Pondicherry)

ABOUT A CENTURY AFTER THE PORTUGUESE ARRIVED TO
trade on the east coast, the English, Dutch, and French followed. The
French bought land from the sultan of Bijapur in 1672, and two years
later, François Martin set up a trading post. Although Pondicherry
was lost to the Dutch once and to the English several times, the
Marquis de Dupleix, who dreamed of a French empire in India,
restored its prestige, and Jean Law laid out the grid-plan town
(1756–1777) that still survives. After independence the French hung
on to their territories, only relinquishing them in 1954. Today, about
14,000 French nationals live here.

Pondicherry
255 C4
**Pondicherry
Tourist Office**
www.tourism.pon.nic.in
Goubert Salai
0413-2339497

**Pondicherry
Museum**
Closed Mon.

You can spend a pleasant day wandering the deserted streets of the
old core, catching a hint of French
colonial times as you pass by old
colonial houses with louvered windows. Start in the main square.
Dupleix's statue (1870) stands
near the gleaming white **Raj
Niwas,** a fine French colonial
house (1752) built as his palace.
(There is a brief but splendidly formal ceremony here each sunset.)
Across the square, **Pondicherry
Museum** occupies the French former Government Library and displays all sorts of bits and pieces,
including Dupleix's bed.

Down on the waterfront, eight
pillars from Gingee and a statue of
Mahatma Gandhi stand at the
entrance to the pier. South of here
is a statue of Joan of Arc, the
**Église de Notre Dame des
Anges** (1855), and, in the cemetery opposite, the tomb of Dupleix's
enterprising follower, Charles,
Marquis de Bussy (1785).

North of the pier, **Sri
Aurobindo Headquarters** is
on Rue de la Marine. Sri Aurobindo
Ghosh (1872–1950), a Bengali
educated at Cambridge, retired here
to practice yoga. He and his disciple, a Parisian known as the Mother
(1878–1973), established the
ashram here. In 1968, she founded
the nearby futuristic city of
Auroville, designed by French

architect Roger Anger. There is a
fascinating handmade **paper
factory** around the corner *(Closes
3 p.m.),* and daily tours go to
Auroville (see p. 282).

Finally, see whether the home of
the 18th-century diarist Ananda
Rangapillai, one of Dupleix's protégés, is open to the public. His
house, at 69 rue Rangapillai, mixes
Indian and French colonial styles. ■

**The pretty
Church of the
Sacred Heart of
Jesus on South
Boulevard**

Thanjavur

LIFE IN THIS MODERATE-SIZED, MODERATELY PACED
town still centers on the monumental royal Brihadishvara Temple
(circa 1010) built by Rajaraja I *(R.* 985–1014), who donated the
gilded pot finial on top of the 217-foot-high (66 m) tower. In the
morning, locals hurry in through the sun-drenched gates to pray
before work. In the evenings they come in their hundreds as the last
rays of sun are glowing on the tower and enliven the whole compound with their prayer, chattering, music, and religious readings.

Thanjavur
🅜 255 C3
**Thanjavur
Tourist Office**
www.tamilnadutourism.org
✉ Hotel Tamu Nadu
Complex
☎ 04362-230984

Thanjavur was Rajaraja I's capital,
built up under previous Chola
rulers, chieftains in the area for
centuries. One leader conquered
Thanjavur in the ninth century and
quickly claimed descent from the
sun. Expansion of land and power
followed under Rajaraja I and his
son Rajendra I (*R.* 1012–1044).
Campaigns in Kerala, the Maldives,
Sri Lanka (Ceylon), and right up to
Orissa brought most of the Indian
peninsula under Chola control
until the Hoysalas of Halebid and
the Pandyas of Madurai expanded
in the 12th century.

Chola trading in cottons, silks,
spices, drugs, jewels, ivory, sandal-

wood, and camphor was lucrative,
while at home agriculture was
made more efficient. Caste differences became stronger. The poor
were encouraged to win spiritual
and social respect by giving their
skills and time to the temple, the
wealthy to acquire prestige by
donating whole villages to the
temples. Church and state became
intertwined: The god-king cult was
promoted through image worship
of past rulers and temple buildings,
and the *raja-guru* (king's priest)
became the king's chief spiritual
and temporal adviser.

The thoroughly royal **Brihadishvara Temple** epitomizes this

increasingly controlled and central-ized state. The biggest and richest Chola temple was conceived as a temple-fort and dedicated to Shiva as the Great Lord. The gateway leads into a large, rectangular court, where a Nandi bull lies in a high pavilion in front of the steep steps up to the temple. Rich sculpture decorates the porch and exterior; see especially the Shiva images on the outside of the sanctum. Inscriptions run all around the platform, like a public notebook documenting the construction of the temple and the donations, together with the names of the donors. Inside, join the faithful to see the colossal *lingum*. There are Chola period paintings here, too, including one of a royal visit to Chidambaram (west wall) and another of Shiva riding in a chariot drawn by Brahma (north wall); many others were overpainted by the Nayakas. The compound has a

delicate 17th-century subsidiary temple dedicated to Subramanya, one of Shiva's sons, and a treasury, museum, and library.

In the royal palace compound is the **Nayak Durbar Hall Art Museum,** a collection of Chola bronzes found in the area, exhibited with beautiful simplicity in open rooms around the palace courtyard, together with fine stone carving. Several show Shiva as Nataraja (see box below); the best were found at Tiruvelvikudi and Jambavanodai. Others show him as the archer, with his consort Parvati, or with their son Skanda. The masterpiece is Shiva with Parvati, one arm out-stretched. ■

Cholas & Shiva Nataraja

Hindu temple sculpture is the most sublime achievement of Indian art, reaching one of several peaks under Chola patronage. Shiva is a favorite deity. He represents dynamic energy, both creative—hence his symbol of the *lingum*—and destructive, which suited the powerful warring temple patrons. His developed per-sonality was at once outrageous, amoral, and wild, yet ascetic and that of the perfect family man.

The Chola rulers worshiped Shiva Nataraja—Lord of the Dance. Shiva dances in a wild, ecstatic frenzy or in a withdrawn yogic state, eyes down-cast or closed, within a ring of flames. With his hands he carries the fire of destruction and the double drum, whose beat summons up creation, and calms and protects the worshiper. Shiva's matted hair contains the Ganga River-goddess; below him, the demon Apasmara, personifying ignorance, looks up in hope. In all, Shiva symbolizes both endings and beginnings. ■

Chola bronze of Shiva as Nataraja

Tiruchchirappalli

THE SMALL TOWN OF TIRUCHCHIRAPPALLI, BETTER KNOWN as Trichy, lies beside the sacred Kaveri River. Just north of the town the waters split to flow on each side of a long island, thus considered especially holy. Here, at Srirangam, one of southern India's largest and most complete sacred complexes, Sri Ranganathaswamy, was built. Founded by the Cholas, it received patronage from both the Pandya and Hoysala rulers, was sacked twice by 14th-century Muslim armies from Delhi, then expanded unabated during the 16th and 17th centuries.

Tiruchchirappalli
🗺 255 C3
Tiruchchirappalli Tourist Office
www.tamilnadutourism.org
✉ Williams Rd.
☎ 0431-2460136

Today, Tiruchchirappalli is a vibrant temple city dedicated to Ranganatha—Vishnu when he is reclining on the serpent Anata. Pilgrims swell the resident population daily, especially at festival time. It is a timeless yet thriving world. The first, huge gateway, with writhing sculptures painted bright yellows, greens, and pinks, was completed only in 1968. As you move forward, past stores selling everything from temple offerings and souvenirs to chilis and light bulbs, the sacred mystery of the temple increases.

The temple itself begins at the fourth wall, where you leave your shoes. Here you see the **Ranganayaki Temple** and the richly carved thousand-pillared **Kalyan Mandapa.** Even more

spectacular carving has transformed the pillars of the **Sheshagiriraya Mandapa** into rearing horses carrying hunters armed with spears, a typical Vijayanaga double symbol of good triumphing over evil—that is, of brave Hinduism protecting the temple against Muslim invaders. In contrast, the Nayaka-period **Venugopala shrine** on the south side is delicately carved with maidens leaning against trees.

At the fourth wall, ask to climb onto the roof to enjoy the splendid view right across all the walls to the gold-encrusted sanctum; the *gopuras* diminish toward the center. Inside the third courtyard, continue to the **Garuda Manadapa,** a hall carved with maidens and donors that surrounds the shrine to Vishnu's man-eagle vehicle. Only Hindus can continue to the inner sanctum to see the image of reclining Vishnu.

As well as its stupendous temple, the town has a Chola-period earthen dam, the **Grand Anicut;** the great rock with temples including the **Lower Cave Temple** (Pandya, eighth century) and **Upper Cave Temple** (Pallava, 580–630); and the **Church of St. John** (1816) in the cantonment. ■

Rooftop level view of the gopuras protecting the gold-roofed inner sanctum and treasury of Sri Ranganatha-swamy Temple

Rural routes from Trichy

THE DRIVES FROM TRICHY TO THANJAVUR AND TO Madurai are not long. If you have time and a good driver, a detour from either one takes you right into peaceful, sometimes dramatic country with magical sites. Take water and snacks.

Tiruchchirappalli
255 C3

Thanjavur
255 C3

Madurai
255 B2

TRICHY TO THANJAVUR
From Trichy, take the road south-east to Kiranur. Along this 34-mile (55 km) route you can stop to look at a group of hundreds of dilapidated, abandoned *ayyanars* on the right. These are heraldic terra-cotta figures of equestrian deities, sometimes with horses and elephants, often brightly colored, found on village outskirts throughout Tamil Nadu. Their functions are to protect the village from calamities such as plague, make barren land fertile, bring good harvests, and protect night watchmen. A priest regularly performs *pujas* at each group. On special occasions, such as the time of sowing seeds, new ayyanars are added and special pujas performed.

At Kiranur, turn right for the village of **Nartamalai.** Once there, leave your car at the far end of the village and walk for about 15 minutes up the granite hill to find a cluster of early Chola temples. One is cut into the granite and has 12 identical high-relief Vishnu figures carved into the back wall. The free-standing temple has guardian figures flanking the door, and fading murals.

It is about an hour's drive from Nartamalai to **Mallaiyadipatti.** Here you find superb late Pallava caves (ninth century), one carved with a huge Vishnu reclining on the Cosmic Ocean, another carved with the nine gods. From here continue to the main Trichy–Thanjavur road, and turn right. Soon you will see on the left a memorial—two standing stones and a crossbar—to a death in childbirth, which travelers use to rest their load. A little farther along,

on the right, a group of ayyanars stands beneath a banyan tree across a small field. The road continues to Thanjavur.

TRICHY TO MADURAI
Leave Trichy on the country road to Madurai (88 miles/140 km), not the main one, toward Kodumbalur. You will pass brightly colored ayyanars, whose creators have kept them up to date by giving them wristwatches. At Kodumbalur, the isolated double **Muvakoil Temple** (ninth century) built by the Cholas is all that remains of the original nine shrines. Their sculptures are glorious; it's worth coming here just to see the Shiva Nataraja on the east side of the south shrine.

Continue to **Sittannavasal** to find a Jain cave temple (ninth century) cut into a long granite outcrop. Inside the hall, find images of Parshvanatha (right), Mahavira (left) on the sides, and more Jinas in the rear walls. Delicate paintings survive, too: dancing maidens and royal figures on the columns, a lotus pond in full blossom on the hall ceiling, a design with knotted patterns on the shrine ceiling. A rocky overhang on top of the hill has a natural cavern with polished beds for Jain monks and an inscription that dates from the second to first century B.C.

Pudukkottai is the next stop: Its Tondaiman rajas supported the British against Tipu Sultan and the French; thus they received titles and security and left a well-built city. In the old area, Tirugorakarna, find the **Gokarneshvara Temple** (begun in the seventh century), with its 18th-century *Ramayana* paintings and rock-cut Pallava inner chamber, whose carvings include a set of Matrikas (mother goddesses).

Near the temple entrance, **Government Museum** (*Closed Mon.*) displays quality local finds.

You can now go direct to Madurai or make four final stops. First is at the village of **Avudaiyarkoil,** where the broad temple passageway has supports carved with Tondaiman royals, their ministers, and, at the end, Shiva in his fierce aspects. Farther into the temple, find a shrine dedicated to the local saint, Manikkavachakar.

A road leads cross-country to **Karaikkudi** in the heart of the Chettinad communities, where merchants made their money in the 19th and 20th centuries in trade and finance with Madras, Burma, and Malaya. Their mansions have some of the finest wood carving in Tamil Nadu but display a masonry facade to orderly streets in small settlements. See them here and in **Devakottai** to the south and **Chettinad** village to the north from where it is about 59 miles (95 km) to Madurai (see pp. 274–75). ■

As you drive through rural areas watch for ayyanars, protective terra-cotta figures grouped outside villages.

The riot of gaily painted, dancing and cavorting gods and goddesses decorating this *gopura* at Madurai's Minakshi temple heralds the richness of color and carving to be found inside.

Madurai

PILGRIMS FLOCK TO MADURAI'S BUSY, COLORFUL, AND HUGE complex of the Minakshi Sundareshvara Temple, dedicated to Shiva's consort, Parvati (Minakshi), giving it a lively yet medieval atmosphere.

Madurai
🗺 255 B2
Madurai Tourist Office
www.tamilnadutourism.org
✉ W. Veli St.
☎ 0452-2334757

Built on the banks of the Vaigai River, Madurai was founded by the Pandyas, who made it their capital while they ruled south Tamil Nadu (7th to 13th centuries). However, in 1323 Malik Kafur's Tughlaq forces from Delhi took Madurai and stayed until 1378, when the Vijayanagas liberated it. Their governors, known as Nayakas, slowly asserted their independence; Tirumala (R.1623–1660) was an especially active builder throughout

his kingdom. Resisting Mughals and Marathas, the Nayakas held on to their throne until the British established control in 1763.

Madurai's temple is thus a testament to Nayaka royal and aristocratic patronage through the 17th and 18th centuries. Remodeling and redecoration continue to keep the ceilings, murals, and *gopura* as colorful as when built. If you can, make both a morning and an evening visit to find *pujas*, elephant processions, music, and singing in the various halls. The 12-day festival in April–May, to celebrate the coronation of Minakshi and her marriage to Shiva, is spectacular.

While simply wandering through the corridors and halls will be rewarding, there are some special things worth seeing. Entering the **Ashta Shakti Mandapa,** notice how elegant and tall the gopuras are. Then find the lively dancing men flanking the corridor to the **Potramarai Kulam** (Golden Lily Tank), behind

which you find superb carvings of the *Mahabharata* heroes in the **Panch Pandava Mandapa.** Just near here, in the gloom, find a beautiful and sensuous freestanding group of Shiva and Parvati. See also the **Kambattadi Mandapa** with its seated Nandi, the huge, corridor-like **Viravasantaraya Mandapa,** the **Temple Art Museum**'s carvings, and the **Pudu Mandapa,** whose columns are sculptured into portraits of all the Nayaka kings up to Tirumala, each with his family and ministers. ∎

MADURAI'S TEMPLE

Madurai's temple is best appreciated by wandering the corridors and halls; only the inner sanctuaries of the shrines are off-limits to non-Hindus. All day, processions, worshipers, and visitors throng the temple. Climb the south gopura for a wonderful overview and don't miss the Temple Art Museum's carvings.

1. **Entrance through the Ashta Shakti Mandapa (Porch of the Eight Goddesses)**
2. **Potramarai Kulam (Golden Lily Tank)**
3. **Minakshi shrine**
4. **Kambattadi Mandapa**
5. **Sundareshvara (Shiva) shrine**
6. **Viravasantaraya Mandapa**
7. **Pudu Mandapa**
8. **South gopura**

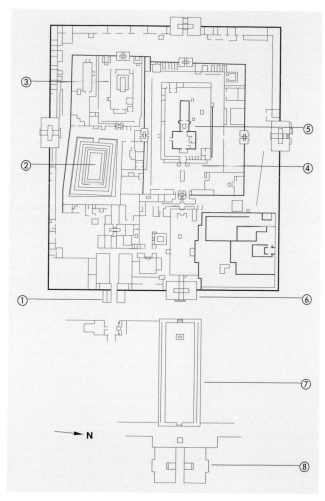

N

Southern Tamil Nadu

WHAT THE SOUTH OF TAMIL NADU LACKS IN ARCHITEC-
turally stunning temples, it makes up for in coastal beauty, some
fascinating offbeat sites, and the chance to visit Kanniyakumari,
where the waters of three seas mingle.

Rameswaram
⚠ 255 C2
**Rameswaram
Tourist
Information**
www.tamilnadutourism.org
✉ Bus Terminus
☎ 04573-221371

Tirunelveli
⚠ 255 B1
**Tirunelveli Tourist
Information**
www.tamilnadutourism.org
✉ Collectorate Complex
☎ 0462-2500104

The far south of India has attracted
devotion rather than war, inspiring
temple-building rather than forts.
Rameswaram, the 35-mile-long
(56 km) peninsula jutting out from
mainland India toward Sri Lanka,
plays a vital role in the climax and
finale of the great Hindu epic, the
Ramayana. The huge **Ramanatha
Temple** (mostly 17th to 18th century) marks the spot where Rama,
having killed the demon Ravana,
worshiped Shiva to purify himself.
Today's pilgrims imitate this by
bathing in the sea and then being
doused with water from the 22 wells
in the temple complex. Many also
visit **Gandhamandana Hill** to see
Rama's footprint, and **Dhanushkodi,**
where Rama received submission
from Ravana's brother.

On the way to the peninsula,
you can stop at the village of
Ramanathapuram to see the
local Setupati rulers' palace, where
the Ramalinga Vilasa rooms are
lavishly decorated with 18th-
century paintings recounting the
Hindu epics and Setupati royal life.
Farther south on the Gulf of
Mannar, huge maritime fossils
have been found on the shores
near Kilakkarai.

Set in the lush valley of the
Tambraparni River, **Tirunelveli**
makes a good base for visiting the
tip of India. If you are driving here
from Madurai, pause at Kalugumalai
to see the monolithic **Pallava
Temple** (eighth century) chiseled
out of a granite outcrop and exten-
sively decorated. In Tirunelveli
itself, a major Nayaka city, the
Nellaiyappa Temple (mostly

16th to 17th century), dedicated to
Shiva and Devi, has a riot of fine
stone and wood carving; in the first
enclosure find donor sculptures of
the Tirunelveli chiefs.

The first stop on a tour southeast from Tirunelveli is the village
of **Krishnapuram,** whose
Venkatachala Temple, dedicated to
Vishnu as Lord of the Venkata Hills,
has glorious 17th- to 18th-century
carvings and fine figural piers in its
Virappa Nayaka Mandapa. The Iron
Age site of **Adichanallur,** beside
the Tambrapani River, has fascinating ancient sepulchral urns. At the
town of Alvar Tirunagari, the high-
ranking Vishnu saint Nammalvar,
born here in the ninth century, was
the inspiration for the **Adinatha
Temple** (mostly 16th to 17th
century) and its lively carvings.
When you reach the coast, there are
three places to visit overlooking the
Gulf of Mannar: **Kayalpattinam,**
with its mosques for locals
descended from Arab traders;
Tiruchchendur's pilgrimage
temple; and **Manapadu,** whose
Catholic associations go back to St.
Francis Xavier's visit in 1542.

The tip of India is a rocky
promontory overlooking the
mingling waters of the Bay of
Bengal, the Arabian Sea, and the
Indian Ocean. The town of
Kanniyakumari is named after
Kumari, the Hindu goddess who
protects the shores, and pilgrims
come here to bathe near the
temple. Two great Indians have
memorials here: Mahatma Gandhi,
whose ashes were thrown into
the ocean here; and Vivekananda,

the Bengali philosopher who came here as a monk in 1892 and founded the Ramakrishna Vivekananda Missions. Headquartered in Kolkata, the missions still thrive today.

West of Kanniyakumari, you can stop at Suchindram to see the **Sthanumalaya Temple** (13th to 18th century) beside the large tank. Dedicated to Vishnu and Shiva, grand and gaily painted *gopuras* and colonnades lead to the earlier shrines. Before Shiva's, see the splendidly carved corner columns of the small pavilion. Similarly, the pavilion housing the image of Vishnu's vehicle, Garuda, has columns carved with portraits of Nayaka donors and their queens. In the corridor inside the perimeter walls, **Alankara Mandapa** has carvings of royals, including Martanda Varma of Tiruvananthapuram (see pp.

212–13). It is an easy drive northwest from Suchindrom to the astonishing palace of the Travancore kings at **Padmanabhapuram.**

Another good route from Tiruneludi goes to Kollam (Quillon). Stop at **Tenkasi** to visit the capital of the Pandya in the 15th to 16th centuries. Their **Vishvanatha Temple** has very fine carvings; see Shiva with the wives of the sages on the gopura walls, and the huge carved piers of the hall in the first enclosure.

A different, more rural route west to Kollam goes through the village of **Tiruppudaimarudur.** Its **Narumbunatha Temple,** on the banks of the Tambraparni River, has unusually well-preserved sculptures and paintings. At **Papanasam,** up in the hills, you simply enjoy the beauty of the spot. ■

Indians travel from all over their huge country, often in village or school groups on subsidized train or bus tickets, to visit Gandhi's memorial at Kanniyakumari.

As Ooty's popularity has grown since independence, its eclectic mix of colonial buildings has been joined by modern Indian housing, stores, and billboards.

Tamil Nadu's hill stations

ALTHOUGH THE EARLY BRITISH ADVENTURERS ADOPTED Indian ways and dress, and had Indian wives, by the 19th century an altogether more powerful and bureaucratic British presence seemed determined to remain as British as possible. Rather than adapting to the hot and humid climate and self-preserving ways of Indians, they wore too many clothes, ate and drank in quantities suited to northern Europe, and dreamed of green hills, gentle rain, and rose gardens.

As a result, they fell ill and many died of typhoid, cholera, and malaria. Soldiers stationed in the hill forts, however, did not. So sanitariums were built in the hills for ailing servants of the empire. Once it had been proved that the hills were healthier, enterprising officers set off to discover suitable sites. British hill stations were born.

Shimla, then called Simla, was the first, dating from 1819 (see p. 124). During the next 30 years more than 80 hill stations were established at elevations of between 4,035 feet (1,230 m) and 8,071 feet (2,460 m), and vast resources were spent on constructing mountain roads and railroads to reach them. Built on open hilltops with no

Scotch trout streams and Lusitanian views." She and her compatriots loved the colder climate, tolerated the leaking houses and discomforts, and built British-style houses with names like Rose Bank and Glenthorn.

But India was never far away. For all the attempts to create a drop of pure "home," every British hill station had a certain Indianness about it. Today, it is the reverse: Every Indian hill station has a certain Englishness about it.

UP TO COONOOR

Leaving the hot, lush, and sparkling paddy fields of the Tamil Nadu plains, roads twist and turn up gentle slopes into the fresh air and forests of the Western Ghats. These are truly spectacular drives, so it is worth allowing time to stop and enjoy panoramic views, do some bird-watching, and visit tea or coffee gardens. From north to south, the Ghats run more than 1,000 miles (1,609 km), reaching their height in the Nilgiris (Blue Mountains) at Ooty, which stands at the foot of the 8,615-foot-high (2,626 m) Doda Betta Peak.

Affluent **Coimbatore** is strategically placed near Palghat, the broadest pass through the hills. Coimbatore serves as a gateway to the Nilgiris. Its industrial wealth soared after hydroelectric power was harnessed from the Pykara Falls in the 1930s, boosting cotton manufacture. Most people drive through because it has no tourist attractions, but if you stay overnight here, you could take a morning stroll in the **Botanical Gardens,** established around 1900.

From Coimbatore drive north to Mettuppalaiyam, where the steep ascent begins, bringing hairpin bends, wonderful views, and a canopy of dark foliage. Northwest of Mattuppailayam is **Coonoor,**

Coimbatore
255 A3

Coonoor
255 A3

The Collector's Office in Ooty is a typical example of colonial British architecture.

fortifications, they represented a British confidence in themselves, their power, and their home culture.

The hill stations were cocktails of ideal British countryside, town activities, and beach town resorts. Highly social, elitist, and yet trapped in an isolated dream far from home, the British in the hill stations lived life to the full. The theater, clubs, churches, sports, flower shows, and promenades along the Mall ensured a continuous whirl of activity and a fair number of romantic flings.

But underneath there was homesickness, too. Lady Betty Balfour wrote from Ooty in 1877 of "such beautiful English rain, such delicious English mud. Imagine Hertfordshire lanes, Devonshire downs, Westmoreland lakes,

Udagamandalam (Ooty)
📍 255 A3

Udagamandalam (Ooty) Tourist Office
www.tamilnadutourism.org
✉ Wenlock Rd.
☎ 0423-2443977

Botanical Gardens
✉ Garden Rd.

Sim's Park
✉ Upper Coonoor

Raj Bhawan
✉ Garden Rd.
🕐 Closed to visitors

Savoy Hotel
✉ 77 Sylks Rd.
☎ 0423-2444142
💲 $

which stands at 6,096 feet (1,858 m). It is at the head of the Hulikal Ravine in the Doda Betta Range and is less wet and cool than "The Queen" (see below). Huge tree-ferns, rhododendrons, and roses flourish in **Sim's Park,** where the prestigious Coonoor Fruit and Vegetable Show is held annually, after Ooty's flower show.

This is a marvelous area for hiking: Visit **Lady Canning's Seat** (2 miles/3 km); **Lamb's Rock** (3½ miles/6 km), with dramatic views; **Dolphin's Nose** (7½ miles/12 km), with views of Katherine Falls and the Coonoor Stream; and **Law's Falls** (3 miles/ 5 km), named after the man who constructed the Coonoor Ghat Road. You can also hike the 2 miles (3 km) up to **The Droog** (Pakkasuram Kottai) for exhilarating views of the plains.

OOTY

At an elevation of 7,349 feet (2,240 m), Udagamandalam (Ootacamund, or Ooty) is the highest Nilgiri hill station and is surrounded by rolling, grassy slopes, natural woodland, and imported eucalyptus and conifers.

The original inhabitants here were four tribes, including the Todas, a tribe who tended herds of sacred buffalo. Today, their few surviving members have, sadly, been turned into something of a tourist curiosity. Following the death of Tipu Sultan in 1799, the East India Company annexed the Nilgiris and their tribes. In 1818 two assistants of John Sullivan, Collector of Coimbature, saw the possibilities of the area; in 1823, Sullivan built his Stone House. Word spread, the British arrived, and Sullivan planted English vegetables and trees. He enlarged the lake and introduced fast-growing eucalyptus trees from Australia.

By 1861 Ooty, as it was known, was the summer capital of the Madras Presidency and "The Queen of Hill Stations." The governor and his staff, servants, and all their families arrived, soon followed by other Europeans and anglophile Indian princes. According to their means and position, they came on foot or on horseback, were carried in palanquins, or, later, took the train; the first passengers arrived in Ooty in 1908. Nowadays the train can be taken from Mettuppalayam or, for a longer journey, from Coonoor.

French botanist M. Perottet introduced tea here; coffee had already been grown near Mysore since the 1820s. Visitors in the early years included the first governor-general of India, Lord William Cavendish Bentinck (1774–1839), and historian Thomas Babington Macaulay (1800–1859). Snooty Ooty, as the hill station was known, has changed radically and now feels more like a midscale Indian town transplanted to the hills; but its popularity is unabated.

To visit some of British Ooty, start with a walk through the orchids, trees, ferns, and medical plants of the glorious hillside **Botanical Gardens,** founded in 1848 by the Marquess of Tweeddale with the help of Mr. MacIvor from Kew Gardens in London. Above the gardens lies **Raj Bhawan** (1877, *closed to the public*), built for the Duke of Buckingham when he was governor of Chennai. Ooty's biggest events, the annual flower and dog shows, are held here.

Among the verdant lanes, you can get a feel of British Ooty by surveying the Ootacamund Club (founded 1843, *closed to non-members*), and the Ooty Gymkhana Gold Club on Wenlock Downs. Then go to **St. Stephen's Church** (1831), full of memorials to those

who could not be saved by Ooty's fresh air, and to the **Savoy Hotel,** whose wood fires burn each night. Go down past the lake to see the racetrack, station, and beyond them, **St. Thomas's Church** (1870). Farther on down is the **Fernhill Palace** (1842), which once belonged to the ruler of Mysore and is now a hotel (*closed for renovation*). In town, find Sullivan's **Stone House** near Charing Cross, the **Nilgiri Library** (1885), and the **District and Sessions Court** (1873).

There are good excursions and hikes, or you can make arrangements through your hotel for an accompanied horseback ride. Try going to Doda Betta Peak for fine views, or to Marlimund Lake, Tiger Hill, Kalhatti Falls, and Pykara Lake or Pykara Falls, 20 miles (32 km) west of Ooty. A scenic road leads to Avalanche, and from Mukerti Lake you can hike up Mukerti Peak.

KODAIKANAL

Set in a natural bowl in the Palani Hills and surrounded by terraced hills, Kodaikanal has only recently lost its peaceful charm in favor of lucrative tourism. Known as "The Princess of Hill Stations," it was founded in 1844 by the American Madurai Mission, whose members moved up here from Madurai in a desperate search for renewed health.

If you can, avoid the two monsoons Kodaikanal receives and arrive here along picturesque Laws Ghat Road between January and March, when there are few visitors. You can rent rowboats from the Boat Club and find good views over the plains along Coaker's Walk.

YERCAUD

Across in the Eastern Ghats, the thickly forested Shevaroy Hills rise sharply. Here, at Yercaud, 4,920 feet (1,499 m) up, the first real hotel opened in 1971, offering a convenient respite from the heat for people living in Madurai and Bangalore. Until then it had been a place for coffee estates since the 1820s and, more recently, for Catholic schools. Leaving the whitewashed, red-tiled houses of the town and its planters' club, there are pleasant walks through the wooded lanes around the coffee estates. ∎

Hike to Dolphin's Nose rock in Kodaikanal, a picturesque hill station in Tamil Nadu. From this point on the edge of a deep gorge, enjoy the peaceful view of the south Indian landscape.

Kodaikanal
🄰 255 B3
Kodaikanal Tourist Office
www.tamilnadutourism.org
✉ Rest House Complex
☎ 04542-241765

More places to visit in Tamil Nadu

ALAGARKOIL
The **Algar Perumal Temple,** beside a forested hill, is dedicated to Vishnu as Kallalagar, Minakshi's brother; so the temple is part of Madurai's great festival (see p. 275). Note the elegant donor figures with Nayaka queen, and the rare Pandya central shrine.
🅼 255 B2 ✉ 7 miles (12 km) north of Madurai

AUROVILLE
Inspired by The Mother (see p. 267), about 800 families live in this ideal coastal city founded in 1968. Houses with names such as Grace form an outward spiral, symbolizing continuous motion and the universality of faith; Matrimandir (meditation house) is central. Stores in the city stock quality homemade goods.
🅼 255 C4 ✉ 6 miles (10 km) north of Pondicherry

CHENGALPATTU (CHILGLEPUT)
Chengalpattu is famous for its fort, which was disputed by the French and English. Roam the remains and, at nearby **Vallam,** see three very early, fascinating Pallava cave temples from the reign of Mahendravarman I (*R*.580–630).
🅼 255 C5 ✉ 36 miles (58 km) west of Chennai

CHENNAI–MAHABILIPURAM DRIVE
There are two places to stop: **Cholamandel** coastal artists' community, with its permanent arts exhibition, and Muttukadu's **Dakshinachitra** (*Tel 04114-24462435, closed Tues.*), to see old vernacular buildings rescued from destruction. A building from each of four southern states is preserved, together with information on their respective ways of life.
✉ 13 miles (21 km) south of Chennai

GINGEE
Tamil Nadu's most spectacular fortified site, Gingee was built by the Vijayanagas and con-tested by most subsequent armies in the south. Climb the steps to the citadel.
🅼 255 C4 ✉ 42 miles (68 km) northwest of Pondicherry

KILAIYUR & TIRUVAIYARU
Kilaiyur's finely finished twin temples, built in the ninth-century by local chieftains, make an interesting combination to visit in conjunction with nearby Tiruvaiyaru's temple, famous more for its music festival than for its architecture.
🅼 255 C3 **Kilaiyur** ✉ 20 miles (33 km) north of Thanjavur

PANAMALAI
On the Villupuram–Vettavalam road, the important hilltop **Talagirishvara Temple** (eighth century), dedicated to Shiva, is built of reddish granite and has a hemispherical roof, some nice sculpture, and traces of paintings.
🅼 255 C4 ✉ 46 miles (75 km) west of Pondicherry

POINT CALIMERE WILDLIFE SANCTUARY
Saltwater tidal swamps are home to flamingoes and other waterbirds. On a trip from Thanjavur, you can return via **Velanganni,** a Catholic pilgrimage center, and **Nagappattinam,** an ancient port and Buddhist center whose Karikop Cemetery has early Dutch tombs.
🅼 255 C3 ✉ 56 miles (90 km) southeast of Thanjavur

PULICAT
Right on the border with Andhra Pradesh, Pulicat Lake attracts resident and migratory waterbirds such as pelicans and flamingoes. The town's Dutch cemetery is especially rich in old tombstones.
🅼 255 D5 ✉ 25 miles (40 km) north of Chennai

PULLAMANGAI
The splendid **Brahmapurishvara Temple** (tenth century), dedicated to Shiva, sits quietly at the end of this rural village where in almost every house there lives a master silk-weaver. Walk around the back to see the fine sculptures on the outside of the sanctuary.
✉ 6 miles (10 km) from Thanjavur

SRINIVASANALLUR
There is fine sculpture on this early Chola temple (927) overlooking the Kaveri River and dedicated to Koranganatha, a form of Shiva. Westward, **Punaji** has a similarly good temple, while **Namakkal's** eighth-century Pandyan shrine, with vigorous and large sculptures, is hidden behind later additions.
✉ 28 miles (45 km) northwest of Tiruchirappalli

SRIPERUMBUDUR
Believed to be the birthplace of the Vaishnava saint Ramanuja, the temple (16th to 17th century) has splendid *Ramayana* friezes.
🅰 255 C5 ✉ 25 miles (40 km) southwest of Chennai

SRIVILLIPUTTUR
This temple town is focused on two temples. One of them, **Vatapatrashayi,** dedicated to Vishnu, has a 17th-century Nayaka period *gopura* 207 feet high (63 m) with an 11-stage tower. Said to be the tallest of all gopuras, it is Tamil Nadu's official emblem.
🅰 255 B2 ✉ 46 miles (74 km) southwest of Madurai

SWAMIMALAI (TIRUVALANJULI)
Find the **Kapardishvara Temple,** dedicated to Shiva, in the hamlet of Tiruvalanjuli; the

Srivilliputtur's Adal Temple, a twin to Vatapatrashayi Temple, has brass-encased portraits of its patrons, the Madurai ruler Tirumala Nayaka and his brother, by the temple swing.

Chola-period hall has unusual bulbous pilasters. In the village, you can watch craftsmen make religious bronzes by the traditional lost wax method; you can buy direct from them.
✉ 5 miles (8 km) west of Kumbakonam
(🅰 255 C3)

TARANGAMBADI (TRANQUEBAR)
From 1620 to 1807 this town was the headquarters of the Dutch East India Company, and the European character survives intact today in the houses, churches, and fort with museum *(Closed Fri.).*
🅰 255 C3 ✉ 39 miles (63 km) east of Kumbakonam

TIRUCHENGODU
There are two Chola foundations to see here, much enlarged by the Nayakas and Wodeyars. Midtown **Kailasanatha** is crowded with stores and temple chariots; walk up the hill to **Ardhanarishvara** for the best entrance, fine woodcarving, and good views.
🅰 255 B3 ✉ 31 miles (50 km) southwest of Salem

TIRUKKALUKKUNDRAM

One of the most ambitious temples to be built by the Nayakas of Gingee, and dedicated to Shiva as Bhaktavatsaleshvara, Tirukkalukkundram's grand *gopura* has fine sculptures and paintings of royal visitors (west gopura).

⛰ 255 D4   ✉ 9 miles (14 km) west of Mahabalipuram

TIRUMANGALAKKUDI

The 18th-century paintings on the corridor ceiling in **Pramanatheshvara Temple,** dedicated to Shiva, make a trip across the Kaveri worthwhile. They depict local legends and, interestingly, the shrines along the river.

✉ 9 miles (15 km) northwest of Kumbakonam (⛰ 255 C3)

THIRUPPARANKUNDRAM

The sacred granite hill of this town is where its **Murugan Temple,** dedicated to Shiva's son Subramanya, began as a fine Pandya-period cave temple (773). To reach it, go through the later additions of painted and sculptured halls. See Travelwise for details of the major 14-day festival *(March–April).*

⛰ 255 B2   ✉ 4 miles (6 km) southwest of Madurai

TIRUTTANI

Follow the path to this hilltop Subramanya temple. Then go through ascending terraces to find a Pallava period shrine with fine images of Subramanya and, in the outer enclosure, a row of stone soldiers as his army.

⛰ 255 C5   ✉ 53 miles (86 km) NW of Chennai

TIRUVADAIMARNDUR

There are two Chola shrines to Shiva here. First, see the grand and large corridors and halls of the **Mahalinga Perumal** temple complex (17th to 18th century), with its Chola shrine, then Tribhuvanam's royal **Kampahareshvara Temple,** built by Kulottunga III *(R.1178–1218).*

✉ 6 miles (10 km) northeast of Kumbakonam (⛰ 255 C5)

TIRUVANNAMALAI

The **Arunachaleshvara Temple** in this town is one of Tamil Nadu's grandest, dedicated to Shiva's fiery *lingum* (phallus). The temple is the focus of a crowded 14-day festival *(Nov.–Dec.),* which coincides with the cattle fair. If you are going north from here, pause at **Tirumalai** to see the 16th-century Jain complex.

⛰ 255 C4   ✉ 23 miles (37 km) west of Gingee

TIRUVARUR

This is one of the area's most important Chola temples, dedicated to Shiva as Tyagaraja, whom Tamil saints such as Appar and Sambandar glorified in their devotional hymns. Massive gopuras lead through halls to the shrine, whose Somaskanda form of Shiva (Shiva, his consort Parvati, and their son Skanda or Subramanya) was a favorite Chola image.

⛰ 255 C3   ✉ 33 miles (53 km) east of Thanjavur

VEDANTANGAL BIRD SANCTUARY

A lake and marshy, low-lying ground attract a variety of waterfowl, including ibises, purple moorhens, gray pelicans, and night-herons.

⛰ 255 C4   ✉ 25 miles (40 km) southwest of Mahabalipuram

VELLORE & ARCOT

Vellore's **fort,** a fine piece of military architecture, has haunting associations with the Vijayanagas (their temple here is superb), Marathas, Mughals, British (courthouse, church), and Tipu Sultan, whose family was kept here after the fall of Srirangapatnam (see p. 246). A mile (1.6 km) northeast, find the **dargah** (tomb) of Tipu's mother and wife. At Arcot to the east, the famous battles fought with the Nawabs of Arcot have left few remains.

⛰ 255 C5

VRINCHIPURAM

Rising grandly above its modest village of lanes and thatched houses, the **Marghabandhu Temple,** dedicated to Shiva, was substantially funded by the Nayakas of Gingee. It has a huge gopura, a columned hall, twin marriage halls possibly inspired by Vellore's superb temple (see above), and with donor portraits of the Nayaka patron and his wife (in the northwest hall).

⛰ 255 C5   ✉ 9 miles (14 km) west of Vellore ■

The Ganga's great delta brought prosperity to empires from the early Mauryas to the British. Trace the legacy of these cultures and visit their distinctive monuments in a verdant land that is home to the Hindus' sacred Varanasi city.

Eastern India

An intricately carved wheel at Konark's Surya Temple

Eastern India

STEEPED IN HISTORY, EASTERN India is surprisingly little visited by foreigners. East of Delhi, India is for the most part quiet and very accessible; there is little of the aggressive tourism found west of Delhi, in Rajasthan.

You can trace the path of the Ganga (see pp. 304–305) through three very different states: Uttar Pradesh, Bihar, and West Bengal. Uttar Pradesh has the highest population of any Indian state—more than 140 million; yet its literacy is just 41 percent, a telling yardstick. Its cities vary from the Mughals' Muslim Agra (see pp. 96–99), the Hindus' sacred Varanasi, and Buddhist Sarnath, to Lucknow, now the state capital. Out in the fields, farmers produce more cereals than any other state and half of all India's sugarcane.

Neighboring Bihar is even more densely populated but less fortunate: Literacy is just 38 percent. However, it is India's richest state in minerals and is responsible for 42 percent of the country's production. Around the capital, Patna, you can follow the story of Buddhism at Bodh Gaya and Nalanda.

Kolkata (Calcutta) is West Bengal's capital and eastern India's commercial and cultural center. The state's recent history is one of reduction: It once stretched to Agra and included Bihar and Orissa, but it was divided in two in 1905, a move that fed the area's awakening patriotism. It was further divided at independence to form East Pakistan (now Bangladesh) and West Bengal. Kolkata has a state literacy rate touching 60 percent, and still maintains Bengal's cultural tradition, while the farmers produce much of India's rice, jute, and, up in the hills, tea.

Between these three states and the Deccan Plateau to the south lie Madhya Pradesh, Tharkand, Chhatisgarh, and Orissa. A vast landscape of dry plains and forested hills, Madhya Pradesh is India's largest state; yet apart from the area around Delhi it is rarely visited by tourists. Orissa, bordered by the Eastern Ghats on one side and the Bay of Bengal to the

other, is home to some of India's most interesting tribal communities. As in Bihar, you can visit vestiges of remarkable early empires in and around the capital, Bhubaneshwar.

The tropical Andaman and Nicobar Islands form India's most remote state, more than 600

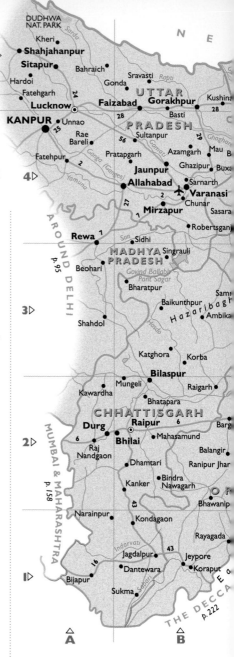

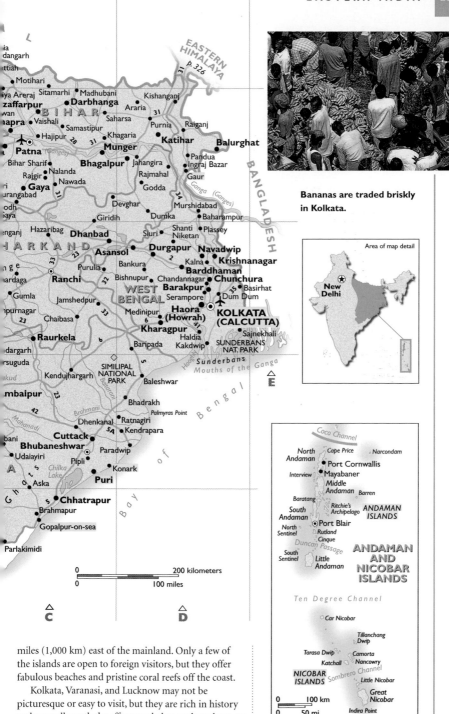

Bananas are traded briskly
in Kolkata.

EASTERN HIMALAYA P. 326

L
dangarh
ttiah
Motihari
iya Areraj Sitamarhi Madhubani   Kishanganj
zaffarpur   **Darbhanga**   Araria
wan   Saharsa   Araria   31
aapra Vaishali   Samastipur   Purnia   Raiganj
Hajipur 28   Khagaria
Patna   **Munger**   **Katihar**   **Balurghat**
Bihar Sharif   Jahangira   Pandua
Bhagalpur   Ingraj Bazar
Rajgir Nalanda   Rajmahal   Gaur
Gaya   Nawada   Godda
urangabad   Murshidabad
odh   Devghar   34
aya   Giridih   Dumka   Baharampur
nganj Hazaribag **Dhanbad**   Shanti Plassey
ARKAND   Siuri Niketan
n g e   **Asansol**   **Durgapur** **Navadwip**
nardaga   Purulia   Bankura   Kalna **Krishnanagar**
Ranchi   Bishnupur **Barddhaman**
Gumla   Jamshedpur Chandannagar **Chunchura**
ipurnagar   **Barakpur** Basirhat
Chaibasa   Medinipur Serampore Dum Dum
Raurkela   **WEST BENGAL** **Haora (Howrah)** **KOLKATA (CALCUTTA)**
dargarh   Kharagpur Haldia Sajnekhali
rsuguda   SIMILIPAL   Baripada Kakdwip **SUNDERBANS NAT. PARK**
akud   NATIONAL PARK Baleshwar
mbalpur   *Sunderbans Mouths of the Ganga*
Bhadrakh   E
Brahmani   Palmyras Point
Dhenkanal Ratnagiri
Cuttack   Kendrapara
bani **Bhubaneshwar** Paradwip
Udaiayiri   Pipli
Chilka Lake Konark
Aska   **Puri**
Brahmapur   **Chhatrapur**
Gopalpur-on-sea
Parlakimidi

BANGLADESH

Ganga (Ganges)

0   200 kilometers
0   100 miles

C   D

Area of map detail

New Delhi

ANDAMAN AND NICOBAR ISLANDS

Coco Channel

North Andaman   Cape Price   Narcondam
Interview   **Port Cornwallis**
Mayabaner
Middle Andaman   Barren
Baratang
South Andaman Ritchie's Archipelago   ANDAMAN ISLANDS
North Sentinel **Port Blair**
Rutland
Cinque
Duncan Passage
South Sentinel   Little Andaman

Ten Degree Channel

Car Nicobar
Tillanchang Dwip
Tarasa Dwip Camorta
Katchall   Nancowry
NICOBAR ISLANDS *Sombrero Channel* Little Nicobar
Great Nicobar
Indira Point

0   100 km
0   50 mi

miles (1,000 km) east of the mainland. Only a few of
the islands are open to foreign visitors, but they offer
fabulous beaches and pristine coral reefs off the coast.

Kolkata, Varanasi, and Lucknow may not be
picturesque or easy to visit, but they are rich in history
and are well worth the effort needed to explore them. ∎

Kolkata (Calcutta)

Former colonial grandeur is the backdrop to contemporary Kolkata life on Bentinck Street, named for Lord William Bentinck, governor-general between 1834 and 1835.

Kolkata, West Bengal
🅰 293
India Tourist Information
✉ 4 Shakespeare Sarani
☎ 033-2421402 or 2421475

THERE IS A STRENGTH AND SPIRIT IN KOLKATA THAT, DESPITE all it has suffered, makes it one of the world's great cities. If you are looking for prettiness, this is not a city for you. But Kolkata allows you to touch the pulse of Bengal's great culture, past and present, and see, through the decay, the grandeur of a great colonial city.

In fact, Bengalis consider themselves, with some justification, the intelligentsia of India. The Bengali Renaissance of the 19th century witnessed a flowering of talent, led by Raja Ram Mohan Roy (1774–1833), which created a new intellectual elite whose legacy continues today; do try to visit one of the city's art centers.

Kolkata is relatively new. In 1690 Job Charnock, a maverick agent for the British East India Company, leased three swampy villages from Mughal Emperor Aurangzeb. Trading began, and six years later the company built Fort William, but times were uncertain. When Suraj-ud-Daula of Murshidabad took the city and incarcerated British soldiers in a dark room later dubbed the "Black Hole of Calcutta," Robert Clive arrived from Madras and crushed him at the Battle of Plassey in 1757. Seven years later, Sir Hector Munro led the British

(Madras) as the British head-quarters in India and appointed its first governor of British India, Warren Hastings. Kolkata's rich hinterland became the main source of the company's vast wealth (which, after 1858, went directly to the British government). Dazzling white stuccoed mansions with a lifestyle to go with them made Kolkata the greatest colonial city of the Orient.

Kolkata's position held until 1931, when New Delhi was inaugurated as the new capital, and kept its commercial prowess until independence, when colonial companies were obliged to become Indian. Since independence, the city's population has swelled first with Hindu immigrants from newly created Muslim East Pakistan, then with refugees from the Indo-Pakistan war of 1965 and the Pakistan-Bangladesh war of 1972, prompting the start of high-profile charity work (see box). Today, Kolkata covers 40 square miles (104 sq km) and has a population of more than 11 million.

To begin your exploration of the city, try driving around downtown (see pp. 292–93). Then explore one of the areas described on pp. 290–291. Early mornings are best, when you can imagine the past elegance of this City of Palaces.

triumph at the Battle of Buxar, wresting most of Bihar from the Nawabs of Bengal, who had recently won it from the weakening Mughals.

The fortunes of the British—and the city—took off. In 1772 Kolkata (Calcutta) usurped Chennai

State Tourist Office
www.kolkata-india.com
www.wb.nic.in
✉ 3/2 BBD Bagh (East)

High Court
🕐 Closed Sat. & Sun.

Town Hall
🕐 Closed Sat. & Sun.

Raj Bhavan
✉ Red Rd.
🕐 Closed to visitors

Writers' Buildings
☎ 033-2215858
🕐 Closed to visitors

Marble Palace
✉ Muktaram Babu St., off Chittaranjan Ave.
🕐 Closed Thurs. & Mon.

Rabindra Bharati Museum
✉ Dwarkanath Tagore Lane, off Chittaranjan Ave.
🕐 Closed Sat. p.m. & Sun.
💲 $

Charity in Kolkata

Despite Kolkata's tremendous spirit, the outward image is one of poverty. In fact, much is being done to help Kolkata's poor. Mother Teresa (1910–1997) was the beacon bringing support for the many charities working in the city. Born in Albania, Mother Teresa joined the Sisters of Loreto. She was sent to Darjiling, where she took her vows in May 1931. Seeing the poverty in Kolkata, she founded the Missionaries of Charity, which focuses on helping the dying. Never shy in criticizing the powerful, she was an outspoken campaigner, who was awarded the Nobel Prize for Peace in 1979.

Some charities help street children and children's homes or women's education; others give inoculations or eye treatments. ■

B.B.D. BAGH & AROUND

Start early in the morning west of Assembly House, by the statue of Khudiram Bose, the first martyr for independent India, who was hanged in 1908 at the age of 19 for killing two British women with a bomb. In front of Walter Granville's very fine Gothic **High Court** (1872), well worth exploring, stands a statue of the revolutionary Surya Sen (died 1930).

John Garstin's **Town Hall** (1813) is a handsome Tuscan-Doric building, remodeled in the 1990s. Beyond it, on your way around the back of Raj Bhavan's huge garden, find the statue of the political leader Subhas Chandra Bose's equally revolutionary brother.

Raj Bhavan (Government House) is the West Bengal governor's residence. Beyond this take Old Court House Street past the Great Eastern Hotel to **B.B.D. Bagh** (Dalhousie Square), renamed for Benoy, Badal, and Dinesh, three freedom-fighters hanged by the British. B.B.D. Bagh was the hub of company power. **Writers' Buildings** (1780, refurbished 1880) spanning the north side of the square, was built for company clerical staff and is still a bureaucratic hive.

On the west side of B.B.D. Bagh is Walter Granville's **G.P.O.** (General Post Office, 1864–68), with its Corinthian columns standing over the site of the Black Hole of Calcutta (see p. 288). Try to imagine the lives of Robert Clive, Warren Hastings, and Clive Francis, who all lived nearby. Francis wrote: "Here I live, with a hundred servants, a country house, and spacious gardens, horses and carriages...."

Finally, down Government Place West, visit **St. John's Church** (1787), designed by Lt. James Agg and based on London's St. Martin-in-the-Fields. In the cool interior, memorials to Kolkata's British heroes include John Bacon's to Maj. James Achilles Kirkpatrick; the altarpiece (now in the south aisle) depicts famous Kolkata residents as Christ's apostles; the churchyard has memorials to the Rohilla War (1794) and Job Charnock (circa 1695), who founded the city.

HAORA (HOWRAH) STATION & BRIDGE

A good way to see this area is to visit the early morning **flower market** under Howrah Bridge (1943), where gymnasts and wrestlers train at Armenian Ghat. Then drive over

Durga Puja

This is the most spectacular of Kolkata's many festivals, which fill the city's calendar. It falls in September–October, generates a near collapse of the city's offices, and brings families together for constant celebrations. The focus is Durga, Shiva's wife in her destructive form. Idol-makers living in the Kumartuli area work all year to create hundreds of Durga images, painting their straw and unbaked clay models gaudy colors to look like the latest film stars. Offices,

local groups, or whole streets then create unashamedly glitzy settings for their goddess, who, fierce and furious with her ten arms, is shown either on or with her lion, slaying the demon Mahisasura, who has deviously taken the form of a buffalo to threaten the gods. For the ten days before Mahadashami, when the images are paraded down to the Hooghly and immersed in the water, Kolkatans take evening strolls to visit as many as possible of these spectacular creations. ■

the bridge to explore Halsey Ricardo's magnificent **Howrah railroad station** (1854–1928), which is always busy. From here you can take a ferry across the Hooghly to land at **Babu's Ghat** on the Maidan, or one upriver to **Kumatuli Ghat** to see craftsmen making inlaid woodwork and the Durga Puja clay deities.

NORTH KOLKATA

North of B.B.D. Bagh was where rich Kolkatans once lived, and some old families still do. Here you can explore narrow alleys and find facades of crumbling mansions. Try **Barabazaar** and its Armenian church (1724). North of M.G. Road, find the vast and decaying **Marble Palace,** begun in 1835 by Rajendra Mullick when he was 16 years old. It abounds with Belgian chandeliers, Venetian mirrors, and paintings by Rubens and others. Northeast of here, visit the restored house of Rabindranath Tagore, which is now the **Rabindra Bharati Museum,** and trace the story of the Tagores and the Bengal Renaissance. Finally, visit College Street in the university area, where the **Ashutosh Museum of Indian History** has Bengali crafts and *kantha* embroidery.

SOUTH KOLKATA

Alipore and Ballygunge, Kolkata's wealthy residential areas, developed around the Deputy Governor's House, now the **National Library.** Alipore's **Horticultural Gardens** are half a mile (1 km) south of here. At the **Kolkata Zoo,** the snake, bird, and big cat collections are especially interesting.

Still farther south **Kalighat,** the temple to Kali, patron goddess of Kolkata, is best reached on India's only underground transit system. Opened in 1984, it is Russian-designed, clean, and efficient. Zip down to Kalighat station, then walk five minutes to the city's most important temple. Indeed, such is its importance that the East India Company servants used to give high-profile but controversial devotional offerings here. Excellent brass is sold in the market outside the entrance. ■

A stallholder finds his wares make a handy pillow.

Horticultural Gardens
- ✉ Alipore
- ⏱ Closed Mon., flower shows in Feb.
- 💲 $

Ashutosh Museum of Indian History
- ✉ Centenary Building, College St.
- ⏱ Closed Sun. & university holidays
- 💲 $

Rabindra Bharati Museum
- ✉ 6 Dwarakanath Tagore Lane

Kolkata Zoo
- ✉ Jawahar Rd.
- 💲 $

A drive around colonial Kolkata

After Clive's victory (see p. 288), the East India Company rebuilt the fort (1757–1770) and cleared thick jungle in front of it to create the defensive Maidan (open space) that is Kolkata's great lung today. This drive takes you past some of the colonial public buildings, churches, monuments, and houses built in Kolkata's heyday.

Ranks of yellow taxis wait among the crowds outside Howrah Station.

Start at **Babu's Ghat ❶,** from where ferries go to Howrah Station (see pp. 290–91). Near the Ghat, **Eden Gardens ❷** contain Kolkata Stadium, where test cricket matches are held. Look across the Maidan to Jawaharlal Nehru and Chowringhee Roads: Enough buildings survive to help your imagination furnish them with 18th- and 19th-century grandeur.

Drive along Esplanade past Col. John Garstin's handsome, refurbished **Town Hall** (1813) and grandiose **Raj Bhavan ❸** (Government House, 1797–1803), begun by Viceroy Lord Curzon and designed by Capt. Charles Wyatt in imitation of Robert Adam's Kedleston Hall in Derbyshire, England.

At the corner with Jawaharlal Road, the **Ochterlony Monument ❹** (1828) is a tall column in remembrance of Sir David Ochterlony, the eccentric British hero of the Nepal War (1814–1816). Your drive down Chowringhee Road begins with the **Oberoi Grand Hotel** (1911, much changed), which stoically holds on to its Raj character through every restoration. Down Lindsay Street bustling lanes are centered around **New Market ❺;** if you want to shop, a coolie will follow you around and carry your purchases on his head.

Proceed to the **Indian Museum ❻** (opened 1814), India's first national museum. Despite its shabbiness, it holds exceptional stone and metal sculptures rescued from eastern Indian sites. See the second-century B.C. sculptures from Vidisha, Sravasti, and Bharhut; the second-century A.D. panels from Mathura; India's finest collection of first- to third-century schist sculptures from Gandhara; and other treats from Khajuraho, Halebid, Konark, Nalanda, and Nagappattinam. Farther down Chowringhee Road, you pass the **Asiatic Society of Bengal,** founded by Sir William Jones in 1784, and the forerunner of such British learned societies.

Turn left on Park Street, then right into Middleton Row to find more buildings from Kolkata's past. The **Convent of Our Lady of Loreto** was once home to the great collector Sir Elijah Impey. On Shakespeare Sarai, the **Royal Calcutta Turf Club** (1820), built as the home of a shipping magnate, is now one of many traditional British clubs that have changed little apart from the nationality of their membership. Stop to take a stroll around **South Park Street Cemetery ❼,** where pyramids, catafalques, pavilions, and obelisks, all saved from destruction, tell the amazing story of the city's growth and heyday. The cemetery guide, sold on site, is worth buying.

🅜 See area map pages 286–87
► Babu's Ghat, Maidan
↔ 6 miles (10 km)
⊕ 4–5 hours: Leave early enough to reach the Indian Museum at 10 a.m., when it opens.
► Victoria Monument

NOT TO BE MISSED
- South Park Street Cemetery
- St. Paul's Cathedral
- Victoria Memorial

Back along Shakespeare Sarai **St. Paul's Cathedral** ❽ (1839), overlooking Chowringhee, is the British Empire's first Church of England cathedral. Treasures inside include Sir Edward Burne-Jones's west window (1880), Clayton and Bell's east window

(1860s), Sir Arthur Blomfield's reredos, the pre-Raphaelite monument to Lord Mayo, and much more.

Finally, you reach the symbol of British imperialism in the east, the now restored **Victoria Memorial** ❾ (1921). Designed by Sir William Emerson and faced in Makrana marble from Jaipur state, it is topped off with a bronze figure of Victory. A statue of Lord Curzon, who conceived it, stands at the unused south entrance. In front, there is Sir George Frampton's striking art nouveau statue of the Queen-Empress Victoria. Inside, find quantities of huge oil portraits of self-regarding servants of the empire, plus an excellent new gallery in the back, which explains Kolkata's history. ■

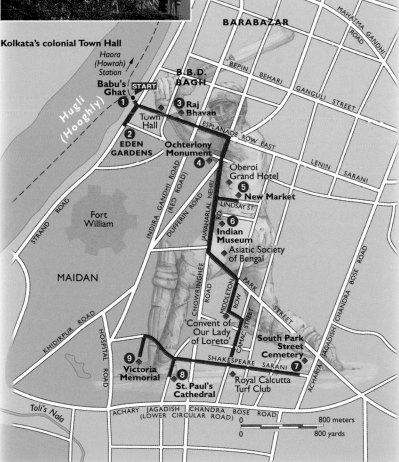

Kolkata's colonial Town Hall

Bhubaneshwar, Orissa

🅐 287 C2

India Tourist Office

✉ B/21 B.J.B. Nagar
☎ 0674-412203

State Tourist Office

www.orissa.gov.in/tourism

✉ 5 Jayadev Marg
☎ 0674-2431299

Orissa State Museum

✉ Lewis Rd.
🕐 Closed Mon.
💲 $

Orissa's capital, Bhubaneshwar, offers relative tranquility and delightful temples, such as the exquisitely carved **Mukteshvara Temple.**

Visitor tip

Both tourist information offices in Bhubaneshwar have information on Orissa's many festivals.

Bhubaneshwar, Puri, & Konark

BHUBANESHWAR, THE STATE CAPITAL OF ORISSA, HAS A long and glorious history. In the fourth century B.C. it was the capital of ancient Kalinga. Ashoka fought here in 260 B.C. before turning to Buddhism (see p. 31); he later placed one of his rock edicts there. During the city's golden age of prosperity and religious fervor, the 7th to 12th centuries, more than 7,000 temples were built around Bindu Sagar (Ocean Drop Tank) by the Bhauma-Kara, Somavansi, and Ganga rulers, as offerings to the gods and symbols of authority.

Many temples survive, including three groups of stunning ones on the town's southern outskirts, best reached by rickshaw. By visiting just five temples in chronological order, you can trace the development of distinctive Orissan style. These are the temples to see: **Parasu-maresvara Mandir** (late seventh century), **Vaital Deul** (late eighth century), **Mukteshvara** (late tenth century), **Lingaraja** (late 11th century), and **Yameshvara** (late 13th century). The curved tower grows higher and more complex; the *mandapa* (hall) becomes larger with a pyramid roof; sculpture is increasingly fully modeled, more elaborate, and focused on the niches.

In town, the **Orissa State Museum** has an excellent collection of Orissa's archaeological finds, as well as ethnographic items and illustrated manuscripts. India's largest zoo is in **Nandankanam Botanical Gardens.**

Farther afield, a one-day trip south to **Puri** winds through quaint villages with decorated houses, including **Pipli,** center of Orissa's colorful cotton appliqué-work. Puri is best known for its soaring Jagannath Temple *(closed to non-Hindus),* and this is a true pilgrim town, especially during the annual Rath Yatra festival *(June– July).* You can also take a prome-nade along the waterfront (the sea is not especially clean here).

Then drive up the coast to **Konark,** whose splendid **Surya Temple** (13th century), built by the Ganga king Narasimha *(R.* 1238–1264) marks the climax of all you saw at Bhubaneshwar: The temple is built as the sun god's chariot drawn by a team of horses. ∎

Orissa's early monuments

ORISSA'S ELABORATE, ROCK-CUT CAVES AND SUBSTANTIAL
Buddhist remains testify to the prosperity of the Kalinga empire of
the fourth century and its mercantile strength, military power, and
opulent lifestyle.

In two sandstone outcrops overlooking Bhubaneshwar are some
remarkable Jain caves left by a large
Jain community that thrived here
in the first century B.C. under the
benevolent Chedi rulers. About 35
massive and austere caves, some
natural and some dug out, provide
our earliest evidence of the art
found here in Orissa.

The dozen caves on the
Khandagiri Hill are fairly simple.
Those on the **Udayagiri Hill**
include **Cave no. 1,** the largest
and most elaborate. Two levels of
cells surround a large courtyard.
See the guardian figures, some in
foreign dress (upper story, right
wing), and the relief carvings over
the doorways that show pious couples, musicians, dancers, and nature
scenes. **Caves no. 3–5, 9,** and **10**
are also interesting.

If these have whetted your
appetite, take a long but rewarding
one-day trip north to find more
caves at Lalitagiri, Udaiayiri, and
Ratnagiri, and to enjoy stunning
countryside. On your way, you pass
through Orissa's former capital,
Cuttack, crammed onto a narrow
island on the Mahanadi River. In
the old quarter's bazaars, find
Orissa's distinctive filigree jewelry
(in Balu and Nayasarak bazaars).

The caves are hidden amid lush
farmland sprinkled with tiny
villages. It is easy to imagine how
each of these hill sites was an
ideal place to found a Buddhist
university with the great expansion
of Buddhist teaching from the 5th
to the 12th centuries. At that time
the sea reached farther inland and

would have been, in the monks'
view, thoroughly appropriate
because their patrons were often
affluent merchants trading by
sea. Some of these monasteries

were training centers for Buddhist
missionaries who were to spread
the word eastward.

At **Lalitagiri,** remains of platforms, shrines, mounds, and
monastic buildings are still being
excavated on Parabhadi and Landa
Hills. At **Udaiayiri,** archaeologists
are finding more of these plus a
colossal image of Buddha seated
and panels of Bodhisattvas. Last
and best of all, **Ratnagiri,** once the
center of Buddhism in Orissa, has a
great hilltop *stupa* and two monasteries; one still has its courtyard,
cells, and a Buddha figure. ∎

**Udayagiri Hill
caves**
✉ 4 miles (6 km) W
   of Bhubaneshwar
💲 $

Cuttack
🅰 287 C2
✉ 30 miles (48 km) N
   of Bhubaneshwar

**Two wonderfully
realistic elephants
stand in the
compound of
Konark's isolated
Surya Temple,
matched by two
rearing horses on
the other side.**

Ratnagiri
🅰 287 D2
✉ 85 miles (135 km)
   NE of Bhubaneshwar
💲 $

India's tribal communities

About 70 million of India's billion inhabitants still live their traditional tribal lives. Known collectively as Adivasis (original inhabitants) or by their official government grouping of Scheduled Tribes, they trace their origins right back to pre-Aryan times. For many, their lifestyle has changed little over the centuries. Until recently, they had remained separate from all the great empires and their developments, and had rarely encountered Hindu, Muslim, Western, or other cultures—even though the British encouraged them to settle so they could be taxed.

Naga tribeswomen living in Nagaland, wearing their distinctive shawls and jewelry

their buffaloes, which has been eroded by close encounters with the British and with Hindu Indians. The Bhils of southern Rajasthan, on the other hand, have for centuries been close allies with the rulers of Mewar, and this symbiotic relationship of mutual respect continues today. The Abors and Apatamis of Arunachal Pradesh in northeast India, however, continue to manage their own affairs.

But the pulls of tradition against modernity are increasingly causing friction. The more than three million Santhals of West Bengal and Bihar, who form the largest tribe of southern Asia, capture best these contrary pulls. Back in the 19th century, rapacious Hindu moneylenders dispossessed them of their land to the extent that they rebelled in 1855–57; yet they wanted high-caste Hindu privileges. In the 20th century they were drawn into the emerging industrialization that arrived on their doorstep, and its attendant education and modernization opportunities: Tata Iron and Steel Company opened at Jamshedpur in Bihar in 1908.

Today India has more than 500 named tribes speaking more than 40 different languages and following ancient customs and religious rituals. Each one has its own lineage or clan. Tribes still live on the periphery of society, with their distinctive lifestyles, although environmental pressure has forced the traditional hunters among them to change to cultivation. Most live in the thickly forested regions of India—where the terrain is unattractive for urban development or just plain inaccessible—such as southern Bihar, western Orissa, parts of Madhya Pradesh, the Andaman Islands, and the northeastern states.

Some tribes, such as the Jarawas of the Andamans, live at subsistence level, hunting and gathering in tiny communities of fewer than 500; others account for almost an entire population, such as the Mizos of Mizoram or the Nagas of Nagaland, who have adopted Christianity and Western lifestyles. India's tribal life has been under threat since the British period. The Todas of the Nilgiri Hills in Tamil Nadu had a rich culture, centered on

Today, with improved communications and a ballooning population, ideas and people reach most of India's tribes. So does outside competition for land where the tribes have lived for centuries; that these people are exposed to secular life and political awareness, and must make choices about them, is unavoidable but acceptable to them. That they are ruthlessly exploited, dispossessed, used as cheap labor, and left hungry is not. However, the Scheduled Castes and Tribes do have a voice in parliament: In each state, the number of constituencies reserved for them is in proportion to the state's total population. ■

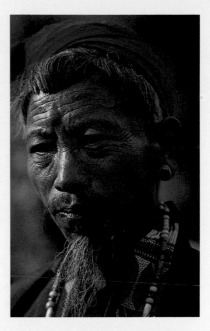

India's Scheduled Tribes, known as Adivasis, are scattered throughout the country. In the Lower Himalayas, a Kulu woman (above) living in Himachal Pradesh shops for a water pot.
In Gujarat, Maghwal *harijans* living in the town of Bhuj (below) lost their beautifully decorated homes in the devastating earthquake of 2001 (see p. 147).

Above: A Naga tribesman from Khonsa district in Arunachal Pradesh state

The Andaman & Nicobar Islands

The Andaman & Nicobar Islands

⚠ 287 box inset

India Tourist Office
www.andamanisland.com
✉ VIP Rd., Jungli Ghat, Port Blair

Port Blair Tourist Office
✉ A&N Administration
☎ 03192-20694

Cellular Jail National Memorial
💲 $

Samudrika Marine Museum
🕐 Closed Mon.
💲 $

Fisheries Museum & Aquarium
🕐 Closed Mon.
💲 $

Anthropological Museum
✉ Gandi Rd.
🕐 Closed Mon.
💲 $

Mini Zoo & Forest Museum
✉ MG Rd.
🕐 Mini Zoo closed Mon.
💲 $

Visitor tip
You can visit some of the islands but not all. Consult the Tourist Office.

IN THE BAY OF BENGAL, IN THE ANDAMAN SEA, MORE THAN 300 tiny islands make up a far-flung Indian possession that is important predominantly for its strategic position. Difficult to reach, these islands offer a complete escape to superb beaches and wonderful underwater sight-seeing on the coral reefs.

These forested islands, some 808 miles (1,300 km) from Kolkata and 746 miles (1,200 km) from Chennai, form two groups: the Andamans in the north, where Port Blair is the capital on Middle Andaman Island, and the Nicobars (which you cannot visit) in the south. Geologically, they were once part of the landmass of southeast Asia. The total population of about 300,000 people live on fewer than 40 of the islands.

In the past, the Portuguese, Dutch, British, and Japanese have controlled the islands; in 1857 the British sent some 4,000 convicted rebels to prison here. In 1956 the Indian government passed the Aboriginal Tribes Protection Act to help protect the island tribes' culture. However, this has not been wholly successful: Many Sri Lankan Tamils have migrated to the islands, swelling the population sixfold in just 20 years, and much forest has been felled in favor of rubber plantations. Even the islands' most valuable possessions—their tribal people and unique ecology—are threatened by mismanagement. Tribal people now account for less than 10 percent of the population, and numbers continue to fall.

Tourism, on the other hand, is doing little damage. So far, just a few of the 260 islands, most with superb beaches and coral reefs, have been developed. This policy works well in the Maldive Islands, lying off the west coast of southern India.

In Port Blair, where all the hotels currently are, there are several places to visit. The **Cellular Jail National Memorial,** once a British jail, is now a shrine to India's freedom fighters. The **Samudrika Marine Museum** provides a good introduction to the islands' geography, archaeology, and marine life. For more specialized information, visit the **Fisheries Museum & Aquarium** to discover more about the Andaman Sea, the little **Anthropological Museum** to learn about the indigenous but threatened tribes, and the **Mini Zoo** and **Forest Museum** to

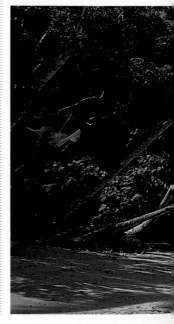

find out about the 200 or so animals exclusive to these islands. Out of town, you can visit **Mount Harriet National Park** and climb its mountain; sometimes you can stay in the Forest Guest House. A trip to **Ross Island** is worthwhile to see the British administrative buildings that are now very overgrown.

But the real joy of the islands lies in the water surrounding them. Beautiful coral reefs and very clear water combine to offer some of the world's best snorkeling. (Diving here is still in its infancy.)

BEACHES NEAR PORT BLAIR

Corbyn's Cove is the nearest beach, 4 miles (7 km) south of Port Blair. **Snake Island** is surrounded by a coral reef; take a boat there rather than swim, since the current can be strong. At Wandoor, the **Mahatma Gandhi National Marine Park** is 15 islands with mangrove creeks, tropical rain forest,

and reefs supporting more than 50 types of coral. From Wandoor village, you can take a boat (*except Mon.*) 18 miles (29 km) southeast to **Jolly Buoy** and **Red Skin** islands to explore coral reefs for a couple of hours. **Chiriya Tapu,** 19 miles (30 km) south of Port Blair, is a tiny fishing village with mangroves and beaches; just over a mile (2 km) south lies an especially attractive beach. From here you can sometimes arrange a boat to the Cinque Islands (see below).

OTHER ISLANDS

Havelock Island, 33 miles (54 km) northeast of Port Blair, has perfect, white sandy beaches, clear turquoise water, and good snorkeling, plus dolphins, turtles, and large fish. **Long Island,** off Middle Andaman, is tiny, with one village and several perfect beaches. **North** and **South Cinque Islands,** some of the most beautiful of all, are part of Wandoor's national park; day visits only. ■

Mount Harriet National Park
🕐 Closed sunset to sunrise
💲 $

Mahatma Gandhi National Marine Park
✉ 19 miles (30 km) SW of Wandoor
💲 $

Port Blair Library
✉ Near the Post Office; reference section 1st floor

Pristine tropical beaches await visitors to these isolated islands.

Tibetan monks pray at Bodh Gaya.

The Buddha trail

NON-BUDDHISTS RARELY VISIT INDIA'S EIGHT SITES associated with Buddha—Sravasti, Sankasya, Lumbini, Kushinagar, Sarnath, Bodh Gaya, Rajgir, and Vaishali—yet these places are as fascinating as Hindu, Muslim, and Jain sites. So consider joining the groups of Buddhists that flock to these fascinating places.

Lucknow, Uttar Pradesh
⚠ 286 A4 & A5

State Tourist Office
✉ Paryatan Bhawan, C-13, Vipin Khand Gomtinagar
☎ 0522-2308017

Sravasti, Uttar Pradesh
⚠ 286 B5

Kushinagar, Uttar Pradesh
⚠ 286 B5

If you have time, and a strong interest, begin your trip from Lucknow by first visiting **Sravasti,** where the Buddha spent 24 rainy seasons: See where he stayed, plus monastic ruins and Jetavana Park. **Sankasya,** west of Lucknow, is where Buddha reputedly descended from heaven. **Lumbini,** just across the border in Nepal, is Buddha's birthplace, and at nearby **Kapilavastu** there is the palace of Buddha's father and a stupa. **Kushinagar** (30 miles/50 km

east of Gorakhpur) is where Buddha died and attained Mahaparinirvana; see the stupa built after his cremation, monastic remains, and a large reclining Buddha made of stone.

Or you could start at the next site, **Sarnath,** near Varanasi in Uttar Pradesh, the leading Buddhist pilgrimage center. Here Buddha preached his first sermon, usually called Dharmachakra ("Setting in Motion the Wheel of Righteousness"), on the July full moon

Leaving G.T. Road, you enter a quiet, rural area. **Bodh Gaya** is where Buddha meditated, was tempted by the demon Mara, and finally received *bodhi* (enlightenment), making the place an important pilgrimage site. The bodhi tree that is believed to spring from the one he sat under stands at the back of a Hindu temple; Buddhists sit here to meditate, chant, and read. There is also an excellent **Archaeological Museum** displaying fine sculptures and some modern temples built by Japanese, Vietnamese, and other Buddhist communities.

Country lanes twist past medieval Gaya to **Rajgir**. Buddha and Mahavira, who spread Jainism, often visited the ancient Magadha kingdom, whose capital was here. Its rulers Bimbisara and Ajatashatru (circa 543–459 B.C.) converted to Buddhism, and the First Council was held here. You may need a guide to help find the many localities associated with Buddha: **Venuvana bamboo grove**, which became the first Buddhist monastery; **Saptaparni Caves**, where the First Council was held; Pippala stone house, where the senior monk Mahakashyapa stayed, and others. Take the walk up **Gridhrakuta Hill** (Vulture Peak) past two caves to the high terrace to experience a peaceful, restorative sunset. Rajgir has a quality hotel.

Nearby, **Nalanda** was a huge monastery and university from the 5th to 12th centuries, and it was the seventh-century Pala rulers' principal seat of learning and place of art patronage. Beneath the farmers' fields, nine brick Buddhist monasteries facing four temples have been unearthed; even some floor tiles survive. Treasures in the **Archaeological Museum** range from a *Naga* deity to ancient rice grains.

Complete the trail at **Vaishali**, 20 miles (32 km) north of Patna, where Buddha preached his last sermon. ∎

night (see p. 58); this was the basis of all future development of the religion. Buddha also founded his *sangha* (monastic order) here. As you wander around the monasteries, the Dharmarajika Stupa (third century B.C.), and Main Shrine (mostly fifth century), you will soak up the strong historical-religious atmosphere. Visit the excellent **Sarnath Museum**; its Ashoka pillar capital is now the official symbol of India.

Now turn eastward into Bihar along the Grand Trunk Road, or G.T. Road, described by Kipling as "the backbone of all Hind…" with "such a river of life as nowhere else exists in the world." After 60 miles (97 km), detour to **Sasaram** to see Sher Shah Sur's five-story, midlake tomb (1540–45), considered by some to be one of India's best buildings.

Sarnath, Uttar Pradesh
▲ 286 B4

Sarnath Museum
✉ Ashoka Mara
🕐 Closed Fri.
💲 $

Sasaram, Bihar
▲ 286 B4

Bodh Gaya, Bihar
▲ 287 C4

Bodh Gaya Archaeological Museum
🕐 Closed Fri.

Rajgir, Bihar
▲ 287 C4

Nalanda, Bihar
▲ 287 C4

Nalanda Archaeological Museum
💲 $

Vaishali, Bihar
▲ 287 C4

Visitor tip
Most facilities in this area are very simple; always carry water and snacks.

For more information, visit the websites for Uttar Pradesh and Bihar states: www.up-tourism.com and www.bstdc.bih.nic.in

Patna

THIS ANCIENT CITY OF GREAT HISTORICAL IMPORTANCE, founded in the fourth century B.C. as Pataliputra, was the center of the legendary Magadhan and Mauryan empires. From Patna, Chandragupta Maurya extended his rule to the Indus, and his grandson Ashoka pushed it even farther (see p. 31). Under the Guptas (fourth century) and Sher Shah Sur (16th century), the city enjoyed revivals. However, this narrow city beside the Ganga has little to offer visitors today.

Patna, Bihar
◪ 287 C4
**India Tourist
Office**
✉ Sudma Palace,
Kankur Bagh Rd.
☎ 0612-345776

**State Tourist
Office**
✉ 9D Hutments, Main
Secretariat
☎ 0612-2224531

Patna Museum
✉ Budh Rd.
🕐 Closed Mon.
$ $

There are few remains to testify to its glory, except in the **Patna Museum.** So, start here. The superb collection includes a wooden Maurya wheel (third century B.C.) and pillar in the entrance hall, which come from Pataliputra's palace. Don't miss beautiful sculptures, such as the woman holding a *chauri* or flywhisk (third century B.C.), recently retrieved from Delhi's National Museum. Another is the woman with a parrot (third to seventh century), which was once part of a door. There are rooms full of gentle Buddhas and Bodhisattvas, Hindu carvings, and, upstairs, prints by the uncle–nephew team of

Sonpur Fair

India's largest livestock fair, held outside Patna at the confluence of the Gandak and Ganga Rivers, lasts a full month and is a parade of nonstop color and amazing sights. It is so big that the local train station has India's longest platform, specially built to accommodate freight trains bringing farmers and their sheep, cows, goats, horses, and other wares for sale. The fair begins on Kartik Purnima, the night of the November full moon, which is the climax of the Chath Festival. After pre-dawn *puja* at the tiny Hari Hari temple, the faithful go down to the river. There you can rent a boat and be punted past saffron-saried women performing their pujas, to see mahouts scrubbing their elephants. Back on land, see the elephants, all painted up to look their best for sale, the animal-trading, and the latest agricultural tools. ■

Elephants for sale are taken for their morning bath in the river during the fair.

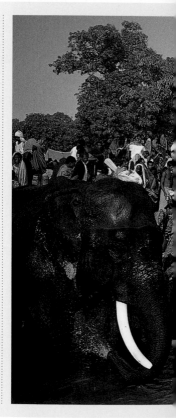

Thomas and William Daniels, superb bronzes, and a hall full of lively proto-Mauryan terra-cottas (2000 B.C.).

To see old Patna, you can avoid the worst of the city's constant traffic congestion by setting off very early and using the Old Bypass Road to reach **Har Mandir Sahib,** one of the four holy temples for Sikhs (see p. 59). It honors the tenth Guru, Guru Gobind Singh, who was born here. As in the temple at Amritsar (see pp. 122–23), there is an aura of peacefulness.

When the British lopped Bihar and Orissa off Bengal to make an independent administrative unit, Patna once again became a capital. New Patna, contemporary with New Delhi, was laid out as a modern imperial town, with wide avenues ending in vistas of grand buildings and a central axis called King George's Avenue. To see it, you need to drive or take a rickshaw and pass by **Raj Bhavan** (Government House), the **Secretariat** (1929) and **Council Chambers** (1920), and the **High Court** (1916).

West of Patna, 17 miles (29 km) along the road to Ara, lies **Munar** (Maner). Here, in a clearing in the woods stands **Choti Dargah** (1616), the tomb of Shah Daulat, built by Ibrahim Khan. Its fine proportions, delicate *jali* (stone lattice) work, and surface ornament make it one of eastern India's finest Mughal monuments. ■

Ganga River

The dominant force of eastern India is the Ganga. Its hundreds of tributaries trickle down the Himalayan slopes, link up into rivers, and create the life-giving Gangetic Plain and Delta. On the map on pp. 286–87 you can see how the Ganga flows past Kanpur, near Lucknow in Uttar Pradesh, then continues to Allahabad, where it takes in the Yamuna River, which has already watered Delhi and Agra. On it flows through Varanasi and into Bihar state. Here, at the city of Patna, major tributaries swell its waters: the Ghaghara, the Son, and the Gandak. Soon the great river begins to split into hundreds of threads to become the vast delta whose blessings of nourishment and punishments of flooding are shared by West Bengal and Bangladesh.

The Ganga is sacred to Hindus. A Hindu's Ganga *yatra* (journey, pilgrimage) begins at the river's source, Gangotri, near Rishikesh, then descends to Haridwar, Allahabad, and Varanasi. At each stop the river's water is revered; just a few droplets, not a hard scrub, can purify. The Ganga's water is especially purifying since Hindus believe it to be the goddess Ganga flowing eternally from the summit of Mount Meru, the abode of the gods, down through Shiva's matted locks. To bathe in the waters is to cleanse oneself of the *karma* of previous and current lives and so be prepared for death and rebirth into a better life. Hindus from all over India attend the mass ritual bathings that take place during the Kumbh Mela festival held every three years at one of Haridwar, Allahabad, Nasik, and Ujjain in turn. Of these, Allahabad, also known as Prayag (confluence) because the Yamuna and Ganga meet there, is especially sacred so the Kumbh Mela held here is known as Maha (Great) Kumbh Mela; the city also has an annual Magh Mela *(Jan.–Feb.)*.

At Chunar, upstream from Varanasi, the Ganga turns sharply north and then makes a great arc through the holy city. This, combined with the high west banks and the flat land on the east banks, creates an extraordinary, almost tangible bowl of light, especially at sunrise. Hindus have for centuries thought of Varanasi as Kashi (City of Divine Light), or as Kashika (The Shining One), referring to the light of Shiva.

Historically, the Gangetic Plain was the hearth of Indian culture, and settlements spread eastward from this core region more than three millennia ago. The Ganga was a highway for east–west trade across the subcontinent, and it irrigated and fed the soil to produce rich farmland. Thus, early cities such as Pataliputra (Patna) grew to be capitals of great empires. Later, the Mughals made Allahabad one of their capitals. The British pushed their influence up the Ganga from Calcutta to protect their vital trading route.

Today the rich alluvial plains formed by deposits from the Himalayan Mountains form one of the world's most densely populated regions. Deforestation of the Himalayan Mountains means additional silt is carried down river and helps cause flooding; more than a third of Bangladesh is flooded annually. Ironically, this rich silt is essential to the nourishment of the rice crops being intensively farmed throughout the Ganga basin. ∎

Devotees wash away their sins by bathing in the Ganga at Haridwar (above). Others (right) bathe at the confluence of the Ganga, Yamuna, and Saraswati Rivers. A Hindu faithful in prayer in the Ganga (far right).

During the Maha Kumbh Mela festival of 2001 (above), more than two million Hindus gathered at Allahabad to witness the moon's eclipse.

Varanasi

A Hindu pilgrim
meditates as he
witnesses the
sunrise at
Varanasi.

**Varanasi,
Uttar Pradesh**
🗺 286 B4
**India Tourist
Office**
www.up-tourism.com
✉ 15-B The Mall
☎ 0542 2343744

**UP Government
Tourist Office**
www.up-tourism.com
✉ Tourist Bungalow,
Parade Kothi
☎ 0542 2206638

THE HINDUS' HOLIEST CITY, VARANASI IS PERPETUALLY
overflowing with pilgrims. To visit it once in a lifetime is every
Hindu's goal; to die here is to have the greatest chance of *moksha* (salvation, release). It is, therefore, not an easy city for a Western person
to visit. But once you do, it may well become one of the most fascinating places of all your travels.

Walk down to the river for a boat
ride (see pp. 308–309), either early
in the morning or in the late
afternoon when the sun's rays are
enjoyable rather than punishing.
Give this city some time; zipping
in for a dawn boat ride and then
out again is rarely satisfying.
Varanasi is about watching a
nonstop pilgrim city going about
its business.

A city as old as Babylon, Varanasi

is, for Hindus, quite simply Kashi
(City of Divine Light). Of the
Hindus' Seven Sacred Cities, it is
the most sacred. The others are
Haridwar, Ujjain, Mathura, Ayodhya,
Dwarka, and Kanchipuram. Each is
dedicated to Shiva or Vishnu,
except Kanchipuram, which is
dedicated to both.

Thus, although it is a center for
Hindu culture and has fine music
and art, Varanasi's daily trade is

pilgrims, India's most numerous and free-spending visitors. From the most humble upward, pilgrims often make their *yatras* (pilgrimages) by bus on an excursion, singing *bhajans* (religious songs) along the way. At their destination, the aim is to receive *darshan* (the meritorious glimpse of the god) and to bathe in the sacred waters. Emotional outpourings of religious fervor are common. Meanwhile, priests, gurus, peddlers, and con-men of all kinds abound, often all too ready to relieve pilgrims, unused to the city and emotionally vulnerable, of their hard-earned money.

Varanasi was already thriving 2,500 years ago when Buddha came to Sarnath to deliver his first sermon (see p. 300), making it sacred to Buddhists, too. Later, Muslims periodically plundered the city; the widowed Shah Jahan forbade temple-rebuilding, and pious Aurangzeb converted one temple into a mosque. Early British arrivals wrote of being intoxicated by Varanasi's exoticism and mystery. Winding your way through the maze of narrow, filthy alleys swarming with cows and pilgrims, you feel something of this as you peek into temples of all sizes, some simple, some flashy, like **Tulsi Manasmunda,** funded by the Birla family. Pilgrims flood in and out of them ceaselessly.

Despite the city's squalor—for no other word will fit—the holiness of Varanasi has been the inspiration for some of the most sublime creations in Hindu culture. Classical music was nurtured in the temples, and today the city produces many of India's top musicians and stages important music festivals. Sanskrit and classical Hindu studies thrive in back rooms, on rooftops, and at the Banaras Hindu University, known as B.H.U.

Top right: A boy dressed as Sita, bride of Rama, in the famous *Ramlila* pageant. This annual outdoor performance, based on an epic poem about an ancient king's life and adventures, lasts roughly 10 to 32 days.

Bharat Kala Bhavan

🕐 Closed Sun.

$ $

Here, too, is the **Bharat Kala Bhavan,** where you can see some exquisite miniature paintings, whose religious message is heightened by the use of a rigid and highly symbolic iconography and intense colors.

Then there is the silk, originally woven to clothe the temple deities. Varanasi's weavers developed Baranasi brocade, a lusciously extravagant weave that includes threads of gold and silver. Much loved by the Mughals, it is still woven today. To see it, go to the daily **silk market,** found through an arch off Thatheri Bazar. In the late afternoon the weavers hurry through the maze of tiny alleys full of motorbikes, with their wooden boxes full of completed saris. They sell them to plump dealers sitting in cubicles on white cotton, their tools of trade a moneybox, a calculator, and a cell phone. Outside the silk market, find the **brass market** and continuous bazaars down to the water, where you can rent a boat and boatman for an evening cruise on the river, your boat lit by tiny oil lamps. ∎

A boat ride on the Ganga at Varanasi

Take this boat ride in the early morning to see the sunrise and morning Hindu rituals, or go in the evening for pretty views of the ghats. Drive a hard bargain for your boat, and do not be persuaded into a short, hurried trip.

If you can do it, get up well before dawn, put on plenty of warm clothes, and go down to **Dasaswamedh Ghat ❶** in the dark. Be on your boat as dawn creeps in, when you may hear the notes of the *shehna* reed instrument played by the musicians of the Shiva Temple to welcome the day. The dawn light is thin, liquid, and like no other light. It is easier to accept the various oil lamps and flowers pressed on you than to spoil the mood by entering into a bargaining session.

First, go upstream (to the right) to **Asi Ghat ❷,** or as far as you can persuade your boatman to go. As the boat slides through the water, the city begins to wake, and pilgrims sleeping beneath the high walls of the maharajas' old riverside palaces rouse themselves.

By the time you turn around to go downstream, a pale sun rises, the light changes, and a steady stream of people flows down to the holy water. From the city's 80 or so *ghats,* each with its Shiva *lingum,* the faithful begin to bathe and do their *puja* (worship) to the new day. Each ghat has its own importance; ideally, a Hindu should worship at each one. Asi Ghat marks the confluence of the Asi and Ganga waters. Right next to it, **Tulsi Ghat ❸** commemorates the 17th-century poet Gosain Tulsi Das, who translated the *Ramayana* from Sanskrit into Hindi and later died here.

A little farther along, **Shivala (or Kali) Ghat ❹** is owned by the former royal family of Varanasi, whose fort across the river at Ramnagar is where the great Ram Lila festival is held annually. The ghat has a large Shiva lingum. Nearby **Hanuman Ghat ❺** attracts pilgrims who worship the monkey god, whereas **Dandi Ghat** is used by ascetics called Dandi Paths. **Harishchandra Ghat** is one of the city's two burning ghats; the other is Jalasai Ghat, which you see later.

Kedara Ghat ❻ has fine linga and a temple. **Mansarowar Ghat** is named after a lake in Tibet near the Gangotri, the Ganga's source. **Man Mandir Ghat ❼** is in front of the Maharaja of Jaipur's palace; beside it Jai Singh built one of his observatories (see pp. 131–32).

As the sun rises over Varanasi, boatloads of pilgrims and visitors share the sacred Ganga water with bathing worshipers.

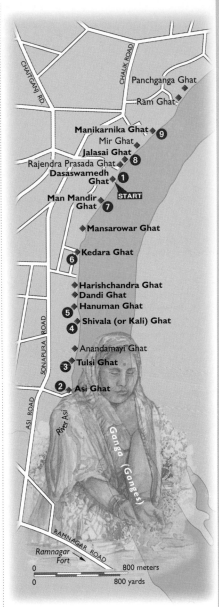

Panchganga Ghat
Ram Ghat
Manikarnika Ghat   9
Mir Ghat
Jalasai Ghat   8
Rajendra Prasada Ghat
Dasaswamedh Ghat   1
Man Mandir Ghat   7   START
Mansarowar Ghat
Kedara Ghat   6
Harishchandra Ghat
Dandi Ghat
Hanuman Ghat   5
Shivala (or Kali) Ghat
4
Anandamayi Ghat
Tulsi Ghat   3
Asi Ghat   2

CHATGANJ RD
CHAUK ROAD
SONAPURA ROAD
ASI ROAD
River Asi
Ganga (Ganges)
RAMNAGAR ROAD
Ramnagar Fort

0   800 meters
0   800 yards

- See area map pages 286–87
- Dasaswamedh Ghat
- 2–4 miles (3–6 km)
- 1–2 hours
- Dasaswamedh Ghat

NOT TO BE MISSED
- Dasaswamedh Ghat
- Asi Ghat
- Man Mandir Ghat
- Jalasai Ghat

(Ask your boatman to point them out)

Moving downstream you pass by **Dasaswamedh Ghat,** your starting point, where *brahmans* are by now setting themselves up for the day's business, sitting cross-legged beneath their shabby umbrellas. Continue to **Jalasai Ghat 8,** the famous burning ghat with a heap of lopsided temples (absolutely no photographs may be taken of this); the ghat is named after Vishnu when he is sleeping on the Cosmic Ocean. It adjoins **Manikarnika Ghat 9,** the most sacred of all ghats, for here Mahadeo (Shiva) dug the tank to find Parvati's

earring. As if to emphasize the Hindus' inequality in death, only the most privileged families are burned on the Charanpaduka slab marked with the imprint of Vishnu's feet.

With the sun warming your back, the boatman will row you back upstream to Dasaswamedh Ghat. ■

Dhobi-wallahs
(washermen) use
Lucknow's free
and spacious
Gomti River and
its banks to do
the citizens'
washing.

Lucknow & Kanpur (Cawnpore)

THE CAPITAL OF INDIA'S MOST POPULOUS STATE, UTTAR
Pradesh, Lucknow is spacious and calm. The relative lack of visitors
and distance from industry make this an easy city to explore. Its key
sites are in two groups: the faded, romantic Muslim buildings of the
old city and the practical brick British buildings of the Residency, a
silent and poignant reminder of a complete breakdown in the two
countries' long relationship, a breakdown that also engulfed Kanpur,
an important British garrison town.

**Lucknow,
Uttar Pradesh**
🅰 286 A5

**State Tourist
Office**
www.up-tourism.com
✉ Paryatan Bhawan
C-13 Vipin Khand
Gomtinagar
☎ 0522-2308017

Great Imambara
🕐 Closed during
prayers

The city's Shia Muslim rulers, called
the Nawabs of Avadh (Oudh, in
Bihar), rose to power in the
vacuum of 18th-century Mughal
decline and made their final capital
Lucknow. The ten lazy, plump,
pleasure-loving, and debauched
rulers set the tone for a distinctly
self-indulgent yet highly sophisticated
Muslim culture, especially under
Asaf-ud-Daula (*R.* 1775–1797) and
Saadat Ali Khan (*R.* 1798–1814).
Today, the fruits of the Nawabs'
extravagant patronage of buildings,
artists, craftsmen, musicians, and
Urdu poetry retain the atmosphere
suitable for a decaying, decadent,

and introverted court that ended in
tragedy: The British deposed the
last incompetent ruler, one of
several actions that triggered the
Rebellion of 1857.

The best of the Nawabs' buildings is the **Great Imambara,** or
House of the Imam (1780s), one of
the world's largest vaulted halls,
entered through the Rumi
Darwaza. Designed by Kifayat-ullah
for Asa'f-ud-Daula as a famine
relief project, its purpose is to be
the focus of the Muharram festival.
This is when Shia Muslims have a
procession in memory of the
martyrdom of Hussain and his

two sons. Inside, see the *tazias,* ornate paper reproductions of the Shia Imam's shrine at Karbala in southern Iraq. Upstairs, there are good views of other buildings worth visiting: the **Jami Masjid,** the **Small Imambara,** the **Tower** for watching the moon at Id, the **Clock Tower,** and various royal tombs and Muslim shrines.

Chowk, the old market area, is a maze of alleys perfumed with the spices of *paan* ingredients, a Lucknow specialty. On Chowpatia Street, near Akbari Gate, you can find the essentials of any Lucknow sophistication: gold leaf being beaten, *bidri* work (see p. 249), gold thread-makers, *chikankara* (white-on-white cotton embroidery), silk brocade, Koran bookstands, heavy *attar* (perfume), and delicious fresh breads, kebabs, and confections. To see taziamakers, go to Hazaratganj area.

The **Residency** complex (see pp. 312–13) is the surreal, frozen reminder of the 1857 Rebellion, which staged some of its bloodiest scenes at Lucknow and Kanpur. This is the site of the epic siege and relief in 1857. The rebellion broke out in Meerut on May 10, when 47 battalions of the Bengal army mutinied. The next day it reached Delhi (see p. 75) and quickly spread to Kanpur, where there was a massacre on June 27, then to Lucknow.

Here the British endured a double siege, then reaped a vile revenge. Events began on June 30, 1857, when *sepoys* (Indian soldiers) poured over the Gomti River to join citizens already angry that their Nawab had been deposed. The British garrison of about 3,000, under the command of Sir Henry Lawrence, quickly took refuge in the Residency. Fighting was both above ground and underneath it in tunnels and mines. Meanwhile, gangrene, scurvy, cholera, and general lack of hygiene took their toll on the British garrison. Gen. Sir Henry Havelock arrived with reinforcements after three months, retaking the fort on September 25 only to lose it immediately. On November 17 Sir Colin Campbell led the final relief. Just 979 of the original 3,000 had survived.

KANPUR

Another significant site of this intriguing period of history, for India and Britain, is **Kanpur,** a two-hour drive away. This, one of the most important British garrisons on the Ganga, was also beseiged during the "mutiny." In the cantonment, Walter Granville's Lombardic-Gothic **All Souls Memorial Church** (1862–1875) has poignant tablets around the apse wall, and the adjoining **Memorial Garden** has equally eloquent angels and a screen that remember the British women and children massacred and put in Bibighar well in revenge for British atrocities. In the nearby scrub find General Sir Hugh Wheeler's entrenchment, where the siege took place. You can also visit nearby **Sati Chaura Ghat,** where British fleeing Fatehgarh down the Ganga were massacred in their boats—a bleak, chilling spot. ■

Small Imambara
🕐 Closed during prayers

The magnificent Great Imambara at Lucknow is dedicated to three imams— Ali, Hassan, and Hussein.

The Residency at Lucknow

THIS IMPORTANT SITE, WHICH MARKED A WATERSHED IN British and Indian history, has been cleaned up but left almost as it was at the end of the siege on November 17, 1857. Under the spreading banyan, neem, and bel fruit trees, you can visit the eerie remains of buildings where men, women, and children survived for five months, from the monsoon of July to the chilly days of November.

**Lucknow
Residency**
💲 $. Free Fri.

Through the Baillie Guard gateway, you find the **Treasury** on the right, whose long central room was used as an arsenal in 1857. Next door, the grand and once sumptuous **Banqueting Hall** was the siege hospital. Dr. Fayrer's House, to the south, is a large, one-story building where women and children stayed; a tablet marks the spot where Sir Henry Lawrence died—there is a memorial cross to him on the lawn, and he is buried in the cemetery. **Begum Kothi** is where Mrs. Walters, a British woman who married the Nawab, once lived.

The elegant **Residency** building itself stands on the northeast side of the complex and was built by Nawab Saadat Ali Khan in 1800. The wives and children of high-ranking officers lived here in appalling and dank conditions in the basements. The second floor

is now a little **museum** with a model of the whole residency complex in 1857, and some horrific prints. On the wall there is a poignant plaque to Susanna Palmer, killed by a cannonball on July 1, 1857. After this incident, the residents buried their snobbery and moved to Dr. Feyrer's House. In the **cemetery** find simple graves of Lawrence and of Brig.-Gen. J. S. Neill, whose frightful revenge on the Kanpur mutineers was not repeated at Lucknow; he was killed here on September 25, 1857. As for the hero Havelock, he died of dysentery a week after Campbell arrived. ■

The poignant remains of the Residency are well-maintained, perhaps to remind Indians of their hard-won freedom, whose beginnings here are called by some "The First War of Independence" rather than the "Mutiny" or the "Rebellion."

More places to visit in Eastern India

BARAKAR, GHURISA, & KABILASPUR

This is a pleasant rural trip northwest from Kolkata into the Bengal countryside. Stop at Barakar for a ninth-century Orissan-style temple with miniature figures adorning its curved tower; at Ghurisa for a Bengali hut-style temple (1633) with terra-cotta panels, with some figures in European dress; and at Kabilaspur for a beautiful temple that lacks all decoration.

BARAKPUR

Once the summer residence of Calcutta's British governors-general, this model cantonment on the east banks of the Hooghly, opposite Serampore (see p. 316), retains its layout and spaciousness, and it is well maintained by the army. Drive around to the many original houses and bungalows, several of them part of the Ramkrishna Vivekananda Mission. Access is restricted to some parts, but try to see **Government House** (1813), the **Temple of Fame, Lady Canning's Grave,** and **Semaphore Tower.**
A 287 D3 ✉ 15 miles (24 km) north of Kolkata

BISHNUPUR

Come to the capital of the cultured Malla rulers of Bengal, now a rural backwater, to see their group of exquisite Bengali hut-style 17th- to 18th-century temples faced with beautiful terra-cotta story plaques, usually showing scenes from the *Ramayana*. See especially the **Shyam Rai Temple** (1643), **Keshta Raya Temple** (1655), and **Madana Mohana Temple** (1694).
A 287 D3 ✉ 93 miles (150 km) northwest of Kolkata, most easily reached by train

BUXAR

This Hindu pilgrimage site on the Ganga was the scene of Sir Hector Munro's decisive victory on October 23, 1764, when he used clever tactics to reverse near defeat against the forces of Shah Alam, Shuja-ud-Daula, and Mir Qasim, taking their entire camp and 160 guns. This built on Clive's victory at Plassey in 1757 (see below) and confirmed Britain's supremacy

in Bengal. On the way here from Patna, pause at Ara, where 12 British and 50 Sikhs held the Little House of Ara from July 27 to August 3, 1857, against more than 2,000 *sepoys* and rebels.
A 286 B4 ✉ 73 miles (117 km) west of Patna, Bihar

GAUR & AROUND

A wonderful trip from Kolkata takes you through rural Bengal to seek out the extensive, fine, and rarely visited Muslim capital of the Afghan rulers of Bengal during the 15th and 16th centuries. Later sacked by Sher Shah Sur (1537), Gaur became part of Akbar's Mughal empire in 1576. Find substantial ruins dotted among villages and farms covering some 20 square miles (52 sq km), there is a central group within huge embankments that includes a fort, mosques, tombs, a victory tower, and gateways. From here the intrepid can continue to **Malda** (Islamic buildings), **Pandua** (the Afghan capital before Gaur),

Bangarh (archaeological site of an ancient city), **Rajmahal** (good Mughal city remains 4 miles/6 km west of the modern city), and **Sultangunj** (eighth-century carvings on granite rocks at Jahangira), ending at Patna.
287 D4 **Gaur** 200 miles (320 km) north of Kolkata

GOPALPUR-ON-SEA & AROUND

A delightful beach, small village, and a few cottages in Orissa make this the best beachside escape from Kolkata. You can reach it by train to Brahmapur, where you may see silk-weavers around the temple. North of here, **Chilka Lake** is a large lagoon rich in migratory birds from December to February.
287 C1

MURSHIDABAD & AROUND

The drive through Bengal from Kolkata to Murshidabad passes Plassey and Brahmapur. At the former, little remains to mark Clive's

Two women sit outside their simple coastal home at Gopalpur-on-sea.

victory beside the Bhagirathi River on June 23, 1757, against the Nawab Suraj-ud-Daula of Murshidabad. At the latter, the early British cantonment is interesting, with its grid-pattern streets interspersed with ditches and water tanks for defense. Murshidabad became the capital of Bengal in 1704 when Murshid Quli Khan moved the capital here from Dacca and Rajmahal. Later, the British moved the law (1772) and then the bureaucrats (1790) to Kolkata. Reminders of past splendor to see include: the **Palace of the Nawab, Imambara, Medina, mosques,** and **tombs.** North again, **Baranagar's** 18th-century hutlike temples contain fabulous terra-cotta story plaques. From here you can link in to the Gaur trip (see p. 314).
287 D4 **Murshidabad** 122 miles (196 km) north of Kolkata

SERAMPORE & NORTH OF KOLKATA

Leave very early to avoid city traffic on this day trip from Kolkata, up the west bank of the Hooghly to visit sites evocative of intrepid European merchants and fine Bengali temples. First stop is Serampore, a Danish settlement (1755) where an English Baptist missionary set up Kolkata's first printing press (1799); see **Serampore College** (1821), **India Jute Mill,** and **St. Olave's Church** (1821). Continue to **Belur Math Temple** (1938), built by Swami Vivekananda, a disciple of Ramakrishna; a mile (1.6 km) or so beyond, Kolkata's popular **Dakshineshwar Temple** (1855) stands across the Bally Bridge. At **Chandannagar,** crumbling yet grand buildings testify to a successful French factory (1688). Beyond Hooghly and Bandel, both early European settlements, find first **Bansberia's** lovely terra-cotta-ornamented Bengali temples, then many more at **Kalna,** maintained by

A gaily painted modern temple decoration

the former royal Burdwan family.
🗺 287 D3 **Serampore** ✉ 13 miles (21 km) north of Kolkata

SHANTI NIKETAN & AROUND

This is a peaceful escape from the steamy city. Founded by Bengal's great writer and poet Rabindranath Tagore in 1921, as a settlement and center of study to promote Bengali cul-

ture, Shanti Niketan was the Bengali Renaissance's most ambitious and successful project. Tagore designed the **Uttaraya** complex of buildings, which includes a **museum** *(Closed Wed.),* **gallery** *(Closed Wed.),* and departments for art, music, and drama.
🗺 287 D3 **Shanti Niketan** ✉ 84 miles (135 km) north of Kolkata

SIMHANATHA & RANIPUR JHARIAL

This is an adventurous trip through Orissa's countryside. Simhanatha's well-preserved temple (eighth century) stands on an island in the Mahanadi River. Continue into the hills to **Ranipur Jharial,** two villages whose rocky outcrop has more than 50 little temples.
🗺 286 B2 **Ranipur Jharial** ✉ 180 miles (290 km) west of Bhubaneshwar

SIMILIPAL NATIONAL PARK

The inhospitable, thickly wooded slopes of Orissa's Eastern Ghats have preserved this park, founded in 1957, from any form of taming—even today, the effort of reaching this very beautiful landscape, and the simplicity of accommodations, mean it has few visitors. However, the mixture of deciduous forest, streams, and open savannah provide the habitat for a varied wildlife, from leopards and tigers to porcupines, elephants, and mugger crocodiles, plus more than 230 species of birds. Permits and reservations with exact dates are essential; otherwise, join an organized tour.
🗺 287 D2 ✉ Field Director Project Tiger, Baripada 757002, Mayurbhunj District, Orissa

THE SUNDERBANS

Where the great Gangetic Delta meets the Bay of Bengal, water and land intermingle. The Hooghly River creates an estuarine delta of more than 965 square miles (2,500 sq km). Here is the Sunderbans Tiger Reserve, a group of mangrove-covered islands whose Royal Bengal tigers have adapted to the landscape and both swim and eat fish. To visit, stay at Sajnekhali Tourist Lodge 75 miles (120 km) south of Kolkata; explore the area by boat and with a Project Tiger guide. Permits available from the West Bengal Tourist Office in Kolkata; best visited November to March.
🗺 287 D3 ■

The great Himalayan range that forms India's dramatic northern border supplies hikers, painters, botanists, and those in search of relief from the plains' heat with lush, cool valleys; sparkling, clear rivers; forested hillsides; and spectacular mountain views.

The Himalaya

**A woman from the western
Himalaya Ladakh Valley**

Kaylong Khardong village sits in the dramatic, bare landscape of the Lahaul district.

The Himalaya

THE HIMALAYA, THE WORLD'S HIGHEST MOUNTAINS, ARE LESS THAN 130 million years old and still growing. When the ancient Indian Plate of the peninsula, some 3,000 million years old, moved under the Asian Plate the dramatic crumpling and fissuring began, the Himalaya began to rise, and they continue to do so.

Looking at the map on the inside front cover, you can see what a formidable barrier the Himalaya are, effectively isolating the subcontinent from the rest of Asia. Varying in width from 93 miles (150 km) to 210 miles (400 km), and with 95 peaks reaching an elevation of more than 24,000 feet (7,500 m), they stretch 1,553 miles (2,500 km) from Pakistan's Pamirs to Assam's Brahmaputra River. Two large chunks of these mountain ranges are in India.

The mountains are made up of several ranges, where some of India's great rivers rise. In the west, the young Indus flows between the Karakoram Range in Pakistan and the Zaskar Range. Moving east, you find many beautiful lakes in the frontier Vale of Kashmir, the region's most famous valley, which suffers from Indo-Pakistan political tensions. Eastward, Himachal Pradesh's hills belong to the Siwalik Range—massively folded and faulted mountains with longitudinal valleys known in the western part as "duns." Lowland

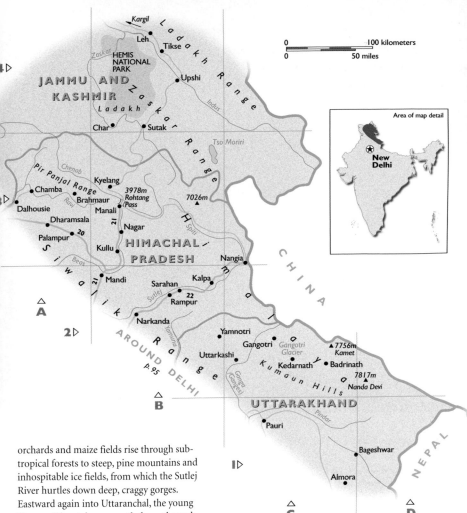

orchards and maize fields rise through sub-tropical forests to steep, pine mountains and inhospitable ice fields, from which the Sutlej River hurtles down deep, craggy gorges. Eastward again into Uttaranchal, the young Yamuna River takes one path down through mighty gorges, while the Ganga River takes another. From Gangotri Glacier it foams and crashes down to Haridwar, where it becomes more sedate for the long journey through the Sarawik Hills, here called the Garhwal.

East of Nepal the mountains of the central Himalayan range receive the full deluge of the annual monsoon rains, and the postmonsoon waters of the Brahmaputra River thunder through Assam. This isolated region has wild rhododendrons and orchids, Kaziranga and Manas wildlife sanctuaries, tea plantations, and individual cultures and peoples.

The Mughals loved Kashmir; later, the British discovered the vast, cool, and expansive beauty of all the Himalayan mountain scenery from lush lowlands to stunning high mountain passes. Today, the best way to experience it is to hike. This is nature in its most raw and awesome condition, with the occasional Buddhist monastery, Hindu shrine, and British hill station. Choose an area that appeals; then make reservations for the right trek for you: anything from gentle day walks to a challenging ten-day journey sleeping in tents (see pp. 332–34 for trekking ideas). The more adventurous you are, and the less fussy about comfortable accommodations, the more rewarding your visit will be. ■

The Suru Valley is a welcome ribbon of green in the high, parched region of Ladakh.

Western Himalaya

AS A CONTRAST TO THE HEADY COCKTAIL OF MONUMENTS, history, heat, and city crowds, a hike in the foothills of the Himalaya invigorates you. The cool air, mountain scenery, culture, and lifestyle offer relaxation after touring the plains, and the lower slopes in Uttaranchal or Himachal Pradesh easily accessible from Delhi. The more ambitious can press on north to Ladakh.

Uttarakhand (formerly Uttaranchal)

Map p. 319

Uttarakhand Tourist Office

www.hill-stations-india.com

http://gov.ua.nic.in/uttaranchaltourism/index.html

UTTARAKHAND

An easy drive or train ride from Delhi, the Garhwal and Kumaun Hills that lie between Uttar Pradesh and Nepal and Tibet and are known as the Uttaranchal, or Uttarkhand. From the fertile plains, or *terai*, they rise through summer mountain meadows called *bugyals* to a series of snowpeaked mountains, including Nanda Devi (25,643 feet/7,816 m), the highest mountain complete-

ly in India. These hills have scenic variety as well as charming hotels (see p. 376); the sacred Hindu pilgrimage center of Haridwar; Rishikesh, made famous by the Beatles; the protected forests of Corbett National Park; and the gentle, still slightly Victorian British hill stations of Mussoorie and Nainital (see pp. 124–126 for all of these).

The history of the area is complex, since each of the deep

river valleys has its own distinct culture, and the Garhwal and Kumaun regions have their own languages. Furthermore, although Hinduism dominates, a shrine may reveal elements of animism and Buddhism; it was through the Himalayan mountains that Buddhism was carried to China. Indeed, so distinct is Uttarkhand that it won autonomy from Uttar Pradesh and became a separate state in 2000.

The sources of the Yamuna and Ganga Rivers give the Garhwal special status and popularity. Here are the four *yatra* (pilgrimage) temples known as the Char Dham: **Badrinath, Kedarnath, Gangotri,** and **Yamnotri.** The hundreds of thousands of pilgrims who come here via Rishikesh from May to November each year have influenced the indigenous culture of this area. To experience purer Garhwal beauty, hike through the **Harki Dun valley** or the **Tehri Garhwal.** The less popular **Kumaun Hills,** however, retain much of their original charm. The temples receive fewer pilgrims, the landscape fewer trekkers, and hill towns such as Almora, with its cobbled alleys and wood and stone houses, fewer visitors.

For trekking ideas, see pp. 332–34. Rewarding trips to consider are the day-long walk to **Gangotri Glacier,** the source of the Ganga, or the varied five-day trek to **Pindari Glacier.**

HIMACHAL PRADESH

The gateway to this small state of hills and mountains, sandwiched to the east and west by Tibet and Pakistan, is **Shimla** (see p. 124), queen of all India's hill stations. North of here the mountains and gorges are the boundaries for remote and distinct districts, boundaries crossed by the Gaddi and Gujjar,

semi-nomadic shepherds. The area has seen Rajputs ruling Kangra, and Tibetans ruling Lahaul and Spiti; and since the 18th century control has passed from the Sikhs of the Punjab to the Gurkas of Nepal and finally to the British until independence.

After the lush valleys of the southern Sirmaur area, including delightful **Nalagar,** the landscape north of Shimla becomes more dramatic. Moving northeast past Narkanda you can follow the Sutlej River to find the wooden temple of **Sarahan** and, with a special Inner Line Permit, the Kinnaur district's isolated and austere beauty up on the Tibetan Plateau. Ambitious treks lead through to Spiti and the Kullu Valley; simpler walks are along the Sutlej Valley.

Just north of Shimla, passengers can enjoy spectacular mountain views.

For places in the Himachal Pradesh
www.himachaltourism.nic.in
www.hill-stations-india.com

Kinnaur area
▲ Map p. 319
Shimla Tourist Office
✉ Railway Station

Dhauladhar Range
▲ Map p. 319
Dharamsala Tourist Office
✉ Main bazaar

Pangi Valley
 Map p. 319
Brahmour
Mountaineering
Institute
✉ Brahmour; Kullu
Tourist Office
✉ Dhalpur maidan,
Kullu; Manali Tourist
Office
✉ The Mall, Manali

Ladakh
 Map p. 319
Leh Tourist Office
www.jktourism.org
✉ Fort Road, Bazaar

Kargil Tourist Office
✉ Hotel area, Kargil

North of Shimla, the road
divides at Mandi. Keeping to the
north, **Manali** is the increasingly
developed base for exploring verdant
Kullu Valley's terraces, forests, and
diminishing apple orchards, and for
white-water rafting at Vashisht. But
farther north, across the treacherous
Rohtang Pass (13,051 feet/3,978 m),
fewer people visit the bare mountains and snowfields of the great
Himalayan Range that encase
Lahaul and Spiti Valleys. The 300-
mile-long (500 km) **Manali–Leh
Highway,** one of the world's great
drives, is open June through
October. The mountain and valley
views are incredible as it switchbacks
through Keylong, Sarchu Serai, and
the passes of Langlacha La (16,597

feet/5,059 m) and Tanglang La
(17,480 feet/5,328 m).

Northwest of Mandi, the well-
trodden trail leads through the
heavily populated Kangra Valley
toward the Dhauladhar mountains,
where the Dalai Lama and his
Tibetan exiles live at **Dharamsala.**
From here, gentle treks lead
through the tea-growing area of
Palampur; more adventurous ones
cross the mountains into the
Chamba Valley toward the Pir
Panjal Range.

LADAKH
High in the Zaskar and Ladakh
mountain ranges and stretching up
to the Karakoram, **Ladakh**
(appropriately meaning "land of

Ecology

**Mountain
farmers have
to terrace their
fields. Seen
from a distance
in the Garhwal
area of Uttar
Pradesh, the
terraces look
like rippling
water.**

India, so rich in resources, faces an
ecology crisis. Rampant population growth is one reason, though
the average Indian consumes a tiny
fraction of resources compared to
the average Westerner; local politics, modernization, and unplanned
development are others. Ancient
forests and their ecosystems are
being destroyed by uncontrolled
lumber industries, mining, cultivation, and dams. An estimated 5,800
square miles (15,000 sq km) are
lost each year. As a result, tribal
groups are losing their means of

survival, as are species of flora and
fauna. As industry increases, so land
is overfarmed for its raw materials—cotton, paper, rubber, jute,
tobacco, and sugar—at the expense
of food. The huge dam projects,
such as the Tungabhadra and
Narmada, have displaced communities totaling more than 20 million
people. They have also affected
fish-breeding, wildlife, and animal
migration; increased the dangers of
waterborne diseases; and often silted
up. Disadvantages, often not fore-
seen, have outstripped advantages.

Meanwhile, despite the green
revolution making India self-
sufficient in food, Western farming
methods, fertilizers, and high-yield
strains of crops have damaged the
soil, demanded extra irrigation,
and affected the environment and
traditional by-products.

But there is hope: An increasingly energetic ecology movement
is making its voice heard, and
successful local projects may soon
have state and national backing. ■

The view from Ladakh's best-known *gompa*, at Tikse near Leh, has changed little since the gompa was built in the 15th century.

high mountain passes") is a high-elevation desert crossed by razor-sharp peaks. Here, where the land is frozen for eight months a year and scorched for four, rainfall is the same as in the Sahara. Yaks, goats, and sheep are essential for wool, milk, and butter, and for bartering in exchange for grain and fuel. Open to general visitors since 1974, the current unrest makes this the only area of Jammu and Kashmir state that it is advisable to visit.

Such an isolated and starkly beautiful spot is one of the large refuges of Mahayana Buddhism (see p. 58), Ladakh's principal religion, which historically has looked to Tibet for its inspiration; the Dalai Lama is head of its most popular sect, the Gelug-pa ("yellow hat"). As you travel through the area, the thin mountain light sparkles on brightly colored prayer wheels, rooftop flags, and whitewashed *chortens* (stupas). Furthermore, Ladakh's medieval monasteries, perched on craggy cliffs and known locally as *gompas*, are still centers of learning and worship. These house remarkable artifacts—brass Buddhas, walls painted with fierce divinities, *thangkas* (scroll paintings), and unusual musical instruments.

If you arrive by taking the Manali–Leh Highway (see p. 322), you go through the most concentrated area of these monasteries as you progress up the Indus Valley from Upshi to Leh, Ladakh's capital and once a staging post on the Silk Road. Having benefited from past trade and religious patronage, Leh is now buffeted by summer visitors. While acclimatizing to the elevation, you can visit the old palace, **Namgyal Tsemo gompa,** and the old quarter. One-day trips down the valley can take in pretty villages, **Shey's** derelict palace, and the stunning **Tikse gompa,** returning via **Hemis gompa** and **Stok palace. Spitok** and **Phyang** gompas lie to the north, as do the 11th-century murals of **Alchi,** best seen during the breathtaking drive to **Kargil,** beyond which lies the beautiful Suru Valley and stunning but remote **Zaskar,** the goal for serious trekkers. The intrepid can visit the stark Nubra Valley, opened to visitors in 1994. ■

VISITOR TIPS

Some of the hill areas are politically volatile, so it is wise to follow your own government's advice; currently, visits to Kashmir are discouraged, except to Ladakh. The Indian government requires foreign visitors to obtain special permits for some northeastern states. It is best to do your research, make your reservations, and obtain your permits before you arrive in India.

Fabrics of India

Until you first visit India, your experience of Indian fabrics may well be limited to seeing pictures of old woolen Kashmir shawls with richly patterned borders. They are glorious. The best were woven in Kashmir from the 15th to the mid-19th centuries, using fleece imported from Central Asia. Sophisticated Mughals and other rulers prized them for their intricate flower designs and precision craftsmanship: Each shawl required a dozen specialists, from pattern-drawers to dyers, and took many months to make. Introduced into European high fashion in the 1770s, the Kashmir shawl became an essential chic fashion accessory, especially in France. A century later, however, the Jacquard looms of Lyons and Paisley made the shawls so inexpensively that they lost their appeal.

Most Hindu women, however modern, choose to marry in traditional clothes.

Today's Western fashion for so-called pashmina shawls (from the Persian word *pashm,* meaning wool) is a pale imitation of past glories and India's present weaving skills. That the variety and quality of India's weaving is unequaled, is quickly evident if you simply keep your eyes open as you travel around India.

The incredible colors, patterns, and weaves both in the markets and being worn by the people are infinite. These remarkable fabrics may be woven in many kinds of cotton, silk, and wool. For instance, cotton may be fine muslin, handspun and handwoven *khadi* made famous by Mahatma Gandhi, or mill-spun but handwoven "handloom" cotton. Indians tend to drape rather than cut and tailor their fabrics, wearing them as shawls, saris, or *lunghis* (or *dhotis,* a cloth worn by a man). Depending

where you travel, you may also see local people in finely woven or intricately embroidered jackets, skirts, tight shirts, hats, and even shoes.

Weaving has been serious business in India since at least the period of the Indus Valley Civilization, from which spindles and pieces of cotton cloth wrapped around a silver vase survive. In the 1630s, the British established their first major foothold in India at Madras expressly to buy cotton from the nearby weavers. Today, textiles are a major part of the economy. India has about three million cotton handloom weavers. Sericulture (silk farming) and silk-weaving, first introduced by Buddhist monks from China, is a government-controlled industry in Karnataka state. Master weavers are revered and receive national awards, and fine silks dress temple deities. A bride-to-be is the focus of a serious family outing to choose her wedding saris; it may be a shopping trip to Varanasi to buy a luxurious Barnasi brocade encrusted with silver and gold threads, or a more modest outing to Jaipur's cotton market.

The best way to buy local weaves is to visit the village and town markets. If you are in a weaving area, maybe traveling through the villages of Tamil Nadu, weavers will welcome you into their homes, where the great wooden looms dominate the living space.

To see the range and quality of traditional Indian fabrics, visit the National Crafts Museum in Delhi (see p. 72), the Calico Museum in Ahmedabad (see p. 148), and the Delhi street lined with fixed-price, high quality stores representing each Indian state, Baba Kharak Singh Marg at Connaught Place. ∎

Traditional dress continues to be popular among Indian women, including this brightly festooned wedding party (above).

Traditionally hot-toned, hand-dyed silk saris are put out to dry in Jodhpur, Rajasthan (above). These colors stand out against the ancient stones of Chittaugarh Fort (right).

Eastern Himalaya

THIS WHOLE HIMALAYA REGION SHARES MOUNTAINS, wildlife, and flora, but the presence of Bangladesh divides it in two— only Indian citizens may take the train from West Bengal to Assam. Getting to the Eastern Himalaya is easiest by plane from Kolkata (see pp. 288–93) or Delhi (see pp. 62–93). The necessary acquiring of permits and the long journey are richly rewarded.

Darjiling, West Bengal

🗺 326 A3

Darjiling Tourist Office

www.wbtourism.com

Gangtok Sikkim

🗺 326 A4

Sikkim Tourist Office

www.sikkiminfo.net

✉ M.G. Rd., Gangtok

Northeastern states India Tourist Office

www.north-east-india.com
www.shubhyatra.com
www.ignca.nic.in

✉ B.K. Kakati Rd., Ulubari, Guwahati

Gawahati Assam Assam Tourist Office

www.assamtourism.org

✉ Station Rd., Guwahati

WEST BENGAL & SIKKIM

The 56-mile (90 km) trip from Siliguri up to Darjiling is spectacular. You can drive or make the nine-hour journey by the Darjiling Himalayan Railway, known as the Toy Train because of its resemblance to a toy train set, built in 1879–1881 and still pulled by steam engines. Less patient people take a short run from Darjiling to Ghoom and back.

Up in the mountains, there are two hill stations to visit. **Darjiling (Darjeeling)** (7,218 feet/2,200 m) makes up for its faded British style with its spectacular mountain views toward Kanchenjunga, the world's third highest mountain. Tiger Hill, an unparalleled viewpoint from which to watch the sunrise, the Ghoom monasteries, and a tea garden are essential visits. In town, get a taste of Victorian Darjiling by walking along Chowrasta, then down the Mall to see The Planters' Club, founded in 1868. At the other end of town, the Botanical Gardens' paths lead down to dilapidated but atmospheric greenhouses filled with ferns and orchids. From here, treks leave to see Everest.

Smaller **Kalimpong** (4,101 feet/1,250 m) is ideal for investigating mountain flora, especially orchids; you can visit commercial orchid nurseries. Nearby Rachela Pass (10,341 feet/3,152 m) leads into **Sikkim,** India's smallest state,

which combines deep valleys and soaring mountains. From the capital, **Gangtok** (5,164 feet/1,574 m), trekkers through the Teesta and Rangit Valleys enjoy orchids, rhododendrons, magnolia blossoms, and other flora. Sikkim has almost 70 Buddhist monasteries, many with fine murals and images; try to see Phodang, Rumtek, Tashiding, and Pemayangtse.

NORTHEASTERN STATES

This region was all Assam until the 1960s, when separatist movements led to the creation of six new states Arunachal Pradesh, Nagaland, Manipur, Mixoram, Tripura, and Meghalaya. These states surround the now reduced but fertile valley of **Assam** and rely heavily on its road, rail, and air transportation routes.

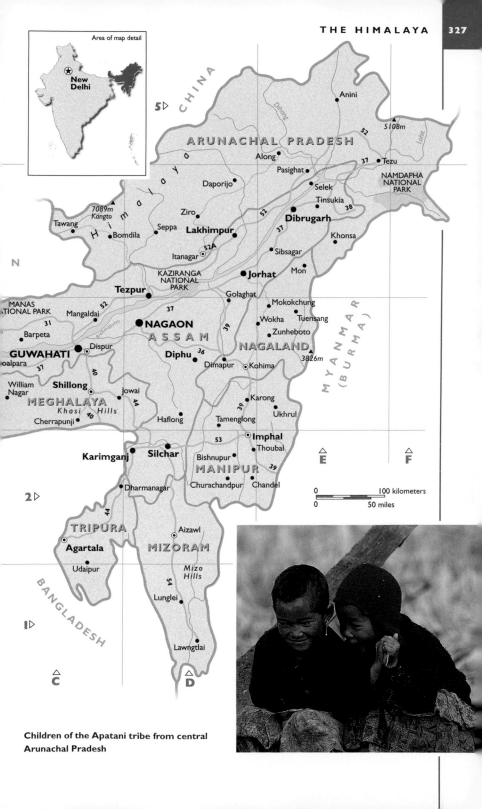

Area of map detail

New
Delhi

5▷

CHINA

Anini

ARUNACHAL PRADESH

Dihong

5108m

Lohit

52

Along

Pasighat

Selek

Tezu

NAMDAPHA
NATIONAL
PARK

37

Daporijo

Tinsukia

38

Ziro

Dibrugarh

52

37

Khonsa

7089m
Kangto

Himalaya

Tawang

Bomdila

Seppa

Lakhimpur

Itanagar

52A

Sibsagar

KAZIRANGA
NATIONAL
PARK

Jorhat

Mon

Tezpur

Golaghat

N

MANAS
NATIONAL PARK

Mangaldai

52

37

Mokokchung

31

Brahmaputra

NAGAON

39

Wokha

Tuensang

Barpeta

Dispur

ASSAM

Zunheboto

GUWAHATI

Diphu

36

NAGALAND

3826m

oalpara

37

Dimapur

Kohima

William
Nagar

Shillong

40

Jowai

MYANMAR (BURMA)

MEGHALAYA

Khasi Hills

44

Karong

39

Ukhrul

Cherrapunji

40

Haflong

Tamenglong

53

Imphal

Thoubal

Karimganj

Silchar

Bishnupur

△
E

△
F

2▷

Dharmanagar

Churachandpur

Chandel

MANIPUR

39

0   100 kilometers
0   50 miles

TRIPURA

Aizawl

Agartala

MIZORAM

Udaipur

Mizo
Hills

BANGLADESH

54

Lunglei

1▷

Lawngtlai

△
C

△
D

**Children of the Apatani tribe from central
Arunachal Pradesh**

Sprawling Gangtok, capital of Sikkim, straddles a hill that was a major India–Tibet trade route.

Arunachal Pradesh Tourist Office
www.arunachaltourism.com
✉ Naharlagun, Itanagar

Nagaland Tourist Office
www.ignca.nic.in
✉ Near Japfu Ashok Hotel, Kohima

Guwahati, Assam's capital until the new one is built at Dispur, sits on the great 1,800-mile-long (2,900 km) Brahmaputra River, which sweeps through the state. Assam is mostly peopled by Hindu Bengalis, mingled with the Ahoms and Bodos originally from Thailand and Tibet. Some 750 tea estates produce half of India's tea (see pp. 330–31), their clipped bushes giving way to rice fields and then the forested slopes of the mountains.

Guwahati's Kali temples and tea auctions are interesting. Out of town, the spectacular national parks of **Kaziranga** and less developed **Manas** both World Heritage sites, deserve every effort to reach them. Kaziranga, home to 1200 rhino, is 172 miles (215 km) from Guwahati; the park offices are in Kohara. Manas is a Project Tiger reserve, contact Assam Tourist Information for details.

The name **Arunachal Pradesh** means "land of the dawn-lit mountains," aptly romantic for this unspoiled wilderness of forested mountains, rushing rivers, and few roads. Out of reach of developers, this is a tantalizing glimpse of how the Himalaya was when Europeans first explored it, not so long ago. From **Itanagar,** the capital, you can take treks through magical scenery rich in flora and fauna.

Nagaland, only recently fully charted, is a state of densely forested mountains inhabited by the fiercely independent Nagas. The British built the capital, Kohima, but for something more ethnic,

Cricket is unavoidable in India: Here, young Buddhist students near Darjiling take a break from their monastic studies.

Imphal (2,575 feet/785 m).

Mizoram state is home to the peaceful, egalitarian, and mostly Christian Mizo people who live on forested and bamboo-covered hills sprinkled with churches and farms. Beautiful handicrafts can be found in and around **Aizawl,** the capital.

A diversity of people, including Bengalis, lives in **Tripura** state, whose Manikya rulers traced their ancestry to Rajput *kshatriyas* (see p. 29). See the capital **Agartala's** Ujjayanta Palace (1901), **Udaipur's** Tripura Sundari Temple, associated with female power, and **Neermahal** water palace.

In **Meghalaya,** orchid forests benefit from the monsoon that makes this one of the world's wettest places. The lakeside capital, **Shillong** (16,102 feet/4,908 m), retains some of the character of its Scots tea-planter founders. ■

visit nearby **Bara Basti.**

The mainly Hindu Meitheis live in **Manipur** state. Their distinct culture includes classical dance, martial arts, and, in September, the colorful Heikru Hitongba Boat race—all found in the capital,

Manipur Tourist Office
www.manipur.nic.in/tourism
✉ Jail Road

Mizoram Tourist Office
www.mizotourism.nic.in

Tripura Tourist Office
www.tripura.nic.in
✉ Ujjayanta Palace, Agartala

Meghalaya Tourist Office
www.igncа.nic.in
✉ Jail Rd., Shillong

Kargyudpa sect monks at Rumtek dress up to parade and dance during the Lohsar (New Year) celebrations.

Tea

When you drink a cup of tea, ponder for a moment on the precision skills required to produce the apparently simple dried tea leaf. It was the British who introduced tea production into northeastern India in the 19th century, using tea seed imported from China. In 1841 Dr. Campbell raised his first tea bushes at his home in Darjiling. Soon the government set up tea nurseries, whose bushes were planted in India's first commercial tea gardens in 1852. By the 1870s there were 113 tea gardens, and tea had joined other cash crops such as cotton, sugar, jute, and coffee, which the British were producing in India for international trading.

While Darjiling planters continued to grow Chinese tea, considered by tea connoisseurs to be the champagne of teas, British adventurers clearing plots of thickly forested land to lay out gardens in Assam discovered a more robust local bush. Land was parceled out on the almost uncharted maps in Kolkata, and many of the men with dreams died before their boats reached Guwahati.

Those who survived faced a tough and isolated life, whose highlight was the weekly gathering at the distant planters' clubs. It changed little until the 20th century when the telephone and television arrived. Still known as tea planters, the gardens' managers work a day that begins before sunrise and ends late. They must oversee their workforce, often composed of whole villages transplanted from Bihar in central India. They build temples and schools for them, and provide child care and medical care. To the workers, the manager is *ma-bapu* (mother-father), the person to whom they bring disputes; who sits in judgment, punishes, and even presides over marriages. Meanwhile, the manager also oversees the job of producing the tea, from trimming the bushes to deciding when to pluck the precious shoots, from keeping rogue elephants from trampling through the gardens to keeping standards high enough to satisfy the frequent visits of the company tea taster.

During the season, women pluck the leaves in the morning, delivering their full baskets to the on-site factory; they do a second picking in the afternoon. At the factory the fresh leaves immediately undergo a succession of carefully monitored processes: They are withered, rolled to bruise them and bring the juices to the surface, and then left to ferment to develop the flavor. They are then dried and sifted into ever more precise grades.

The bigger the leaf, the better the flavor—so the whole and unbroken leaves of Darjiling's Golden Flowery Orange Pekoe is the top grade, and Dust, literally the tea dust, is the cheapest. The tea is sent to auctions in great wooden chests, then on to the blenders. Almost every tea needs to be blended to produce the right balance of color, flavor,

strength, and perfume, and each country has its own preferred blend.

Since independence, ownership of tea gardens has moved into Indian hands, although there is still a strong British interest. Assam's 750 tea gardens produce more than 55 percent of India's tea needs. India and China together produce half the world's tea. However, Kenya and Sri Lanka are rising competitors thanks to low labor costs, younger bushes, and state support. ∎

The manager of the tea garden (right) is up before dawn to inspect the bushes and decide which should be picked that day. For faster picking, some workers hang their baskets high up their backs and toss the tender leaves over their shoulders, into the baskets (below).

Trekking

A WIDE VARIETY OF TREKS IS POSSIBLE—HERE ARE JUST A few. They range from a few days to two weeks, from gentle walks and drives to challenging hikes that demand considerable physical fitness. See p. 381 for more information.

The gentle rhythm of a few days' trekking through the Himalayan landscape is a world away from the country's monument-laden plains.

WESTERN HIMALAYA

The Harki Dun Valley trek is an easy, four-day trek from **Mussoorie** through the beautiful and interesting **Harki Dun** (Valley of the Gods), a sparsely populated area of northwest Garhwal; the local people have their own customs and religious traditions, they live in alpine houses with carved wooden doors. You will stay in bungalows, except for the last night. On the first day, drive or take a bus via Netwar to Purola; the next day,

continue by road to Sankri and trek to Taluka (6,233 feet/1,900 m). On day three, trek beside the Tons River to Osla (7,411 feet/2,259 m). On day four, continue up to Harki Dun (11,679 feet/3,560 m), an excellent base for several days of trekking. From here, either return down or, if physically fit and prepared, continue across the challenging Yamnotri Pass.

The **Pindari Glacier** makes an easy and varied five-day trek from **Bageshwar** into the heart of

the forested Kumaun region; there are simple bungalows along the way. From the pilgrimage town of Bageshwar, drive or take the bus to Bharari and hike through the Sarayu Valley to Song (or bus/drive all the way); from here, walk to Loharkhet. Day two is a hard trek over the Dhakuri Pass (9,301 feet/2,835 m), with its spectacular views, and down to Dhakuri. Days three and four are gentler hikes along the Pindar Valley to Khati, and then beside the Pindar River and its great waterfalls to Dwali and on to Phurkia—worth this last effort to be well-placed for the final day. The culmination of this trek takes you up to Zero Point (12,532 feet/ 3,820 m), marking the foot of the Pindari Glacier, and back down again unless you wish to camp.

The trek through **Kullu Valley,** from Nagar to Jari, with **Manali** as your base, is justly popular. It is the best way to enjoy the alpine scenery and the varied landscape and flora, especially from mid-September to late October. For this five-day route you need to camp, but there are many other simpler and shorter options. From Nagar, hike through a beautiful forest and grazing pastures, and camp above the tree-line or continue to the base of Chandrakani Pass. Day two is a hike over the Chandrakani Pass (12,008 feet/3,660 m) with fine mountain views, and on to Malana, whose people have distinctive houses and follow a strict cultural behavior (your guide will help you on this). You can stay two or three nights in a guest house and do day treks into the surrounding rugged country. Finally, take the steep descent into the Parvati Valley to Rashol, and go on to Jari.

The trek from **Shimla** to **Leh** is a 15-day combination of walking with driving or buses, to the remote mountain reaches of **Kinnaur** and

Spiti. These spectacular drives are not for the faint-hearted. It is essential to acclimatize to the high elevation; possibly you should allow extra days for this. In the first week, drive to Sarahan via Narkanda and Rampur; then trek to Sangla to see wooden Bhimkali Temple and the beautiful temples in the Baspa Valley. Continue to Kalpa via Chitkul, and hike through mountain terrain to the medieval villages of Kothi, Tehlangi, Pangi, Chini, and Peo; see Hubulankar Monastery at Chini. Drive on to Nako (12,008 feet/3,660 m) and visit Lotsabalhakhang Monastery. In the second week, drive on to Tabo, where the frescoes of Chos Khor Monastery (A.D. 996) compare with Ajanta's (see pp. 178–79). Continue through Pin, then on via Ki and Kibber to Rangrik and across the Kumzum La pass (14,931 feet/4,551 m) to Chatru. Keylong lies over the Rohtang Pass (13,057 feet/3,980 m), from where you drive over the Baralacha La pass (15,912 feet/4,850 m) to Sarchu, enjoying breathtaking mountain scenery. The Lachaalang La pass (16,617 feet/5,065 m) and Tanglang La pass lead to Leh.

The **Markha Valley** trek is the classic Ladakh trek. It lasts eight to ten days, goes from **Spiti** or **Stok,** near Leh, to **Hemis,** and there are plenty of camps along the way. Best done mid-June to mid-October (the valley can be crowded during July and August), the trek offers a good variety of landscape, some of it stunning, and mostly keeps within the **Hemis National Park.** Two gentle days start the trek, going through the Markha Valley. From Spiti (10,498 feet/3,200 m), you proceed via Jingchan and Yurutse to Rumbak (12,467 feet/3,800 m), then on to Yurutse and Shingo (13,615 feet/4,150 m). The next stage is through a spectacular gorge to Skiu (11,154 feet/3,400 m). From there you continue to Markha (12,139 feet/3,700 m) and enjoy glorious views of Mount Nimaling (20,9997 feet/6,400 m). Continue to Tahungste, the remote and charming camp at Nimaling (15,485 feet/4,720 m), and so through the Longaru La pass (16,732 feet/5,100 m) to the pretty camp at Shang Sumdo (12,008 feet/3,660 m). End with a visit to Hemis monastery.

EASTERN HIMALAYA

The trek from **Maneybhanjan** to **Rimbik** is a relatively easy six-day trek along the **Singalila Range** to enjoy spectacular views of four of the world's highest mountain peaks: Everest, Kanchenjunga, Makalu, and Lhotse. It is best done in October and November or from February to May. Stay in trekking huts, and take warm bedding.

On day one, drive or take the bus from Darjiling to Maneybhanjan; then hike to Meghma and on up to Tonglu (10,072 feet/3,070 m), or sleep at a lodge in Jaubari; reach Sandakphu (11,929 feet/3,636 m) the next day. On days three and four, enjoy spectacular views along the ridge, first hiking to stay overnight at Molley, then returning to Sandakphu on to Phalut (11,811 feet/3,600 m). On days five and six, trek to Gorkhey and on to Rammam (8,398 feet/2,560 m) for the night, before ending at Rimbik.

More of a tour than a trek, the journey from **Darjiling** to **Kalimpong** involves a gentle week of moving from West Bengal into Sikkim and staying in hotels, mixing drives with walks and visits to monasteries, nurseries, and a botanical garden; excellent for seeing Himalayan flora. It is best enjoyed in October and November or in February and March (orchids are best in March).

First, spend a day in Darjiling (see p. 326), and visit the Himalayan Mountaineering Institute on Birch Hill. On day two, drive through the Teesta River Valley to Gangtok (5,075 feet/ 1,547 m), where you can visit the Orchidarium, the Cottage Industries Institute, and the unique Research Institute of Tibetology the next day, or do a local trek. On day four, drive to Ramtek (5,085 feet/1,550 m), visit its monastery, and the next day enjoy a full day trek. On day six, drive along the Teesta River valley to **Kalimpong** (4,101 feet/1,250 m), the region's floriculture center, for two nights; you can mix local treks with visits to nurseries, Tarpacholing Monastery, and the School of Tibetan Medicine at Brang Monastery.

The **Dzongri Trail** is a nine-day, high-elevation trek through Sikkim's lush forests from **Yoksum** to **Dzongri** and back on a circular route, taking in wonderful mountain views and, in May, rhododendrons in bloom. Do this trek in an organized group, so that food, guides, and other things are arranged for you. On day one, walk from Pelling to the official start, Yoksum. On day two, hike up into the cloud forests to Tsokha (10,000 feet/3,000 m); then spend day three hiking in the area to acclimatize to the altitude. On day four, hike up through pines and rhododendrons to Dzongri (13,221 feet/4,030 m); then again spend a day acclimatizing. On days six and seven, trek on to Thangsing (12,467 feet/3,800 m), then on to Samiti Lake (13,320 feet/4,060 m); camp here or continue to Zemanthang. On day eight, ascend to Gocha La (16,207 feet/4,940m) and return. On day ten, descend directly to Tsokha. ∎

Travelwise

Living a modern life: A sari-clad woman balances on the back of a scooter.

TRAVELWISE INFORMATION

PLANNING YOUR TRIP

India has such a wide range of climates and attractions that you can enjoy a visit at any time of the year. Its variety of history, crafts, monuments, wildlife, and activities can satisfy almost any interest. Spend some time planning your itinerary. Remember that if you spend a few days in one place, you usually experience much more than if you are bouncing from place to place, constantly on the move. India is vast, and no one can see it all in one visit. If you enjoy your first experience there, you will go again.

WHEN TO GO

India has three seasons: October to February is winter, with warm sunny days, but chilly nights in the north. April to June is summer, progressively hot and humid, except in the hills. July to September is the monsoon, which moves up across India from the south (see p. 20).

To visit the forts, temples, and palaces of India, as well as its beaches, the best time to go is from September to March. High season is from October to February, when you'll need to reserve hotel rooms in advance to be sure of a place to stay. To see India's wildlife, visit between February and August, when it gets drier and hotter and the undergrowth is less lush, as you are likely to spot more of the animals going to water holes. Bird-watchers can see an astounding variety of migrating birds in winter, especially from December to February.

The searing heat from April to July, which pushes most visitors up into the hills, breaks with the arrival of the monsoon, which can be a fantastic experience and has the advantage of being a time when India is almost tourist free. Up in the hills, trekkers will find the spring and summer months, from May to October, best. It is worth arranging your itinerary to coincide with one of India's many colorful festivals (see pp. 382-85), although you are likely to bump into delightful minor festivals and village fairs wherever and whenever you go.

TOURIST INFORMATION

For information, maps, brochures, and help planning the trip that matches your interests, contact one of the Government of India Tourist Offices. For a full list, visit www.incredibleindia.org

GENERAL INFORMATION WEBSITES ON A WIDE VARIETY OF SUBJECTS:
www.incredibleindia.org
www.india-tourism.com
www.tourisminindia.com
www.indiasite.com
www.asia-planet.net
www.webindia123.com
www.indianembassy.org
www.hcilondon.net

SPECIAL INTEREST WEBSITES:
Culture:
www.worldheritagesite.org
www.unesco.org
www.intach.org (Indian National Trust for Art and Cultural Heritage)
www.shubhyatra.com (covers religious sites for all religions)
Crafts: www.ignca.nic.in (Indira Gandhi National Centre for the Arts; information on crafts throughout India, state by state)
Hill stations: www.hill-stations-india.com
Judaism in India: www.haruth.com/asiaindia synagogues
Maps: www.mapsofindia.com
Trains: www.indianrail.gov.in www.theluxurytrains.com and see p. 340

Trekking:
www.trekkingindia.com
www.greatindianoutdoors.com
Wildlife: www.ispsquash.com/Link_Wildlife.htm (leads to every kind of Indian wildlife website)

STATE WEBSITES:
There are various websites for India's states and union territories. The most useful and reliable are listed below:
Andaman & Nicobar Islands http://tourism.andaman.nic.in
Andhra Pradesh www.aptourism.in
Arunachal Pradesh www.arunachaltourism.com
Assam www.assamtourism.org
Bihar http://bstdc.bih.nic.in
Chandigarh www.chandigarhtourism.gov.in
Chhatisgarh www.chhattisgarh.nic.in
Delhi www.delhitourism.nic.in/public page/governingdelhi.aspx www.delhitourism.com
Goa www.goatourism.org
Gujarat www.gujarattourism.net
Haryana www.haryanatourism.com
Himachal Pradesh www.himachaltourism.nic.in
Jammu & Kashmir www.jktourism.org
Jharkhand www.jharkhand.nic.in
Karnataka www.karnatakatourism.org www.karnataka.com/tourism www.kstdc.nic.in
Kerala www.keralatourism.org www.karala.gov
Lakshadweep Islands www.lakshadweeptourism.nic.in
Madhya Pradesh www.mptourism.com
Maharashtra www.maharashtratourism.gov.in
Manipur www.manipur.nic.in
Meghalaya www.meghalaya.nic.in
Mizoram www.mizotourism.nic.in
Nagaland www.north-east-india.com/nagaland www.nagaland.nic.in
Orissa www.orissatourism.gov.in
Pondicherry www.tourism.pon.nic.in
Punjab www.punjabtourism.org

Rajasthan
www.rajasthantourism.gov.in
Sikkim www.sikkiminfo.net
Tamil Nadu
www.tamilnadutourism.org
Tripura www.tripura.nic.in
Uttaranchal
www.ua.nic.in/uttaranchaltourism/
Uttar Pradesh
www.up-tourism.com
West Bengal
www.wbtourism.com
www.wb.nic.in

In the United States
3550 Wilshire Blvd., Room 204,
Los Angeles, CA 90010, tel 213-
380-8855, fax 213-380-6111,
email: indiatourismla@aol.com

1270 Avenue of the Americas,
New York, NY 10020, tel 212-
586-4901, fax 212-582-3274,
email: rd@itonyc.com

In Canada
60 Bloor St. (West), Suite 1003,
Toronto, Ontario, M4W 3B8, tel
416-962-3787, fax 416-962-6279,
email: indiatourism@bellnet.ca

In the U.K.
7 Cork St., London, W1X 2AB,
tel 020-7437-3677, fax 020-
7494- 1048, email:
info@indiatourist office.org

TRAVEL AGENTS
To make your holiday in India go
smoothly, use a travel agent who
is experienced in advising on
India and booking holidays there.
If you wish to travel independently, an agent should be able to
work within your budget, and to
cater to your required levels of
adventure, culture, and comfort.
The agent should recommend
sights and tours that suit your
interests—while one person's
dream is to visit temples galore,
another's is to palace-hop in
Rajasthan, walk in the hills, or
explore the fort cities of Karnataka. An agent will handle the
whole booking, using reliable
agents in India, and should save
you time and remove much of
the worry. Once in India, local
agents will ensure that your
bookings for hotels, cars, guides,

and other facilities are honored,
and can amend itineraries and
hotel choices if necessary.

PACKAGE DEALS
However much you may prefer
to plan and make your own
arrangements directly, when
going to India it is definitely
easier to take a tour. That
way, you benefit from other
people's experience and hard
work, and when in India you can
enjoy the sites while someone
else organizes hotel reservations
and transportation.

Nowadays, there is a tour to suit
most interests, most budgets, and
most preferred paces of travel.
Many clubs and museums run
tours to India, too. The price
usually includes the airfare,
transportation, hotels, some
meals, and guide or lecturer;
many are of very good value.
Your local Indian tourist office
(see above) can suggest reliable
travel agents. Since the British
have a particularly long and close
relationship with India, it is well
worth looking at tours departing
from London, both for range and
good prices.

Tours vary from the simple to
the deluxe in content and in
price. Look at a number of the
brochures published by the travel
agents listed below to get an idea
of the range of trips—and prices.
Even if your starting point is the
U.S., do not discount using a
British agent; the British are
enthusiastic and experienced
visitors to India. Finally, should
you find yourself in India wanting
to explore the country, the
agents suggested here all have
countrywide knowledge and can
create itineraries quickly.

U.S. TOUR COMPANIES
**Abercrombie & Kent
International, Inc.**
1520 Kensington Road, Suite 212,
Oak Brook, IL 60523-2156
tel 800-554-7016; fax 630-954-
3324, email: info@abercrombie
kent.com, www.abercrombie
kent.com

Absolute Asia
15 Watts Street, 5th floor, New
York NY 10013, 800-736-8187,
fax 212-627-4090, email:
info@absolutetravel.com,
www.absoluteasia.com

**Academic Arrangements
Abroad**
1040 Avenue of the Americas,
New York, NY 10018-3721, tel
800-221-1944, fax 212-344-7493,
email: info@arrangements
abroad.com, www.arrangements
abroad.com

Asia Transpacific Journeys
2995 Center Green Court,
Boulder, CO 80301, tel 800-642-
2742; fax 303-443-1078, email:
travel@asiatranspacific.com,
www.asiatranspacific.com

Geographic Expeditions
1008 General Kennedy Avenue,
P.O. Box 29902, San Francisco, CA
94129-0902, tel 800-777-8183,
fax 415-346-5535, email:
info@geoex.com
www.geoex.com

**International Ventures and
Travel Inc (IVAT)**
224 West 35th Street, Suite 1401,
New York, NY 10001-2507, tel
800-338-2624, fax 212-563-7048,
email: mary@ivat.com,
212-947-7075,
www.ivattravel.com

Oasis K. Benn Travel
1299 Yonge Street, Toronto,
Ontario, Canada, M4T 1W6, tel
800-563-4181/416-934-0994, fax
416-934-1030,
email: info@kbenntravel.com,
www.oasisjourneys.com

Tauck World Discovery
10 Norden Place, Norwalk, CT
06855, P.O. Box 5020, tel 800-
788-7885, www.tauck.com

Travcoa
4340 Von Karman, Suite 400,
Newport Beach, CA 92660, tel
800-992-2003, 866-591-0070,
fax 949-476-2538,
email: requests@travcoa.com,
www.travcoa.com

U.K. TOUR COMPANIES
Audley Travel
New Mill, New Mill Lane, Witney, Oxfordshire OX29 9SX, tel 01993-838-000, webite www.audleytravel.com

Cazenove & Loyd
9 Imperial Studios, 3-11 Imperial Rd., London SW6 2AG, tel 020-7384-2332, fax 020-7384-2399, email: info@cazloyd.com, www.caz-loyd.com

Exsus
23 Heddon Street, Mayfair, London W1B 4BQ, tel 020-7292-5060, fax 0870-731-9133, www.exsus.com

Scott Dunn
Madgwick Lane, Westhampnett, Chichester, West Sussex, PO18 0FB, tel 020-8682-5000/5075, fax 01243-792-990, email: india arabia@scottdunn.com, www.scottdunn.com

Trans Indus
75 St Mary's Road and the Old Fire Station, Ealing, London W5 5RH, tel 020-8566-2729, fax 020-8840-5327, email: enquiries@transindus.com, www.transindus.co.uk

The Ultimate Travel Company
25-27 Vanston Place, London SW6 1AZ, tel 020-7386-4646, fax 020-7381-0836, email: enquiry@theultimatetravelcomp any.co.uk, www.theultimate travelcompany.co.uk

INDIAN TOUR COMPANIES
The following agents have a good reputation for reliability and financial integrity. They are accredited to the Ministry of Tourism and members of IATO (Indian Association of Tour Operators). All cover the whole of India except Cosmopol, which concentrates on southern India. All have a network of local agents.

First Tours
tel 91-124-406-7722 email: info@firstours.com, www.firstours.com

IVAT India Pvt
tel 91-124-401-7848 email: reet@ivatindia.com, www.ivatindia.com

Peirce & Leslie
tel 91-124-404-9361 email: travel@peirceandleslie .com, www.peirceandleslie.com

Travelscope
tel 91-124-438-1801; 91-11-668-7593, email: travelscope@vsnl .com, www.travelscopeindia.com

WHAT TO TAKE

The old rule applies: The less the better. India has changed hugely in the past decade. Today, if you forget something and you are not far off the beaten track, you can usually buy it easily and far cheaper than back home. This includes quality camera film, face creams, batteries, books, maps, and other essentials. The major exceptions to this rule are high quality sunscreen, quality razor blades, and makeup. Adventurous travelers need to be better pre-pared, but even they can top up supplies with anything from film equipment to mountaineering gear in the main cities in India.

CLOTHES
Cottons, not man-made fibers, are the most comfortable clothes, but you will need extra layers for chilly mornings and nights in the north. Hotel laundries are quick and efficient, so you do not need to take much. Shorts are acceptable, pants best for wildlife parks and trekking, a hat for sun protection, and swimsuits for pools and the sea—topless bathing is frowned upon. Shoes need to be comfortable for walking, yet easy to slip off when visiting religious buildings. On these occasions, some people like to slip on a pair of socks rather than go barefoot. Indian people are

informal, so it is not necessary to dress up in the evenings.

MEDICINES
You may feel happier taking your own selection of pills, potions, and lotions. However, hotel doctors and local drugstores are very good. The best way to remain healthy is to drink plenty of bottled water and to eat freshly cooked vegetarian versions of local dishes. Stomach-calming, nutritious bananas can often provide an effective and simple remedy to minor upsets caused by unfamiliar foods.

There are, however, certain essential precautions. For the latest information on vaccinations or inoculations and malaria prophylaxis you should contact your doctor or travel clinic. Owing to the numbers of migrant workers, no area of India is now free of malaria. You should keep a note of the name of your tablets, so that if you lose them, more can be bought in India. The same applies to most medicines, so carry a copy of your prescription from home.

OTHER ITEMS
Other miscellaneous items that may be useful for your India trip are: sunscreen, rehydration tablets or powders (the local equivalent is Electrol), antiseptic cream, throat lozenges (the dust can irritate your throat), lip balm (the sun dries the skin), sterilized wet wipes, insect repellent, and soft toilet paper.

SPECIAL INTERESTS
Take a pair of binoculars for looking at birds, wildlife, and architectural detail. A notebook is useful to list the order in which you see buildings. This makes identifying your photographs later much easier. Bartholomew's Map of India (not available in India) helps you keep your location in perspective; state maps give more details. Those interested in design and crafts should remember to take small swatches of fabrics or

paints, so that you can match colors when you are buying bargain-priced silks and cottons.

GADGETS

Electricity is now much more reliable than it was. Voltage is 220, occasionally 230. American appliances may require both a voltage transformer and plug adapter. It is worth taking a small, light antimosquito machine and an iPod with favorite music for long journeys. A flashlight is useful for unlit palaces and sculpted temples and caves. Arrange for your cellular phone to operate in India (see p. 341) and remember to pack the battery charger for this and for your digital camera. You can also use public phones (see p. 341). If you need to keep in touch by email, Internet cafés abound. Most hotels have guest computer facilities, and many rooms are wi-fi.

INSURANCE

Be sure to take out adequate insurance policies for health, possessions, and cancellations. If you have opted for a package deal, you may want to have more insurance than is included in the price—always check.

ENTRY FORMALITIES

PASSPORTS & VISAS

You will need a valid passport and a visa. The visa, of which there are many types, ranging from tourist to business, must be obtained before arrival. A tourist visa costs around $30. These and special permits for visiting certain areas (see p. 323) are available from the Indian embassy or consulate in your home country.

CUSTOMS ON ARRIVAL

Items brought into India for personal use are exempt from duty. So are gifts up to the value of Rs4,000, one liter of wine, one liter of spirits, and 200

cigarettes or 50 cigars or 250g of tobacco. Commercial goods must be declared, as must currency over $10,000 or its equivalent. Drugs and narcotics, apart from prescription drugs supplied by your doctor, are strictly prohibited.

CUSTOMS ON DEPARTURE

Several items are prohibited from export without an export license. These include gold jewelry valued above Rs6,000, animal skins and products made from them, art objects over 100 years old, and wild plants. To verify art objects, contact the Archaeological Survey of India, Janpath, New Delhi, tel 011-301 9451.

INDIAN MISSIONS

For detailed information on any of the above, you should contact your nearest Indian mission. These include:

In the U.S.
Embassy of India
2107 Massachusetts Ave., NW,
Washington, DC 20008, tel 202-939-7000, fax 202-265-4351
www.indianembassy.org

Consulate General of India
3 East 6th St., New York, NY
10021, tel 212-861-3788,
fax 212-861-3788,
www.indiacgny.org.
There are also consulates in Chicago, Houston, and San Francisco.

Canada
High Commission of India
10 Springfield Rd., Ottawa, ON
KIM IC9, tel 613-744-3751/
3752, fax 613-744-0913
www.cgitoronto.ca. There is also a consulate in Vancouver.

U.K.
High Commission of India
India House, Aldwych, London,
WC2B 4NA, tel 020-7836-8484,
fax 020-7836-4331
www.hcilondon.net. There are also consulates in Birmingham, Edinburgh, and Belfast.

HOW TO GET TO INDIA

INTERNATIONAL FLIGHTS

Most national carriers fly to India. The main international airports are New Delhi, Mumbai (Bombay), Kolkata (Calcutta), and Chennai (Madras) and some airlines fly into Bangalore. Charter planes fly into Panaji (Goa) and Trivandrum (Thiruvananthapuram, Kerala). It is worth considering flying into one city and home from another, an option offered by many large airlines at no extra cost. Consider, too, whether to fly across the Pacific into Kolkata (Calcutta) or Chennai (Madras), or across Europe into Delhi or Mumbai (Bombay). Shop around for a good deal as prices vary and may be particularly cheap if you travel via Hong Kong or London. Ensure that the price includes all airport taxes.

GETTING AROUND

ON ARRIVAL

Once you have passed through immigration, collected your luggage, and gone through customs (see above), if you are not being met, it is best to go to the official taxi desk (where rates are controlled) rather than accept a ride with one of the many unaffiliated drivers.

TRAVELING WITHIN MAJOR CITIES

India has more transportation options than most countries. The trick is to select the one most suitable for your journey or sightseeing. In Delhi, for instance, you might use a taxi for long journeys, a motorized rickshaw for shorter ones, and a bicycle rickshaw for exploring Old Delhi. In Mumbai (Bombay) you can use a combination of taxis and local trains; in Kolkata (Calcutta) you can choose between taxis, underground trains, river ferries, and, possibly, rickshaws. The adventurous might like to tackle the local buses, but this is challenging.

Taxis may or may not have meters that work. So for these and for all rickshaw journeys, agree on a price with the driver before starting your journey, make stops where you wish, then pay at the end adding extra money for "waiting time." Your hotel concierge should give you a clear idea of the local rates, which vary considerably.

TRAVELING AROUND THE COUNTRY

Traveling is part of your holiday in India. It is fun to collect your methods of transport. See if you can travel by air, car, coach, bus, and train; by camel, pony, and elephant; and by auto-rickshaw and tempo. Air travel is useful for big leaps across the country, but planes can be delayed and are best avoided for short trips such as Delhi–Agra, when the train is fastest and easiest.

India's roads are like no others. Your car, coach, or bus may share the tarmac with a herd of goats, some bicyclists, and overloaded bullock carts carrying farm produce. What appears at first merely to be movement between one palace or temple city and another becomes a colorful and memorable experience.

Riding an animal, though, is quite different. Even the shortest journey on a camel may be too much, so ensure you have tested your endurance before you embark on a five-day camel ride through the desert. Ponies are easier, and often used on treks, and to sit atop an elephant to spot exotic birds and, perhaps, a tiger, is special indeed.

You can hire a car (which comes with a driver; it is madness to drive oneself in India, see p. 342).

BY AIR

Three large domestic airlines plus a handful of small ones service India's extensive network of 120 domestic airports. Your travel agent will have the most up-to-date information, as schedules change in October and April. The major and budget airlines below offer reduced child and youth fares, as well as special discount fares for visitors—usually a 15- or 21-day ticket for unlimited travel at a flat rate, with certain restrictions. Check-in time for all domestic flights is one hour before departure.

Major Airlines:
Air Sahara
www.airsahara.net
Indian Airlines
www.indian-airlines.com
Jet Airways
www.jetairways.com
Kingfisher Airlines
www.flykingfisher.com

Budget Airlines:
Air Deccan
www.airdeccan.net
GoAir
www.goair.in
IndiGo
www.goindigo.in
SpiceJet
www.spicejet.com

BY TRAIN

For many visitors to India, a train journey is essential. India's vast railroad network (see p. 108) operates about 7,800 passenger services each day. Rail schedules and tickets are now available on the net at www.indianrail.gov.in.

At the top end of the market, where tickets should always be reserved well in advance, you can choose between tourist trains such as the Palace on Wheels and regular passenger trains such as the Rajdhani and Shatabdi superfast trains.

Indian Railways offers Indrail passes valid from just half a day up to 90 days, at very good prices.

Tourist trains
The Palace on Wheels circles Rajasthan in eight days, departing from Delhi each Wednesday. www.palaceonwheels.net

The Royal Orient Express operates from September to April, taking passengers from Delhi through Rajasthan and Gujarat over eight days. www.royalorienttrain.com

Deccan Odyssey
Travels from Mumbai's VT station to Goa, hilltop forts, Pune, Ajanta, and Ellora. www.deccan-odyssey-india.com

Superfast regular trains
The deluxe, air-conditioned Rajdhani Express trains connect large cities and have sleeping berths, while the Shatabdi Express trains connect cities less far apart, such as Delhi with Agra, Gwalior, and Bhopal.

The Konkan Railway
India's newest railroad runs down the west coast from Mumbai (Bombay), see p. 204.

Toy trains
With the demise of most steam trains, and India's commitment to making all of its train track broad gauge, the charming, British-built lines up to the hill stations are rare opportunities to evoke earlier times. Routes include the Kalka–Shimla journey, 43 miles (69 km); the **Shivalik Queen**, offering the same run but with private rooms aimed at honeymooners; the **Nilgiri Mountain Railway** to Ooty; the **Matheran Railway;** and the **Darjiling Hill Railway** with the narrowest gauge of all and uninterrupted views of the Himalayan Mountains. **The Fairy Queen,** the world's oldest running locomotive, is now used for weekend trips from Delhi to Alwar and back.

BY CAR & DRIVER

To "drive" in India means to rent a car with a driver. Budget permitting, this is the most luxurious way to travel around India. It is often the easiest way to reach interesting sites. You are free to go where you wish, when you wish, and to stop whenever you see anything interesting.

A good driver knows your route, knows the best restroom stops and the best *dhabas* (roadside cafés), protects you from untrustworthy guides and tiresomely pestering peddlers, keeps the car stocked with bottled water and soft drinks, helps with minor practical shopping, and generally looks after your interests. Many travelers strike up strong friendships with their drivers, who should be well rewarded when you part (see tipping, p. 343).

When you first have your car and driver, it is important that you feel confident about both: If not, be sure to talk to your local agent immediately and request a change.

Your travel agent should arrange a car and driver, and include the cost as part of the price of the travel arrangements they make.

BY BUS

There are several classes of Indian public bus. At the top end of the market, deluxe buses are the most comfortable and have air-conditioning. Good lines include Jaipur's **Pink Line** and **Silver Line.**

BY WATER

Sometimes a boat journey is an integral part of the sightseeing. Sunrise at Varanasi seen from a boat on the Ganga River is magical (see pp. 308–309), as is exploring the backwaters of Kerala by boat (see pp. 210–11); you can even stay on one.

The best way to move from south to north Kolkata (Calcutta) is to take the public ferries on the Hooghly. On the west coast, ferries leave Mumbai (Bombay) for Elephanta Island (see p. 169), while hydrofoils and hovercrafts cross the harbor to the Maharashtran coast.

PRACTICAL ADVICE

COMMUNICATIONS

To bypass the hotel markup on telephone bills, either bring your own cellular phone, or use the local pay phones that usually have yellow advertising boards marked "PCO-STD-ISN." Internet cafés abound.

Note that American cellular phones normally operate on the frequency 1900 mHz. The operating frequency in India is 900/1800 mHz; contact your network operator to check whether your phone will work on those frequencies. It is also possible to rent phones and to buy local SIM cards.

The phone numbers for hotels and restaurants included later in this section include long-distance area codes. The first digit (the zero) of the area code should be omitted when dialing from outside the country. In other words, to dial these numbers from within India, simply dial the number listed; to dial from the U.S., dial 011 then 91 (India's international code), then the number listed, omitting the first zero.

CONVERSIONS

Temperature is measured in degrees Celsius, distance in kilometers, liquids in liters, fabric in meters, gold in grams. However, as some of the world's greatest traders, Indians will be able to adapt any measurement, from shoes to silk, to facilitate your understanding.

ETIQUETTE & LOCAL CUSTOMS

You will almost certainly encounter beggars in India. This can be distressing. The solution is not necessarily to give alms, which may not be kept by the person begging and in any case perpetuates the begging culture. Consider instead giving to one of the many charities based either in India or abroad that are focusing their efforts on a particular aspect that you feel strongly about—health, education, children, village water supplies, etc. If you feel you must give to a beggar, do so just before you leave the site to avoid being mobbed.

Indian people are so polite and so anxious to put visitors at ease that it is easy to be ignorant of causing offense, especially to people in the more traditional, rural areas. To help show your respect for different customs, here are some tips:

Remove your shoes when entering a temple, *gurudwara,* or mosque; dress conservatively in all places of worship.

The left hand and foot are considered unclean, so do not use your left hand to touch a holy object, point to anything, or eat food.

Respect any rules in holy places, such as "no cameras" or "no leather objects."

When shopping, you are expected to bargain hard, except when a store has fixed prices. Bargain when taking public transportation, too, unless the taxi has a working meter.

When things do not run on time, try not to mind too much. See it as an opportunity to write in your diary, read, or take a short walk to look at life around you.

PRACTICAL ADVICE

Indian hospitality is unusually generous, and not to accept it may well cause offense. Furthermore, if you are invited to someone's house, try to arrive with some flowers or with a present brought from your own country. It is a good idea to purchase small, inexpensive items for this purpose before you leave home.

Skimpy T-shirts and short shorts are frowned upon, and on the beach you should wear appropriate swimwear—nudity and topless sunbathing are rarely tolerated. Sleeveless tops are fine.

Some people, especially women in rural places, do not wish to be photographed—respect their wishes.

It is strictly prohibited by law to take photographs in a number of places. These include airports, ports, docks and train stations. It is also forbidden to take photographs of any bridge, law court, or government defense building. If in doubt, ask. Otherwise you may be asked to hand over your camera film or your camera, or even be detained by the police.

HOLIDAYS

In addition to the many festivals (see pp. 382–85), most offices close for the following official public holidays:

Jan. 26, Republic Day
Aug.15, Independence Day
Oct. 2, Mahatma Gandhi's birthday
Dec. 25, Christmas Day

LIQUOR LAWS

Almost all hotels serve beer and spirits in their bars and restaurants. However, depending upon the political party in power, individual states may call for certain days of the month to be "dry." It is important to respect these rules and restrict liquor consumption to your hotel room on these occasions.

MEDIA

More than 40,000 newspapers and periodicals are published in 100 languages and dialects in India each year. Many are in English, including the *Times of India,* the *Hindu,* the *Hindustan Times,* and the *Indian Express,* each with several local editions. One or two will be delivered to your hotel room, and foreign newspapers are usually on sale in hotel shops. *India Today* is India's answer to *Time* or *Newsweek.*

While India's own television networks tell you much about its culture and values—and some are in English—most hotel rooms are also supplied with satellite TV channels including BBC and CNN.

MONEY MATTERS

Indian currency is the rupee. Bills come in denominations of Rs 1000, 500, 100, 50, 20, 10, 5, and 2. The rupee is divided into 100 paise. Small bills and coins are useful for tips. However, visitors will find that large sums are often quoted in U.S. dollars, from hotel rooms to upscale shopping. Major credit cards are accepted in hotels, hotel shops and restaurants, and in larger stores. It is best to carry U.S. dollar traveler's checks and to change them at your hotel, where the rate is usually favorable, as the long lines at banks move slowly. When changing money, ask for an encashment certificate so that you can change back any money that you have left over at the end of your trip—it is not permitted to take rupees out of India. Cities, towns, and even some villages have ATMs.

OPENING TIMES & ENTRANCE FEES

Sites in the care of the ASI (Archaeological Survey of India) usually open sunrise to sunset. Admission fees are minimal except for a handful of notable exceptions such as the Taj Mahal, for which the fees are regularly revised. Museums often have quirky opening hours that vary from week to week; if you are someplace where the museum is known to be good, then check out its opening times upon arrival.

Government offices are open Monday through Friday from 9:30 a.m. to 5 p.m., plus some Saturdays from 9:30 a.m. to 1 p.m. Stores are mostly open between 9:30 a.m. and 6 p.m., but those in hotels and at tourist sites are open whenever there is a chance of business. Bazaars keep longer hours.

PLACES OF WORSHIP

Most towns have active places of worship for Christians, Hindus, and Muslims; many have gurudwaras for Sikhs. The cities historically linked with Jewish people, such as Mumbai (Bombay), Kolkata (Calcutta), Delhi, and Kochi (Cochin), have synagogues.

RESTROOMS

Rest rooms in hotels and upscale restaurants are modern and clean, although water restrictions may mean that the flush is replaced by a bucket and tap. When traveling it may often be more comfortable (and more hygienic) to stop at the roadside near some bushes than to use a modest public lavatory, so carry a roll of toilet paper and packs of antiseptic wipes.

TIME DIFFERENCES

India has one time zone. It is 5.5 hours ahead of GMT; this means that it is 10.5 hours ahead of U.S. Eastern Standard Time, and 13.5 hours ahead of U.S. Pacific Standard Time.

TIPPING

As a general rule any service in India requires a tip. In a hotel, Rs 20–50 (depending on the level of the hotel) is suitable for carrying luggage, delivering room service, returning laundry, etc. In a restaurant, tip 10 percent of the total bill. A good tourist guide deserves Rs600 tip per day, a good driver the same, more if he has driven a hard and long route. In both cases, give the tip at the end of the service, when you say goodbye; do not feel obliged to tip for bad service.

Be careful to note which tips are included in a package deal, checking with the local agent if necessary.

TRAVELERS WITH DISABILITIES

In India, where respect for the infirm and elderly is considerable, travelers with disabilities should have no problem, and there are always plenty of people to help. Being in a wheelchair does not mean you will not be able to ride on an elephant. You should be sure to inform your travel agent of any specific requirements that you might have, and reconfirm these with your Indian agent upon arrival.

VISITOR INFORMATION

There are a number of Government of India Tourist Offices in India, and in other countries, mostly staffed by knowledgeable and helpful people. In addition, each state and union territory has its own web of tourist offices in its area, plus one in the capital, Delhi (see state websites at the beginning of this Travelwise section).

EMERGENCIES

EMBASSIES

U.S. Embassy
Shanti Path, Chanakyapuri, New Delhi 110021, tel 011-2419 8000, fax 011-2419 0017 http://newdelhi.usembassy.gov Branches in Kolkata, Mumbai, Chennai

U.K. High Commission
Chanakyapuri, New Delhi 110021, tel 011-2687 2161, fax 011-2687 0065

ACCIDENTS

If you witness a crime, are involved in an automobile accident, have something stolen, or experience anything that might require police assistance, make a clear note of the event at the time and include any necessary sketches. Then try to go to the local police station with your travel agent, your hotel manager, or, if serious, a representative of your embassy or consulate who will help with the bureaucracy and paperwork. It is important to report a crime if you are intending to make a claim on your insurance.

DIFFICULTIES

If something goes wrong in your hotel, contact the duty manager. If something goes wrong while touring, your driver or guide will deal with it. For any other problems, contact your travel agent's local representative. However, should you suffer a significant robbery, you should go to the local police station with your travel company representative to report it.

If you mislay your passport—and this really does happen!—you will obtain a replacement more quickly by having photocopies of the essential pages and of your visa; so take these with you. To replace your passport, contact your country's local mission; they should send someone with

you to get the required documents from local Indian offices, which may be difficult to do alone.

HEALTH

If you need to use local medical facilities, these are usually of a high standard. In fact, India trains some of the world's finest doctors who are often knowledgeable in both Western medicine and complementary remedies. If you have any health problems, your hotel will have a doctor on call 24 hours a day. Drugstores are well staffed and well stocked and hospitals in the big cities are of a high standard. Keep receipts for all medical help and drugs as they will be needed for insurance claims. Also keep copies of prescriptions to show your doctor at home.

FOOD & DRINK

Eating and drinking are either perpetual worries or perpetual delights. If you worry, then make sure you always carry bottled water with you and, if you are unhappy about the food available away from your hotel, buy and eat a few bananas every day to keep up your strength.

If you find the aromas of cafés too tempting to pass by, then take basic precautions and you should come to no harm. Always eat freshly prepared local food in a popular café with a bustling trade (which means regular clients know it is reliable and food does not hang around). Stick to vegetables, dhal, rice, and bread unless absolutely sure of the storage systems and hygiene levels. Take bottled water, biscuits, and fruit you can peel on a journey or while sightseeing.

HOTELS & RESTAURANTS

India's accommodations and restaurants began to experience a total revolution in the 1990s. With the increase in international tourism and domestic travel, coupled with favorable tax breaks for heritage hotels, there has been a great growth of hotels of all sizes and qualities opening up across the country.

However, the unprecedented economic boom in India has resulted in there being a grossly inadequate supply of hotels at all levels—first class, standard, and moderate. Thus there have been some horrendous hotel room price increases, sometimes 100% over the 2003–2007 period. High prices in some instances do not necessarily mean good hotels; due diligence should be exercised. If the heat goes out of India's economic upward spiral, prices may well drop. Until then, when traveling in the high season try to make hotel bookings well in advance and to have written confirmation of the rates.

Here is just a tiny selection of what is available. As elsewhere in the world, a change of hotel manager may quickly bring even a famous hotel up or down. That said, a well-run palace hotel with plenty of character, old fashioned service, and fine facilities is a very special experience, the stuff of dreams.

If you are planning your own trip, rather than opting for a preplanned package deal, beware: Upscale hotels and their in-house facilities from telephones to bar prices are not cheap, plus there are hefty taxes. Use websites to find the best deals. Consider staying in one or two memorable hotels, then economize with modest ones when you are sight-seeing most of the day.

As for food and drink, the Indian tradition of eating at home where the wife or cook knows just how the family prefers its spice blends is becoming much more liberal. Large hotels often have several restaurants, some highly fashionable with locals, so it is wise to reserve a table; they also have a "coffee shop" that offers informal eating and stays open long hours. The advantages of eating in such hotels is the range of cuisines (Chinese is especially good, Western food is known as Continental), fresh fruits from papaya to pineapple, and drinks—a favorite thirst-quencher is a fresh lime juice with soda, drunk either plain or with added salt or sugar syrup.

India has few stand alone restaurants of note. Highly regarded restaurants and chefs tend to be associated with the good hotels. Furthermore, to keep their local clientele happy, hotels often renovate their restaurants and change both name and cuisine. Where there are local neighborhood restaurants, the current extended government crackdown on illegal buildings is forcing many to close down overnight. Thus, consult with your hotel duty manager for local restaurants. That said, small hotels and independent cafés and restaurants can produce fresher and more authentic local food, especially if asked—Indians love to talk about food. A simple roadside café known as a *dhabba* can be the best of all, especially for a "rice-dhal" meal or a *thali* (a whole meal arrives on one platter) in the south, or a kebab with a *naan* or *paratha* along the Grand Trunk Road in the north, washed down with hot, sweet, milky *chai* (tea) and some bottled carbonated drinks. Drivers and guides, once briefed, are very good at seeking out the best ones.

Suspicion and fear all too often lead foreign visitors to stick to disappointing, format food. It's far better, and safer, to eat freshly cooked local food. Include plenty of rice or bread with your meal; stick to vegetable dishes unless you are sure of the freshness of fish or meat; have a daily bowl of yogurt; and drink lots and lots of bottled water.

TYPES OF ACCOMMODATIONS

The burgeoning of hotels in India is accompanied by the radical and repeated improvement of facilities in older hotels—from in-room wi-fi connections to fusion food and elaborate spas. Some of these upgrades are not easy to understand precisely; some openings are delayed. For up-to-date information, consult the hotel websites, and for specific needs (e.g., type of gym equipment, non-smoking rooms, sophistication of business center), use the website contact information to email or, better still, call the front desk. (Note also that telephone numbers are constantly being upgraded, so consult the websites for the latest on those, too.)

The hotels listed below include the number of rooms, to give an idea of a hotel's size. They also note if there is a swimming pool and a health club. If swimming laps is important to you, check

---

---

the shape and size of the pool. "Health club" can have a broad interpretation in India, ranging from a small gym or a single masseuse to a full-blown international standard spa or ayurvedic center; again, if specific services are important to you, check directly with the hotel for up-to-date information.

There are an increasing number of "eco" hotels in India. Some have only outdoor shower facilities, others restrict alcohol or do not have TVs or telephones in the rooms. Some ban cellphones. If such facilities are important to you, check with the hotels when booking.

India's deluxe hotel chains
Ashok Group:
www.theashokgroup.com
Casino Group:
www.casinogroupkerala.com
HRH Group:
www.hrhindia.com
Heritage hotels:
www.heritagehotelsofindia.com
www.welcomheritagehotels.com
Neemrana Hotels:
www.neemranahotels.com
Oberoi Hotels and Resorts:
www.oberoihotels.com
Palaces: www.tajhotels.com
Park Hotels:
www.theparkhotels.com
Taj Hotels, Resorts, and Welcomgroup:
www.welcomgroup.com

State-run hotel groups
Some of these are very useful, especially in rural areas or for more moderate accommodations. Some include heritage hotels and old British buildings. For more information, visit the state websites listed at the beginning of Travelwise.

International hotel chains
India's globalization and increase in upscale travel mean that familiar hotel groups with hotels in India include Best Western, Country Hospitality (Regent, Radisson, Country Inns, TGIF), Four Seasons, Hilton, Holiday Inn, Hyatt, Inter-Continental, Kempinski, Mandarin Oriental, Marriott, Meridien, Park Plaza, Quality Inns, Sheraton, and Aman.

Heritage hotels
From sprawling palaces to modest hunting lodges, from imposing forts to cozy family homes, the former royals and aristocrats of India have taken full advantage of tax benefits to transform their properties into hotels. India has an increasing number of these, some of which have joined forces for their marketing. A few are part of the big hotel chains or run by businesspeople; most are run by descendants of their creators. The vast majority are in Rajasthan, but there are a growing number in Kerala, Gujarat, and the hill states, including some tea managers' homes. Although romantic and often very beautiful, their success in delivering a comfortable room, hot water, good food, and lively service to their guests varies. That said, the ones that are run well provide a remarkable and personal experience that no big hotel can match—and good local food, too. To find out more: Heritage Hotels Association, 9 Sardar Patel Marg, C Scheme, Jaipur 302001, Rajasthan, tel 0141-381906, fax 0141-382214, www.heritagehotelsofindia.com www.gujaratindia.com www.hill-stations-india.com
See also the previous entry on India's deluxe hotel chains.

Other lodging
Owner-managed hotels can be especially charming, and several are selected below. Individual states run some hotels, indicated in the lists below with their state initials in brackets after the title. Some modest, British-built Tourist Bungalows and Traveler Lodges in off-beat places are also run by the states. Kerala's country boats once used to transport rice are now pretty houseboats. Delhi, Goa, Mumbai, Kolkata, Chennai, and a dozen Rajasthan cities including Jaipur run paying-guest programs where you stay with an Indian family; all reserved through the local tourist offices. India's extensive network of youth hostels are very cheap and often centrally located; contact Youth Hostels Association of India, www.yhaindia.org. The YMCA and YWCA also provide good value for central accommodations. www.indiaymca.com www.ywcaindia.org

STANDARDS & PRICES
Local star ratings have little significance in India; and it would be misleading to imply the membership of upscale international hotel groups means a hotel will be the equivalent of, say, a hotel in New York belonging to the same group; so such information is omitted. All hotels and most enclosed restaurants have air-conditioning of varying types. Nonsmoking rooms are very few and far between, as are nonsmoking areas in restaurants. Most hotels will change foreign currency into rupees; most accept payment with the major credit cards. Hotel rooms above a certain prices are subject to extra luxury taxes. Very often the best restaurants in town are in the hotels.

CREDIT CARDS
Most hotels accept the major credit cards. The situation is changing fast, so check before you depart for India. Unless restaurants are in hotels, you should not expect them to accept credit cards.

ORGANIZATION OF LISTINGS
The hotels and restaurants on the following pages have been grouped according to chapter, first by price category, then alphabetically within those categories.

HOTELS & RESTAURANTS

DELHI

In this sprawling city, location is important. As business areas expand into the suburbs the term "central" has less meaning. To find the best location for you, check on where you will be spending your days. For more modest hotel options, see "Other lodging" on p. 345. Whatever your choice, the capital's hotels are often full, so reserve in advance.

Traditional North Indian cuisines include the rich Mughlai dishes of the Mughal rulers, with plenty of cream, butter, and nuts, and the simpler Northwest Frontier cuisine of the soldier invaders, which is based on meat cooked on a griddle. Punjabi food, the most familiar to Western visitors, includes plenty of *ghee* (clarified butter), meat cooked in a tandoor oven, and hot naan breads.

CLARIDGES
$$$$$
12 AURANGZEB RD.
TEL 011-4133 5133
www.claridges.com
Three-story, 1950s landmark in Lutyens's New Delhi, beside the Diplomatic Enclave. Now renovated into a smart and contemporary but unpretentious and friendly hotel, with Chinese, Mediterranean, and informal outdoor dhaba restaurants.
162

HYATT REGENCY DELHI
$$$$$
BHIKAJI CAMA PLACE, RING RD.
TEL 011-2679 1234
www.delhi.regency.hyatt.com
Located in south Delhi, an upscale business hotel with all conveniences including tennis court and Club Olympus fitness center. Restaurants currently offer Italian and Asian dishes, but none dedicated to Indian cuisine.
508

ITC MAURYA SHERATON HOTEL & TOWERS
$$$$$
DIPLOMATIC ENCLAVE
TEL 011-2611 2233
www.itcwelcomgroup.in
Sited in the Dilpomatic Enclave of southwest Delhi, between the airport and the government and historic areas, this award-winning hotel has three levels of increasingly elite club rooms plus the well-established Bukhara (Northwest Frontier cuisine) and Dum Pukt (Mughlai-Lucknowi cuisine) restaurants. Contemporary Indian art in the public spaces.
484

ITC WELCOMHOTEL
$$$$$
DISTRICT CENTRE, SAKET
TEL 011-4266 1122
www.itcwelcomgroup.in
Located in south Delhi's upscale residential Saket area, convenient for the airports and new business areas, this business hotel has specialist restaurants serving South Indian and Pan-Asian cuisine, and a notable gym.
220

THE IMPERIAL
$$$$$
JANPATH
TEL 011-4150 1234
www.theimperialindia.com
A row of royal palms leads to this lavishly renovated 1930s hotel, part of Lutyens's original scheme for New Delhi. It is the capital's only deluxe heritage hotel and the owners' notable collection of Company School art decorates the walls. Outdoor terrace eating overlooking sprawling lawns; indoors, a rich mixture of bars and restaurants (good Indian in Daniells).
274

OBEROI
$$$$$
DR. ZAKIR HUSSAIND MARG
TEL 011-2436 3030
www.oberoihotels.com
The nearby golf course and historic sites coupled with the elegant renovated public rooms make this a repeat choice for travelers, both businessmen and tourists. In addition to the world cuisines of the spacious Threesixty bar-restaurant, there is a big traditional bar and individual Chinese, Italian, and Northwest Frontier restaurants. Exceptional spa and pools.
279

THE PARK
$$$$$
15 PARLIAMENT ST.
TEL 011-2374 3000
www.theparkhotels.com
India's only chain of contemporary city-center luxury boutique hotels has its Delhi property right in the heart of Lutyens's core. There is a 35-foot-long (11 m) bar designed by Conran, equally modern restaurants inside and poolside, and a good spa.
220

🏨 RADISSON HOTEL
🍴 $$$$$
NATIONAL HIGHWAY-8
TEL 011-2677 9191
www.radisson.com
Convenient airport hotel for overnight stops to catch a few hours of sleep. If you are delayed, there is a nice bar and two good restaurants (Italian and Chinese) plus an indulgent spa.
ⓘ 256 🏊 ♨

🏨 SHANGRI-LA HOTEL
🍴 $$$$$
19 ASHOKA RD.,
CONNAUGHT PLACE
TEL 011-4119 1919
www.shangri-la.com
Inside Lutyens's New Delhi, yet totally contemporary. Rooms are not especially spacious, but the public areas are superb, from the bar and Café Uno's world cuisines at live cooking stations to the 19 Oriental Avenue restaurant's Japanese, Thai, and Chinese cuisines and the luxurious garden space.
ⓘ 232 🏊 ♨

🏨 TAJ MAHAL
🍴 $$$$$
1 MANSINGH RD.
TEL 011-2302 6162
www.tajhotels.com
Benefiting from a total renovation that included a good spa and club floors, this hotel right in Sir Edwin Lutyens's core New Delhi suits businessmen and tourists. Angolie Ela Menon's work decorates Haveli restaurant (Northwest Frontier); other restaurants include House of Ming (Chinese) and Rick's (wok cuisine, plus a martini bar).
ⓘ 269 🏊 ♨

🏨 TRIDENT HILTON
🍴 GURGAON
$$$$
NEW DELHI NATIONAL
CAPITAL REGION, 443 UDYOG
VIHAR, PHASE V, GURGAON
TEL 011-245 0505
www.trident-hilton.com

Contemporary luxury, signature design, delicious food, and a remarkable pool make this more than a convenient airport hotel at Gurgaon, west of Delhi—it also attracts people working in the nearby cyberspace city of call centers and shopping malls. Well worth attending the buffet breakfast—and delaying your next flight.
ⓘ 136 🏊 ♨

🏨 AMBASSADOR
🍴 $$$
SUJAN SINGH PARK,
CORNWALLIS RD.
TEL 011-2463 2600
www.tajhotels.com
This small, relaxed, and friendly hotel is in a residential area built by one of New Delhi's developers, on the edge of Lutyens's core plan, near Humayun's Tomb and Lodhi Gardens. No pool or spa, but nice lawns.
ⓘ 88

🏨 MAIDENS HOTEL
🍴 $$$
7 SHAM NATH MARG
TEL 011-2397 5464
www.maidenshotel.com
Opened in 1903, this is where Lutyens stayed while his garden city was being built. Sited north of New Delhi, its advantages are its spacious classic colonial-style rooms, restaurant hung with original Raj photographs, lush gardens, and easy access to Old and New Delhi's core historic buildings.
ⓘ 54 🏊

🏨 AHUJA RESIDENCY
🍴 $$
193 GOLF LINKS
TEL 011-2461-1027
www.ahujaresidency.com
The main guest house, located in Delhi's affluent deluxe Golf Links residential area, is patronized by many regular Delhi visitors, both diplomats and tourists. Rooms and apartments well maintained, plus the advantage of home

cooking. Two further houses are nearby.
ⓘ 54

🍴 THE GREAT KEBAB FACTORY

Indian trips often end at Delhi with a spare evening before taking a night flight home. This is the best place to spend it. Open only for dinner, the set price menu offers customers vegetables, dhal, pickles, Indian breads, and as many kebabs as they wish chosen from 150 different kinds that they can watch chefs prepare through a glass wall.
$
THE RADISSON HOTEL,
NEAR THE AIRPORTS
NATIONAL HIGHWAY-8
TEL 011-2613 7373

🍴 CAFÉ UNO
$$
SHANGRI-LA HOTEL,
ASHOKA RD., NEW DELHI
TEL 011-2336 8533
This contemporary culinary spectacle runs 24/7, with indoor and outdoor seating. A combination of buffets and chefs at live cooking stations provide Indian, Continental, and Mediterranean dishes, and the desserts are amazing. Upstairs, there is a similar setup for Asian cuisines.

🍴 SHALOM RESTAURANT
$$
N-BLACK,
GREATER KAILASH PART I
TEL 011-5163 2280
Reserve a table to enjoy dinner in this chic, upscale, contemporary restaurant in one of Delhi's wealthier inner residential districts, where sophisticated cocktails precede such dishes as paella and other India-Continental fusion dishes.

🏨 Hotel   🍴 Restaurant   ⓘ No. of bedrooms   🏊 Indoor/🏊 Outdoor swimming pool   ♨ Health club

🍽 THE CULINARE
$
I SHANDAN MARKET,
GREATER KAILASH PART I
TEL 011-2623 8050
A good lunch stop while
shopping in Greater Kailash I
and II districts of south Delhi
(FabIndia, etc.), this simple,
kitchen-style restaurant
serves some of the best
Thai food in town to Delhi's
discerning foodies, at very
cheap prices.

🍽 KARIM'S
$
JAMA MASJID,
GALI KABABIAN,
OLD DELHI
TEL 011-2326 9880
www.karimhoteldelhi.com
If you want to get the feel
for what Old Delhi was
once like, seek out Karim's on
the south side of the Jama
Masjid, where a succession of
little courtyards and rooms
have cooks preparing
khameeri roti bread, *shami*
kebabs, *badam pasanda*
(lamb), and more.

AROUND DELHI

The Delhi–Agra and Delhi–
Jaipur roads are home to
several well-run restaurants
with good restrooms and,
sometimes, gardens. Try the
ones at Hodel and Kosi.

AGRA

🏨 AMARVILAS
🍽 **$$$$$**
TAJ EAST GATE RD.
TEL 0562-2230 1515
www.oberoihotels.com
One of the Oberoi group's
super-deluxe Vilas trio of
hotels at Agra, Jaipur, and
Udaipur. Every room of this
one has views of the Taj
Mahal, which is barely 650
yards (600 m) away, and
some have terraces. Golf
buggies or a ten-minute walk
reaches the Taj, if guests can

tear them-selves away from
the Mughal-inspired hotel,
gardens and pool, good food,
and indulgent spa.
🛈 16 🏊 🏋

🏨 TIKLI BOTTOM
🍽 **$$$$$**
HARYANA, OFF THE
DELHI-JAIPUR HIGHWAY
TEL 0124-276 6556
www.tiklibottom.com
An hour's drive west of Delhi,
Annie and Martin Howard
have created a spacious and
luxurious Lutyens-style
mansion in the countryside,
a tranquil spot to recover
from too much work, city
life, or sight-seeing.
🛈 4 🏊

🏨 MUGHAL SHERATON
🍽 **$$$$**
FATEHABAD RD.,
TAJ GANJ
TEL 0562-233 1701
www.sheraton.com
/mughalagra
Well-designed, low-rise,
brick buildings inspired by
Mughal architecture are set
on 35 acres of gardens in
increasingly built-up Agra.
This welcome oasis provides
peace, tennis courts, and
spa facilities. Restaurants
serve Indian, Asian,, and
speciality Northwest
Frontier cuisines.
🛈 300 🏊 🏋

🏨 TRIDENT HILTON
🍽 AGRA
$$$
TAJNAGARI SCHEME,
FATEHABAD RD.
TEL 0562-233 1817
www.trident-hilton.com
A good value choice, not
least because the hotel is
one of the nearest to the
Taj and thus good for repeat
visits. The rooms are arranged
around a central pool and
courtyard; gourmets may wish
to visit other hotels for dinner.
🛈 138 🏊

🏨 JAYPEE PALACE
🍽 **$$$**
FATEHABAD RD.
TEL 0562-233 0800
www.jaypeehotels.com
This large, low-rise, Mughal-
inspired hotel set in 25 acres
of gardens has its rooms
arranged around a Mughal-
style *char bagh* (four gardens)
complete with dancing
fountains. Restaurants include
Avadh cuisine from Lucknow,
South Indian cuisine, a
poolside barbecue, and a
grand buffet. Ayrvedic spa,
gym and plenty of games.
Ideal for families and hungry
young people.
🛈 350 🏊 🏋

🏨 MANSINGH PALACE
🍽 **$$$**
FATEHABAD RD.
TEL 0562-233 1771
www.mansinghhotels.com
Named after the Amber
ruler who owned the land
on which his ally Emperor
Shah Jehan built the Taj, this
no-frills but reliable hotel has
a Taj view from some rooms.
🛈 100

🏨 TAJ VIEW
🍽 **$$$**
FATEHABAD RD.,
TAJ GANJ
TEL 0562-223 2400
www.tajhotels.com
The top-floor rooms really
do have views of the Taj,
albeit distant ones across
the city. The pool and lawns
are good respites after early
Taj visits, as is the good
Indian food and the shopping
mall's bookstore. Puppets,
games, and other amusements
for families.
🛈 100 🏊 🏋

🏨 HOWARD PARK PLAZA
🍽 **$$**
FATEHABAD RD.
TEL 0562-400 1870/1/2
www.sarovarhotels.com
No-frills hotel well aimed
at businessmen; located
a mile (1.5 km) from the Taj,
so it is possible to walk down

or take a rickshaw. The rooftop barbecues provide lunch with views of the Taj, and, if you are lucky, later moonlit views of it.
① 83 ⊠

AMRITSAR

🏨 HOTEL RANJIT'S 🍴 SVAASA
$$
10 CANTONMENT, MALL RD.
TEL 0183-505 6344
www.welcomheritagehotels.com
Amritsar's heritage hotel is the beautifully restored 18th-century Nanak Shahi haveli (courtyard house)on Mall Road. It doubles as a holistic spa resort, and follows the vaatsu texts for room direc-tions. All rooms have balco-nies, and therapies include ayurveda panchakarma treatments.
① 13 🎔

🏨 MOHAN 🍴 INTERNATIONAL
$$
ALBERT RD.
TEL 0183-222 7801
www.hotelmohaninter national.com
This simple hotel, well located for visiting the Golden Temple, provides clean rooms and wholesome food both indoors and at a poolside barbecue.
① 76 ⊠

🏨 RITZ PLAZA 🍴 $$
45 THE MALL
TEL 0183-256 2836
Simple and clean rooms in this refurbished hotel that was Amritsar's first, opened in the 1960s and conveniently close to the Golden Temple.
① 50 ⊠

BANDHAVGARH NATIONAL PARK

🏨 MAHUA KOTHI 🍴 $$$$$
BANDHAVGARH NATIONAL PARK, VILLAGE TALA, DISTRICT UMARIA

TEL 092123-05607
www.tajhotels.com
Taj Hotels have joined up with experienced wildlife lodges company C C Africa to create a new experience in Bandhavgarh National Park, in Madhya Pradesh. Occupants of the twelve very beautiful, ethnic-gone-chic kutiyes (jungle village huts), each with its private courtyard and bicycles, can enjoy all the usual game park activities, from bird-watching to jungle safari rides when the possibility of spotting a tiger is fairly high.
① 12

🏨 ANANT VAN 🍴 $$$$
MARDARI
TEL 0124-406 8852
www.anantvan.com
This wildlife camp on the edge of Bandhavargh National Park focuses on ecology—reforestation, local communities, regeneration of overgrazed farmland, and organic farming. While staying at Dhruv Singh's two cottages and two tented cottages, guests explore the park to learn as much about its trees as about how to read the pug marks of a tiger.
① 4

🏨 BANDHAVGARH 🍴 JUNGLE LODGE
$$$$
TALA
TEL 011-2685 3760
(Delhi Office)
www.tiger-resorts.com
The 12 cottages and 8 rooms area set out like a village, with an organic vegetable garden and some solar water heating. This ecological awareness is the focus for guests who are encouraged to learn about conservation and to study nature as well as listen to it at night. Plenty of quiet areas, plus games (badminton, chess, etc.) and wildlife videos.
① 20

KEOLADEO GHANA NATIONAL PARK

🏨 THE BAGH 🍴 $$$
BHARATPUR
TEL 05644-228 333
www.thebagh.com
Several elegant buildings are set in a mature old garden, where resident naturalist Vishnu Singh helps guests get their eyes ready for visiting the bird sanctuary. Rooms are individually decorated, the restaurant serves the distinctive local Braj cuisine, and guests can relax in the orchard or gym or while having a massage.
① 23 ⊠

🏨 LAXMI VILAS PALACE 🍴 $$$
KAKAJI-KI-KOTHI, RAGHUNATH NIVAS, AGRA RD.
TEL 0564-231 199
www.laxmivilas.com
An 1880s little rural palace of the Bharatpur rulers, transformed into a small hotel in 1994. Family photographs in quantity, charming period rooms, and a modern pool combine to complement the purpose of being there: spending time watching birds.
① 25 ⊠

HOTELS & RESTAURANTS

🏨 CHANDRA MAHAL 🍴 HAVELI
$$
VILLAGE—PEHARSAR,
JAIPUR AGRA RD.,
TEHSIL NADBAI
TEL 05643-264 336
www.chandramahalhaveli.com
A delightful 19th-century noble's courtyard mansion set in an unspoiled village, this makes a perfect break between Jaipur and Agra's hurly burly. Ideal for observing India's village life, and for reading or sketching. It deserves more than a mere lunch stop.
🛏 23

BHOPAL

🏨 JEHAN NUMA 🍴 PALACE
$$$
157 SHAMLA HILL
TEL 0755-266 1100
www.hoteljehanumapalace.com
Another Bhopal palace, this time built in the 1880s by Nawab Sultan Jehan Begum's second son, General Obaidullah Khan, who was commander-in-chief of the Bhopal state forces. This perhaps accounts for the British colonial style. Today, its rooms are spread through four wings surrounding a lush garden; suitable for families.
🛏 98 🏊

🏨 NOOR-US-SABAH 🍴 PALACE
$$$
VIP RD.,
LOHE-FIZA
TEL 0755-522 3333
www.welcomheritagehotels.com
Built in the 1920s for Nawab Hamid Ulah Khan's daughter, whose family later went to live in Pakistan, this informal palace sits on a cliff overlooking Bhopal Lake. All rooms have lake views, while the lawns transform into a starlit dining room serving good food patronized by locals.
🛏 60 🏊

CHANDIGARH

🏨 TAJ CHANDIGARH 🍴 $$$$
BLOCK NO. 9,
SECTOR 17-A
TEL 0172-651 3000
www.tajhotels.com
All rooms in this newly built hotel in Le Corbusier's city have ergonomic furniture and contemporary amenities, as well as views of the city's Rose Garden and the Shivalik mountain range.
🛏 149 🧖

🏨 HOTEL MOUNT VIEW 🍴 $$$
SECTOR 10
TEL 0172-274 0544
www.nivalink.com/mountviewchandigarh
A functional hotel well located for visiting Chandigarh's Rock Garden.
🛏 156 🏊 🧖

CORBETT NATIONAL PARK

Some basic accommodations (cabins, log huts, etc.) are available within the park, but these are disappointing (see p. 126).

🏨 INFINITY 🍴 RESORTS
$$$$
RAMNAGAR
TEL 011-4160 8509
www.infinityresorts.com
Set amid mango trees on the banks of the Kosi River in the Kumaon Hills, the circular lodge room is where guests chat, drink, eat, and compare sightings after visits into Corbett Park. Other activities include trekking, fishing, and enjoying the holistic nature cures.
🛏 24 🏊 🧖

🏨 CAMP FORKTAIL 🍴 CREEK
$$$
VILLAGE BHAKRAKOT
TEL 05947-287 804
www.campforktailcreek.com

PRICES
HOTELS

An indication of the cost of a double room without breakfast is given by **$** signs.

$$$$$	Over $280
$$$$	$160–$280
$$$	$100–$160
$$	$40–$100
$	Under $40

RESTAURANTS
An indication of the cost of a three-course dinner without drinks is given by $ signs.

$$$$$	Over $80
$$$$	$50–$80
$$$	$35–$50
$$	$20–$35
$	Under $20

Named for the forktail birds that visit in winter, this rural camp focuses on getting close to the jungle. It offers bird-watching hikes, fishing on the Ramganga River, and elephant and jeep safaris through the Kumaon and Garhwal hills staying at old forest bungalows. Camp fires, banyan trees, and hammocks help relaxation.
🛏 11

GWALIOR

🏨 USHA KIRAN PALACE 🍴 $$$$
JAYENDRAGANJ, LASHKAR,
BESIDE JAI VILAS
(CITY PALACE)
TEL 0751-244 4000
www.tajhotels.com
The former guest house of Gwalior state's ruler, called The Scindia, and its 9 acres (3.6 ha) of gardens have all been lavishly renovated to create 40 rooms and suites. The billiards room is now the bar, the restaurant overlooks the courtyard.
🛏 40 🧖

KEY 🏨 Hotel 🍴 Restaurant 🛏 No. of bedrooms 🏊 Indoor/🏊 Outdoor swimming pool 🧖 Health club

HOTELS & RESTAURANTS

KANHA NATIONAL PARK

🏨 SHERGARH
🍴 $$$$
KANHA TIGER RESERVE,
VILLAGE BAHMNI
TEL 07637-226 215
www.shergarh.com
Deeply committed to the
area, Jehan and Katie made a
dream come true: on a piece
of land at the quiet southern
end of the park they have dug
ponds, planted trees, built
beautiful individual tented
rooms, and created a drop of
immaculately run, ecologically
aware paradise where guests
get close to nature and live well.
ⓘ 8

🏨 KANHA JUNGLE
🍴 LODGE
$$$$
MUKKI
TEL 011-2685 3760 (Delhi Office)
www.tiger-resorts.com
Another ecologically aware
lodge on the southern side of
the park, this one with organic
farming, solar energy, and
medicinal herbs. As well as
visiting the park, there is on-
site bird- and butterfly-
watching and nightly astronomy
or simply star-gazing.
ⓘ 20

KHAJURAHO

🏨 JASS RADISSON
🍴 $$$
BYPASS RD., MADHAYA
TEL 07686-272 344
www.radisson.com
Sited near the Taj Chandela,
this hotel is its twin, with
equally satisfactory no-frills
rooms and facilities for relaxing
between temple visits.
ⓘ 90 ⌇

🏨 TAJ CHANDELA
🍴 $$$
JHANSI RD.
TEL 07686-272 355
www.tajhotels.com
A low-rise, practical hotel with
garden, pool, shopping mall,
and friendly staff, five minutes'

drive from the reason for
being here: the temples.
ⓘ 94 ⌇

MAHESHWAR

🏨 AHILYA FORT
🍴 $$$$$
MAHESHWAR
TEL 07283-273 329
www.ahilyafort.com
Built to be the capital of one
of India's celebrated women
rulers, Ahilya Bai Holkar. Her
descendent Richard Holkar has
spent two decades restoring it
and creating its gardens. Guests
staying here pass their days
enjoying the rhythm of the
fort and its on-site temples,
the good food, the local
weaving, and taking boat rides
out on the Narmada River.
ⓘ 11 ⌇

MATHURA

🏨 BEST WESTERN
🍴 RADHA ASHOK
$$
MASANI BYPASS RD.
TEL 0565-253 0395
www.bestwestern.com
Reliable modern hotel with
simple facilities, set among
lawns on the edge of town.
ⓘ 5

MUSSOORIE

🏨 JAYPEE RESIDENCY
🍴 MANOR
$$$
BARLOWGANJ
TEL 0135-263 1800
www.jaypeehotels.com
Enjoying superb views from its
hilltop location, guests can
follow their walks with the
indoor heated swimming pool
and Sansha Ayuvedic Health
Spa, play a wide variety of
games, and eat wholesome
Indian and Continental food.
ⓘ 90

🏨 NABHA PALACE
🍴 $$$
BARLOWGANJ RD.
TEL 0135-263 1426
www.claridges.com

The renovated period rooms
with modern comforts (down
pillows, duvets) open onto
Victorian wraparound
verandas that overlook lush
gardens and wooded valleys.
Ideal for taking a trek and then
curling up with a good book
in the well-stocked library.
ⓘ 22

🏨 KASMANDA PALACE
🍴 $$
THE MALL
TEL 0135-263 3434
www.indianheritagehotels.com
The Kasmanda royal family
have transformed their
summer retreat—built in
1836 by Captain Rennie
Tailour of the Bengal
Engineers, and subsequently a
sanatorium and a school—
into a comfortable hotel for
relaxation mixed with walks,
picnics, and bird-watching.
ⓘ 14

🏨 PADMINI NIVAS
🍴 $$
LIBRARY, THE MALL
TEL 0135-263 2793
www.hotelpadmininivas.com
Among Mussoorie's oldest
buildings and originally called
Rushbrooke Estate, the
Maharaja of Rajpipla gave it
to his wife, Padmini. With
fireplaces inside, a wide
veranda, and deodar and
oak trees in the garden, this
is hill station life revived.
ⓘ 5

NAINITAL

🏨 PALACE BELVEDERE
🍴 $$
AWAGARH ESTATE, MALLITAL
TEL 05942-237 434
www.welcomheritagehotels.com
Formerly the Raja of
Awagarh's summer retreat
built by Raja Balwant Singh in
1897. Royal family treasures
still furnish the rooms of this
red-roofed heritage hotel that
enjoys views down the hills
over Naini Lake.
ⓘ 21

🏨 Hotel 🍴 Restaurant ⓘ No. of bedrooms ⌇ Indoor/⌇ Outdoor swimming pool ♨ Health club **KEY**

HOTELS & RESTAURANTS

ORCHHA

🏨 AMAR MAHAL
🍴 $$
TEL 07680-252 102
A surprisingly grand hotel for such a small village, but the Bundelkund-inspired architecture and characterful rooms are appropriate for exploring Orchha's royal buildings.
🛏 24

RANTHAMBHORE NATIONAL PARK

🏨 AMAN-I-KHAS
🍴 $$$$$
RANTHAMBHORE
TEL 07462-252 052
www.amanresorts.com
Staying at Aman-i-Khas (meaning "special peace") is to understand that camping can be very stylish. Here, the specially designed tents, their furnishings, their service, the spa, and the open fireplace all enhance the perfect rural location.
🛏 10 🧖

🏨 OBEROI VANYAVILAS
🍴 $$$$$
RANTHAMBHORE RD.,
SAWAI MADHOPUR
TEL 07462-223 999
www.oberoihotels.com
Each super-luxurious, well-appointed tent has its own little garden; the dining room is a real room but guests can choose to have their meals where they wish. Great pool and spa..
🛏 25 🏊 🧖

🏨 SHERBAGH
🍴 $$$$
SHERPUR-KHILJIPUR,
SAWAI MADHOPUR
TEL 07462-257 120
www.sherbagh.com
Founded by Jaisal Singh, who regularly camped here throughout his childhood, Sherbagh focuses on how tourism can make man aware of the delicate balance between him and nature. Comfortable tents,

wholesome food, and a friendly atmosphere.
🛏 12

🏨 SAWAI MADHOPUR
🍴 LODGE
$$$
RANTHAMBHORE NATIONAL PARK RD.,
SAWAI MADHOPUR
TEL 07462-220 541
www.tajhotels.com
The former royal hunting lodge, built in the 1930s, has been renovated and its period gardens spruced up; the heritage atmosphere is maintained with croquet, badminton, and table tennis.
🛏 36

RISHIKESH

🏨 ANANDA IN THE
🍴 HIMALAYA
$$$$$
THE PALACE ESTATE
NARENDRA NAGAR
TEL 01378-227 500
www.anandaspa.com
Once the home of the Maharaja of Tehri-Garhwal, this magical location in the Himalaya overlooking the Ganga River is rated a worldwide top spa hotel. While the former palace forms the public area, the rooms are state of the art as is, of course, the spa. For activities there is eco-friendly golf, river rafting, and walking.
🛏 75

🏨 GLASSHOUSE
🍴 ON THE GANGES
$$$
23RD MILESTONE RISHIKESH-BADRINATH RD.
VILLAGE GULAR-DOGI
TEL 01378-269 224
www.neemranahotels.com
This remarkable hotel on the Ganga has its own orchard filled with birds and butterflies, a mineral spring, and a sandy beach. Guests venture out to walk, river raft, and join pilgrims visiting local temples. Vegetarian food and beer, not spirits, in keeping with the sacred location.
🛏 6

🏨 HIMALAYAN
🍴 HIDEAWAY
$$$
NEAR BADRINATH
BOOKING ADDRESS:
N-8, GREEN PARK MAIN,
NEW DELHI
TEL 011-2685 2602
www.hhindia.com
A lovely peaceful lodge set in the Sal forest above the Ganga, where the garden is being planted with specimens of the lower Himalayas. After kayaking or hiking, there is traditional massage and great views from each room's balcony.
🛏 10

SHIMLA

🏨 CHAPSLEE
🍴 $$$$
NEXT TO AUCKLAND HOUSE SENIOR SCHOOL
CENTRAL SHIMLA
TEL 0177-280 2542
www.chapslee.com
Descendents of the Raja of Kapurthala run his former Edwardian summer home, maintaining its Raj flavor in its furnishings, croquet lawn, card room, and warm hospitality. Well located for walking through Shimla and its outlying hills. Restaurant offers

traditional royal cuisine from the palaces of the Maharajas.
ⓘ 6

🏨 WILDFLOWER HALL
🍴 $$$$
SHIMLA-KUFRI RD., 8M/13KM FROM SHIMLA, NEAR CHARABRA
TEL 0177-264 8585
www.oberoihotels.com
At 8,300 feet (2,500 m) up in the Dhauladhar and Garhwal mountains, every room of Lord Kitchener's rebuilt country house has spectacular views. To complement country pursuits, there is quality food, an outdoor heated pool, and a good spa; and Shimla is just a 40-minute drive away.
ⓘ 87 🏊 🏋

🏨 OBEROI CECIL
🍴 $$$
CHAURA MAIDAN CENTRAL SHIMLA
TEL 0177-280 4848
www.oberoihotels.com
This is where the Oberoi group of hotels began a century ago, in a magnificent building on Chaura Maidan in central Shimla, now lavishly and beautifully restored. Glorious views from the rooms, elegant teas to enjoy in the public spaces, immaculate service.
ⓘ 79 🏊 🏋

🏨 WOODVILLE PALACE
🍴 $$$
RAJ BHAWAN RD. CENTRAL SHIMLA
TEL 0177-262 3919
www.welcomheritagehotels.com
The Rana of Jubbal built his finely crafted, chateau-style, fashionable Shimla home in 1938. Its little changed bedrooms, billiards room, Hollywood lounge, and hunting trophies inside, and plant-covered trellises and lush garden outside all evoke those times.
ⓘ 28

RAJASTHAN

This colorful area of India, so popular with first-time visitors to India, has numerous charming heritage hotels, with more opening each year. These hotels should be very much a part of your vacation.

SARISKA NATIONAL PARK, KESROLI AND DEEG

🏨 AMANBAGH
🍴 $$$$$
AMANBAGH AJABGARH, ONE-HOUR DRIVE NE OF JAIPUR
TEL 01465-223 333
www.amanresorts.com
Set in an ancient oasis deep in the countryside about an hour's drive northeast of Jaipur, guests enjoy absolute peace and sublime facilities (some rooms have their own pools), and can explore local villages, fort ruins, or enjoy a sunset picnic.
ⓘ 40 🏊 🏋

🏨 NEEMRANA FORT-
🍴 PALACE
$$$$
NEEMRANA
TEL 01494-246 006
www.neemranahotels.com
This flagship of the successful Neemrana group of heritage hotels, close to Delhi, spreads its many rooms over ten levels. Both rooms and the good cuisine mix Indian and European inspirations, and its size and conference facilities make it a convivial experience.
ⓘ 50 🏊 🏋

🏨 HILL FORT
🍴 $$
VILLAGE KESROLI
TEL 01468-289 352
www.neemranahotels.com
This massive 14th-century fortified palace north of Alwar is set in still unspoiled countryside. With few facilities beyond its own

architecture and situation, this is ideal for time off during the hectic Delhi-Agra-Jaipur circuit.
ⓘ 21

AJMER AND PUSHKAR

🏨 CHHATRASAGAR
🍴 $$$$$
NIMAJ ON THE UDAIPUR-JODHPUR RD.
TEL 02939-230 118
www.chhatrasagar.com
The immaculate and beautiful tents are pitched between a reservoir and an idyllic farm on the Udaipur-Jodhpur road, and micromanagement ensures every detail is perfect from homemade breads at breakfast to hilltop cocktails at sunset.
ⓘ 11

🏨 FORT SEENGH
🍴 SAGAR
$$$$$
3 MILES (5KM) FROM DEOGARH MAHAL
TEL 02904-252 777
www.deogarhmahal.com
The Deogarh family has converted a tiny fort into a villa; ideal for two or three couples to rent and enjoy total peace, the surrounding lake, boating and walking, and a personal staff.
ⓘ 4

🏨 DEOGARH MAHAL
🍴 $$$
DEOGARH ON THE UDAIPUR-AJMER ROAD
TEL 02904-252 777
www.deogarhmahal.com
Set within the triangle of Udaipur, Ajmer, and Jodhpur, the palace is found in a fairytale walled town, once the seat of senior Mewar feudatories. Rooms spread through the palace and its outbuildings are Indian in style, some with lovely period wall paintings.
ⓘ 62

BIKANER

🏨 BHANWAR NIWAS 🍴 PALACE
$$$
BIKANER
www.bhanwarniwas.com
This extravagantly carved pink sandstone palace-mansion mingling Indian and Western styles was built in 1927 by the great Rampuria family of Bikaner. Its interior is strikingly lavish and opulent, its staff thoughtful.
🛏 24

🏨 GAJNER PALACE 🍴 $$$
15 MINUTES' DRIVE OUTSIDE BIKANER
TEL 01534-255 061
www.hrhhotels.com
Sensitively renovated to its 1890s Raj perfection, this elaborate, pink-stone hunting palace of the Bikaner rulers overlooks a lake where grand duck shoots used to entertain Indian royalty and Raj dignitaries. Great for bird-watching, boating, and billiards.
🛏 44

🏨 LALLGARH PALACE 🍴 $$$
LALLGARH COMPLEX, GANGANAGAR RD.
TEL 0151-254 0201
www.lallgarhpalace.com
Sir Swinton Jacobs designed the vast pink sandstone palace for the charismatic Maharaja Ganga Singhji. It has so much public space that you might get lost looking for the bar or the billiards room, or roaming through the splendid collection of period photographs.
🛏 40 ≋

🏨 LAXMI NIWAS PALACE 🍴 $$$
LALLGARH COMPLEX, DR. KARNI SINGHJI RD.
TEL 0151-252 1188
www.laxminiwaspalace.com
Located within Lallgarh Palace gardens, here is yet another Bikaner palace to stay in, this one originally the guest wing

of the main palace. The renovated rooms keep the traditional spacious format of bedroom, dressing room, and bathroom.
🛏 42

BUNDI

🏨 ISHWARI NIWAS 🍴 $$
1 CIVIL LINES
TEL 0747-244 2414
www.ishwariniwas.com
Built at the turn of the 20th century for the Diwan (prime minister) of Bundi state, this delightful, simple, family-run haveli with Bundi-style wall paintings has its rooms ranged around a central courtyard.
🛏 21

DUNGARPUR

🏨 UDAI BILAS PALACE 🍴 $$$
DUNGARPUR, OFF THE UDAIPUR-AHMEDABAD HIGHWAY
TEL 02964-230 808
www.udaibilaspalace.com
Conveniently sited in quiet Dungapur, off the highway, lakeside Udai Bilas was built as a hunting palace by descendants of the Chittorgarh rulers. Enjoy the infinity pool, the home cooking, and a visit to the family's private ancient fort-palace.
🛏 22 ≋

JAIPUR

🏨 OBEROI RAJVILAS 🍴 $$$$$
GONER RD., 30 MINUTES' DRIVE EAST OF JAIPUR
TEL 0141-268 0101
www.oberoihotels.com
A multi-award-winning luxury resort set in a lush oasis estate. Every part displays taste and style and is immaculately managed, from the fortress-style central building to the clusters of rooms and the indulgent pool and spa.
🛏 70 ≋ 🏋

🏨 RAJ PALACE 🍴 $$$$$
JORAWER SINGH GATE, AMER RD.
www.rajpalace.com
One of Jaipur's most evocative places to stay, thanks to the dedicated restoration by Princess Jayendra Kumari who since 1995 has brought the entire palace and its historic contents back to life. The "museum suites" are like fairy-tale Rajput film sets.
🛏 40 ≋

🏨 RAMBAGH PALACE 🍴 $$$$$
BHAWANI SINGH RD.
TEL 0141-221 1919
www.tajhotels.com
The last Maharaja of Jaipur lived here, on the southern side of his Pink City. In 1957 he turned his palace and its extensive terraces and gardens into a hotel. Run by the Taj group since 1972, the entire palace has recently been lavishly refurbished.
🛏 85 ≋ 🏋

JAI MAHAL PALACE
$$$$
JACOB RD.,
CIVIL LINES
TEL 0141-222 3636
www.tajhotels.com
Located in Jaipur's Civil Lines area, Jai Mahal, founded in the 18th century, has totally refurbished rooms, renovated Mughal formal gardens, and a more relaxed tempo than its sister hotel here, the Rambagh Palace.
🛏 100 🏊 �҈

TRIDENT HILTON
JAIPUR
$$$
AMER RD., OPPOSITE JAL MAHAL
TEL 0141-267 0101
www.trident-hilton.com
Every room in this good value yet attractive hotel built in traditional Jaipur style on the Jaipur-Amer road has a balcony so guests can enjoy the view across Mansagar Lake. Its good location makes visiting both Amer and Jaipur easy.
🛏 138

SAMODE HAVELI
$$$$
GANGAPOLE, AN HOUR'S DRIVE NORTH OF JAIPUR
TEL 0141-263 2407
www.samode.com
The spacious town mansion of the Samode courtiers, feudatories of the Jaipur rulers, has restored mural walls and a swimming pool and is right inside the Pink City; ideal for enjoying the bazaars. This and its sister hotel, Samode Palace, have been beautifully restored by family descendents.
🛏 29 🏊 💏

SAMODE PALACE
$$$$
SAMODE VILLAGE
TEL 0141-263 2407
www.samode.com
This sister hotel of the Samode Haveli (see previous entry) is set in Samode

village in the Aravalli Hills an hour's drive north of Jaipur. Guests stay either in the palace or in tents in the walled bagh (garden). All has been beautifully restored by family descendents.
🛏 66 🏊 💏

BARWARA KOTHI
$$$
5 JACOB RD.,
CIVIL LINES
TEL 0141-222 2796
www.barwarakothi.com
Built in the early 20th century, Barwara Kothi's white-washed Lutyens-style building is in the quiet and convenient Civil Lines area. The Barwara family maintains an immaculate yet friendly home and gardens, so the atmosphere is more of a home stay than a hotel.
🛏 7

SOMETHING SPECIAL

LMB
The Jain beginnings of this Jaipur landmark explain its fastidious standards. Locals come to the ground floor café-shop to stock up on the creamiest cashew nuts and best sweetmeats in town, while enjoying delicious fruit juices and snacks. The simple restaurant downstairs serves an excellent Rajasthan thali, which includes *ker sangria* (capers and desert beans) and *bela Rajasthani* (basan dumplings in a yogurt gravy).
$
JOHARI BAZAR
TEL 141-256 5844

GULAB MAHAL
$$
JAI MAHAL PALACE HOTEL, CIVIL LINES
TEL 141-261 6449
To take carefully prepared and authentic Rajasthani dishes, reserve a table amid the cusped arches of the congenial restaurant in this sprawling, restored palace.

For tender meat, consider *maas ka soyeta* (lamb with millet) with *papad ki subji* (spiced lentil wafers) and *hara mattar sisua* (green peas with ginger).

THE CAFÉ
$
ANOKHI SHOP, TILAK MARG
TEL 141-222 9247
Not only do you have the original Anokhi shop, which often has "test" designs for upcoming seasons, but the outdoor café serves delicious soft drinks and homemade sweet and savory pastries.

HANDI RESTAURANT
$
M.I. ROAD, OPPOSITE THE POST OFFICE
TEL 141-236 4839
Well-located on a main shopping street; you should ignore the unpromising surroundings. Enjoy rich Mughal dishes, especially the meat ones such as *kathi* kabab (mutton wrapped in thin bread) and those cooked in the signature *handi* (clay pot), which intensifies the fragrant spices.

MUSEUM CAFÉ
$
ANOKHI MUSEUM OF HAND PRINTING, AMBER
TEL 141-253 0226
Sitting in the forecourt to enjoy homemade lemon and ginger biscuits with freshly brewed chai (Indian tea) or a soft drink complete the visit to one of India's best-run and most fascinating museums.

THE PALACE CAFÉ
$
THE CITY PALACE
TEL 141-261 6449
The perfect spot to relax over a *nimbu* soda (fresh lime juice soda), a samosa snack, or a full meal, following a cultural visit to the extensive City Palace. Tables are either

HOTELS & RESTAURANTS

in an air-conditioned room or—much nicer—outside in a shady courtyard.

JAISALMER

FORT RAJWADA
$$$
JODHPUR-BARMER LINK RD.
TEL 02992-253 233
www.fortrajwada.com
Opera set designer Stephani Engeln helped restore and convert this extensive palace set in 6 acres (2 ha) on the edge of Jaisalmer. Its grand façade and public rooms are in the full tradition of Jaisalmer's lace-like stone carving; its rooms are more contemporary.
95

GORBANDH PALACE
$$$
SAM RD.
TEL 02992-253 801
www.hrhhotels.com
One of the royal retreats that belong to the reliable HRH chain of Rajput heritage hotels (see Udaipur hotels, p. 358), Gorbandh Palace blends Jaisalmer's cultural heritage with contemporary comforts, and has a tented camp.
67

NACHANA HAVELI
$$
GOVERDHAN CHOWK
TEL 02992-252 110
www.sawdays.co.uk
The 17th-century haveli of the Bhatia family, right in Jaisalmer, is now run by two young brothers and a sister who keep the atmosphere informal and home-like.
11

RAWAL-KOT
$$
JODHPUR-JAISALMER RD.
TEL 02992-251 874
www.tajhotels.com
Set on a slight rise, both the rooms and dining room of this purpose built hotel have fine views over Jaisalmer. To

spend a night beneath the stars, the hotel has a tented camp out on the dunes.
31

JODHPUR

UMAID BHAWAN PALACE
$$$$$
TEL 0291-251 0101
www.tajhotels.com
One of the world's finest and grandest art deco palaces is now a destination hotel, with sumptuously refitted bathrooms, numerous public spaces with original furnishings, grand gardens, and great views across the city to Jodhpur's fairy-tale fort.
64

TAJ HARI MAHAL PALACE
$$$$
5 RESIDENCY RD.
TEL 0291-243 9700
www.tajhotels.com
This modern and very comfortable hotel on Jodhpur's city fringes echoes the local Mawar designs in its decoration and the central courtyard, where the pool is located.
93

AJIT BHAWAN PALACE
$$$
TEL 0291-251 0410
www.ajitbhawan.com
One of India's early heritage hotels, well-located Ajit Bhawan has moved with the times. Today it feels less heritage than ethic contemporary, and has a good pool and a spa and some rooms have their own balconies overlooking the garden.
81

KOTA

BRIJRAJ BHAWAN
$$$
TEL 0744-450 057
www.indianheritagehotels.com
This whitewashed, modest heritage hotel stands on the

banks of the Chambal River and keeps its evocative atmosphere thanks to the oil portraits of royals, their hunting trophies, and their regal furniture.

UMED BHAWAN PALACE
$$$
PALACE RD.
TEL 0744-232 5262
www.welcomheritagehotels.com
Sir Swinton Jacob designed the beautifully carved, grandly spacious 1905 royal palace with its strong Raj-Rajput flavor. Keep in tune with it by playing croquet on the lawns.
32

PALKIYA HAVELI
$$
NEAR SURAJ POLE
TEL 0744-238 7497
www.alsisar.com
The flagship of five boutique heritage hotels owned by a branch of the Rajput Kachhwaha clan, this one has fairly small rooms but prettily painted public spaces and a relaxing courtyard.
7

PRICES

HOTELS
An indication of the cost of a double room without breakfast is given by $ signs.
$$$$$ Over $280
$$$$ $160–$280
$$$ $100–$160
$$ $40–$100
$ Under $40

RESTAURANTS
An indication of the cost of a three-course dinner without drinks is given by $ signs.
$$$$$ Over $80
$$$$ $50–$80
$$$ $35–$50
$$ $20–$35
$ Under $20

KUMBALGARH

🏨 AODHI HOTEL
🍴 $$
NEXT TO KUMBHALGARH FORT
TEL 02952-242 341
www.hrhhotels.com
Blending ethnic with contemporary, this isolated hotel located right in the Aravalli hills has a pool, serves good Rajasthani food, and each room has a balcony. Perfect for walking and relaxing.
ⓘ 26 🌊

MOUNT ABU

🏨 CAMA RAJPUTANA
🍴 CLUB RESORT
$$
ADHAR DEVI RD.
TEL 02974-238 205
www.camahotelsindia.com
Built in the 1880s in the traditional hill station style of rooms spread through lush English-style gardens with panoramic views, this renovated club is the place to enjoy British sports, from table tennis, and snooker to cricket, tennis, and swimming.
ⓘ 40 🌊 🏋

🏨 CONNAUGHT HOUSE
🍴 $$
RAJENDRA MARG, MOUNT ABU
TEL 02974-238 560
www.welcomheritagehotels.com
Built in the style of an English country cottage, this quiet unpretentious retreat was once the home of the chief minister of Mewar state, whose capital was nearby Udaipur.
ⓘ 14

🏨 PALACE HOTEL
🍴 BIKANER HOUSE
$$
DELWARA RD.
TEL 02974-235 121
www.heritagehotelsofindia.com
Built in 1893 so the grand Maharaja of Bikaner could escape the summer heat, guests have suitably regal and

spacious rooms and gardens. There is tennis and volleyball and the hotel will also arrange picnics and pony rides.
ⓘ 38

NAGAUR

🏨 ROYAL CAMPS
🍴 $$$$
NAGAUR FORT
TEL 0291-257 1991 (JODHPUR OFFICE)
www.welcomheritagehotels.com
The tented camp is right inside impressive and well-conserved Nagaur Fort, and operates October through March. Each luxury tent has a bedroom, bathroom, and balcony, and evening campfires complete the setting. This is a good stop between Jodhpur and Bikaner.
ⓘ 20

OSIAN

🏨 OSIAN CAMEL CAMP
🍴 $$$$
C/O THE JODHPUR SAFARI CLUB
HIGH COURT COLONY, JODHPUR
TEL 0291-243 7023
www.camelcamposian.com
This is a permanent luxurious camp 37 miles (60 km) from Jodhpur, run by the experienced Reggie Singh. In addition to going on one, two, or three-day camel safaris, guests learn about the surprisingly rich culture of the Thar Desert and visit temples and oasis villages.
ⓘ 51 🌊

RANAKPUR

🏨 FATEH BAGH PALACE
🍴 $$$
RANAKPUR RD.
TEL 02934-228 6186
www.hrhhotels.com
In 2002, Arvind Singh Mewar of Udaipur transplanted and then restored a crumbling palace from Jodhpur to Ranakpur—all 65,000 pieces of it. This good stop on the

rural Udaipur-Jodhpur road is right near India's most exquisite Jain temples.
ⓘ 18 🌊 🏋

🏨 MAHARANI BAGH
🍴 ORCHARD RETREAT
$$$
NEAR RANAKPUR TEMPLES
TEL 02934-285 151
www.welcomheritagehotels.com
Set in an orchard laid out by the Maharani of Jodhpur in the late 19th century, the modest cottage-style rooms are shaded by mature trees and the atmosphere is informal.
ⓘ 15 🌊

SHAHPURA

🏨 SHAHPURA BAGH
🍴 $$$
BETWEEN JAIPUR AND UDAIPUR
TEL 01484-222 077
www.shahpurabagh.com
This whitewashed hideaway and very stylish oasis between Jaipur and Udaipur is set in 30 acres (12 ha) of lakes and woodland. Local skills have been honed to totally renovate the spacious rooms that mingle contemporary with period. Good food; excellent bird-watching.
ⓘ 5

SHEKHAWATI

🏨 CASTLE MANDAWA
🍴 $$
MANDAWA
TEL 01592-223 124
www.mandawahotels.com
Built in 1775, the castle dominates Mandawa town. Despite the number of rooms, there is plenty of peace to be found in the public areas—the Durbar Hall, dining room, courtyard, and up on the terrace where dinner is served. The hotel also runs a desert resort.
ⓘ 51

HOTELS & RESTAURANTS

⌂ MANDAWA HAVELI
⫴ $$
SANSAR CHANDRA RD.,
MANDAWA
TEL 0141-237 1194 OR
01592-223 088
www.mandawahotels.com
Built in 1890 by a Mawari
jeweler, the courtyard of this
classic painted Shekhawati
haveli is especially heavily
decorated. The Marwari
vegetarian thali on the
rooftop is a memorable treat.
ⓘ 28

⌂ PIRAMAL HAVELI
⫴ $$
BAGAR
TEL 05972-221 220
www.neemranahotels.com
Part of the reliable Neemrana
group, this witty and
incongruous 1920s Raj-
colonial mansion is
encapsulated in its elegant
living room, which has cane
furnishings, tiles on the walls,
and ceiling paintings of flying
angels. Good Mawari food.
ⓘ 8 ⊠

UDAIPUR

⌂ DEVIGARH
⫴ $$$$$
DELWARA, 50-MINUTE DRIVE
NORTH OF UDAIPUR
TEL 02953-289 211
www.deviresorts.com
India's most accomplished
hotel renovation blends
historic palace with uncompromising contemporary
hotel. All the rooms,
restaurants, and bars enjoy
rural views. Every detail
breathes the discerning taste
of its creator, Lekha Poddar.
ⓘ 39 ⊠ ⊻

⌂ OBEROI UDAIVILAS
⫴ $$$$$
HARIDASJI KI MAGRI
TEL 0294-243 3300
www.oberoihotels.com
"Extravagant palatial splendor"
might sum up this astounding
hotel built on the banks of
Lake Pichola, with views
across to the City Palace.

Everything is luxurious, from
the towering lobby to the inlaid
furniture and superb spa.
ⓘ 86 ⊠ ⊻

⌂ SHIV NIWAS PALACE
⫴ $$$$$
THE CITY PALACE
TEL 0294-252 8016
www.hrhindia.com
While some of the big palace
hotels have lost their original
flavor, this carefully maintained
one retains its character
thanks to being managed by
the former royal family. Rooms
are arranged around the large
courtyard where guests enjoy
drinks and meals beneath the
trees or beside the pool.
ⓘ 35 ⊠ ⊻

⌂ TAJ LAKE PALACE
⫴ $$$$$
LAKE PICHOLA
TEL 0294-252 8800
www.tajhotels.com
Perhaps India's most famous
hotel location, and certainly
one of its most romantic, the
former royal summer palace
was an early heritage hotel
but has recently undergone a
total and sumptuous
renovation. Guests reach it by
boat across Lake Pichola.
ⓘ 83 ⊠ ⊻

⌂ ATEH PRAKASH
PALACE
⫴ $$$$
THE CITY PALACE
TEL 0294-252 8016
www.hrhhotels.com
Spread over two parts of the
City Palace, 7 rooms are in
Fateh Prakash Palace and have
period Victorian furnishings,
while 21 rooms are in the
Dovecote wing and all of
these have sweeping Lake
Pichola views. Guests use all
Shiv Niwas's facilities.
ⓘ 31

⌂ DEVRA
⫴ $$$
SISARMA-BUJRA RD.,
KALAROHI
TEL 0294-243 1049
www.devraudaipur.com

This colonial contemporary
house up on the hill to the
west of Lake Pichola enjoys
superb views across Lake
Pichola to Udaipur city.
Verandas, rooftop and public
rooms take advantage of this
stunning setting; much of the
food is organically grown.
ⓘ 4

⌂ TRIDENT HILTON
UDAIPUR
⫴ $$$
HARIDASJI KI MAGRI,
MULLA TALAI
TEL 0294-243 2200
www.trident-hilton.com
Set on a 43-acre (17 ha)
estate beside Lake Pichola
about ten minutes' drive
from the city center, this
is worth it for the peace
and space.
ⓘ 143 ⊠ ⊻

⌂ UDAI KOTHI
⫴ $$$
HANUMAN GHAT, O/S
CHANDPOLE
TEL 0294-243 2810
www.udaikothi.com
A purpose-built, immaculate,
and gleaming haveli a short
walk from the old city, its
glories are the rooftop
pool, pavilions, and restaurant

that have panoramic views across Lake Pichola.

ⓘ 24 🏊 🎽

🏨 JAGAT NIWAS
🍴 PALACE HOTEL
$$
23-25 LAL GHAT (BETWEEN THE CITY PALACE AND JAGDISH TEMPLE)
TEL 0294-242 0133
www.jagatniwaspalace.com
This favorite and charming Udaipur lakeside heritage haveli is run by family members. Both guests and visitors enjoy socializing at the rooftop restaurant with its panoramic views.

ⓘ 29

🏨 KANKARWA HAVELI
🍴 $$
26 LAL GHAT, NEAR JAGAT NIWAS (SEE ABOVE)
TEL 0294-241 1457
www.indianheritagehotels.com
Kankarwa haveli has been sensitively renovated and tranquility is preserved by having no phones or TVs in the rooms. Delicious food prepared in the family kitchen is eaten at the rooftop restaurant.

ⓘ 15

GUJARAT

AHMEDABAD

🏨 CAMA HOTEL
🍴 $$$
KHANPUR RD.
TEL 079-2560 1234
www.camahotelsindia.com
Located between the banks of the Sabarmati River and the old battlements, the restaurant of this well-located 1960 hotel is a good place to eat meat in mostly vegetarian Ahmedabad. Be sure to visit the shops at the back of the hotel, too.

ⓘ 40

🏨 FORTUNE LANDMARK
🍴 $$$
ASHRAM RD.
TEL 079-2755 2929
www.fortuneparkhotels.com
This practical, city center hotel aimed at businessmen has two good restaurants: the Orchid serving multi-cuisine buffets and the Khyber serving a la carte Northwest Frontier cuisine.

ⓘ 96

🏨 HOUSE OF
🍴 MANGALDAS
GIRDHARDAS
$$$
OPPOSITE SIDI SAIYAD MOSQUE, LAL DARWAJA
TEL 079-2550 6946
www.houseofmg.com
Renovated to blend historic with contemporary, this merchant's mansion right opposite Sidi Saiyad mosque buzzes with local life. Rooms have family furnishings, and the rooftop restaurant serves superb Gujarati food. Note: This hotel is entirely vegetarian.

ⓘ 12

🏨 TAJ RESIDENCY
🍴 UMMED
$$$
INTERNATIONAL AIRPORT CIRCLE
TEL 079-2286 9999 OR 079-2286 4444
www.tajhotels.com
A reliable hotel with good service located near the airport and about 15 minutes' drive from the city.

ⓘ 91 🏊

🍴 VISHALA
$$
SARKHEJ RD., NEAR VASNA TOLNAKA
TEL 079-643 0357
Designed as a Gujarati village, with potters and weavers working in mud huts and the fine Vechaar Utensils Museum, guests can enjoy all this and local dance, music, and puppetry before and during a very hefty Gujarati thali dinner.

🍴 THE GREEN HOUSE
$
HOUSE OF MANGALDAS HOTEL, OPPOSITE SIDI SAIYAD MOSQUE, LAL DARWAJA
TEL 079-2550 6946
The ground floor of House of Mangaldas, in the center of town, is a great meeting place for locals and buzzes with chat from morning to night. Some just have a fresh juice, local icecream, or cup of tea; others watch the excellent South India *dosas* and *uttapams* being made for them in the open kitchen.

SOMETHING SPECIAL

🍴 AGASHIYE
This is the most congenial place in Ahmedabad to spend lunch when it is not too hot, or dinner any evening. The extensive rooftop is divided into three areas: the arrival area for inventive mocktails (no alcohol here) and hors d'oeuvres among the sculptures and mobiles; the indoor restaurant, or, much nicer, the open-air tables where diners are saved from decision-making and brought a succession of authentic and distinct vegetarian Gujarati dishes served in a kansa thali (round shallow dish).
$$
HOUSE OF MANGALDAS HOTEL, OPPOSITE SIDI SAIYAD MOSQUE, LAL DARWAJA
TEL 079-550 6946

🍴 GOPI RESTAURANT
$
ASHRAM RD., OPPOSITE TOWN HALL, ELLISBRIDGE
TEL 079-657 6388
When you are exploring the west side of the Sabarmati River, this makes an excellent lunch or dinner stop to enjoy both regular Guajarati dishes and the soft specialties of the Kathiawadi peninsula.

HOTELS & RESTAURANTS

🍴 VADILAL SODA FOUNTAIN
$
THREE GATES, OPPOSITE
KARANJ POLICE STATION
TEL 079-535 3032
Gujarat is famed for its fresh
and very creamy ice-cream
made only from fresh
ingredients, its aim to be
"dense, rich, and filling."
At this parlor, founded in
1926, try the almond or
pistachio flavors, or the
Indian mango *kulfi*.

MUMBAI & MAHARASHTRA

A long isthmus with terrible
traffic, Mumbai—still known as
Bombay by repeat visitors—is all
about location. Choose a hotel
that fits with where you will be
during the day, and reserve in
advance because there is a
serious
lack of hotel beds here.
To find the latest restaurants
in this style-conscious and
international city, consult
Time Out Mumbai—you will
find every cuisine of India to
choose from, and many of
the world's.

MUMBAI (BOMBAY)

🏨 THE OBEROI
🍴 **$$$$$**
NARIMAN POINT
TEL 022-6632 5757
www.oberoihotels.com
Downtown Mumbai's most
deluxe, large contemporary
hotel overlooks the Arabian
Sea at Nariman Point. The
historic and banking areas
are right behind; the
upcoming business areas
are a 30-minute drive away.
Restaurants, bars, and shops
are top notch.
ℹ️ 337 🏊 🏋️

🏨 TAJ LAND'S END
🍴 **$$$$$**
BANDRA (WEST)
TEL 022-6668 1234
www.tajhotels.com

Very efficient deluxe business
hotel overlooking the Arabian
Sea, strategically located near
the Bandra-Kurla, Andheri,
and Worli business districts
and 20 to 30 minutes from
the downtown historic area.
Gym, pool, jogging track; golf
and tennis nearby.
ℹ️ 368 🏊 🏋️

🏨 TAJ MAHAL
🍴 PALACE & TOWERS
$$$$$
APOLLO BUNDER
TEL 022-6665 3366 OR
022-5665 3366
www.tajhotels.com
Opened in 1903, the totally
renovated "grand lady of
Bombay" faces the harbor.
Rooms are spread over the
historic Palace Wing and
in a newer tower; all guests
enjoy the great internal
courtyard with its large
pool, loungers and wicker
chairs. The Colaba location
is ideal for sightseeing
and shopping.
ℹ️ 565 🏊 🏋️

🏨 TAJ WELLINGTON
🍴 MEWS LUXURY RESIDENCES
$$$$$
33 NATHALAL PEREKH MARG
TEL 022-6656 9494
www.tajhotels.com
An ideal place for a longer
stay, these deluxe downtown
apartments at Colaba
range from studios to five-
bedroom apartments.
Designed by John Portman
and Sue Freeman, they
have all amenities from
home theater systems to
modular kitchens.
ℹ️ 80 🏊 🏋️

🏨 HILTON TOWERS
🍴 MUMBAI
$$$$
NARIMAN POINT
TEL 022-6632 4343
www.trident-hilton.com
Formerly the Oberoi Towers,
the hotel boasts great
views—especially from the

PRICES

HOTELS
An indication of the cost
of a double room without
breakfast is given by $ signs.
$$$$$	Over $280
$$$$	$160–$280
$$$	$100–$160
$$	$40–$100
$	Under $40

RESTAURANTS
An indication of the cost of a
three-course dinner without
drinks is given by $ signs.
$$$$$	Over $80
$$$$	$50–$80
$$$	$35–$50
$$	$20–$35
$	Under $20

high floors overlooking the
Arabian Sea. The good lively
atmosphere and excellent
facilities, including tennis,
attract a younger crowd
than The Oberoi next door
(see above).
ℹ️ 575 🏊 🏋️

🏨 MARINE PLAZA
🍴 **$$$$**
29 MARINE DR.
TEL 022-2285 1212
www.sarovarhotels.com
Overlooking the Arabian
Sea at Nariman Point, this
unpretentious boutique
hotel is well located for
both tourist and businessman,
and the roof terrace is a
major bonus.
ℹ️ 68 🏊 🏋️

🏨 TAJ PRESIDENT
🍴 **$$$$**
90 CUFFE PARADE
TEL 022-6665 0808
www.tajhotels.com
Located downtown at
Cuffe Parade near the
historic district, this relaxed
hotel—more practical than
stylish—is used as much by
locals as by visitors.
ℹ️ 292 🏊 🏋️

KEY   🏨 Hotel   🍴 Restaurant   ℹ️ No. of bedrooms   🏊 Indoor/ 🏊 Outdoor swimming pool   🏋️ Health club

🏨 GORDON HOUSE
🍴 $$$
5 BATTERY ST.,
APOLLO BUNDER
TEL 022-2287 1122
www.ghhotel.com
Its contemporary rooms
slipped into a period building,
fair room rates, and location
behind the Taj Mahal Palace
& Towers (see above)
make this a great hotel
for exploring downtown
Mumbai. The upbeat
restaurant, bar, and nightclub
attract a young crowd.
🛏 31

MUMBAI/AIRPORT AND BUSINESS DISTRICT HOTELS

If you are either passing through
Mumbai airport and need
overnight accommodations, or
have meetings in the business
areas of north Mumbai, consider
staying in this area to avoid
drives of up to two hours or
more through the city's 24/7
heavy traffic.

🏨 GRAND HYATT
🍴 $$$$$
OFF WESTERN EXPRESS
HIGHWAY, SANTACRUZ (EAST)
TEL 022-6676 1234
www.mumbai.grand.hyatt.com
Mumbai's most stylish and
spacious hotel, ideal for
businessmen and tourists
alike, is notable for its owners'
stunning contemporary Indian
art collection displayed
throughout the open lobby
and lower levels, where the
bars and restaurants are
superb. (See also Hyatt
Regency hotel, below).
🛏 547 rooms, 147
apartments 🏊 🏋

🏨 HYATT REGENCY
🍴 $$$$$
SAHAR AIRPORT RD.
TEL 022-6696 1234 OR
022-5696 1234
www.mumbai.regency.hyatt.com
It is important not to confuse
this hotel with the Grand

Hyatt hotel (see above). The
Hyatt Regency, located by
the international airport, is a
deluxe, efficient business hotel
with club rooms, tennis and
squash courts, and good
meeting areas.
🛏 408 🏊 🏋

🏨 ITC GRAND CENTRAL
🍴 SHERATON
$$$$$
287 DR. BABASAHEB
AMBEDKAR RD., PAREL
TEL 022-2410 1010
www.itcwelcomgroup.in
Located further away from
the airports (9 miles; 15 km),
this business hotel at Parel
has colonial character and is
more cosseting than the
usual business hotel. Five
restaurants include the
exclusive rooftop Point of
View with, as promised, great
city and sea panoramas.
🛏 287 🏊 🏋

🏨 ITC GRAND MARATHA
🍴 SHERATON
$$$$$
SAHAR
TEL 022-2830 3030
www.itcwelcomgroup.in
This huge hotel sited between
the two airports is essentially
for businessmen and provides
four categories of increasingly
well-serviced rooms for them.
It has six restaurants and
copious conference facilities.
🛏 741 🏊 🏋

🏨 LEELA KEMPINSKI
🍴 $$$$$
SAHAR
TEL 022-6691 1234 OR
022-5691 1234
www.theleela.com
Equipped with probably India's
most comfortable beds and
best designed bathrooms, the
Leela sits between the
domestic and international
airports and fully upholds its
group's reputation.
🛏 425 🏊 🏋

🏨 ORCHID HOTEL
🍴 $$$$
NEHRU RD., ADJACENT TO
DOMESTIC AIRPORT
TEL 022-2616 4040
www.orchidhotel.com
Geared to serve guests
arriving and departing from
the airports, this efficient
eco-hotel right near the
domestic airport has practical
rooms, kind service for the
weary, and its Maharashtran
buffet is memorable.
🛏 245

SOMETHING SPECIAL

🍴 SALT WATER GRILL
Imagine this: lazing in a
hammock beneath the stars,
sipping a cocktail and munching
on grilled fresh fish, resting
against brightly colored
cushions, listening to the gentle
lapping of the waves of the
Arabian Sea. There are also deep
sofas, loungers, and tables and
chairs. The staff are friendly and
it is cool to slip off your shoes
and wiggle your toes in the sand.
$$
BESIDE H2O WATER SPORTS
COMPLEX, MARINE DR.
TEL 022-2368 5459

🍴 SOUK AND MASALA
$$$
THE TAJ MAHAL PALACE &
TOWERS, COLABA
TEL 022-6665 3366
The top-of-the-tower Souk
presents a stunning Lebanese
buffet at lunchtime, plus
panoramic views, while a
coveted dinner table at the
bar in the old wing's Masala
lets you to watch one of
three set menus of sublime
contemporary Indian dishes
being cooked before your
eyes. Reserve at both.

🍴 INDIGO
$$
MANDLIK RD., COLABA
TEL 022-5636 8981
Reserve a table to join
Mumbai's most discerning

HOTELS & RESTAURANTS

and design-conscious in a sensitively restored and white-washed Mumbai mansion behind the Taj Mahal. Sip cocktails at the bar or linger over fresh Italian dishes; the risottos are always delicious.

OLIVE
$$
PALI HILL TOURIST HOTEL,
14 UNION PARK, BANDRA
TEL 022-2605 8228
Requiring a reservation and a 30-minute drive from a downtown hotel, this continually popular Mediterranean bar and restaurant has indoor and outdoor tables, plenty of young celebrities, and good pastas and salads.

TRISHNA
$$
7 SAI BABA MARG, BY RHYTHM HOUSE, KALA GHODA
TEL 022-2270 1623
Found down a lane opposite the Wedgwood blue synagogue, this simple café-restaurant is a longtime favorite for Mumbai celebrities. Quiet at lunchtime; crowded and boisterous at night. Be sure to try the signature butter garlic crab and the stuffed pomfret.

MAHESH LUNCH HOUSE
$
8B CAWASJI PATEL ST.
TEL 022-2287 0938
This off-beat, no frills, long established downtown restaurant draws knowing seafood lovers from all over town. They come for the Konkal coastal dishes of the Mangalore area, especially the black pomfret dishes and the amazing tandoor or curried crabs.

PARADISE RESTAURANT
$
SIND CHAMBERS, COLABA CAUSEWAY
TEL 022-2283 2874

This long-established family restaurant, where locals have eaten since childhood, provides a rare chance to taste the Parsi community's very distinctive cuisine. Chicken dhansak is the classic dish.

A NOTE ON MUMBAI'S BARS

This being India's most hip and westernized city, there are plenty of great bars. Consider this handful as a starter pack: The Dome, rooftop of the Inter-Continental hotel, Marine Drive; poolside at the Taj Mahal Palace & Towers (see hotels); Vie Deck and Lounge on Juhu Beach (102 Juhu Tara Rd., tel 022-2660 3003); and all the bars at the Grand Hyatt (see hotels).

MAHARASHTRA

AURANGABAD

TAJ RESIDENCY
$$$
8-N—12, CIDCO,
RAUZA BAGH
TEL 0240-238 1106
www.tajhotels.com
The lush gardens, good pool, and kind staff, who will serve food outside if wished, make this a good base for visiting the astounding ancient sculptures and paintings of Ajanta, Ellora, and Aurangabad itself.
 66

WEST COAST: GOA & KERALA

The hotel selection assumes you will probably be relaxing in this region and will want to be on or very close to a beach or in a beautiful landscape.

PRICES

HOTELS
An indication of the cost of a double room without breakfast is given by **$** signs.

$$$$$	Over $280
$$$$	$160–$280
$$$	$100–$160
$$	$40–$100
$	Under $40

RESTAURANTS
An indication of the cost of a three-course dinner without drinks is given by **$** signs.

$$$$$	Over $80
$$$$	$50–$80
$$$	$35–$50
$$	$20–$35
$	Under $20

GOA

There is a well-organized network of paying guest accommodations in traditional Goan homes; contact the Tourist Office. The following selection of hotels are almost all either right on the beach or a few minutes' walk from it.

NORTH GOA

FORT AGUADA BEACH RESORT & HERMITAGE
$$$$$
SINQUERIM
TEL 0832-664 5858
www.tajhotels.com
Built before the laws existed to keep buildings back from the fragile beachside ecology, the pool, restaurants, and rooms start right on the old Portuguese ramparts and sprawl back up the hill, ending with private villas. Guests can also use the facilities of Taj Holiday Village next door (see next page).
 130

🏨 NILAYA HERMITAGE
🍴 $$$$$
ARPORA
TEL 0832-227 6793
www.nilaya.com
Owners Claudia Derain, Hari Ajwani, and architect Dean d'Cruz have indeed created a contemporary hilltop hermitage and made it a haven for the world's social celebrities. Some find it perfectly dreamy and cosseting, others find it cloying and miss the beach.
🛏 12 🏊 🏋

🏨 POUSADA TAUMA
🍴 $$$$$
PORBA VADDO, CALANGUTE
TEL 0832-227 9061
www.pousada-tauma.com
Set beside Calangute beach, the 12 suites built of Goa's red laterite stone stand in a lush garden. The emphasis is on ecology and ayurvedic treatments, and guests can consult with the doctors before taking single treatments or 7- or 14-day packages.
🛏 12 🏊 🏋

🏨 VILLA AASHYANA
🍴 $$$$$
ESCRIVAO VADDO, CANDOLIM
TEL 0832-248 9225
www.aashyanalakhanpal.com
An immaculate contemporary Goa-inspired villa set in tranquil gardens that go down to Candolim beach, the main house has five bedrooms while three cottages on the grounds each have two more. Guests can rent the villa, a cottage, or everything. Massage on call.
🛏 11 🏊

🏨 PANCHAVATTI
🍴 $$$$
CORJUEM ISLAND, ALDONA
TEL 09822-580 632
www.islaingoa.com
A quiet inland haven, this guest-house retreat sits on a hill outside Mapusa, with expansive views over the gardens to the Mapusa River.

Each room has its own balcony, and guests can enjoy yoga, ayurvedic treatments, good food, and lovely country walks.
🛏 4 🏊

🏨 SIOLIM HOUSE
🍴 $$$$
WADI, SIOLIM
TEL 0832-227 2138
www.siolimhouse.com
This quality boutique heritage hotel at Siolim, quite far north up the coast, is immaculately restored, spacious, well-run and sits in an unspoiled village and near equally unspoiled beaches such as Morjim and Ashwem. Good food; no air-conditioning.
🛏 7 🏊

🏨 TAJ HOLIDAY
🍴 VILLAGE
$$$$
SINQUERIM, BARDEZ
TEL 0832-664 5858
www.tajhotels.com
Like Fort Aguada, this 25-year-old hotel benefits from a beachside setting, and its boardwalk restaurant is nice for beach-gazing. Rooms are situated throughout lush gardens. Guests can use the facilities of the adjoining Fort Aguada hotel.
🛏 140 🏊 🏋

🏨 FORT TIRACOL
🍴 $$$
TIRACOL, PERNEM
TEL 02366-227 631 OR 0832-227 6793
www.nilaya.com
The fairy-tale fort at Tiracol, well up the coast from Panaji, has been transformed into a small boutique hotel. Guests must be prepared to climb a few stairs to enjoy the split-level rooms, superb views, the courtyard with its own church, and the local beaches.
🛏 7

🏨 LAGUNA ANJUNA
🍴 $$$
SORANTTO VADO, ANJUNA
TEL 0832-227 4305
www.lagunaanjuna.com
Another Dean d'Cruz design, this time rustic-style cottages with spacious interiors by SOTOdecor of Switzerland, all arranged in tropical gardens around an old Portuguese mansion that is now the restaurant and bar. Ideal for families; near Anjuna beach.
🛏 15 🏊

🏨 HOTEL
🍴 BOUGAINVILLEA GRANPA'S INN
$$
ANJUNA BEACH
TEL 0832-227 3270
www.granpasinn.com
In a peaceful corner of hip Anjuna, this good-value and well-run home stay is in a sensitively converted old Goan house. Notably helpful family of resident owners. Simple is available, but most guests eat out.
🛏 14 🏊

🏨 PANJIM INN
🍴 $$
E-212 31ST JANUARY RD., FONTAINHAS
TEL 0832-222 6523 OR 0832-222 8136
www.panjiminn.com
Found in the lanes of Fontainhas, the old quarter of Panaji, Goa's capital, this grand old mansion has only 12 simple rooms (another 9 are in the quieter Casa Pousada, nearby). Panjim also has a friendly, informal restaurant that is the nicest place to eat in town.
🛏 12

SOUTH GOA

🏨 THE LEELA
🍴 $$$$$
MOBOR, CAVELOSSIM
TEL 0832-287 1234
www.theleela.com
Set on a luxurious estate in

Goa's deep south, guests can enjoy the on-site 12-hole golf course and the very quiet Mobor beach. All rooms have essential gadgets such as DVD players; Leela Club rooms have butlers, Bose music systems, and private plunge pools.

[i] 152 🏊 ♥

🏨 PARK HYATT
🍴 $$$$$
AROSSIM BEACH, CANSAULIM
TEL 0832-272 1234
www.goa.park.hyatt.com
A convenient 15-minute drive south from the airport, this luxurious hotel sits in 45 acres (18 ha) beside Arossim beach at Cansaulim. On site, it provides quality rooms and services for the whole family, from kids camp to serious spa; off site, Panaji and Old Goa are nearby.

[i] 251 🏊 ♥

A NOTE ON GOA'S RESTAURANTS

In addition to the hotels and the delightful beach cafés, where a plate of freshly grilled shrimp makes a perfect light meal, Goa has a large number of informal, friendly, family-run restaurants serving distinctive Goan dishes such as *balcao* (shrimp with ginger, garlic, and vinegar) and *caldiero* (fish cooked with coconut and coriander). Goa's restaurants tend to come and go with the seasons, so it is best to ask locally for recommendations; or simply walk outside your hotel and try the first one you like the look of—that way, you enter into Goa's informal lifestyle.

🏨 TAJ EXOTICA
🍴 $$$$$
BENAULIM
TEL 0832-277 1234 OR
0832-668 3333
www.tajhotels.com
This family hotel at Benaulim, with lots of sports and activities, is set on a large 50-acre (20 ha) plot that goes down to South Goa's great long beach. Good business and expansive meeting facilities make it a popular conference location.

[i] 140 🏊 ♥

KERALA

South Indian cooking is distinct, lighter, and less rich than northern cuisines. Kerala's is especially good and uses plenty of coconut, mustard seed, and tamarind. Rice predominates over breads. Breakfasts may be dosas (think rice-flour crepes) or *idlis* (steamed rice cakes); main meals can be easily ordered with one word, thali, (leaf) which brings a number of dishes served on a leaf or a circular platter—soup-like *sambar*, vegetables, yogurt, dessert, with plenty of rice. If you are on the coast, the Kerala fish dishes are delicious. Many Kerala hotels give cooking demonstrations.

NORTH AND INTERIORS

🏨 KALARI KOVILAKOM
🍴 $$$$
KOLLENGODE, PALAKKAD
TEL 04923-263 737 OR
0484-266 8221 (BOOKINGS)
http://kalarikovilakom.com
A stunningly beautiful old palace of the Venganad rulers has been restored and transformed into a retreat dedicated to serious ayurvedic treatments. Guests come for 7, 14, or 21 days, leaving behind their cellphones and wearing special clothes and shoes.

[i] 18

🏨 TRANQUIL
🍴 PLANTATION HIDEAWAY
$$$$
ASWATI PLANTATIONS LTD.,
KUPPAMUDI COFFEE ESTATE,
KOLAGAPARA P.O.
TEL 04936-220 244
www.tranquilresort.com
Guests on this working coffee and vanilla plantation in the Wayanad hills have two unusual extra treats: a swimming pool and a tree-house suite for the more adventurous. Activities include visiting the plantation, hiking, bird-watching, and ayurvedic massages.

[i] 8 🏊

🏨 AYESHA MANZIL
🍴 $$$
TELLICHERRY
TEL 0490-234 1590
www.i-escape.com
Built by a British cinnamon planter in 1862 and owned since 1900 by local spice traders, this beautifully furnished colonial hilltop guest house has great food and sea views. The local village and beaches are unspoiled. No children, no alcohol (but beer can be obtained).

[i] 6 🏊

🏨 COSTA MALABARI,
🍴 CANNANORE
$$$
NEAR ADIKADALAYI TEMPLE,
KANNUR
TEL 0497-237 1761
www.costamalabari.com
A six-hour ride north from Cochin or west from Mysore reaches a real hideaway guest house just south of Kannur. Set amid cashew and coconut groves, the home cooking is good and a five-minute walk brings you to empty idyllic beaches.

[i] 5

🏨 FRINGE FORD
🍴 $$$
CHERRAKARRA P.O.,
TALAPOYA POST
TEL 098800 86411
www.fringeford.com
A total escape: no cellphone reception, no road, just comfortable rooms, good food, and the stunning and therapeutic Wayanad hills to walk through. Owned by a

HOTELS & RESTAURANTS

naturalist, the 520-acre (210 ha) former spice plantation has been given back to the forest for him and his guests.
🛈 8

🏨 RAIN COUNTRY 🍴 RESORT
$$$
LAKKIDI P.O., WAYANAD
TEL 04936-251 1997 OR
04936-205 306
www.raincountryresort.com
Inland from Calicut and 1,300 feet (396 m) up in the cool, undulating hills of the little-explored Wayanad district, the beautiful Kerala-style one-, two- and three-bedroom cottages are your eco-friendly base for enjoying a landscape of hills, waterfalls, lakes, and forest; good flora and birds.
🛈 8

🏨 TAJ RESIDENCY 🍴 $$$
P.T. USHA RD.
CALICUT
TEL 0495-276 5354
www.tajhotels.com
On the edge of the busy town, this hotel combines business facilities with therapy, and the ayurvedic spa offers 7 to 35 day packages
🛈 74 🏊 🏋

🏨 THARAVAD, 🍴 THENKURUSSI
$$$
KANDATH THARAVAD,
THENKURUSSI
TEL 04922-284 124
www.tharavad.info
Lying among the paddy fields two hours' drive northeast of Cochin airport, s the beautiful 18th-century ancestral home of the Kandath family, with airy courtyards and verandas. Plenty to do, from visiting sights and trekking to learning to cook local dishes.
🛈 6

🏨 VYTHIRI RESORT 🍴 $$$
LAKKIDI P.O., WAYANAD
TEL 04936-255 366
www.vythiriresort.com

Inland from Calicut's steamy coast and 2,600 feet (792 m) above sea level, the rooms of this simple, eco-aware hotel in the lush forests of the Wayanad district are tribal-style cottages. Escorted day walks into the stunning scenery are a highlight; the spa offers ayurvedic packages.
🛈 28 🏋

KOCHI (COCHIN)

🏨 BRUNTON BOATYARD 🍴 $$$$$
FORT COCHIN
TEL 0484-266 8221 OR
0484-221 4562
www.cghearth.com
Built on the site of a boatyard, this new building and its quality wood furnishings perfectly evoke Dutch and Portuguese colonial styles. Spacious public areas surround a lush courtyard, and all the rooms on the ground and upper floor have harbor views.
🛈 26 🏊 🏋

🏨 MALABAR HOUSE 🍴 $$$$
1/268-1/269 PARADE RD.,
FORT COCHIN
TEL 0484-221 6666
www.malabarhouse.com
This contemporary hotel in a converted colonial bungalow at Fort Cochin is much-patronized by the world's social set. Others prefer to visit for dinner in the courtyard, noting the small public spaces, tiny pool, and lack of water views in this pretty port.
🛈 17 🏊 🏋

🏨 TAJ MALABAR 🍴 $$$$
WILLINGDON ISLAND
TEL 0484-266 6811
www.tajhotels.com
Located on Willingdon Island, which hovers between historic Cochin and its twin city, Ernakulum, little remains of the 1930s house at its core. Guests enjoy grand views

from the upper floors of the high-rise tower and good open-air bayside barbecue.
🛈 96 🏊 🏋

🏨 TRIDENT-HILTON 🍴 COCHIN
$$$$
BRISTOW RD.,
WILLINGDON ISLAND
TEL 0484-266 9595
www.trident-hilton.com
A practical family hotel located on Willingdon Island. The rooms overlook the central courtyard and its pool or the lush gardens; nice poolside barbecue, good ayurvedic spa.
🛈 85 🏊 🏋

🏨 TRINITY HOUSE 🍴 $$$$
1/658 RIDSDALE RD., PARADE GROUND, FORT COCHIN
TEL 0484-221 6666
www.malabarhouse.com
Three contemporary suites skillfully slotted into an old Dutch building at Fort Cochin by designer Soumitro Ghosh. Ideal for a family or group of friends. Guests use Malabar House facilities (see above).
🛈 3 🏊

HOTELS & RESTAURANTS

CASINO HOTEL
$$$
WILLINGDON ISLAND
TEL 0484-266 8221
www.cghearth.com
This modest hotel is where
the excellent, eco-friendly
Casino Group of hotels began
and is still headquartered.
Well located on Willingdon
Island, with restaurants
worth visiting wherever
you are staying.
ℹ️ 67 🏊 💪

SOUTH AND INTERIORS

THE LEELA
$$$$$
KOVALAM BEACH
TEL 0471-248 0101
www.theleela.com
Rooms sprawl down from the
clifftop lobby of Kerala's
largest beach resort, near the
capital, Thiruvananthapuram.
Beach-view rooms have
sundecks; pavilion rooms are
at beach level; rooms in the
discerning Leela Club have
balconies. Facilities are deluxe.
ℹ️ 181 🏊 💪

SURYA SAMUDRA
BEACH GARDEN
$$$$$
PULINKUDI, MULLUR P.O.
TEL 0471-226 7333
www.suryasamudra.com
The name means "sun and
sea." This long-established,
deluxe, German-owned hotel
near Vizhinjam has
contemporary and historic
cottages scattered over its 20-
acre (8 ha) site, each with
privacy and good sea views.
Natural rock swimming pool,
reputed ayurvedic center.
ℹ️ 23 🏊 💪

TAJ GREEN COVE
$$$$$
G.V. RAJA VATTAPARA RD.,
KOVALAM
TEL 0471-248 7733
www.tajhotels.com
Overlooking the backwaters
outside Thiruvananthapuram,
the granite cottages with

elephant grass roofs each
have a balcony and overlook
Kovalam beach. Good
meeting facilities mean
visitors can mix business
with pleasure.
ℹ️ 57 🏊 💪

COCONUT LAGOON
$$$$
KUMARAKOM
TEL 0484-266 8221 OR
0481-252 4491
www.cghearth.com
A collection of beautiful old
Kerala houses saved from
demolition sets the tone
of this backwater retreat
overlooking Vembanad
Lake, near Kottayam. Rooms
have open-air bathrooms;
waterside restaurant serves
quality Kerala cuisines; good
ayurvedic spa.
ℹ️ 50 🏊 💪

KUMARAKOM LAKE
RESORT
$$$$
KUMARAKOM NORTH POST,
NEAR KOTTAYAM
TEL 0481-252 4900
www.klresort.com
This smart hotel is composed
of Kerala-inspired villas, some
opening onto the 250-foot-
long (76 m) meandering
swimming pool, others with
private courtyards and sunken
baths. Guests enjoy the
manicured gardens, infinity
pool, seafood bar, and hotel
rice boats.
ℹ️ 52 🏊 💪

LAKE PALACE,
THEKKADY
$$$$
THEKKADY
TEL 0486-922 2023
www.ktdc.com
A real hideaway in the
Cardamom Hills, this
renovated royal lodge sits on
a peninsula jutting into Periya
Lake. Lucky residents enjoy
good early morning and
sunset bird-watching and
sometimes see elephant, wild
boar, and deer.
ℹ️ 6

MARARI BEACH
$$$$
MARARIKULAM
TEL 0484-266 8221
www.cghearth.com
Kerala-style thatched cottages,
some with private pools, dot
the coconut plantation that
continues to its beach,
bordered by fishing villages.
Good seafood, yoga classes,
ayurvedic center, and
opportunities to visit local
fishing villages. Cochin is 37
miles (60 km) away.
ℹ️ 51 🏊 💪

SPICE COAST
CRUISES/RICE BOATS
$$$$
PUTHENANGADI
TEL 0484-266 8221
www.cghearth.com
The best way to visit Kerala's
extensive network of
backwaters is to spend a
night or two on a *kettuvallom*,
a houseboat of jackfruit
wood inspired by the
local rice boats. Departing
from Kottayam, each has
a full staff; bedrooms have
adjoining bathrooms.
ℹ️ 1–2 (according to the
boat size)

SPICE VILLAGE
$$$$
VILLAGE KUMILY, 5-MIN. WALK
FROM CENTRAL THEKKADY
TEL 0484-266 8221 OR
04869-224 514
www.cghearth.com
Up in the Cardamom Hills,
the spacious thatched
cottages with verandas are
scattered through a mature
spice garden—the resident
naturalist gives afternoon
tours. Quality food and
ayurvedic center and a
commitment to ecology
keep the tranquil ambience.
ℹ️ 52 🏊 💪

TAJ GARDEN RETREAT,
KUMARAKOM
$$$$
1/404 KUMARAKOM,
NEAR KOTTAYAM
TEL 0481-252 5711

HOTELS & RESTAURANTS

www.tajhotels.com
These restored colonial houses in the backwaters near Kottyam were previously called Baker's Bungalow, the original structure on the property. The newly-built rooms range from villas with private pools to cottages and rice boats.

 33 🏊 🏋

🏨 TAJ GARDEN RETREAT, 🍴 THEKKADY
$$$$
AMALAMBIKA RD, THEKKADY.
TEL 04869-222 401 OR
04869-232 240
www.tajhotels.com
For better views over the Cardamom Hills, the cottages are built on stilts and each has a balcony. This hotel keeps nature at bay by providing TVs, meeting rooms, and other city services. Good views from the Hornbill bar.

🛏 32 🏊 🏋

🏨 PARADISA 🍴 PLANTATION RETREAT
$$$
MURINJAPUZHA P.O.
TEL 04692-701 311
www.paradisaretreat.com
Set on the route up to the Cardamom Hills, on an organic coffee and spice plantation, each traditional Kerala wooden guest house has hand-picked furnishings, absolute privacy, and glorious views. Good food, yoga, and serious ayurvedic treatments packages.

🛏 11 🏊 🏋

🏨 RAHEEM RESIDENCY 🍴 $$$
BEACH RD., ALLEPPEY
TEL 04772-223 0767 OR
04772-239 767
www.raheemresidency.com
Its Irish-Indian owners have immaculately restored and furnished this 1860s colonial villa set on the fringes of delightful Alleppey town, making for a stay that mixes elegant comfort with local color. Rooftop restaurant,

good ayurvedic spa, beach across the road.

🛏 7 🏊 🏋

🏨 WINDERMERE ESTATE 🍴 $$$
WINDERMERE HOUSE, THRIKKAKARA
TEL 0484-242 5237
www.windermeremunnar.com
Munnar, Kerala's British hill station for tea and spice planters, retains its Raj feel, as do the unpretentious rooms on this working cardamom estate. Some have views over the lovely Chithirapuram valley. Activities are trekking, visiting the estate, and family dining.

🛏 15

KARNATAKA

🏨 SWASWARA 🍴 $$$$$
NEAR KARWAR
TEL 0484-266 8221
www.swaswara.com
The name means "inner sound." Lying four hours' drive south from Goa airport on a virgin stretch of the Konkan coast, the immaculate Konkan-inspired villas, gardens, and empty beach form a haven of repose. Quality ayurvedic treatments; no meat or spirits served.

🛏 27 🏊 🏋

🏨 DEVBAGH BEACH 🍴 RESORT
$$$
KODIBAGH, OPPOSITE HOTEL BHADRA, UTTAR KANNADA DIST.
TEL 08382-221 603
www.junglelodges.com
Lying just inside Karnataka, across the border from Goa, this eco-friendly beach lodge's simple cottages and log hut rooms are built in a grove of casuarinas trees. Guests can swim, snorkel, parasail, go hiking and bird-watching, and visit the local village.

🛏 12

CHIKMAGALUR

🏨 TAJ GARDEN RETREAT 🍴 $$$
K.M. RD., OPPOSITE PAVITRAVANA, 4 MILES OUTSIDE CHIKMANGALOR
TEL 08262-220 202
www.tajhotels.com
A mixture of rooms and cottages make up this very congenial, modern rural hotel, convenient for visiting the Hoysala temples and coffee plantations and doing some nice hiking.

🛏 29 🏊 🏋

HOSPET

🏨 HAMPI'S BOULDERS 🍴 $$
NARAYANPET, BANDI HARLAPUR P.O.
TEL 08539-265-939
Set among the dramatic boulders of Vijayanagar's landscape, the cottages are reached by coracle, crossing the Tungabhadra River. Guests at this tranquil oasis of bamboo, coconut, and mango enjoy good food, a pool and well-appointed cottages.

🛏 11 🏊

🏨 Hotel 🍴 Restaurant 🛏 No. of bedrooms 🏊 Indoor/🏊 Outdoor swimming pool 🏋 Health club   **KEY**

HOTELS & RESTAURANTS

🏨 **MALLIGI TOURIST**
🍴 **HOME**
$$
6/143 J.N. RD.
TEL 0839-422 8101
www.malligihotels.com
The Malligi is an institution
that has grown along with the
numbers of visitors coming to
see Vijayanagar's magnificent
ruins. Unpretentious, friendly,
with simple rooms and
home-cooked food, it
now has a pool and caters
to conferences.
🛏 100 🏊 🆆

BADAMI

🏨 **BADAMI COURT**
🍴 **$$**
17/2 STATION RD.
TEL 08357-220 230
www.hotelbadamicourt.com
To see some of the best
sites in India requires staying
in simple accommodations.
Badami Court is simple
but can provide welcome
smiles, hot water, and, if
asked, good homemade
country food.
🛏 27 🏊

THE DECCAN

BANGALORE

Since becoming an international
center for information technology,
Bangalore has developed an
extensive restaurant, café, and
bar network. To find the right
place for you, consult the almost
exhaustive listings at
www.karnataka.com/burp/

🏨 **ISTA HOTEL**
🍴 **$$$$$**
1/1 SWAMI VIVEKANANDA RD.,
ULSOOR
TEL 080-2555 8888
www.istahotel.com
Benefiting from great views
across Ulsoor Lake, this
refined, deluxe, contemporary
hotel works well for both
businessman and tourist.
Rooms are spacious; dining

options include Oriental,
Continental, and Italian.
🛏 143 🆆

🏨 **ITC WINDSOR MANOR**
🍴 **SHERATON & TOWERS**
$$$$$
25 WINDSOR SQUARE,
GOLF COURSE RD.
TEL 080-2226 9898
www.itcwelcomgroup.in
A large white stucco hotel
evoking the Raj, sited near
the golf course, its rooms and
facilities designed to keep the
fussiest businessman happy.
Restaurants dedicated to
Anglo-India, Raj, Northwest
Frontier, Lucknowi, and
Chinese cuisines.
🛏 240 🏊 🆆

🏨 **THE LEELA PALACE**
🍴 **$$$$$**
23 AIRPORT RD.
TEL 080-2521 1234
www.theleela.com
This massive, palatial hotel
with gold-leaf domes set in
lush gardens is right by
Bangalore's international and
domestic airports, and is
convenient for city business.
Rooms start deluxe and rise
upward to the Royal Club;
Asian and Indian restaurants.
🛏 358 🏊 🆆

🏨 **THE OBEROI**
🍴 **BANGALORE**
$$$$$
37–39 MAHATMA GANDHI RD.
TEL 080-2558 5858
www.oberoihotels.com
Set in an oasis of gardens
and trees right in the city's
heart on M G Road, this
hotel is what the Oberoi
group does best: efficient
business facilities, professional
service, understated luxury,
and reliable quality food
(Continental, Szechwan, and
Thai cuisines).
🛏 160 🏊 🆆

🏨 **THE PARK**
🍴 **$$$$$**
14/7 MAHATMA GANDHI RD.
TEL 080-2559 4666
www.theparkhotels.com

Part of India's only group of
inspired contemporary, city-
center boutique hotels, this
one designed by Conran and
Partners of the U.K. lies off M
G Road. Rooms and public
areas have plenty of color,
creating an upbeat ambience.
Notable Italian restaurant.
🛏 109 🏊 🆆

🏨 **TAJ RESIDENCY**
🍴 **$$$$$**
41/3 MAHATMA GANDHI RD.
TEL 080-6660 4444
www.tajhotels.com
A good downtown location,
with views of Ulsoor Lake, the
rooms have ergonomically
designed desk chairs by
Herman Miller to keep
businessmen happy. Dining
includes Chinese and
Continental restaurants.
🛏 166 🏊 🆆

🏨 **TAJ WEST END**
🍴 **$$$$$**
RACE COURSE RD.
TEL 080-6660 5660 OR
080-5660 5660
www.tajhotels.com
Located downtown beside
the race course and golf
course, this long-established
hotel maintains its distinctive
Bangalore style in its renovated

form. Businessmen like the club rooms; one restaurant is Vietnamese, another is a poolside barbecue.
🛏 117 ⧈ 🗑

🏨 VILLA POTTIPATI
🍴 $$$
142 8TH CROSS, 4TH MAIN RD., MALLESWARAM
TEL 080-2336 0777
www.neemranahotels.com
The antidote to business hotels, this villa in the Malleswaram area of central Bangalore is a rare case of buildings conservation in this city addicted to the new. Sensitively renovated, beautifully furnished, and set in gardens shaded by gulmohars and jacarandas.
🛏 8 ⧈

SOMETHING SPECIAL

🍴 THE DARSHINIS OF BANGALORE

In 1983, inspired by fast food chains abroad, Mr. Prabhankar started Café Darshini to bring high-quality, low-cost, hygienic South India dishes—crunchy masala dosas, soft idlis, and crispy vadas—to the Bangalore public. Today there are more than 5,000 Darshinis in the city of which the most popular are Upahara Darshini in Netkalappa Circle, Basavanagudi district, and Ganesh Darshini in Jayanagar, Palahara Darshini district.
$
Outlets all over town

🍴 I-T.ALIA
$$$
THE PARK HOTEL, M. G. RD.
TEL 080-2559 4666
The contemporary hotel's restaurant is suitably avant garde Italian, so reserve a table to ensure you can enjoy flavorful salads, remarkable pizzas, fresh artichokes, and gorgonzola cheese, accompanied by Italian wines.

🍴 KARAVALLI
$$
TAJ GATEWAY HOTEL, RESIDENCY RD.
TEL 080-558 4545
Sit outside beneath a beautiful spreading raintree or in a Mangalore-inspired interior and sample coastal Karnataka and Goan delicacies such as baby lobster, black pomfret, pearlspot, ladyfish, tiger prawns, and other fish dishes—and a few meat ones, too.

🍴 VINDU
$$
VAISHNAVI RESIDENCY, KANAKAPURA RD., SOUTH BANGALORE
TEL 080-5760 6685
Vindu focuses on the distinctive cuisine of Nellore on coastal Andhra Pradesh. Meats are marinated in masalas whose spices are sent down from Hyderabad, gravies have their *gongura* (a high-protein vegetable) sourced from the owners' farm.

🍴 MAVALLI TIFFIN ROOMS (MTR)
$
14 LAL BAGH RD.
TEL 080 222 0022
A traditional *tiffin* (light meal) room founded in 1924, last redecorated mid-century. It is always bustling with locals rushing in to gobble their thali meals, which are served by waiters walking from table to table spooning out the food from buckets.

HYDERABAD

The city's rich royal Muslim legacy—Persian, Mughal, Abyssinian—lives on in its cuisine, especially the classic *biryani* (fragrant rice and meat steamed together) and other meat dishes such as kebabs, *kheemas*, *shorvas*, and *khalias*.

🏨 ITC GRAND KAKITIYA
🍴 SHERATON & TOWERS
$$$$$
63-3-1187, BEGUMPET
TEL 040-2340 0132
www.itcwelcomgroup.in
This modern hotel in the Begumpet district is convenient to the airport and for sightseeing and business, and has all the necessary facilities. Especially nice pool area, and a choice of three good restaurants, including Peshawri for northern and Dakshin for southern.
🛏 188 ⧈ 🗑

🏨 TAJ KRISHNA
🍴 $$$$$
ROAD NO. 1, BANJARA HILLS
TEL 040-6666 2323
www.tajhotels.com
Hyderabad's premier hotel sets the tone with a lavish building in the Banjara Hills, overlooking the city. Well-placed for the airport and sightseeing, with great facilities and Taj Club rooms. The Firdaus serves good Hyderabadi dishes.
🛏 260 ⧈ 🗑

🏨 TAJ BANJARA
🍴 $$$$
ROAD NO. 1, BANJARA HILLS
TEL 040-6666 9999
www.tajhotels.com
The smallest of the Taj Group's three hotels in Hyderabad, this one overlooks its own lake in the Banjara Hills. Guests and non-residents can enjoy the notable waterside buffet of India, Chinese, and continental dishes at both lunch and dinner.
🛏 118 ⧈ 🗑

🏨 TAJ DECCAN
🍴 $$$$
ROAD NO. 1, BANJARA HILLS
TEL 040-6666 3939
www.tajhotels.com
Also in the Banjara Hills, this less opulent Taj hotel set in mature gardens has

most of the advantages of the Taj Krishna but in a slightly more modest way. Friendly service includes an upbeat bar and restaurant.

(i) 140

🏨 GREEN PARK
🍴 $$$
GREENLANDS, BEGUMPET
TEL 040-6651 5151 OR
040-5551 5151
www.hotelgreenpark.com
One of a small group of useful business hotels, this Hyderabad one is in the Begumpet district so it is well located for business and pleasure. It has a bar and restaurant that are popular with locals.
(i) 146

🏨 ADITYA PARK INN
🍴 $$
ADITYA TRADE CENTRE, AMEERPET
TEL 040-6678 8888 OR
040-5578 8888
www.sarovarhotels.com
Located in Ameerpet, the business district of the new city, this nicely designed, no-frills business hotel is ideal for those who want a good location but intend to be out and about during the days.
(i) 88

SOMETHING SPECIAL

🍴 ABHIRUCHI
Well worth the journey to a spot near Secunderabad's Parade Ground to join locals and experience the true Andhra thali. For less than five dollars you can savor a medley of local recipes for vegetables and meat. Be sure to have the side order of *gongura* (mutton) and curd-chili (tiny chilies marinated in curd and then fried).
$
1-7-274 A, S.D. RD.,
SECUNDERABAD
TEL 040-2789 6565

🍴 DAKSHIN AND DUMPUKT
$$
ITC GRAND KAKITIYA SHERATON & TOWERS, BEGUMPET
TEL 040-2340 0132
Choose between two top-flight restaurants in this hotel, conveniently located for Hyderabad sightseeing. Dakshin's southern dishes include refreshing *vasantha neer* (coconut water with honey and lime) and the Iyer special (a deluxe thali), while Dumpukt offers fine Hyderabadi and Lucknowi biryani and kebabs.

🍴 FIRDAUS
$$
TAJ KRISHNA, ROAD NO.1, BANJARA HILLS
TEL 040-339 2323
Make a reservation here for the lunch buffet or, much better, a leisurely dinner reminiscent of the days of the Nizam's refined court. Hyderabadi mutton biryani (rice cooked with mutton) and tomato *qoot* are signature dishes.

🍴 MALGUDI
$
6-3-1 1192/2/1-16, 1ST FLOOR, MY HOME TYCOON, BEGUMPET
TEL 040-5563 2277
The same effort put into the decor, which includes jeweled doors, is put into the meticulously prepared southern food served on copper thali plates. The menu lists dishes by state—such as Malabar *parotha*. Or simply order a regional thali.

🍴 SOUTHERN SPICE
$
8-2-350/3/2, ROAD NO. 3, BANJARA HILLS
TEL 040-2335 3802
Well located if you are staying in a Banjara Hills hotel, locals like the way "southern" is interpreted as Andhran and recipes are absolutely authentic—try chicken

Chettinad or *chaapa vepudu* (fish fry), and the essential side dish of *perugannam* (spiced curd rice).

MYSORE

🏨 LALITHA MAHAL
🍴 PALACE
$$$$
TEL 0821-247 0470
www.theashokgroup.com
In this extravaganza of a palace, built in 1931 as the Maharaja's guest house overlooking his city palace on the plains below, guests enjoy spectacular public rooms, a sweeping double staircase, a billiards hall, extensive gardens—and a certain evocative shabbiness.
(i) 54

🏨 ROYAL ORCHID
🍴 METROPOLE
$$$$
5 JHANSI LAKSHMI BAI RD.
TEL 0821-525 5566
www.baljeehotels.com
In another royal guest house turned hotel, this time 1920s Raj-classical white stucco in the town center, the period decor and ambience is mixed with the quality service of this Royal Orchid hotel

group. Good for an in-town restaurant, barbecue, bar, and tea.
(i) 30 🏊 🏋

🏨 GITANJALI FARM
🍴 $$
P.B. #6 SIDDARTANAGAR
TEL 0821-247 3779
www.gitanjalifarm.com
Located near the Lalitha Mahal Palace, this redbrick farmhouse and garden are home for the Kodava family who help their guests to have the experiences they want—home cooking, going to the market, massage, visiting weavers. They also run a cottage deep in the countryside.
(i) 4

NAGARHOLE

🏨 KABINI RIVER LODGE
🍴 $$$$
KARAPURA,
TEL 080-2559 7021
(BANGALORE OFFICE)
www.junglelodges.com
Held in deep affection by all its visitors, this lodge that began as a royal hunting lodge has rooms, cottages, and tents. Guests explore the jungle by Jeep, boat, or coracle, and meet up around the dining table and camp fire to recount their sightings of the day.
(i) 25

TAMIL NADU

CHENNAI (MADRAS)

Madrasis go out to enjoy their city—to the beach for sunset walks, to hideaway places to watch quality dance or listen to incredible musicians, and to eat out. Almost all the restaurants in the streets will be busy and hygienic and serve delicious fresh vegetarian food, and sometimes fish; they make delicious fresh fruit juices and milk shakes, and like to drink frothy, sweet, milky coffee and tea.

🏨 ITC CHOLA SHERATON
🍴 $$$$$
CATHEDRAL RD.
TEL 044-2811 0101
www.itcwelcomgroup.in
Half of the rooms are duplexes, with a separate living area. The hotel is strong on business facilities, and the Welcomgroup's usual high standards in food are maintained at the Northwest frontier and Chinese restaurants.
(i) 92 🏊 🏋

🏨 THE PARK CHENNAI
🍴 $$$$$
601 ANNA SALAI
TEL 044-4214 4000 OR 044-5214 4000
www.theparkhotels.com
Chennai's only contemporary hotel, so far, starts with Hemi Bawa's lotus artwork at the entrance and ends with a rooftop pool. Extra luxury in the residence rooms; designer shop; upbeat bar and restaurants serving Indian, Italian, and Thai dishes.
(i) 215 🏊 🏋

🏨 TAJ CONNEMARA
🍴 $$$$$
BINNY RD.
TEL 044-6600 0000 OR 044-6600 6600
www.tajhotels.com
The city's only heritage hotel, so far, whose colonial origins reveal themselves in the white stucco columns and the central courtyard where the pool is. Low key, with an excellent buffet restaurant for in-town eating while sightseeing; also visit the bookshop, Giggles.
(i) 150 🏊

🏨 TAJ COROMANDEL
🍴 $$$$$
37 MAHATMA GANDHI RD., NUNGAMBAKKAM
TEL 044-6600 2827
www.tajhotels.com
Guests enjoy notable service in Chennai's's leading hotel that keeps business and holiday travelers happy.

Rooms cater to every need; worth considering the club and executive rooms. Exceptional food, be it at the coffee shop, South India or Szechwan restaurants.
(i) 205 🏊 🏋

🏨 TRIDENT HILTON
🍴 CHENNAI
$$$$
1/24 G.S.T. RD.
TEL 044-2234 4747 OR 044-2334 4747
www.trident-hilton.com
Sited near the airport, this efficient hotel is useful for an overnight stay or pre-flight meal. It is also near Chennai's new business districts—Sriperumbudur, Maram-lianagar, and Guindy, and ten-minutes' drive from Chennai's Trade Center.
(i) 167 🏊 🏋

🏨 AMBASSADOR
🍴 PALLAVA
$$$
30 MONTIETH RD., EGMORE
TEL 044-2855 4476
www.ambassadorindia.com
This unpretentious central hotel, whose spacious but simple heritage rooms each have a separate living area, is suitable for economic business and family travel—there is a squash court and snooker table.
(i) 100 🏊 🏋

🏨 GRT GRAND
🍴 $$$
120 SIR THYAGARAYA RD., T. NAGAR
TEL 044-2815 0500
www.grtgrand.com
The good value, high-quality GRT group's well-located Chennai hotel focuses on what many travelers on a budget want today: good service, unpretentious rooms and food, and a particularly good pool and spa.
(i) 133 🏊 🏋

🏨🍴 SAVERA HOTEL
$$$

146 DR. RADAKRISHNAN RD.,
SALAI
TEL 044-2811 4700
www.saverahotel.com
This large, economic, no-frills
hotel works well for the
budget traveler who is happy
to exchange some comforts
for a very central location.
ⓘ 260 🏊 🏋️

SOMETHING SPECIAL

🍴 SARAVANA BHAVAN

It was Mr. P. Rajagopal, known
affectionately as Annachi, who
in 1981 opened the first
Saravana Bhavan to serve quality
South Indian vegetarian food.
Soon joined by his two sons,
today he serves some 350
different dishes at 20 restaurants
in Chennai (find them by asking
almost anyone!) and around the
world. Spotlessly clean and fast,
smiling service adds to the joy of
the crisp dosas, onion uttapams,
superb sambaar sauces, and
freshly squeezed juices.

$
19 VADAPALANI ANDAVAR,
KOIL ST., VADAPALANI,
AND BRANCHES
TEL 044-483 2671

🍴 GOLDEN DRAGON
$$

TAJ COROMANDEL,
M.G. RD.,
NUNGAMBAKKAM
TEL 044-6600 2827
All the restaurants in this
top-flight hotel are worth a
detour. For formal dinner,
Golden Dragon delivers
authentic Szechwan dishes;
alternatively, there is South
Indian cuisine at Southern
Spice. For a more casual meal,
Match Point has a stunning
buffet lunch that includes
offbeat recipes sought out
by the chef.

🍴 THE VERANDAH
$$

THE TAJ CONNEMARA,
BINNY RD.
TEL 044-6600 0000
Located on the ground floor
overlooking the courtyard,
this is an excellent lunch stop
during sightseeing to enjoy
the extensive buffet that
includes a section of Chennai
dishes. For dinner, consider
the Raintree, the hotel's
outdoor speciality restaurant
devoted to Chettinad cuisine.

🍴 KARAIKUDI
$

84 DR. RADHAKRISHNAN
SALAI, OPPOSITE A.V.M.
RAJESHWARI KALYANA
MANDAPAM
TEL 044-826 9122
Even the waiters in this
elegant and atmospheric
restaurant devoted to
Chettinad cuisine dress the
part in their *panchakacham*
(dhoti tied and tucked with
five folds). Signature dishes
include the Chettiar special
chicken pepper roast and the
pigeon *varuval* (fry).

COVELONG

🏨🍴 FISHERMAN'S COVE
$$$$

COVELONG BEACH,
TEL 044-6741 3333
www.tajhotels.com
Set in lush gardens that
stretch down to the beach,
rooms are in the main
building or, much nicer,
individual cottages and
villas—the nicest ones are
nearest the sea where guests
sleep to the sound of the
water. A good rural base for
Chennai and temple visits.
ⓘ 88 🏊 🏋️

KARAIKUDI

🏨🍴 THE BANGALA
$$$

KARAIKUDI
TEL 04565-220 221 OR
04424-934 851
www.thebangala.com

To explore the great
mansions of the Chettinad
district traders, stay at this
heritage hotel. Its fresh and
immaculate decoration and
its delcious home-cooked
Chettinad food is over
seen by the owner,
Meenakshi, who arranges
visits to the mansions.
ⓘ 12

MADURAI

🏨🍴 TAJ GARDEN RETREAT
$$$

PASUMALAI, NO. 40 TPK RD.
TEL 0452-237 1601
www.tajhotels.com
Originally the hilltop home of
the manager of Coats Cotton.
Guest cottages surround the
original house, now the bar
and billards room, while the
62-acre (25 ha) estate has
mature trees, pool, spa, and
great views over the city.
Excellent food in the
restaurant and barbecue.
ⓘ 63 🏊 🏋️

🏨🍴 HOTEL SANGAM
$$

ALAGARKOIL RD.
TEL 0452-253 7531
www.hotelsangam.com
This well-located, good-value
hotel has a welcome
freshness—light, spacious, and
colorful, with both an indoor
restaurant and a congenial
outdoor one which is popular
with locals.
ⓘ 60 🏊

MAHABALIPURAM (MAMALLAPURAM)

🏨🍴 GRT TEMPLE BAY
$$$

KOVALAM RD.
TEL 044-2744 3636 OR
04114-243 636
www.grttemplebay.com
A great location for visiting
Mahabalipuram's extensive
Pallava sculptures and other
nearby treats. Guests enjoy
lovely thatched cottages
beside the sea and good food
at the indoor and beachside

restaurants. If not staying here, this is an ideal meal stop.

🛈 72 ⬛ 🏥

OOTACAMUND (OOTY)

🏨 SAVOY HOTEL
🍴 $$$

77 SYLKS RD.
TEL 0423-244 4142
www.tajhotels.com
With its English cottage-style rooms built in the 1830–60s and set amid English flowerbeds, the Savoy encapsulates Ooty. Plenty of original furnishings evoke the Raj, and on chilly evenings the staff light a log fire in your living room.

🛈 40 🏥

🏨 SULLIVAN COURT
🍴 $$$

123 SELBOURNE RD.
TEL 0423-244 1415
www.fortuneparkhotels.com
Named after John Sullivan, who founded Ooty in 1861, this modern hotel with conference facilities has sweeping staircases, simple rooms, and scenic views. A reliable base for exploring Ooty and its ravishing surrounding countryside.

🛈 67 ⬛

PONDICHERRY

🏨 LE DUPLEIX
🍴 $$$

5 RUE DE LA CASERNE
TEL 0413-222 6999
www.ledupleix.com
One of several restored 18th-century buildings in Pondicherry, this one has been transformed into a courtyard hotel that mixes historic with dramatic contemporary, for the most part with success. Good atmosphere, with bar and courtyard dining for both residents and visitors.

🛈 14

🏨 THE PROMENADE
🍴 $$$

23 GOUBERT AVE.
TEL 0413-222 7750
www.sarovarhotels.com
This freshly built contemporary boutique hotel stands on Beach Road—which has no beach but directly overlooks the Bay of Bengal. Good public spaces include its rooftop bar and restaurant. Same owner as Le Dupleix (above), so guests can use both hotels' facilities.

🛈 35

🏨 HOTEL DE L'ORIENT
🍴 $$$

17 RUE ROMAIN ROLLAND
TEL 0413-234 3067
www.neemranahotels.com
Pondicherry's first heritage hotel is beautifully restored and furnished by the Neemrana group whose specialty is conservation. It is very intimate, with a delightful central courtyard evocative of the town's French colonial days, serves good Creole cuisine.

🛈 10

THANJAVUR

🏨 HOTEL PARISUTHAM
🍴 $$

POST BOX 86, G.A. CANAL RD.
TEL 04362-231 844
www.hotelparisutham.com
This family-run hotel with simple rooms is just two minutes' drive or a pleasant walk from the great Chola temple. The large pool, spa, and outdoor eating make this a good relaxation package after temple visits.

🛈 52 ⬛ 🏥

🏨 HOTEL SANGAM
🍴 $$

TRICHY RD.
TEL 04362-339 451 OR 04362-239 451
www.hotelsangam.com
Part of the reliable Sangam group, this spacious and bright hotel is within sight of the great Brahadeshwara Temple

built by the Chola. Rooms are practical, and the pool and spa are a quality bonus.

🛈 54 ⬛ 🏥

TIRUCHIRAPALLI (TRICHY)

🏨 HOTEL SANGAM
🍴 $$

COLLECTOR'S OFFICE RD.
TEL 0431-241 4700
www.hotelsangam.com
Although a 20- to 30-minute drive from the great temple town at Srirangam, this hotel is very well run and serves good food. Its staff go to great lengths to keep guests happy. For those staying more than one night, there are some good restaurants at the nearby bus stand.

🛈 60 ⬛

KOLKATA (CALCUTTA)

Bengali food is delicious—always fresh, delicately spiced, and especially good for fish. *Dahi maachh*, malai shrimp, is a delightful dish and well worth asking your hotel to prepare, as

---

HOTELS & RESTAURANTS

it is rarely on the menus. Otherwise, eat it out at the few Bengali restaurants in town—Peerless Inn (next to the Oberoi Grand), Suruchi in Elliot Road, or Kewpies Kitchen on Elgin Lane. And go to a sweetmeat shop to taste Bengal's special delicacies, such as *rossogolla* and *rasmalai*, that have inspired sonnets.

🏨 HYATT REGENCY
🍴 $$$$
JA-1 SECTOR III, SALT LAKE CITY
TEL 033-2335 1234
www.kolkata.regency.hyatt.com
This luxurious hotel is located at Salt Lake City, convenient for the airport and the new business areas but out of downtown historic Kolkata. Guests enjoy Malaysian teak floors in their rooms, three stylish restaurants (all worth a detour for visitors), and a great spa.
ⓘ 235 🏊 🏋

🏨 ITC SONAR BANGLA
🍴 SHERATON & TOWERS
$$$$
1 JBS HALDEN AVENUE, OPPOSITE SCIENCE CITY
TEL 033-2345 4545
www.itcwelcomgroup.in
The super-luxurious, talked-about Sonar Bangla is located by Science City in the new business area, away from downtown Kolkata. Overlooking one of the city's greenest areas, it has a stylish pool, tennis courts, golf putting courses and five elegant restaurants.
ⓘ 238 🏊 🏋

🏨 OBEROI GRAND
🍴 $$$$
15 JAWAHARLAL NEHRU RD., CHOWRINGHEE
TEL 033-2249 2323
www.oberoihotels.com
The grand lady of Calcutta, opened in the 1890s, maintains its style and is one of India's finest hotels today. Perfectly located on Chowringhee beside the Maidan, guests enjoy

beautifully furnished and appointed rooms, and colonial-style public spaces, a bar, and tea.
ⓘ 119 🏊 🏋

🏨 THE PARK KOLKATA
🍴 $$$$
17 PARK ST.
TEL 033-2249 9000 OR 033-2249 3121
www.theparkhotels.com
Well located near the Maidan, the city's traditional clubs, and the buzzing shopping district, the Park is a contemporary, elegant, and lively hotel drawing plenty of locals to its bars, restaurants, and clubs including a very congenial al fresco bar-restaurant.
ⓘ 174 🏊 🏋

🏨 TAJ BENGAL
🍴 $$$$
34B BELVEDERE RD., ALIPORE
TEL 033-2223 3939
www.tajhotels.com
A large hotel in leafy Alipore district of south Kolkata, it seems even larger thanks to the busy 11,000-square-foot atrium and the several popular restaurants—French, barbecue, Bangali, Chinese, Italian, and more. It is geared more for businessmen than tourists.
ⓘ 229 🏊 🏋

🏨 THE KENILWORTH
🍴 $$$
1 & 2 LITTLE RUSSEL ST.
TEL 033-2282 3939
www.kenilworthhotels.com
A Calcutta institution, the Kenilworth opened in 1947 as a guest house but is now a successful, well-run, and good value hotel. Very well located downtown, on Little Russell Street near the Maidan. The staff are friendly and helpful.
ⓘ 105

🏨 LYTTON HOTEL
🍴 $$$
14 & 14/1 SUDDER ST.
TEL 033-2249 1875 OR 033-2249 1872
www.lyttonhotelindia.com

PRICES
HOTELS
An indication of the cost of a double room without breakfast is given by $ signs.
$$$$$ Over $280
$$$$ $160–$280
$$$ $100–$160
$$ $40–$100
$ Under $40

RESTAURANTS
An indication of the cost of a three-course dinner without drinks is given by $ signs.
$$$$$ Over $80
$$$$ $50–$80
$$$ $35–$50
$$ $20–$35
$ Under $20

This small, no-frills hotel is usefully located on Sudder Street off the north end of Chowringhee, and is ideal for those who will spend their days out sightseeing. In addition to its own restaurant, the Oberoi and Peerless hotels are nearby.
ⓘ 80

🏨 FAIRLAWN HOTEL
🍴 $$
13/A SUDDER ST.
TEL 033-2252 1510
www.fairlawnhotel.com
Violet Smith continues her family's long tradition of running this heritage. Guests—often writers—chat in the garden or upstairs lounge, enjoy the simple period rooms, and usually return for a second visit.
ⓘ 20

SOMETHING SPECIAL

🍴 KEWPIES
Reserve a table to experience being in this traditional Calcutta home found down narrow Elgin Lane. You sit in the dining room decorated with family furniture and

pictures and enjoy real Bengali home-cooked thalis following traditional recipes for vegetables, fish, and meat. Remember, Bengali food only tastes really delicious when absolutely fresh, like this.

$$
2 ELGIN LN.
TEL 033-2475 9880

∏ AAHELI
$$
THE PEERLESS INN,
JAWAHARLAL. NEHRU RD.
TEL 033-243 0222
Located in the adjacent hotel to the landmark Oberoi Grand, Aaheli takes Bengali food as seriously as it is possible to do so. Old recipes are sought out and prepared meticulously, then served as a set menu thali with soft drinks to accompany. Reservations essential.

∏ SAFFRON
$$
THE PARK HOTEL, PARK STREET
TEL 033-2249 9000
The totally renovated hotel takes contemporary to its kitchens, too. Dishes from various Indian cuisines are served in the beautiful Saffron dining room. For local ones, try Kolkata *bekti* and Bengali *dab*. And have a pre-dinner cocktail at the hotel's chic bar, Roxy.

∏ TRINCA'S
$$
PARK ST.
TEL 033-2229 7825
Of the several good Park Street restaurants, this one is great for sitting outside over a beer and a simple meal, such as a Thai platter, in the early evening, and enjoying the live bands who follow in the footsteps of Freddie Mercury (who was born in this city).

∏ FLURY'S
$
18 PARK ST.
TEL: 033-229 7664
Despite its makeover and uneven food standards, this old-established Swiss tea house remains a Calcutta institution. Join locals who meet here for a cup of tea or a milk shake and tuck into vegetable patties, pineapple pudding, and chocolate cake.

∏ SURUCHI
$
89 ELLIOT RD., PARK CIRCUS
TEL 033-229 1763
If possible, have your driver or someone kind help you locate this apparently straightforward address. Well worth the effort for delicious and totally authentic, freshly made Bengali lunch; try the fish curries with rice.

BHUBANESWAR

∰ MAYFAIR LAGOON
∏ $$$$
8-B JAYDEV VIHAR
TEL 0674-236 0101
www.mayfairhotels.com
Spread over 10 acres (4 ha), the nicely furnished cottages overlook a lagoon. Guests can enjoy sports including tennis and snooker, and restaurants serve Chinese, Thai, Continental, and roadside dhabar food. Near the Trident (see below), so guests can visit either one for meals.
(ℹ) 64 ⊠ 🏋

∰ TRIDENT HILTON
∏ BHUBANESWAR
$$$$
CB-1 NAYAPALLI
TEL 0674-230 1010
www.trident-hilton.com
A whitewashed, low rise, modern and reliable hotel that makes a well-located base for exploring Orissa's distinctive architecture and villages. Good food and pool for post-sightseeing relaxation.
(ℹ) 62 ⊠ 🏋

BODH GAYA

∰ LOTUS NIKKO
∏ BODHGAYA
$$$
BODHGAYA
TEL 0631-220 0700
www.lotusnikkohotels.com
This is the flagship of Lotus Nikko hotels, located at Buddhist sites. As many Far Eastern pilgrims come here, the restaurant serves both Chinese and Japanese food, and some of the rooms are Japanese style while others are traditional European.
(ℹ) 47

PATNA

∰ MAURYA-PATNA
∏ $$$
SOUTH GANDHI MAIDAN
TEL 0612-220 3040
www.maurya.com
Patna's most upscale hotel—and Bihar state's only five-star hotel—is relatively simple and makes a good base for exploring this ancient city and its historic surroundings.
(ℹ) 80

VARANASI

∰ CLARKS VARANASI
∏ $$$
THE MALL, CANTT
TEL 0542-250 1011
www.clarkshotels.com
Varanasi's oldest quality hotel has large colonial-style rooms with simple furnishings; some have verandas overlooking the gardens.
(ℹ) 113 ⊠

∰ TAJ GANGES
∏ $$$
NADESAR PALACE GROUNDS
TEL 0542-250 3001
www.tajhotels.com
The renovated rooms, friendly staff, and expansive gardens make this a welcome retreat from the intensity of this crowded temple city. Guests can snack poolside or while playing croquet, use the buffet restaurant, or, at night,

HOTELS & RESTAURANTS

eat quality Indian food in Varuna restaurant.
🛈 130 🌊

LUCKNOW

The sophisticated heritage of Uttar Pradesh's state capital is evident in its food—the rich and complex Avadh cuisine includes fine kebabs, *romali rotis* (handkerchief bread), and *dum pukht* (sealed and steam cooked meat and rice). Kebabs and breads from stalls in the old market are delicious.

🏨 TAJ RESIDENCY
🍽 $$$
GOMTI NAGAR
TEL 0522-239 3939
www.tajhotels.com
A palatial hotel fit for a nawab, with plenty of marble and set in 25 acres of gardens. In addition to the bar and café, the Oudhyana restaurant serves the rich local Avadh cuisine.
🛈 110 🌊

THE HIMALAYA

These hotels are useful bases for trekking or exploring an area. Many are historic buildings in beautiful settings. If you are trekking, your travel agent will arrange the modest accommodations or tents.

For hotels in Mussoorie, Nainital, Rishikesh, and Shimla, see pp. 351–353.

DARJILING (DARJEELING)

🏨 GLENBURN TEA
🍽 ESTATE
$$$$
RESERVATIONS: KANAK BUILDING, 41 CHOWRINGHEE RD., KOLKATA
TEL 033-2288 5630
www.glenburnteaestate.com
The third generation of the Prakash family manage their tea garden that was first planted in the 1860s an hour's

drive outside Darjeeling. Guests staying in their four immaculate and beautiful suites can learn about tea-growing, take hikes, bird-watch, and much more.
🛈 4

🏨 CEDAR INN
🍽 $$$
JALAPAHAR RD.
TEL 0354-225 4446
www.cedarinndarjeeling.com
Most rooms in this heritage hotel on Jalapahar Road have great Himalayan views and their own fireplaces, useful when the mist comes down. Guests return from hiking to enjoy the billiards, bar and health club and sitting in the garden enjoying the panoramas.
🛈 22 🏋

🏨 WINDAMERE HOTEL
🍽 $$$
OBSERVATORY HILL
TEL 0354-225 4041
www.windamerehotel.com
Set on Observatory Hill in the town center, this heritage hotel that served English and Scottish tea planters is still a real time-warp; some rooms lack TVs and phones. Guests enjoy the nostalgia that includes porridge for breakfast and, of course, Darjeeling tea.
🛈 46

KAZIRANGA NATIONAL PARK

🏨 WILD GRASS LODGE
🍽 $$$$
KAZIRANGA
TEL 03776-266 2085
www.oldassam.com
This is the ideal place to stay for visiting Kaziranga National Park with its elephant and one-horned rhino. The colonial-style lodge is thoughtfully designed, the food imaginative, the pickles homemade, and guests enjoy knowledgeable naturalists and well-arranged park visits.
🛈 18 🌊

PRICES

HOTELS
An indication of the cost of a double room without breakfast is given by $ signs
$$$$$ Over $280
$$$$ $280– $160
$$$ $100–$160
$$ $40–$100
$ Under $40

RESTAURANTS
An indication of the cost of a three course dinner without drinks is given by $ signs
$$$$$ Over $80
$$$$ $50–$80
$$$ $35–$50
$$ $20–$35
$ Under $20

RIVERBOATS

🏨 RV CHARAIDEW AND
🍽 RV SUKAPHA
$$$$
RESERVATIONS: 1ST FLOOR, MANDOVI APARTMENT, GNB RD., AMBARI
TEL 0361-260 2186
www.assambengalnavigation.com
This Indo-British joint venture runs cruises on Indian rivers. Two boats cruise the Brahmaputra River, pausing at Manas and Kaziranga national parks where they have their own lodges. Another cruises the Hugli from Kolkata, pausing at the monuments. Boats have 12 cabins.
🛈 12

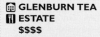 🏨 Hotel 🍽 Restaurant 🛈 No. of bedrooms 🌊 Indoor/🌊 Outdoor swimming pool 🏋 Health club

SHOPPING IN INDIA

Take a tip from second-time visitors to India: Pack an extra duffle bag in the bottom of your suitcase. This is for your inevitable shopping. Indian craftsmanship of almost every kind can be remarkable for its quality and originality, and prices are often lower than in other countries.

If you see something you really want, buy it. If it is specifically local or particularly good, you may not see something similar again. If you have an idea of what you want to buy before you leave home, such as silk furnishing, dress fabrics, or a piece of jewelry to match an outfit, take color swatches with you as the Indian light can confuse the memory. Also, research equivalent prices in your own country to correctly identify bargains.

Shopping opportunities come in various forms: fueled by India's economic boom, boutiques, department stores, and shopping malls are opening all over India every month, some showcasing India's very talented designers. Meanwhile the old established government emporia, run by each state, often in dowdy concrete buildings, should not be ignored. They stock high-quality crafts produced in that state and sell them at fixed prices. They have knowledgeable staff, accept credit cards, and will ship goods (after a bit of form-filling). You do not bargain.

Beware: Do not be seduced by private shops that pose as state-run emporia, giving themselves almost the same title, slipping in words such as "authorized" and "emporium"; they often stock shoddy goods at high prices or nice crafts at outrageous prices.

The hotel shops, unlike many in the West, are often extremely good and are even patronized by discerning locals. Park Hotels have excellent designer in-house shops. Their convenience and their long opening hours compensate for the slightly above average prices; bargaining is perfectly acceptable. Those selling fabric will usually

offer a very fast tailoring service, too; if you are returning to a city, then there is time to order a garment and have a fitting to ensure it is precisely correct.

The markets provide the most shopping fun, even if you only buy small items. A successful purchase demands your own judgment and your own sense of the right cost—remember, however hard you bargain, the trader will always sell for more than cost price.

There are two high-priced items that need special care: carpets and jewelry. Even in a reliable hotel shop, carpet buying should be undertaken with extreme caution. It is wise to research prices at home, compare various local prices, bargain hard and, if making a purchase, sign the carpet on the back, measure it yourself, and take a picture of it. Also get a detailed receipt so that when It arrives home, usually after about three months, you can be sure it is the one you chose.

With few exceptions, stores in deluxe hotels are the safest places to purchase jewelry. Modest buys, either loose or set, include garnets, topazes, amethysts, and black stars, all mined in India. Pearls, sorted and pierced in Hyderabad, are also a good value. A reputable jeweler should always be prepared to give you a certificate of authenticity and be prepared to buy back a piece you later decide you do not want.

The variety of India's fabrics is infinite and impossible to resist. Whether it is a woolen shawl, Karnataka raw silk, or just some dazzlingly bright cotton from Jaipur's market, most people buy something. Silk and cotton are

sold in sari lengths (which vary slightly around the country, so check) or by the meter.

To find out more about traditional master craftspeople, contact Paramparik Karigar, 10 Kumaram, Flat no. 5, Kan Abdul Gaffar Khan Marg, Worli Sea Face, Mumbai, tel 022 56611059, email paramparik@vsnl.net

Note: In Indian law, the sale of an item that is fully paid for by the buyer is deemed to be final. Shopkeepers are not obliged to accept returns. Thus, it is best to think carefully before making a purchase, and if necessary to ask a shopkeeper to reserve an item pending finalizing a purchase.

For the latest designer and high-end outlets' locations and stocks, pick up some of India's many glossy magazines: *Verve* (India's answer to *Vogue* and *Vanity Fair*), *L'officiel-India*, *In Touch with Fashion*, and *Elle—India*. For interiors, seek out *Elle Décor—India*, *Inside Outside*, and *idi* (Indian Design & Interiors).

Here are some shopping ideas, following the areas covered by the chapters of this book. This springboard of ideas will help you get started and include a mixture of markets (called "bazars" in India), government craft shops (known as "emporia") and private stores.

DELHI

For markets, the most traditional are in Old Delhi (pp. 64-67). Around Connaught Place find **Shankar Bazar** (fabrics, cheap tailors), **Palika Bazar** (underground in Connaught Circus), and others.

Delhi is the best place to take advantage of the unglamorous but well-stocked and well-priced government-run emporia. There is **Central Cottage Industries Emporium** on Janpath, opposite the Imperial Hotel, a multistory department store that stocks goods from all over India. Just hunt for what you want; especially for fabrics by the yard/meter. A ten-minute walk away on Baba Kharak Singh Marg are all the individual state emporia where you can focus on, say, Varanasi brocade at the Uttar Pradesh store called **Gangotri.**

Delhi claims to be India's fashion capital. Certainly, it has excellent concentrated shopping areas used by locals, the huge diplomatic corps, and visitors. The following are not too far from the center. Try **Khan Market** for books (**Bahri and Sons**), modest boutiques (**Anokhi**), and general goods (luggage, pharmacy), and nearby **Sunder Nagar** for antique arts and serious textiles. For jewelry, try reliable **Bharany's** at no.14. For designer clothes go to **Santushthi** shopping complex (**Tulsi, Good Earth, Shyam Ahuja,** etc.), and the districts of Hauz Khas (**Ogaan,** etc.), and Mehrauli (**Carma, Ayamik, Malini Ramani**). Visit South Extension Part II for the biggest **FabIndia, Samsara,** and **Orra.** Go to the **Crescent Mall** for India's favorite upscale designers (**Satya Paul, Ritu Kumar, Ranna Gill, Tarun Tahiliani**). Throughout the city, Indian-made leather clothes and goods are worth considering (the Taj's **Khazana, Khan Market,** and **Central Cottage Industries Emporium**).

AROUND DELHI

Most towns are laid back, with local shops and markets to enjoy. But Agra, with its heavy tourism and consequent aggressive shopkeepers, is different. Here, the obvious craft buy is marble inlaid with semiprecious stones, made in ateliers all over the city. It is vital not to confuse this with the cheap, soft soapstone—which can also make a nice gift. For genuine marble inlay work

using genuine semiprecious stones, one of the most reliable stores is the multi-award-winning **Subhash Emporium,** 18/1 Gwalior Road. In addition to traditional designs, they also do the bold, Italian-style work and some contemporary pieces.

RAJASTHAN & GUJARAT

This area is a shopper's paradise for lovers of bright colors, folk art, and tribal textiles. Puppets, embroidered shoes, startlingly bright cloth and jackets, and intricate embroidery are available at low prices as welll as higher for serious collectors who know what they are doing (beware: heavy tourism means some shopkeepers charge high prices).

In Jaipur, find fabrics, bangles, puppets, *bandani* (tie-dyed) cloth and other goods on and around **Johari Bazar, Badi Chopra,** and **Hawar Mahal;** find loose gems on **Gopalji ka Bazar.** Go to MI Road (**Gem Palace, Manglam, Amrapali, Meenu Tholia,** etc). Seek out **Anokhi's** headquarters and cafe and **Leela Bordia's** Jaipur blue pottery, both in **C-Scheme.** Go to **Soma** for contemporary clothes and furnishings, **Hot Pink** in Narain Niwas hotel gardens for colorful high fashion, and **AKFD** opposite the Birla Auditorium for cutting-edge Indian design. Some of the best shawls being woven in Kashmir are sold at exquisite **Andraab's,** 38 Gupta Garden, near Brahampuri police station, on the Jaipur-Amber road just outside Jaipur. At Amber, **Anokhi** block-print has an excellent designer boutique. For big furniture buys, consult **La Voute Exports** in Sanganer.

In Jodhpur, Mehranagah Fort has good boutiques, the multifloor **Maharani Textiles** in the old city has a huge stock, and the new mall on Rani Bagh next to Ajit Bhawan has contemporary fashion (**Tulsi, Anokhi, Amra-**

pali, **Raghu Rathore,** plus Jodhpur crafts).

Udaipur, with so many congenial little shops, has a few specials: in the City Palace square, beside the café, the former ruler's daughter runs **Anshka,** selling items inspired by the royal collection. A branch of **Anokhi** is next door. Two minutes' walk down the main street, on the right, is the warren of rooms that is **Ganesh,** stocking not just fun clothes and fabrics but also museum-quality pieces. **Royal Arts,** on Lake Road, has good fabrics and tailors who can whip up a fitted evening jacket over night. If you visit Devigarh, do not miss their designer boutique—the same is true for **Deogarh's** shop in the palace-hotel compound.

Ahmedabad, an ancient traders' city, is wonderful for shopping. Wander through the old town to find colorful bandani (tie-dye) and other cottons including the distinctive Vadodara block-prints. The **National Institute for Design** has an excellent shop. For books, go to **Art Boo Center** or **Crossways** (where the notable designer fashion store **Bandhej** is in the basement). For quality antique Gujarat, Punjabi, and other textiles, go to **Honeycomb** in the Cama Hotel; they will also help with other dealers for textiles, wooden furniture, etc. If you go into rural Gujarat, buy good embroidery and weaving whenever you see it to support local communities and keep the art alive.

MUMBAI & MAHARASHTRA

Mumbai's ostentatious wealth is served by high-end stores with an alluring buzz. If you stay downtown in the Fort area, explore the some of the very good shops at the Oberoi hotel and the Taj Mahal (**Nalanda** bookstore, the **Indian Textile Co., Joy Shoes,** etc.). Colaba has shoe shops,

Tantra's wacky T-shirts and plenty more, sidewalk stalls, and **Phillips** the reliable, long-established antiques store at the end. Around the synagogue find **Ensemble** (lots of high-end designers) and **FabIndia** (light, cheap cottons). A five-minute walk from the Taj brings you first to **Tarun Tahiliani,** and then **The Courtyard** for a cluster of top designers, very wearable in the West (**Tulsi, Fish Fry, Hot Pink, Rohit Bal,** etc). The keen go further afield to **Kemps Corner, Raghuvanshi Mills Compound, 7 Best Road, Aza, Kimaya, Fuel,** and **Designer Studio.** To buy Parsee embroidery, call Parveez Aggarwal (2352 1337) and arrange a visit. For major jewelry, visit **Dia** and **Gazdar** in the Taj Mahal Hotel, **Tijori** in the Oberoi, or **Moksh, Sat-yani's, Divi, Lalchand, Rose or Jamini Ahluwalia, TBX The Original, Maia,** or **Notandas;** bargain very hard.

Aurangabad note: if you are visiting the caves of Ajanta and Ellora, take note of the revived fine weaving of nearby Paitan, stocked by shops in Aurangabad and along the high roads.

GOA & KERALA

North Goa's seaside shopping reaches a peak of concentration behind Sinquerim, Candolim, and Calangute beaches, outposts of hot young city designers such as **Malini Ramani.**

Kerala, new to mass tourism, is still relatively quieter; most cities have more fresh spices and traditional cream-colored Kerala saris than anything else. Cochi is the exception, where **Jewtown's** spice warehouses are now either "antiques" stores (goods gleaned from all over India; shipping easily arranged) or stocked with run-of-the-mill Rajasthani or Kashmiri products. Exceptions are the bookstores next to the synagogue, the local Catholic nuns or

fishermen's quality embroidery, and, up at the Fort area, some designer boutiques. In Ernakulum, find good silk shops, South Indian jewelry and household stores.

THE DECCAN

Hyderabad is modernizing by the month. However, head for the old Char Minar area for the big bangle bazaar, brass pots, and pearls of all sizes, colors and qualities. Andhra Pradesh state has some of India's finest weavers working in the villages—find local *ikats* in cotton and silk on Tilak Road.

Bangalore's IT and international workforce means high-end fashion shopping like a mini-Mumbai—**QH20, Fflolios, Collage,** etc. And as silk is a state-run industry, this is the place to buy it (plain, wild, stone-washed, chiffon, etc.) at the best prices by the yard/meter and in quantity! Lots of large silk stores line M.G. Road and side roads. You can also find carved local sandalwood and rosewood and chunky Lambani jewelry.

TAMIL NADU

Chennai is a sophisticated shopping city. **Spencers** is the great glitzy mall. Outside the mall, do not miss **FabIndia** and various stylish boutiques often located in heritage buildings, such as **Amethyst** (Sunday Mahal, 14 Padmavathi Rd, Jeypore Colony), which stocks high-end designers and has a garden café. The quality fabric stores have top Kanchipuram silk, Madrasi check, Chettinad weaves, and other Tamil specialities.

Down the coast, Dakshinachitra museum has a good shop; and Pondicherry's phoenix-like rise includes several nice boutiques in heritage houses in the old French quarter, and more in the main town. The **Sri Aurobindo** paper-making factory has glorious stock,

and outside town, **Auroville** has extensive eco-friendly items.

In Mahaballipuram you can commission a granite sculpture to be carved and shipped for your garden; in Thanjavur and Thiruchirapalli bronze ateliers will make you a traditional Nataraja or Parvati and ship it. In Madurai, **Hajeemoosa** stocks all kinds of silk, saris, and linen in its rabbit warren shop opposite Meenakshi Temple's East Tower Gateway; beside it, **Pudumandapam** is a great carved temple hall where local tailors sew garments in a few hours. To see traditional South Indian jewelry, visit **Joy Alukkas** on West Masi Street.

EASTERN INDIA

As Kolkata's fortunes rise, so does its shopping options. In-house hotel shops are increasingly good; as are the small shops on Russell Street in the city center (Ananda has quality Bengali saris and kurtas). For something more dynamic, visit the multistory **Forum** on Lala Lajpat Rai Sarani (Elgin Road)—don't miss **Cima** on the 4th floor, stocking top-quality designer fashions and objects sourced from all over India. For very special dyes and weaves, visit **Kanishka,** 2/1 Hindustan Road, Gariahat; products are dyed locally.

Varanasi is synonymous with silk brocade, known as *baranasi* brocade. Wherever you shop—and it makes little difference, it seems—take some time to learn what brocade is and what makes a good one. Then bargain very hard before you buy. Brass is a good buy here, too.

THE HIMALAYA

India's hills are for relaxing or hiking, not for shopping. Local woollen shawls and walking sticks are good buys.

ACTIVITIES & ENTERTAINMENT

Most people visit India to see its outstanding monuments, experience its fascinating lifestyle, stay in historic hotels, and shop for great crafts. Some visitors may like to spend at least part of their time there taking part in India's two most popular activities: trekking and visiting wildlife sanctuaries and national parks. But India can also offer you plenty of other activities and entertainment to add to your sightseeing. Why not a round of golf in the cool of the morning? Or a visit to a festival performance of dance-drama in the evening?

PERFORMING ARTS

Many artistic performances in India are connected more or less directly to its religions. Although there is plenty going on, it is not always easy to find. Your first stop in a town should be the tourist office where staff are usually very good; some offices even have a printed list of one-off events and festivals (see also the section on festivals pp. 382-85)—a religious festival may well draw top stars in classical music or dance. Tourist offices can book tickets, which are usually modestly priced and readily available; most Indian people do not like to book up their time in advance in the way Western people do. The local English edition of national newspapers such as the *Times of India,* the *Hindustan Times,* the *Indian Express,* the *Asian Age,* or the *Hindu* also list the day's events. Delhi, Mumbai, Bangalore, Chennai, and Kolkata each have their own local events magazines, usually given away free in hotels.

You may expect quality dance, dance-drama, and music to be performed in custom-built halls such as those in Delhi or the Bharat Bhawan in Bhopal. But many top performances are given outside, by or in temples, in ruins, at shrines, in forts, or beneath modest awnings—Delhi's major Ram Lila spectacle is performed on a temporary platform rigged up outside the Red Fort; Chennai's musicians sometimes perform in backstreet gardens. The one place top artists do not like to perform is hotels. Kathakali shows (see p. 207) are a special event in Kerala.

SPORTS & RECREATION

Not only are there plenty of sports in India, they are serviced to a degree rare in the West. Hikers and trekkers have their equipment carried for them, horseback riders have their horses prepared for them, fishermen even have the bait put on the hook for them. In Goa you can enjoy most water sports, while in the lower Himalaya you can ski and river raft.

GOLFING

Golfers are especially well served in India, the first country outside Britain to lay golf courses. The Royal Calcutta Golf Club was founded in 1829. At most clubs visitors are welcome and given temporary membership, and can rent equipment. Spectacularly beautiful courses include Shillong with its wooded dells, Delhi with its Mogul remains, and Gulmarg with a mountain backdrop.

HORSEBACK RIDING

Riders are increasingly well catered to in India, especially at Udaipur and other Rajasthan cities. There are imaginative and well-run expeditions, or you can simply arrange an individual ride when you arrive at your hotel. The adventurous could try a camel ride in a desert area such as Rajasthan. A good travel agent can set up a reliable trip. See p. 337.

SCUBA DIVING

Scuba diving is popular in the Andaman Islands and in Goa. Equipment can be hired from local dive centers, who also run courses from beginner to advanced.

SPECTATOR SPORTS

Indians love to bet, and horse-racing is a favorite source of inspiration. Much of the horse training in India is centered around Bangalore. Here and at Mumbai, Mysore, and Kolkata there are very pretty courses that make an afternoon at the races great fun. So, too, is a polo match. You are most likely to find the latter on a weekend at either Delhi or Jaipur polo grounds.

Cricket, however, is the national obsession. You do not have to understand very much about it; simply enjoy the gentle rhythm of the game. Americans might like to think of it as the ancestor of baseball: Two batsmen take turns defending one of the "wickets" (wooden frames of three uprights and two cross-pieces) from the bowlers of the opposing side. The batsman's aim is to score runs, either by running between the wickets while the ball is out in the field, or by hitting the ball to the boundary (four runs) or over it (six runs). The bowler's aim is to knock down one of the wickets or to cause the batsman to hit the ball into the air where it can be caught by one of the fielding side—that batsman is then "out" and another takes his place. When ten men from one side are all out, the other side bats and the first side fields.

All over India you will see kids putting bat to ball anywhere they can—inside a mosque, on a road, in a field of sugarcane, on a railway siding—even sharing valuable space with another team and having players field for two teams simultaneously.

Other spectator sports are soccer and also field hockey—at which Indians have been champions for decades.

SWIMMING & OTHER WATER SPORTS
Hotels provide some facilities. Many have swimming pools, but these may be closed when there is a big local function using the adjoining terrace. If a pool is important to you, check its availability. Most hotels allow non-guests to use their pools for a small fee (around 550 rupees).

There are long stretches of delightful beaches along India's coasts; Goa in particular is known for its beach resorts. If you are intending to swim in the sea, check carefully for a possible undertow and check that the lifeguard is on the beach when you swim. In areas with few tourists, be sure not to wear a scanty bikini or locals will be upset; put a T-shirt over your usual outfit, and do not go topless.

TENNIS
Some hotels have tennis courts, although their conditions vary, and supply balls and rackets, but keen players should bring their own equipment. Other hotel facilities might include table tennis, badminton, and mini-golf. If the hotel does not have the sports facility you want, the management can usually arrange for you to use a local club.

TREKKING
Trekking can mean a rugged 14-day high-altitude expedition in the Himalaya with a guide and porters or a day hike in the Nilgiri Hills guided by information from the local tourist office.

The toughness of the trek you choose and your own fitness determine the preparation you need to make; age is no barrier. However, if you keep below 11,000 feet (3,360 m) you should need little preparation if you are reasonably fit. In the Himalaya a trek can be a gentle hike with porters and ponies, a climb with just a Sherpa (mountain guide), or a rigorous expedition into the high mountains. Confident and experienced trekkers can arrange a route and porters for themselves, but it is always wise to consult the local tourist office, which will have knowledge of local conditions. Alternatively let the tourist office arrange the trek for you. They should be able to provide an English-speaking leader who will hire porters, deal with problems, and may even be able to tell you something about the history of the area, and about the wildlife that you see on your trek.

For most people it is best to go in a group, organized by a specialist trekking company. This will be more expensive, but such companies have experience of what suits most foreign visitors and have all the necessary back-up should anything go wrong. There are plenty of such companies in India as well as in the U.S. and the U.K. (see p. 337).

It is important that you check your itinerary precisely and do not challenge yourself too much. Ensure you have all your inoculations; mountain air and water may feel healthy but they can carry diseases; and do take malaria prophylactics, even if you are above the transmission cut-off height of 6,500 feet (2,000 m) for most of your trip. As for packing, the less and the lighter the better. Use the expertise of a good mountaineering store to buy all your specialist items, from rucksack to water bottle and boots. Once on your trek, a good Sherpa will ensure you pause to acclimatize as you climb, and will never push you too far. Remember that the Himalaya trekking season can be short and tip generously as your porter may only have a few earning months a year. Your company will advise what is appropriate.

WILDLIFE SANCTUARIES & NATIONAL PARKS
A stay in one of India's many wildlife sanctuaries or national parks may be a highlight of your visit. It is a chance to relax, catch up on your diary, and learn from the usually well-informed guides something about the geography, wildlife, and nature of the extraordinary country you have come to visit. You may arrive thinking only of seeing a tiger, but a successful visit is much more than this.

Park accommodations can be good, although this is not always the case. For a fixed price it usually includes your room and washing facilities, your meals, early morning and afternoon tea, jeep, elephant and boat rides with naturalists as guides (you are not usually allowed to walk in the parks unescorted), and extra nature walks, wildlife films, or talks. Beware of temperature extremes: chilly at dawn and dusk in winter, blisteringly hot at noon in summer.

Best viewing is from March to June, the pre-monsoon period when the animals have less choice of water holes. Do not wear brightly colored clothing; wear a hat; take good binoculars, a camera, and 400 or 800 ASA film; use a cushion or back-pillow for rides in jeeps. Take great notice of your guide's safety instructions. Tipping on departure is important. Consult with the lodge manager for appropriate sums and distribution; tipping is sometimes distributed evenly for fairness.

Beware: some parks now have so many visitors that numbers are restricted and some areas may be closed. This is especially likely in late December and may seriously affect game and bird viewing. Some of India's best park lodges are listed in the hotels section of this book.

FESTIVALS IN INDIA

Traveling through India, you will almost certainly bump into a festival. It may be a small village celebration with the temple deity dressed up and enthroned in a field surrounded by drummers, pipers, a small fair, and some cows with brightly painted horns. It may be a wedding procession, with dancing through the town's back-streets to the accompaniment of a brass band and fancy chandeliers powered by a mobile generator. It may be an arts festival, such as the Bharata Natyam dance season in Chennai. Or you may happen to be in the right place at the right time for one of the great Hindu festivals, such as Durga Puja in Kolkata or Diwali in Rajasthan. Whatever it is, Indian people will welcome your joining them.

Fortunately, many of the most spectacular festivals are held during the cooler winter months when visitors tend to time their India trips. Here is a tiny selection of month-by-month suggestions for especially colorful festivals to look out for. The state where the festival is held (or, for nationwide festivals, the best place to witness each) is given after the name, if relevant; the specific date is given if there is one. Since many festival dates are determined by the lunar calendar, even some of the major festivals can vary their dates from year to year. Other festivals may be arranged with little warning, such as the elephant ones in Kerala. You should check for major dates with the Government of India Tourist Office before you leave home, and then check at local tourist offices to see what is going on as you move around India. Also, beware that apart from such major festivals as Republic Day, when everything closes across the country, such things as closures of local forts or museums at festival times are often unpredictable, so be flexible.

JANUARY

Feast of the **Reis Magos** or Three Kings, Goa, January 6.
Elaborate processions at Cansaulim, Chandor, and Reis Magos churches.

Elephant March, Kerala.
Over 100 caparisoned elephants parade from Trissur to

Thiruvananthapuram over three days, during which snake boat races are held at Alappuzha. The spectacular fourth-day finale involves many otherwise hard-to-see regional Kerala dances and displays of Kalariphayat (local martial arts).

Pongal, Tamil Nadu, mid-January.
This is the celebration of the rice harvest, and is southern India's most important festival. It is at its most colorful in Tamil Nadu where four days of celebrations start with houses and bullocks being scrubbed and painted, and women drawing kolams (elaborate rice patterns) outside their doors. On Pongal, the first dish of newly harvested rice is boiled up with sugarcane and turmeric—according to tradition the more the boiling mixture froths and spills over the pot, the better the next harvest will be. The next day, the bullocks, with their long horns newly painted, are garlanded and raced through the villages by young men.

Delhi Rose Show, Delhi.
An impressive show with serious judges and proud winners, held against the backdrop of Safdarjang's grand tomb.

Kite Festival, northern India, mid-January.
Flimsy, brightly colored paper kites are flown by people of all ages. Kite battles are staged from the rooftops, and for these the kite strings are coated with

crushed glass and gum to turn them into lethal weapons for their handlers to use against their opponents' kites.

Lori, Punjab, mid-January.
Music and dancing to celebrate the height of winter.

Republic Day, nationwide, January 26.
India's principal national holiday celebrates the inauguration of the Republic of India and the adoption of its constitution in 1950. Celebrations are most dramatic in New Delhi, where the president's bodyguard leads a spectacular morning-long public parade of state floats, dancers, camels, elephants, and military equipment. Tickets are on sale at travel agencies, tourist offices, and hotel bell desks. All the events are televised country-wide. Each evening during the week, Rastrapati Bhawan (see p. 86) is illuminated and, once the visiting foreign dignitaries have left Delhi, its spectacular Mughal Gardens are open to the public for about six weeks.

Folk Dance Festival, Delhi, January 27–28.
The capital's public halls are filled with performances of colorful and fascinating dances from all over India.

Beating the Retreat, Delhi, January 29.
A brief but impressive ceremony held at sunset at the bottom of Raisina Hill. Massed bands parade, camels stand at attention on the ramparts, and the Last Post is sounded by a lone trumpet from one high pavilion as the north star comes out. Fireworks then burst into the sky. This, like the Republic Day celebrations, is televised. A few tickets are on sale.

JANUARY–FEBRUARY

Teepam, Madurai.
Known as the Floating Festival, this celebrates the birthday of

the 17th-century ruler Tirumala Nayak. Temple deities are dressed up in silk, garlands, and jewelry, and paraded to the city's large tank. Here, they are put on barges that are pulled through the water, accompanied by plenty of music and chanting.

Desert Festival, Jaisalmer.
First held in 1979, this is a good chance to see some camel polo and races, and some traditional Rajasthani dance, music, and crafts.

Nagaur Fair, Nagaur, near Jodhpur.
This is one of India's biggest livestock fairs, and now augments its traditional trading with dance and entertainment for visitors.

Ulsavom, Ernakulum.
The 8-day festival at Shiva Temple includes an elephant procession, dance, and music.

FEBRUARY

Tansen Music Festival, Delhi.
There are, in fact, two festivals honoring this great musician who was part of the Mogul emperor Akbar's court; the other is held at his home city, Gwalior, in December (see p. 385). Tansen helped to develop and elaborate the stately *dhrupad* form of Hindustani classical vocal and instrumental music, as well as the particular *Gwalior gharana* form of singing. At both festivals, some of India's greatest musicians play for several days and nights.

Dhrupad Music Festival, Delhi and Varanasi.
A chance to hear top musicians who have mastered northern India's demanding and complex classical music. Look out for other classical music and dance arts festivals in Delhi this month.

Delhi Flower Show, Delhi.
Spectacular blooms of all colors and sizes, from marigolds to gladioli and chrysanthemums, are on show at Purana Qila. Around this time, the fiercely competitive gardens created on Delhi's many roundabouts are judged and signs indicate the proud winners.

FEBRUARY–MARCH

Shivratri, nationwide.
Devotees of Shiva spend the whole night worshiping their deity, and major Shiva temples are alive with *puja*, music, bell ringing, processions, and chanting. Good places to witness this include Chidambaram, Khajuraho (which holds a 10-day-long fair), Mandi, Ramaswaram, Udaipur (and Eklingji), and Varanasi.

Holi, Rajasthan and Mathura.
Although this festival is to an extent celebrated across India, Rajasthan is the place to experience it. The festival marks the arrival of spring and the triumph of good over evil. Homes are cleaned, and bonfires sizzle with unwanted possessions. On Holi eve, the first dish of lentils is singed in the communal bonfire, then eaten ceremoniously at home. On the day of Holi itself, social rules are suspended until noon while men and women flirt, dance through the streets, and play holi by squirting pink water at one another and throwing handfuls of pink, red, and mauve powder. Children, elders, and visitors join in the state-wide party—but be sure to wear old clothes. At Mathura and its surrounding villages—associated with Krishna—the celebrations are equally intense and include plays acting out Krishna's life.

Carnival, Goa.
For the four days before Lent, this informal, open-air fancy dress party focuses on a different city each day: Panaji, Margao, Mapusa, and Vasco. Everyone is welcome to join in the celebrations with the processions, dancing, bands, barbecues, and floats that fill city and village streets and continue as all-night beach parties.

MARCH

Khajuraho Dance Festival, Kajuraho.
Each evening for a week, top dancers perform India's classical dances such as Kathak in front of the illuminated western group of temples (see pp. 112–13).

MARCH–APRIL

Gangaur, Udaipur.
Rajasthan's important spring festival, celebrated about two weeks after Holi and best seen at Udaipur. Gauri (a name sometimes used for Shiva's wife, Parvati) is the goddess of abundance and fertility. Women pray in temples to painted images of her, asking for bliss and faithfulness in marriage. Then, dressed in yellow, they parade these images down to Lake Pichola to give them a ceremonial bath, singing all the way. The same festival is celebrated in Bengal and Orissa, where it is called Doljatra.

Mahivir Jayanti, Gujarat.
Jains remember Mahavira, the 24th Tirthankara and founder of their religion, with special pilgrimages to sacred sites such as Palitana. Celebrations also occur at Ranakpur and Shravanabelagola.

Lent Procession, Goa.
The Procession of All Saints of the Franciscan Third Order is held on the Monday after Palm Sunday at St. Andrew's Church, Velha. Over 20 figures of saints are paraded around the streets on decorated floats, a tradition begun in the 17th century.

Hindu New Year, nationwide, April 13.
An official public holiday, with local fairs.

APRIL–MAY

Minakshi Kalyanam, Madurai.
The vast and warrenlike Minakshi temple is thronged with the faithful, who spend ten days celebrating the marriage of Minakshi (a name for Parvati) to Shiva. It ends with a great procession of deities on a huge *rath.* More impressive and inclusive than the similar and better known Puri festival.

Baisakhi, northern India.
This spring festival is celebrated with particular fervor in the hills, with dancing among the almond blossoms of the orchards and in the green wheat fields of the Punjab. There Sikhs also celebrate Guru Gobind Singh's forming of the faithful into Khalso (the pure one) in 1689.

MAY–JUNE

Buddha Purnima, Bodh Gaya.
Celebrated on full-moon night at all sacred Buddhist sites, to remember Buddha's birth, enlightenment, and attainment of nirvana. This is a particularly intense experience at Bodh Gaya, where Buddha received enlightenment.

JUNE–JULY

Hemis Setchu, Leh.
Crowds of locals dressed in their traditional garments watch the two-day pageant that includes wonderful *chaam* dances performed with crashing cymbals and thundering drums, and lamas dressed in silk and ghoulish masks performing mime dance-dramas from Buddhist mythology. The festival ends with a symbolic triumph of Buddhism over ignorance. Every 12 years (next time 2016) the *gompa's* prize *thanka* (painted scroll) is unwound and hung across the entire facade of the building.

JULY–AUGUST

Teej, Rajasthan.
If you have suffered from the pre-monsoon heat and humidity of Rajasthan, you will empathize with locals who celebrate the onset of the monsoon with singing, dancing, and playing on garlanded swings. The women wear striped green veils. The moment also remembers the reunion of Shiva and Parvati, and at Jaipur caparisoned elephants escort Parvati's image and crowds of faithful worshippers from her parents' symbolic home to her husband's.

AUGUST

Independence Day, nationwide.
This is a public holiday across the country in remembrance of the midnight hour on August 14–15, 1947 when Viceroy Lord Mountbatten handed over power to Jawaharlal Nehru and independent India was born. In Dehli each year, the prime minister makes a televised speech from the ramparts of the Red Fort, and Rastrapati Bhavan is illuminated.

AUGUST– SEPTEMBER

Janmashtami, Vrindaban.
Celebrations of Krishna's birthday are best seen in the villages associated with his mythical, flirtatious, and eventful youth, particularly in Vrindaban, just south of Mathura. Here, temple festivities include the lyrical *ras lila* dances which are performed in circles just as they appear in miniature paintings, where Krishna is pictured with his consort, Radha.

Onam, Kottayam.
Kerala's harvest festival and new year are rolled into one for a celebration that lasts for a week leading up to full-moon day. Amid the feasting and dancing,

its highlight is the series of snake boat races held on the back-waters, especially those at Kottayam. Fiercely competitive teams of up to 100 members each row their long, narrow, dug-out boats. The men sing and shout war cries while their fast paddling is kept in time by a man pounding a wooden pole.

SEPTEMBER

Ganpati, Mumbai.
The elephant-headed god of good fortune and prosperity is eminently suited to money-making Mumbai, where his festival brings the city to a standstill. More than 6,000 gaudily painted clay images are made annually, the large ones for factories who display them on top of lorries. Ten days of celebration begin with pujas performed to smaller images in homes and on street corners. On full-moon day, citizens parade their idols down to Chowpatty beach, which is already adorned with multi-colored Ganesh sand-sculptures, amid much dancing, singing, and throwing of pink powder. Finally, the people give up the images to the water and watch them bob out to sea and disintegrate.

SEPTEMBER– OCTOBER

Dussehra, nationwide.
A countrywide celebration of good over evil, which is particularly elaborate in certain cities. In the north, celebrations focus on Rama's defeat of the demon Ravana to save his wife Sita. In Delhi, classical and contemporary plays, dance, and music fill every hall; special nightly play cycles recount the *Ramayana;* and in Old Delhi there are processions and spectacular open-air *Ramayana* shows. In Varanasi, a month of nightly Ram Lila plays and music, each in a different venue, ends with a huge procession and continuous temple readings of

the epic. In Kolkata, where the festival is called Durga Puja, celebrations take over the city for three weeks and focus on Durga, destroyer of evil: Here huge, brightly painted and tinsel-decorated images, made throughout the year, are set up in the streets, and Bengalis visit them on nightly promenades, enjoying plenty of dance, music, and theater until the final day when the images are taken through the decorated streets down to the Hooghly and immersed in the water. At Mysore, this festival is called Dassera and focuses on Chamundeswari's triumph over the demon Mahishasura: Ten days of medieval pageantry and classical and folk dance and drama end with a sumptuous procession and fireworks.

OCTOBER–NOVEMBER

Diwali, nationwide.
This nationwide festival is best seen in the north of the country. About four weeks after Dussehra, Diwali celebrates the return of Rama with his rescued wife, Sita, to his capital city, Ayodhya. Tiny terra-cotta oil lamps symbolically light the way for the couple while also welcoming Lakshmi, goddess of wealth, to the new Hindu financial year (not to be confused with the Hindu New Year on April 13), ending with late-night fireworks. This is a time for families to come together, for giving boxes of sweetmeats, and for going to special cultural events.

NOVEMBER

Sonepur Fair, Patna.
Held just outside the city on the banks of the Ganga, this centuries-old, month-long fair claims to be the world's largest agricultural fair. India's longest station platform allows for trainloads of livestock to be transported here. Starting on

full-moon day, this is the place to see cows, horses, parrots, goats, and often more than a hundred elephants traded. All kinds of agricultural seeds, plants, and equipment are also sold.

Nanak Jayanti, Amritsar.
The birthday of Guru Nanak, founder of the Sikh religion, is celebrated by Sikhs, especially at the Golden Temple in their holy city, Amritsar.

Desert Festival, Bikaner.
This Rajasthan city's desert festival is more modest and less crowded than that in Jaisalmer during February.

NOVEMBER–DECEMBER

Pushkar Cattle Fair, Pushkar.
This was once just a cattle fair, full of natural interest and charm. It is now almost drowned by tourists and their requisite shopping opportunities.

DECEMBER

Tansen Music Festival, Gwalior.
See February (p. 383).

DECEMBER–JANUARY

Chennai Dance and Arts Festival, Chennai.
Four weeks of nightly performances by the country's top classical musicians and dancers, often in deceptively informal settings of simple white awnings in backstreets. A superb opportunity if you are touring southern Indian temples, since the music and dance you see now was developed in the temples and originally only performed in them. Tickets can be bought at the tourist office on arrival at the city.

Kumbh Mela
This great religious cleansing festival is held every three years in one of four places

consecutively: Allahabad, Nasik, Ujjain, and Haridwar—it is at Haridwar in 2010. According to legend, each of these cities is located where a drop of nectar was spilled by Vishnu, thus allowing the devout to cross from this world into that of the gods. Literally millions of Hindu pilgrims and holy men gather for their holy bath, stimulating the arrival of fairs, stalls, and entertainers. Foreign visitors are beginning to take a keen interest in the Kumbh Mela, but facilities are simple and hygiene not always good.

Mohini Alankaram, Tiruchchirappalli.
The huge, rambling Sri Ranganathaswamy Temple fills with the faithful, temple elephants, and worship of all sorts for this festival. Two other festivals are also held here at around the same time: Vaikunta Ekadasi and the Car Festival.

MUSLIM FESTIVALS

Muslim festivals move right around the year and are celebrated with feasts, fairs, fine literature, and revelry. The best places to witness them are the old Muslim centers such as Lucknow, Old Delhi, Hyderabad, and Ahmedabad. The principal ones are:

Id-ul-Fitr (also called **Ramzan-Id**)
Celebrates the end of 30 days of fasting during Ramadan.

Id-ul-Zuha (also called **Bakr-Id**)
Commemorates Abraham's attempted sacrifice of his son.

Muharram
Lasting for ten days, this commemorates the martyrdom of Mohammed's grandson, Imam Hussain, and is best seen at Lucknow where *tazias* (replicas of Hussain's tomb) are paraded by mourning men, accompanied by drummers.

GLOSSARY

English is the connecting language of India, and used by the travel industry, hotel staff, shops, guides and, usually, drivers. You do not need a phrase book for Hindi, the predominant language of northern India, nor for the languages of other areas; even if you go right off the beaten track you are likely to have a guide or driver who will translate. However, it is useful to know the meanings of some everyday words, some words to do with India's religions, and some unfamiliar uses of English words. Words related to food can be found at the front of the book on p. 24.

A
adivasi tribal person
agarbati incense
ahimsa non-violence
apsaras heavenly nymphs who seduce men and escort gods
arak liquor distilled from coconuts or rice
ashram spiritual retreat; center for yoga and meditation
auto-rickshaw two-seater scooter-powered taxi
avatar incarnation of a god, especially Vishnu
ayurveda ancient system of medicine
ayyanar large terra-cotta images of deities

B
baba term of respect for old man
bagh garden
baksheesh bribe to get service; tip to reward service; gift to beggar
Balarama brother of god Krishna
baoli (or *vav*) stepped water well, often elaborately decorated
bandhana tie-dye craft
banyan huge fig tree, often with drooping lateral roots
bazar market, market-place
beedi small, hand-rolled cigarette
betel leaf or nut that is an ingredient of paan
Bhagavad Gita Song of the Lord, see p. 76
Bhagavata Purana Hindu epic, see p. 76
bhakti emotional religious devotion
bharata natyam classical dance of Tamil Nadu
bhavan house
Bhumi earth goddess
bindi (bindu) fashion decoration on a woman's forehead
bodhi enlightenment; pipal tree, see p. 58

Bodhisattva Buddhist saint who shows others the way
Brahma Creator of the universe; head of the Trimurti (Hindu Trinity) of Brahma, Vishnu and Shiva; Saraswati is his consort/daughter; Hamsa, the goose, is his vehicle
brahman highest Hindu caste group, the teachers and priests, see p. 54
Buddha The Enlightened One, see p. 58
burqa body-covering garment worn by orthodox Muslim women

C
cantonment military area of a town
caste broad Hindu social status at birth; see also p. 29
cenotaph tomb
chaat snack
chai tea
chaitya Buddhist shrine
chappals sandals
char bagh garden divided into four symmetrical parts
charpoi string bed with wooden-frame
chhatri tomb, mausoleum, cenotaph, domed pavilion
choli blouse worn with sari
chorten see *stupa*
chowk crossroads; courtyard
chowkidar watchman, caretaker
coolie porter, laborer
crore 10 million
curd yogurt, also called *dahi*

D
dargah Muslim saint's tomb
darshan for Hindus, the merit-winning glimpse of a deity
deepastambha lamp tower
deva god
devi goddess
dhabba roadside café
dhal pulses, especially lentils

dharma religious and social duty (Hindu); Buddha's teachings (Bhuddist)
dhobi laundry
dhoti white cloth worn by men
dhurrie flat-weave rug
dikpalas guardians of the four directions, often sculptures at temple doorways
diwan chief minister
diwan-i-am public audience hall
diwan-i-khas private audience hall
dowry agreed marriage gifts from bride's family to groom's family
Dravidian culture of Southern India, derived from Dravidadesh, the former name for Tamil Nadu
dupatta Muslim woman's veil
durbar government meeting/hall
Durga malevolent aspect of the goddess Parvati

E
emporium shop, often large and selling local crafts

F
feni an alcoholic drink made in Goa by distilling coconut or cashew fruit
fresco a method of painting using colors ground in water, laid on the wall or ceiling while the plaster is still wet

G
gadi throne
gandharvas Indra's heavenly musicians
Ganesh elephant-headed god of learning and good fortune, son of Shiva and Parvati
garbha griha womb of a Hindu temple
garh fort (see also *kot, qila*)
Garuda eagle or mythical sunbird, vehicle of Vishnu
ghaghra skirt
ghat step; stepped mountains
ghazal Urdu song
ghee clarified butter
godown warehouse
gompa monastery
gopi young cowgirls who play with Krishna
gopura temple gateway with tapering tower
guru teacher, mentor
gurudwara Sikh place of worship

gymkhana social club with good sports facilities

H
haj Muslim pilgrimage to Mecca
haldi turmeric
Hanuman the monkey god, Rama's ally in the *Ramayana*
Hanti Panchika's (q.v.) consort
harijans children of God, Gandhi's word for untouchables; see p. 29
haveli courtyard house (mansion)
Hinayana Lesser Vehicle, the Buddhist sect that spread to Sri Lanka, Burma, and Thailand
hookah cooling water pipe for smoking tobacco
howdah elaborate elephant saddle

I
imam Muslim teacher/leader
Indra god of rain and thunder
ITDC India Tourism Development Corporation

J
jali pierced screen
Jangha body of a Hindu temple
jatakas tales about Buddha's life and teachings
-ji name suffix to show respect
Jihad justified holy war for Muslims
jina Jain tirthankara/saint
johar mass self-immolation by women after war defeat

K
Kali fearsome goddess of destruction, an aspect of Parvati
kailasha mountain abode of the gods
karma idea that deeds in previous existences determine one's status at rebirth
kasti wrestling
Kartikeya god of war, son of Shiva and Parvati, also known as Skanda or Subramanya
katcha no good, opposite of pukka
kathak classical dance of N. India
kathakali dance-drama of Kerala
khadi hand-spun and woven cotton
kolam a ritual pattern created using colored rice flour

kot fort (see also *garh, qila*)
Krishna blue-skinned human incarnation of Vishnu
kshatriya warrior caste, see p. 29
kumkum red mark on forehead worn by married women
kurta man's loose-fitting shirt

L
lakh 100,000
Lakshmi goddess of wealth and good fortune, consort of Vishnu
lingam Shiva's phallic emblem symbolizing energy
lunghi similar to dhoti, often colored

M
machan watchtower (hide) in a wildlife park
madrasa Islamic school, often in mosque
Mahabharata Hindu epic, see p. 76
mahal palace
maharaja great king
maharani great queen
Mahatma great soul; epithet of Gandhi
Mahayana Great Vehicle, the Buddhist sect that spread to China, Japan, and Tibet
mahout elephant keeper/driver
maidan large open space
makara aquatic monster, often symbol of sea god or of River Ganga
mala garland
mandala religious diagram
mandapa hall, porch
mandir temple
mantra sacred verse
marg road
masala mixture, as in spices for cooking
masala dosa rice pancake stuffed with vegetables
masjid mosque
mela festival
memsahib term of respect for Western woman
mendhi henna
mihrab prayer niche of a mosque, with *qibla* (indicator) for the direction of Mecca
mimbar mosque's pulpit
minaret tower the faithful are called to prayer from a mosque's minaret

mithuna amorous couple, as in temple sculpture
moksha blissful release from rebirth
monsoon rainy season, see p. 20
mudra hand gestures in rituals, dance, and art (Hindu, Jain); teachings of Buddha (Buddhist)
muezzin man calling Muslims to prayer
muggu colored rice flour
mullah Muslim teacher/scholar

N
naga snake
nala mountain stream, gorge
namaste word of respectful greeting
natak dance
natya drama
nawab Muslim prince
nirvana blissful state when personal identity is extinguished

O
om symbol for the origin of all things

P
paan betel (q.v.) nut and sweet/sour condiments wrapped in a leaf and chewed as a digestive
padma lotus
paise 100th of a rupee
pajama man's baggy trousers
palanquin covered couch carried by servants (litter)
palo decorated end of a sari
Panchika guardian of the earth's treasures (Buddhist)
parikrama ritual walk clockwise round a temple/shrine
Parsee Zoroastrian, see p. 60
Parvati goddess of peace and beauty, symbol of female energy, malevolent aspects include Devi, Kali, and Durga; consort of Shiva
pietra dura patterned stone inlay
pilo head veil
pol gate
prasad food offered in a temple, blessed, then shared by devotees
puja worship
pukka correct
Puranas ancient myths and legends, see p. 76

purdah the practice of women living separately from men, and covering their heads with veils in public

Q

qawwali devotional songs of Muslim *Sufis* (q.v., see p. 60)

qila fort; other words for fort include *garh, kot*

R

ragamala series of music themes, poems or art iconography related to a specific mood, each called a raga or ragini

raj rule The Raj was British imperial rule 1858–1947

raja ruler, king

Rajput kshatriya sub-caste that dominated north and west India

Rama incarnation of the god Vishnu, hero of the *Ramayana*; brother of Bharata and Lakshmana; his wife is Sita

Ramayana Hindu epic, see p. 76

rangoli geometric pattern of rice powder

rath chariot for parading temple deities

S

sadhu Hindu holy man free from caste or family ties

sagar lake, ocean

sahib term of respect for a man

salwar kameez baggy trousers and long shirt worn by women

samadhi site of Hindu saint's death or burial

samsara the spirit's movement across the generations enduring a cycle of rebirths, whose liberation is nirvana or moksha

sangam academy

sangeet music

sannyasi homeless ascetic; final stage of a Hindu's life

sarai inn, originally on the trade routes

Saraswati goddess of knowledge, music, arts; daughter or consort of Brahma

sari length of fabric worn by women

Sat truth, the Sikh idea of God revealed through the gurus

sati a widow's honorable self-immolation, often on her husband's funeral pyre

satya truth

satyagraha grasping truth; Gandhi's campaign of non-violent protest

scheduled castes official name for untouchables (q.v.)

sepoy Indian soldier in European service

serai medieval equivalent of a motel

Seven Sacred Cities Varanasi, Haridwar, Ujjain, Mathura, Ayodhya, Dwarka, and Kanchipuram are sacred pilgrimage centers for Hindus

Shaivite worshipper of Shiva

shakti life force

shastra Hindu treatise

Sherpas Nepalese people renowned as high-altitude mountaineers

Shesha serpent on whom Vishnu reclines on the Cosmic Ocean

shikar hunting

shikara tapering temple tower

Shiva (Siva) The Auspicious, third member of the Hindu Trinity, symbol of destructive and creative energy, manifested in Nataraj (Lord of the Dance), etc.; consort Parvati, sons Ganesh and Kartikeya; vehicle Nandi the bull; emblem the lingam

Sita wife of Rama

shri title of respect

shudra laborer caste, see p. 29

singh lion

stupa Buddhist funerary mound signifying Buddha's presence

Surya god of the sun; Arjuna, symbol of dawn, is his charioteer

swami title of holy man

swaraj self-rule, Gandhi's word for independence

T

tandoor clay oven

tank water reservoir, artificial lake

tazia multi-colored tinsel, silver or brass replicas of Hussain's tomb, paraded at the Muslim festival of Muharram

tempera a method of painting on plaster or chalk with powder colors mixed with the yolk or white of egg, often used on internal walls

thangka scroll painting

tilak red dot priest puts on the forehead during worship

Tirthankara ford-makers, the 24 Jain saints and teachers

thali platter, usually used for vegetarian meals

tiffin light meal

tiffin can lunch box

tulsi basil

U

uba dando straight rod

untouchable lowest strata of Hindu society; see also *harijan* (q.v.) and p. 30

urs Muslim saint's festival

V

vahana deity's vehicle

Vaishnavite worshipper of Vishnu

vaishya merchant caste, see p. 29

vav see *baoli*

vedas Hindus' sacred early texts

vihara Buddhist or Jain monastery

vimana principle temple or central shrine of a Hindu temple; tower above temple

Vishnu The Preserver, second member of the Hindu Trinity; symbol of preservation to maintain the balance of the universe; incarnations include Rama and Krishna; consort Lakshmi; vehicle Garuda

W

wallah fellow, e.g. dhobi-wallah

wazir chief minister

Y

yatra pilgrimage

yoga psycho-physical discipline involving the practice of meditation, exercise positions, and breathing control to achieve spiritual peace

yoni symbol of the female sexual organ, often depicted in a temple as a circular shape surrounding a central lingam (q.v.)

Z

zenana women's quarters

CREDITS

ILLUSTRATIONS CREDITS

Illustrations credits
Abbreviations for terms appearing below:
(t) top; (b) bottom; (l) left; (r) right; (c) center

Cover (l), Photographer's Library. (c), Images Colour Library. (r), Gettyone/Stone. Spine, Gettyone/Stone. 1, Wolfgang Kaehler. 2/3, Andrea Booher/Gettyone/Stone. 4, Catherine Karnow. 9, Steve McCurry/National Geographic Society. 11 & 12/13, Joe McNally/National Geographic Society. 14/15 & 16/17, Steve McCurry/National Geographic Society. 18/19, Hans Georg Roth/Corbis. 21, R. Ian Lloyd Productions. 22/23, Steve McCurry/National Geographic Society. 25, Bennett Dean/Eye Ubiquitous. 27, David Cumming/Eye Ubiquitous. 28/29, Steve McCurry/Magnum Photos. 30, Steve McCurry/National Geographic Society. 31 & 33, Anne & Bury Peerless Picture Library. 34/35, Wolfgang Kaehler. 36, Maxine Cass. 37, Anne & Bury Peerless Picture Library. 38, Wolfgang Kaehler. 41, Art Directors & Trip Photo Library. 43, Gettyone/Stone. 44/45, Mary Evans Picture Library. 47, By Courtesy of the National Portrait Gallery, London. 48/49, Royal Geographical Society, London. 50, Hulton Getty Picture Collection Ltd. 50/51 & 52, Steve McCurry/National Geographic Society. 53, Raghu Rai/Magnum Photos. 55, Steve Jones/Axiom. 56/57, Steve McCurry/National Geographic Society. 58, Art Directors & Trip Photo Library. 59, Steve McCurry/National Geographic Society. 61, Dinodia Photo Library. 62, AA Photo Library/D. Corrance. 64/65, Peter Sanders Photography. 66, Mecky Fögeling/travimage.com. 67, www.copix.co.uk. 68, Mecky Fögeling/travimage.com. 69t, Steve McCurry/National Geographic Society. 69b, Jeremy Horner/Corbis. 70, Wolfgang Kaehler. 70/71, Peter Sanders Photography. 72, C. Wormald/Art Directors & Trip Photo Library. 73, AA Photo Library/D. Corrance. 74, www.copix.co.uk. 76/77, AA Photo Library/D. Corrance. 77, John D. McHugh/AFP/Getty Images. 78, T. Bognar/Art Directors & Trip Photo Library. 80, Maxine Cass. 81, Eye Ubiquitous/Hutchison. 82, Anne & Bury Peerless Picture Library. 83t, Gerald Cubitt. 83b, SuperStock Ltd. 84/85, Peter Sanders Photography. 85, AA Photo Library/D. Corrance. 86, Victoria & Albert Museum, London/Bridgeman Art Library. 87, National Museum of India, New Delhi, India/ Bridgeman Art Library. 88 & 89t, René Burri/Magnum Photos. 89c, F. Good/Art Directors & Trip Photo Library. 89b, David Forman/Eye Ubiquitous. 90/91, John Elk III. 92, Images Colour Library. 93, Bennett Dean/Eye Ubiquitous.

94, Eye Ubiquitous. 96/97, Wolfgang Kaehler. 98, AA Photo Library/D. Corrance. 99, Robert Holmes. 100/101, Steve McCurry/National Geographic Society. 102l, David Cumming/Eye Ubiquitous. 102r, Raghu Rai/Magnum Photos. 103l, AA Photo Library/D. Corrance. 103r, Robert Holmes. 104 & 105t, Terry Harris. 105b, Wolfgang Kaehler. 106, Gerald Cubitt. 107, M. Powles/Eye Ubiquitous. 108, Eye Ubiquitous/Hutchison. 109, Steve McCurry/Magnum Photos. 110 & 111, Robert Harding Picture Library. 112/113, Dinodia Photo Library. 113, Art Directors & Trip Photo Library. 114 & 115, Eye Ubiquitous/Hutchison. 116, Art Directors & Trip Photo Library. 117, Dinodia Photo Library. 118/119, Wolfgang Kaehler. 120, Dinodia Photo Library. 122/123, Bennett Dean/Eye Ubiquitous. 123, H. Rogers/Art Directors & Trip Photo Library. 124 & 124/125, John Elk III. 126, Gerald Cubitt. 127, Eye Ubiquitous/Hutchison. 128, Robert Holmes. 129, Eye Ubiquitous/Hutchison. 130/131, SuperStock Ltd. 131, John Elk III. 132 & 133, AA Library/D. Corrance. 134, David Sanger. 135t, Eye Ubiquitous. 135b, Robert Harding Picture Library Ltd./Alamy. 136, Axiom. 137t, Eye Ubiquitous. 137b, Art Directors & Trip Photo Library. 138 & 139, AA Photo Library/D. Corrance. 141, Steve McCurry/National Geographic Society. 142, AA Photo Library/D. Corrance. 143, Art Directors & Trip Photo Library. 144, Eye Ubiquitous. 145t & 145c, Eye Ubiquitous. 145b, Eye Ubiquitous/Hutchison. 146-149 (all), Art Directors & Trip Photo Library. 150, Dinodia/ Art Directors & Trip Photo Library. 151, Hulton Getty Collection Ltd. 152/153, Art Directors & Trip Photo Library. 153, Bennett Dean/Eye Ubiquitous. 154/155, Art Directors & Trip Photo Library. 156, Gerald Cubitt. 157, Eye Ubiquitous/Hutchison. 159-162 (all), Catherine Karnow. 163, D. Constantine/Axiom. 164/165 & 166/167, Catherine Karnow. 168, Christine Pemberton/Eye Ubiquitous/Hutchison. 169, Anders Blomqvist/Alamy. 170/171 & 171, Eye Ubiquitous/Hutchison. 172, Travel Ink. 173, Robert Leon/www.robertleon.com. 174, SuperStock Ltd. 175, R. Francis/Eye Ubiquitous/Hutchison. 176/177, Anne & Bury Peerless Picture Library. 177, D. Shaw/Axiom. 178, Eye Ubiquitous. 179, Jean-Louis Nou/akg-images. 180, Anne & Bury Peerless Picture Library. 181, Bibliothèque Nationale, Paris, France/Bridgeman Art Library. 182, René Burri/Magnum Photos. 183-185 (all), Robert Leon/www.robertleon.com. 186, H. Rogers/Art Directors & Trip Photo Library. 187 & 188, Robert Leon/www.robertleon.com. 189, Terry Harris. 190, Axiom. 192/193, Aspect Picture Library. 194, Robert Harding

World Imagery/Getty Images. 195-197 (all), www.copix.co.uk. 198, Art Directors & Trip Photo Library. 199, Terry Harris. 200/201, S. Jones/Axiom. 201, Art Directors & Trip Photo Library. 202 & 203, Terry Harris. 204 & 205bl, www.copix.co.uk. 205br, Art Directors & Trip Photo Library. 205t, Robert Leon/www.robertleon.com. 206, Anne & Bury Peerless Picture Library. 207, Barbara Lloyd. 208, Wolfgang Kaehler. 210, Eye Ubiquitous/Hutchison. 211, Tom Hanley/Alamy. 212, David Sanger. 213, Hornbil Images/Alamy. 214, Vera Bogaerts/Shutterstock. 215t, www.copix.co.uk. 215bl, Harry Gryaert/Magnum Photos. 215br, Bennett Dean/Eye Ubiquitous. 216 & 217, Terry Harris. 219, Leon Schadeberg/Eye Ubiquitous. 220, Barbara Lloyd. 221, Jeremy Horner/Corbis. 223t, Art Directors & Trip Photo Library. 223b, Travel Ink. 224/225, Axiom. 226, Walter Bibikow/Getty Images. 227, Eye Ubiquitous/Hutchison. 228, Axiom. 229 (both), Eye Ubiquitous/Hutchison. 230, Nicholas Sumner. 231, Travel Ink. 232, Danita Delimont/Alamy. 233, Art Directors & Trip Photo Library. 234, Eye Ubiquitous/Hutchison. 235, C. Caldicot/Axiom. 236/237, Simon Reddy/Alamy. 238, Barbara Lloyd. 238/239, Michael Freeman 2006. 240, Claude Renault/age fotostock. 241, Eye Ubiquitous. 242, Tim Beddow/Eye Ubiquitous/Hutchison. 245, Jehangir Gazdar/Woodfin Camp. 247, Barbara Lloyd. 248, Eye Ubiquitous/Hutchison. 249, Art Directors & Trip Photo Library. 251, Anne & Bury Peerless Picture Library. 253, Barbara Lloyd. 254, Eye Ubiquitous. 256, Art Directors & Trip Photo Library. 257, Hornbil Images/Alamy. 258, Eye Ubiquitous/Hutchison. 260, Barbara Lloyd. 261, Anne & Bury Peerless Picture Library. 262, Art Directors & Trip Photo Library. 263t, Anne & Bury Peerless Picture Library. 263b, Eye Ubiquitous/Hutchison. 264, Anne & Bury Peerless Picture Library. 266 & 267, Eye Ubiquitous. 268, Anne & Bury Peerless Picture Library. 269 & 270/271, Art Directors & Trip Photo Library. 271, Eye Ubiquitous/Hutchison. 272/273, Barbara Lloyd. 274, Eye Ubiquitous. 277, David Sanger. 278/279 & 279, Eye Ubiquitous/Hutchison. 281, Bjanka Kadic/Alamy. 283, F. Good/Art Directors & Trip Photo Library. 285, Eye Ubiquitous. 287 & 288/289, Paul Harris Photography. 291, Eye Ubiquitous/Hutchison. 292, T. O'Brien/Art Directors & Trip Photo Library. 293, Eye Ubiquitous/Hutchison. 294, Lindsay Hebberd/Corbis. 295, Eye Ubiquitous. 296, Art Directors & Trip Photo Library. 297tl, John Elk III. 297tr, Paul Harris Photography. 297b, F. Good/Art Directors & Trip Photo Library. 298/299, John S. Callahan/Photo Resource Hawaii. 300/301, Michael Freeman 2006. 302/303, Eye Ubiquitous/Hutchison. 304, Francis Bacon/Axiom. 305t, Dinodia/Art

Directors & Trip Photo Library. 305bl, Raghu Rai/Magnum Photos. 305br, Fredrick Renander/Alamy. 306/307, Robert Holmes. 307, John Wilson/Robert Harding World Imagery/Getty Images. 308/309, Axiom. 310, F. Good/Art Directors & Trip Photo Library. 311, Michael Freeman 2006. 312/313 & 313, Gerald Cubit. 314/315 & 316, Bennett Dean/Eye Ubiquitous. 317 & 318, John Elk III. 320, Gerald Cubitt. 321, Ian Cumming/Axiom. 322 & 323, Art Directors & Trip Photo Library. 324, Mecky Fögeling/travimage.com. 325t, Vera Bogaerts/Shutterstock. 325bl, Robert Holmes. 325br, S. Carpenter/Axiom. 327, Paul Harris Photography. 328/329, AA Photo Library/F. Arvidsson. 329t, Steve McCurry/National Geographic Society. 329b, Art Directors & Trip Photo Library. 330/331, Blaine Harrington III/Corbis. 331, Paul Harris Photography. 332/333, Axiom. 335, Wolfgang Kaehler.

Founded in 1888, the National Geographic Society is one of the largest nonprofit scientific and educational organizations in the world. It reaches more than 285 million people worldwide each month through its official journal, NATIONAL GEOGRAPHIC, and its four other magazines; the National Geographic Channel; television documentaries; radio programs; films; books; videos and DVDs; maps; and interactive media. National Geographic has funded more than 8,000 scientific research projects and supports an education program combating geographic illiteracy.

For more information, please call 1-800-NGS LINE (647-5463) or write to the following address:

National Geographic Society,1145 17th Street N.W.,Washington, D.C. 20036-4688 U.S.A.

Visit us online at: www.national geographic.com/books

For information about special discounts for bulk purchases, please contact National Geographic Books Special Sales: ngspecsales@ngs.org

Published by the National Geographic Society
John M. Fahey, Jr., *President and Chief Executive Officer*
Gilbert M. Grosvenor, *Chairman of the Board*
Nina D. Hoffman, *Executive Vice President; President, Book Publishing Group*
Kevin Mulroy, *Senior Vice President and Publisher*
Leah Bendavid-Val, *Director of Photography Publishing and Illustrations*
Marianne Koszorus, *Director of Design*
Elizabeth L. Newhouse, *Director of Travel Publishing*
Carl Mehler, *Director of Maps*
Barbara A. Noe, *Series Editor*
Cinda Rose, *Art Director*
Jennifer A. Thornton, *Managing Editor*
Gary Colbert, *Production Director*
Ric Wain, *Production Manager*

Staff for 2007 Edition
Lawrence M. Porges, *Project Manager*
Susan Straight, *Editor*
Connie D. Binder, *Indexer*
Kay Kobor Hankins, Sonia Harmon, Lynsey Jacob, Mapping Specialists, Val Mattingley, Michael McNey, Christine Tanigawa, Ruth Thompson, Maura Walsh, Meredith C. Wilcox, *Contributors*

Edited and designed by AA Publishing (a trading name of Automobile Association Developments Limited, whose registered office is Norfolk House, Priestley Road, Basingstoke, Hampshire, England RG24 9NY. Registered number: 1878835).
Virginia Langer, *Project Manager*
David Austin, *Senior Art Editor*
Victoria Barber, *Senior Editor*
Inna Nogeste, *Senior Cartographic Editor*
Richard Firth, *Production Director*
Steve Gilchrist, *Prepress Production Controller*
Cartography by AA Cartographic Production
Maps © 2001. Based upon Survey of India maps with the permission of the Surveyor General of India
Picture Research by Zooid Pictures Ltd., & Carol Walker, AA Picture Library
Area maps drawn by Chris Orr Associates, Southampton, England
Cutaway illustrations drawn by Maltings Partnership, Derby, England

ISSN 1536-8637

National Geographic Traveler: India, Second Edition (2007)
  ISBN: 978-1-4262-0144-8

Printed and bound by Mondadori Printing, Toledo, Spain.

Visit the society's Web site at http://www.nationalgeographic.com

NATIONAL GEOGRAPHIC
TRAVELER

A Century of Travel Expertise in Every Guide

  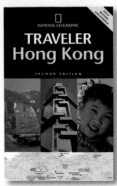

AVAILABLE WHEREVER BOOKS ARE SOLD